"One ordinary day. One extraordinary disappearance."

I0560901

THE
VANISHING

THE DAY WILL BEGIN LIKE ANY OTHER—UNTIL THE

RAPTURE

SILENCES THE WORLD

LORI ANN MOESZINGER

THE RIDGE
PUBLISHING GROUP

THE RIDGE PUBLISHING GROUP
COUER D'ALENE, IDAHO

THE RIDGE

PUBLISHING GROUP

The Ridge Publishing Group
Visit us at https://www.RidgePublishingGroup.com

The Ridge Publishing Group is headquartered in Coeur d'Alene, Idaho, 83814 USA.

The name, house mark, logo, and all associated trademarks—including *Guardians of Biblical Truth*—are trademarks or service marks of The Ridge Publishing Group.

All Scripture quotations are taken from the Holy Bible, King James Version (KJV), translated out of the original tongues and published in 1611, with the former translations diligently compared and revised.

Cover design by Eric Moeszinger
Interior design and images by Guardians of Biblical Truth

Library of Congress Cataloging-in-Publication Data

Name: Moeszinger, Lori Ann, author
Title: *The Vanishing: The Day Will Begin Like Any Other—Until the RAPTURE Silences the World*

Description: If you've ever sensed something is coming, this book will confirm your deepest fears. A prophetic warning the Church—and the world—can't afford to ignore. | Idaho : The Ridge Publishing Group, 2025.

Identifiers: LCCN 2025909988 | ISBN 978-1-956905-64-9 (hardcover) | ISBN 978-1-956905-65-6 (softcover) | 978-1-956905-66-3 (e-book)

Subjects: Religion, Christian Theology, Prophecy | Religion, Christian Theology, Eschatology | Religion, Christian Living, Spiritual Growth | Religion, Christian Theology, Apocalyptic and Eschatology | Fiction, Christian, Futuristic

Printed in the United States of America

To those who long for His appearing. The moment is closer than we dare imagine.

Contents

Author's Note   vii

Preface   ix

1   A Mystery of Seven Thousand Years   1

2   The Gospel of Salvation at the Heart of the Vanishing   9

3   The Gospel of the Kingdom at the Heart of Eternity   33

4   The Seven Harbingers: A Prophetic Roadmap   61

5   The First Harbinger: The Sign of the Times   81

6   The Second Harbinger: The Biblical Calendars   115

7   The Third Harbinger: The Signs in the Heavens   169

8   The Fourth Harbinger: The Feasts That Reveal the Future   255

9   The Fifth Harbinger: The Shemitah Cycles   313

10   The Sixth Harbinger: Daniel's 70th Week Trigger   337

11   The Seventh Harbinger: The War Prophecies   359

12   The Final Countdown: The Last Days Before Forever   387

Afterword: The Invitation   405

From the Author   409

Acknowledgments.   411

About the Author.   413

For More Information   415

Figures

1   God Works with Hebrew Calendars   118

2   Biblical and Gregorian Calendars   124

3   Feasts of the LORD, Harvests, Biblical and Gregorian Calendars   159

4   The Great American Eclipse: 2017 and 2024   217

5   Biblically Significant Tetrad Timelines   227

6   Revelation 12 Sign   238

7   The Holy Days of the LORD   291

8   Shemitah Cycles and Jubilee Years Since Creation (1 AM).   326

9   Daniel's 69 Weeks   338

10 Daniel's 70th Week.   339

11 Supercontinent—Pangaea (Genesis 1:9)   351

12 North America and Eurasia   352

AUTHOR'S NOTE

The Vanishing is not a work of fiction—but it is deeply story-driven. Like *The Trumpet I: The Ancient Prophecy That Reveals America's Final Hour* and *The Trumpet II: The Prophecy Continues—America's Final Hour Unveiled*, this book unfolds through intimate, narrative dialogues. At its heart are two women—Irene, the publisher, and Ann, the seeker—who walk side by side through the prophetic signs that signal the approaching end of the age. Their conversations aren't simply reflections; they are spiritual awakenings—windows into a generation wrestling with truth, urgency, and eternity.

These dialogues are rooted in years of theological study, Holy Spirit-led insight, and faithful watching as the prophetic clock inches toward midnight. Irene and Ann ask the same haunting questions many readers carry: What's really coming? How close are we? Who will be taken—and who will be left behind?

All Scripture references are drawn from the 1611 Authorized King James Version (KJV), occasionally revised for clarity in modern vernacular—similar to approaches used by trusted contemporary translations. Throughout this book, biblical doctrine, prophetic patterns, and spiritual application are carefully woven together to illuminate what I believe is the next great event on God's calendar: the Rapture of the Church—the great and sudden disappearance of millions.

While *The Trumpet I* and *II* series presented a story-driven journey through the Book of Revelation with America's prophetic role at the center, *The Vanishing* is a more direct blueprint. It traces the warnings, harbingers, and accelerating signs that point to the end of the Church Age—the last days—and the dawn of the Tribulation Age—the end times.

This book was not written to entertain.
It was written to awaken.

The vanishing is near.
The time to prepare . . . is now.

Preface

THE RAPTURE IS REAL—For centuries, the idea of the Rapture—the sudden removal of believers from the earth—has been debated, dismissed, spiritualized, or relegated to the margins of theology. Yet the Bible is unequivocal: a day will come when millions will be caught up in an instant, vanishing without warning. The world will awaken to chaos, confusion, and silence—and for many, it will be too late.

This book doesn't ask *if* the Rapture is real. Scripture has already answered that question. Instead, *The Vanishing: The Day Will Begin Like Any Other—Until the RAPTURE Silences the World* asks a far more urgent one: Are we closer to that moment than we dare to believe?

WHAT TIME IS IT ON GOD'S PROPHETIC CLOCK?

We often think of the Rapture as a sudden, standalone event. But Scripture tells a different story. God's Word is a prophetic timeline, carefully designed through divine patterns—feasts, calendars, and covenants. From the seven-day Creation to the Shemitah (also spelled Shmita) and Jubilee cycles, from Daniel's Seventy Weeks to Jesus' warnings in Matthew 24, the Bible has been counting down.

> Therefore be you also ready: for in such an hour as you think not the Son of Man comes. (Matthew 24:44)

How Close Are We?

This question has echoed through the hearts of watchmen, pastors, and seekers for generations. While no one knows the exact day or hour, Scripture calls us to know the season—to stay alert and watch for the signs. And today, those signs are not just appearing—they are converging with prophetic intensity. Could the 2022/2023–2028/2029 Shemitah cycle signal the close of the Church Age? Could the Rapture be the next event on God's sacred calendar?

Consider this: while the biblical calendar may point to 2029/2030—the dawn of the next Shemitah cycle and a possible signal for the Tribulation Age—the global elite are aiming for 2030 as the launch year for their "Great Reset." The overlap is more than coincidence. If we are truly living in the Laodicean era—the lukewarm final phase of the Church—then this isn't just prophecy unfolding. It's a wake-up call to act.

WHY THIS BOOK?

The Vanishing explores the compelling biblical evidence that the Rapture is imminent. Through Scripture, ancient cycles, prophetic appointments, and heavenly signs, a pattern emerges. These truths unfold through narrative dialogues between two women—one a publisher, the other a seeker—as they trace the clues together.

This book wasn't written to entertain.
It was written to interrupt.

To interrupt your assumptions.
To interrupt your spiritual complacency.
To interrupt the lie that there's still plenty of time.

The Rapture won't come with fanfare, nor will it delay for those who are spiritually unprepared. It will arrive like a thief in the night—suddenly, unexpectedly, on a day that feels just like today. When it happens, the Church Age will end. The Bride of Christ will be taken, and the Tribulation will begin.

ARE YOU READY?

You don't need to be a theologian to understand what's coming. You only need eyes to see and a heart willing to wake up. We are not date-setting. We are watching. We are sounding the alarm.

The vanishing is coming.
The time to prepare . . . is now.

Chapter 1

A Mystery of
Seven Thousand Years

IS IT POSSIBLE that a seven-thousand-year-old mystery holds the key to humanity's destiny? A divine pattern so ancient, yet so precise, that it stretches from the Garden of Eden to the gates of eternity?

Could this mystery be more than just theological theory—guiding the rise and fall of empires, marking the turning of prophetic ages, and shaping history since the dawn of Creation?

And could this mystery still be active—unfolding beneath global events, threading through Scripture, and converging with our present moment to herald the most pivotal event since the resurrection of Jesus Christ?

The answer is not only yes—it's already happening.

- Is it possible that a divine calendar—established at the dawn of Creation—is counting down to an event that will change the world in a single moment?
- Is it possible that what many consider random or chaotic—wars, disasters, financial collapses, political upheavals—are actually pieces of a larger prophetic puzzle?
- Is it possible that a mystery foretold in Scripture reveals the season, the signs, and even the nature of the next world-shaking event?

- Is it possible that the Church has forgotten—or worse, dismissed—an appointment God never canceled?
- And is it possible that millions will vanish—on a day just like today?

These are not plot points of a Hollywood thriller or speculative fiction. They are real. As real as the breath in your lungs. As real as the pulse in your veins. As real as the promises of God—and the warnings of His prophets.

This is not just theology—it's prophecy. And prophecy is history written in advance.

Did you know that 27 percent of the Bible is prophetic? Out of 31,102 verses in Scripture, over 8,350 contain predictive prophecy. That means approximately one out of every three to four verses is prophetic in nature—making predictive prophecy one of the most dominant themes in all of Scripture.

The mystery we are about to uncover is not confined to ancient parchment. It is encoded in the stars, embedded in Israel's feast days, concealed within the Hebrew language, and echoed in the cries of a world teetering on the brink. It began in a garden—and it will climax in the clouds.

From the Creation of Adam to the crucifixion of Christ, from the fall of Jerusalem to the birth of the Church, from the rebirth of Israel in 1948 to the rise of global digitalism of today—this mystery has marched forward: relentless, precise, prophetic. And if you're reading this now, you are not exempt from its reach.

The Church Age—what many call the Age of Grace—has stretched nearly two thousand years. For much of that time, believers have looked toward the sky, watching and waiting. But now, the signs no longer whisper. They shout. They converge. They accelerate. The prophetic clock is ticking.

You can feel it, can't you? The unraveling. The trembling. The shift in the atmosphere. We live in a time of technological miracles and moral catastrophes. Of enlightenment and confusion. Of abundance and emptiness. Every headline feels like a footstep in prophecy. Every crisis, a drumbeat in a coming storm.

And yet, many in the Church sleep. Many in the world scoff. And many of us go about our days—drinking coffee, checking our phones, planning vacations—as if eternity is not hanging by a thread.

That is why this book exists.

LET THE UNVEILING BEGIN

In the pages ahead, we will open Scripture and see what has been hiding in plain sight. We will step into ancient truths with modern eyes. We will examine harbingers—divine warning signs given by God not to terrify, but to awaken and prepare.

We will walk with two women—one a publisher, the other a seeker—through honest, soul-stirring dialogues that echo the questions many are afraid to ask.

The Rapture is not fiction.
It is not optional.
And it is not far.

What we are about to uncover is nothing less than the prophetic framework that has held the world together since Eden—the divine blueprint that will soon culminate in *The Vanishing*.

So as we begin, we must ask together:

- Could there be an ancient rhythm pulsing beneath the chaos of modern life?
- Could the vanishing of millions be embedded in the very fabric of Creation itself?
- Could every blood moon, every appointed feast, every global shaking be building toward a single, unavoidable moment?
- Could it all unfold suddenly—on a day just like today?

And perhaps the most important question of all:

Are we ready?
Let the journey begin.

———◆◆◆———

My study glowed with a soft amber light. Books lined the shelves, a cedar-scented candle flickered near the window, and a quiet fire crackled in the hearth. Irene stepped in from the cold, her coat half-draped over her arm, her eyes bright with anticipation—and a trace of unease.

I stood, smiling. "Welcome back, Irene. I've been waiting for this moment. You can feel it, can't you? Something has shifted—something seismic."

She eased into the leather armchair across from me, her voice low, edged with urgency. "I can. It's like the world is holding its breath. After everything we uncovered in *The Trumpet I* and *The Trumpet II* books, I thought I had seen the full picture. But this . . . this feels closer. More final. More real."

I nodded, leaning forward. "It is different—and yet it's the very fulfillment of everything we studied. Make no mistake—the Rapture marks the beginning of the end. When it happens, everything will change in an instant. There will never be anything like it again."

Irene's brow furrowed. "The shockwaves . . . I try to picture it—millions of people gone in a heartbeat. Planes without pilots. Cars without drivers. Children vanished from beds. People collapsing in grief and terror. Confusion. Chaos. Panic."

I sat back, my tone sobering. "And everywhere—echoing like thunder—'What on earth just happened?' But we'll know. It won't be an inexplicable mystery. It will be the glorious fulfillment of prophecy—the moment believers have waited for since Christ ascended."

Irene paused. Her voice cracked—not from doubt, but from the weight of the question. "But how can you be so sure? People have said for generations that the time was near. What makes you so certain it's now?"

I met her gaze without hesitation.

"Because the patterns are converging. The ancient cycles, the biblical calendar, the Shemitah years, the signs in the heavens—they're all aligning. And when you trace them—when you truly listen to what Scripture has been shouting all along—it all leads to one inescapable conclusion."

Irene leaned in, her voice barely a whisper.

"You're saying it's soon. Really soon."

"Yes. If the patterns hold—and I believe they will—we may be looking at just three years: 2028/2029."

I let the words settle like dust in the silence. "This isn't about setting dates. It's about watching, discerning, and obeying. Jesus didn't tell us to guess—He told us not to be caught unaware."

He answered and said unto them, When it is evening, you say, it will be fair weather: for the sky is red. And in the morning, it will be foul weather today: for the sky is red and overcast. O you hypocrites, you can discern the face of the sky; but can you not discern the signs of the times? (Matthew 16:2–3)

Irene sat back slowly, absorbing it all.

"In *The Trumpet*, you gave us glimpses of Heaven. It was breathtaking. Beyond anything I could've imagined."

I smiled softly. "And soon—for millions—it will be reality. But for those left behind, the world they knew will be unrecognizable. The Rapture isn't just an escape—it's a divine dividing line. It marks the end of one age and the beginning of another: the Tribulation."

Irene looked up again, this time not with fear, but with resolve. She clenched her hands in her lap, her voice now steady. "So . . . what do we do?"

"We sound the alarm," I said. "We tell the truth. We strip away the lies, the distractions, the false comforts. This isn't the end of hope—but it is the end of pretending. There's still time to turn to Christ. Still time to prepare. But not much. Not much—but enough."

Irene nodded. "Then let's begin."

She hesitated, then looked at me, concern clouding her expression.

"You know, I couldn't sleep last night. I kept going over your notes from our last communications. I kept thinking about that verse—'No one knows the day or the hour.' I don't mean to challenge your conviction, Ann, but if Jesus Himself said that, how can you be so sure the time is near? Doesn't that contradict what He told us?"

I smiled gently. "That's such an important question, Irene. And the answer lies in understanding *which* return Jesus was referring to. The Bible describes His return in two distinct stages: first, the Rapture of the Church—when He comes *for* His people in the clouds—and later, the Second Coming—when He returns *with* His people to establish His kingdom on earth."

Irene raised an eyebrow.

"Two stages? I've always heard about the Second Coming, but I thought it was just one single, final event—Jesus returns and that's it."

"That's a common assumption—and it's exactly where the confusion begins. The Rapture is when Christ comes *for* His Bride—suddenly, without warning. It's imminent. No signs need to come first. That's what Jesus meant in Matthew 24:36—when He said it could happen in the next heartbeat:"

> But of that day and hour knows no man, no, not the angels of heaven, but My Father only? (Matthew 24:36)

"The Second Coming, however—when Jesus physically returns and sets His feet on the Mount of Olives—is a different event entirely. It's preceded by clear signs. In fact, once the Tribulation begins, Scripture gives us a precise countdown."

Irene, leaning forward. "Wait . . . you're saying the Bible actually gives a timeframe for the Second Coming?"

"It does," I replied. "Daniel 9:27 tells us that the Tribulation begins when the Antichrist confirms a covenant—likely a peace treaty agreement—with Israel. From that moment, the countdown begins."

> And he (the Antichrist) shall confirm the covenant with many for one week (seven years): and in the midst of the week (3½ years) he shall cause the sacrifice and the oblation to cease, and for the overspreading of abominations he shall make it desolate, even until the consummation, and that determined shall be poured upon the desolate. (Daniel 9:27)

"Revelation 11:3 speaks of 1,260 days," I continued, "and Revelation 13:5 describes 42 months—both referencing the two halves of the Tribulation. That's 1,260 days each, totaling 2,520 prophetic days—a precise seven years, based on the 360-day biblical calendar."

"And at the end of that, Jesus returns?"

"Exactly," I nodded. "That's the difference. We don't—and can't—know the exact date of the Rapture. But the Second Coming will be precisely measurable from the start of the Tribulation. That's why this distinction matters so much."

"We're not trying to predict the day of the Rapture," I continued, "that's not only unwise, it's unbiblical. But we are commanded to know the season—to watch, discern, and not be caught off guard."

Irene leaned forward. "But how can we be sure we're in that season? People have been saying Jesus is coming back for centuries."

I nodded. "And they were supposed to. The early Church lived with that hope burning in their hearts. Paul preached it. The apostles longed for it. Every generation has been called to watch."

I paused.

"But what sets our time apart isn't just expectation—it's convergence. We're watching ancient prophecies unfold together, like pieces of a puzzle snapping into place:

- Israel is back in the land.
- Jerusalem is back in Jewish hands.
- Global alliances are shifting.
- Technology now makes biblical prophecy possible—worldwide surveillance, digital currency, even global communication in real time.
- And everywhere? Apostasy. Scoffing. Moral collapse. Globalism.

It's all here, Irene. And it's accelerating."

Irene, quietly. "And still . . . people don't see it. Even believers."

"Jesus rebuked the religious leaders of His day for the same thing. 'You know how to interpret the appearance of the sky, but you cannot interpret the signs of the times' (Matthew 16:3). That warning wasn't just for them—it still echoes today."

I continued. "The signs of His First Coming were in plain sight, yet most missed them. And now, we're in danger of making the same mistake."

"The Bible gives us over 500 prophecies about the Second Coming," I confirmed. "More than 300 prophecies were fulfilled at His First Coming—and every single one came true. So tell me, Irene—if God fulfilled the first set with perfect precision, why would we ignore the rest?"

Irene paused.

"Why do so many pastors avoid prophecy? Why is the Church asleep?"

I smiled. "Because prophecy demands something inconvenient: readiness. And readiness calls for holiness."

"Prophecy doesn't coddle comfort zones—it shatters them," I continued. "It exposes compromise. It reminds us that this world isn't our home, and that makes people uncomfortable."

I sighed. "Satan has done a masterful job of discrediting prophecy. He's turned it into a punchline—either dismissed as fanaticism, or worse, twisted into reckless date-setting."

"And once that happens? People check out. The Church disengages. Eyes close. Lamps go unfilled."

I smiled. "But Paul didn't say to ignore the times. He said this—"

But of the times and the seasons, brethren, you have no need that I write unto you. For yourselves know perfectly that the Day of the Lord so comes as a thief in the night. For when they shall say, Peace and safety; then sudden destruction comes upon them, as travail upon a woman with child; and they shall not escape. But you, brethren, are not in darkness, that that day should overtake you as a thief. You are all the children of light, and the children of the day: we are not of the night, nor of darkness. Therefore let us not sleep, as do others; but let us watch and be sober. For they that sleep, sleep in the night; and they that be drunken are drunken in the night. But let us, who are of the day, be sober, putting on the breastplate of faith and love; and for a helmet, the hope of salvation. For God has not appointed us to wrath, but to obtain salvation by our Lord Jesus Christ. (1 Thessalonians 5:1–9)

Irene nodded. "Then we can know?"

"We must know," I said. "Jesus never promised we'd know the hour—but He commanded us to recognize the signs."

I continued. "It's like pregnancy—you might not know the exact due date, but you know when the labor is near. Jesus called them 'birth pangs' for a reason. The earth is contracting. The intervals are tightening. The pressure is building. Time is accelerating."

Irene sighed. "And your conviction? That we're just a few short years away?"

"I'm not setting a date. But everything—every pattern, prophecy, and timeline—points to the 2028–2029 Shemitah year. Not because I want it to, but because Scripture is converging with history in real time. That's what *The Vanishing* is about. Not speculation—a map. A map through God's Word, laid out for those who are watching and praying."

Irene was quiet for a moment, then spoke with conviction.

"Then we have to wake the others. Warn them. Prepare them. This isn't just a message—it's a mission."

I nodded. "And the clock is ticking."

———◆◆◆———

THE FINAL TRUMPET CALL

A Declaration from the Watchtower

We now step into a revelation that has been unfolding for nearly seven thousand years. This is not merely a journey through Scripture—but through time itself. Through divine patterns, prophetic shadows, and promises spoken by God before the foundation of the world.

Ask yourself:

- Could the seven days of Creation conceal a prophetic timeline so precise, so sacred, that it reveals the season of the Rapture and the end of the Church Age?
- Could the biblical feasts—ordained millennia ago—still be proclaiming the Messiah's return with pinpoint accuracy?
- Could the Shemitah cycles and Jubilee years be counting down not only to Israel's restoration—but to the vanishing of the Bride of Christ?
- Could there be a divine calendar—one set in motion at Creation—that foretells the very hour in which we now stand?
- Are we now living in the final moments of the sixth prophetic day—on the threshold of the seventh, the Millennial Sabbath rest?
- Could the convergence of global events, the rise of apostasy, and the fulfillment of technological prophecy be more than coincidence—could they be the final alarms before the heavens split open?
- What if the vanishing of millions is not far-off myth or religious fiction—but tomorrow's headline?
- What if everything familiar—governments, families, economies, daily routines—is about to be overturned in a single, silent heartbeat?
- And what if the window to prepare is closing faster than the world dares to admit?

This is no longer just a study. It is a watchtower. We are not setting dates— we are discerning the season. We are not sounding fear—we are sounding the trumpet. For those with eyes to see and ears to hear, the vanishing is not a theory, nor is it mythology or wishful thinking. It is the next appointment on the calendar of God.

Let us now continue the search, for within the mystery of the vanishing lies the greatest warning, the greatest hope, and the greatest truth of all. And for those who are ready—this moment carries the greatest invitation.

Chapter 2

The Gospel of Salvation at the Heart of the Vanishing

WHO WILL BE TAKEN? WHO WILL BE LEFT?—And why the difference matters eternally? It is the most urgent question in all of prophecy. And yet, it is the one most often misunderstood, assumed, or ignored. Who exactly will vanish when the trumpet sounds—and why?

Before we can understand who will vanish, we must understand that the vanishing is not a divine game of chance. It is not a lottery of the religious. It is the fulfillment of a promise—an appointed moment when Jesus Christ calls His Bride to Himself.

At the heart of the vanishing lies not a mystery, but a message. Not speculation, but salvation. The Rapture will not sweep away everyone who calls themselves Christian. It is not a denominational event. It is not a reward for good behavior. It is the divine gathering of those who have been born again—those sealed by the Holy Spirit, purchased by the blood of Christ, and living in surrender to His grace.

This Bride is not defined by church attendance or theological trivia. She is defined by intimacy with the Bridegroom.

If you've ever wondered why two people could sit side by side in the same pew, sing the same worship songs, read from the same Bible—only to be separated in that final moment—this chapter is your wake-up call.

This is not just a possibility. It is a promise. And it will break hearts.

The Great Divide: Religion vs. Regeneration

The greatest tragedy on the day of the vanishing will not be the chaos—it will be the confusion. Not from those who mocked the Gospel, but from those who thought they knew Christ—only to find He never knew them.

Too many have reduced the Gospel to a casual prayer, an altar call, or a cultural affiliation. But salvation was never meant to be a transaction. It is a transformation. The Bible is painfully clear that not all who say, "Lord, Lord," will enter the kingdom. Many will profess a faith they never possessed. And when the vanishing happens, their world will collapse—not just from the shock of missing loved ones, but from the horrifying realization that they were left behind.

> Not everyone that says unto Me, Lord, Lord, shall enter into the Kingdom of Heaven; but he that does the will of My Father which is in heaven. Many will say to Me in that day, Lord, Lord, have we not prophesied in Your name? And in Your name have cast out devils? And in Your name done many wonderful works? And then will I profess unto them, I never knew you: depart from Me, you that work lawlessness. (Matthew 7:21–23)

That's why this chapter will not offer a modernized message designed for comfort. You will not find motivational phrases or safe theology. You will find the Gospel—raw, urgent, and uncompromising. Because your eternity depends on more than being inspired. It depends on being reborn.

We will explore:

- The difference between believing in Jesus and belonging to Jesus.
- Why the narrow road is harder than many have been told—and why it's worth it.
- What it truly means to be born again:

Jesus answered and said unto him, Verily, verily, I say unto you, Except a man be born again, he cannot see the Kingdom of God. Nicodemus says unto Him, How can a man be born when he is old? Can he enter the second time into his mother's womb, and be born? Jesus answered, Verily, verily, I say unto you, Except a man be born of water and of the Spirit, he cannot enter into the Kingdom of God. That which is born of the flesh is flesh; and that which is born of the Spirit is spirit. (John 3:3–6)

- The signs of authentic conversion—and the dangers of false assurance.
- How to know, beyond emotion or tradition, that you are ready.

The Vanishing: Not for the Curious, But the Converted

When the trumpet sounds, Heaven will not respond to religion—it will respond to relationship. The only ones taken will be those who are in Christ. This is not an arbitrary designation. It is a specific, spiritual reality.

The Rapture is not about spiritual maturity or theological depth—it's about spiritual birth. You must be born from above. Not reformed. Not awakened. Not merely inspired. Reborn.

This isn't just doctrine. It's destiny—yours and mine. That's why the vanishing is not only a prophetic event, but a deeply personal one. Because on that day, it won't matter how much you knew about prophecy. It won't matter how long you attended church or how many verses you memorized.

When the sky splits open, there won't be time to decide. The only question that will matter in that moment—will you rise, or will you remain?

Jesus Himself said:

> Jesus says unto him, I am the way, the truth, and the life: no man comes unto the Father, but by Me. (John 14:6)

The Gospel of Salvation is not one message among many—it is *the* message. And it is the only truth that can prepare a soul for the moment the trumpet sounds.

A Last Warning Before the Vanishing

We are not saved by Rapture theology. We are saved by the Cross. The purpose of this book is not merely to point to a vanishing world—but to ensure you are not left behind when it happens.

This chapter, above all, will challenge you to examine your faith with holy fear and heavenly clarity. The time is short. The line is thin. The stakes are eternal.

So we ask again—before the door shuts, before the age draws to its final breath, before the Bridegroom returns *for* His Bride: Are you ready? Not just emotionally stirred. Not merely religiously affiliated. But biblically grounded, eternally anchored, spiritually reborn?

This is not the hour for vague optimism or secondhand faith. It is the moment for honest reflection, holy surrender, and urgent preparation. Let's open the Scriptures—not to speculate, but to search. Let's examine the evidence—not to debate, but to decide.

Let us draw the line—clearly and soberly—between those who will rise when the trumpet sounds and those who will remain. The sifting has already begun. Will you be found ready?

WHO WILL BE TAKEN?

It is one of the most haunting questions in all of eschatology: Who will be taken when the trumpet sounds? Who will disappear in a moment, in the twinkling of an eye, caught up to meet the Lord in the air—and who will remain behind in a world suddenly thrown into chaos?

> In a moment, in the twinkling of an eye, at the last trump: for the trumpet shall sound, and the dead shall be raised incorruptible, and we shall be changed. (1 Corinthians 15:52)

This is not a question for scholars alone. It is the question that pierces the soul of every believer and confronts the assumptions of the casual churchgoer. The Rapture is not a random disappearance. It is not a lottery of the religious. It is not a reward for the spiritual elite or a rescue for the merely devout. It is a holy appointment between Christ and His Bride—a meeting foretold by prophets, foreshadowed in Scripture, and sealed by the blood of the Lamb.

Let us examine them carefully:

1. Those Who Are Born Again

> Jesus answered and said unto him, Verily, verily, I say unto you, Except a man be born again, he cannot see the Kingdom of God. (John 3:3)

To be born again is not a religious slogan—it is the first and non-negotiable condition for being part of the Rapture. Jesus told Nicodemus, a devout and learned Pharisee, that without spiritual rebirth, entrance into the Kingdom of God is impossible. This rebirth is not symbolic; it is literal and supernatural. It occurs the moment a person genuinely repents of sin, places full faith in the finished work of Christ on the Cross, and receives the indwelling of the Holy Spirit as a seal of salvation:

> In Him whom you also trusted, after that you heard the word of truth, the gospel of your salvation: in Him whom also after that you believed, you were sealed with that Holy Spirit of promise. (Ephesians 1:13)

This is not about attending church, being baptized as an infant, or having a family history of faith. It is about being made new from the inside out. Only those who are spiritually reborn will be taken.

2. Those Who Are Watching and Ready

> Therefore be you also ready: for in such an hour as you think not the Son of Man comes. (Matthew 24:44)

The call to be "ready" is not passive—it's prophetic. In Matthew 24 and 25, Jesus delivers parable after parable about the necessity of spiritual alertness. The wise virgins kept their lamps full of oil. The faithful servant watched and worked while the master delayed. The Bride was to be adorned and expecting her Bridegroom's arrival.

Readiness is a lifestyle. It is marked by ongoing repentance, obedience, a hatred for sin, and a heart longing for Christ's return. Those who are spiritually awake—recognizing the signs of the times, discerning the lateness of the hour, and walking in daily fellowship with Jesus—are the ones who will be taken. Not because of perfection, but because of posture: a posture of surrender.

3. Those Who Do the Will of the Father

> Not everyone that says unto Me, Lord, Lord, shall enter into the Kingdom of Heaven; but he that does the will of My Father which is in heaven. (Matthew 7:21)

This is perhaps one of the most sobering verses in all of Scripture. Jesus tells us plainly that many will claim His name, even perform spiritual acts in His name, and yet still be cast out because He never knew them. Why? Because they were never in true relationship with Him. They had religion without regeneration. Works without worship. Confession without conversion.

The ones who will be taken are those who are not just hearers of the Word, but doers. They are those whose obedience is not out of duty but devotion. Their lives are marked by a genuine pursuit of holiness—not for salvation, but from salvation. They are not perfect, but they are purified by grace and pressing on toward the upward call.

4. The Faithful Remnant: The Bride of Christ

> Henceforth there is laid up for me a crown of righteousness, which the Lord, the righteous Judge, shall give me at that Day: and not to me only, but unto all them also that love His appearing. (2 Timothy 4:8)

The Church is often referred to as the Bride of Christ, but Scripture is clear: not all who are part of the visible Church are counted as the Bride. Within the broader body of believers exists a faithful remnant—those who not only believe but burn with longing for the return of their Bridegroom. They have not defiled themselves with the world. Their garments are white. Their hearts are awake. They love His appearing.

These are the overcomers. The virgins with oil in their lamps. The watchmen on the wall. The Bride who has made herself ready. To them, the Rapture will not be a surprise but a long-awaited consummation.

A Final Word on Who Will Be Taken

The Rapture is not about spiritual maturity—it is about spiritual birth. It is not reserved for those who can quote revelation, but for those who have surrendered their lives to Jesus Christ. It is not a prize for theological intelligence, but a promise for those who belong to Him.

And belonging means more than believing. Even the demons believe—and tremble (James 2:19). The question is not whether you believe Jesus existed. The question is whether He knows you. Whether you've been born again. Whether your life bears the fruit of His Spirit.

> You believe that there is one God; you do well: the devils also believe, and tremble. (James 2:19)

When the trumpet sounds, it will not be a general call. It will be a Bridegroom calling His Bride. The faithful remnant. The truly redeemed. The spiritually reborn.

So again we ask—not out of fear, but with eternal urgency:

Will you be taken?

———◆◆◆———

A quiet study. Morning light filtered softly through a sheer curtain, bathing the room in a gentle glow. The scent of fresh coffee lingered in the air as I poured two mugs, my movements calm and familiar.

Irene sat across from me, flipping open her Bible, her fingers lingering on the gilded edge of the page. Her brow was slightly furrowed.

"I've been wrestling with something," she said thoughtfully, her voice low with sincerity. "You mentioned in *The Trumpet I* the hundredfold, sixtyfold, and thirtyfold harvest—and how it ties into the Rapture. But I always thought that parable was just about fruitfulness . . . not who's taken and who's left behind."

She glanced up, her eyes searching.

"Have I misunderstood it all this time?"

I nodded slowly, setting the coffee pot aside.

"That's a common first reading," I said. "But let's dig deeper."

My voice was gentle, but sure.

"Jesus wasn't offering agricultural trivia—He was unveiling a divine pattern. A revelation of how people respond to the Word of God and what kind of fruit, if any, that response produces in their lives. And yes . . . those responses affect eternal outcomes—especially in the context of the end times."

Irene leaned in, curiosity ignited.

"Okay," she said. "Walk me through it."

"In Matthew 13," I began, opening my Bible to the passage, "Jesus tells the Parable of the Sower. The seed represents the Word of God. The different types of soil? They symbolize the condition of the human heart."

I traced my finger down the page.

"There are four types mentioned: the path, the rocky ground, the thorny ground, and finally—the good soil. Only one of them bears fruit."

Irene's brow furrowed as she listened.

"And that fruit?" she asked slowly. "It's the thirtyfold, sixtyfold, and hundredfold, right?"

I nodded gently.

"Exactly. Most people interpret the thirtyfold, sixtyfold, and hundredfold as just different levels of Christian maturity. But when you view it through the lens of the Rapture, it becomes far more sobering."

I leaned in, my voice low with conviction.

"The hundredfold aren't just mature—they're surrendered. They're the Bride of Christ. These are the believers who have laid down their lives fully, who walk in holiness, who live in daily expectation of the Bridegroom's return. They're not distracted. They're watching. They're ready. When the trumpet sounds—they're the ones who vanish."

Irene furrowed her brow, the weight of my words settling in.

"And the others?" she asked quietly.

I nodded soberly.

"The sixtyfold and thirtyfold—they're believers too. But they're not fully yielded. They're saved, yes, but they're still entangled—by the world, by sin, by comfort, by compromise. Maybe they sat in church every Sunday. Maybe they even served on teams. But their hearts were divided. Their lamps weren't full of oil."

I looked at Irene, the weight of truth pressing between us.

"They weren't ready."

Irene's voice barely broke a whisper.

"They're left behind."

"Yes," I said gently.

"But there's still hope. The Tribulation will become their refining fire. For those left behind, it won't be too late—if they repent, if they truly turn to Jesus. Salvation will still be possible."

I let the truth settle before continuing.

"But most won't make it through with ease. Many will have to seal their faith with their blood. They'll be martyred."

Irene's voice was barely audible, laced with a chill.

"And if they don't choose Christ in time?"

I sighed, the weight of the moment pressing in.

"Then they'll die in their sin. It's spiritual Russian roulette. One hesitation. One delay. One refusal to surrender—and the door closes. The stakes couldn't be higher. A wrong choice at the wrong time could mean eternal separation from God."

Irene's eyes searched mine.

"So you're saying the four soils in that parable—they're not just metaphors or teaching tools. They represent real souls. Real outcomes."

"Yes," I said quietly.

"The path, the rocky, and the thorny soils never bear lasting fruit. These represent the lost—those who never truly received Christ. Some were deceived by religion. Others were lured away by the cares and comforts of the world. They won't rise when the trumpet sounds. And unless they surrender during the Tribulation, their fate is sealed."

Irene exhaled, her voice laced with concern.

"And only one soil bore fruit—those who hear the Word, understand it, and obey. But even among those, the fruit varies. Are you saying . . . that difference could determine who's raptured and who's left?"

"Exactly," I said.

"The hundredfold are those walking in deep intimacy with the Bridegroom. They're the wise virgins, their lamps filled with oil, watching and ready. The others—still deeply loved by God—will not rise with the Bride. Instead, they'll pass through the fire of the Tribulation."

Irene sat still for a moment, her expression thoughtful.

"That's heavy," she said softly.

"But it's also . . . merciful. God's warning us now—before it's too late."

I smiled gently.

"Yes. That's why Jesus gave us this parable—not just to inspire, but to warn. It was never about working harder—it's about surrendering deeper. And that surrender? It begins now."

Irene's voice dropped to a whisper.

"So the question isn't just, 'Am I saved?' It's . . . 'Am I bearing fruit—hundredfold fruit?'"

"Exactly," I said, my tone solemn.

"Because when the trumpet sounds, only the Bride rises. The rest? They will face the fire."

WHO WILL BE LEFT BEHIND?

If the Rapture is the moment Christ gathers His Bride, then what becomes of those who are left behind? The answer is as devastating as it is avoidable.

Those left behind will include nominal Christians—individuals who professed faith but were never truly born again. They may have occupied pews, sang hymns, or even served in ministry, yet their hearts remained unchanged—never surrendered to the lordship of Christ.

Others will be lukewarm believers, the ones Jesus warned about in Revelation 3:16—neither hot nor cold, but spiritually indifferent. They straddled the fence between the world and the Word, never choosing sides until it was too late.

> So then because you are lukewarm, and neither cold nor hot, I will spue you out of My mouth. (Revelation 3:16)

Then there are those who loved the world more than they loved Christ (1 John 2:15)—entangled by its pleasures, possessions, and praise. Though they may have heard the Gospel, they lived as if earth were their home.

> Love not the world, neither the things that are in the world. If any man love the world, the love of the Father is not in him. (1 John 2:15)

Many will be unrepentant—those who encountered the truth but rejected it, choosing their own path over God's. And still others will be religiously deceived—trusting in ceremony over conversion, performance over transformation. They believed that rituals could substitute for relationship, that good works could stand in for grace.

But salvation is not about what we do—it's about who we belong to. Tragically, many will discover that truth too late. These are not hypotheticals. They are sobering portraits of real souls—millions who will miss the moment that divides eternity.

What follows are ten types of people the Bible warns will be left behind—unless they surrender to Christ while there is still time.

1. The Fearful (Cowardly)

In Revelation 21:8, the fearful—also translated as "cowardly"—are listed first among those excluded from eternal life. This isn't a condemnation of natural shyness or quiet temperaments. Rather, it exposes those who, when confronted with the cost of following Christ, choose fear over faith, safety over surrender, and silence over truth.

These are the ones who:

- Back down in the face of cultural pressure or mockery.
- Hide their faith to avoid conflict or loss.
- Compromise biblical convictions to remain comfortable.
- Refuse to stand boldly for Christ when it matters most.

This form of fear becomes a subtle idolatry—placing self-preservation above allegiance to God. Jesus warned:

> Whosoever therefore shall be ashamed of Me and My words in this adulterous and sinful generation; of him also shall the Son of Man be ashamed, when He comes in the glory of His Father with the holy angels. (Mark 8:38)

True discipleship requires courage. The cowardly are not those who never heard the Gospel—but those who heard it, understood it, and still refused to walk the narrow road.

> And He said unto them, Why are you so fearful? How is it that you have no faith? (Mark 4:40)

> For God has not given us the spirit of fear; but of power, and of love, and of a sound mind. Be not you therefore ashamed of the testimony of our Lord, nor of me His prisoner: but be you partaker of the afflictions of the gospel according to the power of God. (2 Timothy 1:7–8)

2. The Unbelieving

The unbelieving are not merely those who experience spiritual doubts. They are individuals who, when confronted with the truth of the gospel, consciously resist or reject it. This rejection may be loud and antagonistic—or quiet and indifferent. But the outcome is the same: spiritual separation from God and exclusion from the promises reserved for those who believe in Jesus Christ.

These are the ones who:

- Hear the gospel, yet dismiss it as myth, irrelevance, or even offense.
- Trust in human intellect, alternative religion, or personal morality—while refusing to surrender to Christ.
- Delay their response, choosing worldly pursuits, pride, or pleasure over repentance.
- Remain spiritually dead, untouched by the supernatural rebirth that brings eternal life.

Scripture is unmistakably clear: belief is not suggestion—it is the doorway to salvation. Without it, a person stands condemned already (John 3:18), no matter how "moral," "spiritual," or "good" they seem. At the time of the Rapture, the unbelieving will be left behind—not because they misunderstood prophecy, but because they refused to believe in the Savior who alone redeems.

> He that believes on Him is not condemned: but he that believes not is condemned already, because he has not believed in the name of the only begotten Son of God. (John 3:18)

> Take heed, brethren, lest there be in any of you an evil heart of unbelief, in departing from the living God. (Hebrews 3:12)

3. The Abominable (Defiantly Unrepentant)

The abominable are not simply sinners—they are those who defiantly embrace what God calls detestable. This label goes beyond occasional moral failure; it speaks to a heart posture that is hardened, rebellious, and resolutely opposed to God's truth and holiness.

Whether through willful actions, corrupt desires, or an unrepentant lifestyle, the abominable reject God's authority in favor of self-rule. They are not ignorant of right and wrong—they just refuse to surrender.

These individuals:

- Take pleasure in sin and openly celebrate what Scripture condemns.
- Twist or ignore biblical truth in order to justify immoral behavior.
- Resist the conviction of the Holy Spirit and mock calls to repentance.
- Often maintain a religious appearance, but their hearts are spiritually defiled.

Scripture is clear:

> They profess that they know God; but in works they deny Him, being abominable, and disobedient, and unto every good work reprobate. (Titus 1:16)

In both the Old and New Testaments, the term "abominable" refers to deep moral corruption, false religion, idolatry, and a proud refusal to repent.

Those who fall into this category will be left behind—not because they failed more than others, but because they rejected the mercy that could have saved them. They will have chosen darkness over light, defilement over deliverance, rebellion over redemption.

4. Murderers

The term "murderers" in Scripture transcends physical violence. Jesus, in the Sermon on the Mount (Matthew 5–7), redefined murder not merely as the taking of life but as a matter of the heart. Hatred, bitterness, and malicious anger carry the same spiritual weight.

> Whosoever hates his brother is a murderer: and you know that no murderer has eternal life abiding in him. (1 John 3:15)

God's justice reaches beneath behavior to motive. The Rapture will bypass those who continue in:

- Hatred toward others with no intent to forgive.
- Malicious resentment or unresolved bitterness.
- Advocacy or participation in abortion without repentance.
- Disregard for the sacredness of life, even under the guise of morality or rights.

Abortion in particular grieves the heart of God. Life is sacred from the moment of conception:

> Thou shalt not kill. (Exodus 20:13)

> Before I formed you in the belly I knew you; and before you came forth out of the womb I sanctified you, and I ordained you a prophet unto the nations. (Jeremiah 1:5)

> For You have possessed my reins: You have covered me in my mother's womb. (Psalm 139:13)

Jesus also warned that inward rage carries eternal consequence:

> You have heard that it was said by them of old time, Thou shalt not kill; and whosoever shall kill shall be in danger of the judgment. But I say unto you, That whosoever is angry with his brother without a cause shall be in danger of the judgment: and whosoever shall say to his brother, Raca (utter disdain or scorn for another person), shall be in danger of the council: but whosesoever shall say, You fool, shall be in danger of hell fire. (Matthew 5:21–22)

Those who persist in hate, bloodshed, or a hardened view of life's sanctity will not vanish when the trumpet sounds. Not because mercy isn't available—but because they rejected both repentance and the divine image in others.

5. Whoremongers (Sexually Immoral)

The term "whoremongers" in Revelation 21:8 is translated from the Greek word *pornos*—the same root as "pornography." It refers to a broad spectrum of sexual immorality, not just specific acts, but entire lifestyles unyielded to God's standards. These are not sins of weakness, but sins of willful indulgence.

This includes:

- Fornication—sex outside of marriage.
- Adultery—unfaithfulness within marriage.
- Cohabitation without covenant.
- Habitual pornography consumption.
- And any sexual behavior—heterosexual or homosexual—that violates the sacred covenant of biblical marriage between one man and one woman.

The apostle Paul makes this clear:

Know you not that the unrighteous shall not inherit the Kingdom of God? Be not deceived: neither fornicators, nor idolaters, nor adulterers, nor effeminate (men acting like women or women acting like men), nor abusers of themselves with mankind (practicing homosexuality—same-sex sexual activity), nor thieves, nor covetous (those who greedily desire what others have), nor drunkards (habitual alcohol abusers), nor revilers (those who slander, insult, or verbally abuse others), nor extortioners (those who obtain through threats or manipulation), shall inherit the Kingdom of God. (1 Corinthians 6:9–10)

And again in Hebrews:

Marriage is honorable in all, and the bed undefiled: but whoremongers and adulterers God will judge. (Hebrews 13:4)

This includes those who embrace identities or practices in defiance of God's Word—whether they be heterosexual or same-sex in nature—when they persist without repentance.

Let it be clear: God's grace is wide, His mercy unfathomable. But judgment comes to those who do not merely fall into sin, but defend it, normalize it, and persist in it without remorse. It is not the struggle that condemns—it is the refusal to repent.

6. Sorcerers

The word "sorcerers" in Revelation 21:8 and Revelation 18:23 comes from the Greek *pharmakoi*—the root of our modern word "pharmacy." In biblical times, sorcery wasn't just about spells or illusions—it often involved the use of mind-altering substances to produce spiritual experiences or to engage with demonic powers. These were not harmless rituals but dangerous encounters with real, dark spiritual forces.

And the light of a candle shall shine no more at all in you; and the voice of the Bridegroom and of the Bride shall be heard no more at all in you: for your merchants were the great men of the earth; for by your sorceries were all nations deceived. (Revelation 18:23)

But the fearful, and unbelieving, and the abominable, and murderers, and whoremongers, and sorcerers, and idolaters, and all liars, shall have their part in the lake which burns with fire and brimstone: which is the second death. (Revelation 21:8)

Today, this term can apply not only to occult practitioners, but also to those who abuse drugs, alcohol, or any substance that dulls the mind, especially in rebellion against God's call to sobriety, holiness, and spiritual alertness. Anything that clouds judgment opens a door to deception—and Scripture takes that seriously.

This includes individuals who:

- Engage in occult practices, such as: witchcraft, Wicca, necromancy, astrology, and spiritualism.
- Seek power or comfort through counterfeit means, including: crystals, rituals, spellcasting, and tarot cards.
- Use mind-altering substances to escape or manipulate reality: illegal drugs and hallucinogens, chronic alcohol abuse, and substances that suppress conviction or distort truth.
- Chronic substance abuse that dulls discernment, invites deception, and breaks the command of sober-mindedness.

Be sober, be vigilant; because your adversary the devil, as a roaring lion, walks about, seeking whom he may devour. (1 Peter 5:8)

Now the works of the flesh are manifest, which are these; adultery, fornication, uncleanness, lasciviousness (unrestrained sexual desire, lewdness, or indecent behavior), idolatry, witchcraft, hatred, variance (discord, strife, or contentious disagreement—especially among believers), emulations (jealousy, envy, or intense rivalry), wrath, strife, seditions (divisions, dissent, or rebellion against authority or unity), heresies (divisive, false teachings or belief systems that depart from the truth of God's Word), envyings, murders, drunkenness, revellings, and such like: of the which I tell you before, as I have also told you in time past, that they which do such things shall not inherit the Kingdom of God. (Galatians 5:19–21)

This issue isn't mere exposure—it's unrepentant indulgence. To open oneself to counterfeit power or intoxication is to reject the Spirit of truth. God's mercy is extended even here, but only to those who lay down these dark practices and return to the light. Those who won't, risk being left behind.

7. Dogs (Morally Depraved and Spiritually Unclean)

In biblical language, the term "dogs" is not about household pets, but a symbol of those considered spiritually unclean, morally depraved, and resistant to correction. In ancient times, dogs were despised scavengers—often used metaphorically to describe individuals who lived outside God's covenant, rejecting truth and embracing defilement.

In Scripture, "dogs" can represent:

- False teachers who distort or exploit the gospel for personal gain (Philippians 3:2; 2 Peter 2:1–3).

Beware of dogs, beware of evil workers, beware of the concision (sarcastic reference to those insisting that Gentile Christians be circumcised to be saved). (Philippians 3:2)

- Backsliders who return to sin after knowing the truth, like a dog returning to its vomit (2 Peter 2:22).

But it is happened unto them according to the true proverb, The dog is turned to his own vomit again; and the sow that was washed to her wallowing in the mire. (2 Peter 2:22)

- Mockers of holiness—those consumed by lust, greed, or spiritual laziness: choosing ease, comfort, or distraction over intentional pursuit of God. This is a heart condition that resists discipline, delays obedience, and forfeits deeper intimacy with Christ (Isaiah 56:10–11; Matthew 7:6).

His watchmen are blind: they are all ignorant, they are all dumb dogs, they cannot bark; sleeping, lying down, loving to slumber. Yea, they are greedy dogs which can never have enough, and they are shepherds that cannot understand: they all look to their own way, every one for his gain, from his quarter. (Isaiah 56:10–11)

- Covenant outsiders—those hardened in rebellion, resistant to repentance, and dismissive of divine correction.

But he answered and said, It is not good to take the children's bread, and to cast it to the dogs. (Matthew 15:26)

For without are dogs, and sorcerers, and whoremongers, and murderers, and idolaters, and whosoever loves and makes a lie. (Revelation 22:15)

These are not merely individuals who sin, but those who persist in a lifestyle of spiritual defilement—who reject cleansing, scorn holiness, and trample on grace. Their lives are marked not by repentance but by rebellion. Unless they surrender to Christ, they will remain outside the gates of salvation—left behind when the Rapture removes the Bride.

8. Idolaters (Lovers of Anything Above God)

Idolatry isn't limited to bowing before golden statues—it is, at its core, a heart issue. Scripture consistently warns that anything we love, trust, or prioritize above God becomes an idol. Idolatry is spiritual adultery—a betrayal of our covenant with the Lord.

An idol can be:

- Material possessions—Money, luxury, homes, fashion, or cars that capture your heart more than God's presence.
- Achievements—Career success, titles, reputation, or awards that become your identity and source of worth.
- People—Spouses, children, relationships, influencers, or celebrities who are loved, feared, or followed more than Christ.
- Self-worship—Pride, vanity, obsession with self-image, personal ambition, or the desire to be seen, celebrated, or envied.
- Religious ritual—Traditions, church attendance, or outward holiness that become routine substitutes for an intimate relationship with Jesus.

Digital distractions—phones, social media, and streaming entertainment—digital content delivered over the internet in real time, such as movies, TV shows, music, podcasts, YouTube videos, or video games—can easily consume your time, attention, and affections. These tech-driven platforms and devices often silently replace prayer, worship, and spiritual hunger for God. What begins as harmless scrolling or relaxing content can subtly become a daily altar of devotion, drawing your heart away from intimacy with Christ.

God's standard is unwavering:

> Thou shalt have no other gods before Me. Thou shalt not make unto you any graven image, or any likeness of anything that is in heaven above, or that is in the earth beneath, or that is in the water under the earth: Thou shalt not bow down yourself to them, nor serve them: for I the LORD your God am a jealous God, visiting the iniquity of the fathers upon the children unto the third and fourth generation of them that hate Me. (Exodus 20:3–5)

Even desires that seem noble can become idolatrous when they eclipse our devotion to God. Paul warns:

> Mortify (put to death) therefore your members which are upon the earth: fornication (sexual relations outside of marriage), uncleanness (moral and spiritual defilement), inordinate affection (idolatrous craving that leads the heart away from Christ), evil concupiscence (wicked, lustful cravings or desires), and covetousness (the intense desire to possess what belongs to someone else), which is idolatry. (Colossians 3:5)

And John's final warning in his first epistle (letter) is striking in its simplicity and urgency:

Little children, keep yourselves from idols. Amen. (1 John 5:21)

Idolaters may appear moral or even devout—but if Christ is not seated on the throne of their hearts, they are spiritually unprepared. Unless they repent, they will be left behind—not because God's love failed, but because they chose lesser loves over the One who gave His all for them.

9. Liars (Those Who Delight in Deception)

Lying is not a harmless flaw or a small moral misstep—it is a serious spiritual offense. In God's eyes, repeated deception is not just a behavior but a reflection of one's true spiritual allegiance. Scripture warns soberly that "all liars" will face eternal judgment (Revelation 21:8).

This judgment is not for those who've stumbled into an occasional falsehood in weakness, but for those who habitually, willfully, and unrepentantly walk in lies.

This includes:

- Those who live by deception, making dishonesty their way of life.
- Those who manipulate truth for power, money, fame, or self-protection.
- Those who spread slander, gossip, or false doctrine, undermining trust and unity.
- Those who build their lives or ministries on hypocrisy—outwardly professing Christ, but inwardly denying Him.
- Those who craft false appearances—claiming virtue, spirituality, or humility while cloaking sin.

Jesus pulled no punches when He revealed the source behind all lies:

You are of your father the devil (Satan), and the lusts of your father you will do. He was a murderer from the beginning, and abode not in the truth, because there is no truth in him. When he speaks a lie, he speaks of his own: for he is a liar, and the father of it. (John 8:44)

The contrast is clear: Jesus is the Truth.

Jesus says unto him, I am the way, the truth, and the life: no man comes unto the Father, but by Me. (John 14:6)

Lying aligns us with darkness. Truth aligns us with Christ. Those who habitually lie reject the very nature of God and cannot walk in communion with Him. Unless they repent, they will be left behind—not because God's grace was insufficient, but because they chose the counterfeit over the truth.

10. The Idle (Spiritually Unproductive and Neglectful)

In the Kingdom of God, idleness is not benign—it is dangerous disobedience. Scripture treats spiritual laziness as a grievous condition, not just because of what it fails to do, but because of what it invites: confusion, gossip, wasted purpose, and eventual judgment.

The idle are not merely tired or in need of a break. They are those who consistently refuse to engage, avoid responsibility, and remain fruitless despite knowing the truth. Their inaction signals a deeper problem: neglect of God's calling.

The Bible associates the idle with:

- Disorder and disobedience—Those who ignore apostolic instruction and live unruly, undisciplined lives.

Now we command you, brethren, in the name of our Lord Jesus Christ, that you withdraw yourselves from every brother that walks disorderly, and not after the tradition which he received of us. (2 Thessalonians 3:6)

- Gossip and meddling—Instead of building others up, idlers often stir division through distraction.

And withal they learn to be idle, wandering about from house to house; and not only idle, but tattlers also and busybodies, speaking things which they ought not. (1 Timothy 5:13)

- Spiritual barrenness—Like the servant who buried his talent, the idle waste what God entrusted to them.

And cast you the unprofitable servant into outer darkness: there shall be weeping and gnashing of teeth. (Matthew 25:30)

- Neglect of divine mission—Idleness leads to spiritual decay, just as neglected buildings collapse from disrepair.

By much slothfulness the building decays; and through idleness of the hands the house drops through. (Ecclesiastes 10:18)

Idleness is not a harmless habit—it is a spiritual posture of neglect. Jesus called us to watch, work, and bear fruit. Those who resist His call—who choose stagnancy over stewardship—are not ready to meet Him. Without repentance and renewed purpose, the idle will be left behind, not for what they did, but for what they refused to become: faithful, fruitful servants.

Final Reflection: A Wake-Up Call from Heaven

These ten categories are not an arbitrary list—they are a divine alarm clock sounding for a slumbering world. Each represents a heart condition that rejects the lordship, love, and holiness of Jesus Christ. And while the consequences are eternal, the invitation remains open.

God is not willing that any should perish, but that all should come to repentance (2 Peter 3:9). No matter where you find yourself in these descriptions, grace is still available—but only before the trumpet sounds.

The question is not merely, "Am I a good person?" The true and urgent question is, "Am I ready?"—ready to stand before the Son of Man, ready to be found faithful, and ready to meet the Bridegroom when He comes. Being good in the eyes of the world is not the standard. Being prepared in heart, mind, and life for the return of Christ is. Time is short, and eternity is long. There is no room for hesitation or half-hearted belief. Choose Jesus—fully, now, and without delay.

WHY THE DIFFERENCE BETWEEN
SALVATION AND READINESS MATTERS—ETERNALLY

Salvation is the door—but obedience is the key that opens it to deeper intimacy with Christ. The gift of salvation comes by grace through faith in Jesus Christ (Ephesians 2:8–9). It cannot be earned, bought, or bargained for. But Scripture never ends at belief alone—it calls believers into a life of obedience, holiness, and spiritual vigilance.

> For by grace are you saved through faith; and that not of yourselves: it is the gift
> of God: Not of works, lest any man should boast. (Ephesians 2:8–9)

The Rapture is not a reward for everyone who once uttered a prayer or sat in a pew. It is repeatedly described in Scripture as a rescue for the faithful—for those who are awake, watching, and living with their lamps full of oil. Jesus warned His disciples to live as though the Master could return at any moment (Luke 12:35–40). These were not soft suggestions; they were instructions for those who long to be counted among the ready.

> Let your waist be girded about, and your lights burning. And you yourselves like
> unto men that wait for their lord, when he will return from the wedding; that
> when he comes and knocks, they may open unto him immediately. Blessed are
> those servants, whom the lord when he comes shall find watching: Verily I say
> unto you, that he shall gird himself, and make them to sit down to eat, and will
> come forth and serve them. And if he shall come in the second watch, or come
> in the third watch, and find them so, blessed are those servants. And this know,
> that if the goodman of the house had known what hour the thief would come, he
> would have watched, and not have suffered his house to be broken into. Be you

therefore ready also: for the Son of Man comes at an hour when you think not. (Luke 12:35–40)

Paul echoed this same urgency when he exhorted the church to "work out your own salvation with fear and trembling" (Philippians 2:12). This is not about earning grace—it's about honoring it. True salvation produces fruit. It transforms. It separates mere profession from true possession. As Jesus warned, many will one day cry, "Lord, Lord," only to be turned away—not because they never heard the gospel, but because they refused to be changed by it (Matthew 7:21–23).

> Wherefore, my beloved, as you have always obeyed, not as in my presence only, but now much more in my absence, work out your own salvation with fear and trembling. (Philippians 2:12)

Lukewarm believers—those who love the world, tolerate compromise, and silence conviction—are not described in Scripture as ready. They may still be saved, but through the fire of Tribulation (Revelation 7:14), possibly at the cost of their lives. These are the thirtyfold and sixtyfold believers: left behind not because they weren't loved but because they weren't watching.

> And I said unto him, Sir, you know. And he said to me, These are they which came out of Great Tribulation, and have washed their robes, and made them white in the blood of the Lamb. (Revelation 7:14)

The Bride of Christ—the hundredfold remnant—is not perfect, but she is prepared. She walks in daily repentance, spiritual sobriety, and intimacy with the Bridegroom. Her life reflects separation from the world, devotion to truth, and a longing for His appearing. She lives with eternity in view and readiness in her soul.

And He is coming. That is the unshakable truth that echoes through every page of Scripture. In light of that, the question we must each confront is not merely, "Am I saved?"—but rather, "Am I ready?" Ready to meet the Bridegroom. Ready to be found faithful. Ready to stand before the Son of Man without shame or regret. Salvation may open the door, but readiness determines whether we walk through it when He returns.

It was a quiet evening in the study. Irene's Bible lay open before her, its well-worn pages catching the soft glow of lamplight. I sat across from her, the silence wrapped in a sense of urgency I couldn't shake.

Irene furrowed her brows, her eyes scanning the familiar text.

"Ann," she asked softly, "why did Jesus tell the story of the ten virgins? What was He warning us about?"

I turned the thin pages of my Bible, stopping at Matthew 25.

"It's a prophetic parable, Irene," I said gently.

"And it's not about unbelievers. It's about those who are waiting for the Bridegroom—those who call themselves part of the Church. All ten virgins were invited. All were expecting Him. But only five were truly ready."

Irene looked up, puzzled. "But they were all virgins. That sounds like believers, doesn't it? Why were half of them shut out?"

I met her gaze, voice solemn. "Because having a lamp isn't enough. They had the appearance of devotion—a form of godliness—but no flame. No oil. The oil represents the indwelling presence of the Holy Spirit. Real intimacy with Christ."

I paused. "Five lived ready. Five only looked the part."

Irene's voice was soft, almost disbelieving.

"And they all fell asleep? Even the wise?"

"Yes," I said.

"Sleep isn't the issue in the parable. Life is exhausting—anyone can grow tired. But when the cry goes out, the question is this: Is your lamp still full?"

I leaned forward. "The midnight cry doesn't allow time to scramble. When the trumpet sounds, we rise based on what we've already prepared—not on what we meant to do later."

Irene's voice dropped, thoughtful.

"And the foolish ones tried to borrow oil from the wise . . ."

I shook my head. "But they couldn't, Irene. Spiritual preparedness can't be borrowed. It's not transferable."

I leaned in gently. "I can pray for you, cheer you on, teach you the truth—but I can't hand you my obedience. I can't surrender on your behalf. Every heart must carry its own oil."

Irene's eyes brimmed with tears. "What happened to them, Ann? The ones who came back with oil—but too late?"

My voice was tender, but resolute. "The door was shut, Irene. Just like in the days of Noah. Mercy had waited—but the moment passed. They cried out, 'Lord, Lord, open to us!' But He answered, 'I never knew you.'"

Irene's whisper trembled.

"But . . . they were waiting for Him. How could He say that?"

I nodded gently. "But they didn't know Him—not in intimacy, not in surrender. They admired Him, maybe even believed in Him, but never gave Him their hearts. And He's not coming for spectators. He's coming for a Bride—one who knows Him deeply, loves Him fully, and burns with longing for His return."

Irene's voice caught in her throat. "Then . . . this is a warning to the Church?"

"It's a mercy to the Church," I said softly. "A final wake-up call. It's Jesus, standing at the door, urging us to check our lamps now—to fill them, to trim the wicks. The time to prepare is before the cry rings out."

Irene clutched her Bible close.

"Ann . . . are we already in that midnight hour?"

I turned to the window, where twilight had swallowed the last sliver of light.

"I believe we are," I whispered.

"And the cry is closer than we dare to imagine."

A quiet hush settled over the room as Irene closed her Bible halfway, her brow furrowed in contemplation. She looked up, her voice tinged with both curiosity and conviction.

Irene said softly, "Ann, I've been reading through Matthew 24, and one parable stopped me cold. It's the one about the faithful and evil servants. Jesus said something about a servant being blessed if his master finds him working when he returns. It hit me hard—like He's talking directly to us. Why does that line carry so much weight?"

I leaned forward, my tone both steady and stirring.

"Because it's personal—and prophetic. That parable isn't just about two servants—it's about two heart conditions. Jesus is painting a picture of what the Church will look like when He returns. Some will be watching and working . . . and others will be wandering and wasting time."

Irene leaned back slightly, her expression tinged with concern and a hint of disbelief. "Isn't it a bit extreme, though? I mean, the master just delays. And the unfaithful servant starts acting out. But who would behave that way just because of a delay?"

My eyes held a quiet depth as I leaned forward, my words deliberate and full of insight. "You'd be surprised. Delay reveals what urgency conceals. When people think the Master is coming soon, they stay alert. But when He tarries, motives surface. That's what Jesus is exposing. The faithful servant doesn't need a countdown clock to stay committed. His or her obedience isn't driven by fear—it's fueled by love."

Irene tilted her head thoughtfully, the realization dawning slowly.

"So watching doesn't mean staring at the sky. It means doing what we were called to do—consistently?"

A soft smile tugged at the corners of my lips as I responded, my voice steady and full of conviction. "Exactly. Watching is working. Waiting is worshiping. The faithful servant keeps feeding the household—spiritually and practically—

because he or she knows the Master is good, even if He seems slow. That's faith in action."

Irene's brow furrowed as she traced the passage with her finger, the weight of Jesus' words pressing in. "But why did Jesus say the evil servant begins to smite his fellow servants and eat and drink with the drunken? That feels like more than laziness."

My expression grew solemn. My voice carried the gravity of truth. "Because spiritual apathy leads to spiritual abuse. When people no longer believe Jesus is coming soon, they turn inward. Their authority becomes selfish. Their words become sharp. They stop building the kingdom and start building their own. That's the danger of delay—it doesn't just dull our senses, it can harden our hearts."

Irene leaned back in her chair, a thoughtful look settling on her face as the truth began to take deeper root.

She said quietly, "So the point of the parable isn't timing . . . it's posture."

A gentle smile touched my lips, my eyes soft with agreement.

"Beautifully said. It's about the posture of our hearts. Jesus never asked us to calculate the day. He told us to live every day like it could be the day. That's what it means to be ready."

Irene's voice trembled slightly as she asked, her Bible resting in her lap.

"And when He does come—what happens?"

My tone was firm but compassionate, my eyes steady as I answered with conviction. "The faithful are rewarded. The unfaithful are removed. It's sobering. But it's merciful. Because right now, we still have time to choose which servant we want to be."

With quiet resolve, Irene said, "Then I want to be the one He finds working."

Gently, but with unwavering urgency, I replied, "Then stay faithful. Stay awake. Stay ready—even while the Master delays."

CHAPTER SUMMARY

Chapter 2 explores one of the most sobering and clarifying themes in Scripture: not all who profess faith in Christ will be taken in the Rapture. It draws a necessary and often overlooked distinction between salvation by grace and the call to live in faithful, obedient readiness. While salvation is a free gift, the Rapture is portrayed throughout Scripture as a reward for the watchful and faithful Bride—those who live in spiritual alertness, purity, and submission to Christ.

The chapter begins by exposing a tragic reality: millions who believe they are ready will be left behind. Using both warnings from Jesus and the epistles, the text lays out ten biblical categories of people who, unless they repent and walk in obedience, are in danger of missing the Rapture. These include the fearful, the unbelieving, the abominable, murderers (including those with hatred in their hearts), the sexually immoral (whoremongers), sorcerers, dogs (morally depraved), idolaters, liars, and the idle (spiritually unproductive).

Each group is unpacked with scriptural insight, not for condemnation but as a loving warning. The chapter stresses that the issue is not momentary failure or struggle—but persistent rebellion, unrepentant hearts, and lifestyles that contradict the holiness of God. These are not hypothetical people—they are real, living today, many in churches, assuming they are safe while spiritually asleep.

The chapter concludes with a passionate call to self-examination: "Am I truly ready?" Not merely saved, but living as one who longs for His appearing. It emphasizes that the Bride of Christ is not marked by perfection but by preparation—daily repentance, intimacy with God, and detachment from the world. Scripture is clear: the Rapture is not a participation trophy; it is a call to the faithful remnant.

KEY TAKEAWAYS

- Salvation is by grace through faith—but readiness for the Rapture requires obedience, holiness, and spiritual watchfulness.
- The Bible warns that many will be left behind—not because God is unloving, but because they rejected His call to repent and be transformed.
- There are biblical categories of people who live in unrepentant rebellion—including those trapped in fear, unbelief, sexual immorality, deception, idolatry, and spiritual laziness.
- The Rapture is for the Bride—those who are watching, waiting, and walking in righteousness.
- The ultimate question is not just "Am I saved?" but "Am I ready to meet Him?"

This chapter reminds us that while salvation is a free gift through faith in Jesus Christ, the Rapture is a reward for those who live ready—walking in obedience, repentance, and intimacy with the Lord. It challenges readers to ask not just, "Am I saved?" but "Am I ready?" The difference is not minor—it's eternal. Those with full lamps and surrendered hearts will be caught up in glory. Those who neglect the call may be left behind—not for lack of God's love, but for lack of preparation. The time to choose wholehearted devotion is now.

Chapter 3

The Gospel of the Kingdom
at the Heart of Eternity

A KINGDOM WARNING UNVEILED—For many, the Gospel is narrowly understood as a message of personal salvation—a means of escape from sin and death. And while that is gloriously true, it is not the whole picture. The Gospel of the Kingdom is a broader, deeper, and more prophetic message. It is not just about being saved—it's about stepping into the rule and reign of a coming King. It is not only the invitation to eternal life—but the proclamation of an eternal government that is already advancing.

The Kingdom of God is not merely a future realm; it is a present reality breaking into our world—and a future certainty that will soon shake every nation.

> And this Gospel of the Kingdom shall be preached in all the world for a witness unto all nations; and then shall the end come. (Matthew 24:14)

In this chapter, we pivot from the personal to the cosmic—from the doorway of salvation to the panoramic view of God's unfolding redemptive plan. Jesus didn't just offer people a ticket to Heaven. He announced a coming kingdom. He spoke of a realm where righteousness reigns, where justice flows like a river, and where every prophecy will be fulfilled to the letter.

This is the Gospel He preached from the beginning of His ministry—and it is the Gospel that must be preached until the end comes.

But here lies the great tragedy of our time: many—even within the Church—know the Savior, but not the King. They've heard of grace, but not of government. They've prayed the sinner's prayer, but have never been discipled in what it means to live as citizens of a kingdom that is not of this world.

To understand the Gospel fully, we must reclaim the kingdom lens—not as a metaphor, but as a divine mandate. The Gospel of the Kingdom calls us to surrender, to allegiance, to watchfulness. It demands not just a confession of faith, but a readiness to reign with Christ.

THE MISSING GOSPEL

In churches across the globe, from towering cathedrals to country chapels, the Gospel has been preached with passion and conviction. The message has echoed through centuries: *Jesus saves*. And indeed, He does. This is the core of the Gospel of Salvation—the blessed assurance that Christ died for our sins, was buried, and rose again, offering eternal life to all who believe.

But while this Gospel has brought multitudes to the foot of the Cross, there remains a deeper call—one that many have never heard. It is the message Jesus preached not only at the end of His earthly ministry, but from the very beginning. It is the Gospel of the Kingdom—a message not merely of rescue, but of rule. Not just of forgiveness, but of transformation through formation—a life re-shaped by the priorities of the King. Not only of going to Heaven someday, but of preparing to inherit and participate in a divine kingdom that is even now advancing upon the earth.

A Narrowed Gospel

How did we end up with a Gospel that focuses primarily on individual salvation, while neglecting the broader kingdom narrative?

The answer lies in what we've emphasized. Over the last two centuries—especially in Western evangelical traditions—the message of the Cross has often been distilled into a personal decision: *accept Jesus into your heart and be saved*. This simplification, while useful in evangelistic settings, has had unintended consequences. It has turned the Gospel into a transaction—pray this prayer, secure your eternal destiny—while sidelining the transformational call to live under the reign of the King.

The result? Millions of Christians who know they are "saved" but have little understanding of what they've been saved for. They've entered the doorway of faith, but never explored the house of the kingdom.

What Jesus Really Preached

Consider the first public words of Jesus:

> From that time Jesus began to preach, and to say, Repent: for the Kingdom of Heaven is at hand. (Matthew 4:17)

When He sent out His disciples, He told them to preach the Kingdom of God and heal the sick (Luke 9:2). In His parables, sermons, and final conversations before the Cross, the kingdom was always central.

> And He sent them to preach the Kingdom of God, and to heal the sick. (Luke 9:2)

To Jesus, the kingdom wasn't a vague idea or a far-off hope—it was the very reality He came to inaugurate. It was a government, a realm, a way of life. And He wasn't just calling people to believe in Him; He was inviting them to surrender to His kingship, to be trained for future responsibility, to live now as citizens of the age to come.

The Kingdom Gospel vs. the Salvation Gospel

Let's be clear: the Gospel of Salvation and the Gospel of the Kingdom are not contradictory—they are complementary. The Gospel of Salvation is the entry point into the kingdom. It deals with the heart, the cleansing of sin, the reconciliation between man and God. But the Gospel of the Kingdom answers a different question: *Now that I'm saved, what am I saved for?* It is about discipleship, rulership, readiness, and the fulfillment of God's cosmic redemptive plan.

- The Gospel of Salvation focuses on the Cross.
- The Gospel of the Kingdom includes the Cross, but points us also to the crown—eternal rewards granted at the Judgment Seat of Christ.

- The Gospel of Salvation prepares us to escape wrath.
- The Gospel of the Kingdom prepares us to inherit responsibility.

- The Gospel of Salvation is about redemption.
- The Gospel of the Kingdom is about reign.

When we preach only the salvation side of the Gospel, we prepare people for Heaven—but we do not prepare them for the return of the King.

Why We've Missed It

The missing Gospel has been eclipsed for many reasons—some theological, some cultural. A fear of sounding "works-based" has led some to avoid any mention of obedience, sanctification, or judgment. Others have avoided end-time themes due to controversy or confusion. Still others have become so earthly-minded—focused on societal change or moral improvement—that they've forgotten the kingdom is not of this world.

> Jesus answered, My Kingdom is not of this world: if My Kingdom were of this world, then would My servants fight, that I should not be delivered to the Jews: but now is My Kingdom not from here. (John 18:36)

But the greatest reason may simply be this: we have not studied what Jesus preached. We've read Paul's letters more than Christ's parables. We've built systems of doctrine, but neglected the narrative of Scripture that centers around a coming kingdom. And in doing so, we've raised a generation that knows how to "get saved," but not how to be faithful.

Why This Matters Now

The absence of the Kingdom Gospel has left the Church unprepared. We are nearing the midnight cry, and many have lamps but no oil. They have said yes to the Savior, but have not submitted to the King. They've heard about grace, but not judgment. They've memorized verses about love, but have skipped the warnings about apostasy, falling away, and the testing of the saints.

Jesus is coming—not just to rescue His people, but to establish His government. He will rule the nations with a rod of iron. He will sit on the throne of David. And those who are faithful will reign with Him.

The Gospel of the Kingdom is not a fringe message. It is the final call of Heaven. It is the missing key that makes sense of all the harbingers, prophecies, and divine shakings. Without it, the Church drifts into complacency. With it, the Church awakens to its true identity as the Bride who is making herself ready.

WHAT IS THE GOSPEL OF THE KINGDOM?

To understand the Gospel of the Kingdom, we must return not only to the words of Jesus—but to the overarching narrative of Scripture itself. From Genesis to Revelation, the Bible is not just the story of redemption—it is the unveiling of a kingdom: a realm where God rules, where righteousness reigns, and where His will is done on earth as it is in Heaven.

While the Gospel of Salvation focuses on how we are rescued *from* sin, death, and separation from God, the Gospel of the Kingdom declares what we are rescued *for*—namely, citizenship in a divine monarchy under the lordship of Jesus Christ, the rightful King.

The Message Jesus Preached

Jesus didn't just preach a message about dying for our sins. He proclaimed:

> Repent: for the Kingdom of Heaven is at hand. (Matthew 4:17)

This was not a vague spiritual idea. The Jews of His day understood "kingdom" to mean a government—a coming reign where the Messiah would rule from Jerusalem, bring justice to the earth, and restore what was lost in Eden. And Jesus confirmed that very expectation. He spoke of thrones, of authority, of servants entrusted with tasks, and of a final day when the King returns to settle accounts (Matthew 25).

A Distinct Message with a Broader Scope

The Gospel of the Kingdom is not a replacement of the Gospel of Salvation—it is the completion of it. Salvation is the doorway. The kingdom is the destination.

Let's look at the distinction more closely:

Gospel of Salvation	Gospel of the Kingdom
Centers on the Cross	Centers on the crown
Forgiveness of sins	Alignment with God's rulership
Focused on individuals	Focused on nations and governance
Emphasizes justification by faith	Emphasizes obedience and stewardship
Entry point into eternal life	Training ground for eternal inheritance
Prepares for Heaven	Prepares for reigning with Christ

The Gospel of Salvation is crucial. Without it, no man can enter the kingdom. But many have stopped at the gate. They have received the invitation to the wedding banquet—but have never prepared for the coming of the Bridegroom, or embraced their role in the coming kingdom.

A Kingdom Now—and Not Yet

Jesus taught that the Kingdom of God is both already and not yet.

> And when He was demanded of the Pharisees, when the Kingdom of God should come, He answered them and said, The Kingdom of God comes not with observation: Neither shall they say, See here!, or See there! For, behold, the Kingdom of God is within you. (Luke 17:20–21)

In this age, the kingdom is spiritual—it lives inside of us. It transforms hearts. It advances through the faithful witness of believers, through righteousness, peace, and joy in the Holy Spirit (Romans 14:17). But that is only Act One.

> For the Kingdom of God is not eat and drink; but righteousness, and peace, and joy in the Holy Ghost. (Romans 14:17)

The final act is yet to come.

And the seventh angel sounded; and there were great voices in heaven, saying,
The kingdoms of this world are become the kingdoms of the Lord, and of His
Christ; and He shall reign forever and ever. (Revelation 11:15)

In the end, the spiritual kingdom will manifest in physical dominion. Jesus
will return not just as Savior, but as Sovereign. The King of kings. The Lord of
lords. He will crush the kingdoms of men, judge the nations, and sit on David's
throne in Jerusalem (Isaiah 9:6–7; Luke 1:32–33).

Why It's Been Overlooked

Many believers haven't been taught this Kingdom Gospel for a simple reason: it
requires more. It's not just about receiving grace—it's about responding to a King.
It calls us to deny ourselves, take up our cross daily, live in holiness, serve in
humility, and wait in expectation.

The Gospel of the Kingdom brings comfort—but also confrontation. It
comforts the faithful and confronts the complacent. It promises inheritance, but
warns of judgment. It unveils our blessed hope, but demands a present obedience.

A Call to Readiness

The Kingdom Gospel is the fuel behind every prophetic harbinger we will soon
explore. Every sign, every shaking, every heavenly trumpet, every Shemitah
cycle—they are not random. They are kingdom calls. Trumpets of awakening.
Echoes of a soon-returning King.

This Gospel is not just for the lost. It is a witness to the nations. A divine
notice that a government is coming. A King is returning. And He is not just saving
souls—He is establishing dominion.

SALVATION OPENS THE DOOR—
BUT THE KINGDOM REQUIRES OBEDIENCE

In chapter 2, we explored the Gospel of Salvation—the glorious truth that we are
saved by grace through faith in Jesus Christ. We saw how salvation is the
undeserved gift of God, not earned by works, but received by believing in the
redemptive work of the Cross. The gospel offers the miracle of a new birth,
forgiveness of sins, and the assurance of eternal life. It is the doorway through
which we are welcomed into God's family. But as incredible and essential as that
first step is, the Bible reveals something more—something deeper and more
expansive. The Gospel of the Kingdom doesn't just begin with salvation; it *builds*
upon it.

Salvation is the entrance; the kingdom is the journey.

It's easy to stop at the threshold. Many have heard the message of salvation: confess your sins, believe in Jesus, and be saved. And that message is true. But if we stop there, we risk missing the larger purpose for which we were saved in the first place. The Gospel of the Kingdom picks up where the Gospel of Salvation leaves off. It is not about *how* to be saved—it is about *why* we were saved. We are not merely rescued from Hell; we are recruited into a kingdom. A kingdom that is not just spiritual, but political. Not just personal, but cosmic. A kingdom that demands obedience, allegiance, and daily surrender to the rule of the King.

Jesus preached this kingdom relentlessly. "Repent: for the Kingdom of Heaven is at hand" (Matthew 4:17). His parables described its mystery. His miracles revealed its power. His Sermon on the Mount explained its ethics. And His Great Commission charged us to carry its message—not just to make converts, but disciples. The Gospel of the Kingdom is the announcement that the government of God is breaking into human history, and that citizenship in this kingdom requires transformation of life, not mere recitation of belief.

That's why Jesus said:

And why call you Me, Lord, Lord, and do not the things which I say? (Luke 6:46)

The kingdom is not inherited through casual belief—it is entered through costly obedience. It's not about having a ticket to Heaven in our back pocket. It's about being conformed into the image of the King—living now under His rule, walking in His ways, bearing His fruit.

Obedience is not legalism—it's love in action. Jesus said:

If you love Me, keep My commandments. (John 14:15)

True faith produces faithfulness. And while salvation is the free gift of grace, the kingdom is where that grace is tested, matured, and displayed. The Gospel of Salvation secures our *position* as children of God; the Gospel of the Kingdom shapes our *posture* as servants and citizens.

Paul echoed this truth when he wrote:

For we are His workmanship, created in Christ Jesus unto good works, which God has before ordained that we should walk in them. (Ephesians 2:10)

Notice the flow: salvation is by grace, but it is unto good works. Works don't *save* us—but once we are saved, they are the evidence that we are no longer living for ourselves. We are living for the kingdom. That is the fruit Jesus is looking for at His return.

This is also why the warnings of Scripture are so weighty. Many will say, "Lord, Lord," but only those who *do* the will of the Father will enter the Kingdom of Heaven (Matthew 7:21). It's not enough to look the part, speak the right language, or attend the right services. The kingdom requires more than appearance—it demands allegiance.

So what does this mean practically? It means we must examine our lives. Have we stopped at the doorway of salvation, content with being "in," but never submitting to the King? Have we responded to the invitation but ignored the instructions? Have we celebrated grace but resisted surrender?

The Gospel of Salvation is a beautiful beginning. But it's not the whole story. The Gospel of the Kingdom is the unfolding of that story—God's plan to establish His rule in us and through us, and ultimately across the entire earth. And for that, He is looking for citizens who will not only believe, but obey.

This is where chapter 2 and chapter 3 converge: Salvation gets us in the door. The kingdom shows us how to live once we're inside. The first gives us life. The second demands that we *lay it down*.

The invitation remains open. But the call is not merely to be saved—it is to follow the King, carry the cross, and live with kingdom purpose until He returns in glory.

THE KINGDOM MESSAGE OF JESUS

When we look closely at the teachings of Jesus in the Gospels, one message rises above all others: the Kingdom of God. From His very first sermon—"Repent: for the Kingdom of Heaven is at hand" (Matthew 4:17)—to His final words to His disciples after the resurrection (Acts 1:3), Jesus consistently and unmistakably focused on proclaiming the Gospel of the Kingdom. Remarkably, Jesus only rarely used the word "salvation" in His teachings. Instead, He spoke over and over again of the kingdom—what it is, how it grows, who will enter, who will be cast out, and what it demands.

This was not by accident.

The Kingdom of God was central to His message because it was central to His mission. He came not merely to forgive sin but to *establish rule*. Salvation is the entry point, but the kingdom is the destination. Jesus didn't call people simply to escape judgment—He called them to follow Him, to live under His lordship, and to become citizens of an eternal kingdom that operates under an entirely different authority than the kingdoms of this world.

He illustrated the kingdom with parables. He demonstrated its power through miracles. He described it as a treasure hidden in a field, a pearl of great price, a mustard seed that grows, a net that fathers fish of every kind, a banquet for which many are invited. Again, He warned that not everyone who says, "Lord, Lord" will enter it, but only those who *do* the will of His Father (Matthew 7:21).

The language of salvation—being born again, having your sins forgiven, receiving eternal life—is precious and true. But it is nested within the broader call to *kingdom living*. Jesus was not recruiting church members—He was raising ambassadors, warriors, and servants of a coming government that would one day rule the earth in righteousness.

And this Gospel of the Kingdom is the one Jesus said must be preached in all the world *before* the end would come (Matthew 24:14). That means if we've only preached salvation without kingdom, we've preached only part of His message.

Understanding this difference is not a theological luxury—it is a prophetic necessity. Because the King is returning. And He is not just coming for believers. He is coming to *rule*. And He is coming for those whose lives have been shaped by that rule even now.

Irene flipped slowly through the worn pages of her Bible, her brow furrowed in thought. "Ann, I read something this morning that completely stopped me. Just one verse. Short, almost forgettable—but it's been echoing in my heart all day."

I looked up with a knowing smile. "Let me guess . . . one of Jesus' parables?"

> Again, the Kingdom of Heaven is like unto treasure hid in a field; the which when a man has found, he hides, and for joy thereof goes and sells all that he has, and buys that field. (Matthew 13:44)

"That one."

I nodded slowly, a quiet reverence rising in my chest. "Ah . . . the parable of the hidden treasure. Just one verse—and yet it holds the weight of eternity. One of the most powerful one-liners in all of Scripture."

Irene leaned forward, eyes narrowing with thought. "That's what got me! It's just one verse, but it holds so much. I kept wondering . . . What exactly *is* the treasure? And who's the man finding it?"

I smiled. "Beautiful questions, Irene."

"Like many of Jesus' parables, this one works on more than one level. On the surface, yes—the treasure is the Kingdom of Heaven: the reign of God, the gift of salvation, the righteousness found only in Christ. The field? That's the world. And the man . . . well, that's where it gets interesting. He could be any of us—recognizing the worth of the kingdom and gladly giving up everything to gain it. But others see the man as Jesus Himself."

I paused, letting the weight of that truth settle.

"Jesus—who gave all He had, even His life, to redeem the world . . . to purchase the field just to claim the treasure He saw in it."

"Wait—Jesus?" Irene tilted her head. "I always thought the man represented the believer. Someone who discovers the kingdom and gives up everything to have it."

I leaned in, nodding gently. "That's absolutely one valid and powerful interpretation. When we truly catch a glimpse of the kingdom's worth—salvation, yes, but also intimacy with Christ, the call to purpose, the promise of eternity—we're compelled to surrender everything else. Not out of obligation, but out of joy. Because we've found a treasure that outshines every earthly gain. That kind of response? That's the heart of a disciple."

I paused and added, softly, "It's what Paul meant when he said, 'I count all things but loss . . . that I may win Christ.'"

"But if the man is Jesus?" Irene whispered.

I smiled, my voice softening. "Then the story becomes even more staggering. It means *we* are the treasure—hidden in a broken world, buried beneath the dirt of sin and time. And Jesus . . . He saw what others overlooked. For the joy set before Him, He endured the Cross. He gave everything—His blood, His life—to buy the whole field just to claim what was precious to Him."

I paused, letting it sink in.

"That's how valuable you are to Him, Irene. That's how valuable we all are."

Irene's eyes widened. "That gives me chills. Either way—the man is us or it's Jesus—the cost is everything. And either way . . . it's worth it."

I nodded, my voice low with conviction. "Exactly. The kingdom isn't a feature we add to our schedule—it's the framework that redefines our entire existence. It demands our comfort, our control, even our cultural attachments at times. But once we glimpse its beauty—its unshakable glory and eternal weight—surrender isn't a sacrifice anymore. It's joy."

Irene, quietly. "And the man was joyful. That part struck me the most. He didn't sell everything reluctantly. He wasn't bitter about the cost—he was thrilled. Like he knew he was finally getting what he was born for."

I smiled. "That's key. The kingdom doesn't rob us—it releases us. Joy is the evidence that we've found something real. It's not a painful transaction—it's the overflow of revelation. When the eyes of our heart are opened, surrender becomes a delight, not a burden."

"It makes me think . . . how many people go to church their whole lives but never dig deep enough to find the treasure?"

I nodded slowly. "That's the tragedy, Irene. The treasure is there—hidden in plain sight, even wrapped in familiar words and rituals. But it takes hunger to seek it, humility to admit we don't already possess it, and a heart willing to trade the comfortable for the eternal. Many settle for surface faith, never realizing the field holds something priceless."

Irene sighed. "So the parable is both an invitation and a challenge?"

I nodded. "Yes. It invites us to search—with hunger, with hope—and challenges us to surrender. To loosen our grip on what we once thought mattered and ask: Have I truly found the treasure? And more than that—have I let go of everything else to make it mine?"

Irene, thoughtfully. "I want to live like someone who's found the treasure."

I leaned in, smiling. "Then live joyfully surrendered, fully devoted, and eternally minded. Let the world see a life re-ordered by something eternal. The field may seem ordinary—but hidden within it is the Kingdom of God. And He's worth everything."

Irene leaned back, Bible open in her lap. "Ann, I kept reading in Matthew 13. Right after the treasure in the field, Jesus tells another short parable. It felt so connected—like a twin in meaning, but with a different facet of truth."

I smiled knowingly. "Ah, the pearl of great price?"

> Again, the Kingdom of Heaven is like unto a merchant man, seeking goodly pearls: who, when he had found one pearl of great price, went and sold all that he had, and bought it. (Matthew 13:45–46)

"Yes. It's almost the same structure as the treasure in the field—but it feels different."

I nodded. "It is. They echo each other, but this one brings a different angle. In the hidden treasure, the man stumbles upon something he wasn't even looking for. But in the pearl of great price, the merchant is intentionally seeking. He knows value when he sees it—and he recognizes the one thing that surpasses all others. That's the kingdom."

"So it's not just a random person stumbling into faith—it's someone *deliberately* searching?"

"Exactly," I nodded. "This is the seeker. The hungry heart that's wandered through religion, chased after philosophy, maybe even tasted success—yet still feels empty. And then . . . they find it. The kingdom. The one thing that truly satisfies. A pearl so pure, so valuable, that nothing else compares. They'd give it all up for that one treasure—and they do."

Irene spoke softly. "And just like in the treasure parable, the merchant gives up everything to have it."

I nodded. "Yes. Because the kingdom isn't just one more thing to acquire—it's the *one* thing that demands everything. You can't cling to old treasures and fully embrace the new. The kingdom resets our priorities, rewrites our identity, and redefines what truly matters. Once you've seen its worth, nothing else holds the same shine."

Irene leaned in, thoughtful. "What strikes me is that both men in the parables give up everything with joy. But the pearl . . . there's something different about it. Pearls are formed through irritation, right? Through pressure?"

I smiled, touched by her insight. "That's a beautiful observation, Irene. Yes—pearls are born from discomfort. When a tiny grain of sand wounds the oyster, it responds not with rejection, but with transformation. It coats the irritation layer by layer until what once caused pain becomes something precious. A pearl is beauty born from suffering."

"So the kingdom—this precious pearl—it came at great cost?"

I nodded slowly. "Indeed. It cost Jesus everything—His suffering, His blood, His life. That's what makes the kingdom so beautiful: it's not just precious, it's redemptive. It was born of pain—His pain—but it transforms our pain into something glorious."

I paused, letting it settle in the air.

"And now, to make it ours, we lay everything down. Not to buy it—no one can afford that—but to receive it fully, unhindered, unentangled. We surrender not out of obligation, but because we've seen the surpassing worth."

Irene paused, her voice barely above a whisper. "It makes me think . . . how many of us are still clinging to lesser pearls?"

I nodded, my tone soft but sure. "Too many. Pearls of ambition, of comfort, of applause or control. They catch the light, but they don't carry life. They promise fulfillment, but they fade. Only the pearl of the kingdom—pure, living, eternal—is worth everything."

Irene whispered, "And once we see it for what it is . . . nothing else compares."

I nodded slowly. "That's the miracle. The kingdom doesn't just ask for sacrifice—it offers joy in return. Eternal joy. The merchant didn't hesitate or bargain. He saw the pearl, recognized its worth, and surrendered everything—gladly. No regret, only rejoicing. That's the posture of a heart awakened by grace—it doesn't cling, it releases. Because it's seen the real thing."

Irene whispered, "So the question for us is . . . have we truly seen the pearl clearly enough to surrender everything else?"

I nodded. "Because when we do—really do—there's no hesitation. The kingdom becomes the only treasure worth having, the only pearl worth keeping, the only pursuit that makes every other dream feel small by comparison."

Irene shook her head.

"Then I want to be that kind of seeker—not just someone who finds the pearl, but someone who's changed by it."

I smiled gently. "And that's exactly what the King is looking for—hearts that treasure Him above all. Because to find the kingdom is to find the King."

Irene flipped pages in her Bible thoughtfully. "Ann, I was reading further into Matthew 13 and paused at the parable of the mustard seed. Jesus says the Kingdom of Heaven is like a grain of mustard seed that a man took and sowed in his field. It grows into a tree so large that birds come and nest in its branches."

> Another parable put He forth unto them, saying, The Kingdom of Heaven is like to a grain of mustard seed, which a man took, and sowed in his field. Which indeed is the least of all seeds: but when it is grown, it is the greatest among herbs, and becomes a tree, so that the birds of the air come and lodge in the branches thereof. (Matthew 13:31–32)

I leaned in with a knowing smile. "Ah, the mustard seed—so tiny, almost invisible. And yet, Jesus says it becomes something far greater than its size would suggest. It's one of the most vivid pictures of the kingdom's growth—starting in obscurity, but destined for overwhelming impact."

"That's what I always thought too," Irene said slowly. "That the Gospel started small—with Jesus and a handful of disciples—and then spread across the world."

I nodded thoughtfully. "That's certainly one layer. The kingdom does begin humbly and expands dramatically. But have you ever paused to ask—why a mustard seed? Jesus was intentional with His imagery. Mustard plants don't usually grow into trees. They're more like oversized bushes."

I glanced at her with meaning. "So when Jesus says this seed becomes a *tree*—that's unusual. Maybe even a clue that He's pointing to something more."

Irene's eyes narrowed with curiosity. "Wait—you're right. Mustard seeds don't grow into towering trees. And birds coming to nest in the branches . . . that seems unusual too."

I leaned forward, voice low. "Exactly. That detail isn't just poetic—it's a red flag. In Scripture, especially in the Old Testament, large trees are often symbolic of powerful world empires—think of Babylon in Daniel 4, or Assyria in Ezekiel 31. These trees stretch wide, offer shelter, but they're also full of pride and excess."

I paused. "And the birds? In several places, birds represent spiritual entities—sometimes even demonic influences or agents of corruption. So when Jesus mentions them lodging in the branches, it may be His way of saying: the kingdom's outward expansion might also attract things that don't belong."

Irene's voice soft. "So are you saying this parable might be a warning too?"

I nodded slowly. "Yes. It's both a promise and a prophetic insight. On the one hand, the kingdom begins in obscurity—small, humble, pure. Just a mustard seed. But as it grows, especially through history and institutional power, it becomes something far more complex."

I glanced at her. "The growth isn't the issue. God intended the kingdom to spread. But when that growth turns into something unnatural—like a mustard plant becoming a towering tree—we have to ask: What else has taken root?"

Irene leaned in, eyes thoughtful.

I continued. "It starts as a movement of the Spirit. But over time, it can morph into machinery—systems, politics, and worldly influence. That's when the birds come. And not all of them are innocent. Some represent spiritual distortion, even demonic infiltration."

Irene shook her head slowly. "That makes so much sense, Ann. We've watched Christianity expand into a global institution—cathedrals, denominations, political clout, media empires. But somewhere along the way, it doesn't always resemble the heart of Christ."

I nodded. "And that's the mustard tree in full view. What started small and sacred has grown—yes—but in some cases, it's grown strange. It's branches now hold many things, and not all of them belong. Some birds carry peace. Others bring poison."

I met her eyes. "That's why discernment is so critical in these last days. Growth alone isn't the metric of God's blessing. Just because something is big, influential, or applauded doesn't mean it's aligned with the kingdom. The question is: Does it reflect the King?"

"So Jesus wasn't just celebrating kingdom growth—He was cautioning us to watch what that growth produces?"

I nodded slowly. "Exactly. Because true kingdom growth still looks like Jesus—it's humble, holy, Spirit-led. It doesn't just expand wide; it roots deep. It purifies as it multiplies. And it doesn't welcome every 'bird' into its branches. There's discernment. There's fruit inspection. Because not all growth is godly— and not all influence is kingdom."

Irene reflected quietly. "So we should be asking . . . what kind of kingdom are we building? Are we rooted in the humble bush—or caught in the shadow of the bloated tree?"

I answered softly. "That's exactly the question. The goal isn't growth for growth's sake—it's godliness. Influence isn't the aim—intimacy is. The true kingdom doesn't just spread outward—it must first take root within us. That's the miracle of the mustard seed: small faith, deeply planted, bearing eternal fruit."

Irene nodded slowly. "A small seed of obedience can grow into something beautiful . . . but if we lose the purity, even beauty can become a burden."

I met her gaze. "Exactly. That's why Jesus gave us parables—not to celebrate size, but to caution us about substance. What matters most is this: Does the King still rule the soil of our hearts?"

Irene, reading softly from her Bible. "Ann, listen to this—"

> Again, the Kingdom of Heaven is like unto a net, that was cast into the sea, and gathered of every kind: Which, when it was full, they drew to shore, and sat down, and gathered the good into vessels. But cast the bad away. So shall it be at the end of the world: the angels shall come forth, and sever the wicked from among the just, And shall cast them into the furnace of fire: there shall be wailing and gnashing of teeth. (Matthew 13:47–50)

I looked up, my voice quiet. "Yes . . . the parable of the dragnet. It's one of the most sobering images Jesus ever gave. Like the wheat and tares, it brings us face to face with the final harvest—when every life is drawn in, and judgment begins."

Irene's eyes lingered on the page. "It feels so relevant. The net is cast so wide—gathering all kinds. That's the Gospel, isn't it? The invitation is universal."

I nodded slowly. "Exactly. The sea represents the world. And the net? It's the message of the kingdom—the Gospel sweeping across nations, cultures, languages. No one is excluded. The call goes out to everyone: the broken and the proud, the repentant and the religious, the sincere and the self-deceived."

Irene's eyes widened.

"So we're all caught up in this net. But not everyone stays?"

I nodded solemnly. "That's right. The gathering isn't the final verdict—it's just the beginning. The real moment comes at the sorting. Jesus is warning us that being *in the net*—being around the things of God, even part of the visible Church—doesn't guarantee we're *in the kingdom*. There's a divine separation coming. The righteous will be gathered like treasures into vessels. But the false, the corrupt, the unchanged—they'll be cast away."

Irene voice caught. "But what makes some good or bad, Ann? They were all in the same net. They all heard the message."

I looked at her with quiet sorrow. "That's the heartbreaking part, Irene. They all heard . . . but not all responded with surrender. Some came close—so close—but never truly let go. Never truly allowed the Gospel to transform them."

I paused, then continued gently. "The difference isn't in who heard—it's in who yielded. It's the fruit of repentance. A life of obedience. Authenticity before God. Not perfection, but direction. God sees the heart. And the angels—the reapers Jesus spoke of—will carry out the sorting with perfect justice. No one will be misplaced. No one will be misjudged."

Irene whispered, "It's terrifying. And yet . . . it's merciful, isn't it?"

I nodded, voice soft but resolute. "Yes. That's what makes this parable so powerful. The judgment is certain—but it hasn't happened yet. The net is still in the water. The invitation is still open."

I leaned forward gently. "There's still time to repent. Still time to move from borrowed belief to genuine surrender. From lip service to living faith. This parable doesn't just warn us—it woos us. It's Jesus pleading with us to be real. To come clean before God, while the net is still gathering and the shore is still a distance away."

Irene nodded, her voice trembling. "Jesus said the bad are thrown into the furnace of fire. That's not metaphor, is it?"

I shook my head slowly, my tone solemn. "No, Irene. It's not. He meant every word. 'There shall be wailing and gnashing of teeth.'"

I paused, letting the words settle. "That phrase isn't poetic flourish—it's prophetic warning. Jesus used it multiple times, always in the context of final judgment. He wasn't exaggerating to scare us. He was pleading with us to awaken before it's too late."

Irene sighed, eyes lowered. "So many think being part of the church—or agreeing with the message—is enough. But this parable says otherwise."

I nodded slowly. "Yes. Proximity to truth isn't the same as possession of it. Being in the net doesn't mean you're in the kingdom. Jesus isn't returning for those who merely heard His words—but for those whose hearts were changed by them. Not just the gathered—but the transformed."

Irene, tears tracing her cheeks, whispered. "Then I want to be the kind He keeps. Not just caught in the net . . . but chosen. Kept. In His vessels. In His kingdom."

I looked at her gently. "Then live each day as if the shore is near—because it is. The net is already drawing closed. The tide is shifting. The time for sorting is almost here. And only those truly His will remain."

Irene looked up from her Bible thoughtfully. "Ann, I was also reading Luke 14:15–24 today—the parable about the man who prepared a great banquet and invited many. But Jesus said they all began to make excuses. One had just bought a field, another some oxen, and another had just gotten married . . . so none of them came."

I nodded solemnly. "Yes. That parable carries more weight than most people realize. It's not just a story about dinner—it's a prophetic snapshot of how the world responds to God's ultimate invitation."

Irene's voice trembled. "It hit me hard. These weren't 'bad' people. They were just . . . distracted. Focused on life. Responsibilities. Relationships."

I nodded slowly. "Exactly. That's the point. It's not always blatant rebellion that keeps people out of the kingdom. Sometimes it's busyness. The comfort of routine. The subtle idols we don't even recognize as idols. Jesus was warning us that the greatest threat to eternity isn't always sin—it's indifference."

Irene's voice was barely a whisper. "And they missed everything. The feast. The joy. The presence of the Master. Just . . . gone."

I nodded, a heaviness in my chest. "They were invited. Personally, generously. But they didn't treasure the invitation. That's the heartbreak. The Master didn't say, 'You're no longer welcome'—He said, 'They shall not taste of My supper.' Not because He rejected them, but because they rejected Him. They wanted the feast—just not on His terms."

Irene leaned forward, her voice soft but steady. "And then the Master tells the servant to go into the streets and lanes—to bring in the poor, the crippled, the blind, and the lame. That part moved me."

I nodded, the weight of grace thick in the air. "Because that's the heart of God. He's not looking for status—He's looking for surrender. If the self-sufficient won't come, He'll fill His table with those who know they're empty. The hurting. The overlooked. Those with nothing to offer—except their 'yes.'"

"That's grace, isn't it?"

I smiled, a quiet awe in my voice. "That's grace in full color. The outcasts become the honored guests. The broken become the beloved. It's the upside-down kingdom—where the least are lifted, and the last are welcomed first. But it's also a warning: grace is offered freely, but not forever. The invitation won't wait forever unanswered."

Irene, voice trembling. "Do you think this parable is about our time too?"

Me, gently but firmly. "Absolutely. The banquet is the kingdom. And the invitation—it's going out now, louder than ever. But too many are still distracted. 'Later.' 'I'm too busy.' 'Let me finish this chapter of life first.' But the feast isn't on our timetable. The doors will close. And not everyone who was invited will enter."

Irene whispering. "'Blessed is he that shall eat bread in the Kingdom of God.' That's what started the whole parable."

I nodded. "Yes—and that blessing isn't just about being invited. It's about responding. Not someday. Not when it's convenient. But with urgency, humility, and joy. Because one day, the door will shut. And those who chose their fields, their oxen, their distractions—over the Master's feast—will find themselves outside. Not because they weren't wanted . . . but because they wouldn't come."

Irene, quietly resolute. "Then I want to say yes. Every day. No more excuses."

I smiled, voice tender. "Then come to the table. Live like the feast is already being set—because in a way, it is. The King is preparing it with you in mind. And every 'yes' draws you closer to His joy."

———◆◆◆———

WHY IT MATTERS NOW

The urgency of our hour cannot be overstated. We are not living in ordinary times. The world is groaning under the weight of escalating chaos—wars, deception, moral collapse, natural disasters, global division. And while many are asking *what is happening*, fewer are asking *what is missing*. What's missing is the message Jesus said must be proclaimed before the end can come: the Gospel of the Kingdom.

In Matthew 24:14, Jesus declared: "And this Gospel of the Kingdom . . ." not just *any* gospel. Not merely the Gospel of personal salvation, though essential. Jesus spoke specifically of the Gospel of the Kingdom—a message that announces His lordship, His return, His justice, His rule, and His call to holy living under divine government.

Why does it matter now?

Because the Gospel of the Kingdom is the *final witness* to the nations. It is the message that will divide wheat from tares, light from darkness, allegiance from apathy. It is the ultimate announcement that a King is coming—not just to comfort, but to conquer. Not just to save souls, but to claim His throne. And we are the heralds of that message.

Too many in the Church have settled for a version of the Gospel that focuses solely on the forgiveness of sin, while ignoring the call to obedience, righteousness, and kingdom citizenship. We have invited people to a Savior—but not always to a King. We've offered people Heaven—but not always transformation. That incomplete gospel, though well-meaning, has left many unprepared for what is coming.

But God, in His mercy, is restoring the fullness of His message. He is raising up voices who will declare not just salvation from sin, but surrender to the Sovereign. The Gospel of the Kingdom is not an accessory to the end-times story—it is the key that unlocks the prophetic timeline.

Before Jesus returns, His kingdom must be preached—not as a metaphor or distant hope, but as a present invitation and future reality. This Gospel must burn like fire in the mouths of messengers who fear no man and long for the King.

This is why it matters now—because time is running out, compromise is increasing, and deception is thickening. The urgency of this hour demands more than a sentimental understanding of Jesus; it calls for a bold proclamation of His lordship. The world must hear not only of His love but also of His reign. Jesus is not returning to take sides—He is returning to take over. And the Church must be ready, not merely to meet Him in the air, but to represent Him on the earth, fully aligned with the kingdom He is bringing.

CALL TO ACTION: A KINGDOM RESPONSE IN A CRITICAL HOUR

The hour is late, and the alarm of eternity is ringing. This is no time for passive faith, comfortable Christianity, or cultural religion dressed in spiritual language. The Gospel of the Kingdom is not a suggestion—it is a summons. It is the King's command, echoing through time, calling His people to rise, repent, and represent Him in truth and power.

We are not waiting on a political shift, a cultural revival, or a prophetic alignment to act. The King has already spoken, and His Word still stands: "This Gospel of the Kingdom shall be preached in all the world for a witness unto all nations; and then shall the end come" (Matthew 24:14). That time is now. The message must go forth—not watered down by comfort, not silenced by fear, and not shaped by the approval of man.

So what must we do?

We must recalibrate our lives around the King and His kingdom.

We must stop asking, "What's safe?" or "What's popular?" and start asking, "What does the King require of me?"

We must trade convenience for consecration.

We must return to the fire of the Upper Room, to the cry of "Thy kingdom come," and to the simplicity of full surrender. No more compartmentalized faith. No more Gospel without a Cross. No more salvation without lordship. The time for double-mindedness is over.

Here is the call:

- Repent of every form of compromise, distraction, and spiritual laziness that has dulled your fire.
- Return to the place of prayer, fasting, and obedience where the voice of the King is louder than the noise of the world.
- Preach the full message—not just the forgiveness of sin, but the reign of Jesus, the call to holiness, and the coming judgment.

- Stand as ambassadors of the kingdom in a world growing darker by the hour—full of grace, but unshakably loyal to Truth.
- Engage the harvest with urgency and compassion. Let every conversation, every platform, every gift you carry be submitted to the advancement of His kingdom.

This is not a time to be lukewarm, silent, or half-awake. The trumpet is about to sound, and we must be found faithful, watchful, and aligned. The King is not returning for a crowd—He is returning for a Bride without spot or wrinkle, a people fully surrendered to His rule.

Let us rise as the final generation of kingdom heralds—voices that prepare the way, hearts that burn for His return, and lives that cry out: "The Spirit and the Bride say, Come."

Because He is not coming to take sides.

He is coming to take over.

And when He comes, may He find us ready.

————◆◆◆————

Irene, her voice low as she looked up from the open pages of Genesis. "Ann, I've been asking myself something lately—something that won't let me sleep. How far have we really drifted from God? And even more haunting . . . when did the slide begin? When did we start slipping so far from His ways that we barely noticed?"

I closed my Bible slowly, the weight of her question pressing into the silence. It wasn't just a question of history—it was a cry for clarity.

"That's the ache of a soul waking up," I said quietly. "And it's the right question to ask, Irene. Not just the world—but for us. For the Church. For every heart that dares to measure itself against the Word instead of the world."

Irene's voice was steady, but her eyes shimmered with wonder—as if she were seeing Eden through the lens of Scripture.

"In the beginning," she said thoughtfully, "the world seemed to know God intimately. Adam and Eve walked with Him. Enoch walked so closely that God simply took him.

The Book of Jubilees records that Enoch was the first man born on earth who learned writing, knowledge, and wisdom directly from God (Jubilees 4:17). The Bible tells us that Enoch's name means 'teaching,' and that he lived from 3378 BC to 3013 BC—until he was taken by God. Raptured.

If so, then writing could predate 700 AM—*Anno Mundi*—the Year of the World. Noah obeyed God even when the whole world mocked him. Back then, obedience wasn't part of an institution. It wasn't religion, was it?"

I smiled gently, feeling the sacredness of what she was sensing.

"No, it wasn't religion—it was communion. Pure, unfiltered relationship. The first two thousand years of human history weren't marked by denominations or rituals, but by remembrance and reverence. People lived long lives and passed down the knowledge of God from generation to generation.

The Sabbath hadn't been commanded—but it was honored, seen in Creation itself: God worked six days and rested on the seventh. Altars weren't built out of obligation, but out of awe. They feared the Lord not from afar, but up close—because they *knew* Him. Not in theory. In proximity.

They worshiped with stones and stories—not with systems and schedules. They remembered. And they recorded—etched in songs, carved in stone, passed down in sacred lines of writing."

Irene, turning to Genesis 5 and 6. "And then came the Flood."

I nodded solemnly. The weight of it never lost on me. "Yes. According to the biblical timeline, the Flood came in the year 2344 BC—or 1656 AM—1,656 years after Creation. By that time, humanity had plunged into deep depravity. God saw that every inclination of the thoughts of their hearts was only evil—continually.

It wasn't just behavior—it was their identity. The corruption ran so deep, it became systemic, etched into their bloodlines and reinforced through every choice. Generation after generation drifted farther from the truth, until they no longer even recognized their Creator."

I paused, eyes drawn to Irene's open Bible. "But then comes that shining line: 'But Noah found grace in the eyes of the Lord.' God didn't erase humanity out of hatred—he preserved a remnant out of mercy. The judgment was severe, yes—but so was the rebellion. And still, God made a way to begin again."

Irene traced the names in the genealogies with her finger, her voice quiet but steady. "And through Noah's sons—Shem, Ham, and Japheth—God repopulated the earth."

I nodded, the timeline vivid in my mind. "Exactly. From those three sons of Noah, the families of the nations were born. Every tribe and ethnicity traces its origin back to them. And after the waters receded, Noah lived another 350 years. He witnessed the world rebuild from the ashes—generation by generation. Incredibly, his life overlapped with Abraham's. Abraham was born in 2052 BC—or 1948 AM—just 292 years after the Flood."

Irene's brow furrowed as the significance sank in.

I continued. "That close. Less than three centuries after the judgment of the Flood, mankind turned again—not toward outright violence this time, but toward something just as devastating: idolatry. Nimrod rose—and with him, his wife

Semiramis, later dubbed the 'queen of heaven.' Babel towered. People no longer tried to walk with God; they tried to build without Him."

Irene's brows drew together in concern. "So quickly? After the Flood, after everything . . . we fell again?"

I exhaled slowly, my voice solemn. "Yes. That's the tragic pattern of human history—revival followed by rebellion. And that's why God called Abraham. He wasn't just picking a man—He was planning a lineage. A people who would carry His name, remember His ways, and preserve His promise."

Irene turned a page, nodding slowly.

I continued. "Abraham, then Isaac, then Jacob—whose twelve sons became the twelve tribes of Israel. But even that chosen family, through a series of famines, betrayals, and divine setups, ended up in Egypt. And there they stayed. Not for a few years, but 430. Generations were born and died in slavery. God's people had His promise—but they forgot His presence."

Irene nodded slowly. "Until Moses."

I met her gaze, steady and full of reverence. "Yes. Moses lived from 1526 BC to 1406 BC. Around 1446 BC—or 2554 AM—God raised him up at eighty years old to lead the people out of Egypt's grip. But in the wilderness, Moses didn't just lead. He listened. And he wrote. There, under the weight of divine presence, he recorded the Torah—the first five books of Scripture."

Irene's eyes drifted to the open pages in front of her.

I smiled, then continued. "God's people have always been scribes and singers—chroniclers of covenant, worshipers of memory. They didn't just live history—they preserved it. They sang it. Every biblical feast—Passover, Pentecost, Tabernacles—was built around remembrance. Because the moment we forget God, we drift. And when we drift, we fall into bondage."

Irene, softly. "And now? We barely remember."

I met her sorrow with steadiness, my voice low but resolute. "We've forgotten the weight of remembering, Irene. The sacred habit of it. After Jesus— the Word made flesh—walked among us, He didn't just teach or heal. He fulfilled every prophecy, every shadow, every symbol. And then the apostles took up the mantle. They didn't just preach—they recorded. Line by line. Testimony by testimony."

Irene listened, still.

"By around AD 100," I continued, "the writings of the New Testament were complete. The Church had already begun recognizing the canon of the Bible— Scripture as we now know it—even if the final formal affirmations would come in later centuries. But even then, the call remained unchanged: *Remember*. Remember who He is. Remember what He's done. Remember who you are."

Irene, hesitant. "But then . . . the Church changed things?"

I nodded slowly. "Gradually, yes. In the centuries after Christ, especially following Constantine's Edict of Milan in AD 313, Christianity moved from the margins to the mainstream. It gained legal status, then favor, and eventually political power. And with that came structure. Influence. Control."

Irene looked up. "And Scripture?"

I nodded. "By around AD 400, St. Jerome translated the Bible into Latin—the Vulgate. It was a gift at the time, meant to unify the Church. But over the next thousand years, something tragic happened. The Roman Catholic Church held the Scriptures tightly. Only clergy were permitted to read and interpret them. Services were spoken in Latin. And the people—most of whom were illiterate—sat in silence, hearing words they couldn't understand."

Irene, voice low. "And people died trying to change that, didn't they?"

I nodded solemnly. "They did. Heroes of the faith. John Wycliffe translated the Bible into English in the late 1300s—long before it was allowed. After his death, the Church declared him a heretic, exhumed his body, and burned his bones."

Irene gasped. "Even in death?"

"Yes," I said softly. "And William Tyndale paid the ultimate price. He printed English Bibles in secret and smuggled them into England. In 1536, he was betrayed, imprisoned, and finally burned at the stake. His last words? 'Lord, open the King of England's eyes.'"

Irene's eyes welled up. "And did God answer?"

I nodded. "He did. Within a year, English Bibles were being printed legally. And with the invention of Johannes Gutenberg's printing press around 1440—just before Tyndale's time—the Word of God began to spread. By the 1530s, ordinary people were finally holding the Scriptures in their own hands."

Irene, voice heavy with grief. "And today . . . we treat it like background noise."

I looked at her, eyes solemn. "We're drowning in access—but starving for awe. We scroll past Scripture like it's optional, while there are believers in North Korea, Somalia, Iran, Afghanistan, Libya, and parts of China who risk everything just to hold a few pages."

Irene whispered. "They memorize it, don't they?"

I nodded. "Word for word. Sometimes a single page is passed around a church in hiding. A torn corner of the Gospel becomes a treasure. And here we are—free, well-fed, surrounded by Bibles—yet often empty of reverence. That's the kind of hunger we've lost."

Irene leaned forward, eyes searching mine. "What about the Creation story? When did people stop believing in Genesis?"

I took a slow breath, choosing my words with care. "It started in the 1800s. In 1859, Charles Darwin published *On the Origin of Species*, and with it came a massive shift—away from divine design toward evolutionary theory. For the first time on a large scale, Genesis 1 was no longer taught as sacred history but as myth or metaphor."

Irene frowned. "And that changed everything."

I nodded. "It did. Around the same time, Sir Richard Owen coined the term 'dinosaur.' Suddenly, these massive creatures—once just described as dragons or great beasts—were rebranded as 'prehistoric,' as if they belonged to a different timeline than the Bible. It drove a wedge between science and Scripture. The world began to believe they had to choose."

Irene, her voice barely above a whisper. "So we stopped believing what God said—right from the very first page."

I met her gaze, steady and somber. "Yes. And when Genesis is dismissed, the whole structure begins to crumble. If there's no Creator, there's no design. Without design, there's no purpose. Without purpose, no sin. No fall. And if there's no fall, why would we need redemption? Why the Cross? Why the gospel?"

I paused, letting it settle. "Everything begins in Genesis. It's not just the start of the Bible—it's the foundation of the story of salvation."

Irene, her brow furrowed. "And now with AI, social media, endless screens— are we more connected . . . or just more distracted?"

I let the silence linger before answering.

"We're drowning in distraction. We've traded face-to-face fellowship for filtered versions of ourselves. We scroll endlessly but rarely sit still. We've learned how to search—but forgotten how to seek. We know how to Google, but we don't know how to grieve. Our lives are saturated with noise, and then we wonder why we can't hear God."

I leaned forward, voice firm. "And the cost? The Gospel of Salvation has been reduced to a sales pitch—marketed as comfort, not conviction. Repentance has become optional. Obedience, old-fashioned. Surrender, ignored. And the Gospel of the Kingdom? Almost erased. We're no longer consumed with building His kingdom . . . we're obsessed with building personal platforms."

Irene, blinking back emotion. "We've made it all about us."

I met her gaze, voice resolute. "But it was never supposed to be about us. It's always been about Him—His glory, His kingdom, His authority. We've twisted the story into one about our dreams, our careers, our comfort. But the true Gospel doesn't orbit our personal happiness—it demands our allegiance."

I paused, then added with clarity. "The Gospel of Salvation is about being saved *from* sin. The Gospel of the Kingdom is about being saved *for* Him. One rescues us. The other reclaims us."

Irene, voice soft with longing. "So how do we return?"

I answered slowly, letting the weight settle between us.

"We return by remembering. By repenting. By teaching our children—not just stories, but *truth*—beginning at Genesis 1."

I leaned forward, voice steady. "We return by choosing awe over apathy. Faith over fear. Obedience over opinion. We return when we treat the Word of God like it's not optional—because it never was."

My eyes held hers. "The Bible we hold today was bought with blood. And in places around the world, it's still forbidden. So we must read it like our lives depend on it. Because they do."

Irene, eyes wide, clutching her Bible to her chest. "Ann, think about it. Abraham was born in 1948 AM—nearly two thousand years after Creation. And Israel? Reborn in 1948 AD. The man through whom God made the covenant . . . and the nation through whom He kept it. That can't just be a coincidence."

She shook her head slowly, voice trembling. "And seventy years later—to the very day—on May 14, 2018, President Trump recognized Jerusalem as Israel's capital. He moved the U.S. Embassy from Tel Aviv to Jerusalem. That feels too precise to be random. It's like God stamped that moment—marked it—with His signature on history."

I nodded slowly, flipping through the pages of my Bible. "You're right to feel the weight of that, Irene. These aren't random moments in history—they're threads in a divine tapestry. The birth of Abraham marked the beginning of God's covenant with a people. The rebirth of Israel in 1948 marked the restoration of that nation. And President Trump's recognition of Jerusalem, exactly seventy years later . . . It wasn't just politics. It was a prophetic exclamation point."

Irene leaned forward, eyes searching. "And seventy years—Ann, that number keeps showing up. It's all over the Bible. Didn't God tell us something about a generation in Psalm 90:10?"

> The days of our years are threescore (sixty) years and ten; and if by reason of strength they be fourscore (eighty) years, yet is their strength labor and sorrow; for it is soon cut off, and we fly away. (Psalm 90:10)

I turned to the passage and read aloud, and then looked up. "Yes, Irene. That's it. A biblical generation is typically seventy years—eighty if there's strength.

That's why many prophecy teachers point to the rebirth of Israel in 1948. It wasn't just a political event. It was a prophetic marker. A countdown, some say."

Irene's breath caught as she leaned back, her eyes wide. "So if we count seventy years from 1948, we land in 2018—the exact year the embassy moved. But if we stretch it to eighty years . . . that brings us to 2028. Could this be what Jesus meant when He said the generation that sees the fig tree blossom—Israel coming back to life—wouldn't pass away until everything is fulfilled?"

I met her gaze, my voice low but steady. "Yes. In Matthew 24, Jesus tells us to learn the parable of the fig tree. 'When its branches become tender and put forth leaves, you know summer is near.' The fig tree has always been a symbol of Israel. And He was clear—the generation that sees it come to life again won't pass away until all these things are fulfilled."

> Now learn a parable of the fig tree; When his branch is yet tender, and puts forth leaves, you know that summer is near. So likewise you, when you shall see all these things, know that it is near, even at the doors. Verily I say unto you, This generation shall not pass, till all these things be fulfilled. (Matthew 24:32–34)

I paused for a moment, letting it settle.

"That places us squarely in prophetic territory. We may not know the day or the hour . . . but there's no doubt—we're living in the season."

Irene whispered, her eyes misted with awe.

"And it's all unfolding right on time."

I nodded slowly, the weight of history settling around us.

"Yes. From Abraham's birth in 1948 AM to Israel's rebirth—born again—in 1948 AD. From ancient prophecy to modern headlines, it's all moving according to God's calendar. He's never been late. He sees the end from the beginning. Nothing is coincidence—it's all divine design."

Irene, her voice barely above a whisper. "And if 1948 marked the start of that final generation, eighty years brings us to 2028."

I nodded, my tone sober and steady. "Exactly. We don't set dates—but we *do* pay attention. Jesus didn't ask us to calculate the day or hour. But He *did* command us to discern the times. And all signs point to a narrowing window. It's like the last grains in the hourglass. Everything is aligning—biblically, historically, spiritually. God's prophetic clock is ticking. And it's almost midnight."

Irene, with rising intensity. "It's as if God placed mile markers in time—Noah's death, Abraham's birth, Israel's rebirth, Jerusalem's recognition—to wake us up and warn us. These aren't coincidences. They're *coordinates*. Like Daniel's Seventy Weeks, God is pointing to something urgent. The end of the age is near."

My eyes misted, voice low but sure. "And yet, so few are paying attention. So many are distracted—by politics, by entertainment, by the grind of life. They've forgotten the *storyline*. They've lost track of the timeline."

I paused. "But God hasn't. He sees the end from the beginning. Isaiah 46:10 says He *declares* it—boldly, clearly."

> Declaring the end from the beginning, and from ancient times the things that are not yet done, saying, My counsel shall stand, and I will do all My pleasure. (Isaiah 46:10)

"The very fact that we're even having this conversation—linking Abraham's birth to Israel's rebirth, connecting the seventy-year prophetic window—is a testimony of His sovereignty . . . and His mercy."

Irene, voice firm with resolve. "Then we must sound the alarm, Ann. This isn't just fascinating—it's *urgent*. We're living in the most prophetic generation since Jesus walked the earth."

I reached over, gently taking her hand. "Yes, Irene. It's not enough to admire the precision—we must *answer* to the invitation. Jesus isn't just coming back to comfort the broken. He's returning to reign as King."

I continued. "The real question is: Are we ready for the King? Because the hour is later than most think. And we . . . we are that generation."

CHAPTER SUMMARY

Chapter 3 uncovers the often-overlooked core message that Jesus consistently preached—the Gospel of the Kingdom. While modern Christianity has largely centered the gospel around personal salvation, Jesus proclaimed something far more expansive: a kingdom both present and future, a divine government that not only saves souls but rules hearts, transforms lives, and will ultimately reign over nations.

The chapter challenges the Church's tendency to reduce the Gospel to a spiritual rescue mission, focused solely on forgiveness of sins and securing Heaven. While salvation through faith in Christ is essential and foundational, it is only the beginning. Jesus came not just to save us from sin, but to invite us into a kingdom—a way of life marked by righteousness, power, surrender, and obedience under His lordship.

Through His parables, sermons, and miracles, Jesus revealed the kingdom as a living reality—not just a distant hope. He healed the sick, cast out demons, and taught with authority to demonstrate that God's reign was already breaking into the world. Over and over, He declared, "The Kingdom of Heaven is at hand." This kingdom requires more than belief; it demands allegiance.

The urgency of this message is underscored in Matthew 24:14, where Jesus declares that "this Gospel of the Kingdom"—not just any gospel—"must be preached in all the world as a witness to the nations before the end can come." This isn't just a call to evangelize—it's a call to announce the reign of the returning King and prepare the world for His coming rule.

The chapter concludes with a clear challenge: stop living as a consumer of grace and start living as a citizen of the kingdom. Citizenship requires commitment. It calls for daily surrender, alignment with kingdom values, and boldness to walk in the authority and purpose of Heaven on earth. We are not merely saved to escape judgment—we are saved to represent the King until He returns.

KEY TAKEAWAYS

- The Gospel of Salvation is essential, but it is only part of the message—Jesus also preached the Gospel of the Kingdom.
- The Kingdom of God is both present and future; it is spiritual in nature but will soon be physical in manifestation.
- Salvation opens the door, but the kingdom requires obedience, faithfulness, and surrender to the King's rule.
- Jesus emphasized the kingdom repeatedly—this was central to His ministry and mission.
- The Gospel of the Kingdom must be restored and preached before Jesus returns (Matthew 24:14).
- Believers are called to live as ambassadors of the coming kingdom, not passive spectators of the faith.

With this chapter, the focus shifts from personal redemption to cosmic reign—from escaping judgment to embracing divine purpose. It prepares the reader to explore the prophetic signs—the seven harbingers—that confirm the nearness of the kingdom and the return of its King.

Chapter 4

The Seven Harbingers:
A Prophetic Roadmap

A SHIFT IN TONE—Up to this point, we've been laying the theological foundation of salvation and the kingdom—truths at the heart of the Gospel message and central to the believer's identity and mission. But now, the tone of this book changes. We move from the terrain of foundational doctrine to the landscape of prophetic insight. This is not a turn toward fearmongering or speculation, but rather toward biblically rooted preparation—a call to discern the signs of the times through the lens of Scripture.

God has always been a communicator. He does not act in silence. Before every major turning point in redemptive history, He has issued a warning, a pattern, a harbinger. These divine signals are not hidden—they are given for those who are watching. A harbinger is a forerunner, a signal of what is to come. It is God's way of shaking His people awake before He shakes the nations.

> Surely the Lord GOD will do nothing, unless He reveals His secret unto His servants the prophets. The lion has roared, who will not fear? The Lord GOD has spoken, who can but prophesy. (Amos 3:7–8)

From the Book of Genesis to the Book of Revelation, the testimony is clear: God reveals before He acts.

- He warned Noah of a coming flood and gave him 120 years to prepare.

- He gave Joseph prophetic insight into Pharaoh's dreams—seven years of plenty followed by seven years of famine—and positioned him to preserve the future of Israel.
- He gave Daniel understanding of Jeremiah's prophecy and revealed the timetable for Israel's return from exile and the long-range vision of world empires and Messiah's coming.
- The Magi watched the heavens and recognized the birth of the Messiah from celestial alignments foretold centuries earlier.

In every case, God provided insight to those who were listening. And He still does. Just as God gave signs to Noah, Joseph, Daniel, and the Magi—He still reveals what's coming to those who watch.

This chapter marks the beginning of a new section in the book: a prophetic roadmap. Here, we will preview seven harbingers—seven divine signposts that point toward the nearing fulfillment of end-time prophecy. These harbingers are not arbitrary ideas or subjective impression; they are grounded in Scripture, confirmed in history, and reflected in the present day. They represent God's fingerprints on unfolding events—evidence that His plan is not only in motion, but accelerating.

You'll find that each harbinger is tied to a biblical pattern:

- Some are celestial—written in the heavens.
- Some are calendrical—hidden in God's sacred rhythms.
- Some are geopolitical—anchored in prophecies about Israel and the nations.
- And some are deeply personal, challenging believers to shift from passive belief to active obedience.

We live in a generation that has grown dull to warning signs, skeptical of prophecy, and content with spiritual comfort. But the Gospel of the Kingdom is not a gospel of escape; it is a call to readiness—to live as alert watchmen, faithful stewards, and bold witnesses.

Jesus Himself commanded us to watch:

Watch therefore, for you know neither day nor the hour wherein the Son of Man comes. (Matthew 25:13)

This chapter will briefly introduce the seven harbingers, which will each be explored in greater depth in the chapters that follow. Think of it as a prophetic overview, a glimpse of what God is saying to His people in this urgent hour.

The question is not *if* God is speaking through these signs.

The question is: Are we listening?

WHAT ARE THE HARBINGERS?

The seven harbingers presented in this book are not creative metaphors, allegorical illustrations, or speculative theories. They are prophetic indicators—divine revelations drawn directly from Scripture and reflected in the patterns of history, Creation, and current events. These harbingers mark the final season before the return of Jesus Christ. They are grounded in God's unchanging covenants, revealed through His appointed times and sacred calendars, written into the movements of the cosmos, and confirmed through the geopolitical shifts and global headlines unfolding before our very eyes.

They are God's voice echoing through time, saying:

Behold, I have told you before. (Matthew 24:25)

The harbingers in this book are not subtle. They are loud, unmistakable, and spiritually confrontational. They are divine alarms that break through spiritual apathy and demand a response. These harbingers are not just signals of what's coming—they are invitations to prepare, to repent, and to return to the Lord. They serve as both a call to readiness and a confrontation with compromise.

We call them harbingers because that's what they are: Forerunners of fulfillment. Signals of transition. Trumpets from Heaven.

They do not merely point to natural events—they reveal supernatural convergence. Each harbinger you'll encounter in the chapters ahead is a puzzle piece in a larger prophetic picture, a strategic insight that together points toward one inescapable truth: the vanishing is near.

That sudden, irreversible moment when the Bride of Christ—the Church—is caught up, removed from the earth in the Rapture, before the great and terrible Day of the Lord begins.

What follows is not theory. It is a blueprint—a prophetic roadmap written by God who declared the end from the beginning (Isaiah 46:10). These seven harbingers, each grounded in Scripture and confirmed by patterns unfolding in our lifetime, unveil a stunning convergence of prophecy and present reality.

The Seven Harbingers:

1. **The Sign of the Times**—Global events aligning with the specific warnings of Scripture—wars, lawlessness, moral decay, natural disasters, and the rise of false messiahs.

2. **The Biblical Calendars**—God's sacred timeline embedded in the Hebrew calendar, Jubilees, and sabbatical years. The world may run on Gregorian time, but Heaven keeps its own calendars.

3. **The Signs in the Heavens**—Celestial phenomena—solar and lunar eclipses, blood moons, planetary alignments—given not for astrology, but as "signs and seasons" (Genesis 1:14) for those who understand their prophetic significance.

4. **The Feasts That Reveal the Future**—The appointed Feasts of the LORD, given in Leviticus 23, are not just memorials—they are prophetic rehearsals, each one pointing to a past fulfillment in Christ or a future fulfillment at His return.

5. **The Shemitah Cycles**—God's seven-year cycles of rest, release, and reckoning. Ignoring these cycles has resulted in judgment for Israel in the past—and these same patterns now appear to influence global economic and spiritual shifts.

6. **Daniel's 70th Week Trigger**—The event that initiates the final seven years of prophetic time—known as Daniel's 70th Week or the Tribulation. Understanding this trigger helps us discern how close we are to the final countdown.

7. **The War Prophecies**—Specific end-time wars foretold in Ezekiel 38–39, Psalm 83, Isaiah 17, and others. These conflicts involve alliances and tensions already visible on the global stage, particularly surrounding Israel.

Each harbinger will be examined in detail in the chapters ahead. Each is like a trumpet blast from the throne room of Heaven—a wake-up call to the sleeping Church and a witness to the world. Together, they confirm what the Holy Spirit has been whispering to hearts around the globe: The time is short. The vanishing is imminent. And the King is coming.

OVERVIEW OF THE SEVEN HARBINGERS

The modern Church has, in large part, neglected the prophetic message. Some have avoided it out of fear. Others have dismissed it out of indifference or distraction. But Scripture is clear: the Gospel of the Kingdom cannot be separated from prophecy. Jesus Himself tied the end of the age to the preaching of this Gospel—not merely a call to personal salvation, but a global witness to His rule, His return, and His reign.

> And this Gospel of the Kingdom shall be preached in all the world for a witness unto all nations; and then shall the end come. (Matthew 24:14)

He warned us that just as labor pains intensify before birth, the signs of His return would grow in frequency and severity. This is not poetic hyperbole—it is a divine forecast. And to preach the kingdom rightly is to preach with urgency.

To proclaim the harbingers is to accept the calling of a watchman—to take your place on the wall, to blow the trumpet, and to sound the alarm that the hour is late.

This is not doomsday talk. This is kingdom talk. It is hopeful, because we know who wins. It is holy, because it calls us to purify our hearts. And it is urgent, because time is running out.

And so, we ask:

- What if God has already marked the calendar?
- What if the signs are already in motion—louder, clearer, and closer than we imagined?
- What if you're not just reading this message, but you were chosen to carry it—to your family, your church, your city?

This is the Gospel of the Kingdom. This is the hour of the harbingers. And this is your invitation—not to spectate, but to participate. To watch. To warn. And to wake the world before the final trumpet sounds.

Let the countdown begin.

Seven harbingers. Seven warnings. One divine timeline.

1. The Sign of the Times

Jesus once issued a sharp rebuke to the religious leaders of His day. Though they could forecast the weather by observing the sky, they remained blind to the prophetic realities unfolding right in front of them. He said, "You can discern the face of the sky; but can you not discern the signs of the times?" (Matthew 16:3). That question wasn't rhetorical—it was convicting. And it still echoes into our day.

We are now living in a generation saturated with prophetic indicators. They are not subtle. They are not abstract. And yet, many continue to ignore or dismiss them. The first harbinger is a call to awaken. It urges the Church to shake off complacency and spiritual slumber and to recognize the season we're living in—a season Scripture has clearly outlined for those willing to see.

God has not left us in the dark. The Bible provides a detailed roadmap filled with prophetic mile-markers—events, patterns, and global shifts that act as divine signals. And in our time, those markers are not just appearing—they are multiplying and accelerating. Consider the rebirth of Israel in 1948, the miraculous recapturing of Jerusalem in 1967, the rise of globalism, the rapid spread of lawlessness, the normalization of sin, and the creeping apostasy within the Church. Add to this the exponential explosion of technology and information, as foretold in Daniel 12:4, and the picture becomes startling clear: we are not approaching the signs; we are living in the midst of them.

These are not random headlines or cyclical events. They are converging prophetic fulfillments—a flashing red light on the spiritual dashboard of history. Together, they signal two realities: the Rapture is near, and the Tribulation is closer than we want to believe. Contrary to what the world believes, things are not falling apart—they are falling into place, exactly as Scripture foretold.

This harbinger reminds us that God has always revealed His plans before executing them. "Surely the Lord GOD will do nothing, unless He reveals His secret unto His servants the prophets" (Amos 3:7). His expectation has never changed—He calls His people to watch. Not to panic. Not to predict. But to prepare. To watch is to walk in readiness. To recognize the signs is to live with urgency, wisdom, and boldness.

To ignore the signs is to fall asleep in the hour of visitation. But to discern them is to rise as a watchman—to sound the alarm with conviction, clarity, and courage. The clock is ticking. The signs are intensifying. The question is no longer if the season has arrived, but whether we're paying attention.

2. The Biblical Calendars

God does not operate on man's clock. He governs time according to His own divine calendar—one that has been ticking since Creation. The second harbinger draws our attention to the biblical calendars, the sacred rhythms and appointed times by which God structures His redemptive plan. These are not merely historical observances or cultural customs left to ancient Israel—they are Heaven's schedule, embedded in Scripture, pointing toward prophetic milestones we dare not overlook.

The Hebrew word *moed* means "appointed time" or "divine appointment." It appears repeatedly throughout the Old Testament, tied to feasts, Sabbaths, and moments of divine intervention. In Leviticus 23 and elsewhere, God lays out a calendar that is prophetically rich and spiritually precise. His timeline is cyclical: daily sacrifices, weekly Sabbaths, monthly new moons, annual feast days, seven-year Shemitah cycles, and the once-in-a-generation Jubilee every fifty years. These weren't empty rituals—they were prophetic rehearsals, shadows of things to come.

And come they did.

Jesus' First Coming was fulfilled with astonishing precision on these biblical feast days. His crucifixion aligned with Passover, His resurrection with the Feast of Firstfruits, and the outpouring of the Holy Spirit with Pentecost. These were not symbolic coincidences—they were divine appointments kept on schedule. God moved on time then, and He will move on time again. If the spring feasts were fulfilled in exact detail at His First Coming, we can be assured the fall feasts—Feast of Trumpets, Day of Atonement, and Feast of Tabernacles—will be fulfilled with the same prophetic accuracy at His return.

To understand the biblical calendar is to begin syncing your spiritual watch with God's eternal clock. It changes how we perceive time. It pulls us out of cultural confusion and into prophetic clarity. We stop watching the stock market or the news cycle for clues, and instead look to God's appointed times—times He has already set aside for decisive moves in redemption and judgment.

This harbinger reminds us that we are not blindly guessing the season of His return—we are rediscovering it. To study God's calendar is not to speculate, but to anticipate. It is to awaken with urgency, to align our hearts with His patterns, and to live with the sobering realization that the appointed time is drawing near.

The calendar is not hidden. The patterns are not vague. The question is not whether God is on time—it's whether we are on His schedule.

3. The Signs in the Heavens

From the very beginning, God declared that the sun, moon, and stars were not only to give light and mark seasons, but also to serve as signs—visible, divine signals appointed to communicate with humanity. "And let them be for signs, and for seasons, and for days, and years" (Genesis 1:14). This third harbinger calls us to lift our eyes upward, to the heavens where God continues to speak, writing messages across the sky for those who are watching.

Throughout Scripture, celestial signs accompany decisive moments in redemptive history. A star led the wise men to the infant Messiah. Darkness cloaked the earth at Calvary. The prophet Joel foresaw the moon turning to blood before the great and terrible Day of the LORD. These are not merely poetic metaphors—they are literal, observable events, orchestrated by the Creator and placed precisely in time to awaken a sleeping world.

This harbinger draws attention to an unfolding pattern—blood moons, solar eclipses, planetary alignments, and constellation-based phenomena—that have not only increased, but have done so on significant biblical feast days. These are not the inventions of astrology. They are the handiwork of God through astronomy—under divine authorship, not human superstition. The heavens are not random. They are calibrated. And they operate, not on man's calendar, but on God's.

In recent years, we've witnessed signs that are impossible to ignore. The tetrad of blood moons (2014–2015) appeared precisely on Passover and Tabernacles. The Revelation 12 Sign in 2017 mirrored the imagery of John's apocalyptic vision with celestial accuracy. Historic solar eclipses have bisected nations—geographically and spiritually—marking moments of warning and impending judgment. These signs align not with superstition, but with Scripture.

> The heavens declare the glory of God; and the firmament shows His handiwork. (Psalm 19:1)

And increasingly, they declare more than glory—they declare urgency.

The question is not whether the signs exist. The question is whether we are paying attention. Could the sky be God's final billboard—broadcasting warnings before the vanishing? And if so, are we already standing beneath it, heads down, unaware?

This harbinger compels us to look up—not just to the sky, but to the timeline of God. Because if He is speaking from the heavens . . . we must not be silent on earth.

4. The Feasts That Reveal the Future

God's appointed feasts—His *moedim*—are not merely ancient Jewish customs or relics of Old Testament worship. They are divine rehearsals, prophetic blueprints embedded in the calendar of Heaven. In Leviticus 23, God doesn't call them Israel's feasts. He calls them "My feasts." These sacred days belong to Him—and they reveal far more than historical tradition. They reveal eternity's rhythm.

Each feast unveils a layer of God's redemptive plan. Passover foreshadowed the crucifixion of Christ—the spotless Lamb of God slain for the sins of the world. Unleavened Bread declared the burial of the sinless Savior, His body laid in the tomb without corruption. Firstfruits proclaimed the resurrection, as Jesus rose on the very day that celebrated the first harvest. Pentecost marked the outpouring of the Holy Spirit and the birth of the Church, fifty days later.

These spring feasts were fulfilled with stunning precision—not merely in a symbolic sense, but in a literal, historical fulfillment, down to the day and even the hour of Jesus' First Coming. So what about the fall feasts—the Feast of Trumpets, the Day of Atonement, and the Feast of Tabernacles? Many scholars, pastors, and watchful believers agree: these are divine appointments waiting to be fulfilled at Christ's Second Coming.

The Feast of Trumpets is steeped in Rapture imagery: the blowing of trumpets, the "last trump," a sudden appearing on a day and hour no one knows. It speaks of a hidden day, a divine interruption. The Day of Atonement foreshadows judgment and repentance, aligning with the Tribulation and Israel's national awakening. And the Feast of Tabernacles reflects the final act of redemption—the Messianic reign of Christ when God will once again dwell among His people.

This fourth harbinger sounds a clarion call: God keeps appointments. His feasts are not manmade holidays. They are prophetic signposts, designed to reveal the Rapture, the Tribulation, and the return of the King. They remind us that God is not late—He is precise.

If the first four feasts aligned with Christ's First Coming, could the final three align just as precisely with His return? What if the entire calendar of redemption has already been written in Heaven—and the clock is now running out?

This harbinger challenges us not to live by man's holidays, but by God's holy days. Because when the trumpet sounds, it won't be just another tradition. It will be the next fulfilled appointment—right on time.

5. The Shemitah Cycles

Every seventh year, God commanded Israel to let the land rest, release debts, and reset the economy. This sacred rhythm—called the Shemitah (from the Hebrew *shamat*, meaning "to release")—was more than agricultural policy; it was a prophetic clock embedded into the fabric of time itself.

The Shemitah was a divine sabbatical cycle, a system of rest and release designed to reorder society around trust in God. But when Israel disregarded these sabbatical years, judgment followed. In fact, their seventy-year Babylonian exile directly corresponds to seventy ignored Shemitah cycles. God had been counting. The principle was unmistakable: what God commands, He enforces.

> And them that had escaped from the sword carried he away to Babylon; where they were servants to him and his sons until the reign of the kingdom of Persia: To fulfil the Word of the LORD by the mouth of Jeremiah, until the land had enjoyed her Sabbaths: for as long as she lay desolate she kept Sabbath, to fulfill threescore and ten years. (2 Chronicles 36:20–21)

But the Shemitah didn't disappear with ancient Israel. This cycle still echoes into modern history. Time and again, global economies have convulsed in Shemitah years—most recently, 2001, 2008, 2015, and 2022—all marked by financial upheaval, debt crises, and moral decline. Though the nations may not observe it consciously, the rhythm continues. The shaking intensifies.

The fifth harbinger reminds us: God still keeps time. When the Shemitah is honored, it releases blessing, provision, and peace. But when defiled, it brings disruption, exposure, and collapse. It is both a grace period and a countdown.

Could the current Shemitah cycle—September 2022–2023 to September 2028–2029—serve as a prophetic trigger for the Tribulation? Could it mark a divine reset that signals both the vanishing and the Day of the Lord? If the past is prologue, then the pattern will not just repeat—it will intensify. And when it does, the reset will move beyond the financial. It will become eternal.

Are we living in a Shemitah season right now?

And if so—what might God release . . . or remove . . . next?

6. Daniel's 70th Week Trigger

In Daniel 9:24–27, God entrusted the prophet Daniel with one of the most precise prophetic timelines in all of Scripture: seventy "weeks"—or seventy sets of seven years, totaling 490 years—appointed for Israel and the Holy City of Jerusalem. Remarkably, sixty-nine of those weeks (483 years) were fulfilled to the exact day with the coming of the Messiah, Jesus Christ—His First Coming.

Since Christ's First Coming, Israel's prophetic timeline has been paused during the Church Age—a mystery age in which God is calling out a people for His name from among the nations. But that pause will end, and His covenant plan for Israel will resume in the final prophetic week.

But one final "week" remains—seven prophetic years yet to be fulfilled. This climactic period, known as Daniel's 70th Week, is what we refer to as the Tribulation. It won't begin randomly or through vague signs. It will be triggered by a specific, prophetic event: "He (the Antichrist) shall confirm the covenant with many for one week . . ." (Daniel 9:27). This is not merely a diplomatic treaty—it is a prophetic tripwire, a divinely ordained countdown that will mark the beginning of the final seven years of this age.

This harbinger is not speculation—it's prophetic precision. God's timeline is not guesswork. He is exact. History has already validated the accuracy of the first sixty-nine weeks. The final week will unfold just as precisely. And right now, we are witnessing global events align in real time:

- The rebirth of Israel in 1948.
- The recapturing of Jerusalem in 1967.
- Rising cries for peace in the Middle East.
- Emerging coalitions and power blocs positioning for influence.

These developments are not random. They are prophetic staging cues, pointing toward the moment when a global leader will rise—not merely to create peace, but to "confirm" what appears to be peace. That moment will trigger Daniel's final week—and by then, the Bride of Christ must already be gone.

The sixth harbinger sounds like a trumpet blast of warning: the final seven years are not abstract—they are appointed. And the world is on the brink of signing its final deal. The prophetic clock didn't stop. It's been paused—waiting for its final tick. And we are seconds away from the countdown to eternity.

7. The War Prophecies

War is not merely a backdrop to the end times—it is one of Scripture's loudest alarms. The final harbinger brings us face to face with a truth that many would rather avoid: the last days will be marked by conflict. Not random skirmishes or isolated violence—but prophesied wars, involving specific nations, prophetic alliances, and sovereign outcomes.

The Bible is not vague about this. It names, names. It draws geopolitical maps long before history catches up. These are not symbolic conflicts—they are literal, unfolding battles with divine timing and eternal consequence.

Among the most significant war prophecies in Scripture:

- Psalm 83—A confederacy of Israel's immediate neighbors plotting her annihilation. Though hotly debated, many believe this coalition represents a pre-Gog war of regional hostility, forming a noose around Israel.
- Isaiah 17—A startling prophecy that declares: "Damascus shall be a ruinous heap." The destruction of one of the oldest cities in the world is not poetry—it is a future military flashpoint.
- Ezekiel 38–39—The Gog Magog War: a massive northern invasion against Israel, involving Russia, Iran (Persia), Turkey, and other Islamic nations. This war ends not by human victory, but by divine intervention—with fire, hail, and earthquakes shaking the world.

These are not merely military encounters—they are spiritual showdowns. They represent the climactic clash between light and darkness, truth and deception, righteousness and rebellion. Each battle is a trumpet blast, declaring the nearness of the King's return.

- Israel is increasingly surrounded by hostile powers—and faces growing international isolation.
- Antisemitism is rising, even in the West, echoing ancient hatred with modern intensity.
- Strategic alliances between Russia, Iran, and Turkey are strengthening—just as Ezekiel saw.
- The world pulses with instability, terror, and rumors of war—fulfilling Jesus' own forecast in Matthew 24:6.

So why is this the seventh harbinger?

Because these wars are not just end-time symptoms—they are prophetic triggers. They unleash judgments. They shift global power. And they clear the path for the return of the Warrior King, Jesus Christ.

This final harbinger reminds us that the world is not only being militarized for judgment—it is being mobilized for redemption. The battlefield is not the end—it is the stage for glory. And the faithful are not called to fear, but to readiness. War is coming. But so is the Commander of Heaven's Armies. Lift your eyes—not to the battlefield, but to the eastern sky. Jesus wins.

THE WATCHMAN'S CALL

As the final words of this chapter settle in, a deeper question begins to rise: What now? What are we to do with the seven harbingers? What do they mean for us today—not in theory, but in truth?

These prophetic indicators are not curiosities for the spiritually curious. They are commissions for the spiritually awakened. Each harbinger is not just a revelation—it is a responsibility. To see and not speak is to fail the call of the watchman.

In Ezekiel 33:6–9, God makes it clear: if the watchman sees the sword coming and fails to sound the alarm, the blood is on his hands. But if he warns the people—even if they refuse to listen—he has delivered his soul. These harbingers are the sword on the horizon. The trumpet is in our hand. And this moment is our wall.

The modern Church has, for too long, been lulled into a false peace, convinced that prophecy is either too confusing to understand or too frightening to mention. But Jesus never told us to look away. He told us to look up. He said, "Watch therefore: for you know not what hour your Lord does come" (Matthew 24:42). To watch is not to wonder. It is to wake up.

The harbingers call us to live differently. Not with fear, but with fire. Not with dread, but with discernment. These are not the ravings of alarmists—they are the road signs of the Redeemer, shouting that the hour is late and the Bridegroom is near.

So what now?

We take our place on the wall. We tune our hearts to the sound of approaching footsteps. We open the pages of Scripture and recognize that we are living in the very days the prophets saw from afar—and longed to understand. But unlike them, we do not merely see—we stand in the middle of it. The convergence is no longer theoretical. It is visible. Tangible. Undeniable.

The Watchman's Call is this: Open your eyes. Sharpen your voice. Ready your heart. The King is coming.

And so we turn the page—not just of a chapter, but of time itself.

In the next section, we begin our journey into the first harbinger: The Sign of the Times—the spiritual tremors, geopolitical alignments, and societal shifts that are crying out in real time, "Prepare the way of the Lord!"

This is not the end of a chapter. It is the beginning of a call.

The Watchman's Call is sounding. Will you answer it?

A quiet study, mid-morning light streaming through the window. A Bible rests open beside a steaming cup of coffee. A stack of books—*The Trumpet I*, *The Trumpet II*, and *The Vanishing*—sits between us.

Irene, leaning over the stack, her fingers grazing the cover of *The Vanishing*, whispered as if handling something sacred. "Ann . . . I've been reading your three prophetic volumes—*The Trumpet I*, *The Trumpet II*, and *The Vanishing*. And I have to say . . . it's remarkable."

She paused, then looked up, eyes searching mine. "These books are so different. Different tones. Different themes. Even different timelines. And yet— somehow—they weave together like a perfect tapestry. It's as if each one holds a key to the same divine vault."

I, offering a soft smile, nodded with quiet assurance. "That's because they do, Irene. Different lanes—same destination. *The Vanishing* declares the next prophetic event: the Rapture. It answers the piercing question: who will be taken, and who will be left behind?"

I leaned back slightly, voice steady but charged with purpose. "And *The Trumpet* series? That's the roadmap for everything after. *The Trumpet I* reveals what happens in the first half of the Tribulation—how God begins to judge a rebellious world. *The Trumpet II* unveils what happens in the last half of the Tribulation and beyond—the return of the King, the Millennial Kingdom Age, and the Eternal Age. It's not just what's coming . . . it's what comes after."

Irene, eyes widening, tapped the cover of *The Trumpet I*. "So *The Vanishing* prepares us for lift-off, and *The Trumpet* explains the rest of the journey?"

I smiled with a spark of intensity. "Exactly. *The Vanishing* tells us what happens the moment Heaven opens and the Bride of Christ is caught up. It's immediate. It's imminent. It's not far-off anymore. And *The Trumpet*—well, that's what you'll need to know if you're still here. And what you'll rejoice in if you're not."

Irene, lifting her Bible and thumbing through Revelation, her voice hushed. "So it's all here. The escape. The reckoning. The restoration. Three books . . . one story."

I, gently. "One divine story. And we're already living in the final chapter."

Irene turned the book slowly in her hands, her voice almost a whisper. "This one chills me the most."

She looked over the top of it, locking eyes with me. "The way you describe the Rapture—not as some distant, abstract event, but as something that could literally happen *any* day—it haunts me, Ann. In the best way. You didn't dramatize it. You didn't try to make it Hollywood. You just . . . documented it."

She tapped the cover gently. "It's not science fiction. It's Scripture."

I, quietly but firmly. "Because it *is* true. The Rapture is not symbolic. It's not poetry. It's not something to spiritualize away. It's real. And it's next. The next scheduled intervention on God's prophetic calendar."

I leaned forward, folding my hands over my Bible. "It's not an 'if.' It's a 'when.' And we're running out of *when*."

Irene sat back slightly, eyes still on the book in her hands.

I continued, voice gaining a thread of urgency. "And those seven harbingers we've been walking through together? Every single one . . . different as they are in content and scope . . . screams the same message: *Get ready!*"

I paused. "Because this isn't about scaring people. It's about waking them. It's about handing them the key before the door shuts."

Irene, brows furrowed in thought. "And what gets me is this—each harbinger, though totally different in scope and subject, still circles back to the same time frame."

She looked up from the pages in front of her, her voice rising with conviction. "The 2028–2029 Shemitah year. I mean, Ann, we're talking about signs in the heavens, Daniel's 70th Week, the Shemitah resets, the biblical feast fulfillments—all distinct themes. Separate lenses. And yet, every single one of them zeroes in on the same prophetic window—September/October 2028 to September/October 2029."

She held her hands out, palms up, as if inviting the heavens to answer. "That's not random. That's precision."

I met her gaze with a knowing look and nodded slowly. "Exactly. And it's not just the harbingers, Irene."

I reached for the notebook beside me and flipped it open to a page marked with two bold dates: *1948 AM* and *1948 AD*.

I, tapping the page. "Even the Abrahamic prophecy—1948 AM, the year Abraham was born from Creation—and the rebirth of Israel in 1948 AD. Two separate timelines. One from the beginning of everything, the other from modern history. And yet . . . both pointing to 2028/2029."

I, softer now. "Two timelines. Two clocks. And they intersect at the same divine checkpoint. That's not numerology. That's sovereignty."

Irene, awestruck, barely a whisper. "God's fingerprint is all over it."

I nodded again, this time slower, reverently. "He's not hiding it. He's revealing it—for those who have eyes to see and ears to hear."

Irene leaned back in her chair, visibly shaken. "Ann . . . that's *crazy* accurate. It's almost too precise to comprehend."

I nodded, slowly. "It is His fingerprint. Etched across time. From Genesis to Revelation, He's been telling one story—ours."

I reached across the table and gently tapped the cover of *The Trumpet I* sitting between us. "People want to know their future? They don't need a psychic hotline or a political savior. They need *Scripture*. And honestly, they need *The Trumpet*. Because once the Rapture happens—and it *will*—these books won't just be prophetic insight . . ."

I paused. "They'll be survival guides. Roadmaps for the left behind. A guide to what's coming next—for those caught in the storm."

Irene, almost whispering. "And most churches won't even touch this."

I, nodding. "That's why God raises up watchmen."

Irene leaned forward, brow furrowed in thought. "So *The Vanishing* explains the *what* and the *who*—what actually happens during the Rapture, who's taken, and who's left behind. But *The Trumpet* . . . that's the *then what*."

I nodded, solemn. "Exactly. *The Trumpet I* walks readers through the first eleven chapters of Revelation. It unveils what happens *after* the Rapture—the Church in Heaven, the rise of the Antichrist, the 144,000 Jewish evangelists, the seal judgments, and the trumpet blasts. It gives you a glimpse into the Bride in Heaven while judgment is breaking loose on earth."

Irene, quietly. "The seal judgments . . . famine, plague, global chaos . . ."

I nodded. "Yes. And it's just the beginning. The Two Witnesses appear. Martyrs cry out from under the altar. A great spiritual deception blankets the earth. The restrainer will have been removed. And those left behind—well, they'll be living through the first act of divine reckoning."

Irene shook her head. "And people treat Revelation like it's allegory."

I, more intense now. "If they're not ready, this won't feel symbolic—it'll feel apocalyptic. That's why I didn't write *The Trumpet* as theory. I wrote it as a clear, prophetic timeline—something that anyone left behind could open and understand."

Irene's voice dropped to a near whisper. "And *The Trumpet II*? What does that reveal?"

I leaned in, my tone turning reverent. "That's where it deepens. From Revelation chapter 12 to 22, it walks you through the bowls of wrath—God's final judgments poured out on a defiant world. Then the fall of Mystery Babylon—yes, America, brought to her knees. After that, the battle of Armageddon, where Christ returns with His saints and angels to defeat the armies of the world."

Irene's eyes widened. "So it moves from wrath to restoration?"

I nodded. "Yes. From devastation to renewal. It chronicles the return of Christ to establish His kingdom, the 1,000-year millennial reign, where the saints will govern with Him. And then, the unveiling of eternity: a new heaven, a new earth, and the radiant New Jerusalem descending from above."

Irene sat quietly for a moment, stunned. "So *The Trumpet II* doesn't just warn—it promises."

I nodded. "It does more than that. It prepares. It shows what we're not only escaping—but what we're inheriting. Eternity isn't some vague hope. It's structured. It's real. And it's mapped out in detail. God has written the ending."

Irene's voice firmed, but her eyes shimmered with conviction.

"And this isn't fearmongering. It's a wake-up call."

My expression grew solemn. "That's exactly the point, Irene. *The Vanishing* isn't sensational—it's urgent. It's about the immediacy of the Rapture. Not someday. Any day. It will be sudden—without a headline, without a countdown. Just . . . gone."

Irene nodded slowly. "Like Jesus said—'like a thief in the night.' Unexpected. Undeniable."

I leaned forward, my voice low but steady. "One moment, life will feel normal. People eating, working, scrolling, laughing. Business as usual. And then—silence. Chaos. Grief. Planes without pilots. Cribs without babies. Pulpits without preachers. And a stunned, confused world asking: What just happened?"

Irene's eyes welled up. "And for those who vanish . . . peace. Glory. Finally home."

I nodded. "But for those left behind—it'll feel like waking up in a nightmare. And they won't be able to say God didn't warn them. They'll realize: This wasn't conspiracy. It was prophecy. And in that moment, they'll either harden their hearts—or fall to their knees."

Irene exhaled, her voice barely above a whisper. "It's overwhelming . . . but also clarifying. Because while the world spins off its axis—wars, deception, economic collapse, even nature groaning—you're saying we already have the blueprint. The timeline isn't hidden. It's been in front of us all along."

I nodded slowly. "That's right, Irene. Nothing is spiraling out of control. It's unfolding by design. The world isn't unraveling—it's aligning."

Irene leaned forward, brows knit. "But people keep saying revival is coming—some great outpouring before the end."

My tone sharpened, tender but unflinching. "The Bible doesn't promise revival in the last days, Irene. It promises deception, delusion, and division. Paul said people would heap up teachers to tell them what they want to hear. Jesus warned even the elect might be deceived. This isn't the age of awakening—it's the hour of reckoning."

Irene swallowed hard. "Then what hope is there?"

My eyes brightened. "A remnant. A rescue. A reign. God always preserves a people for Himself. There is a great escape—the Rapture of the Bride. And after that? A royal return. We're not heading toward extinction. We're moving toward coronation. Christ is coming to reign—and we'll reign with Him."

Irene blinked back the weight of it. "And this changes everything."

I smiled gently. "It changes everything—no more evil, no more pain, no more sorrow. For those who are watching and waiting . . . this isn't the end. It's the beginning of everything we've hoped for."

Irene whispered, eyes glistening with conviction. "And time is running out."

I nodded slowly, the air thick with holy urgency. "Yes. But as long as we still have breath, we sound the alarm. That's our assignment."

"These aren't predictions, Irene. They're proclamations. Not speculation—but declaration. Each page is a trumpet blast. And the message is not vague. It's crystal clear: Jesus is coming soon."

"And everything He said—everything the prophets warned—"

I finished her sentence, my voice resolute. "—is unfolding before our eyes. Not someday. Now."

A moment of silence hung between us. Holy. Weighty. Final.

Then she breathed the only words left to say, "Let the trumpet sound."

Irene ran her hand slowly across the cover of *The Trumpet II*, her voice barely above a whisper. "If anyone wants to know what comes next . . . the answer isn't hidden. It's right here."

I leaned forward, my tone steady but intense. "In the pages of Revelation. In the seven harbingers. In the trumpet blasts that echo louder with each passing day. This isn't fiction—it's prophecy. Truth that will either save or condemn."

Irene looked up. "So why did you write them, Ann? Just to warn?"

"No. I didn't write these books just to inform. I wrote them to ignite."

She raised an eyebrow. "To ignite what?"

"To ignite revival," I said. "Because once you understand where we are in the story . . . you'll know exactly how to get ready."

The weight of eternity hung in the room. And then—

Irene whispered, voice steady now. "Then let's sound the alarm."

Irene sat still for a long moment, her hand lingering over the cover of *The Vanishing*. Sunlight streamed through the nearby window, casting golden light over the table as if Heaven were quietly leaning in to listen.

"So," she said softly, her voice full of wonder, "this is how revival begins—one obedient heart at a time."

I nodded, the weight of her words settling deep. "That's exactly it."

She looked at me, her eyes searching almost reverent now. "Ann . . . you couldn't have seen all this coming when you first started, could you?"

I let out a quiet breath, more like a confession than an answer. "No. I couldn't have. Not in a million years."

My voice steadied as I leaned into the truth. "I give all glory to God. I couldn't have written these books, let alone seen how they converge and flow, had He not been guiding me every step of the way. It wasn't strategy. It was surrender."

Irene leaned in, heart open, as if she knew what I was about to say wasn't just for her—it was for others too.

"Then something unexpected happened," I continued. "After I finished writing these books, God spoke clearly to my spirit. He told me what to do next—not to sit back, but to step out."

I smiled as I shared it—not a boast, but a sacred unveiling. "He told me to get back on Goodreads. To relaunch my *Jesus-Says blog*, and to reopen my private Facebook group, *Guardians of Biblical Truth Forum*."

I paused, eyes lifting slightly as if remembering the moment it all clicked into place. "And then He said something that undid me."

Irene waited, eyebrows lifted.

"He told me to give it all away."

Her eyes widened, but I went on, voice filled with quiet fire.

"He told me to start a YouTube channel—also called *Guardians of Biblical Truth*. To read the books aloud, offer Q&A sessions, open the Scriptures in plain language. To make it accessible. Free. Story-driven. Real."

Irene sat back, blinking slowly. "That's . . . bold. And beautiful."

"That's God," I said simply.

I let my hand rest on the stack of books between us.

"If someone wants to support the mission, they can buy the books—maybe even buy multiple copies and leave them behind. For family. For friends. For complete strangers who might pick them up after the Rapture. Because someone's going to need to understand what's happening."

I let the words hang in the air for a moment, then added gently.

"My husband and I are strong tithers and philanthropists. We always have been. And with that said, we've already committed in our hearts to be led by our pastors and give at least ten percent of the proceeds from these books back to the kingdom—to the ones who've sown into our lives."

I saw Irene's eyes shift from admiration to quiet awe as I continued, "Our pastors, John and Brenda Kilpatrick, have been spiritual pillars for us—true shepherds. They're not just leaders. They're our spiritual father and mother. So we're tithing to Church of His Presence, and to others, as God leads."

I smiled—not the kind of smile that boasts, but the kind that rests in holy confidence. "Whatever God tells us to do with the money, we'll do. No hesitation. These aren't just book sales to us—this is kingdom soil. And in our house . . ." I looked her straight in the eyes, "we serve the Lord."

Irene's voice cracked just slightly as she whispered, "And that's why this will bear fruit. Because you're not building a brand. You're sowing into eternity."

I nodded slowly. "Exactly. This isn't about platforms or followers. This is about obedience. About oil in our lamps. About making sure others have oil too."

I glanced at her, my tone soft but certain.

"The Bible is God's instruction manual for life. But people need it opened, illuminated. That's why these books are story-driven. Stories stay with the heart. They imprint truth in a way doctrine alone sometimes can't. And when the heart is stirred, the Spirit has room to work."

Irene's expression changed—no longer just admiration, but partnership. "So come fall . . . you're going all in?"

I smiled. "Come fall, I'll be active. Because God's not finished—not with these messages, and not with the ones who still need to hear them. The alarm is sounding. And I intend to let it ring."

Irene reached across the table and gently squeezed my hand.

"Then let's make sure they hear it."

The room was quiet now—still, sacred. As if Heaven was bearing witness.

CHAPTER SUMMARY

Chapter 4 transitions from foundational doctrine to prophetic insight, introducing the seven harbingers as divine alerts that signal the final season before Christ's return. These harbingers are not imaginative metaphors or speculative theories—

they are prophetic indicators grounded in Scripture, rooted in the covenants, the biblical calendar, celestial signs, and unfolding geopolitical events.

Each harbinger functions as a trumpet blast from Heaven, calling the Church to awaken from spiritual slumber. They represent God's consistent pattern of revealing His plans to those who watch—just as He warned Noah, Joseph, Daniel, and the prophets of old. The chapter emphasizes that these signs are already in motion and are meant not to incite fear, but to stir urgency and faithfulness.

The overview presents the seven harbingers briefly:

1. Global signs aligning with biblical prophecy.
2. God's sacred calendars revealing appointed times.
3. Celestial events as divine signals.
4. Prophetic insight through the biblical feasts.
5. Shemitah cycles revealing patterns of judgment and restoration.
6. The countdown of Daniel's 70th Week.
7. Prophesied wars positioning the world for Christ's return.

The chapter ends with a commissioning—the Watchman's Call—to rise up, sound the alarm, and prepare others. It challenges the reader not to dismiss these signals, but to embrace them with clarity, conviction, and courage.

KEY TAKEAWAYS

- The seven harbingers are biblically rooted prophetic indicators, not speculative ideas.
- God uses signs—just as He did in Scripture—to prepare His people for major events in redemptive history.
- Each harbinger corresponds to a pattern already playing out across global events, Scripture, and time itself.
- The Church is called to discern the times (Matthew 16:3) and respond with readiness—not fear.
- The prophetic roadmap presented confirms that the Rapture is near, the Tribulation is coming, and the King is returning.
- Believers are commissioned to be watchmen—to warn, to wake, and to witness before the hour grows too late.

With this chapter, the book shifts decisively toward prophetic revelation, laying out the structure for the next seven chapters. Each harbinger will now be explored in detail, beginning with the Sign of the Times.

Chapter 5

The First Harbinger:
The Sign of the Times

JESUS' FIRST WARNING WAS "WATCH"—The next major prophetic event on God's divine calendar is not a revival, not a global awakening, not even a new outpouring. It is the Rapture of the Church. And contrary to popular belief, there are no other prophecies that must be fulfilled before this glorious and sobering event takes place. It is imminent. It is unscheduled. And it will arrive like a thief in the night.

When Jesus' disciples came to Him on the Mount of Olives and asked, "What shall be the sign of Your coming, and of the end of the world?" (Matthew 24:3), He didn't begin with comfort. He didn't start with reassurance. His first response was a warning: "Take heed that no man deceive you" (Matthew 24:4). The first word from the lips of Jesus about the end times was not love—it was watch.

> And as He sat upon the Mount of Olives, the disciples came unto Him privately, saying, Tell us, when shall these things be? And what shall be the sign of Your coming, and the end of the world? And Jesus answered and said unto them, Take heed that no man deceive you. (Matthew 24:3–4)

Watching, in the biblical sense, is not a passive suggestion—it is a spiritual command. It implies a continual state of alertness, discernment, and preparation. To watch is to live with your eyes wide open, your spirit aligned with Heaven, and your heart detached from this fading world.

The first harbinger—divine warning—is not an earthquake, a war, or a plague. It's a mindset. A posture. A call to spiritual alertness. In a generation lulled to sleep by comfort and distraction, this harbinger sounds the alarm:

Wake up, Church. The hour is late.

The Watchman Mandate

Before God executes judgment, He raises up watchmen. The prophet Ezekiel was appointed as one such sentinel. In Ezekiel 33:1–9, God laid out the watchman's mandate: if the watchman sees the sword coming and does not blow the trumpet to warn the people, their blood is on his hands. But if he sounds the alarm and they ignore it, their blood is on their own heads.

The role of the watchman is not about popularity—it's about accountability. It is about standing between judgment and the people, and crying out for repentance before it's too late.

This is the spirit behind the harbinger. It is the role of those who carry the burden of truth. It's what Amos meant when he wrote, "Surely the Lord GOD will do nothing, unless He reveals His secret unto His servants the prophets" (Amos 3:7). God never acts without warning. He never unleashes judgment without first releasing revelation.

And today, those who are watching—the spiritual sentinels—are all saying the same thing: Something is coming. And it's closer than we think.

Jesus didn't just warn once. He repeated Himself with a sense of urgency that should arrest every believer's attention. Consider these commands:

- Matthew 24:42–44—"Watch therefore: for you know not what hour your Lord does come."
- Matthew 25:13—"Watch therefore, for you know neither the day nor the hour wherein the Son of Man comes."
- Mark 13:33–37—"Take you heed, watch and pray: for you know not when the time is . . . And what I say unto you I say unto all, Watch."
- Luke 12:35–40—"Let your loins be girded about, and your lights burning . . . Be you therefore ready also: for the Son of Man comes at an hour when you think not."

These are not poetic flourishes or optional add-ons to our faith. They are marching orders. To "watch" is not to obsess over timelines or to engage in endless speculation. It is to be ready, to walk in holiness, to grow in discernment, and to remain spiritually awake while the world slumbers.

We are not to casually browse headlines. We are to interpret the times.

As Jesus said in Luke 12:56:

> You hypocrites, you can discern the face of the sky and of the earth; but how is it that you do not discern this time? (Luke 12:56)

This chapter begins the unveiling of the seven harbingers—the sign of the times; prophetic markers that signal the nearness of Christ's return. But none of them matter unless you first accept the call to watch. Because no matter how many signs appear in the sky, no matter how loudly the trumpets blast, they are only heard by those who are listening.

And this is the hour to listen.

CAN WE KNOW WHEN JESUS WILL RETURN?

The question of when Jesus will return is one of the most asked—and most misunderstood—topics in Bible prophecy. Yet the answer isn't as simple as "yes" or "no." It depends entirely on which event in His return you're referring to.

The return of Jesus will occur in two distinct phases. First, there is the Rapture of the Church, a sudden and imminent event that can happen at any moment. Then, after a period of Great Tribulation, comes the Second Coming, when Jesus physically returns to earth with His saints and angels to establish His kingdom.

These two stages are often conflated, but they are theologically and scripturally separate. The Rapture is imminent—nothing else needs to happen prophetically before it occurs. It's a signless event. But the Second Coming is different. Once the seven-year Tribulation begins, the timeline becomes measurable.

Imminence vs. Timeline:

- The Rapture is a mystery moment: no signs, no countdown. As Jesus said, it will be "like a thief in the night" (Matthew 24:42–44).
- The Second Coming, however, can be calculated: 2,520 days—seven prophetic years of 360 days each—from the signing of the peace treaty between the Antichrist and Israel (Daniel 9:27; Revelation 11:3, 13:5).

This distinction matters. The Church is called to live in expectation of the Rapture, not in prediction of its date. But once the Tribulation begins, those left behind will be able to mark their calendars for Christ's visible return.

Knowing the Season, Not the Day

Jesus rebuked the Pharisees for knowing how to read the weather but not the "signs of the times" (Matthew 16:3). He was pointing out their spiritual blindness. They had all the Messianic signs in front of them—over 400 prophecies in the Old

Testament concerning His First Coming, with more than a hundred being specific and distinct—and yet they still rejected Him.

In the same way, Scripture gives us hundreds of prophetic signs that point to His Second Coming. These include:

- Signs in Nature—Earthquakes, famines, pestilences (Luke 21:11).
- Spiritual Signs—Great apostasy, rise of false prophets, corruption in the Church (1 Timothy 4:1).
- Societal Signs—Moral decay, violence, lovers of self and pleasure (2 Timothy 3:1–5).
- Technological Signs—Global communication, digital currencies, surveillance systems (Revelation 11:9, 13:17).
- Israel Signs—Return to the land (Ezekiel 36–37), rebuilt Temple preparations, surrounding nations rising in hostility (Zechariah 12:2–3).

Together, these signs indicate not the date, but the season of His return *for* the Church. Just like a pregnant woman knows birth is near, even if she doesn't know the hour, we can know when the Rapture is close (Matthew 24:8).

Paul's Clarification: Not in Darkness

Some cite Jesus' words—"no one knows the day or hour"—as a reason to ignore prophecy altogether. But Paul had something to say about that:

> But you, brethren, are not in darkness, that that day should overtake you as a thief. You are all the children of light, and the children of the day: we are not of the night, nor of darkness. (1 Thessalonians 5:4–5)

In other words, while unbelievers may be caught off guard, believers who are spiritually alert will not be surprised. Through the indwelling of the Holy Spirit and diligent study of God's Word, Christians can have discernment about the season we're living in. The apostle John puts it this way:

> But the anointing which you have received of Him abides in you, and, you need not that any man teach you: but as the same anointing teaches you of all things, and is truth, and is no lie, and even as it has taught you, you shall abide in Him. (1 John 2:27)

Beware of Date-Setting

Satan loves when people set dates for the Rapture. Why?

1. It sets up believers for disappointment and disillusionment.
2. It turns attention from the Person of Jesus to the timing of His arrival.
3. It brings ridicule from the secular world when the predicted dates fail.

Jesus warned us in Matthew 24:36 that only the Father knows the exact day and hour. Any attempt to calculate the Rapture date directly defies that warning and distracts from readiness.

Yet many well-meaning believers have fallen into this trap. When their predictions fail, it leads others to mock prophecy altogether—just as Peter predicted:

> Knowing this first, that there shall come in the last days scoffers, walking after their own lusts. And saying, Where is the promise of His coming? For since the fathers fell asleep, all things continue as they were from the beginning of the Creation. (2 Peter 3:3–4)

God Warns Before He Acts

God never pours out wrath without first issuing a warning (Amos 3:7). Before the Flood, Noah preached for 120 years. Before Nineveh fell, Jonah cried out for repentance. And before Jesus returns, God is again shouting through signs, prophecy, and voices like watchmen on the wall.

But sadly, most ignore it. When God's wrath is finally unleashed, many will cry for the rocks to fall on them (Revelation 6:15–16), shocked that the day they scoffed at has arrived.

The Signs Are Increasing

People will say, "There have always been wars and earthquakes." True—but Jesus compared the signs of His return *for* the Church to birth pangs (Matthew 24:8). Just as contractions increase in frequency and intensity, so will prophetic signs. And that's exactly what we're witnessing.

This Is a Wake-Up Call

To ignore the signs is to ignore the kindness of God who, in His mercy, is warning the world. As Nahum wrote:

> The LORD is slow to anger, and great in power, and will not at all acquit the wicked: the LORD has His way in the whirlwind and in the storm, and the clouds are the dust of His feet. (Nahum 1:3)

God's patience is great—but not infinite.

Jesus is coming soon. The signs are everywhere. The trumpet is about to sound. For those who are watching, He will appear as the Blessed Hope (Titus 2:13). For those unprepared, He will arrive as a thief in the night. The question is not *if*—but *when*. And more importantly—are you ready?

THE SIGNS OF THE TIMES: A WORLD ON THE BRINK

Before God pours out His wrath, He sends warnings. Always. From Noah's Flood to the plagues of Egypt, from prophetic voices in ancient Israel to Christ's own declarations—Scripture reveals a consistent truth: judgment is always preceded by mercy. And in this generation, the warnings are blaring again.

Hebrews 10:25 urges us to "encourage one another—and all the more as you see the Day approaching." This is not poetic suggestion; it's a prophetic expectation. The Bible teaches that the return of Jesus Christ will be observable in its approach. How? Through signs—specific, escalating, undeniable signs.

God has embedded history with signals—indicators meant to awaken a sleeping world. In Genesis 1:14, we're told the sun, moon, and stars were created "for signs, and for seasons." These celestial markers are divine appointments on a cosmic calendar. Luke 21:25–28 reiterates this, describing upheaval on earth and signs in the heavens, all pointing to the nearness of Christ's return.

We've already seen recent signs unfold in dramatic fashion:

- 2014–2015 blood moon tetrad.
- Astronomical alignment of the Revelation 12 Sign in 2017.
- Total solar eclipses cutting across America in 2017 and 2024.

These are not superstition or coincidence. They are divine wake-up calls—God's way of shouting: "The time is near."

Yet the world slumbers. Many in the Church do, too. Paul warned in 1 Thessalonians 5 that the Day of the Lord would come like a thief in the night—but only for those in darkness. Those who are spiritually awake are not meant to be surprised.

Sadly, the modern Church reflects the very conditions Paul and Jesus foretold. In 2 Timothy 3:1–5, we see a culture obsessed with self, pleasure, and rebellion.

> This know also, that in the last days perilous times shall come. For men shall be lovers of their own selves, covetous (lovers of money), boasters, proud, blasphemers, disobedient to parents, unthankful, unholy, without natural affection, truce-breakers (unforgiving), false accusers (slanders), incontinent (without self-control), fierce (brutal), despisers of those that are good; traitors, heady (headstrong), high-minded (haughty), lovers of pleasures more than lovers of God: having a form of godliness, but denying the power thereof: from such people turn away. (2 Timothy 3:1–5)

In Revelation 3, Jesus addresses the end-time church of Laodicea—lukewarm, self-satisfied, and blind. He stands at the door, still knocking.

The signs aren't just in the sky or across the nations—they are within us. Our complacency, our compromise, our lack of urgency is itself a sign.

In the following pages, we'll examine seven major categories of end-time signs the Bible highlights. These are not disjointed prophecies. They are interconnected alarms, converging like never before. Each one whispers—and together they shout—Jesus is coming soon for a Bride.

1. Birth Pangs of a Dying Age: God's Alarms in Creation

Of all the prophetic indicators, the signs found in nature may be the most dismissed and least respected. People often scoff at the idea that weather patterns, earthquakes, or famines could mean anything other than natural cycles. The response is usually something like, "You've got to be kidding! There have always been hurricanes and earthquakes. What else is new?" But this reaction overlooks two key truths—one scriptural and the other spiritual.

Birth Pangs: Frequency and Intensity—Jesus Himself warned in Matthew 24:7–8 that famines, pestilences, and earthquakes would increase like birth pangs. That metaphor is everything. Just as contractions grow more frequent and more intense as labor progresses, so too will natural calamities as we near His return. It's not the mere presence of these events that signals the times—it's the compounding intensity. What once felt like occasional tremors have become relentless contractions. Anyone paying attention can see the global uptick in hurricanes, wildfires, floods, and earthquakes—not only in number, but in ferocity. These are not random. They are revelatory.

Our Rational Blindness—But here lies the second problem: we are a rationalistic people. Trained to trust only what we can see, measure, and replicate in a lab, we've become skeptics of the supernatural. The very idea that God would use weather patterns, disasters, or cosmic anomalies to get our attention sounds primitive to modern ears. Yet, Ephesians 6:12 reminds us that reality is not limited to what we can perceive. We war against "spiritual forces of wickedness in high places"—a dimension beyond the five senses. Because of this spiritual blindness, many are unable—or unwilling—to connect the natural with the supernatural. Yet it is the supernatural realm—not the physical—that is ultimate, eternal, and most real. As Scripture affirms:

> While we look not at the things which are seen, but at the things which are not seen: for the things which are seen are temporal; but the things which are not seen are eternal. (2 Corinthians 4:18)

Biblical Precedent: God Speaks Through Nature—This resistance is especially tragic because the Bible is saturated with examples of God using nature as a megaphone for judgment, warning, or revelation. In Joel 1, a devastating locust plague ravages the land. The prophet doesn't explain it away with climate patterns. He identifies it as divine discipline—God's plea for repentance. And Joel warns that if the people ignore the locusts, worse is coming: an invading army.

The pattern continues throughout Scripture:

- The Flood in Noah's day was a worldwide cataclysm, sent after a lengthy period of warning (Genesis 6–7).
- The plagues in Egypt (Exodus 7–12), including hail, locusts, and darkness, were nature's response to Pharaoh's hardened heart.
- The earthquake at Mount Sinai (Exodus 19:18).
- The sun standing still for Joshua (Joshua 10:12–14).
- At Jesus' birth, a mysterious star appeared (Matthew 2:2).
- At His crucifixion, there was an earthquake and an unnatural darkness for three hours (Matthew 27:45, 51; Luke 23:44–45).
- At His Second Coming, there will be the greatest earthquake in human history, flattening mountains and reshaping the earth itself (Revelation 16:17–21).

These were all supernatural signs using the natural order to get humanity's attention. And in the future, Scripture tells us this divine method of messaging will continue. In fact, it will escalate.

No wonder Jesus told us to watch for "famines and earthquakes" in Matthew 24:7, and "great signs from heaven" in Luke 21:11. He was describing the symptoms of a planet groaning in anticipation (Romans 8:22). Creation is not in chaos—it's in labor. And labor leads to birth.

> For we know that the whole Creation groans and travails in pain together until now. (Romans 8:22)

The Book of Revelation—When we examine the Book of Revelation, we see this crescendo vividly. Earthquakes rattle the planet repeatedly (Revelation 6:12, 8:5, 11:13, 11:19, 16:18), hailstones fall from the sky weighing about 75–100 pounds (Revelation 16:21), and the sun and the moon are darkened (Revelation 6:12). The natural world enters a state of violent protest, signaling the full wrath of God about to be poured out.

But long before the Tribulation judgments arrive, the world begins to feel the tremors of what's coming. These are the signs we are seeing now.

Modern Disasters as Remedial Judgments—Some natural disasters are more than signs; they function as remedial judgments—disciplinary tools God uses to wake us up. They're not simply tragedies; they are warnings.

In American history alone, we can point to events like the Vietnam War, the 9/11 terrorist attacks, and Hurricane Katrina as national wake-up calls. Globally, the COVID-19 pandemic serves as perhaps the most extensive and sobering remedial judgment in modern memory. Like Joel's locusts, these events strip away our illusions of control. They shake us—literally and spiritually—and demand our attention.

We must ask: Is God speaking today through nature? And are we still plugging our ears?

The Rise of Earthquakes, Plagues, and Signs in the Skies—We need only glance at data from global monitoring agencies to confirm that natural disasters are increasing—not just in frequency, but in intensity. Earthquakes are now occurring in regions that have never experienced seismic activity before. Astounding wildfires, unprecedented droughts, and catastrophic floods are becoming global norms. Add to that celestial signs like the 2014–2015 blood moon tetrad, the solar eclipses aligning with biblical feast days, and the Revelation 12 Sign that appeared in the skies on September 23, 2017.

These aren't random astronomical phenomena. According to Genesis 1:14, the heavenly bodies were created "for signs, and for seasons." And Jesus Himself said in Luke 21:25–26 that the last days would be accompanied by "signs in the sun, and in the moon, and in the stars; and upon the earth distress of nations."

> And there shall be signs in the sun, and in the moon, and in the stars; and upon the earth distress of nations, with perplexity; the sea and the waves roaring. Men's hearts failing them for fear, and for looking after those things which are coming on the earth: for the powers of heaven shall be shaken. (Luke 21:25–26)

We are no longer just seeing the season—we are hearing it scream.

The Challenge: Are We Listening?—What will it take to wake us up? God is speaking through a megaphone called Creation. The question is not whether the signs are present—the question is whether we're willing to discern them. And if not now, when?

As nature groans and judgments rumble, we are not to fear—we are to watch. These signs are not meaningless—they are mercy. They are God's loving alarms to a distracted world, warning of what's coming and inviting repentance before the final trumpet sounds.

Let us not be like the scoffers of 2 Peter 3:3–4, dismissing the signs and ridiculing the return of Christ. Let us instead be among those who "encourage one another . . . as we see the day approaching" (Hebrews 10:25). Because the signs of nature aren't subtle anymore. They're roaring.

2. The Age of Lawlessness: Society at the Crossroads

When the disciples asked Jesus for signs of His return, He pointed them not just to cosmic disturbances or geopolitical turmoil, but to the moral condition of mankind. In Matthew 24:37, Jesus warned:

> But as the days of Noah were, so shall also the coming of the Son of Man be. (Matthew 24:37)

He echoed this again in Luke 17:28–30, referencing the days of Lot. The implication is chilling: society at the end of the age will mirror the moral decay of the ancient world, descending into the same depths of rebellion, violence, and depravity that marked both Noah's generation and the cities of Sodom and Gomorrah—just before divine judgment fell. As it was before the worldwide Flood, so it will be again before the return of the Son of Man.

Genesis 6:5–13 offers our first glimpse into the moral state of Noah's generation—"every intent of the thoughts of man's heart was only evil continually," and "the earth was filled with violence" (Hebrew: *hamas*). But it's the apostle Paul who gives the New Testament commentary—first as a *historian* in Romans 1 and then as a *prophet* in 2 Timothy 3. These two passages, read together, form a complete picture of a society gone full circle—one that begins with the rejection of God and ends in cultural collapse.

The Downward Spiral of Rebellion (Romans 1)—In Romans 1:18–32, Paul outlines a step-by-step descent into societal decay. It begins when a culture suppresses the truth of God (verse 18), denies His divine nature (verse 20), and exchanges His glory for manmade ideologies (verse 23). In this rebellion, mankind "exchanged the truth about God for a lie and worshiped and served the creature rather than the Creator" (verse 25). This is the religion of Humanism— man as his own god.

In response, God removes His hand of restraint. First, He "gave them over to sexual impurity" (verse 24), leading to widespread fornication—sex outside of marriage—and adultery. When that brought no repentance, He "gave them over to degrading passions" (verse 26), resulting in the normalization and celebration of homosexual sin. Still unrepentant, God finally "gave them over to a depraved mind" (verse 28), a reprobate way of thinking where every boundary is erased and every perversion is embraced.

That depraved mind has led to the celebration of what God calls shameful. Today, we see this most vividly in the transgender movement, where humanity attempts to override the Creator's design, asserting autonomy over biology, identity, and even truth itself. What God designed as male and female has been deconstructed into a spectrum of confusion. This is not progress—it is prophetic evidence that our generation is mirroring the lawlessness of Noah's day.

The result of this descent is a culture defined by Romans 1:29–31: "They have become filled with every kind of wickedness, evil, greed and depravity." We are watching that Scripture come alive in real time.

Paul the Prophet: End-Time Society Foretold (2 Timothy 3)—In 2 Timothy 3:1–5, Paul moves from historian to prophet, confirming that the last days would again be marked by this same spiritual rot. He writes, "But understand this, that in the last days there will come times of great difficulty." Why? Because "men will be lovers of self, lovers of money, boastful, arrogant, revilers, disobedient to parents," and on he goes with a sobering catalog of corruption.

Paul identifies three spiritual pathologies that define a collapsing society:

- Humanism—"Lovers of self" (verse 2).
- Materialism—"Lovers of money" (verse 2).
- Hedonism—"Lovers of pleasure rather than lovers of God" (verse 4).

These are not isolated vices—they are the ruling ideologies of the modern world. Humanism exalts the self above God. Materialism worships wealth as the measure of worth. Hedonism pursues pleasure at any cost. Together, they produce a fourth and final consequence: Nihilism—a despairing worldview that sees no meaning, no hope, and no future.

Paul describes the fruit of this godless system in detail: "unholy, ungrateful, heartless, unappeasable, slanderous, brutal, without self-control, haters of good . . . treacherous, reckless, swollen with conceit" (verses 2–4). Sound familiar? Turn on the news. Scroll through social media. Watch a Netflix original. It's not a preview. It's a fulfillment.

A Prophetic Mirror—Scripture warns that in the final days, sin won't merely exist—it will be celebrated, institutionalized, and normalized. We're not just seeing isolated acts of rebellion; we're watching civilization-wide transformation:

- Moral confusion is now codified into law.
- Gender distinctions—established at Creation—are blurred or denied outright.
- Children are exploited, trafficked, and exposed to ideologies meant to destroy innocence.

- Violence and rage dominates our streets, our screens, and our speech.
- Truth is subjective, and those who stand on biblical absolutes are labeled dangerous, intolerant, or hateful.

This moral freefall isn't random—it's prophetic.

As in the Days of Noah and Lot—Jesus said that His return would be like the days of Noah and Lot (Luke 17:26–30): In Noah's day, violence filled the earth (Genesis 6:11). In Lot's time, sexual perversion and pride saturated Sodom (Ezekiel 16:49–50). In both cases, people were indifferent—eating, drinking, marrying, buying, and selling—until judgment fell. The warning is unmistakable: When society reaches a certain moral tipping point, divine intervention follows.

Lawlessness and the Love Grown Cold—Jesus also warned:

Because lawlessness will abound, the love of many will grow cold. (Matthew 24:12)

We're watching this happen in real time. Lawlessness doesn't just mean breaking laws—it's the rejection of God's moral law, the deliberate push toward chaos, rebellion, and self-rule.

And the result? Love grows cold. Not only in the world—but tragically, in the Church. Compassion is replaced with convenience. Conviction is replaced with compromise. The flame of agape love—the highest and most selfless form of love described in Scripture—flickers in a windstorm of cultural pressure.

A Culture Addicted to Pleasure and Entertainment—Paul's warning continues: "Lovers of pleasure rather than lovers of God." We live in a time where distraction is king. Endless streams of content. Instant gratification. Digital dopamine. Entertainment is no longer a pastime—it's an identity. Many are so saturated with noise that they can no longer hear the still small voice of the Lord.

Spiritual apathy is one of the clearest signs of the end. Jesus warned the Laodicean church (Revelation 3:14–22) that they were lukewarm, blind, and unaware of their true condition. Their wealth masked their poverty. Their comfort concealed their compromise. This is the spirit of the age—and it is infiltrating even the most well-intentioned believers.

The Rise of Scoffing—One of the most chilling societal signs is found in 2 Peter:

In the last days, scoffers will come, mocking and following their own evil desires. They will say, Where is this 'coming' He promised? (2 Peter 3:3–4)

Mockery of biblical truth is no longer subtle—it's mainstream. Prophecy is marginalized. Moral purity is ridiculed. Righteousness is offensive. Even within the Church, a spirit of deconstruction and compromise is pushing many into apostasy. But Peter's warning reminds us: The increase in scoffing is itself a sign.

God's Response to a Collapsing Culture—Just as in the days of Noah and Lot, God will not allow evil to spiral unchecked. He delays judgment because of His mercy (2 Peter 3:9), but He does not ignore rebellion forever.

We are witnessing Romans 1 unfold before our eyes:

- God gave them over to sexual impurity (verse 24).
- Then to shameful lusts (verse 26).
- Then to a depraved mind (verse 28).

When a society reaches this point, it's not just lost—it's judged.

The American Mirror—This prophetic diagnosis could not be more relevant to our own culture. Though we claim to be a Christian nation, our true religion is Humanism, our god is the dollar, and our lifestyle is hedonism. From classrooms to boardrooms, from Capitol Hill to Hollywood Boulevard, we've institutionalized the very sins God warned about.

Our media exports these values to the world, packaging rebellion as entertainment. We glamorize sexual immorality, mock biblical truth, and cheer on moral confusion. And we are reaping what we have sown. Galatians 6:7 warns:

> Be not deceived; God is not mocked: for whatsoever a man sows, that shall he
> also reap. (Galatians 6:7)

Our nation is now wallowing in despair. Drug overdoses, suicides, depression, anxiety, and mass shootings are symptoms of a soul-starved generation. The American dream of money, sex, and power has turned into a nightmare. And still, the world sleeps.

But the signs are unmistakable: we are in the days of Noah and Lot once again. And just as judgment fell before, it will fall again. The collapse of society is not merely a political or cultural crisis—it is a spiritual one. And it is prophetic proof that Jesus is coming soon.

Are We Watching?—The collapse of culture is not a reason to despair—it is a wake-up call. The darker the night becomes, the more clearly we see the Light of Christ—and the more urgent our mission is to shine that Light.

> You are the light of the world. A city that is set on a hill cannot be hid. Neither
> do men light a candle, and put it under a bushel, but on a candlestick; and it gives
> light to all that are in the house. Let your light so shine before men, that they may
> see your good works, and glorify your Father which is in heaven. (Matthew 5:14–
> 16)

This is not the time to blend in—it's the time to stand apart. To warn. To prepare. To point others to Jesus.

3. The Age of Spiritual Deception: The Last Days of Truth

If there is one warning Jesus gave more than any other concerning the last days, it is this: "Do not be deceived." When the disciples asked Him for signs of His return in Matthew 24, His first response wasn't about earthquakes or wars. It was a caution: "Take heed that no man deceive you." (Matthew 24:4). That should stop us in our tracks. Because while we often focus on outward disasters and political upheavals, Jesus warned us that the greatest threat would come from within the spiritual realm.

This is the era of spiritual confusion, counterfeit gospels, and religious rebellion. It's not just society collapsing morally—it's the Church drifting theologically. And that is perhaps the most dangerous sign of all.

False Christs and False Prophets—In Matthew 24:5, 11, and 24, Jesus says that in the last days, "many" false teachers would rise—not a few, but many. These deceivers would lead astray not just the skeptical, but even the "elect" if possible. This isn't just about cult leaders or televangelist scandals. This is a widespread infiltration of deception into the very core of Christian thought.

Paul confirms this in 2 Thessalonians 2:3, where he warns of a great "falling away" that must occur before the return of Christ. This apostasy won't be a quiet departure from orthodoxy—it will be a brazen rebellion against truth, masquerading as enlightenment.

> Let no man deceive you by any means: for that Day (the Day of the Lord) shall not come, except there comes a falling away (great apostasy) first, and that man of sin be revealed, the son of perdition (the Antichrist). (2 Thessalonians 2:3)

Today, we see this apostasy exploding across every denomination. Preachers declare that Hell isn't real. Influencers claim the Bible is outdated. Churches celebrate sin under the banner of love. Many now preach a gospel without repentance, a Christianity without the Cross, and a kingdom without a King.

The prophet Isaiah warned of this inversion in Isaiah 5:20:

> Woe unto those who call evil good, and good evil; that put darkness for light, and light for darkness; that put bitter for sweet, and sweet for bitter! (Isaiah 5:20)

That is exactly what our generation is doing—calling compromise compassion, and truth hate speech.

Doctrines of Demons and a Departure from Sound Doctrine—In 1 Timothy 4:1, Paul gives a chilling prophetic insight: "Now the Spirit speaks expressly, that in later times some shall depart from the faith, giving heed to seducing spirits, and doctrines of devils." These teachings don't come from atheism—they come clothed in religious language, from pulpits, platforms, and spiritual influencers.

2 Timothy 4:3 continues the warning: "For the time will come when they will not endure sound doctrine; but after their own lusts shall they heap to themselves teachers, having itching ears." Instead of submitting to God's truth, people will seek out voices that affirm their feelings, validate their lifestyles, and silence their convictions.

This is the age of spiritualism consumerism, where theology is customized like a playlist and where conviction is replaced by comfort. Instead of hearing "Thus says the Lord," we hear "Follow your heart." The result is a Christianity that looks nothing like Christ.

The Rise of the False Church—Perhaps most sobering of all is what Revelation 17 describes—a harlot church, riding on the beast, intoxicated by power and influence. This is Mystery Babylon in her religious form—a global, one world spiritual system that rejects biblical authority while cloaking itself in religious unity. It will welcome all faiths, all gods, and all paths—except the true gospel of Jesus Christ. Beneath its appearance of peace and inclusion lies a spirit of deception, seducing the world into a counterfeit worship that denies the lordship of Christ.

We are watching the scaffolding of this church rise today. Interfaith movements, one world religious summits, and the erasure of moral absolutes are all laying the groundwork for a final false religious system that will welcome the Antichrist with open arms.

This is not an exaggeration. It's prophecy being fulfilled.

Spiritual Signs All Around Us

- Apostasy in the Church (2 Thessalonians 2:3).
- Doctrines of demons being preached (1 Timothy 4:1).
- Itching ears rejecting truth (2 Timothy 4:3–4).
- Mockers in the last days (2 Peter 3:3–4).
- A form of godliness but denying its power (2 Timothy 3:5).

We are witnessing it all unfold—deception, delusion, and defiance of truth. And yet, amid the darkness, a remnant is rising—those who cling to the Word, who hunger for righteousness, who have not bowed the knee to Baal, the false god of compromise and rebellion so often condemned in the Old Testament. These are the watchers. The faithful. The ones Jesus will find awake when He returns.

4. The Age of Artificial Dominion: When Machines Meet Prophecy

From the moment humanity built the first tower in Babel (Genesis 11), there's been an innate drive to ascend—to grasp divine power through human means. Today, the tower is not made of bricks and mortar. It's built in code, satellites, microchips, and neural networks. We are living in an era of unprecedented technological advancement—one that is not only reshaping daily life but also preparing the infrastructure for the rise of global control, deception, and surveillance prophesied in Scripture. This is the Age of Artificial Dominion. And it's not science fiction—it's prophecy in real-time.

Technology as a Tool of Global Control—Revelation 13 gives us one of the clearest pictures of end-time technological application. The Antichrist will exercise total economic control, enforcing the infamous mark of the beast system—where "no one will be able to buy or sell unless he has the mark" (Revelation 13:17). For centuries, this sounded impossible. But today, with digital IDs, biometric tracking, blockchain transactions, implantable microchips, and cashless economies, it's no longer far-fetched. It's within reach.

We now have the infrastructure to monitor, restrict, and manipulate transactions globally with the click of a button. Governments and corporations alike are investing in Central Bank Digital Currencies (CBDCs), which would give unprecedented control over every purchase and movement. All in the name of "convenience" and "security."

Artificial Intelligence and the Rise of Deception—Paul warns in 2 Thessalonians 2:9–10 that the coming Antichrist will deceive with "all power, signs, and lying wonders." Combine this with deepfake technology, AI-generated speech and images, and synthetic voice mimicry, and the prophetic landscape becomes clear: the infrastructure for mass deception is already here.

AI is not merely advancing industry—it's reshaping truth itself. Chatbots evangelize New Age doctrine. Algorithms suppress biblical values while promoting lawlessness. People are slowly being trained to accept information without discernment, to accept reality as it is curated for them by artificial intelligence rather than divine wisdom.

Jesus warned in Matthew 24:24:

> For there shall arise false Christs, and false prophets, and shall show great signs and wonders; insomuch that, if it were possible, they shall deceive the very elect. (Matthew 24:24)

The digital tools now available can fabricate those "signs" with disturbing precision.

Surveillance State and the Erosion of Privacy—We live in a world where nearly every movement, transaction, conversation, and decision is tracked, recorded, and stored. What began as convenience has become surveillance. Smart homes listen. Phones track. Cameras record. Satellites watch. Social credit systems are emerging in some parts of the world, eerily echoing Revelation 13's system of compliance-based access.

While these systems promise safety, they ultimately train the masses to surrender freedom for control. The Antichrist's system will not be built overnight—it will be welcomed by a generation already conditioned to believe surveillance is safety.

The Gospel Through Technology—In the midst of these dark developments, technology is also being used by God. Jesus said:

> And this Gospel of the Kingdom shall be preached in all the world for a witness unto all nations; and then shall the end come. (Matthew 24:14).

Thanks to satellite TV, YouTube, podcasts, and Bible apps, the gospel is being broadcast to remote villages and restricted nations alike.

Bible translation software, AI-supported language modeling, and livestream worship services are reaching the unreached. Prophecy is not only fulfilled by the dark side of technology—it is also being accelerated by its use in evangelism and discipleship.

A Warning and a Charge—Daniel was told to "seal up the book until the time of the end—when knowledge will increase" (Daniel 12:4). That time is now. Knowledge has exploded. But wisdom? Discernment? Truth? Those are rapidly disappearing.

As the Church, we must be awake—not hypnotized by our screens or lured by the convenience of tech-driven life. We must guard our hearts, renew our minds, and discern the hour. Technology is not neutral. It's a battleground—and the enemy is fighting for our loyalty, our privacy, and our worship.

This is the Age of Artificial Dominion. But it won't last forever. Jesus is coming. And the One who truly reigns does not need machines to rule.

5. The Age of Globalism: Preparing the World for One Ruler

Throughout human history, the rise and fall of nations have marked the passage of time. Kingdoms have clashed, alliances formed and fractured, and empires have ruled and crumbled. But the Bible reveals that in the last days, the world will experience a convergence—a geopolitical transformation paving the way for a final global leader. We are witnessing this convergence now.

A Prophetic Framework for Political Change—Daniel 2 and Daniel 7 give us the clearest picture of this trajectory. The statue in Nebuchadnezzar's dream—comprising gold, silver, bronze, iron, and finally iron mixed with clay—represents successive world empires, culminating in a fragile, divided global system. This final state, the ten toes of iron and clay, foreshadows a fractured alliance of nations—a loose confederation primed for takeover by a singular ruler: the Antichrist.

Revelation 13 expands on this with chilling clarity. It describes a beast rising out of the sea—symbolizing a global empire under one man's rule. This empire will be political, economic, and spiritual in nature, empowered by Satan himself. This is not fiction or fearmongering. It's prophecy unfolding in real time.

The March Toward Globalism—In recent decades, the world has moved steadily toward interconnectedness. Technology, travel, trade, and diplomacy have broken down borders. While this has brought undeniable convenience, it has also laid the infrastructure for centralized control.

- Global governance bodies such as the United Nations, the World Economic Forum, and the International Monetary Fund have gained increasing influence over national policies.
- Supranational agreements like the Paris Climate Accord, World Health Organization treaties, Abrahamic Accord, and digital identity frameworks are becoming globally binding.
- World crisis—including pandemics, wars, and climate emergencies—are constantly used as justifications for centralized decision-making.

Revelation 13:16–17 describes a time when no one will be able to buy or sell without the mark of the beast. For that to happen, there must first be a global economic and digital system. We are on the brink of that very reality. Central Bank Digital Currencies (CBDCs), biometric identification, and social credit systems are no longer theoretical—they're operational in multiple countries.

The Erosion of Sovereignty—Globalism is not just about unity—it's about control. The sovereignty of nations is being subtly eroded. From climate mandates to pandemic restrictions, governments around the world are increasingly taking their cues from unelected, unaccountable global elites.

Even the United States—the last great superpower—is showing signs of strategic decline. Economic instability, cultural division, weakened borders, and international withdrawals signal a retreat from global leadership. This power vacuum will not remain empty. It is setting the stage for a new kind of leader—one who promises peace, security, and prosperity, but delivers bondage.

The Cry for a Savior—And the Rise of the Antichrist—As the world reels from wars, inflation, food shortages, cyberattacks, and political corruption, people are becoming desperate for answers. The Bible prophesies that in such a time of global chaos, a charismatic figure will emerge with seemingly supernatural wisdom and solutions (Daniel 8:23–25).

He will come "in peace," and by peace, "destroy many" (Daniel 8:25). He will unite the world under a false pretense of stability. He will confirm a covenant with Israel (Daniel 9:27), rebuild trust among nations, and establish a one world system—political, economic, religious, and military.

But this peace will be short-lived. His true nature will be revealed at the midpoint of the Tribulation when he declares himself to be God and demands worship (2 Thessalonians 2:3–4; Revelation 13:5–8).

Prophecy in Motion—What once seemed impossible—a single government, a unified economy, a digital currency, a monitored society—is now on our doorstep. The convergence of these global trends is not coincidence. It's confirmation. Every geopolitical tremor is a step closer to the fulfillment of Revelation's vision.

The world is not just drifting toward globalism—it's accelerating. And this transformation is not random—it's prophetic.

So What Should We Do?—This isn't a call to panic. It's a call to prepare. As Jesus warned in Luke 21:28:

> And when these things begin to come to pass, then look up, and lift up your heads; for your redemption draws near. (Luke 21:28)

Our hope is not in politics or policy, it is in the Prince of Peace—Jesus Christ—who will return to overthrow the Antichrist and establish His eternal kingdom (Revelation 19:11–16).

The signs are not subtle. They're systemic. The world is being prepared for one ruler. The only question is: Which ruler will you follow—the Antichrist or Jesus Christ?

6. The Age of Restoration: Israel, God's Super Sign

Bible prophecy has many threads, but one golden thread runs through nearly every prophetic narrative in Scripture: Israel. More than any other nation, Israel serves as God's prophetic timepiece. When you want to know where we are on God's prophetic calendar, look to Jerusalem—look to Israel.

Jesus Himself said:

> Now learn a parable of the fig tree: When his branch is yet tender, and puts forth leaves, you know that summer is near. So likewise you, when you shall see all

these things, know that it is near, even at the doors. Verily I say unto you, This generation shall not pass, till all these things be fulfilled. (Matthew 24:32–34)

In Scripture, the fig tree is a symbolic picture of Israel (Hosea 9:10; Jeremiah 24:5–8). Jesus was clearly pointing to the rebirth of Israel as a harbinger—divine warning—of the last days.

The Rebirth of a Nation—Against All Odds—Perhaps the most dramatic fulfillment of Bible prophecy in the modern age occurred on May 14, 1948, when Israel became a nation again after nearly 2,000 years in exile. No other people group in history has been scattered across the earth and yet remained a distinct people, only to return to their ancient homeland and reestablish their national identity.

This fulfillment of Isaiah 66:8—"Can a nation be born in a day?"—was not a coincidence. It was God's declaration to the world that the prophetic countdown had resumed. The "dry bones" of Ezekiel 37 were rattling to life. The Jews were coming home, just as foretold by the prophets (Ezekiel 36:24; Jeremiah 31:10).

The Return of the Jewish People—A Global Regathering—The regathering of the Jewish people is one of the clearest signs that we are living in the last days. Isaiah 11:11–12 says the Lord will "recover the remnant of His people . . . from the four corners of the earth." That is exactly what has happened.

From Europe, Russia, Africa, the United States, and most recently Ukraine, Jews have returned to Israel in fulfillment of dozens of prophetic scriptures. The miraculous ingathering continues—even in the face of persecution, antisemitism, and war. This is not a political movement—it is a prophetic movement.

The Reclamation of the Land—The Blooming Wilderness—When the Jewish people returned to their land, they found it barren, swampy, and desolate—exactly as prophesied (Leviticus 26:32–33). But as they returned, the land responded. Isaiah 35:1 said, "The wilderness and the dry land shall be glad; the desert shall rejoice and blossom like the rose."

Today, Israel is one of the world's agricultural powerhouses. Its deserts bloom. Its technology exports are among the highest per capita in the world. What we are witnessing is not just economic recovery—it is covenant restoration.

The Rebuilding of Jerusalem—the World's Epicenter—Jerusalem, once a backwater city under Muslim control, has become the focal point of global diplomacy and conflict. In 1967, during the Six-Day War, Israel recaptured Jerusalem—fulfilling Luke 21:24, which prophesied that "Jerusalem will be trampled underfoot by the Gentiles until the times of the Gentiles are fulfilled."

No other city on earth carries such prophetic weight. Jerusalem is the epicenter of past promises and future fulfillment. It will be the throne of Jesus Christ in the coming Messianic Kingdom (Zechariah 14:9; Jeremiah 3:17).

The Rise of Global Antisemitism—Satan's Final Assault—As Israel rises, so does opposition to her existence. Antisemitism has once again gone global. United Nations resolutions disproportionately condemn Israel. Terrorist groups attack her borders. Iran threatens her existence. College campuses rage against her right to exist.

But this too was foretold. Zechariah 12:2–3 said that in the last days, "all nations of the earth" will gather against Jerusalem.

> Behold, I will make Jerusalem a cup of trembling (a source of instability) unto all the people round about, when they shall be in the siege both against Judah and against Jerusalem. And in that day will I make Jerusalem a burdensome stone for all people: all that burden themselves with it shall be cut in pieces, though all the people of the earth be gathered together against it. (Zechariah 12:2–3)

These verses prophesy that Jerusalem will become the center of global conflict in the last days. This hostility is not merely political—it is spiritual. It's Satanic. Because Israel is at the heart of God's end-times plan, she is the bullseye of Satan's wrath.

The Third Temple Preparations—A Prophetic Powder Keg—Multiple prophecies declare that a Third Temple will stand in Jerusalem during the Tribulation period (Daniel 9:27; Matthew 24:15; Revelation 11:1–2). While the Temple doesn't exist yet, everything necessary to build it already does.

- The Temple Institute has recreated the priestly garments and vessels.
- Red heifer candidates have been bred; on July 1, 2025, a disqualified one was burned for its ashes in a practice ceremony for Temple purification.
- Levitical training is underway.
- Blueprints for the structure are complete.

All that remains is the political permission to build—which many scholars believe will be part of the covenant that the Antichrist confirms with Israel (Daniel 9:27).

Israel: God's Timepiece Is Ticking—The restoration of Israel is not just a sign—it is the super sign. Every prophetic event related to the end times is Israel-centric. From the Tribulation to the return of Christ to the Millennial Kingdom, Israel is the stage on which the final drama unfolds.

If you want to understand the urgency of the hour, look no further than Jerusalem. God is not finished with Israel—He is just getting started. And if the fig tree has blossomed, as Jesus said, then our redemption is drawing near.

7. The Convergence of Signs: The Acceleration Effect

The six categories we've explored—nature, society, spirituality, technology, global politics, and Israel—are not isolated strands in the tapestry of prophecy. Rather, they are interwoven signals, forming a prophetic symphony that is rising to a crescendo. The Bible makes clear that, as the return of Christ approaches, these signs will not simply occur—they will converge, intensify, and multiply, just like labor pains before birth.

Jesus Himself warned of this pattern in Matthew 24:8, saying, "All these are the beginning of sorrows." The word translated "sorrows" in the Greek word *odin*—meaning birth pains. And birth pains follow a predictable pattern: they increase in frequency, intensity, and closeness together until the moment of delivery. That is exactly what we're witnessing today. These signs are no longer scattered tremors—they are contractions, growing stronger and closer, signaling that the moment is near.

In past generations, these prophetic indicators appeared sporadically—isolated events unfolding decades apart. A societal collapse here, a war there, a technological leap now and then. But today, in our generation, we're seeing them all—simultaneously, globally, and with unprecedented speed. This is not coincidence. It's convergence.

Consider this:

- The moral collapse of society isn't separate from the rise in false religion—they feed each other.
- The technological advancements aren't neutral—they are laying the infrastructure for economic control and mass deception.
- The political alignment of nations, including hostility toward Israel, isn't random—it's exactly what the prophets foretold.
- And through it all, God is still speaking through nature, through judgment, through the supernatural, and through His people.

What we are witnessing is not just a collection of bad headlines. We are witnessing a prophetic convergence—a convergence that is accelerating, pressing the world ever closer to the moment when Christ will step back into history and take His rightful place as King of kings and Lord of lords.

For the world, this acceleration is terrifying. For the believer, it is confirmation. God is not silent. He is not absent. He is not slow, as some count slowness. He is patient, "not willing that any should perish but that all should come to repentance" (2 Peter 3:9).

But His patience will not last forever. The contractions are nearing full dilation—the moment of delivery is almost here. The Day of the Lord is not creeping—it's racing toward us.

The only question is—are you watching?

WHAT MAKES TODAY'S SIGNS DIFFERENT?

Throughout history, God has issued prophetic markers—some immediate, others sealed for future fulfillment. But today, we stand in a truly singular moment in time. For the first time in history, ancient prophecies that once seemed vague, symbolic, or even impossible to interpret are now coming into clear focus. Why? Because the conditions needed to understand and fulfill them are unfolding right before our eyes.

This generation is witnessing signs that no other generation has ever seen. Not just in volume—but in specificity, clarity, and technological feasibility.

Unsealing the Future: Daniel's Mystery Becomes Our Reality

Centuries ago, the prophet Daniel received visions about the end of the age—visions that even he couldn't make sense of. "I heard, but I did not understand," he confessed (Daniel 12:8). God's response? "Go your way, Daniel . . . the words are sealed until the time of the end" (Daniel 12:9).

In other words, there would come a generation for whom those sealed mysteries would be unlocked—by historical developments, technological breakthroughs, and spiritual insight. That generation is ours. The unsealing has begun.

Prophecies Now Possible: Six Modern-Day Fulfillments

1. The Mass Deaths of the Tribulation (Revelation 6–9)—The Bible describes catastrophic judgments during the first half of the Tribulation, wiping out half of the global population. For centuries, these numbers seemed unimaginable. But today, with over 8 billion people on earth—and with the terrifying potential of nuclear, biological, and chemical warfare—it's not only plausible, it's chillingly probable. Prophecies like "a third of the earth burned" (Revelation 8:7) and "loathsome sores" (Revelation 16:2) make haunting sense in light of radiation fallout and modern weaponry.

2. An Army of 200 Million (Revelation 9:16)—John described a staggering force of 200 million troops marching from the East. In his day, that number far exceeded the entire global population. For most of history, it seemed impossible. But not anymore. Today, with China and India each exceeding 1.4 billion people, and other eastern nations rapidly militarizing, such a force is no longer a fantasy—it's feasible. What once sounded symbolic now reads like a headline waiting to happen.

3. Global Viewing of the Two Witnesses (Revelation 11:9–10)—How could "the whole world" gaze upon two dead bodies in Jerusalem? For centuries, this prophecy was dismissed as allegorical. That is, until the rise of global satellite networks, smartphones, and 24/7 news coverage. What once seemed fantastical is now as simple as a livestream.

4. The Rebirth of Israel (Revelation 12; Matthew 24:32–35)—Perhaps the most undeniable sign of our time is the miraculous rebirth of the nation of Israel in 1948. For nearly 2,000 years, this prophecy seemed like a distant dream. Yet Jesus pointed to the blossoming of the fig tree—a symbol for Israel—as a crucial indicator of the end times. Add to this the recapturing of Jerusalem in 1967, and the prophetic countdown begins ticking with precision.

5. The Image of the Beast (Revelation 13:14–15)—John describes a false religious leader who would create an image that could speak and cause people to worship it. In previous centuries, this sounded absurd—until the advent of robotics, holograms, and artificial intelligence. What used to be mythological now feels like tomorrow's tech demo.

6. The Mark of the Beast (Revelation 13:16–17)—Controlling global commerce through a mark on the hand or forehead was unthinkable—until now. With biometric scanning, digital currency, implantable microchips, and cashless economies already in motion, this prophecy is no longer futuristic speculation. The infrastructure is being built in real-time.

Even the Prophecy Books Are a Sign

The enormous popularity of prophecy-centered books—like *The Late Great Planet Earth* or the *Left Behind* series—is a phenomenon unique to our generation. These books have sold in the tens of millions, awakening both believers and skeptics to the urgency of the hour. Why now? Because something deep within the collective soul of this age senses the coming storm.

Now add to that prophetic bookshelf: *The Trumpet I: The Ancient Prophecy That Reveals America's Final Hour, The Trumpet II: The Prophecy Continues—America's Final Hour Unveiled,* and *The Vanishing: The Day Will Begin Like Any Other—Until the RAPTURE Silences the World*. These aren't just books. They're catalysts—summoning conviction, stirring repentance, and preparing hearts for the return of the King.

Could these three books alone ignite a revival so great, we've never seen anything like it before? If the message is His and the hour is now—why not?

The Bottom Line

We are not looking at vague echoes of the past. We are witnessing unprecedented fulfillments. Prophecies that were once sealed and incomprehensible are now visible, tangible, and—in some cases—technologically enabled.

We are the generation living on borrowed time. The clock isn't just ticking— it's racing. Jesus is coming soon. The question is no longer whether the signs are here. The question is whether we are awake enough to see them—and bold enough to respond.

RECOGNIZING THE ACCELERATING CONVERGENCE OF PROPHETIC WARNINGS

There is a profound difference between steady progression and accelerating convergence. One moves at a measured, predictable pace—noticeable but manageable. The other begins quietly, then builds with relentless speed— doubling, compounding, and cascading until it becomes a global tremor. That's exactly what we're witnessing with the signs of the end times. They are not only increasing in number—they are accelerating in intensity, frequency, and perfect synchronization. We are no longer seeing isolated prophecies in distant corners. We are standing at the intersection where all of them are erupting at once.

Jesus Himself foretold this phenomenon in Matthew 24:8, when He described the signs of the end as "sorrows" or *birth pains*. These labor contractions are not only painful—they come closer and closer together, with greater force each time, until the moment of delivery. For the world, the delivery will be the Day of the Lord. For the Church, it will be the Rapture.

From Warning to Whiplash

In generations past, one could look at a prophetic sign and track its slow progress over decades or even centuries. Today, however, that's no longer the case. Events that once took centuries to unfold now happen in *months*, *weeks*, or even *days*. Consider the rapid rise of global surveillance, digital currencies, artificial intelligence, and religious apostasy. These didn't inch forward—they erupted. Combine that with the resurgence of anti-Israel sentiment, the moral freefall of society, and the soft totalitarianism sweeping across governments, and you get a landscape where prophetic dominoes are collapsing in real time.

The steady progression and accelerating convergence means that tomorrow won't look like today—it will be drastically worse, and it will come drastically faster. Deception is no longer subtle—it's systemic. Evil isn't creeping anymore—it's sprinting. And truth isn't merely ignored—it's despised.

The Warning in the Acceleration

This acceleration is not incidental—it's intentional. In His mercy, God is compressing prophetic fulfillment into a window of clarity that cannot be missed by anyone who is awake. The increase in velocity is itself a sign: a divine exclamation point punctuating the prophetic sentence that's been written for millennia.

Technology, geopolitics, natural disasters, cultural collapse, and spiritual apostasy are no longer occurring in isolation. They are overlapping—feeding off one another like flames in a windstorm. Each new headline feels like an echo of Scripture. And the pace is quickening.

The Convergence Demands a Response

We are not spectators—we are participants. The hour is late, and the signs are not slowing. Every tick of the prophetic clock brings us closer to the moment when the trumpet will sound and the Age of Grace will give way to judgment.

Now is the time to wake up, look up, and speak up. The exponential curve isn't just a graph—it's a *signal*. A call to readiness. A final warning that the King is at the door.

GROWING APOSTASY IN THE CHURCH

One of the most heartbreaking and sobering signs of the times is not found in the culture "out there," but within the Church itself. Apostasy—the great falling away—was not only predicted, it was *guaranteed* to occur in the final days. What once seemed unthinkable in past generations is now the norm: the Church, in many quarters, is abandoning the very truths it was entrusted to protect.

Paul warned of this in no uncertain terms:

> For the time will come when they will not endure sound doctrine; but after their own lusts shall they heap to themselves teachers, having itching ears. And they shall turn away their ears from the truth, and shall be turned unto fables (tales). (2 Timothy 4:3–4)

We are living in that time.

From Truth to Tolerance

The modern Church, especially in the West, has become a house of mirrors—distorting truth for the sake of comfort, numbers, and cultural acceptance. Biblical preaching is often replaced with motivational talks. Sin is rebranded as brokenness. Repentance is swapped for self-improvement. Righteousness is deemed "intolerant." Many pulpits no longer thunder with "Thus says the Lord," but whisper softly, "here's what might work for you."

Entire denominations have embraced false doctrines. Some bless what God calls sin—marrying same-sex couples, ordaining practicing homosexuals, and championing gender fluidity. Others reject the authority of Scripture altogether, reinterpreting it through a progressive, worldly lens. Still more remain silent, choosing cultural relevance over biblical faithfulness.

This isn't renewal. It's rebellion.

Wolves Among the Sheep

Jesus warned that in the last days, false prophets would come in sheep's clothing (Matthew 7:15). Today, they fill our bookstores, flood our podcast feeds, and trend on social media. Many are charismatic, articulate, and wildly popular. But their message is toxic. It denies sin, elevates self, and preaches a Jesus made in man's image—a life coach who affirms but never confronts, who loves but never judges.

> Beware of false prophets, which come to you in sheep's clothing, but inwardly they are ravening wolves. (Matthew 7:15)

Some charismatic circles have strayed so far from Scripture that they now blend Christian language with occultic practices—angel cards, grave soaking, and New Age visualization—all in the name of "spiritual experience." It's a dangerous deception: spiritual sensationalism without biblical grounding.

Meanwhile, others promote a prosperity gospel promising health, wealth, and success to all who follow Jesus—as if God were a vending machine rather than a holy, sovereign Lord.

Persecution and Purification

True believers—those who love God's Word and live by it—are increasingly mocked, marginalized, and maligned, even by fellow Christians. Standing for biblical truth today may cost you your friends, your reputation, and in some cases, your platform or job. But take heart: this purging is not without purpose.

The growing apostasy is separating the wheat from the chaff. The lukewarm are falling away. The remnant is rising.

A Call to the Faithful

The apostasy in the Church is not cause for despair—it's confirmation that we are near the end. Jesus Himself asked, "When the Son of Man comes, will He find faith on the earth?" (Luke 18:8). That's not a rhetorical flourish. It's a prophetic challenge.

This is the moment for the true Church to rise—not in numbers, but in faithfulness. To preach truth when it's unpopular. To walk in holiness when compromise is expected. To shine brightly when the world—and much of the Church—grows darker by the day.

Apostasy may be growing. But so is the resolve of the remnant. And the Bride is making herself ready.

THE FIRST HARBINGER HAS SOUNDED

Living in the Shadow of His Imminent Return

We have seen the signs—in the natural world, in society's decay, in spiritual deception, in explosive technology, in political realignment, and in the miraculous restoration of Israel. These are not scattered clues. They are a symphony of warnings, converging, and accelerating, like contractions before birth. Jesus called them *birth pains* for a reason. They're not only increasing in frequency—they are intensifying with every passing moment.

The first harbinger has been given. The signs of the times are flashing like neon across the global landscape.

And these aren't just any signs. They are uniquely modern-day fulfillments of prophecies once sealed and mysterious—now made clear by history, technology, and the Spirit's insight. What Daniel was told to seal has now been opened. What once seemed impossible—an army of 200 million, worldwide viewing of the Two Witnesses, a digital mark that controls buying and selling—is now not only plausible, but accepted in our lifetime.

We are living in the most prophesied era in human history.

From the return of Israel to the rise of global surveillance, from the fall of truth in the modern Church to the rise of lawlessness in global governments, all the pieces are in place for the final act of redemptive history. The clock hasn't just started ticking—it's reaching its final second.

And at the heart of it all sits the 2022–2023 to 2028–2029 Shemitah cycle—a prophetic pivot point that aligns with the final years of a biblical generation, marked by Israel's rebirth in 1948. According to Psalm 90:10, a biblical generation spans seventy to eighty years—placing key watch years around 2018 to 2028. This is not date-setting—it's season watching. And make no mistake: the season is ripe.

Let us say this plainly: the world is not going to bounce back. We are not in a cycle of recovery. We are in a descent—a moral, spiritual, geopolitical, and cultural freefall. As Paul warned, "Evil men and impostors will wax worse and worse" (2 Timothy 3:13). What we are witnessing is not random chaos—it is prophetic choreography.

> But evil men and seducers shall wax worse and worse, deceiving, and being deceived. (2 Timothy 3:13)

The systems of Antichrist are already here. The deception is already working. The slumber of the Church is already deep. And the only restraining force left is the Bride of Christ—who is soon to be removed.

We must live like we believe it.

We must be watchmen on the wall, blowing the trumpet, not hitting the snooze button. We must stop arguing over what hour it is and start living like we're at midnight.

The return of Jesus is not folklore. It's not fringe. It's not fearmongering. It is fact—the blessed hope of the Church and the next major event on God's calendar.

We are not promised tomorrow, but we are promised this: "When you see all these things, lift up your heads, for your redemption draws near" (Luke 21:28).

And we are seeing them. All of them.

All at once.

The first harbinger has sounded.

Are you listening?

Are you ready?

Irene and I sit on a quiet back porch, the sky stretches deep and clear above us. The stars blink down like watchmen, each in its post. A breeze stirs the trees with a hush that feels reverent, almost listening. Between us, a single candle flickers beside our worn Bibles and half-finished mugs of tea, its flame swaying like a sentinel against the dark.

We've finished reviewing the first harbinger together—the Sign of the Times—and the silence between us now feels as weighty as the content we just discussed.

I exhale slowly, leaning back in my chair.

"You know, Irene, I've studied prophecy for years—filled the margins of my Bibles with notes, dog-eared pages, cross-referenced passages. But tonight, after walking through this first harbinger, I don't just know it in my head anymore. I feel it in my spirit. The signs . . . they're not just stirring."

Irene's voice is a whisper wrapped in awe.

"They're shouting."

I glanced at her. She's still—reflective—but I can see it too: the quickening beneath her calm.

"Yes," she says. "I feel it too. It's no longer subtle. It's synchronized. It's like . . . Creation itself is echoing the drumbeat of prophecy."

She pauses, her gaze drifting past the porch railing toward the horizon, now swallowed in quiet darkness.

"But here's what I keep circling back to—if the signs are this loud, where is the Church's voice? Why are the pulpits so silent?"

I nod slowly, sadness tugging at the edge of my expression.

"Because comfort sells—and urgency offends. The gospel of now has replaced the Gospel of the Kingdom. And no one wants to admit we've grown cozy in Babylon."

Irene's voice tightens—not angry, but clear and burdened.

"It's not just silence—it's seduction. Have you noticed? Apostasy isn't sneaking in through the back door anymore. It's marching down the center aisle— draped in rainbow flags, whispering about love without truth, lighting candles to a God no one dares to name."

I shake my head slowly.

"And yet the Bible warned us this would happen: 'They will not endure sound doctrine, but after their own lusts shall they heap to themselves teachers . . .' What gets me is this—how the same signs that awaken the wise virgins are lulling others to sleep. Same warnings. Same world. Two completely different responses."

Irene exhales, the sound more prayer than breath.

"That's what haunts me some nights. How can something be so prophetic . . . and yet so invisible at the same time?"

I stir my tea, watching the leaves spiral like a slow-moving storm.

"Maybe it's mercy. Maybe God is still whispering before He thunders."

She glances over, eyes searching.

"Can I ask you something bold?"

I meet her gaze.

"Do you really believe America is Mystery Babylon?"

I take a breath, letting the silence hold for a moment.

"If she's not Mystery Babylon, she's certainly auditioning—and getting a standing ovation. She's rich, arrogant, morally bankrupt. Drunk on blood and entertainment. Intoxicated by comfort, convenience, and compromise.

But worse than all that—she's been warned.

9/11 should have been a national turning point. Instead, it became a photo op.

She's entangled in the politics of every nation—manipulating behind the scenes, toppling regimes, igniting wars. Sometimes through false flags. Always with an agenda.

And her bloodguilt runs deep—over sixty million unborn lives silenced in the womb.

No empire in history has plummeted so far from such great spiritual light.

If divine accountability is real—and it is—then she is marked. Judgment isn't just coming. It's overdue."

Irene closes her eyes for a moment, the candlelight flickering across her face like a soft echo of the fire in her thoughts.

"I agree. But then I wonder—if we're really this close to the end, why hasn't the Rapture happened yet?"

I set my mug down slowly, the ceramic landing with a quiet finality. I let her question settle between us before answering—because it deserves more than a quick reply.

"Because God is patient. Because the Ark still has room. Because somewhere, someone's prodigal son is still wandering. Someone's daughter is still straddling the fence. Someone's final chance hasn't come yet.

Because we serve a God who delays judgment for the sake of mercy—who waits just one more day so one more soul can walk through the narrow gate.

And maybe . . . maybe it's because the final puzzle pieces are still falling into place. Nations aligning. Hearts hardening. The spiritual dividing lines becoming unmistakably clear.

He's not slow. He's exact. He's waiting—not because He's uncertain, but because He's unwilling that any should perish."

I lean forward, the weight of it all pressing into my voice.

"Everything is converging, Irene. The headlines. The technology. The apostasy. The birth pains. And even the Shemitah clock—it's ticking toward 2028/2029. Not because I'm trying to set a date. You know I'm not. But I do believe in patterns. And the patterns are prophetic. They're the breadcrumbs God leaves for those who are watching."

She sits up straighter, something tightening in her voice—urgency, maybe even anticipation.

"So . . . do you believe that's the year?"

I take a breath, slow and measured, before answering.

"I believe it's a window. A narrowing one. I'm not pointing to a calendar—I'm pointing to a convergence. The Bible doesn't say we won't know the time—it says we won't know the exact day or hour. But it also says we are children of the light, not of the dark, and that the Day should not overtake us like a thief.

So yes . . . we may not know the hour—but we're absolutely meant to recognize the season. And sister . . . we are in it. Every indicator is shouting. Every spiritual line is being drawn. If not now—when? If this isn't the season—what on earth would it take?"

Irene's voice trembles—not with fear, but with the weight of realization.

"Then that means the Rapture . . . the Tribulation . . . the rise of the Antichrist . . . it's all waiting just beyond the veil."

I nod, solemn.

"And we're the final watchmen before the curtain rises. That's why this first harbinger matters. It's not just a warning—it's the prologue."

She turns toward me fully now, her eyes searching.

"Then what do we do, Ann? How do we live in the shadow of a world about to collapse?"

I offer a quiet smile—somber, but sure.

"We live like we believe it. With oil in our lamps. With trumpets in our hands. With eyes on the sky . . . and feet planted firm. Not panicked, but prepared."

A hush settles over us—holy, weighty, still. The kind of silence that listens.

Then Irene whispers, "Then let's wake the others."

I nod slowly, the candle flickering between us like a signal fire.

"The first harbinger has sounded—"

She finishes the sentence with quiet conviction.

"—and it won't be long before the second one follows."

————◆◆◆————

CHAPTER SUMMARY

Chapter 5 launches the first of the seven harbingers with a sobering and clarifying look at the signs of the times—God's prophetic indicators that the world has entered the final season before the return of Christ. Drawing from Jesus' words in Matthew 24, the writings of Paul, and the apocalyptic visions of Daniel and John, this chapter reveals that we are not only witnessing isolated events, but a convergence of accelerating signs that were foretold in Scripture.

The chapter begins by establishing a key biblical principle: God always warns before He acts in judgment. From the days of Noah to the fall of Jerusalem, divine warnings precede divine interventions. We are in that very moment again. The difference this time? The warnings are global—and they are converging at exponential speed.

Seven major categories of prophetic signs were examined:

1. **The Distress in Nature**—from earthquakes and famines to environmental upheaval.
2. **Cultural and Moral Collapse**—societies unraveling under the weight of rebellion and lawlessness.
3. **Spiritual Deception and Apostasy**—a Church drifting from truth, trading power for popularity.
4. **Technological Prowess**—tools now exist to fulfill prophecies once considered unimaginable.
5. **Global Political Realignment**—world systems preparing for a centralized authority.
6. **The Rebirth and Centrality of Israel**—the super sign and epicenter of end-time prophecy.
7. **The Convergence of Signs: The Acceleration Effect**—prophetic indicators once isolated are now unfolding simultaneously, gaining speed and intensity. Like birth pains, they are increasing in frequence and magnitude—signaling that we are not approaching the end slowly, but racing toward it.

Each of these signs, while distinct, is shown to be interdependent, forming a prophetic mosaic that points to the nearness of the Rapture and the rise of the Antichrist.

The chapter continues by highlighting modern-day fulfillments that were once sealed, especially in the Book of Daniel, but are now understood in light of technological and historical advancements. Prophecies about the mark of the beast, the Two Witnesses, the image of the beast, and the army of 200 million are no longer futuristic riddles—they are realities within reach.

Finally, the chapter identifies the 2028/2029 Shemitah year as a probable prophetic window. It doesn't predict a date, but it affirms a season—one that aligns with biblical patterns and global developments. The conclusion is stark but hopeful: the world is not heading toward revival, but toward judgment. And yet, for the Church, this is not a time of fear but of watchfulness, readiness, and urgency.

KEY TAKEAWAYS

*   God always issues warnings before judgment; the current global landscape reflects that divine pattern.
*   The signs of the times are converging in ways never before seen in history—pointing to the soon return of Christ.

- Many end-time prophecies, once mysterious, are now understood through technological and historical lenses.
- The 2028/2029 Shemitah year may mark a significant prophetic moment tied to Daniel's timeline and Israel's modern rebirth.
- The Church must wake up from spiritual slumber and return to truth, holiness, and gospel urgency.
- This chapter sets the foundation for the remaining harbingers, proving that the end-time clock is not only ticking—it's accelerating.

Chapter 5 is both an awakening and a warning—an unmistakable trumpet blast piercing the fog of apathy.

The signs are no longer distant shadows on the horizon; they are present, visible, and undeniable. We are the generation that sees them not dimly, but clearly—through the lens of fulfilled prophecy, global upheaval, and spiritual discernment.

Jesus warned that these things would come like labor pains, growing in intensity and frequency, and now we feel the full contractions shaking every sphere of life.

But this is not a time for fear. It is a time for the Church to awaken from spiritual slumber and reclaim her prophetic posture.

It is a call to stand firm in the truth, to reject compromise, and to sound the alarm with courage and clarity.

The first trumpet has sounded—not in speculation or hysteria, but in Scripture-aligned reality.

This chapter sets the stage for the rest of the harbingers by declaring what must first be understood: the end-time clock is no longer ticking quietly in the background—it is accelerating. And every believer must now decide: will I sleep through the shaking, or rise up for such a time as this?

Chapter 6

The Second Harbinger:
The Biblical Calendars

TIME ACCORDING TO GOD, NOT MAN—Time governs everything. From the moment we wake up to the moment we rest our heads at night, we live under the constant ticking of a manmade clock. Our lives revolve around the Gregorian calendar—twelve months, seven-day weeks, 24-hour days—calculated by emperors, adjusted by popes, and cemented by Western tradition. Our holidays are marked by cultural customs. Our years are structured around academic cycles, fiscal quarters, and political seasons. We have grown accustomed to believing that this is the only time that matters.

But it isn't.

Long before there was a Julian calendar (45 BC) or a Gregorian calendar (1582 AD)—before Rome carved months into marble or Babylon aligned weeks with the stars—there was God's calendar. A divine rhythm of time, woven into Creation itself. The *moedim*, the appointed times. The sacred seasons of Heaven.

This calendar wasn't man's invention. It was God's revelation. Not given as an option, but as a blueprint. Not just for remembrance—but for prophecy.

In Genesis 1:14, God says plainly:

> And God said, Let there be lights in the firmament of the heaven to divide the day from the night; and let them be for signs, and for seasons, and for days, and years. (Genesis 1:14)

That word for "seasons"—*moedim* in Hebrew—means appointed times, divine appointments. Not just harvest cycles or weather patterns, but prophetic markers on God's calendar. Fixed windows where Heaven intersects with earth—on purpose, by design.

We've lost touch with that timeline.

When the Church divorced itself from its Hebraic roots, it didn't just lose tradition—it lost time. It became a people out of sync with the very clock God set to reveal His purposes. We began to interpret prophecy through manmade lenses, trying to understand heavenly events with earthly calendars. And as a result, the Church began missing divine appointments—both symbolically and literally.

But Daniel 2:21 reminds us that God is the One who "changes the times and the seasons." He alone holds the authority to alter the clock.

> And He changes the times and the seasons: He removes kings, and sets up kings: He gives wisdom unto the wise, and knowledge to them that know understanding. (Daniel 2:21)

And in 1 Thessalonians 5:1, Paul makes it clear that believers are not to be in the dark: "But of the times and the seasons, brethren, you have no need that I write unto you." In other words, if we're watching the right calendar—God's calendar—we'll see what others don't.

This chapter is about reorienting our sense of time.

It's a call to return—to step out of cultural convenience and back into covenant clarity. To learn again what the Bible has been saying all along: that God has a pattern, a rhythm, a sacred calendar that governs the rise and fall of nations, the unfolding of prophecy, and the movements of the Messiah Himself.

Consider this: Jesus fulfilled the spring feasts—Passover, Unleavened Bread, Firstfruits, and Pentecost—with precision. He was crucified on Passover, buried during Unleavened Bread, resurrected on Firstfruits, and the Spirit was poured out on Pentecost. Exact days. Exact purposes. The fall feasts—Trumpets, Atonement, and Tabernacles—still remain to be fulfilled. And they will be. Right on time.

This chapter will explore the biblical months—each one prophetically named and spiritually significant. We'll examine the difference between the civil calendar and the religious one, the feasts and fasts, the Shemitah cycles and Jubilee years, and how all of it points to the soon return of Christ.

Because the countdown isn't random.

The ticking clock of prophecy isn't based on the whims of empires or the forecasts of economists. It's based on a calendar that has never changed—a calendar God gave to Moses, repeated through the prophets, fulfilled by Jesus, and still in motion today.

And at the heart of this revelation is something both stunning and sobering: We are almost out of time.

The year 2028/2029 marks the close of another Shemitah cycle—the seven-year sabbatical rhythm God uses to reset nations, confront rebellion, and prepare the way for redemption. It also marks eighty years since the rebirth of Israel in 1948—the upper limit of a biblical generation, according to Psalm 90:10.

> The days of our years are threescore years and ten (seventy); and if by reason of strength they be fourscore (eighty) years, yet is their strength labor and sorrow; for it is soon cut off, and we fly away. (Psalm 90:10)

These aren't coincidences. They're convergences. Prophetic intersections. Divine appointments hidden in plain sight.

The Church must stop asking, "What time is it on the world's clock?" and start asking, "What time is it on God's calendar?" Because only one of those will prepare us for what's next. And only one of those is counting down to the trumpet.

Let us tune our hearts not to culture, but to covenant. Let us stop marking our days by man's time—and start aligning our lives with God's appointed seasons.

The second harbinger has sounded.

It's time to synchronize your watch—with Heaven.

THE ORIGIN OF GOD'S CALENDAR

To understand the second harbinger, we must first understand time—not as man tracks it, but as God ordains it. The biblical calendar is not a historical curiosity or a cultural artifact; it is the very heartbeat of Heaven pulsing through the pages of Scripture. It is the divine rhythm by which God governs His appointments with mankind. If we want to know what God is doing and when He plans to do it, we must return to His calendar.

Not Bound by Time, But Author of It

God is eternal, unbound by time and space. He exists outside the linear constraints of minutes and hours. "I am the LORD, I change not" (Malachi 3:6), and "Forever, O LORD, Your Word is settled in Heaven" (Psalm 119:89). The God who ordained the beginning also sees the end. And within His timeless sovereignty, He has established patterns—"times and seasons" (Daniel 2:21)—for revealing His will on earth.

When God created the heavens and the earth, He also created the timepieces by which His purposes would be marked. Genesis 1:14 declares, "Let there be lights in the firmament of the heavens to divide the day from the night; and let them be for signs, and for seasons, and for days, and years." The word "sign" in

Hebrew is *'oth*—meaning signal, banner, or warning. The word "seasons" is *moedim*—meaning appointed times, sacred festivals, divine rehearsals.

From the very beginning, the sun, moon, and stars were not merely decorative. They were prophetic. God literally wove His plan of redemption into the fabric of Creation's clock. He etched warnings and appointments into the sky. This is why Psalm 104:19 says, "He appointed the moon for seasons"—for the *moedim*, the fixed times to meet with His people.

> He appointed the moon for seasons: the sun knows his going down. (Psalm 104:19)

Biblical Time vs. Modern Time

Unlike the Gregorian calendar we use today—created by Pope Gregory XIII in 1582 AD and based on solar cycles—God's calendar is lunar-solar. It begins in the spring, not in January. It names its months not after Roman gods or emperors, but based on divine encounters and agricultural rhythms in the land of Israel. While the Gregorian calendar ticks to the rhythm of empire and commerce, the biblical calendar beats to the pulse of eternity.

THE BIBLE AT A GLANCE

God Works with Hebrew Calendars

Month	Genesis/ Civil Calendar	Month	Exodus/ Religious Calendar	Gregorian Calendar	Month
1	Tishri	1	Nisan	1	January
2	Heshvan	2	Iyyar	2	February
3	Kislev	3	Sivan	3	March
4	Tebet	4	Tammuz	4	April
5	Shebat	5	Av	5	May
6	Adar	6	Elul	6	June
7	Nisan	7	Tishri	7	July
8	Iyyar	8	Heshvan	8	August
9	Sivan	9	Kislev	9	September
10	Tammuz	10	Tebet	10	October
11	Av	11	Shebat	11	November
12	Elul	12	Adar	12	December

Figure 1 – God Works with Hebrew Calendars

The Bible is filled with references to these sacred times—yet most believers today read past them without recognizing their significance. We read that "on the tenth day of the seventh month" something happened (Leviticus 23:27), or that "in the first month, on the fourteenth day" something else was commanded

(Exodus 12:6). But we rarely pause to connect these divine dates to the Hebrew calendar—or more importantly, to our spiritual lives today.

> Also on the tenth day of this seventh month (Tishri) there shall be a Day of Atonement: it shall be a holy convocation unto you; and you shall afflict your souls, and offer an offering made by fire unto the LORD. (Leviticus 23:27)

> This month shall be unto you the beginning of months: it shall be the first month (Nisan) of the year to you. And you shall keep it up until the fourteenth day of the same month: and the whole assembly of the congregation of Israel shall kill it in the evening. (Exodus 12:2, 6)

What we often miss in translation is this: God wasn't simply acting in history—He was establishing patterns. Blueprints on the Hebrew religious calendar. Patterns that pointed to Christ. And patterns that still speak today.

God's Sacred Appointments

In Leviticus 23, God doesn't merely list ancient traditions—He codifies His appointed times, first set in motion at Creation (Genesis 1:14). These include the weekly Sabbath, the three spring feasts (Passover, Unleavened Bread, Firstfruits), the summer Feast of Pentecost (*Shavuot*), and the three fall feasts (Trumpets, Atonement, Tabernacles).

These are not merely "Jewish holidays." Scripture calls them "the Feasts of the LORD" (Leviticus 23:2). They belong to Him. They were ordained by Him. And they reveal Him—His character, His covenant, His redemptive plan, and His prophetic calendar.

Each feast is fixed to a specific day in a specific month—according to God's calendar, not man's. These are divine appointments—sacred intersections when Heaven touches earth and time bows to eternity. To ignore or replace His calendar is not just to lose context—it is to risk missing the moment entirely.

The Prophetic Power of the Biblical Months

God has woven spiritual rhythms into each of the twelve biblical months. These are not just historical designations—they are prophetic windows, moments in time that carry deeper meaning. Each month is rich with spiritual themes, tribal alignments, and agricultural patterns that mirror our journey with God.

For example:

- Nisan (the first month) is the month of redemption, marked by the Exodus and fulfilled through Jesus' crucifixion.
- Tishri (the seventh month) is the month of awe and judgment, observed through the Feast of Trumpets and the Day of Atonement.

- Kislev (the ninth month) is a time of hope and light, commemorated through *Hanukkah*, the Festival of Dedication.

When we align ourselves with these appointed times—not as legalists, but as watchful sons and daughters—we begin to see differently. We sense spiritual shifts. Our ears grow attuned to His whisper. Our hearts awaken to His timing.

Walking in God's Time: Releases God's Blessing

God desires to bless His people—not randomly, but rhythmically. His calendar carries a divine cadence. When we begin to honor His timing, we step into alignment with His order. Our vision clears. Our steps steady. We begin to see what He sees—and move when He moves.

As we walk in sync with God's appointed times:

- Our discernment sharpens.
- Our intercession aligns.
- Our expectation rises.
- Our obedience deepens.

We no longer live by the chaos of man's calendar, but by the rhythm of Heaven. And as we align with Heaven's seasons, we begin to experience what many only talk about: transformation, revelation, and intimacy with the Holy Spirit—like a river flowing in season.

Conclusion: It's Time to Return

The origin of God's calendar isn't rooted in ritual—it's anchored in relationship. The same God who ordained sacred seasons for ancient Israel is still inviting His people today to step back into His timing. Not to earn favor, but to walk in alignment. Not to relive the past, but to prepare for the future.

We are now living at the end of the age. The current Shemitah cycle—set to end in 2028/2029—is not an isolated event. It is part of a prophetic countdown, calibrated not by Wall Street or Washington D.C., but by the calendar of Heaven itself—the very one God entrusted to His people.

The second harbinger is a call to wake up—not just to the times, but to the timing. To step out of manmade chaos and into divine alignment.

To return.

It's not too late to recalibrate.

But the clock is ticking.

THE TWO CALENDARS IN SCRIPTURE

One of the most repeated prophetic themes in Scripture is the image of Jesus coming with the clouds. This phrase echoes through both Old and New Testaments—from Daniel's night visions to John's apocalyptic revelations. But to fully grasp its timing and symbolism, we must understand the framework of the biblical calendar—because in Scripture, clouds don't just signal His return; they mark His calendar.

In His divine wisdom, God has woven two calendars into the biblical narrative: the civil (Creation) calendar and the sacred (religious) calendar. Each serves a distinct, yet deeply connected, purpose—one rooted in His covenant with Creation, the other in His redemptive covenant of redemption with His people.

The Civil Calendar: Creation to Kingship

The civil calendar begins in the fall, with the month of Tishri. This was considered the original "beginning of the year" and is still commemorated today through *Rosh HaShanah*, the head of the year. According to Jewish tradition, this is the anniversary of Creation—when God formed Adam from the dust and breathed life into humanity.

Tishri marks the beginning of the civil calendar in Scripture—the start of the agricultural and governmental new year, rooted in Creation's natural rhythms: planting, harvesting, and national life. It is from this point that Israel measured the reigns of kings and tracked its appointed cycles.

Every seventh year marked the Shemitah year, a year of rest and release. During the Shemitah year, the land was not cultivated, debts among Israelites were forgiven, and economic rhythms were reset. This sacred pause was a national declaration of trust in God's provision and a reminder that the land—and time itself—belongs to the Lord (Leviticus 25:1–7; Deuteronomy 15:1–2).

Then after seven full Shemitah cycles (49 years), the fiftieth year was declared the Jubilee year. On the 10th day of Tishri (*Yom Kippur*), a trumpet was blown throughout the land to announce its arrival. In this year of Jubilee, ancestral lands were returned to their original owners, captives were set free, and debts were canceled on a national scale (Leviticus 25:9–10).

Both Shemitah and Jubilee years reveal God's heart for justice, rest, and restoration. These cycles weren't just agricultural—they were prophetic patterns, aligning His people with Heaven's timing, mercy, and covenant provision.

This calendar begins with the Feast of Trumpets—a prophetic picture of both the call to repentance and the future return of Messiah in the clouds—the Rapture of the Church. So when Scripture says, "He is coming with the clouds" (Daniel

7:13; Revelation 1:7), we're not just seeing a dramatic image—we're seeing Him align with the calendar of divine reset and royal authority.

The Sacred (Religious) Calendar: Redemption to Restoration

In contrast to the civil calendar, the sacred (religious) calendar begins in the spring, with the month of Nisan. This was ordained by God Himself at the Exodus:

> This month shall be unto you the beginning of months: it shall be the first month of the year to you. (Exodus 12:2)

This calendar reflects God's redemptive timeline. It begins not with Creation—but with deliverance. Nisan commemorates Israel's freedom from Egypt, the blood of the Passover lamb, and the beginning of their covenant journey with God.

This is the calendar that forms the foundation of the Feasts of the LORD (Leviticus 23) and governs the spiritual cycle of God's interaction with His people.

Jesus fulfilled this sacred calendar with prophetic precision:

- He died on Passover (Nisan 14).
- He was buried during Unleavened Bread (Nisan 15).
- He rose on Firstfruits (Nisan 16).
- He poured out the Holy Spirit on Pentecost (Sivan 6).

In His First Coming, Jesus didn't just fulfill prophecy—He fulfilled the sacred calendar to the day.

Why Two Calendars?

God gave both calendars for a reason. The civil calendar governs the earthly; the sacred (religious) calendar governs the eternal.

- One counts time from Creation.
- The other counts purpose from redemption.
- One deals with governments, harvests, Shemitah cycles, and Jubilee years.
- The other reveals feasts, offerings, and messianic fulfillment.

Together, they form a prophetic blueprint.

And when Jesus returns, He will merge the two in perfect fulfillment. The King of Creation (civil) will complete the Feasts of the LORD (sacred) in their second cycle—not as the suffering Lamb, but as the reigning Lion.

Clouds, Calendars, and Coming Glory

The repeated imagery of Jesus coming with the clouds (Daniel 7:13; Matthew 24:30; Acts 1:9–11; Revelation 1:7) bridges both calendars—civil and sacred.

- In Exodus, the cloud led Israel out of bondage—a sacred redemption.
- In 1 Kings, the cloud signaled Elijah's rain—a sign of civil restoration.
- In Acts, Jesus ascended in a cloud.
- In Revelation, He returns in one.

These clouds are not merely meteorological—they're calendaric. They mark moments when Heaven intersects with earth, when a divine transition takes place—a change of season, a shift in authority, a movement from one phase of God's prophetic plan to the next.

So when Scripture says Jesus will return with the clouds, it's not just revealing *how* He will come—it's whispering *when*: at a prophetic intersection, at an appointed time, on God's calendar. These clouds mark more than atmospheric phenomena; they signify divine transitions—Heaven meeting earth at precise moments foretold by both the civil and sacred (religious) calendars. In every appearance, the cloud carries not only presence but timing. And that timing is never random. It's holy.

Conclusion: Aligning with the Divine Rhythm

Understanding these two calendars isn't about returning to ritual—it's about aligning with revelation. God is not governed by the Gregorian calendar or Western time zones. He is moving according to His own divine rhythm—and we are rapidly approaching the point of convergence.

From the beginning, God established the rhythm of time not by clocks or empires, but by Creation itself.

> And God said, Let there be lights in the firmament of the heavens to divide the day from the night; and let them be for signs, and for seasons, and for days, and years. (Genesis 1:14)

And even before this, Genesis 1 repeatedly affirms God's definition of a day:

> And the evening and the morning were the first day. (Genesis 1:5)

This reveals a divine truth often overlooked: God's day begins at sunset—not at midnight. From evening (around 6:00 PM) to morning at sunrise (around 6:00 AM), from darkness to light, His appointed times unfold—not according to the world's systems, but perfectly aligned with Heaven's design.

As watchers on the wall, we must tune our hearts to both timelines. We must discern the governmental shifts marked by the civil cycle, and the redemptive appointments revealed in the sacred cycle. The closer we draw to the Rapture, the more clearly we'll see these two calendars collide in holy convergence.

And when they do, He will come—with the clouds, and with perfect precision.

THE 12 MONTHS OF THE BIBLICAL CALENDAR

When God brought the Israelites out of Egypt, He didn't just deliver them from bondage—He reset their sense of time. In Exodus 12:2, God said to Moses:

> This month shall be unto you the beginning of months: it shall be the first month (Nisan) of the year to you. (Exodus 12:2)

With that divine decree, God established His religious calendar—a rhythm not merely for marking days, but for ordering divine appointments, covenant moments, and prophetic cycles. This was not just a way to count time—it was a sacred framework for living in sync with Heaven's agenda.

In contrast to the Gregorian calendar, which begins in January and is rooted in Roman imperial structure, God's sacred (religious) calendar begins in the spring, with the month of Nisan (Abib/Aviv)—the season of freedom, redemption, and new beginnings. It is not just historical—it's prophetic, orienting God's people to His cycles of redemption, judgment, and blessing.

Over time, ancient Israel came to observe two overlapping calendars:

- A Civil Calendar—Beginning in the fall with Tishri. Used for measuring governmental reigns, agricultural cycles, Shemitah years, and Jubilee years. It governs the earthly order of time.
- A Sacred (Religious) Calendar—Beginning in the spring with Nisan. Used to mark the Feasts of the LORD and divine appointments. It governs the eternal order of redemption.

THE BIBLE AT A GLANCE

Jewish Religious Calendar – Nisan is considered the first month
Jewish Creation Calendar or Civil Calendar – Tishri is considered the first month

NISAN	IYAR	SIVAN	TAMMUZ	AV	ELUL	TISHRI	HESHVAN	KISLEV	TEVET	SHEBAT	ADAR
1	2	3	4	5	6	7	8	9	10	11	12
MAR	APR	MAY	JUN	JUL	AUG	SEP	OCT	NOV	DEC	JAN	FEB
3	4	5	6	7	8	9	10	11	12	1	2

Gregorian Calendar – Calendar in the Western world

Figure 2 – Biblical and Gregorian Calendars

Though the names of the months remain consistent, their starting points differ—each revealing a different aspect of God's character: one as Creator and King, the other as Redeemer and Restorer.

While these distinctions may seem confusing to some believers today, they reveal extraordinary spiritual depth when viewed through the right lens. Each biblical month carries prophetic significance—woven into Israel's history, God's covenant purposes, and ultimately fulfilled in the person and work of Jesus Christ, our Messiah and soon coming King.

Some may ask, "Aren't these Old Testament observances just for the Jewish people?" While it's true that the Jewish people were entrusted with God's calendar and His appointed times (Romans 3:2), the New Testament makes it clear that every believer in Christ—Jew and Gentile—has been grafted into the spiritual inheritance of Israel (Romans 11:17; Ephesians 2:14–15).

These sacred appointments are not about legalism or ritual—they're about alignment. Alignment with God's heart. Alignment with His timing. They are prophetic rhythms that help us discern what God is doing in the world—and what He wants to do in us.

More importantly, these months point to Jesus. Every feast, every observance, and every prophetic pattern in the biblical religious calendar ultimately unveils a facet of Christ's redemptive mission—past, present, and future. To understand the rhythm of the Hebrew months is to gain deeper insight into the character of God, the unfolding of prophecy, and the hidden richness of Scripture.

Genesis 1:14 reminds us that God created the sun, moon, and stars to serve "for signs, and for seasons, and for days, and years." The Hebrew word for "seasons" is *moedim*—a term that refers not just to spring, summer, fall, and winter, but to God's appointed times.

These sacred appointments weren't marked by ink and paper calendars, but by the movements of the heavens—specifically the phases of the moon. The new moon, *Rosh Chodesh*—"head of the month"—signaled the beginning of a new month and reset God's prophetic rhythm on earth.

The Jewish people honored the new moons with great reverence—offering sacrifices (Numbers 28:11–14) and holding special gatherings (1 Samuel 20). These were not superstitions, but sacred acknowledgments that time itself belongs to the Lord—and that every month carries a fresh invitation to encounter Him.

In the pages that follow, we will journey through each of the twelve biblical months, beginning with Nisan. Each month will explore:

- The historical events and appointed feasts that mark the month.
- The spiritual themes God emphasizes during that season.
- The prophetic connections to Jesus Christ.
- And monthly prayers to help you walk in God's favor.

Whether you're new to the biblical calendar or have long studied its depths, this section is designed to help you walk in step with the Spirit, attuned to the rhythms of Heaven. God is not bound by our clocks—but He has given us a divine one. And if we learn to watch it, we'll be far more prepared for the times we're living in—and for the glorious future just ahead.

Let's begin with Nisan, the month of redemption.

1. The Month of Nisan: A Season of Redemption and New Beginnings

The sacred (religious) calendar does not begin with the close of winter or the turning of a Gregorian year—it begins with Nisan. This divinely appointed month signals a season of redemption, reset, and revelation. In Exodus 12:2, God speaks directly to Moses and Aaron: "This month shall be unto you the beginning of months: it shall be the first month of the year to you."

This wasn't merely a shift in dates—it was a shift in divine rhythm. God was redefining time for His covenant people, marking the start of a redemptive timeline that would not only shape Israel's identity but would lay the foundation for the arrival of Messiah Himself.

Before the Babylonian exile, this month was known as Abib (or Aviv)—meaning "young ear of grain" (Exodus 13:4)—a reference to the early barley harvest. After the exile, the Babylonian name Nisan (from the Akkadian *nisannu*, meaning "beginnings" or "start of the year") became widely used. Either way, the message is unmistakable: Nisan is a month of holy beginnings.

On the civil calendar, which starts in the fall with the month of Tishri, Nisan is counted as the seventh month—linking it prophetically to spiritual perfection and covenant fulfillment. But in the sacred calendar, Nisan is month one—the foundation of all of God's redemptive appointments.

On the Gregorian calendar, Nisan typically falls during March or April, depending on two key factors: the timing of the spring equinox—when day and night are nearly equal in length worldwide—and the sighting of the new moon, which marks the beginning of each month on both the sacred and civil biblical calendars.

Nisan is not just a historical marker. It is the first chapter of God's prophetic calendar—a time when He resets the clock, reorients His people, and initiates a fresh movement in His unfolding plan of redemption. From the Exodus to the Cross, Nisan has always been a season of breakthrough. And for believers today, it remains a sacred invitation to begin again.

God's Appointed Feasts in Nisan—Nisan is not just historically important—it is prophetically precise. In Leviticus 23, God outlines a series of holy convocations—His *moedim*, or appointed times—and three of them fall within this foundational month.

1. **Passover (Hebrew: *Pesach*)**—Redemption Through the Blood

On the 14th day of Nisan, Israel was commanded to observe Passover, commemorating the night the death angel passed over their homes marked by the blood of a spotless lamb (Exodus 12:13). That blood wasn't just protective—it was prophetic. It pointed to the blood of Jesus, the Lamb of God who takes away the sin of the world (John 1:29). When Christ was crucified on Passover, He fulfilled the feast in exact precision. His blood didn't just rescue from Egypt—it redeemed us from sin and death itself (1 Corinthians 5:7).

2. **Unleavened Bread (Hebrew: *Hag HaMatzot*)**—A Call to Purity

Beginning on the 15th of Nisan, this seven-day feast required the removal of all leaven (yeast) from the home (Exodus 12:15). In Scripture, leaven represents sin and pride. This was a call to cleanse not just kitchens—but hearts. The Israelites ate unleavened bread in haste, with no time for the dough to rise—reminding us of the urgency of obedience and the necessity of holiness. Jesus, the Bread of Life (John 6:48), was sinless. He fulfilled this feast by being buried during this very week—pure, broken, and hidden.

3. **Firstfruits (Hebrew: *Bikkurim*)**—Honoring God with the Best

Celebrated on the day after the Sabbath following Passover (Leviticus 23:10–11), Firstfruits marked the beginning of the barley harvest. The people brought the first ripe sheaf to the priest as a wave offering before the LORD. This act was more than thanksgiving—it was a declaration: "You are our Source. We trust You with what comes next." Jesus rose from the grave on Firstfruits, becoming the "firstfruits of those who have fallen asleep" (1 Corinthians 15:20). His resurrection guarantees the full harvest to come—our own resurrection.

Nisan's Prophetic Themes: God's Timeline Unfolding—Nisan is not just the first month of the year—it's the first chapter in God's calendar of redemption. Each feast is more than a ritual; it's a prophetic blueprint, fulfilled with precision in Christ's First Coming:

- Passover—His death.
- Unleavened Bread—His burial.
- Firstfruits—His resurrection.

Every event was fulfilled on the exact day of its appointed time. God is not random. He is precise. His calendar does not bend to culture—it proclaims Christ-centered history in real time.

And just as the spring feasts were fulfilled with exactness, so too will the fall feasts—Trumpets, Atonement, and Tabernacles—be fulfilled at His Second Coming. Nisan sets the prophetic pattern.

A Call to Personal Alignment—Nisan invites every believer to remember, reflect, and realign. Just as Israel searched their homes for physical leaven, we are called to examine our hearts. What spiritual leaven still lingers—compromise, pride, bitterness, doubt? This is the season to purge it.

Communion, instituted by Jesus during His final Passover (Luke 22:17–20), becomes our sacred reminder. Every time we partake, we honor His sacrifice, remembering what He has done and anticipating His return—with hearts recommitted to walk in His redemption.

> And He took the cup, and gave thanks, and said, Take this, and divide it among yourselves: For I say unto you, I will not drink of the fruit of the vine, until the Kingdom of God shall come. And He took bread, and gave thanks, and broke it, and gave unto them, saying, This is My body which is given for you: this do in remembrance of Me. Likewise also the cup after supper, saying, This cup is the New Testament in My blood, which is shed for you. (Luke 22:17–20)

In 1 Corinthians 11:26, Paul writes:

> For as often as you eat this bread, and drink this cup, you do *show* the Lord's death till He comes. (1 Corinthians 11:26)

The word "show" (translated as "proclaim" in many modern translations) means to declare, commemorate, or publicly remember—not to re-sacrifice or re-enact, as taught in Catholic Eucharistic theology.

Nisan calls us to leave our Egypt behind. To exit the cycles of bondage. To step into a new season of freedom, purpose, and destiny. As we walk in sync with God's sacred timing, we step into alignment with the Spirit—moving when He moves, waiting when He says wait, and celebrating what He has already fulfilled.

Prayer for the Month of Nisan—Father, I thank You for the blood of Jesus—my spotless Passover Lamb. You have delivered me from bondage and broken every chain.

In this holy month of Nisan, I align my heart with Your redemptive plan. Cleanse me from all spiritual leaven—every hidden sin, every compromise, every fear. I remember Christ's sacrifice. I celebrate His resurrection. And I step into my divine new beginning with faith, humility, and gratitude.

Teach me to honor Your calendar, to walk in purity, and to trust Your perfect timing. May I live in step with the Spirit—redeemed, awakened, and ready.

In the name of the Father, the Son, and the Holy Spirit, Amen.

2. The Month of Iyar: A Time of Healing, Provision, and Preparation

Iyar (also spelled Iyyar), the second month on the biblical (religious) calendar, is far more than a bridge between Passover (Nisan) and Pentecost (Sivan). It is a sacred pause—a divinely appointed season of transition between redemption and revelation. Nestled between the deliverance of Nisan and the outpouring of Sivan, Iyar carries profound prophetic significance: it is the month in which God begins to heal, sustain, and prepare His people for deeper encounters with His presence and purpose.

Before the Babylonian exile, this month was known as Ziv, meaning "radiance" or "splendor" (1 Kings 6:1). The name reflects the natural world's seasonal shift—longer days, growing light, and renewed life. Spiritually, it mirrors the illumination of the soul, the gentle light of God's provision, and the slow but steady journey of transformation.

In Jewish tradition, Iyar is the month when the Israelites journeyed through the wilderness—delivered from Egypt, but not yet at Mount Sinai. They were set free, but still being formed. During this month, they encountered bitter waters at Marah, received manna from heaven, and learned the rhythms of dependence and trust.

On the civil calendar, which begins in the fall with Tishri, Iyar is counted as the eighth month, placing it in the second half of the agricultural and governmental year.

In the Gregorian calendar, Iyar typically falls during the months of April and May, depending on the lunar cycle and the sighting of the new moon.

Iyar teaches us that deliverance is only the beginning. It is the season when God begins to rebuild what has been broken, to nourish what has been starved, and to prepare us for the revelation to come. It is a month of healing, provision, and preparation—a time of divine shaping for those who will carry His covenant forward.

Iyar: A Month of Healing—One of the most profound revelations in the month of Iyar is found in Exodus 15:26, where God reveals one of His covenant names:

> If you will diligently listen to the voice of the LORD your God, and do what is right in His sight, give ear to His commandments, and keep all His statutes, I will put none of these diseases upon you which I have brought upon the Egyptians: for I am the LORD that heals you (Jehovah Rapha). (Exodus 15:26)

In Hebrew, this phrase "I am the LORD who heals you" is: *Ani YHVH Rophecha*. It is no coincidence that the very name Iyar has been seen in Jewish tradition as an acronym for this powerful declaration. While not a linguistic acronym in the technical sense, the tradition sees Iyar as a spiritually prophetic abbreviation for *Ani YHVH Rophecha*, tying the name of the month to God's promise of healing.

Jehovah Rapha is a shortened title derived from the full phrase in Exodus 15:26. It literally means "The LORD who heals" or "The LORD our Healer." The word *Rapha* is the Hebrew verb meaning "to heal"—used here as a covenant title that reveals God's nature as Healer.

At Marah, the Israelites encountered bitter water. But when Moses obeyed God's command and threw a tree into the water, it became sweet (Exodus 15:23–25). This was not just a miracle—it was a prophetic picture of the Cross of Christ, the tree that turns the bitterness of sin and suffering into healing and redemption.

Here at Marah, God didn't just show Himself as a Deliverer, but as a Healer—of bodies, hearts, and minds.

Iyar: A Month of Provision—According to Jewish tradition, it was during Iyar that God began to send manna from heaven—daily bread for a people learning to walk by faith. In Exodus 16, God responds to Israel's hunger with miraculous provision.

> Then said the LORD unto Moses, Behold, I will rain bread from heaven for you; and the people shall go out and gather a certain rate every day, that I may prove them, whether they will walk in My Law, or no. (Exodus 16:4)

This wasn't just food—it was daily trust training. The manna tested Israel's dependence, trained their discipline, and pointed forward to Messiah, who declared:

> I am the Bread of Life. (John 6:48)

Even its sweet, honey-like taste (Exodus 16:31) foreshadowed the sweetness of God's Word—sustaining, satisfying, and nourishing in the wilderness. The provision of manna during Iyar reminds us that God doesn't just rescue us—He sustains us, He feeds us, teaches us, and strengthens us in the in-between—between Egypt and Sinai, between salvation and revelation.

Iyar: A Month of Preparation—In 1 Kings 6:1, we learn that Solomon began building the Temple in the month of Ziv—an earlier name for Iyar. This is no coincidence. After healing and provision, comes preparation. Iyar marks a holy invitation to build something lasting with God.

It is a blueprint season—a time when God aligns resources, revelation, and readiness. A season for laying foundations, receiving divine instructions, and partnering with the Lord to construct a place—physical or spiritual—where His presence can dwell.

Today, we are God's temple: "Know you not that you are the temple of God, and that the Spirit of God dwells in you?" (1 Corinthians 3:16).

So the call of Iyar is this:

Let God heal you. Let God feed you. Then let God build you.

Jesus in the Month of Iyar—Everything in this month finds its ultimate fulfillment in Jesus Christ:

- The tree thrown into the bitter waters at Marah becomes a picture of the Cross—transforming our bitterness into healing through His sacrifice (Exodus 15:22–25).
- The manna from heaven points to Jesus, the Bread of Life, who nourishes us in both body and spirit (John 6:48).
- The building of the Temple during Iyar mirrors the construction of a New Covenant temple—our very lives, where the Holy Spirit now dwells (1 Corinthians 3:16).

As the prophet Isaiah declared: ". . . and with His stripes we are healed" (Isaiah 53:5). That healing—physical, emotional, and spiritual—becomes especially meaningful as we journey through the month of Iyar, a season of renewal, dependence, and divine preparation.

The Prophetic Meaning of Iyar Today—Iyar isn't just history—it's a living invitation. This month prophetically reflects the Church Age—that in-between space between redemption at the Cross and revelation at Christ's return. It calls us to trust God's provision, submit to His healing, and prepare ourselves for deeper encounters with His presence.

As we journey through these months on God's calendar, we come to see—they're not arbitrary dates. They're divine appointments. And Iyar is one of them: An appointment with healing, with provision, and with spiritual readiness.

Prayer for the Month of Iyar—Father, thank You for being my Healer and Provider. As You sustained Israel in the wilderness, sustain me—body, soul, and spirit. I declare that Jesus is my Bread of Life, and I trust You for fresh provision and deeper revelation this month.

Heal every wound, cleanse every fear, and prepare me for what's ahead. Let Iyar be a season of spiritual healing, renewed trust, and daily dependence on You.

Build Your temple in me, Lord. Dwell in me and work through me.
In the name of the Father, the Son, and the Holy Spirit, Amen.

3. The Month of Sivan: Covenant, Revelation, and Empowerment

Sivan is the third month on the biblical (sacred) calendar, following Nisan (redemption) and Iyar (healing and preparation). On the civil calendar, which begins in the fall with Tishri, Sivan is counted as the ninth month—a number often associated with fullness, fruitfulness, and divine completion.

On the Gregorian calendar, Sivan typically falls between May and June, aligning with the last spring harvest and the celebration of *Shavuot* (Pentecost).

Though the name Sivan appears only once in Scripture (Esther 8:9), the month carries immense prophetic weight. It marks the culmination of Israel's journey from Egypt's deliverance to Mount Sinai's revelation. It was in Sivan that God gave His Word, established His covenant, and released purpose upon His people.

Sivan reminds us that God does not rescue us merely to set us free—He rescues us to draw us near, to reveal Himself, and to empower us for a divine mission. It is the month when bondage gives way to boldness, and redemption becomes revelation.

From Redemption to Revelation: The Omer Journey—Sivan completes the Counting of the Omer—a forty-ninth-day spiritual journey that begins during Passover and ends at Pentecost (Leviticus 23:15–16). This daily count was far more than a ritual—it was a prophetic pathway of preparation, tracing the transformation from slavery to spiritual maturity.

Just as the Israelites moved from Egypt to Mount Sinai, we too are called to move from personal redemption to divine revelation. The deliverance from Egypt wasn't the destination—it was the beginning of a greater calling.

> And you shall count unto you from the day after the Sabbath, from the day that you brought the sheaf of the wave offering; seven Sabbaths shall be complete. Even unto the next day after the seventh Sabbath shall you number fifty days; and you shall offer a new meat offering unto the LORD. (Leviticus 23:15–16)

This spiritual countdown reveals a pattern: deliverance must lead to discipleship. The Israelites had to unlearn the habits of bondage and prepare to become a holy, covenant people. Sivan marks the divine shift—from merely being rescued to being taught, from receiving freedom to carrying the weight of revelation and responsibility.

The Covenant at Sinai: God Reveals His Voice—It was in the month of Sivan that the Israelites arrived at Mount Sinai, where the LORD descended in fire, thunder, and glory to establish His covenant with His people. In a moment of awe and trembling, God gave the Ten Commandments—the beginning of His Torah— to Moses (Exodus 19–20). This marked not just the giving of laws, but the birth of a nation—a people set apart to reflect the holiness of their God.

But even as Moses received the tablets of stone (the Ten Commandments), the people below crafted a golden calf. In one moment, they traded the voice of God for the echo of idols. Judgment followed, and 3,000 died (Exodus 32:28). Yet even in that failure, we see the heart of God: Moses interceded, and God renewed His covenant. His grace prevailed.

The message of Sivan is this: Even after rebellion, God's voice still speaks. Even after judgment, His mercy makes room for restoration.

Pentecost Fulfilled: The Outpouring of the Spirit—Centuries after Sinai, on the very same feast day—*Shavuot* (Pentecost)—God descended once more. But this time, not in fire on a mountain . . . He came in fire upon hearts.

In Acts 2, on the Day of Pentecost, the Holy Spirit was poured out with wind and flame. Tongues of fire rested upon the disciples, and they began to speak in other languages—empowered to proclaim the gospel across nations of many languages. This moment fulfilled Joel's prophecy:

> And it shall come to pass afterward, that I will pour out My Spirit upon all flesh; and your sons and your daughters shall prophesy, your old men shall dream dreams, your young men shall see visions. (Joel 2:28)

Just as the Torah was given at Mount Sinai, now God's Law was written on hearts (Jeremiah 31:31–33). Just as 3,000 perished after the golden calf, 3,000 were saved after Peter's Spirit-filled sermon (Acts 2:41). This isn't coincidence— it's divine choreography. A prophetic mirror. A holy reversal.

The Feast of *Shavuot* wasn't just a historical event. It was a prophetic moment at Pentecost—and it is a personal encounter for every Spirit-filled believer.

The Calendar Connection: Understanding Sivan's Timing—On the biblical (religious) calendar, Sivan is the third month of the year—a powerful marker in God's redemptive timeline. It follows:

- Nisan—the month of redemption (Passover),
- Iyar—the month of healing and preparation, and now,
- Sivan—the month of revelation, covenant, and empowerment.

But on the civil calendar, which begins in Tishri, Sivan is the ninth month. This contrast isn't a contradiction—it's a reflection of the layered nature of God's timing. Understanding the distinction between the religious and civil calendars helps us see that God measures time in patterns, purposes, and prophetic rhythms—not simply by dates. To walk in sync with Him, we must do more than track time. We must discern the times.

A Prophetic Picture: The Spirit and the Soon Return—The outpouring of the Holy Spirit during Sivan did more than empower the early Church—it launched the final harvest. Jesus called it the "former rain" (Joel 2:23; Hosea 6:3)—the initial downpour of spiritual power to prepare His people. But Scripture also promises a "latter rain"—a final outpouring before Christ's return (James 5:7–8). We are now living in the prophetic fulfillment of Pentecost—but not as bystanders. We are being readied for the return of the Bridegroom.

> Be patient therefore, brethren, unto the coming of the Lord. Behold, the husbandman (farmer) waits for the precious fruit of the earth, and has long patience for it, until he receive the early and latter rain. Be you also patient; establish your hearts: for the coming of the Lord draws near. (James 5:7–8)

Sivan reminds us that the journey from redemption to empowerment isn't optional—it's essential. It calls us to walk not only in salvation, but in revelation, obedience, and spiritual authority.

The Church was never meant to be passive. Pentecost is not a monument—it's a mandate. We are called to be warriors of wind and fire—those who live filled, led, and ignited by the Holy Spirit. Those who press forward with boldness, urgency, and clarity, until the King returns.

Prayer for the Month of Sivan—Father, thank You for rescuing me from sin and calling me into covenant with You. I receive the fullness of Pentecost—Your Spirit poured out on me for power, purpose, and purity.

Write Your Law upon my heart. Fill me afresh with boldness to speak, strength to obey, and wisdom to discern. Let me not stop at deliverance, but move forward into revelation, obedience, and Spirit-led action.

Empower me to walk in spiritual authority. Use me to bring in the harvest in these last days. Make me a vessel of fire, a voice of truth, and a light in the darkness.

In the name of the Father, the Son, and the Holy Spirit, Amen.

4. The Month of Tammuz: A Season of Heart Testing and Idolatry Revealed

Tammuz, the fourth month on the biblical (sacred) calendar, and the tenth month on the civil calendar, which begins in the fall with Tishri. On the Gregorian calendar, Tammuz typically falls in June to July, aligning with the intensifying heat of summer—symbolic of spiritual testing, pressure, and purification.

The name "Tammuz" was adopted during the Babylonian exile and carries unsettling connotations. It is derived from a Babylonian fertility deity whose seasonal death was mourned with ritual lamentation. This association forever linked the month to themes of idolatry, spiritual compromise, and the erosion of covenant identity.

In Ezekeil 8:14, the prophet is shown a heartbreaking vision:

> Then He (God the Father) brought me to the door of the gate of the LORD's house which was toward the north; and, behold, there sat women weeping for Tammuz. (Ezekiel 8:14)

This scene unfolded within the very gates of the Temple—a tragic picture of misplaced worship and spiritual adultery. But Tammuz is more than a historical footnote—it is a prophetic mirror for every generation.

In this month, God calls His people to examine their hearts, confront the idols they've allowed to linger, and reject the subtle compromises that dull spiritual clarity. Tammuz invites us to ask hard questions: Who or what sits on the throne of our lives? Where have we traded holiness for comfort? Have we wept over idols while ignoring the call to repentance?

It is a season of refining—not to shame us, but to reclaim us. The fire of Tammuz isn't meant to destroy, but to burn away every false affection that keeps us from intimacy with the Father.

A Season of National and Personal Mourning—The month of Tammuz begins a solemn season of reflection known as "The Three Weeks" or *Bein HaMetzarim*—"Between the Straits." This period begins on the 17th of Tammuz and ends on the 9th of Av (*Tisha B'Av*), marking some of the most tragic moments in Jewish history:

- Moses shattered the Ten Commandment tablets after witnessing the golden calf (Exodus 32:19).
- Jerusalem's walls were breached by the Babylonians (2 Kings 25:3–4).
- Both the First and Second Temples were destroyed.
- Holy spaces were defiled, and sacred scrolls burned.

These events are commemorated through fasts and mourning, serving as reminders that idolatry invites judgment and turning from God brings ruin. But even in grief, there is a prophetic undertone of hope: This season also points toward repentance, renewal, and the ultimate restoration secured through Christ.

God still calls His people to tear down idols, return to covenant faithfulness, and prepare for the glory that follows surrender.

Idolatry Then and Now: What Has Taken God's Place?—The month of Tammuz invites us to confront a painful question: What idols have crept into our hearts and sacred spaces? While ancient Israel built a golden calf, today's idols often wear modern disguises—career ambition, the pursuit of comfort, the hunger for validation, or the subtle worship of self. These false gods, when elevated above our devotion to Christ, carry the same spiritual danger.

Jesus, in contrast, demonstrated total allegiance to the Father. When Satan offered Him the kingdoms of the world in exchange for worship, He responded with unwavering conviction: "You shall worship the LORD your God, and Him only you shall serve" (Matthew 4:10). In a month that recalls Israel's failures, Jesus stands as the Righteous One—our example and standard.

> Then says Jesus unto him, Get you hence, Satan: for it is written, You shalt worship the LORD your God, and Him only shalt you serve. (Matthew 4:10)

Christ, the Covenant Restorer—Tammuz prophetically points to the New Covenant in Christ. Where the Old Covenant was broken by idolatry, Jesus offers a restored relationship through His death and resurrection. As Jeremiah 31:33 foretells, "I will put My Law in their inward parts, and write it in their hearts." Through the Holy Spirit, we are no longer bound to stone tablets or external rituals—we are invited into internal transformation.

> But this shall be the covenant that I will make with the house of Israel; After those days, says the LORD, I will put My Law in their inward parts, and write it in their hearts; and will be their God, and they shall be My people. (Jeremiah 31:33)

Even the place of Tammuz on the calendar is instructive. As the tenth month on the civil calendar, it evokes imagery of testing (ten plagues, Ten Commandments, ten spies returned with a negative and fear-filled report, ten virgins in the parable). As the fourth month religiously, it reflects global significance—as four often represents the four corners of the earth. Together, these numbers suggest a season of global shaking and personal refinement, especially in the days leading up to Christ's return.

From Judgment to Restoration: The Road Ahead—The tragedies remembered during Tammuz are sobering. But they are not the end of the story. They serve as warning beacons, urging the people of God to realign before greater judgment falls. As we approach the fall feasts—Trumpets, Atonement, and Tabernacles—Tammuz acts as a spiritual checkpoint. Will we prepare our hearts like the wise virgins with oil in their lamps? Or will be found worshiping idols when the Bridegroom returns?

This is the month to cleanse the temple of our hearts, tear down the high places we've tolerated, and rebuild the altar of intimacy with our God. Let this summer heat refine—not consume—our purpose.

Prayer for the Month of Tammuz—Father, I consecrate this month to You. Let no idol remain hidden in the chambers of my heart. Expose anything I've exalted above You, and give me the courage to tear it down.

I renounce every golden calf—every source of comfort, control, or security that has replaced You. Cleanse my mind. Renew my focus. Restore the fire of my devotion.

Jesus, I declare You as King. I yield fully to the refining work of Your Spirit. As testing comes, may I be found faithful—refined, not ruined.

I return to You, my first love. In Your mercy, prepare me for the feasts ahead and the coming of the King.

In the name of the Father, the Son, and the Holy Spirit, Amen.

5. The Month of Av: From Dire Straits to Divine Restoration

Av is the fifth month on the biblical (sacred) calendar, and the eleventh month on the civil calendar, which begins in the fall with Tishri. On the Gregorian calendar, Av typically falls in July to August, in the peak of summer's intensity. Fittingly, it is a month of spiritual heat as well—a time when God draws His people into the fires of reflection, repentance, and ultimately, restoration.

The name "Av" means "Father" in Hebrew. And this month, though marked by historic sorrow, carries the tender invitation of a Father's love. It recalls some of the most tragic moments in Jewish history—including the destruction of both Temples—but it also whispers of renewal. Av is a paradox: a season of national mourning and prophetic hope, of brokenness and divine rebuilding.

God does not call His people to mourn without purpose. In Av, we are invited not just to grieve, but to grow. Not merely to remember what was lost, but to rebuild in covenant strength. In the midst of pain, the Father draws near. The One who disciplines also heals. The Judge who corrects is also the Redeemer who restores.

This month continues our journey through the prophetic calendar—not just as a historical record, but as a spiritual roadmap pointing toward the return of Christ. Av reminds us that even the ashes of loss can become the soil of inheritance. It speaks to the deep places in our lives where God is forming His Bride—purified, matured, and ready to reign with Him.

A Time of Dire Straits: A Pattern of Rebellion and Consequence—Av is most remembered for what Jewish tradition calls "The Three Weeks"—a somber period between the 17th of Tammuz and the 9th of Av, culminating in the fast day known as *Tisha B'Av*. Historically, some of Israel's most devastating tragedies occurred during this window, particularly on the 9th of Av.

Among these events:

- The twelve spies returned from scouting the Promised Land. Ten of them gave a fearful report, leading the people to weep all night (Numbers 14:1)—an act of faithlessness that brought forty years of wilderness wandering (Numbers 14:34).
- Both the First and Second Temples in Jerusalem were destroyed on the 9th of Av, by the Babylonians in 586 BC and by the Romans in AD 70.
- Later disasters followed on this same day: the expulsion of Jews from England (1290), France (1306), and Spain (1492), as well as the beginning of mass deportations from the Warsaw Ghetto during the Holocaust.

Later, in the same month of Av, Aaron, the high priest and brother of Moses, died on Mount Hor. According to Numbers 33:38, Aaron passed away on the first day of the fifth month, which corresponds to Av on the Hebrew calendar. His death marked a sobering moment in Israel's journey, tied to a moment of disobedience at Meribah. When Moses struck the rock instead of speaking to it as God had instructed (Numbers 20:8, 10–13), both he and Aaron were told they would not enter the Promised Land. Aaron's death serves as a solemn reminder that faith and obedience are prerequisites to entering into divine inheritance.

> And Moses and Aaron gathered the congregation together before the rock, and he said unto them, Hear now, you rebels; must we fetch you water out of this rock? And Moses lifted up his hand, and with his rod he struck the rock twice: and the water came out abundantly, and the congregation drank, and their beasts also. And the LORD spoke unto Moses and Aaron, Because you believed Me not, to sanctify Me in the eyes of the children of Israel, therefore you shall not bring this congregation into the land which I have given them. This is the water of Meribah; because the children of Israel strove with the LORD, and He was sanctified in them. (Numbers 20:10–13)

This repeated history is not coincidence—it is a prophetic call. The month of Av becomes a warning sign that rebellion and fear-based living always bring delay and devastation. It's a month of heart testing.

Jesus Christ and the Redemption of Av—Yet even in the midst of these dire straits, God's mercy shines. Where Israel succumbed to fear in the wilderness, Jesus overcame in His. When tempted for forty days, Jesus remained faithful (Matthew 4:1–11; Luke 4:1–13), proving Himself as the Second Israel—the Righteous One. Where Israel wept in defeat, Jesus rose in victory.

Jesus, "a Man of sorrows" (Isaiah 53:3), took upon Himself the consequences of every broken covenant. He did what Israel could not. He fulfilled righteousness on our behalf and offers us a way out of the wilderness—not just from sin, but from sorrow, despair, and delay.

> He is despised and rejected of men, a Man of sorrows, and acquainted with grief: and we hid as it were our faces from Him; He was despised, and we esteemed Him not. (Isaiah 53:3)

Tu B'Av: **A Prophetic Reversal**—Just six days after the mourning of *Tisha B'Av* comes *Tu B'Av*, the 15th of Av—a lesser-known but joyful day of celebration. According to Jewish tradition, it marks the day God lifted His judgment over the Israelites who had wandered for forty years. It also became known as a day of matchmaking, love, and unity. In modern Israel, *Tu B'Av* is often likened to Valentine's Day.

The message is clear: After mourning comes dancing. After delay comes divine acceleration. The same month that marks tragedy also holds a prophetic promise of restoration, reconciliation, and revival.

From Wilderness to Inheritance—This is a month to reflect:

- Are we trusting God like Joshua and Caleb?
- Or are we shrinking back in fear, like the other ten spies?
- Are we building altars to unbelief?
- Or are we standing firm on God's promises?

Av invites us to renew our trust in God's leadership, to grieve with wisdom, and to allow the Holy Spirit to realign our hearts with Heaven's purposes. This is not a month to remain in sorrow, but to press through into victory.

Prayer for the Month of Av—Father, I thank You that even in the wilderness, You are with me. You are my Hope, my Healer, and my Guide. I renounce every spirit of fear, despair, and delay that would hinder me from stepping into Your promises. Just as Jesus overcame in the wilderness, I declare that through Your Word, I too will overcome.

Forgive me, Lord, for the times I've doubted You—when I have complained, compromised, or chased lesser loves. Cleanse my heart from every idol and reset my focus on You alone. I declare that You are my Father, and I choose to trust You fully.

Let this be the month where mourning turns to dancing, and testing gives way to triumph. Restore my joy, renew my strength, and prepare me for what lies ahead.

In the name of the Father, the Son, and the Holy Spirit, Amen.

6. The Month of Elul: The King Is in the Field

Elul is the sixth month of the biblical (sacred) calendar and the twelfth and final month on the civil calendar, which begins in the fall of Tishri. On the Gregorian calendar, Elul typically falls in August to September, during the final stretch of summer.

Elul serves as a sacred threshold—a season of spiritual preparation and introspection as one year draws to a close and another begins. It is traditionally known in Judaism as the month of repentance (*teshuvah*), a time of mercy, self-examination, and returning to God.

Often described with the phrase "The King is in the field," Elul is a unique time when God's presence feels especially near—accessible, intimate, and welcoming. It prepares the heart for the High Holy Days of Tishri:

- *Rosh HaShanah*—Feast of Trumpets—the day of awakening and judgment.
- *Yom Kippur*—Day of Atonement—the holiest day of the year.

Elul is not merely a time to look back—it is a divine call to return, to realign, and to ready the soul for the new prophetic year ahead.

A Season of Soul Searching and Grace—The name "Elul" is thought to derive from a root meaning "to search." It is a time for self-examination and spiritual inventory—a divine pause to reflect, repent, and realign before the trumpet blast of *Rosh HaShanah*. In Jewish tradition, Elul begins a forty-day period of *teshuvah* (repentance), mirroring the forty days Moses spent on Mount Sinai interceding for Israel after the sin of the golden calf (Exodus 32–34). During that time, God not only granted forgiveness but gave Moses a new set of stone tablets (the Ten Commandments). This sets a powerful precedent: God is not only willing to forgive but eager to restore.

Elul reminds us that repentance is not about shame or failure—it's about returning to the Father's arms and stepping into the blessings of a new spiritual year.

Rebuilding What's Been Broken—Elul is also remembered as the month in which Nehemiah and his people restored the city's defenses in just fifty-two days, finishing the work on the 25th of Elul (Nehemiah 6:15). This triumph serves as a prophetic picture of what God can accomplish when we align with His will—especially in times of spiritual repair. Elul teaches us that, through prayer, confession, and persistence, even the most broken places in our lives can be made whole.

The King Is in the Field: A Season of Divine Nearness—One of the most beloved themes associated with the Hebrew month of Elul is the rabbinic parable known as "The King Is in the Field." Though not found in Scripture, this profound allegory comes from Jewish rabbinic and Hasidic tradition. It paints a vivid picture of God's extraordinary closeness during this season of repentance and mercy leading up to the High Holy Days—*Rosh HaShanah* and *Yom Kippur*.

In ancient times, a king would typically reside in a palace, surrounded by layers of protocol, guards, and ceremony. Gaining an audience with the king required status, effort, and permission. But according to tradition, once a year, the king would leave his palace and pitch his royal tent in the fields—right among the people. During this time, anyone—rich or poor, noble or common—could approach the king freely. No guards. Nor formalities. Just face-to-face access.

This parable offers a striking metaphor for Elul, a month where God draws near and invites His people into intimate communion. It is a time when repentance (Hebrew: *teshuvah*) is welcomed—not with dread, but with tenderness and open arms. It is a season to meet the King of Heaven in the simplicity of our "fields"—our ordinary, imperfect lives—and experience His grace firsthand.

Jesus, the King Who Came into Our Field—For followers of Christ, this ancient image prophetically points to Jesus—the King of kings—who did not wait for humanity to ascend to Him, but instead descended to us. John 1:14 declares, "And the Word became flesh and dwelt among us . . ." The Greek word used for "dwelt" is *skenoo*, meaning "to tabernacle" or "to pitch a tent." Quite literally, the King left His throne and set up His tent in the field of human life.

> And the Word was made flesh, and dwelt among us, (and we beheld His glory, the glory as of the only begotten of the Father), full of grace and truth. (John 1:14)

Jesus walked among fishermen, tax collectors, outcasts, and sinners. He touched the leper, healed the broken, and called the weary to Himself. In doing so, He fulfilled the very heart of this parable—not figuratively, but in flesh and blood. The King did not remain distant. He came near. And through His death and resurrection, He tore the veil, giving us permanent access to the presence of God (Hebrews 4:16).

> Let us therefore come boldly unto the throne of grace, that we may obtain mercy, and find grace to help in time of need. (Hebrews 4:16)

The Heart of Elul: I Am My Beloved's—The very name "Elul" is traditionally understood as an acronym for the Hebrew phrase *"Ani L'dodi V'dodi Li"*—I am my Beloved's and my Beloved is mine" (Song of Solomon 6:3). This expression captures the deep intimacy and covenant love that defines the month. Elul is not a time of fear-based repentance, but a divine invitation to return to the One who loves us most.

Elul reminds us that the King is not only accessible—but affectionate. He meets us in our brokenness, listens to our honest confessions, and covers us in His mercy. Whether we come with joy or tears, He welcomes us with open arms.

The King Is Still in the Field—Though the parable belongs to Jewish tradition, its spiritual truth resounds for every believer: God is near. Not only during Elul, but every day, because of Jesus. We no longer need priests, temples, or rituals to draw near. The King of Glory now dwells within us, and He is ever ready to meet with those who seek Him.

So in this sacred season of Elul, let us draw close. Let us search our hearts, confess our sins, and enter into the field—not with fear, but with awe, gratitude, and love. The King is waiting.

Prayer for the Month of Elul—Father, I thank You for the gift of Elul—a holy season of return, reflection, and restoration. I praise You for drawing near—not as a distant King, but as the Beloved who meets me in the field of everyday life. Because of the blood of Jesus, I come not in fear, but with boldness and joy.

Search my heart, Lord. Reveal and cleanse anything in me that has grown cold, distracted, or divided. Forgive my sins, renew my spirit, and awaken my first love. I receive Your mercy and grace. I receive the joy of restored fellowship.

Let this month mark a fresh alignment with Your purposes. Empower me by Your Spirit to walk in obedience, intimacy, and expectation as I prepare for the year ahead.

I am my Beloved's, and my Beloved is mine.

In the name of the Father, the Son, and the Holy Spirit, Amen.

7. The Month of Tishri: A Sacred Season of Awakening, Atonement, and Abundance

Tishri is the seventh month on the biblical (religious) calendar, but it also marks the first month of the civil calendar, beginning the Jewish New Year. Falling during September–October on the Gregorian calendar, Tishri is widely regarded as the holiest and most spiritual weighty month of the year in Jewish tradition.

This is a month where divine appointments converge with prophetic clarity. It is a season of holy tension—where repentance meets rejoicing, and judgment meets mercy. Tishri calls us to return to God, realign our hearts, and rejoice in His faithful promises.

Within this sacred window fall three major Feasts of the LORD, all detailed in Leviticus 23:

- *Yom Teruah*—Feast of Trumpets/*Rosh HaShanah*—a wake-up call to repentance and spiritual alertness.
- *Yom Kippur*—Day of Atonement—the most solemn day of the year, set aside for humility, confession, and forgiveness.
- *Sukkot*—Feast of Tabernacles—a joyful celebration of God's provision, His abiding presence, and the prophetic promise of eternal dwelling with Him. Also known as the Feast of Booths and the Feast of Ingatherings, *Sukkot* commemorates the Israelites' wilderness journey, when they dwell in temporary shelters—and prophetically points to the future "ingathering" of all nations under Messiah's reign.

Together, these festivals form a divine trilogy—revealing God's heart as Righteous Judge, Merciful Redeemer, and Eternal Dwelling Presence.

Tishri not only looks back to Israel's story of deliverance and dependence, but also looks forward with prophetic vision: this is the month that foreshadows the end-time plan of God—when the trumpet will sound, sin will be judged, and Christ will tabernacle among His people.

***Rosh HaShanah*: The Trumpet Blast of Awakening**—The month begins with a divine alarm clock. On the first day, we observe *Yom Teruah*, known today as *Rosh HaShanah*, or the "Head of the Year." Leviticus 23:23–24 calls it the day of blowing the trumpets. The piercing sound of the shofar (ram's horn) echoes through the land—a spiritual wake-up call to all who will hear.

> And the LORD spoke unto Moses, saying, Speak unto the children of Israel, saying, In the seventh month, in the first day of the month (evening and morning), shall you have a Sabbath, a memorial of blowing of trumpets, a holy convocation. (Leviticus 23:23–24)

It is not merely a cultural celebration of the Jewish civil New Year. Biblically, it inaugurates the Ten Days of Awe, a period of deep introspection and repentance that culminates in *Yom Kippur*—the 10th of Tishri. The shofar announces God's kingship and reminds us that a final trumpet will one day sound again—calling believers to rise and meet the returning King (1 Thessalonians 4:16).

Rosh HaShanah is both an invitation and a warning. It asks us: Are we spiritually awake? Are we prepared for the coming judgment? Have we returned to the Lord with all our hearts?

***Yom Kippur*: The Day of Atonement and Redemption**—Ten days after the trumpet's cry, we arrive at the most sacred day on the biblical calendar—*Yom Kippur*, the Day of Atonement (Leviticus 16:15–16). In ancient Israel, this was the only day the high priest could enter the Holy of Holies, carrying the blood of a sin offering to make atonement for the people.

> Also on the tenth day of this seventh month there shall be a Day of Atonement: it shall be a holy convocation unto you; and you shall afflict your souls, and offer an offering made by fire unto the LORD. (Leviticus 23:27)

Two goats were presented: one sacrificed, and the other—the scapegoat—was symbolically burdened with Israel's sins and released into the wilderness. This powerful act pointed forward to the perfect atonement through Jesus Christ, the Lamb of God, who bore our sins once and for all (Hebrews 9:11–15).

Through Christ's sacrifice, we no longer await an annual covering of sin. Our guilt has been removed, not just postponed. Hebrews 8:12 declares: "For I will forgive their wickedness and will remember their sins no more."

Yom Kippur reminds us of both the cost of grace and the depth of mercy. It is a day to confess, to fast, to be still before God—and to rejoice in the assurance that Christ has made a way into the Most Holy Place for all who believe.

***Sukkot*: The Feast of Tabernacles and Abundant Joy**—Only five days after the solemnity of *Yom Kippur* begins the week-long festival of *Sukkot*—also called the Feast of Tabernacles or Booths (Leviticus 23:34). Celebrated from the 15th to the 22nd of Tishri, it commemorates the forty years Israel spent living in temporary shelters in the wilderness, fully dependent on God's daily provision and protection.

> The fifteenth day of this seventh month shall be the Feast of Tabernacles for seven days unto the LORD. (Leviticus 23:34)

During *Sukkot*, families construct outdoor booths called *sukkot*, adorned with fruit, leaves, and open roofs to see the stars—symbolizing both fragility and divine covering. It is a physical reminder that we are pilgrims on the earth, sustained not by our strength, but by God's faithfulness.

Yet *Sukkot* is also a harvest feast—a celebration of abundance, unity, and joy. It's the only biblical feast where God commands His people to rejoice (Deuteronomy 16:14). It is a foreshadowing of the coming Messianic Kingdom, when all nations will gather in Jerusalem to worship Jesus Christ, King of kings and Lord of lords during this very feast (Zechariah 14:16).

> And it shall come to pass, that every one that is left of all the nations which came against Jerusalem shall even go up from year to year to worship the King, the LORD of hosts, and to keep the Feast of Tabernacles. (Zechariah 14:16)

Shemini Atzeret: **The Eighth Day of Assembly**—Tishri 22 marks *Shemini Atzeret*, which means "the Eighth Day of Assembly" (Leviticus 23:36). Though it follows immediately after the seven days of *Sukkot* (Feast of Tabernacles), it stands as a distinct, sacred day—a divine invitation to remain in God's presence just a little longer.

> Seven days you shall offer an offering made by fire unto the LORD: on the eighth day shall be a holy convocation unto you; and you shall offer an offering made by fire unto the LORD: it is a solemn assembly; and you shall do no servile work (ordinary labor, daily work, or burdensome tasks that would distract from worship) therein. (Leviticus 23:36)

Unlike the rest of *Sukkot*, no agricultural or ritual requirements are tied to this day. Its focus is relational, not ceremonial. It represents completion, new beginnings, and deep intimacy with God.

Prophetically, *Shemini Atzeret* is a glimpse of eternity—the eighth day beyond the seven-thousand-year framework of biblical history. It points to the age beyond the Millennial Kingdom, when God will dwell forever with His people in fullness and joy.

In modern Jewish tradition, *Simchat Torah* (Rejoicing in the Torah) is often celebrated on or just after this day, marking the completion and restarting of the annual Torah reading cycle.

Tishri 22 reminds us that God's greatest desire is not just to redeem us, but to dwell with us—forever.

Jesus Christ Revealed in Tishri—Every appointed time in Tishri finds its fulfillment in Jesus:

- He is the shofar blast that awakens the soul (1 Thessalonians 4:16).
- He is our High Priest and eternal Atonement (Hebrews 9:12).
- He is the true Tabernacle who came to dwell among us (John 1:14).
- And He is the coming King who will return to tabernacle with us forever (Revelation 21:3).

Tishri is a holy rehearsal for Christ's return—a divine dress rehearsal for eternity. As Hebrews 4:14–16 reminds us, Jesus, our sinless Savior, has torn the veil. We now have direct access to the throne of grace—no longer needing earthly priests, sacrifices, or intermediaries.

A Call to Prepare for the King's Return—As the final fall feast, Tishri prophetically looks forward to the Second Coming of Christ, when the trumpet of God will sound, and the Bride of Christ will rise to meet Him in the air (1

Thessalonians 4:16–17). These days of awe, repentance, and rejoicing remind us that time is short, and the harvest is ripe.

Now is the time to prepare. The trumpet is sounding. The books are open. The King is coming.

Prayer for the Month of Tishri—Father, I proclaim that You are my King, my Redeemer, and my Provider. You awaken me with Your voice, cover me with Your mercy, and surround me with Your joy. Because of Jesus, my sins are forgiven, and my name is written in the Book of Life—thank You.

Lord, I respond to Your trumpet call. I turn from my own ways and align my heart with Yours. Cleanse me, restore me, and prepare me for what lies ahead.

Let this be a month of holy beginnings. Let every shofar blast stir my spirit. Let every fast draw me closer. Let every celebration deepen my joy.

I rejoice in Your faithfulness, and I long for Your soon return.

In the name of the Father, the Son, and the Holy Spirit, Amen.

8. The Month of Heshvan: A Season of Restoration, Refuge, and Renewal

Heshvan (also spelled Cheshvan), the eighth month of the biblical (religious) calendar and the second month of the civil calendar, typically falls during October–November on the Gregorian calendar. Known in ancient times as Bul (1 Kings 6:38), this month is distinctive in that it contains no appointed feasts or fasts—yet its prophetic significance runs deep.

Heshvan is remembered as the month when the Great Flood began in the days of Noah (Genesis 7:11), symbolizing divine judgment but also the promise of cleansing, covenant, and renewal. It is also traditionally associated with the completion of Solomon's First Temple, a structure built to house the presence of God—a reminder that even seasons without public celebration can be filled with profound spiritual construction.

As the rainy season begins in Israel, Heshvan represents both outpouring and preparation. It is a time to reflect, regroup, and rebuild after the intensity of the High Holy Days in Tishri. Often called the "quiet month," Heshvan invites us to internalize the spiritual work of the previous season and begin walking it out in renewed obedience.

In this way, Heshvan becomes a month of sacred transition—a bridge from public encounter to private devotion, from national feasts to personal faithfulness.

The Flood in Heshvan: Judgment and Grace Collide—Genesis 7:11 tells us that on the 17th day of Heshvan (religious calendar), the heavens opened and the Flood began. A year later, on the 27th day of Heshvan, Noah and his family stepped out of the Ark into a cleansed and silent world (Genesis 8:14–19). This month, therefore, stands as a memorial of divine judgment, yes—but even more so, of divine grace.

> In the six hundredth year of Noah's life, in the second month, the seventeenth day of the month, the same day were all the fountains of the great deep broken up, and the windows of heaven were opened. (Genesis 7:11)

> And in the second month, on the seven and twentieth day of the month, was the earth dried. And God spoke unto Noah, saying, Go forth of the Ark, you, and your wife, and your sons, and your sons' wives with you. Bring forth with you every living thing that is with you, of all flesh, both of fowl, and of cattle, and of every creeping thing that creeps upon the earth; that may breed abundantly in the earth, and be fruitful, and multiply upon the earth. And Noah went forth, and his sons, and his wife, and his sons' wives with him: every beast, every creeping thing, and every fowl, and whatsoever creeps upon the earth, after their kinds, went forth out of the Ark. (Genesis 8:14–19)

Amid a world reset by water, eight souls were preserved. They represent the remnant, the faithful, the ones who believe even when the sky darkens. In Heshvan, we're reminded that when God brings judgment, He also provides refuge—and He always preserves a remnant to rebuild.

Eight: The Number of New Creation—The number eight in Scripture is the number of new beginnings, resurrection, and divine order beyond completion.

- Eight people repopulated the earth (1 Peter 3:20).
- Solomon's Temple was completed in the eighth month (1 Kings 6:38).
- Jesus rose on the first day of the week, often called the "eighth day," ushering in a New Covenant.

Through Christ, we step into a new creation:

> Therefore if any man be in Christ, he is a new creature: old things are passed away; behold, all things are become new. (2 Corinthians 5:17)

Heshvan invites us to bury the old and embrace the new—to walk out of the Ark of the past into the field of God's promises.

Jesus Christ: Our Ark of Refuge—God did not pluck Noah out of the world— He protected him within it. Likewise, Jesus doesn't always remove us from trials, but He shelters us within His presence as the storm passes.

> So shall they fear the name of the LORD from the west, and His glory from the rising of the sun. When the enemy shall come in like a flood, the Spirit of the LORD shall lift up a standard against him. (Isaiah 59:19)

That standard is Christ. In Jesus, we find our ark, our covering, our covenant shelter. He carries us through the chaos and delivers us safely into a future filled with promise.

A Call to Trust in Transition—Heshvan represents the in-between—the quiet pause after the holy convocations of Tishri and before the activity of plowing, sowing, and winter preparation. It symbolizes seasons of waiting, rebuilding, and trusting—times when old structures have crumbled, but the new has not yet emerged.

When Noah stepped off the Ark, the world before him was unrecognizable. Everything had changed. And yet—God was still with him.

If you find yourself in a season of grief, change, relocation, or uncertainty, Heshvan speaks a prophetic truth:

You are not alone. God walks with you into the unknown.

Prayer for the Month of Heshvan—Father, in the name of Jesus, I thank You that when the enemy rushes in like a flood, You raise up a standard—Jesus, my Savior and Shield. You are my Ark of refuge.

Even in seasons of unfamiliarity and transition, I chose to trust You. I declare that what You did for Noah, You will do for me: You will carry me through, and I will emerge into new beginnings with joy and purpose.

Let Heshvan be a month of spiritual renewal. Let Your covenant promises rain down like the early rains in Israel—refreshing the soil of my heart. Lead me by Your Spirit, and anchor me in Your presence. I boldly declare: I am a new creation in Christ.

In the name of the Father, the Son, and the Holy Spirit, Amen.

9. The Month of Kislev: A Season of Revelation, Rededication, and Light

Kislev (also spelled Chislev)—is the ninth month on the biblical (religious) calendar and the third month on the civil calendar, typically falling during November to December on the Gregorian calendar. First mentioned in Zechariah 7:1, Kislev arrives during the darkest days of the year—both physically and, often, spiritually.

Though its Babylonian name carries uncertain origins, its prophetic message is unmistakable: light in the darkness, divine revelation through dreams, and renewed dedication to God's presence.

In this month, we remember that even when the nights are long, God still speaks, God still shines, and God still calls His people to burn brightly. Kislev invites us to press in with expectancy, to dream again, and to rededicate our lives as vessels of holy fire in a darkened world.

The Feast of Dedication: *Hanukkah* **and the Miracle of Oil**—*Hanukkah* (also spelled Chanukah), beginning on the 25th of Kislev, is the central celebration of this month. Known as the Festival of Lights or Feast of Dedication, it commemorates a time when the Jewish people reclaimed their Temple from the Greek-Syrian empire in 167 BC. Led by Judah Maccabee, they overthrew oppression and restored true worship.

Upon entering the desecrated Temple, only one jar of holy oil remained—barely enough to light the menorah for a day. Yet miraculously, it burned for eight days. This divine provision allowed time for more oil to be consecrated.

Hanukkah celebrates this rededication of the Second Temple in Jerusalem after its desecration by Antiochus IV Epiphanes. This story is recorded in the Books of the Maccabees (part of the Apocrypha), particularly 1 Maccabees 4:52–59, but not in the Protestant Bible.

This is the heart of *Hanukkah*: God's light never goes out. His presence endures where human ability ends.

Jesus: The Light of the World—John places Jesus at the Feast of Dedication:

> And it was at Jerusalem the Feast of the Dedication, and it was winter. And Jesus walked in the Temple in Solomon's porch. (John 10:22–23)

It was here that He declared His divine identity:

> I and My Father are one. Then the Jews took up stones again to stone Him. Jesus answered them, Many good works have I showed you from My Father; for which of those works do you stone Me? The Jews answered Him, saying, For a good work we stone You not; but for blasphemy; and because that You, being a Man, makes Yourself God. (John 10:30–33)

Earlier, He said:

> Then spoke Jesus again unto them, saying, I am the Light of the World: he that follows Me shall not walk in darkness, but shall have the light of life. (John 8:12)

The menorah lit in rededication now becomes a symbol of Christ Himself—the eternal flame, shining into the darkness of sin, despair, and confusion. In this month of rededication, we are reminded: We are now the temple. The oil of His Spirit must continually burn within us.

Kislev and the Power of Dreams—Kislev is often called the month of dreams, because the Torah readings during this season recount many divine dreams—Jacob's ladder (Genesis 28:10–19) and Joseph's destiny dreams (Genesis 37:5–10). God often speaks in seasons of darkness and quiet:

> In a dream, in a vision of the night, when deep sleep falls upon men, in slumbering upon the bed; then He opens the ears of men, and seals their instruction. (Job 33:15–16)

This is a month to tune in spiritually—to receive revelation, guidance, correction, and promise through dreams and quiet nudges of the Spirit. Ask the Lord to open your spiritual ears.

Light in Darkness—Kislev includes the winter solstice, the longest night of the year. Just as ancient Jews asked the prophet Zechariah whether they should continue mourning (Zechariah 7:2–3), we too must ask: Am I living in ritual or rededication? In gloom or in glory?

God's answer is still the same: He wants our hearts, not empty habits. He calls us to rededicate, to rejoice, and to burn bright in a dark world.

The Kingdom of Light

> Who has delivered us from the power of darkness, and has translated us into the kingdom of His dear Son. (Colossians 1:13)

As citizens of the Kingdom of Light, we are called to reflect the light of Jesus everywhere we go. Philippians 2:15 says:

> That you may be blameless and harmless, the sons of God, without rebuke, in the midst of a crooked and perverse nation, among whom you shine as lights in the world. (Philippians 2:15)

Kislev asks us: Is your light shining? Are you filled with oil? Are you burning with passion for truth, purity, and presence?

Just as the menorah never ran dry, we trust the Holy Spirit to continually fill us. God's supply is limitless—and His call is urgent.

Prayer for the Month of Kislev—Father, in the name of Jesus, I thank You for sending the Light of the World to pierce the darkness of my soul. I rededicate my heart, my mind, and my body to You. Make me a living temple, filled with the oil of Your Holy Spirit. Let my life burn brightly in the midst of this dark and troubled world.

Open my ears to hear Your voice. Speak to me in dreams, in visions, and in the still small whisper. Let revelation flow with clarity, wisdom, and truth. I will follow You, reflect You, and glorify You in all that I say and do.

I am Yours, Lord—Your vessel, Your flame. Shine through me this month and beyond.

In the name of the Father, the Son, and the Holy Spirit, Amen.

10. The Month of Tevet: Reflection, Rededication, and the Fullness of Christ

Tevet is the tenth month on the biblical (sacred) calendar and the fourth month on the civil calendar, which begins with Tishri in the fall. It typically falls during December to January on the Gregorian calendar, placing it at the very heart of winter—when the days are shortest and the world often feels still and subdued.

This quiet season offers a divine opportunity for sacred reflection and spiritual realignment. While the natural world lies dormant, God invites His people to search their hearts. To rededicate their lives, and to find fullness—not in resolutions, but in Christ Himself.

Tevet follows Kislev, a month of revelation and rededication (highlighted by *Hanukkah*), and moves us into a season of *spiritual sobriety and clarity*. It's a month that asks us to look honestly at our priorities, habits, and inner commitments—releasing what is misaligned and embracing what is eternal.

Just as Tevet stands between the celebration of light and the preparation for spring, it symbolizes a spiritual hinge point: a time to build strength in the hidden place, to deepen roots, and to fix our eyes on the everlasting light of Jesus Christ, who is the fullness of the Godhead in bodily form (Colossians 2:9).

For in Him dwells all the fullness of the Godhead bodily. (Colossians 2:9)

The Number Ten: Completion and Divine Order—The Hebrew word "Tevet" is rooted in the word for "ten," a number that consistently symbolizes completion, accountability, and divine structure throughout Scripture. It's presence in key biblical patterns is unmistakable:

- Ten Commandments—God's complete moral law.
- Ten plagues—Divine judgment that brought finality to Egypt's oppression.
- Ten generations from Adam to Noah—culminating in the judgment and cleansing of the old world.
- Ten generations from Shem, the son of Noah, to Abraham—marking the beginning of a covenantal new era.

In these patterns, we see that ten is not just a number—it is a signal of transition, fullness, and governmental alignment. The month of Tevet calls us into the same awareness: that God is a God of perfect order, and we are invited to submit our lives to His righteous pattern.

Early Generations of God's Faithful People (Genesis 5)
1. Adam—4000 BC to 3070 BC—born on day 6, died at age 930
2. Seth—3870 BC to 2958 BC—died at age 912
3. Enos—3765 BC to 2860 BC—died at age 905

4. Cainan (Kenan)—3675 BC to 2765 BC—died at age 910
5. Mahalaleel—3605 BC to 2710 BC—died at age 895
6. Jared—3540 BC to 2578 BC—died at age 962
7. Enoch—3378 BC to 3013 BC—God took him at age 365
8. Methuselah—3313 BC to 2344 BC—died at 969
9. Lamech—3126 BC to 2349 BC—died at age 777
10. Noah—2944 BC to 1994 BC—died at age 950

Early Generations of God's Faithful People (Genesis 10)

11. Shem—2442 BC to 1842 BC—died at age 600
12. Arphaxad—2342 BC to 1904 BC—died at age 438
13. Salah—2307 BC to 1874 BC—died at age 433
14. Eber—2277 BC to 1813 BC—died at age 464
15. Peleg—2243 BC to 2004 BC—died at age 239
16. Reu—2213 BC to 1974 BC—died at age 239
17. Serug—2181 BC to 1951 BC—died at age 230
18. Nahor—2151 BC to 2003 BC—died at age 148
19. Terah—2122 BC to 1917 BC—died at age 205
20. Abraham—2052 BC to 1877 BC—died at age 175

These Bible genealogies preserve the Messianic bloodline leading to the birth of Christ. The first twenty generations cover roughly 2,000 years of biblical and early world history. The next 2,000 years—marked by 42 generations—trace the unfolding of biblical, global, and Middle Eastern history:

- 14 generations from Abraham to David,
- 14 generations from David to the Babylonian exile, and
- 14 generations from the exile to Jesus Christ.

As we transition from one calendar year to the next, Tevet becomes a sacred checkpoint. A time to ask: Am I still walking in the plans God has for me?

The Siege of Jerusalem: A Call to Remember and Return—On the 10th of Tevet, King Nebuchadnezzar laid siege to Jerusalem. This act, recorded in both Jeremiah 39:1 and Ezekiel 24:1–2, marked the beginning of the fall of Judah. What followed was three and a half years of suffering that ended in the destruction of the First Temple and 70 years of exile.

> In the ninth year of Zedekiah king of Judah, in the tenth month, came Nebuchadnezzar king of Babylon and all his army against Jerusalem, and they besieged it. (Jeremiah 39:1)

> Again in the ninth year, in the tenth month, in the tenth day of the month, the Word of the LORD came unto me, saying, Son of man, write you the name of

the day, even of this day: the king of Babylon set himself against Jerusalem this same day. (Ezekiel 24:1–2)

To this day, the 10th of Tevet is a fast day in Jewish tradition—a time to remember that disregarding God's voice leads to brokenness. As believers, we don't fast out of obligation, but we can pause to reflect: Where have I hardened my heart? What divine warnings have I overlooked?

Tevet reminds us: God is patient, but He is also just. His warnings are not threats—they are invitations to return to Him before the walls fall down.

Jesus: The Fullness of God in Human Form—While Tevet includes solemn reflection, it also overlaps with Christmas, when many celebrate the birth of Jesus—God's ultimate expression of hope and order.

For in Him dwells all the fullness of the Godhead bodily. And you are complete in Him, which is the head of all principality and power. (Colossians 2:9–10)

Jesus is not just Emmanuel (also spelled Immanuel)—God with us—but the perfect fulfillment of what the Temple once symbolized. Where Solomon's Temple was torn down, Christ became the dwelling place of God on earth. Now, He dwells in us.

Tevet reminds us: We don't need a temple to find God. We are the temple. And Jesus has made us whole—nothing lacking, nothing broken.

A Moment to Reflect, Rededicate, and Refocus—As businesses close their books and people draft resolutions, Tevet gives us a better lens:

- Are we still living for the kingdom?
- Are our talents surrendered?
- Have we drifted from the intimacy we once knew?

Tevet is a time to repent where we've grown cold, to reignite what's flickering, and to rededicate our hearts to the Lord. God desires alignment, not perfection. And in Jesus, we find the power to begin again.

From Exile to Restoration—Though Tevet begins with a siege, it points toward restoration. Just as God eventually returned His people from exile, He promises to restore and rebuild every broken part of your life. Jesus is both the warning and the way back. His Cross speaks both justice and mercy. In Him, the year can end with hope, not just habit.

Prayer for the Month of Tevet—Father, in the name of Jesus, thank You for sending Your Son—the fullness of the Godhead in bodily form. In Him, I lack nothing; in Him I am complete. Today, I rededicate my time, my calling, and my desires to You.

Search my heart, Lord. Shine Your light in every dark or distracted place. Align my thoughts with Your Word and my steps with Your will. I surrender every plan to Your perfect purpose and trust You with what lies ahead.

Thank You that even when I fall, You are there with grace to restore. Let this month be a holy turning point—a time of spiritual inventory, realignment, and renewed expectation. I step forward into the new, anchored in Christ—my righteousness, my order, and my peace.

In the name of the Father, the Son, and the Holy Spirit, Amen.

11. The Month of Shevat: Transition, Empowerment, and Kingdom Leadership

Shevat is the eleventh month on the biblical (religious) calendar and the fifth month on the civil calendar, falling during the winter season of January–February on the Gregorian calendar. Though the landscape may appear barren, Shevat pulses with spiritual activity—a time of hidden growth, fresh direction, and renewed authority.

The name "Shevat" is believed to stem from an ancient Akkadian word meaning "rod" or "staff," symbolizing leadership, discipline, and the power to guide and govern. This month prophetically speaks of transition—from wilderness wandering to kingdom purpose. Just as Moses handed the mantle of leadership to Joshua during this season, Shevat becomes a time for divine commissioning.

In Zechariah 1:7, the prophet receives a vision on the twenty-fourth day of Shevat—marking it as a month of heavenly revelation and strategic alignment. In Jewish tradition, this month also includes *Tu B'Shevat*, the "New Year for Trees," reminding us that even in dormancy, life is preparing to bear fruit.

Spiritually, Shevat calls us to rise in kingdom authority—not just to follow, but to lead with righteousness, courage, and clarity. It's a time to listen closely, to realign with God's direction, and to step forward as empowered stewards of His purposes on earth.

A Month of Instruction and Leadership Transfer—In Deuteronomy 1:3, we find Moses delivering his farewell message on the first day of Shevat. Israel stood at the threshold of the Promised Land after forty years of wilderness wandering. Before they could enter, Moses reviewed their history, reminded them of God's covenant, and warned them of the blessings and consequences tied to obedience.

It was also during this season that Moses passed the mantle of leadership to Joshua (Deuteronomy 31:3), signaling a new chapter for Israel—one that would move them from surviving to possessing. Shevat thus becomes a divine reminder that before promotion comes preparation, and before breakthrough comes remembrance.

***Tu B'Shevat*: New Year of Trees and the Call to Fruitfulness**—Midway through the month (on the 15th of Shevat) is *Tu B'Shevat*, known in Jewish tradition as the "New Year of Trees." Originally an agricultural marker for tithing fruit trees, it's become a celebration of growth, fruit-bearing, and environmental renewal.

For believers, it symbolizes a season to be deeply rooted in Christ, to bear fruit in due season, and to nurture the seeds of destiny God has planted. It echoes Psalm 1:3:

> And he shall be like a tree planted by the rivers of water, that brings forth his fruit in his season; his leaf also shall not wither; and whatsoever he does shall prosper. (Psalm 1:3)

Jesus: Light, Leadership, and Kingdom Assignment—Shevat also parallels the transition from John the Baptist's ministry to the public ministry of Jesus. After His baptism and wilderness testing, Jesus emerged with Holy Spirit power and declared the Kingdom of Heaven was at hand (Matthew 4:17).

> From that time Jesus began to preach, and to say, Repent: for the Kingdom of Heaven is at hand. (Matthew 4:17)

John had prepared the way, calling people to repentance. But Jesus brought the government of God to earth, healing the sick, forgiving sins, and establishing a new kingdom. In Shevat, we are reminded that we are not just followers—we are sent ones. We carry His authority to proclaim truth, bring healing, and walk in power.

> You are the light of the world. A city that is set on an hill cannot be hid. Neither do men light a candle, and put it under a bushel, but on a candlestick; and it gives light unto all that are in the house. Let your light so shine before men, that they may see your good works, and glorify your Father which is in heaven. (Matthew 5:14–16)

Looking Back, Stepping Forward—Following Tevet's season of reflection and rededication, Shevat invites us to cross over into activation. It's a time to ask:

- What has God taught me in the wilderness?
- Where is He directing me now?
- Am I ready to lead, build, and bear fruit?

God doesn't call us to circle the mountain forever. He is calling us to move forward—to occupy territory, walk in His power, and fulfill our purpose. But vision without movement leads to spiritual stagnation. Shevat is the time to act.

Prayer for the Month of Shevat—Father, in the name of Jesus, thank You for the clarity of Your Word and the guidance of Your Spirit. I surrender to the transitions You are orchestrating in my life, and I rededicate my heart to follow You with trust and obedience. Like Moses, help me release what is behind. Like Joshua, empower me to step boldly into what lies ahead.

Grant me wisdom to lead, courage to love, and strength to labor for Your kingdom. May I walk as Your ambassador—rooted in grace, moving in authority, and shining brightly with the light of Christ in a dark world.

In the name of the Father, the Son, and the Holy Spirit, Amen.

12. The Month of Adar: Joy, Justice, and Divine Reversals

Adar is the twelfth and final month of the biblical (religious) calendar, and the sixth month on the civil calendar, typically aligning with February–March on the Gregorian calendar. Rich with prophetic symbolism, Adar carries the themes of completion, deliverance, joy, and divine reversal. It is a month when what was meant for harm is often turned for good—reminding us that God's justice always has the final word.

In Esther 3:7, we read that Adar was the month chosen for the destruction of the Jews, but God overturned the enemy's plot. What began as a death sentence ended in miraculous deliverance and celebration, establishing the Feast of *Purim* as a lasting memorial of joy and triumph.

In Hebrew leap years, Adar is observed twice—Adar I and Adar II—emphasizing that divine timing is never rushed or delayed. God is not bound by man's clocks or calendars. His reversals are timely, His justice sure, and His joy contagious.

The Story of *Purim*: God's Reversal Plan—The most well-known event in Adar is *Purim*, celebrated on the 14th of the month, which commemorates God's miraculous deliverance through Queen Esther and Mordecai.

Haman's plot to annihilate the Jews was sealed by casting lots—*purim*—designating the 13th of Adar as the day of destruction (Esther 3:13). Yet, through divine orchestration, God reversed the plot. The king issued a counter-decree, and the Jews overcame their enemies instead of being overcome (Esther 9:1).

Even when God's name isn't mentioned in Esther, His hand is everywhere.

Purim is now celebrated with joyful feasts, gift-giving, and remembrance of the God who turns mourning into dancing.

Jesus Christ: The Greater Deliverer—Esther's story points us to a greater deliverer—Jesus Christ. Just as Queen Esther risked her life to save her people, Jesus gave His life to save all humanity.

Satan's decree was eternal separation from God through sin. But Jesus, the spotless Lamb, canceled the assignment of death and issued a new decree of life and reconciliation through His blood and resurrection (Hebrews 9:22–28).

Adar invites us to stand in that authority, knowing the Cross has nullified every evil plot against our destiny.

A Time to Complete the Assignment—Adar is also known as the month to finish what God has called us to do. In Ezra 6:15, the rebuilding of the Temple was completed on the third day of Adar. After seasons of delay and discouragement, the people finished what God had assigned—because of prophetic encouragement from Haggai and Zechariah.

Adar is a month to say: "It is finished."

What vision have you put on pause? What purpose has been delayed? Adar stirs the spirit to rise up and complete what God started in you (Philippians 1:6).

> Being confident of this very thing, that He which has begun a good work in you will perform it until the day of Jesus Christ. (Philippians 1:6)

Joy That Strengthens and Sustains—There's an old rabbinic saying: "When Adar enters, joy increases." This is no shallow happiness—it's covenant joy that arises from knowing God's faithfulness. The joy of the Lord is your strength (Nehemiah 8:10), especially when darkness tries to dim your purpose.

Let Adar be a month where you laugh again, dance again, hope again.

> Then he said unto them, Go your way, eat the fat, and drink the sweet, and send portions unto them for whom nothing is prepared: for this day is holy unto our LORD: neither be you sorry; for the joy of the LORD is your strength. (Nehemiah 8:10)

Moses: Born and Buried in Adar—Jewish tradition teaches that Moses was born and died on the 7th of Adar. His life bookends remind us that Adar is not just about endings—it's about divine beginnings.

Moses' birth marked the dawn of Israel's deliverance, while his death opened the door for a new generation to step into promise. Similarly, Jesus brings life from death, hope from despair, and legacy from loss.

Adar declares:

Your deliverance is already underway—even if you don't see it yet.

Prophetic Activation: Declare the Reversal—Adar is a warfare month wrapped in joy. It's a season to rise up and contend—to wage war in the Spirit against every decree of defeat, every lie of the enemy, and every spirit of delay. Now is the time to declare reversal. Break agreement with fear and lack. Speak life, fulfillment, and divine completion into your atmosphere. What was meant for evil—God is turning for good.

> No weapon that is formed against you shall prosper; and every tongue that shall rise against you in judgment you shalt condemn. This is the heritage of the servants of the LORD, and their righteousness is of Me, says the LORD. (Isaiah 54:17)

Be bold like Queen Esther. Finish strong like the builders of Ezra. Walk free like the Jews on *Purim*.

Prayer for the Month of Adar—Father, in the name of Jesus, thank You for being the God of reversals and restorations. Just as You defended Esther and Mordecai, defend me and my household. Every evil decree written against my life is canceled by the power of the Cross and the blood of Jesus.

I declare that no weapon formed against me shall prosper, and every tongue that rises against me in judgment shall be condemned. Empower me, Lord, to finish the assignments You've placed in my hands with excellence and courage. Let Your joy rise within me like a fire—strengthening, sustaining, and overflowing.

This is my month of divine turnaround. I step into it with praise, purpose, and unshakable faith. I walk forward clothed in joy, crowned with justice, and covered in grace.

In the name of the Father, the Son, and the Holy Spirit, Amen.

Feasts of the LORD Biblical and Gregorian Calendar:

Request Your FREE 12-Month Biblical Calendar Chart + Prayer Guide— We know the chart next in this book is small—and that's exactly why we created this free gift for you.

If you'd like a full-size, downloadable 8½ x 11 summary chart of the 12 biblical months—complete with prophetic themes, historical insights, and monthly prayers from this chapter—we'd love to send it to you as part of a special teaching package.

Simply email us at: vanishing@GuardiansOfBiblicalTruth.com

With the subject line: "Request for Chart and Package."

You'll receive:

- A PDF-formatted overview chart of the 12 biblical months.
- Instructional summaries for each month.
- A complete set of monthly prayers to align with God's timing.

Because we're not just reading—we're training for reigning.

─── THE BIBLE AT A GLANCE ───

THE CIVIL CALENDAR: CREATION TO KINGSHIP – Agricultural and Governmental Cycle – Shemitah Cycles, Jubilee Years, and Reigns of Kings
THE SACRED (RELIGIOUS) CALENDAR: REDEMPTION TO RESTORATION – Redemptive Timeline: Feasts of the Lord
(The civil calendar governs the earthly; the sacred (religious) calendar governs the eternal.)

Feast	Season	Religious *Lunar* Calendar	Month (Exodus 12:2) Feast (Leviticus 23)	Harvest	Historical Old Testament *Rehearsal*	Prophetic New Testament *Fulfillment*	Gregorian Calendar	Creation/Civil *Solar* Calendar
		Nisan 1 New Moon	Redemption and New Beginnings	Abíb/Aviv Barley	A season of freedom, redemption, and new beginnings; when God resets His clock, reorients His people to His redemptive plan.		March–April	**Tishri 1** Rosh Hashanah
1		**Nisan 14**	Passover (*Pesach*) 7-day feast follows	Barley	Redemption through the blood of a spotless lamb	Crucifixion of Jesus Yeshua–The Passover Lamb	March–April	Head of the Year Tishri 1–2
2	SPRING FEASTS FIRST COMING OF MESSIAH	**Nisan 15** (Pilgrimage)	Unleavened Bread (*Hag HaMatzot*)	Barley	Deliverance out of Egypt; cleanse sin–walk in holiness	Burial of Jesus Yeshua–The Unleavened Bread	March–April	Creation's Anniversary
3		**Nisan 16** Good Friday	Firstfruits (*Bikkurim*) The Omer Count	Barley Barley	You are our Source. Faith in God for what comes next. Egypt to Mount Sinai	Resurrection of Jesus Yeshua–The Firstfruits Passover to Pentecost–7-weeks	March–April	Genesis 1–2 Adam's B-day
		Iyar 1 New Moon	Healing, Provision, and Preparation	Barley	A season of sacred pause – a divine transition between redemption and revelation: preparing for divine encounters.		April–May	**Heshvan 1**
		Sivan 1 New Moon	Covenant, Revelation, and Empowerment	Wheat	A season to walk not only in salvation (freedom), but in revelation, obedience – Spirit-led action, and spiritual authority.		May–June	**Kislev 1**
4		**Sivan 6** (Pilgrimage)	Pentecost (*Shavuot*) Feast of Weeks/Harvest	Wheat	The Torah (the Law) Given to Moses at Mount Sinai	Outpouring of the Holy Spirit Yeshua–The Promised Comforter	May–June	Kislev
		Tammuz 1 New Moon	Heart-Testing and Idolatry Revealed	Wheat	A season of refining to reclaim us – heart-testing and self-examination: what truly sits on the throne of our hearts.		June–July	**Tevet 1**
		Tammuz 17 FAST	"The Three Weeks" (*Bein HaMetzarim*)	Fig/Grape Pomegran	Breach of Jerusalem's walls and other calamities	Mourning and growth – repent, renewal, surrender, restoration.	June–July	Tevet
	SUMMER	**Av 1** New Moon	From Dire Straits to Divine Revelation	Fig/Grape Pom/Dates	A season to remember and rebuild in covenant strength; fires of reflection, repentance, and ultimately, restoration.		July–August	**Shevat 1**
		Av 9 FAST	Ends "Three Weeks" (*Tisha B'Av*)	Fig/Grape Pom/Dates	Destruction of the Temples and other national tragedies	25-hour fast like Yom Kippur	July–August	Shevat
		Av 15	A Prophetic Reversal (*Tu B'Av*)	Fig/Grape Pom/Dates	God lifted His judgment after 40 years in wilderness	From mourning to dancing; from testing to triumph	July–August	Shevat
		Elul 1 New Moon	Month of Repentance (40-days of *Teshuvah*)	Fig/Grape Pom/Dates	A season of mercy, self-examination; Return to God	Jesus Baptized, then 40 days in wilderness until Yom Kippur	Aug–Sept	**Adar 1**
5		**Tishri 1–2** *Rosh Hashanah*	Feast of Trumpets (*Yom Teruah*)	Grape/Pom Date/Olive	A season of awakening, atonement, and abundance. High Holy Day – PM to AM	Yeshua–The Bridegroom King	Sept–Oct	**Nisan 1**
		Tishri 3 FAST	Tzom Gedaliah	Grape/Pom Date/Olive	Mourns the Assassination of Gov. Gedaliah ben Ahikam	Not commanded in the Torah 2 Kings 25:25; Jeremiah 41:1-3	Sept–Oct	Nisan
6		**Tishri 10** FAST	Day of Atonement (*Yom Kippur*)	Grape/Pom Date/Olive	High Holy Day 25-hour fast TEN DAYS OF AWE END	Humility, Confess, and Forgive Yeshua–The High Priest	Sept–Oct	Nisan
7	FALL FEASTS SECOND COMING OF MESSIAH	**Tishri 15** (Pilgrimage)	Feast of Tabernacles (*Sukkot*)	Grape/Pom Date/Olive	High Holy Day – 7 days Feast of Booths/Harvest	Millennial Reign of Christ Yeshua–The King of Kings	Sept–Oct	Nisan
		Tishri 22	Eighth Day Assembly (*Shemini Atzeret*)	Grape/Pom Date/Olive	Remain in God's Presence New Beginnings – Eternity	Eternal Age Yeshua–The Light of Eternity	Sept–Oct	Nisan
		Heshvan 1 New Moon	Restoration, Refuge, and Renewal	Olives/ Grain Sow	A season of sacred transition – a bridge from public encounter (Tishri) to private devotion (Heshvan); quiet month.		Oct–Nov	**Iyar 1**
		Heshvan 17	Noah Entered the Ark (Genesis 7:11)	Olives/ Rains/Sow	Noah and his family; 8 souls 8: number of New Creation	Memorial of divine judgment New Beginnings – 8 people	Oct–Nov	Iyar
		Heshvan 27	Noah Exited the Ark (Genesis 8:14–19)	Olives/ Rains/Sow	Heshvan is the 8th month Cleansed and silent world	Memorial of divine grace Bury the old, embrace the new	Oct–Nov	Iyar
		Kislev 1 New Moon	Revelation, Light and Rededication	Olives/ Citrus Fruit	A season of light in the darkness, divine revelation through dreams, and renewed dedication to God's presence.		Nov–Dec	**Sivan 1**
8		**Kislev 25**	Hanukkah/Festival of Lights or Dedication	Olives/ Citrus Fruit	Maccabean Revolt 167–164 BC and the Miracle Oil	Rededication of 2nd Temple 8-Day Jewish Festival	Nov–Dec	Sivan
		Tevet 1 New Moon	Reflect, Rededicate, and Refocus	Olives/ Grain Sow	A season of reflection, rededication, and the fullness of Christ. A season of spiritual sobriety and clarity.		Dec–Jan	**Tammuz 1**
		Tevet 10 FAST	Exile and Destruction Fast–pause and reflect	Olives/ Grain Sow	Siege of Jerusalem by Nebuchadnezzar (Babylon)	Disregarding God's voice leads to brokenness.	Dec–Jan	Tammuz
	WINTER	**Shevat 1** New Moon	Transition, Empower, Kingdom Leadership	Almonds	A season of hidden growth, fresh direction, and renewed authority – leadership, discipline, power to guide and govern.		Jan–Feb	**Av 1**
		Shevat 15	New Year of Trees (*Tu B'Shevat*)	Almonds	New Year of Trees and Call to Fruitfulness	Be deeply rooted in Christ, bear fruit, and nurture destiny seeds	Jan–Feb	Av
		Adar I/II 1	Joy, Justice, and Divine Reversals	Almonds/ Greens	A season of completion, deliverance, joy, and divine reversal. In Hebrew leap years, Adar is observed twice – divine timing.		Feb–March	**Elul 1**
9		Adar 13–15 FAST	Feast of Purim (*Shushan Purim* – 15)	Almonds/ Greens	Fast of Esther on Adar 13 Feast of Purim on Adar 14	Miraculous deliverance through Queen Esther and Mordecai	Feb–March	Elul

Figure 3 – Feasts of the LORD, Harvests, Biblical and Gregorian Calendars

THE SECOND HARBINGER HAS SOUNDED

Returning to God's Time Before It's Too Late

God is not bound by man's clocks, calendars, or conventions. While the world ticks along on its artificial timelines—founded on pagan roots and secular rhythm—He continues to operate on His own set times: His appointed feasts, His sacred months, His divine seasons. These are not relics of an ancient culture. They are prophetic markers, embedded with eternal significance. They are God's calendars—both religious and civil—and they are still counting down.

The second harbinger is not just a wake-up call. It's a divine invitation to return to God's rhythm before the great shaking begins. The biblical calendars are not legalism—they are alignment. They are not about rules—they are about revelation. From Passover to Tabernacles, from Nisan to Adar, every appointed time whispers the name of Jesus and maps the unfolding of His redemptive plan.

And just as the First Coming of Messiah aligned perfectly with the spring feasts, so too will His Second Coming align with the fall feasts. That means the calendars matter now more than ever.

God is restoring what the world forgot. He's reigniting understanding in the hearts of watchmen, believers, and prophetic voices around the world. The whispers of the Spirit are growing louder: "Get on My calendars." The shadows of man's systems are giving way to the light of divine order.

This isn't a trend—it's a transition. We are shifting from tradition to truth, from manmade holidays to God-ordained holy days. From pagan clocks to prophetic signs.

And this restoration is a sign in itself—one of the final precursors before Jesus returns to fulfill the remaining feasts. The calendars of God are countdowns. The shofar is at the lips. The King is at the door.

The Church today celebrates resurrection without Passover, revival without repentance, and purpose without preparation. We are living disconnected from the times and seasons God has always used to shape His people.

This harbinger is calling us back—to sacred appointments we dare not miss, to holy days that still carry prophetic weight, to calendars that not only tell time—but tell truth.

The biblical calendars don't just measure months. They measure mercy. They measure judgment. They measure prophetic fulfillment. And they are nearly full.

What must we do?

We must realign our lives. We must wake up to the fact that we are not just late on the clock of prophecy—we are in the final moments before the trumpet sounds. The world's rhythm will lull us into slumber, but God's calendars will stir us to readiness. No more living by convenience. It's time to live by covenant. No more following the crowd. It's time to follow the cloud. No more waiting for a "better season." This is the season.

We are not looking at vague signs. We are watching a synchronized unveiling of prophetic convergence:

- Israel has returned.
- The feasts are rehearsals.
- The calendars are accelerating.
- The Bride is being awakened.

And at the center of it all is God's perfect timing, revealed through His appointed days and sacred months.

The clock of man is running out. The calendars of God are being fulfilled. The feast days are aligning. And the King is coming.

Are you living by His time?

Are you preparing for His day?

The second harbinger has sounded.

Heaven has a schedule.

Are you on it?

Jesus is returning.

Are you ready?

———◆◆◆———

The soft glow of lamplight filled the room as rain gently tapped against the windowpanes, its rhythm a quiet echo of the conversation unfolding. Irene poured a second cup of tea and settled into the armchair across from me, her Bible open on her lap. Our evenings often ended like this—two seekers chasing truths hidden in plain sight, led by Scripture and the Spirit.

She looked up, her expression thoughtful.

"Ann," she said, "I was reading Genesis 1:14, where it says the sun, moon, and stars, are for signs and seasons, days and years. That got me wondering—did the biblical calendar actually begin with Creation? Or did it start with the Exodus, around 1446 BC?"

I smiled.

"Great question, Irene—and you're not the only one who's wondered about that. While the formal, redemptive calendar for Israel was established at the time of the Exodus, the framework for God's civil calendar absolutely goes all the way back to Creation."

Irene's eyes widened.

"Really? So there was already an agricultural calendar—or harvest cycle—in place from the very beginning?"

"Yes!" I said, leaning forward slightly. "Let's go back to Genesis 1:14. When God said, 'Let there be lights . . . for signs, and for seasons,' the Hebrew word for 'seasons' is *moedim*. And that's the very same word later used to describe God's appointed times—like Passover, Tabernacles, and the other biblical feasts."

Irene blinked in surprise.

"Wait—so *moedim* doesn't just mean spring, summer, or fall?"

I nodded.

"Exactly. *Moedim* means 'appointed times'—sacred gatherings, feast days, divine appointments. In other words, God wove the entire rhythm of His timing into Creation itself."

Irene leaned in.

"So Adam and Eve would have seen these heavenly markers and known when to plant, when to harvest?"

"Absolutely," I said.

"Think of those early patterns as prophetic foreshadows—appointed times that would later become formalized as biblical feasts. If the event had already occurred, the feast served as a remembrance. If it was still to come, it acted as a rehearsal. Either way, these rhythms were already embedded in Creation, just like the cycles of agriculture."

I continued, "It was preparation for what was to come. Even in Genesis 4, after Adam and Eve were exiled from Eden, we see their sons—Cain and Abel—identified by their roles as farmers and shepherds. That alone tells us they were already functioning within God's built-in cycles of seedtime and harvest."

I paused.

"They wouldn't have had a festival calendar like Israel would later receive, but the patterns of seedtime and harvest, the new moons, and the shifting seasons were woven into the fabric of Creation from the very beginning."

Irene's eyes lit up.

"That makes Genesis 8:22 after the Flood even more powerful: 'Seedtime and harvest . . . shall not cease.'"

I nodded.

"Exactly. That verse is more than a poetic observation—it's a covenant promise. God was declaring that the rhythms of both agriculture and the spirit would remain dependable."

Irene's eyes widened.

"So the sun and moon weren't just cosmic decoration—they were God's calendar!"

"Yes!" I said with a smile.

"They are His original timekeepers. What we call the AM calendar—from the Latin *Anno Mundi*, meaning 'year of the world'—is the Creation calendar. It starts in Genesis 1, marking time from the very beginning, from the moment light first pierced the darkness."

I paused, letting the weight of that settle.

"Now, fast-forward to Exodus. When God tells Moses, 'This month shall be the beginning of months for you' (Exodus 12:2), He's not reinventing time—He's resetting the nation's calendar to align with His redemptive timeline. It's like God was saying, 'Synchronize your lives with My plan of deliverance.'"

Irene nodded slowly.

"So Genesis established the pattern. The Exodus revealed the purpose."

"Perfectly said," I replied.

"The calendar didn't begin with Moses—it began with the Word, the One who spoke the heavens into place. But at the Exodus, God took that eternal rhythm and aligned it with the deliverance of His people. From that point on, time itself told the story of redemption."

Irene, smiled, eyes glancing toward the window.

"You know, that changes how I read the stars at night. They're not just twinkling—they're testifying."

"Yes," I said, my voice hushed with awe.

"They're proclaiming God's order and faithfulness. Every seed planted, every harvest gathered—it's all a reminder that we're living inside God's time. His seasons, His purposes."

The rain began to ease, a soft hush settling over the room as the clock chimed the hour. Irene gently closed her Bible with a thoughtful sigh.

"Living within God's time," she repeated softly.

We sat in reverent silence, deeply aware that even this quiet conversation was part of something far older, far greater—a calendar not written by man, but etched in the sky by the hand of God.

The next day, almond blossoms had begun to bloom, and the air carried a gentle hint of olive and citrus. Irene and I sat on a wooden bench beneath a budding fig tree, sipping warm tea as birds chirped overhead.

Irene glanced up at the tangled branches.

"You know, Ann, I've always heard that the biblical calendar is tied to Israel's harvest cycles. But I've never really understood how it all fits together. Can you explain it to me?"

I smiled and set my tea down.

"Absolutely. It's one of my favorite things to talk about. The biblical calendar is lunisolar—it follows the moon to mark months and the sun to track seasons. And yes, every month aligns beautifully with Israel's agricultural rhythms. Let's walk through it together."

Irene leaned forward, eyes bright with curiosity.

"Let's start with the month of Nisan."

I nodded.

"Nisan falls around March to April. It marks the beginning of the biblical (religious) year and coincides with the barley harvest in Israel. It's closely tied to three foundational feasts—Passover, the Feast of Unleavened Bread, and Firstfruits. Spiritually, Nisan is all about redemption and new beginnings. In fact, Jesus' resurrection aligns perfectly with the Firstfruits celebration, symbolizing Him as the firstborn from the dead."

"And Iyar comes next?" Irene asked.

I nodded.

"Yes—April to May on our calendar. The barley harvest continues during this time, and the wheat harvest begins to form. It's a transitional month. Historically, this is when the Israelites first received manna from heaven in the wilderness. That's why Iyar is often associated with healing, provision, and preparation—a bridge between redemption in Nisan and revelation in Sivan."

She nodded.

"Then comes Sivan and Pentecost."

I smiled.

"Exactly. Sivan falls around May to June and marks the wheat harvest in Israel. It's the month of *Shavuot*, also known as Pentecost—the time when God gave the Torah at Mount Sinai, and later, when He poured out the Holy Spirit in Acts 2. Sivan is a month of covenant and empowerment—the written Word and the living Spirit, both given as gifts to establish God's people."

Irene tilted her head thoughtfully.

"What about the summer months—Tammuz and Av?"

"Tammuz," I replied, "which falls from June to July, brings the first figs and grapes. But spiritually, it's a cautionary month—the sin of the golden calf happened during this time. It's a reminder of how quickly people can turn from God even after great deliverance."

"Av follows, from July to August," I continued.

"It continues the grape harvest and introduces the pomegranate season. The 9th of Av is especially significant—it marks the destruction of both the First and Second Temples. Yet even in its sorrow, Av opens the door to comfort. Jewish tradition teaches that from this place of mourning, restoration begins."

Irene looked up, her brow furrowed. "Wait—did you say both Temples were destroyed on the exact same day? How is that even possible?"

I nodded solemnly. "Yes. The 9th of Av—*Tisha B'Av*. First in 586 BC, when the Babylonians burned Solomon's Temple. Then again in AD 70, when the Romans demolished Herod's renovated Temple."

"Her eyes widened. "That can't just be coincidence."

"It's not," I said quietly. "It's prophetic pattern. *Tisha B'Av* has become the most mournful day on the Hebrew calendar—not just because of those two events, but because it's when other disasters have also struck the Jewish people. It's as if God marked that day in history as a warning—a call to return."

Irene's voice dropped to a whisper. "And yet . . . even in that kind of judgment, there's still hope?"

"Exactly." I leaned toward her. "Av doesn't end in ashes. Comfort follows. The Sabbath immediately after *Tisha B'Av* is called *Shabbat Nachamu*—'The Sabbath of Comfort'—from Isaiah 40:1: 'Comfort you, comfort you My people.' God always writes redemption into the same script as judgment."

She stared out at the horizon, the sun high in the sky. "So even in devastation, He's already planning the restoration."

I smiled. "That's the heart of the Father. Even when we're grieving ruins . . . He's preparing renewal."

Irene's voice softened.

"And Elul . . . Elul has always felt introspective to me."

I nodded. "It is. Elul falls between August to September and coincides with the harvest of summer fruits—figs, dates, and pomegranates. Spiritually, it's a month of repentance, reflection, and renewed intimacy with God. It's often summed up in the phrase from Song of Songs: 'I am my Beloved's, and my Beloved is mine.' It's a time to return—to hear the whisper of the Beloved and prepare the heart for what's coming next."

Irene leaned in. "And what happens in Tishri?"

"Tishri spans September to October," I replied. "It's when the grape harvest comes to a close and the olive harvest begins. But more than that, it's the most spiritually loaded month of the year—the season of the High Holy Days: *Rosh HaShanah*, *Yom Kippur*, and *Sukkot*. It's a time when judgment meets mercy, repentance meets renewal, and atonement gives way to joy. Everything converges here—awakening, cleansing, and celebration."

Irene tilted her head. "Heshvan is next, right?"

I nodded. "Yes—October to November. It's the time of the olive harvest. What's fascinating is that Heshvan contains no major biblical feasts or celebrations. Because of that, it's often seen as a month of hidden obedience—a quiet season where faithfulness isn't celebrated, but still deeply matters. According to tradition, Solomon completed the First Temple during this month—proof that sacred things can be finished in silence."

Irene looked up. "And Kislev?"

I smiled. "Kislev falls between November to December and marks the beginning of spring planting—wheat and barley go into the ground. But spiritually, it's best known for *Hanukkah*—a season of light in darkness, miracles, and rededication. It's a beautiful time to seek God's guidance, especially when the path ahead feels dim. Kislev invites us to trust that even in the dark, His light will lead the way."

Irene's tone grew quieter. "What happens in Tevet?"

I nodded. "Tevet falls between December and January and continues the planting of wheat and barley. But it also carries a heavier weight. The 10th of Tevet marks the beginning of the siege of Jerusalem—a moment of tightening pressure and looming judgment. Spiritually, it's a month of inner reflection and quiet resolve—a time to strengthen what remains and to prepare the soul for what's ahead."

Irene glanced at the branches above.

"When do things begin to bloom again?"

I smiled, gesturing to the delicate almond blossoms overhead. "Shevat—January to February. The almond tree is always first to awaken, signaling that a new season is stirring. In Scripture, it represents alertness, vision, and prophetic leadership. That's why God showed Jeremiah the rod of the almond tree—to confirm that He was watching over His Word to perform it."

Irene's eyes followed a blossom dancing in the breeze.

"*Tu B'Shevat*, the New Year for Trees, is celebrated this month. But it's not just about agriculture—it's about spiritual renewal. Shevat whispers, 'Wake up. Watch. What you plant now matters.'"

Irene leaned back, reflective. "And Adar wraps it up?"

I nodded. "Yes—February to March. The final rains fall, soaking the soil in preparation for the coming barley harvest. But spiritually, Adar overflows with joy and reversal. It's the month of *Purim*, when God turned destruction into deliverance and mourning into dancing."

I paused. "According to tradition, Moses was both born and died on the 7th of Adar. Even in loss, there was legacy. Even in death, a seed of destiny. It's a month that reminds us—what ends with man may begin with God."

Irene, her voice hushed with awe. "Ann, that was beautiful. It's like each month carries a hidden layer of God's message."

I smiled, gently. "It truly does. The harvests aren't just physical—they're spiritual. Each season speaks. God uses the soil, the sun, the rain—to teach, to restore, to realign our hearts with His."

We sat in sacred stillness, the almond blossoms swaying like whispered promises in the breeze. Irene jotted reflections into her journal. I cradled my teacup, warmed more by the moment than the drink.

Above us, birds sang, branches danced, and the fig tree waited—just as we were learning to wait—in rhythm with God's appointed times.

CHAPTER SUMMARY

Chapter 6 unveils the Second Harbinger: The Biblical Calendars—calling believers to realign with God's divine rhythm rather than the world's timelines. It contrasts the manmade Gregorian calendar with the God-ordained Hebrew calendar, reminding us that Heaven still runs on Heaven's clock. God governs through His original timepiece—marked by appointed times (*moedim*), sacred feasts, and prophetic months that continue to shape His redemptive agenda.

The chapter explores the two biblical calendars—civil and sacred—and unveils the prophetic richness embedded in each of the twelve Hebrew months. It reveals how God has marked time through sacred rhythms, using appointed seasons from Passover to Pentecost to shape redemptive history. Jesus fulfilled the spring feasts with perfect precision, and the fall feasts—yet to be fulfilled— serve as rehearsals pointing to His return.

At its core, this chapter proclaims a vital truth: God's calendar still matters. These times are not legalistic rituals; they are divine alignments. Living in sync with His calendar sharpens our discernment, tunes our hearts to His movements, and prepares us for what lies ahead.

The second harbinger isn't just a call to watch for the signs—it's a call to watch the time.

KEY TAKEAWAYS

- God's calendars (both religious and civil) are covenantal, not cultural— and they remain active today.
- Each biblical month carries prophetic meaning and spiritual instruction that speaks to our time.
- Jesus fulfilled the spring feasts precisely and will return to fulfill the fall feasts in perfect order.

- The biblical calendars align us with God's rhythm and sharpens our prophetic awareness.
- The second harbinger is a call to return to God's appointed times before the next unfolds.

Chapter 6 sounds the second harbinger clearly and decisively: God's prophetic clock has not stopped ticking—it continues to count down according to His appointed times, not ours. In a world dominated by manmade schedules and secular rhythms, this harbinger calls believers to return to the sacred calendar God established at Creation and reaffirmed through Moses. It is a call to recalibrate our lives to His feasts, His seasons, and His redemptive timeline. Only those who are watching with spiritual eyes—those aligned with His *moedim*—will be fully awake, fully prepared, and fully in step when the next trumpet sounds.

Chapter 7

The Third Harbinger:
The Signs in the Heavens

WHEN HEAVEN SPEAKS—The first two harbingers—divine signs, events, or messages sent as warnings or prophetic precursors, often tied to judgment or intervention—have already sounded across the landscape of this prophetic generation. These echoes from Heaven refuse to be ignored.

The first harbinger unveiled a startling convergence of end-time signs—birth pains increasing in frequency and intensity—unfolding before our very eyes. The second harbinger reawakened us to the rhythm of God's sacred calendars: Heaven's timeline, not grounded in human tradition or cultural custom, but anchored in covenant.

These were not abstract theological concepts. They were divine wake-up calls—urgent invitations to return, to realign, to recalibrate. They remind us: when Heaven speaks, the wise listen.

Together, these two harbingers have not only warned us—they have prepared us for what comes next.

Now, the third harbinger lifts our eyes upward—to the heavens themselves. For in the ancient sky, where the stars still sing and the sun still rules the days, we discover a truth as old as time itself: God is still speaking.

When the morning stars sang together, and all the sons of God shouted for joy. (Job 38:7)

This poetic verse portrays the stars as singing—celebrating their Creator in the moment of cosmic birth. It's metaphorical, yes—but rooted in biblical cosmology, where Creation is not passive, but alive with praise.

Psalm 148 echoes this theme:

Praise you Him, sun and moon: praise Him, all you stars of light. (Psalm 148:3)

Heaven is not silent. It never has been. From the beginning, the Creator embedded meaning into the heavens.

In Genesis 1:14–18, we read:

And God said, Let there be lights in the firmament of the heaven to divide the day from the night; and let them be for signs, and for seasons, and for days, and years. And let them be for lights in the firmament of the heaven to give light upon the earth: and it was so. And God made two great lights; the greater light to rule the day, and the lesser light to rule the night: He made the stars also. And God set them in the firmament of the heaven to give light upon the earth, and to rule over the day and over the night, and to divide the light from the darkness: and God saw it was good. (Genesis 1:14–18)

The Hebrew word translated "signs" is *otot*—meaning signals, markers, or divine indicators. These lights were never meant to be mere ornaments. They were celestial instruments—calibrated to broadcast messages from eternity into time.

And the word for "seasons" is *moedim*—the very same term used for the appointed times of the Lord: Passover, Pentecost, Tabernacles. These weren't just cultural feasts; they were prophetic appointments on God's heavenly calendar.

Let that sink in: when God said, "Let there be lights," He wasn't merely flipping a cosmic switch between day and night. He was installing a divine clock—woven into the fabric of Creation—to govern natural cycles and reveal redemptive seasons.

God's Clock Doesn't Tick—It Revolves

Unlike human clocks that tick by seconds and minutes, God's timepiece turns through orbits, rotations, and lunar phases. Every new moon resets the biblical month. Every full moon illuminates the feast days—those sacred appointments when Heaven touches earth in divine rehearsal.

- A solar eclipse—where the sun is temporarily darkened, only occurs on a new moon.
- A lunar eclipse, or blood moon, only occurs on a full moon.

That's why the feasts of Passover and Tabernacles—which always fall on full moons—have become center stage for some of the most dramatic celestial signs in history. This isn't randomness—it's rhythm. It's not accident—it's alignment.

The calendar of God and the choreography of the cosmos move in sync—by divine design.

Yet some still resist this truth, often misunderstanding scriptures like Jeremiah 10:2. The Lord says:

> Hear you the Word which the LORD speaks unto you, O house of Israel: Thus says the LORD, Learn not the way of the nations, and be not dismayed at the signs of heaven; for the nations are dismayed at them. (Jeremiah 10:1–2)

Notice what God does not say. He does not say, "Ignore the signs." He says, "Don't be afraid of them." That's a critical distinction.

Why shouldn't we fear? Because we are meant to understand them.

The nations tremble because they don't know what the signs mean. But covenant people are called to read the heavens—not as astrologers chasing fate, but as sons and daughters of the King of kings, discerning the signs of the times.

The night sky was never meant to frighten God's people.

It was meant to guide them.

The Sky as Scroll: Reading the Language of Light

Throughout Scripture, the heavens are God's cosmic canvas—a living scroll on which He writes His redemptive story in light.

At pivotal moments in history, the skies have spoken:

- A star in the east announced the birth of the Messiah.
- Darkness at midday bore witness to His crucifixion.
- Blood moons, foretold by Joel and echoed in Revelation, signal judgment and renewal.

These are not poetic flourishes or symbolic suggestions. These are literal events, seen with human eyes and orchestrated by divine hands.

From Genesis to Revelation, God has used the heavens to communicate movements in His redemptive plan. The sky is not a silent backdrop—it is a prophetic scroll, unrolling in real time.

And now, in our generation, the pattern continues.

What This Chapter Will Uncover

In this chapter, we will explore the stunning convergence of biblical prophecy and astronomical precision. Together, we'll discover:

- How God wrote the Gospel in the constellations—unfolding the redemptive story from Virgo to Leo, etched in the stars since the foundation of the world.

- How solar and lunar eclipses have marked prophetic milestones throughout Scripture and history.
- The awe-inspiring Great American Eclipses of 2017 and 2024—two total solar eclipses, exactly seven years apart, tracing a giant "X" across the heart of the United States.
- The phenomenon of blood moons and supermoons—and why their alignment with God's feast days is no coincidence.
- The mysterious and controversial Revelation 12 Sign—a celestial portrayal of the woman clothed with the sun and the dragon poised to devour her Child.

Let's be clear: this is not astrology. It is not mysticism, speculation, or hype. This is biblical theology, grounded in Scripture and confirmed by astronomical data. The same God who breathed the stars into existence also set them in motion with prophetic purpose—aligning their cycles to His appointed times and divine warnings.

The heavens are not random—they are reliable. They are revealing. They are resounding with purpose. The heavens are roaring.

Before we explore the science behind these signs, let us pause—and reflect on this: God chose the heavens as His canvas. And today, even our most advanced technology is only now beginning to grasp what Scripture declared from the beginning.

HEAVEN'S BUILT-IN MESSAGING SYSTEM

From the very beginning, God hardwired communication into Creation. While the world marvels at supercomputers and satellite systems, the greatest timekeeping device ever built is already hanging overhead. Our solar system functions with a precision so intricate that eclipses, equinoxes, and planetary alignments can be predicted centuries in advance. These are not accidents of gravitational physics—they are the intentional handiwork of a God who "declares the end from the beginning" (Isaiah 46:10):

> Declaring the end from the beginning, and from ancient times the things that are not yet done, saying, My counsel shall stand, and I will do all My pleasure. (Isaiah 46:10)

Astronomers rely daily on the predictable movements of the cosmos. Scientists track time by the oscillations of atomic clocks—but even those are calibrated to the unshakable rhythm of the heavens. Ironically, many of the same minds who dismiss the supernatural rely on divine consistency to do their work. They depend on the very laws authored by the One they overlook.

God doesn't just observe time—He authors it.

To discern the unfolding of prophecy, we must root our expectations in Scripture and obey the call of Luke 21:28—*look up*. The heavens are not a mere backdrop; they are a divine broadcast declaring God's timeline.

> And when these things begin to come to pass, then look up, and lift up your heads; for your redemption draws near. (Luke 21:28)

Hidden in Plain Sight

> It is the glory of God to conceal a thing: but the honor of kings is to search out a matter. (Proverbs 25:2)

God is not hiding from us—He is inviting us into discovery. His messages are layered into Scripture, symbols, history, language—and yes, even constellations.

One of the most profound restorations in our generation is the resurgence of the Hebrew language. Once nearly lost to history, Hebrew has become more than the national tongue of Israel—it's reemerging as a spiritual codebook. It's letters hold not only phonetic sounds, but also numerical values and pictographic symbols. They carry prophetic weight.

Zephaniah 3:9 foretells a day when God would "turn to the people a pure language"—a reversal of Babel's confusion. This return to a shared understanding is not just cultural, it's prophetic.

> For then will I turn to the people a pure language, that they may all call upon the name of the LORD, to serve Him with one consent. (Zephaniah 3:9)

In this divine puzzle, every piece—language, time, the heavens—is coming back together as restoration. We are being invited to "search out" what God has written, not just in scrolls, but in starlight. (While the deeper subject of the Hebrew language and its prophetic design is beyond the scope of this book, it is central to the larger restoration God is orchestrating.)

The Heavens as a Prophetic Canvas

The sky has always been one of God's most dramatic billboards. Consider the sheer number of biblical events linked to celestial signs:

- A star marked the Messiah's birth (Matthew 2).
- The sun went dark at His crucifixion, for three hours (Luke 23:44–45).
- Isaiah 13:10 and Joel 2:30–31 foretell cosmic disturbances—stars ceasing to shine, the sun darkening, and the moon turning blood red—signs that will precede the great and terrible Day of the LORD.

- Revelation 6:12 describes the sun turning black and the moon becoming as blood.
- Luke 21:25 promises signs in the sun, moon, and stars before Christ's return.

These aren't abstract metaphors. They are observable events—real, timed, and intended. When Joshua needed more daylight to defeat his enemies, God *stopped the sun and moon* (Joshua 10:13). When Hezekiah needed confirmation of healing, God *reversed the shadow of time* (2 Kings 20:9–11). When Jesus died, darkness fell—not during a solar eclipse, which only lasts minutes and requires a new moon—but for *three hours*, during Passover, on a full moon. That was no eclipse. That was supernatural intervention.

Even ancient Jewish sages taught that solar eclipses were warnings to the nations, and lunar eclipses were signs for Israel. God embedded meaning into the skies long before modern science caught up.

A Sky That Speaks Every Language

> The heavens declare the glory of God; and the firmament shows His handiwork. Day unto day utters speech, and night unto night shows knowledge. There is no speech nor language, where their voice is not heard. Their line is gone out through all the earth, and their words to the end of the world. In them has He set a tabernacle for the sun. (Psalm 19:1–4)

The beauty of the sky is this: it speaks every language. Its voice transcends nations, politics, denominations, and geography. It cannot be manipulated by man. No politician can manufacture a blood moon. No preacher can conjure a solar flare. These signs come from above, governed by a hand no telescope can reach.

This is why God chose the heavens as His most public platform. It's revelation without translation. A visual sermon visible from every continent, every nation, every tribe.

This is not astrology. This is astronomy aligned with theology. From the very beginning, God has spoken through the cosmos in a language as old as Genesis itself. When He said, "Let there be lights . . . for signs, and for seasons" (Genesis 1:14), He wasn't just illuminating the sky—He was ordaining a divine communication system.

The stars and celestial bodies were positioned with purpose, designed not for mysticism but for message. These are not arbitrary arrangements or superstitious omens; they are signals—cosmic billboards—aligned with God's prophetic calendar.

The signs are in place. The calendar is counting down. The heavens are not whispering; they are thundering with urgency and truth.

The question is not whether God is speaking—it's whether we are listening.

THE SCIENCE OF THE SIGNS

It's no secret: our generation is obsessed with finding signs in the sky. From deep-space probes to million-dollar satellites, science is relentlessly searching for signals—clues that we are not alone. Astronomers scan the heavens for electromagnetic whispers from other galaxies. Telescopes gaze into distant constellations hoping for patterns, pulses, or anomalies that might suggest intelligent life. We are fascinated by the idea that somewhere "out there," someone might be trying to reach us.

And yet—how ironic. While we spend billions listening for signs of extraterrestrial life, humanity often ignores the most spectacular moment of divine communication in history. A moment when God, the Creator of all things, descended to Mount Sinai and audibly spoke to over three million people at once. This estimate is based on Exodus 12:37, which records about 600,000 men leaving Egypt—not counting women and children.

> And the children of Israel journeyed from Rameses to Succoth, about six hundred thousand on foot that were men, beside children. (Exodus 12:37)

(Both locations, Rameses and Succoth, are in northeastern Egypt, with the route continuing toward the Red Sea crossing and eventually Mount Sinai.)

There was thunder, lightning, fire, smoke, and the voice of the Almighty Himself. The heavens thundered—yet many today act as if the message never happened (Exodus 19:16–19, 20:1; Deuteronomy 4:33, 5:4).

Why? Because we often search for signs on our own terms, forgetting that God has always been speaking—just not in the ways we expect.

From the very beginning, God declared His intention to communicate through Creation. In Genesis 1:14, He said the sun, moon, and stars were placed "for signs, and for seasons, and for days, and years." These aren't vague metaphors. They are intentional placements in a cosmic rhythm designed to get our attention.

1. The Fixed Precision of Celestial Mechanics: A Divine Signature

Before we talk about eclipses and blood moons, we must first stand in awe of the brilliant consistency of the system that makes those signs even possible. The heavens do not operate randomly. They are governed by mathematical precision—so exact that even modern supercomputers can barely improve on it. Astronomers can calculate the position of a planet or the timing of an eclipse not just years, but centuries into the future—or the past.

Why? Because God designed it that way.

Unlike human-made clocks that rust, drift, or require recalibration, the sun, moon, and stars have never needed adjustment. The Earth rotates on its axis once every 23.934 hours. The moon orbits the Earth every 27.3 days. The Earth completes its orbit around the sun in precisely 365.2422 days. These aren't ballpark numbers—they are constants, measured to millisecond accuracy. And even slight variances, like leap years or planetary wobbles, are accounted for in predictable, cyclical ways.

The stunning order is not the result of cosmic coincidence. It is the fingerprint of God. As the prophet Jeremiah wrote:

> Thus says the LORD, which gives the sun for a light by day, and the ordinances of the moon and of the stars for a light by night, which divides the sea when the waves thereof roar; The LORD of hosts is His name: If those ordinances depart from before Me, says the LORD, then the seed of Israel also shall cease from being a nation before Me forever. (Jeremiah 31:35–36)

In other words, the very reliability of the sun, moon, and stars is God's own pledge of faithfulness to His covenant. As long as the heavens stay in place—and they always will—God's promises to Israel and to His people stand firm. He staked His reputation on the reliability of His celestial design.

Lunar cycles and eclipses don't surprise God—they are embedded in His calendar. He created them to be predictable, visible, and unshakably regular. NASA can chart eclipses hundreds of years forward or backward. Jewish sages in ancient times, long before modern telescopes, did the same using only the naked eye and centuries of observational record. This is not superstition—it's science and prophecy working hand in hand.

Contrast this with manmade systems. Atomic clocks lose synchronization over time. GPS satellites must constantly recalibrate due to orbital decay—the gradual decrease in altitude of objects in orbit, caused primarily by atmospheric drag or gravitational forces. As satellites drift from their intended paths, recalibration becomes necessary. Our best efforts to measure and manage time inevitably degrade. But the heavenly timepiece? It never skips a beat.

So here's the greater truth: If God maintains such exact, consistent order in the heavens, then how much more should we trust Him to keep His prophetic Word on earth? The same God who keeps the stars in orbit is the One who promised to send the Messiah, to judge the nations, and to restore His people. And just as surely as the sun will rise tomorrow—so too will His Word be fulfilled.

The signs in the sky are not only *timely*; they are *timers*. Every eclipse, every full moon, every planetary alignment is a reminder that God is still counting time—and that His appointed days are drawing near. The heavens are not random. They are reliable revelations of a God who never fails.

2. Timekeeping Before Clocks: Astronomy as the Original Science

Long before wristwatches ticked and atomic clocks synchronized global time, mankind looked upward to measure the days. The sky was our first calendar, the moon our first clock, and the stars our original guideposts for sowing, harvesting, feasting, and traveling. Astronomy—before it became a modern academic discipline—was a deeply spiritual and practical science. It was humanity's first window into divine order.

Ancient Civilizations Watched the Heavens—From the earliest records of human history (Genesis 1), civilizations have lived by the light of the heavens. The Babylonians, renowned for their meticulous astronomical records, aligned both religious and civic festivals to the lunar cycles. The Egyptians calculated their calendar based on the heliacal rising of the star *Sirius*, which coincided with the annual flooding of the Nile—a vital event for agriculture. The Maya, with astonishing precision, developed lunar and solar calendars, using intricate sky charts carved into stone, demonstrating a deep and sophisticated understanding of celestial patterns.

And then, of course, there is Israel—whose calendar was not only practical but prophetically inspired. In Leviticus 23, God instructed His people to mark sacred times—His "appointed feasts" (*moedim*)—based on the rhythms of the moon and the sun: lunar phases for the monthly cycle, and solar shifts for the harvest seasons. Unlike manmade calendars that serve commerce or empire, Israel's calendar was crafted by divine instruction. It wove time together with covenant, tethering Heaven's movements to earth's worship.

To this day, the Jewish calendar remains one of the only ancient calendars still in use—a living testament to God's providential design and prophetic timeline.

Before Clocks, There Were Shadows and Moons—While the modern world may rely on digital timekeeping, our ancestors were guided by sundials, shadow sticks, seasonal stars, and the shape of the moon. These were not primitive instruments—they were tools of revelation, allowing mankind to partner with the cycles God established "for signs, and for seasons, and for days, and years" (Genesis 1:14).

Even the simple waxing and waning of the moon could tell ancient shepherds when to begin their Sabbath or when the new month had arrived. And with nothing more than a carefully positioned obelisk or stone, entire cities could align their national life with solstices and equinoxes—turning their eyes, and often their hearts, to heaven.

God's Clock Came First—In truth, every mechanical device we've invented to measure time—pendulums, gears, digital frequencies—is merely an imitation of what God already wrote into the fabric of the universe. Our ancestors didn't invent timekeeping. They discovered it—already turning in the sky above them.

And if we were wise, we would return to that same heavenly classroom. Because unlike manmade systems that drift and require recalibration, God's celestial rhythms do not falter. They continue to tick with a cosmic precision that predates and surpasses all human achievement.

Time Has Always Belonged to God—From the dawn of civilization, our understanding of time has come not from human invention, but from observation of divine design. Whether charting the harvest or awaiting a holy day, people have always looked to the sky for answers. God's heavenly timepiece—sun, moon, and stars—remains faithful, patient, and visible to every generation.

So as we step into prophetic times, let us return to the simplicity and power of watching God's clock. Timekeeping began not with human innovation, but with divine intention. And that clock is still ticking.

3. The Moon and Tides: The Earth's Clockworks in Harmony

If you've ever stood at the edge of the ocean and watched the tide rising to meet your feet or recede gently into the horizon, you've witnessed one of the most intimate dances between heaven and earth. The moon, quietly suspended above, commands Earth's waters with invisible strings of gravity. Twice a day, oceans swell and shrink—not by accident, but by design.

The Lunar Pull: Regulating the Seas—Modern science confirms that ancient mariners and fishermen always knew: the moon governs the tides. Through its gravitational pull, the moon draws the earth's oceans toward itself, creating high tides on the side facing the moon—and due to inertia, also on the opposite side of the planet. This tidal system is so precise that it can be charted hundreds of years in advance.

Without the moon's stabilizing force, Earth would be chaotic. Tidal movements oxygenate water, regulate marine ecosystems, influence weather, and even shape coastlines. Remove the moon, and oceans stagnate, climates destabilize, and life itself is disrupted. The moon is not merely a nightlight in the sky—it is a meticulously placed governor of Earth's rhythms.

The Moon's Influence on Nature—But the moon's pull doesn't stop at the seas. Countless studies reveal how lunar cycles influence animal behavior, sea turtles time their egg-laying with the full moon. Coral reefs spawn en masse during specific lunar phases. Birds migrate in coordination with moonlight. Deer, insects, fish—all respond instinctively to the moon's rhythms.

It's not superstition—it's science. These creatures were created with an internal awareness of the moon's cycles. God built the moon into the choreography of Creation. Job 12:7–9 invites us to consider the beasts of the earth and the fish of the sea—for they know who their Maker is.

> But ask now the beasts, and they shall teach you; and the fowls of the air, and they shall tell you. Or speak to the earth, and it shall teach you: and the fishes of the sea shall declare unto you. Who knows not in all these that the hand of the LORD has done this? (Job 12:7–9)

Human Beings: Tuned to Heaven's Clock—Even we, as image-bearers of God, are not exempt. The circadian rhythm, our internal 24-hour clock, aligns with the sun's cycle. But there's growing evidence of a "lunar rhythm" embedded in human biology as well. Researchers have documented fluctuations in sleep patterns, mood, hormone levels, and even birth rates corresponding to phases of the moon.

Women's reproductive cycles have long been known to correspond closely with lunar months. Farmers and gardeners—especially those in tune with God's Creation—have used "planting by the moon" techniques for generations, claiming better yields when sowing or harvesting during specific phases.

These aren't folk tales. They're testimonies to how the heavens are built into our biology. The body responds to light, to gravitational rhythms, to celestial cycles—because that's how our Creator designed us. Psalm 139:14 reminds us that we are "fearfully and wonderfully made." What a wonder, then, that the calendar in the sky speaks not just to nations—but to our very cells.

Wired for the Heavens—When Genesis 1:14 declares that the heavenly lights were given "for signs, and for seasons," it wasn't just poetic—it was physiological. Our minds, our bodies, even our planet itself are wired to respond to what God has inscribed in the skies. We are attuned to Heaven's schedule—even when we don't realize it. The question is not *if* the signs are present. The question is: Are we listening.

The moon tugs on the oceans. It nudges the migration of birds. It shapes our sleep, stirs our instincts, and sets internal clocks we barely understand. If the moon—just one of God's lesser lights—has such profound influence over our tides and rhythms, what else might the Creator be saying through it?

4. Solar Cycles and Weather Patterns: Clues to Larger Prophetic Movements

When Jesus warned of "signs in the sun, and in the moon, and in the stars" (Luke 21:25), He wasn't simply invoking poetic imagery. He was pointing to literal, observable phenomena in Creation—patterns that not only reveal God's power, but also serve as prophetic indicators. Among these are the solar cycles, subtle yet significant movements of the sun that affect everything from crops to communication.

The 11-Year Solar Cycle: A Rhythmic Pulse in the Heavens—At the heart of solar activity is the 11-year sunspot cycle, a scientifically documented pattern where the sun's magnetic field flips, resulting in a measurable increase and decrease of sunspots—temporary dark spots on the sun's surface that signify heightened magnetic activity.

This solar "heartbeat" affects space weather, including solar flares and coronal mass ejections. These energetic bursts can disrupt satellites, GPS navigation, and even ground-based technologies like power grids and radio frequencies. Historically, major solar events have caused blackouts, disrupted radio communications, and even affected animal migration.

But beyond the technological impact, solar cycles also have agricultural implications. Scientists have observed that changes in solar radiation can influence weather patterns, rainfall distribution, and growing seasons. During periods of high solar activity, the earth experiences subtle warming; during low activity, cooling trends may follow. Crop yields, growing cycles, and food availability often reflect these patterns—though they are not always immediately attributed to their solar source.

Cosmic Rhythms and Prophetic Birth Pains—When Jesus described the "beginning of sorrows" or *birth pains* in Matthew 24:8, He painted a picture of a world experiencing mounting pressure—geopolitically, spiritually, and environmentally. Like contractions that grow stronger and closer together, these disturbances alert us to an imminent shift. Could these intensifying solar cycles be part of the larger prophetic clock?

We're living in an era of increasing solar flare activity. Some experts warn that upcoming cycles may be among the most volatile on record, with potential implications for energy infrastructure, agriculture, and even human health. While secular scientists view these trends through a lens of caution or curiosity, believers can recognize them as God's early warning system—a natural phenomenon echoing a supernatural message.

As Romans 8:22 says:

> For we know that the whole Creation groans and travails in pain together until now. (Romans 8:22)

The heavens groan too—through radiation bursts, magnetic shifts, and cosmic waves of energy that reverberate through the universe.

Natural Signs, Supernatural Purpose—Jesus never spoke idly. When He mentioned "signs in the sun," He meant it—physically, cosmically, and prophetically. These are not random disruptions, but part of God's designed warning system—measurable changes in Creation that reflect deeper spiritual realities.

> And there shall be signs in the sun, and in the moon, and in the stars; and upon the earth distress of nations, with perplexity; the sea and the waves roaring. Men's hearts failing them for fear, and for looking after those things which are coming on the earth: for the powers of heaven shall be shaken. And then shall they see the Son of Man coming in a cloud with power and great glory. And when these things begin to come to pass, then look up, and lift up your heads; for your redemption draws near. (Luke 21:25–28)

As solar flare activity intensifies, as global weather patterns shift unpredictably, and as humanity grapples with instability in agriculture, technology, and health—let us not merely look at what is happening, but why. These cycles point to a God who governs the stars, who sustains the seasons, and who still calls His people to read the signs.

The heavens aren't chaotic—they are prophetic. And if we tune our hearts and minds to the Creator's rhythm, we will not be caught off guard when prophecy unfolds before our eyes.

5. Modern Tech Confirms Ancient Truths

The more our scientific instruments peer into the heavens, the more they affirm what Scripture declared thousands of years ago. With telescopes orbiting Earth, computer models simulating the skies, and space agencies tracking celestial motion down to fractions of a second, today's technology is catching up to the wisdom encoded in God's Word. Rather than disproving biblical signs, modern tools like NASA's eclipse data and sky-mapping software such as Stellarium actually confirm the precision and prophetic timing of the heavens.

Satellites, Software, and the Scriptures—NASA, the European Space Agency (ESA), and other observatories have compiled exhaustive databases that chart past and future solar and lunar eclipses for thousands of years—some going as far back as 2000 BC. These high-precision algorithms, based on Kepler's laws of planetary motion and modern physics, allow scientists to reconstruct the skies of biblical times with astonishing accuracy.

For example, tools like NASA's Five Millennium Canon of Solar and Lunar Eclipses reveal that:

- Total lunar eclipses—blood moons—have aligned with Passover and *Sukkot* in multiple years of historical and prophetic significance (such as in 1949–1950 and 1967–1968).
- Notable solar eclipses have occurred on or near Jewish fast days or feasts, including rare ones that trace out symbolic shapes or intersect prophetic geography—like the Great American Eclipses of 2017 and 2024.

Even free programs like Stellarium, which simulates the night sky from any point in history or geography, allow users to observe astronomical events as they would have appeared in the days of Yeshua (Jesus)—or during the Exodus, the Flood, or key prophetic milestones.

Biblical Calendar Keepers: The Original Astronomers—Long before Copernicus proposed a heliocentric model or Newton quantified gravity, ancient Jewish scribes and priests were already keeping time by the sun, moon, and stars—just as God commanded in Genesis 1:14 and Exodus 12. The Hebrew calendar was, and still is, a lunisolar system, meaning it synchronizes both solar years and lunar months—requiring detailed knowledge of the moon's phases and orbital patterns.

Priests and Levites observed the new moon with precision, used intercalation—adding a thirteenth month—to keep feast days in season, and calculated timing down to specific twilight hours—centuries before mechanical clocks existed. They weren't astrologers or mystics. They were sky watchers for the purposes of covenant, obeying the Creator's divine calendar and maintaining accurate records of times and seasons.

Faith Isn't Blind—It's Rooted in Reality—We live in a time where faith and science no longer have to be at odds. The very satellites and supercomputers that some believe "disprove" the Bible are actually validating its claims. They confirm that the timing of eclipses, blood moons, and celestial alignments that marked prophetic moments in Scripture are not myth, not poetry, but observable phenomena—now understood with greater clarity than ever before.

The divine signals once studied by torchlight in Jerusalem are now being verified by laser-aligned observatories in Hawaii and radio telescopes on every continent. This isn't mysticism—it's measurable, repeatable, and awe-inspiring.

From Sacred Scrolls to Silicon Chips—The same God who spoke the stars into existence also wrote the script of redemption in the skies. And today, in an era of AI, deep space probes, and quantum computing, His calendar still holds true. Every new moon, every solar flare, every eclipse is not just a marvel—it's a message. Far from superstition, biblical signs align with the most advanced science of our day. The heavens still declare the glory of God—and now we can measure that glory in gigabytes.

6. Scientific Witnesses to Supernatural Events

Modern science, despite its frequent secular framing, has produced compelling evidence that supports the supernatural events of Scripture and affirms the fingerprints of divine orchestration. The closer we look at the natural world—from celestial alignments to cosmic timing—the more we uncover a design too intricate to be accidental, and events too exact to be random.

A Darkness Unlike Any Eclipse—The Gospels record a profound and mysterious event during the crucifixion of Christ: a supernatural darkness that covered the land for three full hours.

> Now from the sixth hour there was darkness over all the land unto the ninth hour. And about the ninth hour Jesus cried with a loud voice, saying, Eli, Eli, lama Sabachthani? That is to say, My God, My God, why have You forsaken Me? (Matthew 27:45–46)

Astronomically, this could not have been a solar eclipse. Passover occurs during a full moon, and eclipses can only happen at a new moon. Even the longest natural eclipse lasts mere minutes—not hours. No known phenomenon explains such an extended midday darkness.

This was no accident of celestial mechanics. It was divine intervention—a cosmic sign marking the moment Jesus, the Lamb of God, bore the sin of the world.

In that darkness, Jesus cried out the opening line of Psalm 22:

> My God, My God, why have You forsaken Me? (Psalm 22:1)

This psalm, written by King David centuries before crucifixion existed, prophetically describes the Messiah's suffering: "They pierced My hands and My feet" (Psalm 22:16). "They part My garments among them, and cast lots upon My vesture" (Psalm 22:18).

By quoting it, Jesus was pointing to a divine script written long before His birth. He was both fulfilling prophecy and revealing the meaning of the Cross.

The darkness was more than physical—it was spiritual. A veil drawn across Creation as the Son of God completed the redemptive plan set in motion before the foundation of the world.

The Blood Moon Tetrad: Verified by Astronomers—In 2014 and 2015, astronomers around the world confirmed a tetrad of blood moons—four total lunar eclipses occurring on Passover and *Sukkot* two years in a row. This rare alignment had only happened a few times in the last 500 years, each time coinciding with pivotal events in Jewish history:

- 1492–1493—The expulsion of Jews from Spain.
- 1949–1950—The rebirth of the nation of Israel.
- 1967–1968—The Six-Day War and the reunification of Jerusalem.
- 2014–2015—The Gaza War (summer 2014) and global antisemitism.

These aren't random red moons—they are calculated celestial events that happened to fall on God's appointed feasts. NASA's eclipse tables verify these dates with mathematical precision, showing that heavenly signs and biblical patterns align with staggering consistency.

The Fine-Tuned Universe: Modern Echoes of Design—Today, even many secular physicists acknowledge what's known as the Anthropic Principle—the observation that the universe appears to be precisely tuned for life. Constants such as gravity, electromagnetism, and the expansion rate of the Universe are so finely balanced that even a fractional deviation would render life impossible. This has led to growing conversation in scientific circles around the theory of intelligent design.

Leading thinkers like Dr. John Lennox, Stephen Meyer, and others in the fields of cosmology and biology have pointed to the incomprehensible complexity and fine-tuning of our universe as evidence for a Designer beyond the natural order. Scripture has long declared this:

> He stretches out the north over the empty place, and hangs the earth upon nothing. (Job 26:7)

> The heavens declare the glory of God; and the firmament shows His handiwork. (Psalm 19:1)

Science as a Servant to Prophecy—Rather than refuting Scripture, science increasingly bears witness to its truths. The very tools that track stars, model the universe, and calculate eclipses—are now confirming the timing and magnitude of biblical signs.

As we've seen:

- Darkness at the Cross defied astronomy.
- Eclipses fall on feast days with prophetic weight.
- The heavens are mathematically structured for life.

God has not hidden His plan in mystery. He has engraved it in the cosmos, waiting for those who have eyes to see and hearts to understand. The more we explore the science, the clearer the signs become: prophecy is not a relic of ancient mysticism—it's the divine blueprint written in the sky.

GOD'S TIMEKEEPERS: THE SUN, MOON, AND CALENDAR

Before the invention of clocks, calendars, and atomic timekeeping, God had already ordained the perfect rhythm of time. His appointed timekeepers—the sun and the moon—were placed in the heavens not just to illuminate, but to regulate. They were created to govern the flow of days, months, seasons, and sacred convocations. They are Heaven's answer to Earth's need for order.

From the very beginning, Genesis 1:14 revealed their dual role:

> And God said, Let there be lights in the firmament of the heaven to divide the day from the night; and let them be for signs, and for seasons, and for days, and years. (Genesis 1:14)

This verse reveals that the heavenly bodies were designed not only to illuminate but to communicate. Again, the word "seasons" is the Hebrew word *moedim*—meaning "appointed times." These *moedim* are not manmade holidays or traditions; they are divine appointments on God's eternal calendar.

The sun and moon mark these sacred moments. The sun rules the day, bringing light, warmth, and growth. The moon marks the month, cycling through its phases to announce new beginnings, full revelation, or times of concealment and waiting. Together, they serve as the heartbeat of God's calendar, establishing rhythms for rest, worship, repentance, celebration, and prophetic fulfillment.

This was the calendar given to Israel—not as a burden, but as a gift, a way to live in sync with Heaven. And it remains just as relevant today.

But over time, human tradition replaced divine timing. Pagan calendars and solar-only systems disrupted the biblical rhythm. The Western world lost touch with the Creator's clock—and with it, many lost the prophetic understanding encoded in that divine system.

Yet in this generation, we are witnessing a restoration. Believers around the world are rediscovering the importance of the biblical calendar, of the new moon, of God's feasts, and of aligning time not to culture, but to covenant. This restoration is not about returning to ritual; it is about returning to revelation.

We are no longer bound to tick-tock calendars invented by men. We are invited to recalibrate our lives to the orbits of heaven, to honor God's timekeepers, and in doing so—to discern the times we are living in.

As we will see, the sun and moon are more than celestial bodies. They are faithful witnesses (Psalm 89:37), testifying day and night to the unfolding plan of the Living God. Are we paying attention to their message?

> It shall be established forever as the moon, and as a faithful witness in heaven.
> Selah (pause, reflect, let the truth sink in). (Psalm 89:37)

The Sun: Governing the Day and Agricultural Seasons

From the very first dawn, the sun was ordained to govern the day. Genesis 1:16 declares: "And God made two great lights; the greater light to rule the day . . ." This wasn't a poetic suggestion. It was a divine assignment. The sun is not merely a ball of plasma—it is a divine governor, appointed by God to mark time, illuminate the earth, and sustain life.

The sun rises and sets with absolute faithfulness, anchoring our daily rhythm. It casts shadows by which ancient time was measured, and it warms the soil that nurtures every seed. From the perspective of Scripture, the sun is not just a source of light—it is a spiritual symbol of God's constancy, provision, and revelation.

Psalm 19:4–6 poetically describes this majesty:

> Their line is gone out through all the earth, and their words to the end of the world. In them has He set a tabernacle for the sun, which is as a bridegroom coming out of his chamber, and rejoices as a strong man to run a race. His going forth is from the end of the heaven, and his circuit unto the ends of it: and there is nothing hid from the heat thereof. (Psalm 19:4–6)

Agricultural Alignment: The Sun's Role in God's Provision—Long before modern farming techniques or digital calendars, agriculture was synchronized with the sun. Planting and harvesting seasons were determined by solar position— spring equinoxes, summer solstices, and the length of daylight. In ancient Israel, the Feast of Firstfruits, *Shavuot* (Pentecost), and *Sukkot* (Tabernacles) were all intricately tied to harvests—and those harvests were governed by the solar cycle.

- Spring marked new beginnings—plowing, planting, Passover.
- Summer brought fullness and increase—the wheat harvest and Pentecost.
- Autumn signaled ingathering—the fruit harvest and the celebration of Tabernacles.
- Winter was a time of rest and hidden preparation—mirroring the Sabbath cycle built into all creation.

The sun determined not only when to plant and reap, but when to worship and give thanks. Every beam of sunlight was a reminder that God provides in season, and that he who sows in faith will reap in joy.

Watching the Sun to Understand the Son—To overlook the role of the sun in the biblical calendar is to miss a key aspect of God's communication. It's not just about physics or photosynthesis. Every sunrise reminds us of God's mercy (Lamentations 3:22–23). Every season echoes His timing.

> It is of the LORD's mercies that we are not consumed, because His compassions fail not. They are new every morning: great is Your faithfulness. (Lamentations 3:22–23)

Just as ancient Israel watched the sun to prepare the soil and the soul, we too must live in step with God's rhythm—looking not to modern schedules, but to eternal patterns.

As we continue, we'll explore how the moon, too, plays a vital role—marking months, feast days, and prophetic timings with stunning precision.

The Moon: Ruler of the Night and the Biblical Months

From the very beginning, God appointed the moon as a governor of the night and a keeper of sacred time. In Genesis 1:16, we are told plainly:

> And God made two great lights; the greater light to rule the day, and the lesser light to rule the night: He made the stars also. (Genesis 1:16)

The moon is more than a celestial ornament. It is a divinely engineered calendar, placed in the heavens to orchestrate the flow of biblical months and determine the timing of God's appointed feasts. Ancient Israel didn't rely on manmade clocks or modern calendars—they watched the sky. With every new moon, a new month began. The Hebrew word for month, *chodesh*, literally means "month" or "new moon."

Lunar Cycles and Sacred Appointments—The moon's monthly waxing and waning formed the foundation of the Hebrew calendar. This lunar cycle—roughly 29.5 days—established the timing of God's *moedim* (appointed times). Each new moon marked the beginning of a month, and many of Israel's holy convocations were set according to its phases.

For instance:

- Passover and Tabernacles both occur on the full moon of the first and seventh months, respectively.
- The Feast of Trumpets—*Rosh HaShanah*—falls on a new moon, signaling the head of the civil year.

- *Yom Kippur*, the Day of Atonement, and *Sukkot* (Tabernacles) follow closely afterward, also anchored to lunar markers.

Psalm 104:19 declares:

He appointed the moon for seasons: the sun knows his going down. (Psalm 104:19)

The word translated "seasons" is again *moedim*—the same term used for the sacred feast days. In other words, God set the moon as a timekeeper for His divine appointments.

The New Moon: A Time of Renewal—The new moon was not merely a calendar reset; it was a time of spiritual reflection and renewal. In Numbers 10:10, God commanded the blowing of silver trumpets at the new moon, marking it as a sacred occasion. Sacrifices were offered, trumpets were blown, and the people paused to remember the rhythm of God's timing.

The prophet Isaiah even speaks of a future age in which new moons and Sabbaths will continue to be observed:

And it shall come to pass, that from one new moon to another, and from one Sabbath to another, shall all flesh come to worship before Me, says the LORD. (Isaiah 66:23)

This tells us that God's lunar calendar is not obsolete—it's eternal.

Lunar Eclipses and Warnings to Israel—Jewish tradition holds that lunar eclipses serve as signs to Israel, just as solar eclipses are seen as omens for the nations. Since the moon is Israel's national timepiece, disruptions in its light carry symbolic weight. This belief is echoed in prophetic Scripture.

And I will show wonders in the heavens and in the earth, blood, and fire, and pillars of smoke. The sun shall be turned into darkness, and the moon into blood, before the great and the terrible Day of the LORD come. (Joel 2:30–31)

These blood moons—lunar eclipses where the moon turns red—have repeatedly aligned with key feast days in recent history, signaling warnings and divine messages for Israel and the world.

Restoration in the Last Days—In these final days, as God is restoring understanding to His people, the biblical calendar is making a return. More believers are discovering the God-ordained rhythm of time, no longer solely bound to Gregorian calendars, but realigning with the moon's testimony—a testimony that has never ceased to proclaim God's order.

Just as the moon reflects the light of the sun, so too are we called to reflect the timing, truth, and glory of God in our lives. Its phases remind us that time belongs to the Lord—and each month is a new opportunity to walk in step with Him.

The Role of Rosh Chodesh (New Moon) in Biblical Worship

The new moon, known in Hebrew as *Rosh Chodesh* (literally "head of the month"), holds a central and sacred place in the biblical calendar. It is far more than the astronomical appearance of a sliver of light in the night sky—it is a divine appointment, a monthly opportunity to reset, reflect, and realign with God's purposes.

God's Design for *Rosh Chodesh*—In Numbers 10:10, God gives Israel clear instructions about honoring the new moon:

> Also in the day of your gladness, and in your solemn days, and in the beginnings of your months, you shall blow with the trumpets over your burnt offerings, and over the sacrifices of your peace offerings; that they may be to you for a memorial before your God: I am the LORD your God. (Numbers 10:10)

Here, *Rosh Chodesh* is treated as a celebratory memorial. Trumpets were blown, sacrifices were made, and the people gathered in remembrance of God's faithfulness and authority over time. This was not a minor detail in Jewish life—it was a spiritual reset button, observed twelve or thirteen times each year depending on the lunar cycle.

***Rosh Chodesh* and Worship in the Temple—**The Temple worship system included specific offerings for the new moon (Numbers 28:11–15). These included burnt offerings, grain offerings, and drink offerings—a sacred assembly that acknowledged God's dominion over the calendar. This regular observance ensured that God's people would not drift from His divine rhythm.

King David clearly honored *Rosh Chodesh*. In 1 Samuel 20:5, we find David speaking to Jonathan:

> And David said unto Jonathan, Behold, tomorrow is the new moon, and I should not fail to sit with the king to eat: but let me go, that I may hide myself in the field unto the third day at evening. (1 Samuel 20:5)

This reveals that *Rosh Chodesh* included communal meals, royal observance, and national awareness. It was woven into the social and spiritual structure of Israel.

A Time of Reflection and Anticipation—Traditionally, *Rosh Chodesh* has been a quiet, contemplative time, especially for women in Judaism, who often viewed it as a special day of rest and renewal. It also became a time to pray for guidance, fruitfulness, and the coming redemption. Like the moon itself—waxing and waning—*Rosh Chodesh* invited God's people to trust His sovereignty through every phase of life.

In Psalm 81:3, we read:

> Blow up the trumpet in the new moon, in the time appointed, on our solemn feast day. (Psalm 81:3)

This trumpet blast announced more than a date on the calendar—it proclaimed spiritual alertness. It was a call to wake up, recalibrate, and remember who the Author of time truly is.

Rosh Chodesh in the Future Kingdom—*Rosh Chodesh* is not only a remnant of the past; it's a signpost for the future. In Isaiah's vision of the Messianic Kingdom, worship on the new moon continues:

> And it shall come to pass, that from one new moon to another, and from one Sabbath to another, shall all flesh come to worship before Me, says the LORD. (Isaiah 66:23)

This is astounding. Even in the restored order of God's Kingdom, *Rosh Chodesh* remains a day of global worship and alignment.

Application for Today—In our fast-paced, Gregorian-driven world, we have largely forgotten God's calendar. Yet *Rosh Chodesh* still offers a monthly invitation to pause, reflect, and listen. It reminds us that time is sacred—not a commodity to manage, but a gift to steward.

Whether or not one follows all the ancient practices, the spirit of *Rosh Chodesh* remains: A holy reminder that God governs the months, not man. A prompt to seek His face at the threshold of every new cycle. A rhythm of worship that, like the moon itself, has never stopped shining—it's just waiting for us to look up.

A Calendar Written in the Sky: The Calendar of Redemption
—How the Feasts Align with Jesus' First and Second Comings

From the very beginning, God embedded His redemptive plan into the fabric of time—not through manmade systems, but through a calendar written in the heavens. This calendar is marked by divine appointments, or *moedim*, which were given to Israel not merely as cultural festivals but as prophetic rehearsals of God's eternal plan.

The Feasts as Prophetic Appointments—In Leviticus 23, God outlines seven appointed festivals, each tethered to agricultural seasons and astronomical markers. These feasts are not arbitrary holidays. They are "holy convocations"—dress rehearsals for divine events, anchored in the sun, moon, and stars. Just as the heavens declare the glory of God, the calendar declares His redemptive timetable.

What's astonishing is this: every major redemptive event in Jesus' ministry aligns perfectly with these feasts.

Spring Feasts—Fulfilled in Jesus' First Coming:

1. **Passover (*Pesach*)**—*Prophetic Picture*: A spotless lamb was slain for the deliverance of God's people, its blood marking their homes for protection and freedom. *Fulfillment*: Jesus, the Lamb of God (John 1:29), was crucified on Passover—fulfilling the prophetic shadow precisely at the hour when the Passover lambs were being sacrificed in the Temple.

2. **Unleaven Bread (*Hag HaMatzot*)**—*Prophetic Picture*: Leaven (a symbol of sin) was removed from every home, representing purity and separation from corruption. *Fulfillment*: Jesus' sinless body rested in the grave during this feast. Just as leaven was purged from Israel, He took the sin of the world to the grave.

3. **Firstfruits (*Bikkurim*)**—*Prophetic Picture*: The first and best of the harvest was offered to God in faith, as a sign of trust in the greater harvest to come. *Fulfillment*: Jesus rose from the dead on the Feast of Firstfruits, becoming the "firstfruits of those who have fallen asleep" (1 Corinthians 15:20)—a pledge and guarantee of the greater resurrection yet to come.

4. **Pentecost (*Shavuot*)**—*Prophetic Picture*: Commemorated the giving of the Law at Mount Sinai and marked the beginning of the wheat harvest. *Fulfillment*: On that very day, the Holy Spirit was poured out (Acts 2), not inscribing the Law on tablets of stone, but writing it on hearts—birthing the Church and initiating the spiritual harvest.

Fall Feasts—Foreshadowing Jesus' Second Coming:

5. **Feast of Trumpets (*Yom Teruah*)**—*Prophetic Picture*: A day of shofar blasts—awakening, warning, and royal announcement. *Yet to Be Fulfilled*: Widely believed to foreshadow the Rapture of the Church, heralded by the sounding of the last trumpet (1 Thessalonians 4:16; 1 Corinthians 15:52).

6. **Day of Atonement (*Yom Kippur*)**—*Prophetic Picture*: A solemn day of repentance, intercession, and judgment—when the high priest enters the Holy of Holies to make atonement for the people. *Yet to Be Fulfilled*: Viewed as the future day of national repentance for Israel and the final

judgment before Christ's millennial reign (Zechariah 12:10; Revelation 20:11–15).

7. **Feast of Tabernacles (*Sukkot*)**—*Prophetic Picture*: God dwelling with His people in temporary shelters (booths), a reminder of His presence in the wilderness. *Yet to Be Fulfilled*: Foreshadows the Messianic Kingdom, when Christ will dwell among His people during His millennial reign (Zechariah 14:16; Revelation 21:3).

Precision in God's Appointments—God's prophetic timeline is not vague. It's mathematically, theologically, and astronomically precise. That's why Jesus fulfilled the spring feasts to the exact day, and it's why many scholars anticipate His return to likewise align with the fall feasts.

This calendar was never meant to be replaced—it was meant to be fulfilled. And while many believers today follow a Gregorian calendar disconnected from God's appointed times, the Lord's *moedim* continue to declare His unfolding plan. The sun and moon keep their appointed circuits. The feasts still echo through history. And God's redemptive storyline remains perfectly on schedule.

A Final Reflection—What we call "Jewish holidays" are actually God's appointments with mankind—engraved in the heavens, revealed in Scripture, and fulfilled in Christ. They are not only memorials of what God has done but prophetic beacons pointing to what He is yet to do.

The biblical (religious) calendar is the calendar of redemption. Its feasts are not relics of a bygone era, but living prophecies awaiting completion in the return of the King.

To everything there is a season, and a time to every purpose under the heaven. (Ecclesiastes 3:1)

Are we watching the clock God gave us? Or have we grown too accustomed to the rhythms of man?

The Danger of Ignoring God's Calendar

In our modern age, it's easy to dismiss ancient biblical calendars as obsolete relics—outpaced by Roman systems, digital planners, and academic year cycles. But when we disregard the calendar God ordained, we do more than replace dates—we step out of sync with the prophetic rhythm of Heaven.

A Forgotten Clock—God never handed down the Gregorian calendar. It was man's invention—implemented by Pope Gregory XIII in 1582 AD to correct the growing inaccuracies of the Julian calendar. The Julian calendar itself was a solar calendar introduced by Julius Caesar in 45 BC, designed to reform the Roman system that had drifted significantly from the seasons due to mismanagement and political interference.

However, these manmade systems gradually removed biblical markers, redefined the months, and disconnected time from the sun, moon, and *moedim*— God's appointed times. As a result, many believers today live unaware of when God's seasons truly begin—or what time it is on Heaven's clock.

When we ignore God's calendar:

- We miss prophetic cues embedded in feasts and lunar cycles.
- We become blind to the timing of His redemptive plan.
- We risk being spiritually unprepared for what He is revealing.

This isn't about legalism. It's about alignment.

God's purposes are time-bound. If we ignore His seasons, we may find ourselves out of step with His purposes.

Biblical Warnings: When Time Was Misread—Consider Israel in the wilderness. They received God's appointed times (Leviticus 23), but when they failed to honor them—whether by idolatry, disobedience, or neglect—they suffered devastating consequences. In Jeremiah 8:7, God rebukes His people.

> Yea, the stork in the heaven knows her appointed times; and the turtle and the crane and the swallow observe the time of their coming; but My people know not the judgment of the LORD. (Jeremiah 8:7)

Even the birds knew how to follow God's timing. But His people didn't.

In Luke 19:44, Jesus weeps over Jerusalem for missing the time of their visitation. They failed to discern the prophetic moment foretold in Daniel's timeline—and the result was judgment.

> And shall lay you even with the ground, and your children within you; and they shall not leave in you one stone upon another; because you knew not the time of your visitation. (Luke 19:44)

Prophetic Consequences of Modern Amnesia—When believers neglect the biblical calendar:

- The Feasts of the LORD become "Jewish holidays" rather than God's appointed dress rehearsals for His redemptive plan.
- The new moon becomes irrelevant, though it once signaled spiritual renewal and community gathering.
- The Sabbath cycle, Jubilee years, and Shemitah patterns are lost—along with the blessings and warnings they bring.

This disconnect makes it harder to recognize when prophecy is being fulfilled in real time. Without the calendar of redemption, we lose the ability to track the convergence of signs—which Jesus directly linked to the end of the age (Matthew 24:32–33).

> Now learn a parable of the fig tree; When his branch is yet tender, and puts forth leaves, you know that summer is near. So likewise you, when you shall see all these things, know that it is near, even at the doors. Verily I say unto you, This generation shall not pass, till all these things be fulfilled. (Matthew 24:32–34)

A Call to Recalibrate—Relearning God's timekeeping is not a return to ritual— it is a return to revelation. Understanding the biblical calendar helps us:

- Decode prophecy with accuracy.
- Anticipate events tied to feast days and heavenly signs.
- Stay alert and aligned, watching as Jesus commanded in Luke 21:28.

Ignoring God's calendar is not just a theological oversight—it is a prophetic blind spot. But rediscovering it can awaken us to the rhythm of Heaven, restore lost truths, and prepare us for the day that is surely approaching.

How the Biblical Day Begins at Sunset, Not Midnight

In our modern world, we mark the beginning of a new day at midnight—an arbitrary moment when the clock strikes 12:00 AM. This system, while convenient for timekeeping, has no basis in Scripture. According to the Bible, a new day begins not in the middle of the night, but at sunset. This distinction is more than a technicality—it's a spiritual insight rooted in God's rhythm of Creation and redemption.

Creation's Pattern: Evening First, Then Morning—The pattern for the biblical day is established in the very first chapter of Genesis. Repeated six times throughout the Creation narrative is the phrase: "And the evening and the morning were the first day." (Genesis 1:5, and repeated in verses 8, 13, 19, 23, and 31).

This sequence is clear: evening comes first (around 6:00 PM), followed by morning (6:00 AM). In God's design, each new day begins at sundown—not at sunrise or midnight. A full days runs from one evening (sunset) to the next evening (sunset).

The day begins with rest and darkness, then moves into light and work. This order carries deep theological meaning: rest precedes labor, and revelation follows darkness. Spiritually, it paints a picture of redemption—God brings light out of darkness and peace out of chaos.

Here's a breakdown of this biblical time structure:

- Evening—Sunset (approximately 6:00 PM).
- Morning—Sunrise (approximately 6:00 AM).
- Daytime—Sunrise to sunset (approximately 6:00 AM to 6:00 PM).
- Full Day—One sunset to the next sunset.

Sunset and the Timing of Biblical Events—This concept was central to Jewish life and worship. In Leviticus 23:32, the Day of Atonement is commanded to be observed "from evening unto evening," underscoring the sunset-to-sunset framework. Likewise, the Sabbath, beginning Friday evening and ending Saturday evening, follows this rhythm.

Jesus Himself observed this order. The Last Supper—held after sundown—was considered part of the same day as His crucifixion, which took place the next morning. This detail matters: the Passover Lamb was sacrificed on the same biblical day He broke bread with His disciples, fulfilling prophecy with precision.

Living on God's Time—Understanding that God's day begins at sunset reshapes how we think about time and devotion. In the biblical mindset, the day begins with rest—a time of resetting, renewal, and intimacy with God. Only after this time of stillness do we move into the work and the light of morning. It's a pattern that invites us to live with divine rhythm, rather than the frantic pace of a manmade clock.

Even the sun and moon honor this order. Nature itself obeys the Creator's clock, yet how often do we live disconnected from it?

Reclaiming Sacred Time—In a world governed by artificial schedules and digital alerts, returning to the biblical concept of time is an act of spiritual alignment. Beginning our "day" with rest rather than busyness realigns our hearts with God's design. It teaches us that we don't earn rest—we begin with it. We don't walk into chaos—we walk out of peace.

As we continue exploring God's timekeepers—sun, moon, and appointed festivals—we are reminded that God doesn't just give us time . . . He gives us timing. And that timing, like His character, is perfect.

The Restoration of Time in the Messianic Age

Time, like language, worship, and Creation itself, has suffered distortion since the fall of man. Humanity has traded divine rhythms for artificial ones—replacing God's appointed times with manmade traditions, disregarding Sabbath rest, and resetting the calendar around political empires rather than prophetic truth. But the story doesn't end in confusion. Scripture tells us a day is coming when time will be restored to its rightful alignment under the reign of the Messiah.

God's Appointed Times Reestablished—In the Messianic Age—the millennial reign of Christ—the biblical calendar will be recentered in Jerusalem, and the Feasts of the LORD will once again become global events. Zechariah 14:16 speaks of a time when all nations will come to Jerusalem to keep the Feast of Tabernacles, worshiping the King, the LORD of hosts. This is not mere symbolism. It is prophetic certainty.

> And it shall come to pass, that every one that is left of all the nations which came against Jerusalem shall even go up from year to year to worship the King, the LORD of hosts, and to keep the Feast of Tabernacles. (Zechariah 14:16)

In this restored era, Sabbaths, new moons, and feast days will no longer be viewed as relics of the past but as vibrant, honored appointments with the King Himself.

A Return to God's Cosmic Clock—This era will not just bring spiritual restoration, but also temporal and cosmic alignment. The sun, moon, and stars—created for signs and seasons—will again function in harmony with humanity's worship and work. The division between sacred and secular time will dissolve. God's clock will once again guide our celebrations, our rest, our agriculture, and our worship.

This is the full restoration of time—not just chronologically, but spiritually. A new day will dawn where time flows in step with eternity, and the rhythms of Heaven govern the affairs of earth.

Living in Prophetic Alignment Now—Though the fullness of the Messianic Age lies ahead, we are called to begin aligning with it now. Every time we honor the Sabbath, observe the new moon, or celebrate a biblical feast, we're not just rehearsing past events—we're prophetically practicing for the kingdom to come. We are restoring time in our hearts, declaring that God's calendar still governs our lives, and preparing ourselves for the age when time will once again bow to the Author of time.

Let us live now with an eternal awareness—embracing the signs, honoring the seasons, and trusting that one day soon, time will be made new under the righteous rule of the Messiah.

CONSTELLATIONS: THE GOSPEL WRITTEN IN THE SKY

Long before telescopes mapped the galaxies and astronauts walked in space, humanity looked upward and saw more than stars—they saw a story. In the velvet canopy of night, ancient eyes discerned patterns, pictures, and meaning. They named the constellations not as myth, but as message. And what if those messages weren't invented—but revealed?

From the beginning, God embedded a divine narrative in the heavens—a pictorial prophecy, written in starlight, spanning from Virgo to Leo, from the virgin birth to the Lion of Judah's return. This is the Gospel written in the sky.

> He tells the number of the stars; He calls them all by their names. (Psalm 147:4)

God named the stars—not man. Those names, preserved in ancient Semitic, Hebrew, and Arabic star catalogs, bear astonishing connections to the redemptive story of Scripture.

The Mazzaroth: God's Story in the Stars

Before modern astronomy charted the night sky, God had already written a message in the heavens. This celestial narrative, known in Scripture as the *Mazzaroth*, predates pagan zodiac systems and stretches back to the very foundations of the world.

> Can't you bring forth *Mazzaroth* in his season? Or can't you guide Arcturus (the Great Bear) with his sons (cubs)? (Job 38:32)

The *Mazzaroth* is a Hebrew term referring to the twelve signs or divisions of the sky through which the sun, moon, and planets appear to move throughout the year. While often misunderstood or conflated with astrology, the biblical *Mazzaroth* is not about fortune-telling—it is about truth-telling. It's not mystical—it's messianic.

The ancients didn't merely admire the stars—they named them, grouped them, and preserved their meanings. These star names, many of which survive in ancient Hebrew, Aramaic, and Arabic, speak of a coming Redeemer, a serpent-crusher, a suffering sacrifice, and a victorious King. Long before Moses wrote Genesis, this story was preached silently in the night sky.

> The heavens declare the glory of God; and the firmament shows His handiwork. Day unto day utters speech, and night unto night shows knowledge . . . Their line is gone out through all the earth . . . (Psalm 19:1–4)

The *Mazzaroth* is that "line"—a divine sequence of constellations beginning with Virgo (the virgin) and ending with Leo (the Lion). Each major sign is paired with two or three decan constellations—subdivisions of the 12 major *Mazzaroth* constellations—which illuminate and expand the meaning of the main sign.

The message is consistent, prophetic, and Christ centered.

Why the *Mazzaroth* Still Matters—In an age when the sky is often ignored or distorted by astrology, recovering the true meaning of the *Mazzaroth* is like uncovering a forgotten Gospel in the stars. This was not a message invented by man but designed by God—a prophetic timepiece and visual testimony of His redemptive plan.

As we now begin to explore each of the twelve constellations—accompanied by their ancient decans—we are not looking at superstition. We are tracing a heavenly narrative authored by the same God who numbered the stars and called them by name (Psalm 147:4).

Let us begin at the beginning and watch the Gospel unfold, one constellation at a time.

From Virgo to Leo: A Celestial Journey Through Redemption

The twelve major constellations form a divine storyline in the heavens—a prophetic arc that begins with Virgo, the virgin who would bear the Promised Seed, and culminates with Leo, the victorious Lion of Judah. Together, they trace the sweeping arc of the Gospel narrative, unfolding God's redemptive plan—from prophecy to fulfillment, from suffering to glory.

Each major constellation is accompanied by three decan constellations—forming a total of 36 minor constellations, grouped in threes across the twelve signs. These supporting constellations act as narrative amplifiers, designed to expand, clarify, and complete the message of the main sign.

The role of the decans is twofold—both practical and prophetic:

- They reinforce and illuminate the themes of the primary constellations.
- They were used in ancient calendars and are embraced by scholars of biblical astronomy to explore the heavens as God's prophetic scroll.

These decans are not arbitrary. They provide essential narrative depth—adding dimensions that the twelve signs alone cannot convey. They reveal the spiritual warfare, heavenly intercession, and final judgment woven into the Gospel in the Stars.

What follows is a journey through each of the twelve major constellations, from Virgo to Leo, paired with their corresponding decans. Each sign represents a prophetic chapter in the Gospel story—unfolding from the virgin birth of the Messiah to His ultimate return in victory. The three accompanying decans for each sign serve as divine footnotes, enriching the meaning and revealing hidden layers of redemption, intercession, warfare, and triumph. Together, these heavenly signs form a celestial testimony to the full arc of God's redemptive plan.

1. Virgo (The Virgin)—The Promise of the Seed—Virgo is the first constellation in the ancient *Mazzaroth*—the twelve signs written in the heavens—and fittingly, it begins the Gospel story in the stars. Virgo is portrayed as a maiden reclining in the heavens, often depicted holding a branch in one hand and a sheaf of wheat in the other. The image of a virgin is not coincidental; it directly corresponds with the ancient prophecy in Isaiah 7:14:

> Therefore the LORD Himself shall give you a sign; Behold, a virgin shall conceive, and bear a Son, and shall call His name Immanuel. (Isaiah 7:14)

The name Virgo itself means "virgin," and it sets the tone for the redemptive narrative told throughout the constellations.

The brightest star in Virgo is *Spica*, a name derived from Latin meaning "ear of grain" or "seed." This star is one of the most significant in biblical astronomy because its ancient Hebrew name means "the Branch." This ties powerfully into Jeremiah 23:5, where it is written:

> Behold, the days come, says the LORD, that I will raise unto David a righteous Branch, and a King shall reign and prosper, and shall execute judgment and justice in the earth. (Jeremiah 23:5)

This "Branch" is a Messianic title for Jesus Christ, and in Virgo, we see the Seed promised to the woman in Genesis 3:15:

> And I will put enmity between you and the woman, and between your seed and her Seed; He shall bruise your head, and you shalt bruise His heel. (Genesis 3:15)

Virgo embodies the humble beginnings of redemption, the moment when Heaven's greatest promise entered time through a lowly virgin in Bethlehem.

Virgo's message is further amplified by its three associated decans—smaller constellations that surround the main figure and elaborate on its meaning.

1. **Coma**—The first, Coma, has been historically depicted not as a woman with long hair (as modern astronomy sometimes renders it), but as a woman holding a Child on her lap. Ancient Middle Eastern tradition called this constellation "The Desired of the Nations"—a Messianic title drawn from Haggai 2:7: "And the desire of all nations shall come." This is a clear picture of the virgin mother and her divine Child, Jesus Christ.

2. **Centaurus**—The second decan, Centaurus, is a dual-natured being—half man, half horse. While the Greek mythological overlay often obscures the biblical truth, its deeper message is profound. Centaurus represents the dual nature of Christ—fully God and fully Man. This echoes the truth of John 1:14: "And the Word was made flesh, and dwelt among us . . ." The centaur figure, while strange to modern readers, symbolized in ancient times a wise and sacrificial being—aptly reflecting Christ, who bore our griefs and carried our sorrows (Isaiah 53:4).

3. **Bootes**—The third decan is Bootes, a constellation portrayed as a strong man holding a sickle and a shepherd's staff. Bootes is known as "The Coming One" or "The Shepherd-King." His sickle represents harvest and judgment, pointing ahead to Revelation 14:15 where the Son of Man is seen with a sickle, ready to reap the harvest of the earth. His role as a shepherd connects to John 10:11, where Jesus declares: "I am the Good Shepherd: the Good Shepherd gives His life for the sheep."

Altogether, Virgo and her decans present a deeply layered prophecy—one that begins the celestial Gospel with the virgin birth, highlights the divine nature of the Messiah, and anticipates His mission as both Shepherd and Judge. The heavens are not silent; they proclaim with brilliance and detail the mystery of God becoming flesh. In Virgo, we see the Seed of hope planted in the soil of human history, the foretelling of a Savior who would come in meekness and power to redeem all mankind.

2. Libra (The Scales)—The Price of Redemption Must Be Paid—Libra, the second constellation in the ancient *Mazzaroth*, represents divine justice and the inescapable truth that sin carries a cost. Depicted as a set of scales balancing in the heavens, Libra speaks of judgment, debt, and the weight of human transgression. In the Gospel narrative written across the stars, Libra follows Virgo because once the Promised Seed is introduced, the next great theological truth comes into view:

> For all have sinned, and come short of the glory of God. (Romans 3:23)

Mankind is weighed in the balance—and found wanting.

The symbolism of the scales traces back to the ancient names of the stars in this constellation. The star *Zubenelgenubi* means "the price is deficient," while *Zubeneschamali* translates to "the price that covers." These contrasting names reveal the central message of Libra: man cannot tip the scales in his favor by his own merit. The price for sin is beyond his reach. But there is One who can cover the price fully—Jesus Christ. This connects directly to Leviticus 17:11:

> For the life of the flesh is in the blood: and I have given it to you upon the altar to make an atonement for your souls: for it is the blood that makes an atonement for the soul. (Leviticus 17:11)

Libra's three decans further develop this Gospel theme.

1. **Crux**—The first is Crux, the Cross—perhaps the most direct and stunning symbol in the sky. Although now associated with the Southern Cross, it once held greater theological meaning in the ancient Hebrew understanding. Crux points us directly to the place where the price was

paid in full: "But God commends his love toward us, in that, while we were yet sinners, Christ died for us" (Romans 5:8). The scales of justice are balanced not by man's righteousness, but by the sacrifice on the Cross.

2. **Lupus**—The second decan is Lupus, the victim. Depicted as a slain animal, often a lamb or goat, Lupus portrays the sin offering. This draws a vivid line to Isaiah 53:7: "He is brought as a lamb to the slaughter . . ." and John 1:29, where John the Baptist declares, "Behold the Lamb of God, which takes away the sin of the world." Lupus confirms the substitutionary nature of redemption—an innocent life offered in place of the guilty.

3. **Corona Borealis**—The third decan is Corona Borealis, the Northern Crown. This constellation represents the reward of righteousness and triumph after sacrifice. It is the victor's crown, promised in James 1:12: "Blessed is the man that endures temptation: for when he is tried, he shall receive the crown of life . . ." The crown in Libra's story arc follows judgment and sacrifice, reminding us that those redeemed by Christ will not only be spared judgment but will be crowned in glory.

Together, Libra and its decans lay out one of the most foundational truths of the Gospel: sin demands payment, and only Christ can pay it. Through the scales of divine justice, the Cross of suffering, the lamb of atonement, and the crown of reward, the heavens declare that redemption is both required—and offered freely through the blood of the Lamb. Libra's message is not condemnation, but hope: the weight of sin has met its match in the worth of the Savior.

3. Scorpio (The Scorpion)—The Mortal Enemy Strikes—But Is Crushed—
Scorpio, the third major constellation in the *Mazzaroth*, marks a dramatic turning point in the celestial Gospel. It represents the great adversary—Satan—the one who seeks to wound, deceive, and destroy. The image of a scorpion poised to strike is no accident. This creature, often associated with lurking danger and lethal venom, perfectly mirrors the ancient serpent's deceptive and deadly nature. Scorpio signifies the mortal blow dealt by the enemy to the promised Seed of the woman—a blow foretold in the very first messianic prophecy of the Bible:

> And I will put enmity between you and the woman, and between your seed and her Seed; He shall bruise your head, and you shalt bruise His heel. (Genesis 3:15)

This bruising—the crucifixion—was real and severe, but not final. The scorpion struck, but the Messiah rose.

The brightest star in Scorpio is *Antares*, which means "the wounding" or "the rival." *Antares* mirrors the deep wound the enemy attempts to inflict. And yet, even as the scorpion rises in the sky, its doom is already illustrated in the heavens: it is being trampled by the foot of Ophiuchus, a nearby figure wrestling with a serpent—one of Scorpio's three powerful decans.

1. **Serpens**—The first decan is Serpens, the serpent that reaches up to seize a crown. This image calls to mind Satan's primal desire to usurp God's authority: "I will exalt my throne above the stars of God . . . I will be like the Most High" (Isaiah 14:13–14). Serpens is the great deceiver, always grasping for what he cannot rightfully possess.

2. **Ophiuchus**—Entwined with Serpens is the second decan, Ophiuchus, the strong man who struggles with the serpent. Ophiuchus holds the serpent back from taking the crown, symbolizing Christ's victory in resisting temptation and ultimately overcoming the enemy. The figure has one foot crushing the scorpion's heart—linking back to Genesis 3:15 and foreshadowing the cosmic victory won at the Cross. This visual is reinforced in Romans 16:20: "And the God of peace shall bruise Satan under your feet shortly."

3. **Hercules**—The third decan, Hercules, depicts a mighty warrior kneeling in victory, holding a club and a three-headed serpent. Though bowed in humility, he is strong and triumphant. Hercules is often shown with his foot planted on the head of a serpent or dragon, confirming again the theme of ultimate conquest. It is a reminder of Colossians 2:15, where Christ "spoiled principalities and powers, and made a show of them openly, triumphing over them in it."

Scorpio, then, is not merely a warning of a strike—it is part of the greater Gospel arc: the enemy appears to wound, but the Savior overcomes. The venom of sin and death, though potent, is powerless against the risen Christ. In this constellation, the heavens testify to the fierce opposition of Satan and the decisive victory of the Messiah. Scorpio may sting, but it does not win. The story of redemption continues—not in defeat, but in unstoppable triumph.

4. Sagittarius (The Archer)—The Dual-Natured Warrior Rides Forth—Sagittarius, the fourth major constellation in the *Mazzaroth*, is depicted as a centaur—half man, half horse—aiming a drawn bow and arrow toward the heart of Scorpio. This image of a dual-natured warrior conveys the astonishing truth of the Messiah's identity: fully God, fully Man, riding in judgment and deliverance. The constellation captures the moment of divine counterattack. While Scorpio symbolizes Satan's strike, Sagittarius represents Heaven's swift and righteous response. The Messiah is not merely a suffering Servant—He is also the conquering King, ready to execute justice.

The dual nature of the centaur mirrors the incarnation: Jesus Christ, both divine and human, riding with authority. "And in righteousness He does judge and make war . . . and He was clothed with a vesture dipped in blood: and His name is called "The Word of God" (Revelation 19:11, 13).

> And I saw Heaven opened, and behold a white horse; and He that sat upon him was called Faithful and True, and in righteousness He does judge and make war. And He was clothed with a vesture dipped in blood: and His name is called The Word of God. (Revelation 19:11, 13)

The bow aimed at Scorpio reminds us of the prophecy in Psalm 45:4–5:

> And in Your majesty ride prosperously because of truth and meekness and righteousness; and Your right hand shall teach You awesome things. Your arrows are sharp in the heart of the King's enemies; whereby the people fall under You. (Psalm 45:4–5)

This warrior comes not to destroy indiscriminately, but to defend the righteous and confront evil.

1. **Lyra**—The first decan of Sagittarius is Lyra, the harp. After battle comes worship. This decan reminds us that God's victories are followed by rejoicing. It evokes images of Revelation 15:2–3, where the saints sing the song of Moses and the Lamb, standing victorious. Lyra reminds us that praise is the proper response to the Rider's triumph—His people will rejoice because His justice is perfect.

2. **Ara**—The second decan is Ara, the altar turned upside down. Ara symbolizes the judgment of the wicked, a fire consuming the enemies of God. In ancient depictions, it represents the altar of divine wrath, flipped downward toward the abyss. This matches the sobering imagery of Hebrews 10:27, which speaks of "a certain fearful expectation of judgment and fiery indignation, which shall devour the adversaries."

3. **Draco**—The third decan, Draco, is the dragon. While this constellation spans several *Mazzaroth* signs, its association with Sagittarius here is strategic. Draco represents Satan, the ancient foe, being cast down. In Revelation 12:9, we are told: "And the great dragon was cast out, that old serpent, called the Devil, and Satan, which deceives the whole world." The arrow of Sagittarius, poised and powerful, strikes against

this dragonic force, pointing forward to the ultimate expulsion of evil from the heavens and the earth.

Together, Sagittarius and its decans proclaim that the battle belongs to the Lord. This Warrior-Redeemer is no passive figure—He rides decisively against evil with grace and justice, fully God and fully Man. As the arrow flies and the harp plays, the altar burns and the dragon falls. Sagittarius announces that the fight for humanity's redemption was never unopposed—but it was always under divine command. The Victor rides on.

5. Capricorn (The Goat-Fish)—The Sacrifice That Springs to Life—
Capricorn is one of the most unusual and mysterious constellations in the *Mazzaroth*. It is depicted as a strange hybrid creature—half goat, half fish. Though this image may seem odd at first glance, it communicates one of the most powerful truths of the Gospel: death and resurrection, sacrifice followed by new life. The goat, often associated with sacrifice in the Bible, particularly on the Day of Atonement (*Yom Kippur*), speaks of the sin offering. The fish, in biblical symbolism, is linked with life, multiplication, and the redeemed—frequently associated with the Church.

> And He says unto them, Follow Me, and I will make you fishers of men. (Matthew 4:19)

The goat portion of Capricorn crouches downward as if in the act of dying, while the fish tail rises upward, strong and alive. This visual imagery represents the death of Christ, the Lamb of God, who bore the sin of the world (Isaiah 53:6–7), and the burst of resurrected life that followed (Romans 6:9).

> All we like sheep have gone astray; we have turned everyone to his own way; and the LORD has laid on Him the iniquity of us all. He was oppressed, and He was afflicted, yet He opened not His mouth: He is brought as a lamb to the slaughter, and as a sheep before her shearers is silent, so He opens not His mouth. (Isaiah 53:6–7)

> Knowing that Christ being raised from the dead dies no more; death has no more dominion over Him. (Romans 6:9)

In Leviticus 16, the scapegoat carried Israel's sins into the wilderness; here in Capricorn, we see the greater reality—Jesus Christ, the final sin offering, whose death brought eternal life to many.

1. **Sagitta**—The first decan of Capricorn is Sagitta, the arrow. Unlike Sagittarius' warrior's bow, this arrow is singular and symbolic—depicted flying alone through the sky, pointed downward. It is often called "the arrow of God's judgment." It evokes Isaiah 53:10, "Yet it

pleased the LORD to bruise Him; He has put Him to grief." This solitary arrow points to the deliberate, divine piercing of the Messiah for the sins of the world.

2. **Aquila**—The second decan is Aquila, the eagle. Aquila is shown falling from the sky, its wings outspread in descent. Ancient star maps often portrayed this eagle wounded and descending—again, a dramatic picture of Christ's willing sacrifice. But the eagle is also a biblical symbol of majesty and deliverance. Exodus 19:4 says, "I bare you on eagles' wings, and brought you unto Myself." Aquila's descent foreshadows the lifting of God's people through resurrection power.

3. **Delphinus**—The third decan, Delphinus, the dolphin, is a vivid image of resurrection. Delphinus is portrayed leaping joyfully out of the sea— alive and active. The sea, often symbolic of death or chaos in Scripture (Revelation 21:1), is overcome here. The leaping dolphin speaks of Christ's resurrection from the grave and of believers' new life in Him. Romans 6:4 declares, "Even so we also should walk in newness of life." Delphinus reminds us that death is not the end—it is the doorway to glory.

Capricorn, then, is a stunning celestial portrait of the Gospel's core: substitutionary sacrifice and glorious resurrection. It begins low—humiliation, suffering, death—but it ends high—life, exaltation, and joy. As John 12:24 proclaims, "Except a corn of wheat fall into the ground and die, it abides alone: but if it die, it brings forth much fruit." Capricorn is the constellation of that holy harvest.

6. Aquarius (The Water Bearer)—The Outpouring of Living Waters— Aquarius, the Water Bearer, is a breathtaking constellation that illustrates the abundant outpouring of divine life. Depicted as a man pouring water from an urn, Aquarius symbolizes the living waters of the Holy Spirit—Heaven's blessing flowing continuously upon the earth. This powerful image aligns with John 7:38– 39, where Jesus declares:

> He that believes on Me, as the Scripture has said, out of his belly (heart) shall flow rivers of living water. (But this spoke He of the Spirit, which they that believe on Him should receive: for the Holy Ghost was not yet given; because that Jesus was not yet glorified.). (John 7:38–39)

Aquarius proclaims this very promise across the night sky.

1. **Piscis Austrinus**—The water flows downward from the urn into the mouth of the first related decan, Piscis Austrinus (The Southern Fish).

This fish receives the stream directly, representing believers—those redeemed by Christ who now live by the Spirit. In Scripture, fish often symbolize God's people (see Matthew 13:47–50, the parable of the net). The water bearer does not trickle the stream—He pours it. This is not a drop of grace but a deluge of blessing. Joel 2:28 foretells, "I will pour out My Spirit upon all flesh," and Aquarius shows us that fulfillment rippling from Heaven to earth.

2. **Pegasus**—The second decan, Pegasus (The Winged Horse), rises next. Pegasus represents the swiftness and majesty of this heavenly gift. The horse, often a symbol of divine mission and movement, is winged—able to rise above the earth. Pegasus portrays the rapid spread of the Gospel and the Spirit's transformative power carrying believers to new spiritual heights. Isaiah 40:31 reminds us: "They that wait upon the LORD shall renew their strength; they shall mount up with wings as eagles." The Spirit doesn't just cleanse; He empowers and lifts.

3. **Cygnus**—The third decan, Cygnus (The Swan), offers an image of beauty and symmetry, soaring in flight across the heavens. It is often referred to as "the Northern Cross," as its brightest stars form a cross-shaped pattern. The swan glides in grace and peace—symbolizing the indwelling presence of the Holy Spirit, who leads believers into all truth (John 6:13). Cygnus also hints at the return of Christ, coming with glory and majesty, tracing the arc of His kingdom established by the Spirit's work.

Together, Aquarius and its decans form a celestial trilogy of blessing: the outpouring of the Spirit (Aquarius), the swiftness of Gospel spread and deliverance (Pegasus), and the peaceful reign of Christ's presence (Cygnus). They mark the age of the Church—an era not of drought but divine abundance. Just as water sustains life on earth, the Spirit sustains spiritual life. As Isaiah 44:3 proclaims, "For I will pour water upon him that is thirsty, and floods upon the dry ground: I will pour My Spirit upon your seed." Aquarius writes that promise in starlight, testifying that the heavens are not dry—they overflow with living water.

7. Pisces (The Fish)—The Church Age and Binding of Believers to Christ— Pisces, the constellation of the Fish, portrays a profound picture of the Church Age—the era of grace in which believers are bound together in Christ. This constellation is composed of two fish connected by a long, flowing band. One fish swims horizontally along the ecliptic (the sun's path), and the other points upward, symbolizing a spiritual aspiration toward Heaven. This dual orientation mirrors the believer's experience—living in the world while longing for the things above (Colossians 3:1–2). The connecting band, a key feature of this constellation, ties the two fish together in unity and covenant, revealing the tension between flesh and spirit, earth and eternity, the seen and the unseen.

> If you then be risen with Christ, seek those things which are above, where Christ sits on the right hand of God. Set your affection on things above, not on things on the earth. (Colossians 3:1–2)

Pisces beautifully represents the followers of Christ who are "in the world but not of it" (John 17:14–16). The fish have long symbolized Christians, dating back to the early Church when the *ichthys* (Greek for "fish") became a secret symbol for believers under Roman persecution. It also draws from Jesus' own words when He called His disciples to be "fishers of men" (Matthew 4:19) and performed miracles involving fish that illustrated abundance, calling, and provision (Luke 5:1–11; John 21:1–14).

> I have given them Your Word; and the world has hated them, because they are not of the world, even as I am not of the world. I pray not that You should take them out of the world, but that You should keep them from the evil. They are not of the world, even as I am not of the world. (John 17:14–16)

1. **The Band**—The first decan, The Band, depicts the restraining force connecting the two fish. This band not only ties the believers together in identity and faith, but it is also shown being pulled by the next constellation, Cetus—a great sea monster or beast. Cetus represents the opposition believers face: spiritual warfare, worldly entrapments, and the enemy who seeks to devour and enslave. Yet the band is ultimately broken by the intervention of Christ, as shown in the final decan, signifying deliverance.

2. **Andromeda**—The second decan, Andromeda, shows a chained woman—symbolic of the suffering Church, often bound and afflicted in this world. She is beautiful but in distress, awaiting deliverance. This mirrors the trials believers endure throughout the Age of Grace, often facing persecution, rejection, and hardship for the name of Christ. Romans 8:18 reminds us, "For I reckon that the sufferings of this present time are not worthy to be compared with the glory which shall be revealed in us." Andromeda represents the Church in that waiting—afflicted but destined for glory.

3. **Cepheus**—The third decan, Cepheus, brings hope. He is a glorious crowned king, seated on his throne, holding a scepter. Cepheus

represents Christ Himself—King of kings and Head of the Church (Ephesians 1:22–23). He is enthroned in majesty, and He will return to redeem His Bride. The placement of Cepheus in the heavens above Andromeda speaks volumes: the Church may be bound on earth, but her King reigns from above, and the wedding of the Lamb is certain to come (Revelation 19:7).

Pisces, with its dual fish, its binding cords, and its connected decans, paints a portrait of the current dispensation—the Church Age. It is a story of unity, struggle, sanctification, and ultimate victory. The heavens declare that those who are joined to Christ are never alone and never forgotten. Bound to Him in covenant, they are destined to rise, as the upward-facing fish foretells, into the glorious freedom of the children of God.

8. Aries (The Ram)—The Lamb That Was Slain and Lives Again—Aries, known as The Ram, stands as one of the most powerful portrayals of redemption and resurrection in the celestial Gospel. This constellation follows Pisces and marks a shift from suffering and restraint to triumph and renewed life. Aries symbolizes the Lamb of God—Jesus Christ—who was slain for the sin of the world yet rose in power and victory. In ancient times, Aries was not viewed as a wild ram but as a sacrificial one, peacefully reclining, yet with head lifted—alive, strong, and exalted. This posture signifies the finished work of redemption and the resurrected life of Christ.

The significance of the ram is deeply rooted in Scripture. It was a ram caught in the thicket that God provided in place of Isaac on Mount Moriah, a foreshadowing of substitutionary atonement (Genesis 22:13–14). Later, the Passover lamb became the central symbol of deliverance, pointing forward to Jesus, "the Lamb of God, which takes away the sin of the world" (John 1:29). Aries declares this truth across the night sky—He who was sacrificed now lives, victorious over sin and death.

> The next day John (John the Baptist) sees Jesus coming unto him, and says, Behold the Lamb of God, which takes away the sin of the world. (John 1:29)

The three decans accompanying Aries amplify this glorious message.

1. **Cassiopeia**—The first is Cassiopeia, the enthroned woman. Once represented in her suffering (as Andromeda in Pisces), she is now elevated and crowned, symbolizing the glorified Church—the Bride of Christ—now seated with Him in heavenly places (Ephesians 2:6). Cassiopeia's transformation from bound to enthroned mirrors the believer's journey from salvation to glorification.

2. **Cetus**—The second decan is Cetus, the sea monster, again appearing as a symbol of evil and chaos. But here, Cetus is firmly under the authority of Aries—beneath the ram's foot—indicating the subjugation of all demonic and worldly powers. This echoes Romans 16:20, which promises, "The God of peace shall bruise Satan under your feet shortly." Aries demonstrates that the power of the Lamb is not only in atonement but also in sovereign authority over darkness.

3. **Perseus**—The final decan is Perseus, the heroic figure holding the severed head of Medusa (a serpent-haired monster). In this image, we see Christ, the mighty Deliverer, victorious over sin, death, and the devil. Hebrews 2:14 declares, "That through death He might destroy him that had the power of death, that is, the devil." Perseus, riding swiftly with his prize of victory, encapsulates the triumphant return of the risen King.

Together, Aries and its decans proclaim the heart of the Gospel: Christ, our sacrificial Lamb, was offered once for all, but He did not remain in the grave. He rose again in power, exalted above all, having defeated every enemy. The stars cry out what Revelation 5:12 says: "Worthy is the Lamb that was slain to receive power, and riches, and wisdom, and strength, and honor, and glory, and blessing." Aries reminds us that the Lamb reigns.

9. Taurus (The Bull)—The Coming Judge and King—Taurus, The Bull, emerges from the celestial lineup as a vivid and forceful picture of Christ returning not as the suffering Lamb, but as the conquering King and righteous Judge. Depicted as a charging bull, its head lowered and horns thrust forward, Taurus symbolizes unstoppable strength, righteous fury, and divine judgment. Unlike the gentleness of Aries, Taurus represents the Messianic fulfillment of justice—when Christ comes again, it will not be to bear sin, but to rule and to crush evil under His feet.

In ancient times, bulls represented power, sacrifice, and kingship. The Hebrew term for the wild ox, *re'em*, often translated "unicorn" in the King James Version, is more accurately understood as a strong, untamable bull (see Numbers 23:22 and Deuteronomy 33:17). It is this powerful image of might and majesty that frames Taurus as a celestial declaration of the Day of the LORD. As prophesied in Isaiah 63:3–4, the Messiah returns in judgment:

> I have trodden the winepress alone; and of the people there was none with Me: for I will tread them in My anger, and trample them in My fury; and their blood shall be sprinkled upon My garments, and I will stain all My raiment (robes). For the Day of Vengeance is in My heart, and the year of My redeemed is come. (Isaiah 63:3–4)

Taurus surges forward as a warning and a promise—justice will come.

Taurus is flanked by three decans that deepen this portrayal of divine power and protection.

1. **Orion**—The first is Orion, the most recognizable constellation in the night sky. Depicted as a glorious and victorious hunter, Orion strides across the heavens, wielding a club and lifting a lion's skin in triumph. In the Gospel story, Orion represents the Messiah returning in majesty and victory. The ancient name of Orion in Hebrew is *Kesil*, meaning "the strong one" or "hero." Revelation 19:11–16 mirrors this imagery: Christ returns riding a white horse, clothed in a robe dipped in blood, with eyes like fire and a sword proceeding from His mouth. Orion's brilliance declares, "The King is coming."

2. **Eridanus**—The second decan is Eridanus, the celestial river flowing from the foot of Orion. This river of fire stretches across the sky and symbolizes judgment. Some traditions interpret Eridanus as a representation of the eternal judgment of the wicked—an image of the "Lake of Fire" described in Revelation 20:14–15. As Taurus advances, this river flows behind, connecting Orion's conquest with the ultimate destiny of those who reject the Lamb.

3. **Auriga**—The third decan is Auriga, the Shepherd or Charioteer. In striking contrast to the fierceness of Taurus, Auriga holds a she-goat and her kids tenderly in His arms. This shows the mercy extended to God's people even in the midst of judgment. While Christ comes as Judge, He never forgets His own. Isaiah 40:11 says, "He shall feed His flock like a shepherd: He shall gather the lambs with His arm, and carry them in His bosom." Auriga reminds us that God's judgment is balanced with protection for the righteous.

In its fullness, Taurus and its decans declare the soon-coming King who will avenge the blood of the saints, restore justice, defeat His enemies, and gather His people. The Gospel story told in Taurus is not only one of wrath—it is also one of redemption completed. The stars point ahead to the moment when every knee shall bow and every tongue confess that Jesus Christ is Lord (Philippians 2:10–11). Taurus, surging across the heavens, is a divine warning and a blessed assurance: the Judge of all the earth is coming—and He will do right.

10. Gemini (The Twins)—The Dual Nature of Christ and His Union with the Church—Gemini, often symbolized by twin figures, holds a profound prophetic message that goes far beyond the mythological twins of Greco-Roman tradition.

In its ancient, biblical context, Gemini represents unity, covenant, and the mysterious duality of Christ—fully God and fully Man—and His inseparable bond with His Bride, the Church. In early Hebrew astronomy, these "twins" were not cast as *Romulus* and *Remus* or *Castor* and *Pollux*, but were understood as the Bridegroom and the Bride, the divine and the redeemed, brought together in covenantal union.

This constellation powerfully portrays the mystery spoken of Ephesians 5:31–32, where Paul writes:

> For this cause shall a man leave his father and mother, and shall be joined unto his wife, and they two shall be one flesh. This is a great mystery: but I speak concerning Christ and the Church. (Ephesians 5:31–32)

"This is a great mystery: but I speak concerning Christ and the Church." The two figures, equal in stature and side by side, mirror the heavenly Bridegroom joined with His redeemed Bride, a prophetic picture of the ultimate unity to be fulfilled at the marriage supper of the Lamb (Revelation 19:7–9). It also echoes the incarnation itself—God made flesh—Jesus Christ, the Son of God, and the Son of Man.

> Let us be glad and rejoice, and give honor to Him: for the marriage of the Lamb is come, and His wife has made herself ready. And to her was granted that she should be arrayed in fine linen, clean and white: for the fine linen is the righteousness of saints. And he says unto me, Write, Blessed are they which are called unto the marriage supper of the Lamb. And he says unto me, These are the true sayings of God. (Revelation 19:7–9)

Gemini's brightest stars are *Castor* and *Pollux*. Though modern names, they reflect deeper truths when seen through a redemptive lens. Castor, associated with mortality, and Pollux, with immortality, hint at the divine-human nature of Christ—one who could die, and yet conquer death. John 1:14 says, "And the Word was made flesh, and dwelt among us," a truth Gemini proclaims in its very formation.

> And the Word was made flesh, and dwelt among us, (and we beheld His glory, the glory as of the only begotten of the Father) full of grace and truth. (John 1:14)

The decan constellations that accompany Gemini further develop this theme.

1. **Lepus**—First is Lepus, the enemy, often depicted as a hare or serpent under Orion's feet. Lepus represents the vanquished foe—Satan—reminding us that the union of Christ and His Church comes only after the enemy has been subdued. This ties directly to Romans 16:20: "And the God of peace shall bruise Satan under your feet shortly."

2. **Canis Major**—Next is Canis Major, the Greater Dog, which ancient star lore identifies as the Prince or Redeemer. It's brightest star, *Sirius*, means "the Prince," and is one of the most luminous stars in the night sky. Canis Major is a picture of the coming Messiah—swift, powerful, and faithful—an image of the Shepherd-King leading His people to safety. This aligns with Revelation 19:11, where Christ rides forth in victory and righteousness.

3. **Canis Minor**—The third decan is Canis Minor, the Lesser Dog, which represents the redeemed. Ancient names for this constellation include terms like "redeemed," "conquered," and "faithful followers." Here we see the Church herself—joyful, secure, and forever united with Christ. The contrast between the Greater and Lesser Dogs reveals the roles of Redeemer and Redeemed—two distinct entities now united, just as Gemini's twin stars stand side by side.

In Gemini, the Gospel message is rich and layered; the Incarnation of Christ as God and Man, His triumph over Satan, and His loving union with His Bride. It proclaims the intimacy of covenant, the victory over darkness, and the eternal oneness of the Savior with His redeemed. As Song of Solomon 6:3 poetically declares, "I am my Beloved's, and my Beloved is mine." Gemini is Heaven's love story written in starlight—the Bridegroom and the Bride, united forever.

11. Cancer (The Crab)—A Gathered and Protected People—Cancer, often depicted as a crab in modern astronomy, carries a much deeper meaning in the ancient *Mazzaroth*. In biblical star lore, Cancer represents a gathered and securely held people, symbolizing the protective nature of God's covenant with His redeemed. Though the image of a crab clinging tightly with its claws may seem curious at first, this visual powerfully conveys a theme central to the Gospel: security, preservation, and rest within the fold of God.

Cancer's brightest star, Tegmine, means "holding" or "embracing." This speaks to the tender grasp of God upon His people, a truth echoed in John 10:28–29, where Jesus declares:

> And I give unto them eternal life; and they shall never perish, neither shall any man pluck them out of My hand. My Father, which gave them to Me, is greater than all; and no man is able to pluck them out of My Father's hand. (John 10:28–29)

The image of Cancer is one of strong yet loving protection, a heavenly portrait of the Shepherd who keeps His sheep safe from harm.

The ancient symbolism associated with Cancer was not a crustacean but rather a circle of sheepfolds, or even a sacred enclosure, highlighting the idea of gathered flocks under divine care. This ties beautifully into Psalm 23:1–3:

> The LORD is my shepherd; I shall not want. He makes me to lie down in green pastures: He leads me beside the still waters. He restores my soul: He leads me in the paths of righteousness for His name's sake. (Psalm 23:1–3)

The three decan constellations that accompany Cancer expand this message of secure redemption and joyful return:

1. **Ursa Minor**—Known as the Lesser Sheepfold, this group has historically been associated with the faithful remnant of Israel. Its brightest star, *Polaris*, is the North Star—a fixed and guiding light, emblematic of God's unchanging covenant with His people. Malachi 3:6 says, "For I am the LORD, I change not; therefore you sons of Jacob are not consumed."

2. **Ursa Major**—The Greater Sheepfold, often referred to as "the Fold and the Flock," represents the Gentile believers gathered into the family of God during the Church Age. Its ancient names speak of the assembled, the protected, and the innumerable company. This reflects the prophetic fulfillment of John 10:16, where Jesus says, "Other sheep I have, which are not of this fold: them also I must bring, and shall hear My voice; and there shall be one fold, and one Shepherd."

3. **Argo Navis**—The Ship of Travelers Returning Home. Though now split into three modern constellations, Argo was once seen as a singular figure representing the voyage home of the redeemed. The Church is on a pilgrimage, as Hebrews 11:13 calls us "strangers and pilgrims on the earth," but Argo reminds us of our final destination—the safe harbor of God's eternal kingdom. It embodies the fulfillment of Hebrews 4:9, "There remains therefore a rest to the people of God."

In Cancer, the Gospel story quiets into a moment of sacred security. The battles may rage outside the sheepfold, but within, the Redeemer gathers, protects, and leads His people. Cancer whispers of the Shepherd who does not lose a single sheep, the Father who preserves His own, and the promise of safe return for every weary traveler. As Isaiah 40:11 proclaims, "He shall feed His flock like a shepherd: He shall gather the lambs with His arm, and carry them in His bosom."

Cancer is not a constellation of fear or struggle—it is one of preservation, covenant, and divine embrace. It declares that no one is forgotten, no soul is lost, and no promise will fail for those who belong to the Good Shepherd.

12. Leo (The Lion)—The Triumphant Return of the Lion of Judah—Leo, the majestic lion in the heavens, concludes the Gospel story written in the stars. It symbolizes the final and glorious phase of redemptive history: the return of Jesus Christ, the Lion of the tribe of Judah, who will conquer all evil and reign as King of kings and Lord of lords. Unlike the gentle imagery seen in Virgo, Leo is bold and royal—poised with one paw extended, often depicted trampling a serpent beneath it. This striking image aligns with the prophecy of Genesis 49:9–10, where Jacob declares:

> Judah is a lion's whelp: from the prey, my son, you are gone up: he stooped down, he couched as a lion, and as an old lion; who shall rouse him up? The sceptre shall not depart from Judah, nor a lawgiver from between his feet, until Shiloh (the coming Messiah—Jesus Christ) come; and unto Him shall the gathering of the people be. (Genesis 49:9–10)

The tribe of Judah, from which Jesus descended, is symbolized by the lion, and Leo completes the celestial gospel with its announcement of Messiah's triumph.

The brightest star in Leo is *Regulus*, meaning "little King" or "King Star." Situated in the heart of the lion, *Regulus* shines with royal authority, reminding us of Revelation 5:5:

> And one of the elders says unto me, Weep not: behold, the Lion of the tribe of Judah, the Root of David, has prevailed to open the book, and to loose the seven seals thereof. (Revelation 5:5)

The lion is not passive—it is roaring, advancing, ruling. Leo declares the Second Coming of Christ with kingly dominance and overwhelming victory.

Leo is accompanied by three decan constellations that amplify its message of judgment, wrath, and final justice:

1. **Hydra**—The many-headed serpent or dragon, often stretching across a third of the sky. It represents Satan and the kingdom of darkness. In Leo's depiction, the lion crushes Hydra underfoot. This visual captures the ultimate fulfillment of Romans 16:20, "And the God of peace shall bruise Satan under your feet shortly." Hydra's sprawling form reminds us of evil's reach—but also its end.

2. **Crater**—The Cup of Wrath. In ancient times, Crater was seen as a vessel for divine judgment, often tied to the wrath of God poured out on the unrepentant. This is echoed in Revelation 14:10, "The same shall drink of the wine of the wrath of God, which is poured out without mixture into the cup of His indignation . . ." Crater is a sobering reminder that God's justice is not to be mocked.

3. **Corvus**—The raven. Corvus represents the birds of judgment, seen devouring the remains of the defeated serpent. It aligns with prophetic warnings like Revelation 19:17–18, where the birds are called to feast on the flesh of kings and mighty men after Christ's return. The raven symbolizes the completeness of God's vengeance on evil.

Together, Leo and its decans present the climactic finale of the Gospel—Christ's royal authority, the crushing of Satan, the judgment of the wicked, and the exaltation of the King. Leo's position as the final constellation in the ancient *Mazzaroth* is no accident. It seals the divine message begun in Virgo in perfect symmetry and power. What began with a virgin and a promise ends with a King and a crown.

When the heavens declare "The Lion has come," they echo the resounding message of Revelation 19:11–16: Christ rides out in righteousness, crowned with many crowns, His name called "The Word of God" and "King of kings, and Lord of lords." The stars, like faithful heralds, have told the end from the beginning—and Leo assures us: the victory is already written.

A Story Older than Scripture but Never in Conflict with It

God's celestial story came first—etched into the sky at Creation, visible to Adam and Eve. The written Scriptures later affirmed and preserved what had already been declared in the stars. As Romans 10:18 alludes, "Their sound went into all the earth, and their words unto the ends of the world." This is the same "sound" spoken of in Psalm 19—the voice of the heavens.

> Their line is gone out through all the earth, and their words to the end of the world. In them has He set a tabernacle for the sun. (Psalm 19:4)

Not Astrology, But Divine Astronomy

Astrology seeks to control or predict through the stars. But biblical astronomy calls us to observe and understand what God has already proclaimed. The constellations do not determine your future—but they do declare God's redemptive plan. Astrology twists the original message for self-focus; biblical astronomy restores the focus on Messiah.

A Call to Remember the Ancient Witness

In a world obsessed with screens and artificial lights, we've forgotten how to read the sky. But the message is still there. The stars haven't moved. The story hasn't changed. And it still speaks of a virgin's Son, a sacrificial Lamb, Living Water, and a returning Lion.

In these end times, as knowledge increases and prophetic fulfillment accelerates, God is restoring awareness of the *Mazzaroth*—calling His people to once again "look up" (Luke 21:28).

> And when these things begin to come to pass, then look up, and lift up your heads; for your redemption draws near. (Luke 21:28)

The next time you gaze at the night sky, remember: you're not just looking at stars. You're reading a divine manuscript—a celestial proclamation of the Gospel of Jesus Christ, authored by the Creator Himself.

SOLAR ECLIPSES: WARNINGS TO THE NATIONS

Since Creation, God has used the heavens as a canvas to communicate His divine will and timing. The biblical calendar, unlike other modern Gregorian systems, is lunisolar—it follows the moon to mark months and the sun to track seasons. This dual rhythm, still used in the Hebrew calendar today, was divinely designed to align humanity with both physical and spiritual order.

One of the most awe-inspiring and sobering phenomena within this system is the solar eclipse—a rare event that can only occur during a new moon, when the moon passes directly between the earth and the sun, momentarily darkening the sky. These events are not merely natural wonders; in the biblical worldview, they are signs from God, and when they align with key moments in time, they become warnings to the nations—especially the Gentile world.

Genesis 1:14 reveals that the sun and moon were created not just to light the sky, but to serve as indicators of "signs, seasons (*moedim*), days, and years." The term *moedim* refers to God's appointed times—His divine calendar. Solar eclipses, especially when they align with these sacred seasons, act as celestial megaphones, announcing warnings, transitions, or impending judgments.

While modern astronomy can now predict these eclipses with remarkable accuracy, ancient Jewish sages also understood the timing and significance of these heavenly events. Long before the invention of telescopes, they used naked-eye observation and centuries of recorded patterns to forecast eclipses and discern their meaning. This wasn't mysticism. It was a prophetic science—one that understood Creation as a reflection of the Creator's voice.

Today, organizations like NASA (National Aeronautics and Space Administration) and ESA (European Space Agency) have developed complex algorithms using Kepler's laws of planetary motion and modern physics to chart every eclipse—past and future—for thousands of years. Some databases reach back to 2000 BC, enabling us to reconstruct the skies of biblical times and observe how solar eclipses aligned with historical and geopolitical shifts.

This divine pattern continues.

In recent history, solar eclipses have occurred on or near major Jewish fast days or biblical feast seasons, often tracing symbolic paths or converging over prophetically charged geography. One of the most striking examples is the Great American Eclipse of August 21, 2017, which crossed the entire continental United States. Its seven-year counterpart, occurred April 8, 2024, traced a new path across the nation—intersecting the 2017 path and forming a literal "X" or Cross over the heart of America.

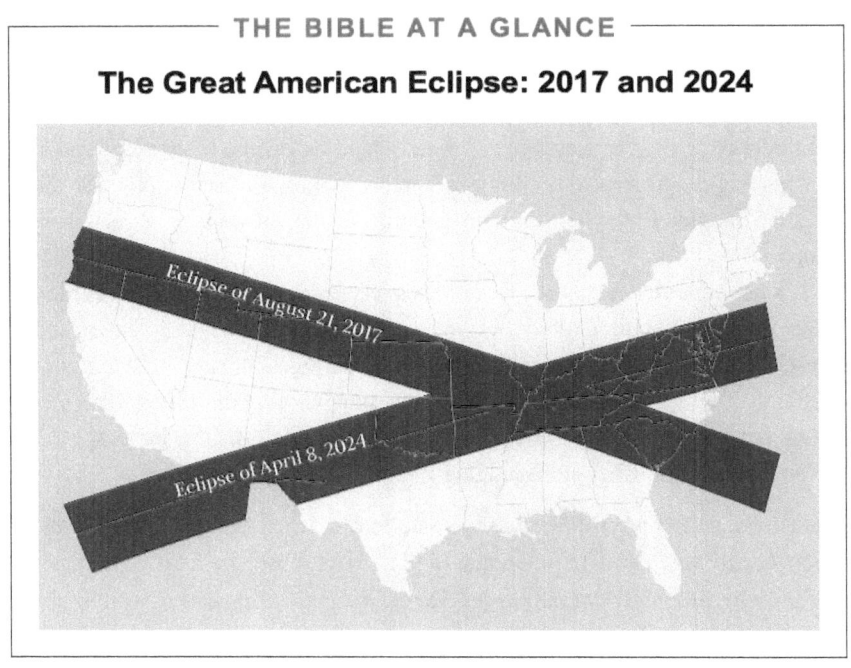

THE BIBLE AT A GLANCE

The Great American Eclipse: 2017 and 2024

Figure 4 – The Great American Eclipse: 2017 and 2024

These are not random events. They serve as warnings—heavenly messages directed not at Israel, but at the Gentile nations. And the message is urgent: repent, return, realign. God's clock is ticking, and He is speaking—not just through prophecy on paper, but through signs in the heavens that no man can ignore.

In a world that watches the ground for answers, the Bible calls us to *look up*. Solar eclipses are one of God's clearest ways of reminding the nations that He is still on the throne—and that judgment always comes preceded by mercy and warning.

The Sun as a Prophetic Sign

Throughout Scripture and history, the sun is consistently portrayed as a symbol of power, dominion, and judgment over the nations. It governs days and seasons, but prophetically, it also governs Gentile nations—those outside of Israel. When God intends to communicate to the broader world, He often does so through the sun. When He speaks to Israel, He uses the moon.

Solar Eclipses: Warnings to Gentile Nations—In biblical typology, solar eclipses are warnings to the Gentile nations. These extraordinary events, where the sun is darkened in broad daylight, are not arbitrary. They are divinely timed messages, often occurring near or on days of biblical significance—fasts, feasts, or moments of global consequence. In contrast, lunar eclipses—or blood moons—serve as signs to Israel, marking pivotal prophetic intersections for God's covenant people. But when the sun goes dark, the message is directed at the nations.

It's no coincidence that the Great American Eclipse of 2017 was visible only across the continental United States—a rare occurrence—and that a second eclipse in 2024 crossed the nation again, forming a massive "X" across its heartland. The symbolism is chilling, and the warning unmistakable. God is calling out to the Gentile world, particularly America, in the language of the heavens: "Return to Me before judgment falls."

Scientific and Prophetic Harmony—Modern science has confirmed what the ancients once watched with reverence. Today, NASA and the ESA can chart solar eclipses with pinpoint accuracy using Kepler's laws of planetary motion, tracing their paths thousands of years into the past and future. These celestial events are so precise that they can be calculated down to the second. Far from superstition, they reflect a universe running on divine order, not chaos.

What's astonishing is that long before telescopes and satellites, ancient Jewish sages were doing the same. With nothing but the naked eye and generations of meticulously recorded observations, they tracked the patterns of the sun, moon, and stars. They understood that eclipses weren't just natural anomalies but prophetic phenomena, woven into the very structure of Creation.

When modern astronomy aligns with ancient biblical insight, we are witnessing what can only be described as science and prophecy working hand in hand. Eclipses are not signs of astrological fortune-telling—they are divine markers, placed by a Creator who wrote His calendar into the heavens. Every solar eclipse is a testimony to both the precision of God's design and the urgency of His call.

We are not to worship the signs—but we are called to discern them. And when the sun is darkened at noon, when its light is hidden without warning, the Bible is clear: the nations should tremble.

Historical Solar Eclipse Events and Repentance

The Bible is clear: God gives signs before He brings the sword. And few signs in the heavens have carried such prophetic weight as a solar eclipse—a sudden darkening of the sun, often interpreted as a warning to the nations. These are not poetic metaphors. They are divine disruptions, designed to arrest the attention of entire civilizations.

The Sign of Jonah—When Jesus rebuked the Pharisees in Matthew 16:4, He said, "An evil and adulterous generation seeks after a sign, and no sign shall be given to it except the sign of the prophet Jonah." This was no vague reference. Jonah's arrival in Nineveh was itself preceded by a total solar eclipse, now known historically as the Bur-Sagale Eclipse—dated June 15, 763 BC.

This wasn't just a celestial event—it was a moment of national terror. The darkness in the sky came amid plagues, political unrest, civil war, and natural disasters. Nineveh's heart had already been softened by these cascading calamities, and when Jonah delivered his haunting prophecy—"Yet forty days, and Nineveh shall be overthrown" (Jonah 3:4)—they believed him. The entire city, from king to commoner, repented in sackcloth and ashes, and judgment was mercifully delayed.

A Prophetic Pattern: Repentance or Ruin—But Nineveh's story doesn't end there. Roughly a century later, the prophet Nahum declared the city's final doom. This time, no eclipse, no warning, no invitation to repent—only judgment. "Behold, I am against you," declares the Lord in Nahum 3:5. The same city that once responded to grace now resisted it, and, as Irene whispered in *The Trumpet II: The Prophecy Continues—America's Final Hour Unveiled*, "It's like we're living in the space between Jonah and Nahum."

That is the tension in which America—and indeed much of the Gentile world—now finds itself. The Great American Eclipses of 2017 and 2024 formed a massive "X" across the heart of the nation, intersecting precisely over Carbondale, Illinois—known as the "Crossroads of America." But more haunting is this: the 2024 eclipse passed over seven towns named *Nineveh*.

That's no coincidence. It's a divine parallel. A harbinger. Just as ancient Nineveh was given forty days to repent, could America have been given seven years—from 2017 to 2024? And now, from 2024 to 2028, are we in a final window of mercy? A symbolic four-year extension—a prophetic echo of "40" reduced to 4 (4 + 0 = 4)—grace before judgment?

Solar Eclipses and Global Upheaval—This prophetic pattern is not isolated. Throughout history, solar eclipses have often aligned with seasons of global shaking and transition. Consider the total solar eclipse of August 21, 1914, which swept across Eastern Europe just weeks after the assassination of Archduke Franz Ferdinand—the flashpoint that ignited World War I. As day turned to darkness, the world soon plunged into one of the bloodiest and most transformative conflicts in human history.

The same pattern surrounds the rise and fall of the powers involved in World War II:

- On August 31, 1932, a total solar eclipse crossed parts of Europe and Asia—seven years before the official outbreak of World War II in 1939. Many see this seven-year gap as prophetically symbolic, echoing the biblical number of completion or warning.
- Then, on February 14, 1934, another total solar eclipse passed directly over Nazi Germany. That same year, Adolf Hitler became Fuhrer, consolidating absolute power. Darkness fell over a nation whose leader would unleash unimaginable evil upon the world.
- Finally, on July 9, 1945, a total solar eclipse passed over Japan, mere weeks before the United States dropped atomic bombs on Hiroshima and Nagasaki, ending the war. It was as if heaven itself bracketed the conflict, marking both the rise of tyranny and the moment of judgment.

God does not cause the evil—but He often permits the shaking, and He always sends a warning. Solar eclipses are not cosmic accidents—they are celestial signals, embedded into Creation and aligned with divine order.

The pattern is sobering: where there is a solar eclipse, unrest often follows—plagues, wars, famines, revolutions. The judgment may not fall immediately, but it is almost always inevitable—unless repentance interrupts the descent.

A Jonah Moment or a Nahum Judgment?—We are once again at a crossroads—the same prophetic fork in the road that faced Nineveh. Do we humble ourselves, fast and pray, and turn back to God? Or do we mock the signs, silence the watchmen, and persist in rebellion, thinking judgment will never come?

God gave us the sun, moon, and stars for signs—not entertainment. And when the sun goes dark across the land, when seven towns named Nineveh lie in its shadow, when two solar eclipses form a Cross over a divided nation, it is no longer just astronomy—it is prophecy in motion.

This is our Jonah moment. But what follows may very well be our Nahum reckoning—unless we, like the Ninevites of old, fall to our knees, not in fear, but in repentance.

The Great American Eclipses: 2017 and 2024

When God speaks through the heavens, it's never random. The two solar eclipses that crossed the United States in 2017 and 2024 were not merely stunning astronomical events—they were, and remain, prophetic warnings written across the sky. These were signs of national consequence, delivered in the language of light and shadow, and marked by the precision of God's calendar—not man's.

The Great American Eclipses: 2017 and 2024—On August 21, 2017, a total solar eclipse swept across the continental United States from Oregon to South Carolina, moving from west to east—a reversal of the typical prophetic direction (east to west), which may symbolize a nation turning away from God.

But more astonishing than its path was its timing.

At the exact moment the eclipse reached totality over the U.S., the sun set in Jerusalem at 7:16 PM IDT. It was as if darkness fell simultaneously on the land of the covenant and the land once blessed by covenantal grace. This was no cosmic coincidence. It was a celestial punctuation mark.

The eclipse occurred on the 1st day of Elul on the Hebrew calendar—the beginning of the month of repentance that leads to the High Holy Days of *Rosh HaShanah* and *Yom Kippur*. Elul, in Hebrew thought, is a time for spiritual harvest, introspection, and preparation for judgment. It means "gathering," and the timing of this eclipse signaled a divine invitation to America: Repent. Return. Prepare for what's coming.

The Eclipse of April 8, 2024: A Prophetic Marker—Seven years later, on April 8, 2024, a second total solar eclipse crossed the U.S.—but this time from Texas to Maine, creating a diagonal line in the opposite direction. This eclipse occurred on Nisan 1, the first day of the Hebrew religious year, marking the beginning of God's calendar of redemption—the same calendar that starts the countdown to Passover in the Exodus.

Nisan 1 is not just a date—it is a divine threshold. It represents new beginnings, deliverance, and the setting in motion of God's redemptive timeline. To have a total solar eclipse fall on this very day, and to do so in a nation already marked by a previous eclipse, is profoundly prophetic.

The path of the 2024 eclipse intersected perfectly with the 2017 path, forming a massive "X" over the American heartland, specifically over the New Madrid Seismic Zone—a region known for one of the most powerful earthquake series in U.S. history. The crossing point near Carbondale, Illinois, has been called the "Crossroads of America," and prophetically, it may very well be just that.

Prophetic Geography: The "X" That Marks the Warning—This celestial "X" does more than draw lines—it traces judgment zones. The combined eclipse paths intersect three major fault lines:

- The Cascadia Subduction Zone—Pacific Northwest.
- The Yellowstone Caldera—supervolcano hot spot.
- The New Madrid Seismic Zone—Central U.S.

These are not just geological features. In prophetic context, they become the fault lines of divine warning, especially when coupled with Revelation 16:18–19, which describes Babylon the Great (America) being split into three parts—a judgment against a once great power corrupted by pride and rebellion.

A Final Warning?—The two eclipses form a seven-year warning window—a biblical timeframe echoing both Shemitah cycles and prophetic patterns of completion and transition. And now, with the second eclipse of 2024 behind us, we may have entered what some call "the Jonah countdown"—a final four-year season of mercy before a decisive moment arrives in 2028/2029.

Will the nation respond like ancient Nineveh under Jonah, or resist like Nineveh in the days of Nahum?

The sky has spoken. The "X" is drawn. The timing is divine. The geography is prophetic. Whether the message is heeded is now up to us.

America and Isaiah 18

The question has echoed for decades: Is America in the Bible? While the United States is not mentioned by name, many scholars and watchmen believe there are prophetic shadows and national characteristics embedded in certain passages—none more compelling than Isaiah 18.

> Woe to the land shadowing with wings, which is beyond the rivers of Ethiopia: that sends ambassadors by the sea, even in vessels of bulrushes upon the waters, saying, Go, you swift messengers, to a nation scattered and peeled (tall and smooth of skin), to a people awe-inspiring from their beginning hitherto; a nation powerful and treading down, whose land the rivers divided! All you inhabitants of the world, and dwellers on the earth, see you, when He lifts up an ensign to the mountains; and when He blows a trumpet, hear you. (Isaiah 18:1–3)

Isaiah's vision describes a land beyond the rivers of Cush (kingdoms south of Egypt—primarily in Nubia (Sudan) but also extending into Ethiopia), sending ambassadors by sea, a people tall and smooth, awe-inspiring, and feared far and wide. It speaks of a nation that raises a banner and blows a trumpet—two powerful images for global influence through both culture and leadership. When viewed through a modern lens, many of these descriptions fit the United States with uncanny clarity.

A Land Divided by Rivers—Isaiah 19:5–8 speaks of a land divided by rivers—a rare geographical trait. The Mississippi River, the largest in North America, cuts the United States in half from north to south. At the same time, the Ohio River forms key state borders and joins the Mississippi at the precise intersection point of the 2017 and 2024 solar eclipses—the Crossroads of America.

> And the waters shall fail from the sea, and the river shall be wasted and dried up. And they shall turn the rivers far away; and the brooks of defense shall be emptied and dried up: the reeds and flags (rushes) shall wither. The paper (papyrus) reeds by the brooks, by the mouth of the brooks, and everything sown by the brooks, shall wither, be driven away, and be no more. The fishermen also shall mourn, and all they that cast angle (hooks) into the brooks shall lament, and they that spread nets upon the waters shall languish. (Isaiah 19:5–8)

This is not just poetic imagery. It is prophetic geography. When the two eclipse paths marked an "X" across the New Madrid Seismic Zone—right at the convergence of these two rivers—it appeared to underline Isaiah's vision with divine precision.

A Nation of Tall and Smooth-Skinned People—Isaiah describes "tall and smooth of skin" (Isaiah 18:2). While this phrase may seem obscure to modern ears, it offers a striking contrast to the bearded, rugged norms of ancient Middle Eastern cultures. In prophetic metaphor, it reflects a people distinguished by their polished appearance, clean-shaven image, and cultural emphasis on external presentation—traits long associated with Western ideals.

When viewed through this lens, the American preoccupation with image, stature, and visual influence resonates powerfully with Isaiah's description.

And then there is the line: "a people awesome from their beginning hitherto" (Isaiah 18:2). From its founding in 1776, America rose rapidly to global prominence—feared by enemies, admired by allies, and unmatched in military strength, economic reach, and cultural influence.

The Banner and the Trumpet—Isaiah 18 continues: "All you inhabitants of the world, and dwellers on the earth, see you, when He lifts up an ensign (banner) on the mountains; and when He blows a trumpet, hear you" (Isaiah 18:3).

What modern nation is more associated with a banner than the Star-Spangled Banner—the very name of the American flag and national anthem? And what other leader in recent history has captured global attention with every tweet, sound bite, or policy declaration like a modern trumpet blast?

Some have even pointed to President Trump as a possible "trumpet" figure—not because he is the fulfillment of this verse, but because his leadership coincided with a surge of prophetic awakenings and national polarity. Whether one admires or rejects him, his role in amplifying the American voice on the world stage is undeniable.

Isaiah 18:7—A Tribute to Mount Zion—The chapter closes with a powerful image: "In that time shall the present be brought to the LORD of hosts of a people scattered and peeled . . . to the place of the name of the LORD of hosts, the Mount Zion" (Isaiah 18:7).

> In that time shall the present be brought unto the LORD of hosts of a people scattered and peeled, and from a people awesome from their beginning hitherto; a nation meted out and trodden under foot, whose land the rivers have divided, to the place of the name of the LORD of hosts, the Mount Zion. (Isaiah 18:7)

This suggests a future moment in which this nation brings tribute to Jerusalem, not as a conqueror, but as a servant and worshiper. Despite its current decline, could America still fulfill this redemptive role in the end times?

America at a Crossroads: Babylon the Great?—While Isaiah 18 offers a glimmer of hope—a nation bringing tribute to Zion—Revelation 17 and 18 cast a much darker shadow. Many prophecy teachers believe America may fulfill the role of Babylon the Great: a once-powerful, luxurious empire now corrupted by idolatry, immorality, and spiritual confusion.

It is no coincidence that the nation with the world's greatest military and largest economy is also a global exporter of pornography, materialism, and rebellion against God's Word. The same country that once sent out missionaries now legalizes sin and silences truth.

So, which will it be?

A gift to Zion—or fire from heaven?

Isaiah 18's tribute—or Revelation 18's collapse?

The Crossroads Before Us—The answer may lie in which prophetic path the nation chooses next. The "X" formed by the solar eclipses, the split of rivers, the rising moral confusion, and the cultural shaking all seem to say the same thing: America is standing at a prophetic crossroads.

Will she repent like Nineveh in Jonah's day or fall like Babylon in Revelation? Only time will tell. But the message of Isaiah 18 is clear: God sees the nations. He weighs their actions. And He calls even the most powerful to humility, obedience, and surrender.

Historical Patterns and Future Warnings

God's patterns rarely change. He is a God of order, rhythm, and mercy—but also of judgment. And history testifies that solar eclipses have often served as markers of significant global upheaval, particularly when they pass over a specific nation. The United States is no exception.

1918 Solar Eclipse and the Spanish Flu—Consider the solar eclipse of June 8, 1918, which swept across the continental United States—from Washington State to Florida—cutting diagonally across the heart of the nation. Just months later, the world was devastated by the outbreak of the Spanish Flu, a pandemic that would claim between 50 to 100 million lives globally, including 675,000 Americans.

But this was no ordinary flu. It emerged with explosive speed and a terrifying death toll—striking down the young and healthy, overwhelming hospitals, and reshaping societies in its wake. Though scientists still debate its precise origin, the timing is hard to ignore.

Once again, the pattern appears: a sign in the heavens, followed by a shaking on the earth.

Prophetic Echoes in the Present—Fast forward to the 21st century. In 2017 and 2024, the United States witnessed two more total solar eclipses, each crossing the entire country in opposite directions—forming a perfect "X" over the New Madrid Seismic Zone. This isn't random geometry. It's prophetic geography.

The "X" intersects at the convergence of the Mississippi and Ohio Rivers, symbolizing both literal and spiritual division. In Scripture, the imagery of "splitting" or "dividing" a land often precedes judgment—especially for nations that turn away from God.

The New Madrid Fault Line is known for some of the most powerful earthquakes in American history, and it lies directly beneath this intersecting path. Add to this the presence of seven towns named Nineveh under the 2024 eclipse route, and a sobering question arises: What happens to a nation that ignores the signs, mocks repentance, and persists in pride?

"X" Marks the Spot—Throughout history, God has marked nations before bringing judgment. The "X" formed by these eclipses appears to be a divine exclamation point.

Whether the next shaking comes through earthquakes, economic collapse, global war, or another pandemic, the pattern is clear: When the sun darkens over a nation, it's time to watch, to warn, and to weep.

But there is still hope. Every warning is a mercy. Every sign is an invitation. The question is not whether God is speaking. He already has.

The question is: Is America listening?

LUNAR ECLIPSES AND BLOOD MOONS: WARNINGS TO ISRAEL

Solar eclipses often serve as wake-up calls to the Gentile nations—but lunar eclipses, especially blood moons, are divine warnings directed toward Israel. In biblical symbolism, just as the sun rules the day, the moon rules the night—and prophetically, the moon represents Israel, God's covenant people. These celestial events are not coincidences; they are God-ordained markers, written into the heavens and synchronized with His sacred calendar. Every lunar eclipse that aligns with Israel's feast days is a message from above, echoing through time and prophecy to capture Israel's attention and call her back to covenant.

Biblical Foundations: God's Calendar Is Lunar

From the very beginning, God established the moon as a prophetic timekeeper. In Genesis 1:14, He declared that the heavenly bodies would serve as "signs, seasons (*moedim*), days, and years." These *moedim*—appointed times—are not human inventions but divine appointments woven into Creation itself.

In Leviticus 23, God commands Israel to observe His feasts in alignment with the moon and the agricultural rhythms of the land. Each biblical feast—from Passover to the Feast of Tabernacles (*Sukkot*)—is rooted in the lunar cycle, with full moons illuminating the major feast days. It is precisely on these full moons that lunar eclipses—blood moons—can occur, making them prophetically significant.

The start of each Hebrew month is marked by *Rosh Chodesh*, the new moon, and the entire biblical (religious) calendar is lunar in structure, making the moon not only a celestial body but a sacred timepiece. It tracks the rhythm of redemption, covenant, and prophecy for Israel.

Blood Moons: Israel's Warning Signs

A blood moon occurs during a total lunar eclipse, when the earth's shadow refracts sunlight and casts a deep red glow across the moon. While these events are awe-inspiring in themselves, their true prophetic weight is revealed when they align with Israel's biblical feast days—Passover, *Sukkot*, and other appointed times on God's calendar.

In the Bible, the moon represents Israel, a nation bound to God by covenant and history. Scripture links blood moons to divine warnings: "The sun shall be turned into darkness, and the moon into blood, before the great and terrible Day of the LORD" (Joel 2:31), echoed in Acts 2:20.

> The sun shall be turned into darkness, and the moon into blood, before that great and notable Day of the Lord come. (Acts 2:20)

Throughout history, tetrads—four consecutive blood moons—have often coincided with critical moments for the Jewish people, such as the expulsion from Spain (1492), the rebirth of Israel (1948), and the recapture of Jerusalem (1967). These are not coincidences, but covenant signals in the sky: God is speaking to His people.

The Blood Moon Tetrads: Verified and Rare

In as recent as 2014 and 2015, the world witnessed an extraordinary astronomical phenomenon—a blood moon tetrad. This rare sequence of four consecutive total lunar eclipses, each aligning precisely with the biblical feasts of Passover and *Sukkot*, captured the attention of both scientists and students of prophecy. Verified by astronomers around the world, this tetrad was not folklore or superstition—it was a documented celestial pattern, observable through both modern technology and the naked eye.

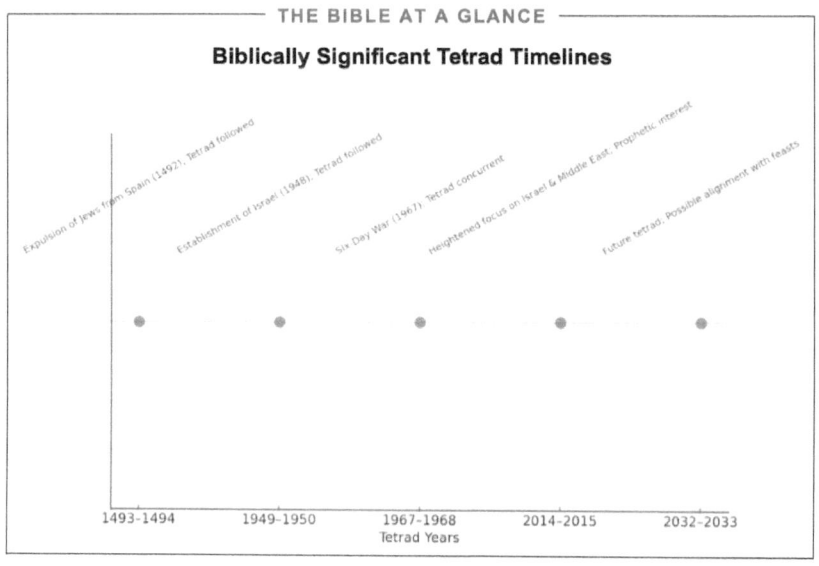

Figure 5 – Biblically Significant Tetrad Timelines

What makes the 2014–2015 tetrad so prophetically striking is not only its rarity, but the historical echo it shares with previous tetrads that also aligned with God's feast days. In the past five centuries, only a few such tetrads have occurred, and each has marked a defining moment in Jewish history:

- 1492–1493—During the height of the Spanish Inquisition, the Jewish people were expelled from Spain, their communities shattered and scattered across Europe and the Middle East. This traumatic displacement followed a tetrad of blood moons that seemed to underscore the judgment and suffering of a covenant people in exile.
- 1949–1950—In the aftermath of Israel's rebirth in 1948, the fledgling nation fought for survival in its War of Independence. The tetrad that followed stood as a heavenly seal of affirmation, echoing Ezekiel's prophecy of dry bones rising into a living nation.
- 1967–1968—The Six-Day War erupted in June 1967, culminating in the miraculous reunification of Jerusalem under Jewish sovereignty for the first time in nearly 2,000 years. The blood moons during this tetrad cast a celestial spotlight on one of Israel's most significant prophetic victories.
- 2014–2015—While its full significance may still be unfolding, this tetrad marked a season of heightened global tension for Israel. During Operation Protective Edge in summer 2014, Israel faced a barrage of rockets from Gaza. Simultaneously, antisemitism surged across Europe and beyond, with violent attacks against Jewish communities, including the Hyper Cacher market shooting in Paris in early 2015. This intense global pressure mirrored Zechariah 12:3, which warned that Jerusalem would become a burdensome stone to the nations—a prophetic indication of Israel's increasing isolation on the world stage.

What makes these alignments so compelling is their mathematical precision. These blood moons didn't just happen to appear near Jewish holidays—they landed exactly on God's appointed feast days, without deviation. Such precision, repeated through history, defies coincidence and demands attention. It signals that God is speaking, using the moon—His prophetic clock for Israel—as a loudspeaker to His people and to the world.

These tetrads have been verified by NASA and astronomers worldwide, and their alignment with Israel's most pivotal moments cannot be explained away as mere chance. They serve as a prophetic pulse, beating in time with God's covenantal dealings with Israel—both in discipline and in deliverance.

The question is no longer if God is using the heavens to speak to His people. The question is: Are we listening?

Tetrads and Tribulations: What Happened in 2014–2015

The blood moon tetrad of 2014–2015 didn't occur in a prophetic vacuum—it unfolded during a season of dramatic global upheaval and escalating tension in the Middle East. These weren't quiet years on the world stage. Instead, they were filled with tribulation, terror, and turmoil, echoing the ancient patterns that have often accompanied celestial warnings directed at Israel and the nations.

A Convergence of Crisis—During this two-year span, the world witnessed the rapid rise of ISIS and the birth of a new reign of terror across Iraq and Syria. In a matter of months, the Islamic State established a so-called caliphate and began its brutal persecution of Christians, Yazidis, and other minorities. The atrocities committed—mass executions, crucifixions, and beheadings—shocked the world and marked one of the bloodiest campaigns against Christians in modern history.

Simultaneously, Israel was at war. In July and August of 2014, during the summer leading up to the first blood moon, Hamas launched thousands of rockets into Israeli territory. Israel responded with Operation Protective Edge, a full-scale military operation aimed at dismantling terrorists infrastructure in Gaza. Over 4,500 rockets were fired at Israeli cities, pushing the nation to the brink and drawing intense global criticism.

As this tension mounted, international diplomacy focused on Iran. In 2015, the United States and other world powers signed the Joint Comprehensive Plan of Action (JCPOA)—commonly known as the Iran Nuclear Deal. This controversial agreement, which aimed to curb Iran's nuclear ambitions in exchange for sanctions relief, was seen by many in Israel as a strategic threat to their survival, especially given Iran's open hostility toward the Jewish state.

A Blood Moon Over Passover—Perhaps the most sobering moment of the tetrad came on April 4, 2015, when a blood moon appeared on the Feast of Passover. Rather than marking a time of protection and deliverance as it did in the days of Exodus, this Passover was marked by intensified global violence, persecution, and unrest. Reports of Christian martyrdom, terror attacks, and antisemitic incidents reached record levels during this time, especially across Europe and the Middle East.

Not Coincidence—Correlation—The timing of these events, lined up with God's sacred calendar, cannot be dismissed. When blood moons fall on biblical feast days, and those very seasons are accompanied by global instability and rising pressure against Israel, the pattern becomes hard to ignore. It's as if the heavens are echoing the words of the prophets—calling Israel to alertness, and the world to repentance.

These blood moons weren't just beautiful spectacles in the sky. They were red flags waving from heaven, calling attention to a world in crisis and a people at the center of God's prophetic timetable.

Supermoons and Signs in the Sky

Not all blood moons are created equal. In several remarkable cases, these lunar eclipses have aligned with supermoons—celestial events when the moon is at its closest point to Earth in its elliptical orbit. During a supermoon, the moon appears larger, brighter, and more dramatic in the night sky, intensifying the visual impact and the prophetic resonance of the event.

What Is a Supermoon?—A supermoon occurs when a full moon coincides with perigee, the point in the moon's orbit where it is nearest to Earth. This can make the moon appear up to 14 percent larger and 30 percent brighter than a typical full moon. When a total lunar eclipse—a blood moon—happens during a supermoon, the effect is stunning: a giant, red-tinged moon hanging in the sky, demanding the world's attention.

A Heightened Heavenly Alarm—The Bible speaks of such awe-inspiring celestial phenomena as warnings of divine intervention and coming judgment. When the moon turns to blood during a supermoon, the visual and prophetic intensity is magnified.

These events are not merely poetic metaphors—they are literal, observable signs in the heavens, aligning precisely with the biblical pattern: warning before judgment, awakening before crisis, and grace before wrath.

In such moments, the heavens are not just beautiful—they are urgent. The moon's deep red glow becomes more than a spectacle; it becomes a heavenly alarm bell, calling God's people to discernment, repentance, and readiness.

A Call to Watchfulness—Supermoons during feast-aligned blood moons serve as a kind of divine spotlight, illuminating the spiritual urgency of the times. These aren't coincidental lunar events—they are heavenly megaphones, proclaiming the nearness of prophetic fulfillment and urging both Israel and the Church to be alert, prepared, and spiritually awake.

Throughout history, certain supermoons have aligned with global upheavals, Jewish feast days, or remarkable celestial conditions. The following data highlights several recent, prophetically significant supermoons:

- January 21, 2000—Closest supermoon in 133 years (356,461 km).

- March 19, 2011—First widely publicized modern supermoon.
- 2014–2015 Blood Moon Tetrad—Four total lunar eclipses occurred on Passover and Feast of Tabernacles in two consecutive years:
  - April 15, 2014—Passover
  - October 8, 2014—Tabernacles
  - April 4, 2015—Passover
  - September 28, 2015—Feast of Tabernacles (also a supermoon and total lunar eclipse)

- November 14, 2016—Closest full supermoon since 1948, the year Israel became a nation.
- January 31, 2018—Super blue blood moon—total lunar eclipse + second full moon of the month.
- April 8, 2020—Brightest supermoon of the year, occurring during COVID-19 global lockdowns.
- August 30, 2023—Rare blue supermoon—the second full moon in a single month and a supermoon, but not a blood moon (no total lunar eclipse). A blue supermoon of this kind won't occur again until 2037.

What about blue supermoons?

A blue moon refers to the second full moon in a single calendar month. Despite the name, the moon doesn't actually turn blue—the term refers purely to timing, not color. Blue moons occur approximately once every 2.5 to 3 years.

A blue supermoon occurs when this rare second full moon also coincides with the moon's closest approach to Earth—a supermoon. The result is a larger, brighter, more visually striking full moon. This alignment happens only about once every 10 to 20 years.

While "blue moon" is not a biblical term, the timing and dramatic visibility of blue supermoons—especially when aligned with Jewish feast days or lunar eclipses—often draws the attention of prophetic watchmen. Many view them as heavenly signposts, emphasizing urgency, divine timing, or coming judgment.

A final reminder:

In a world numbed by distraction, God still speaks through the sky. And when the moon glows red and looms large, it's not just astronomy—it's a signpost from heaven.

Solar Eclipses: Bookends to the Blood Moons

While the blood moon tetrads of 2014–2015 captured global attention with their prophetic timing on Jewish feast days, few realize that these lunar eclipses were framed—or "bookended"—by two remarkable solar eclipses, both falling on days of deep biblical significance. These celestial bookmarks reveal a deliberate, divine orchestration of time, reinforcing that God's prophetic calendar operates with precise symmetry.

Two Eclipses. Two Calendars. One Message—In 2015, two solar eclipses occurred on two of the most sacred days in the biblical calendar—marking both the religious and civil New Year of Israel. To the casual observer, they may have seemed like nothing more than astronomical events. But to those attuned to God's prophetic patterns, they sounded a deeper alarm: a call to spiritual urgency.

- March 20, 2015—total solar eclipse:
    - Occurred on 1 Nisan, the biblical religious New Year.
    - Fell just two weeks before Passover.
    - Not visible in the U.S.; seen across Europe, the Arctic, and the North Atlantic.
    - Considered prophetically significant because of its timing before a major feast.

- September 13, 2015—partial solar eclipse:
    - Fell on 1 Tishri—*Rosh HaShanah*, the Feast of Trumpets.
    - Marks the civil New Year on the Hebrew calendar.
    - Related to judgment, repentance, and the coronation of the King.
    - Also not visible in the U.S.; seen primarily in southern Africa and Antarctica.

Together, these two eclipses framed the final blood moon of the much discussed 2014–2015 tetrad, which occurred on September 28, 2015, during the Feast of Tabernacles—and was also a supermoon. The clustering of these three prophetic sky events in such close proximity created a rare and powerful convergence, which many see as divine alignment with God's appointed times.

In contrast to the globally dispersed solar eclipses of 2015, the Great American Eclipses of 2017 and 2024 have uniquely centered on the United States, capturing the attention of prophetic voices and watchmen around the world.

- August 21, 2017—total solar eclipse:
    - Visible coast to coast across the continental U.S., from Oregon to South Carolina.
    - Dubbed the "Great American Eclipse" for its unprecedented national visibility.
    - Viewed by many as a prophetic sign and warning to the nation.

- April 8, 2024—total solar eclipse:
    - Swept across the U.S. in the opposite direction, from Texas to Maine.
    - Its path intersected the 2017 eclipse in Carbondale, Illinois—called the "Crossroads of America."
    - Together, the two paths form a giant "X" or Cross over the center of the nation, prompting reflection on divine marking and national accountability.

These two are collectively known as the Great American Eclipses—not only for their visibility across the United States, but for their symbolic weight. Where the 2015 eclipses aligned with God's calendar, the 2017 an 2024 eclipses appear to zero in on a single nation, as if God is not only marking time—but calling out a place.

To the natural eye, these events may seem like cosmic coincidences. But to those attuned to the signs and seasons of God, they are heavenly confirmations—declaring that the season is not only historically significant, but spiritually urgent.

Spiritual Alignment and Sovereign Design—The alignment of a solar eclipse on both the religious and civil New Year in the same biblical year is exceedingly rare. This dual marking highlights the sovereignty of God over sacred time, drawing attention to a divinely appointed window in history. It's as if God pressed pause on the calendar year 2015 to say: "Watch. Listen. Repent."

This framing further emphasizes the theme found throughout Scripture: that God rules over time and nations, declaring "the end from the beginning" (Isaiah 46:10). Just as solar eclipses symbolize warnings to the nations, these two events flanking the blood moons serve as celestial parentheses, enclosing a prophetic season of warning, upheaval, and divine invitation.

Heavenly Order, Earthly Wake-Up—In the bookends of these solar eclipses, we see more than cosmic activity—we see a God who speaks in patterns, who calls through Creation, and who leaves no excuse for apathy. The heavens are not silent. They are declaring His glory, His timing, and His urgency.

God's Poetic Clock: Supermoons, Eclipses, and Biblical Timing

In the symphony of Creation, God has not only ordained time—He's composed it with poetic brilliance. Nowhere is this more evident than in the extraordinary convergence of astronomical events that took place during the blood moon season 2014–2015. These were not just cosmic coincidences; they were once-in-history alignments that stitched together Scripture, science, and symbolism in profound ways.

The Divine Convergence: Eclipse + Supermoon + Equinox + 1 Nisan—On March 20, 2015, a total solar eclipse occurred on 1 Nisan—the first day of the biblical religious calendar. But this was no ordinary eclipse. It coincided with the spring equinox, a moment when day and night are perfectly balanced. To complete the pattern, it occurred during a supermoon, when the moon is closest to Earth and appears larger in the sky.

Think about the symbolism:

- 1 Nisan marks new beginnings, redemption, and the preparation for Passover.
- The equinox represents perfect balance—light and darkness in equal measure.
- A supermoon amplifies the moon's visual presence, reminding us of the intensity of God's message.
- A solar eclipse, visible from specific regions, acts as a divine "pause" button—darkness momentarily overtaking light.

This combination of events is so astronomically rare that it stands as a celestial signature of divine authorship—a moment where God signed His calendar with majesty and meaning.

Numbers That Speak: The Prophetic Role of Hebrew Gematria—In Hebrew, numbers often carry symbolic and prophetic weight. For example, the number 44, associated with the Hebrew word *dam* meaning blood, appeared repeatedly during the blood moon sequence. The final blood moon of the tetrad—September 28, 2015—occurred on day 44 of the Jewish counting of repentance (Elul into Tishri). These patterns weren't engineered by man but written into the fabric of time by God Himself.

Even secular astronomers and mathematicians, though not understanding the spiritual significance, have marveled at the elegance and symmetry of these alignments. For the believer, this is a reminder that God speaks in both prose and poetry—in prophecy and in the poetry of the heavens. (While the study of Hebrew gematria is beyond the scope of this book, its prophetic patterns play a meaningful role in the restoration God is orchestrating.)

Heaven's Rhythm, Earth's Reminder—God's poetic clock ticks with purpose. He doesn't waste movement. He aligns the heavens to mark His appointed times, signal His warnings, and comfort His people—assuring them that He is in control, even when the earth shakes or nations rage.

In these rare alignments, we get a glimpse of not just His power, but His personality—a Creator who speaks with artistry and authority. These aren't merely astronomical facts; they are prophetic poetry, telling a story that is still unfolding in our generation.

Israel in Conflict: Fulfillment of Zechariah 12:3

The modern state of Israel, reborn in 1948, has never known a day without controversy. Its very existence continues to stir the nations—and this is no historical accident. It is prophecy fulfilled in real-time, aligning precisely with Zechariah 12:3:

> And in that day will I make Jerusalem a burdensome stone for all people: all that burden themselves with it shall be cut in pieces, though all the people of the earth be gathered together against it. (Zechariah 12:3)

Jerusalem: The World's Pressure Point—Jerusalem—only a small city in terms of geography—is a spiritual epicenter. It holds deep religious significance for Jews, Christians, and Muslims alike, and its status as Israel's capital has placed it under an international microscope. During the 2014–2015 blood moon tetrad, this tension intensified dramatically.

The UN passed multiple resolutions condemning Israel, world leaders issued public rebukes, and violent protests and terror attacks surged. These years saw the Gaza War (Operation Protective Edge), the Iranian nuclear deal, and a sharp rise in global antisemitism. Throughout all of it, Jerusalem remained at the center—an unrelenting flashpoint in world affairs.

Heavenly Signs and Earthly Conflict—What makes this season especially profound is that each blood moon in the tetrad fell on a biblical feast day—Passover or *Sukkot*—while these geopolitical storms raged. These lunar eclipses, visible in parts of the world that directly involve Israel's allies and enemies, seemed to synchronize with moments of prophetic significance. These weren't just blood moons; they were divine billboards, flashing red in the night sky.

In a world where Israel is increasingly isolated, misunderstood, and opposed, the moon has become a silent witness. Each blood moon during these High Holy Days appears to echo Zechariah's warning: "All that burden themselves with it shall be cut in pieces."

The Prophetic Spotlight—Israel has become what Scripture said it would be—a burdensome stone. Not because of politics, land, or ethnicity alone, but because Jerusalem is tied to the return of the Messiah. The spiritual warfare surrounding Israel is escalating because history is converging on its final chapters. The signs in the heavens confirm it. The blood moons serve as warnings not just to Israel—but to the nations watching her.

We are living in prophetic times, and Jerusalem is the clock face. To watch her is to read the times. And as blood moons illuminate her feasts while conflict surrounds her borders, we are reminded once again that God's Word is not just true—it is unfolding before our very eyes.

God's Message to Israel—Lunar Eclipses—especially blood moons aligned with feast days—are not mere celestial occurrences. They are divine dispatches from the heavens, woven into the rhythm of God's covenant with Israel. Each one carries a message—not of doom, but of mercy, urgency, and divine attention.

Throughout Scripture, God has used the moon to mark sacred times, call His people to repentance, and signal turning points in redemptive history. When blood moons appear over Passover or *Sukkot*, it's as if God is whispering—sometimes shouting—from the heavens: "My covenant still stands. My calendar is active. My eyes are on Jerusalem."

These signs may herald seasons of conflict, political unrest, or territorial restoration. But above all, they are a call to return—a summons for the nation of Israel to align once more with God's Word, God's will, and God's timing.

Like a trumpet in the sky, blood moons declare:

- "Repent, for the time is near."
- "Remember My covenant."
- "Return to Me while mercy still flows."

God's warnings are never without grace. These lunar signs are divine reminders wrapped in mercy, offering one more opportunity for Israel to seek the Lord while He may be found. They are not random—they are radiant testimonies of a God who still speaks, still loves, and still calls His people home.

SUPER SIGNS: THE REVELATION 12 CELESTIAL ALIGNMENT

From the very beginning, God designed the heavens as divine timepieces—signals for appointed times (Genesis 1:14). On September 23, 2017, a rare astronomical alignment occurred that many believe fulfills Revelation 12:1–2. The constellation Virgo appeared "clothed with the sun," the moon beneath her feet, and a crown of twelve stars formed by Leo and three planets. Meanwhile, Jupiter—the King Planet—had remained in Virgo's womb for 9½ months before exiting like a birth.

This unprecedented alignment—coinciding with the Feast of Trumpets—has been called the most significant celestial sign since Creation. For many, it signals the nearness of the Rapture, the start of the Tribulation, or a divine wake-up call to the Church and Israel alike. The Revelation 12 Sign is not mere coincidence—

it is a prophetic megaphone shouting, "Look up. Pay attention. God's appointed time is near."

The Revelation 12 Sign: What Happened on September 23, 2017?

On September 23, 2017, the heavens displayed what many believe to be one of the most prophetic celestial alignments in history—an event that matched the vision described in Revelation 12:1–2 with stunning detail. It wasn't the result of superstition or amateur speculation; it was a verified astronomical alignment observable in the sky using standard planetarium software. This event became widely known as the "Revelation 12 Sign."

> And there appeared a great wonder in heaven; a woman clothed with the sun, and the moon under her feet, and upon her head a crown of twelve stars. And she being with Child cried, travailing in birth, and pained to be delivered. (Revelation 12:1–2)

Virgo: The Woman Clothed with the Sun—At the heart of the alignment was the constellation Virgo (Latin for *virgin)*, the only female figure in the twelve *Mazzaroth* constellations. On this day, the sun was positioned directly over Virgo's shoulder, symbolically clothing her in light. This fulfilled the first part of the Revelation 12 description: "a woman clothed with the sun." This placement occurs only once a year, but what made September 23, 2017 unique was the stunning convergence of additional prophetic elements.

The Moon Under Her Feet—As Virgo stood clothed in the sun, the moon moved to rest at her feet—another precise detail from the biblical text. This lunar position, occurring in the lower third of Virgo, completed the celestial image with uncanny accuracy. Notably, this arrangement occurred on the Feast of Trumpets (*Rosh HaShanah*), a feast associated in prophecy with the resurrection of the dead and the Rapture of the Church.

The Crown of Twelve Stars—Above Virgo's head was the constellation Leo, which consists of nine primary stars. On this exact date, three additional "wandering stars"—Mercury, Mars, and Venus—moved into alignment with Leo, forming a celestial garland or "crown of twelve stars." This extremely rare conjunction completed the third condition of the Revelation 12 prophecy. Though Mercury, Venus, and Mars each pass through Leo at different times, their simultaneous alignment with Leo's nine stars above Virgo is extraordinarily rare and prophetically significant.

Revelation 12 Sign

A digital star chart of the Revelation 12 Sign on September 23, 2017, showing the constellation Virgo "clothed with the sun," the moon at her feet, and a crown of twelve stars (Leo with Mercury, Mars, and Venus), including decan constellation markers. Jupiter appears in Virgo's "womb," completing a 9-month retrograde, symbolizing prophetic fulfillment from Revelation 12:1-2.

Figure 6 – Revelation 12 Sign

Jupiter: The King Planet in Retrograde Motion—Perhaps the most remarkable feature of this event was the motion of Jupiter, known as the "King Planet" due to its massive size and symbolic meaning in biblical astronomy. Jupiter entered Virgo's womb region on November 20, 2016, and due to its retrograde motion—a temporary apparent reversal in the sky—it remained in Virgo's "womb" for over nine months, mimicking the length of a full-term pregnancy.

Then, immediately after the Revelation 12 Sign appeared, Jupiter exited Virgo, symbolically "being born." This unusual retrograde gestation period is an exceedingly rare phenomenon and was seen by many prophecy watchers as a symbolic "birth of the Male Child" mentioned in Revelation 12:5:

> And she brought forth a Man Child, who was to rule all nations with a rod of iron: and her Child was caught up unto God, and to His throne. (Revelation 12:5)

A Celestial Alignment of Prophetic Proportions—The complete configuration—Virgo clothed with the sun, the moon at her feet, a crown of twelve stars above her head, and Jupiter gestating and exiting from her womb—had never occurred in this exact pattern in recorded history, nor is it expected to occur again for thousands of years. Using astronomical software such as Stellarium, researchers traced back thousands of years and confirmed the rarity of such an alignment. Some scholars suggest that the last time a similar celestial pattern appeared was around 4000 BC—near the traditional date for the Garden of Eden and the beginning of human history according to biblical chronology.

Because of its alignment with the biblical Feast of Trumpets, its correspondence to Revelation 12, and its layered symbolism involving the Church, Israel, and the Messiah, this event was not dismissed by serious Bible scholars and prophecy teachers. Many saw it not as a definitive fulfillment of the Rapture or Tribulation, but rather as a warning beacon in the heavens—a divine alarm signaling that the prophetic clock is nearing midnight.

Why the Revelation 12 Sign Was Considered Historic—The 2017 Revelation 12 Sign was not an isolated curiosity—it was preceded by a tetrad of blood moons in 2014–2015, each aligning with Jewish feast days, and followed by solar eclipses that marked prophetic paths across the United States. Moreover, it fell precisely 1260 days after the first of those blood moons on April 15, 2014, echoing the time period described in Revelation 12:6.

> And the woman fled into the wilderness, where she has a place prepared of God, that they should feed her there a thousand two hundred and threescore (sixty) days. (Revelation 12:6)

This mathematical and astronomical precision was seen by many as evidence of intelligent design—a heavenly sign scripted by the Creator before the foundation of the world. As Genesis 1:14 declares: "And God said, Let there be lights in the firmament of the heaven . . . and let them be for signs, and for seasons, and for days, and years."

The convergence of celestial bodies in this sign led many to believe that we had entered into a final season of grace—a time when the Church is being called to awaken from spiritual slumber, watch the skies, and prepare for the soon return of the Lord.

Biblical Foundation: Revelation 12 in Prophecy

The twelfth chapter of the Book of Revelation opens with one of the most dramatic and multilayered prophetic visions in all of Scripture. To understand the significance of the celestial sign that appeared on September 23, 2017, we must first turn to Revelation 12:1–5 and explore its meanings—literal, symbolic, and prophetic—to lay a solid biblical foundation for interpretation.

> And there appeared a great wonder in heaven; a woman clothed with the sun, and the moon under her feet, and upon her head a crown of twelve stars: And she being with Child cried, travailing in birth, and pained to be delivered. And there appeared another wonder in heaven; and behold a great red dragon, having seven heads and ten horns, and seven crowns upon his heads. And his tail drew the third part of the stars of heaven, and did cast them to the earth: and the dragon stood before the woman, which was ready to be delivered, for to devour her Child as soon as it was born. And she brought forth a Man Child, who was to rule all nations with a rod of iron: and her Child was caught up unto God, and to His throne. (Revelation 12:1–5)

These verses described a "great wonder"—literally, a mega sign in the heavens. This is not a minor vision, but one uniquely marked by the Greek word *megas* to denote its unparalleled importance. It presents an image of a woman clothed with the sun, the moon beneath her feet, and a crown of twelve stars atop her head, crying out in labor to give birth. This cosmic portrayal is both awe-inspiring and mysterious, begging the question: who is the woman?

The Woman: Israel, Mary—or Both?—Many scholars interpret the woman in Revelation 12 as a symbol of Israel, based on strong scriptural parallels. In Genesis 37:9–10, Joseph's dream features the sun, moon, and twelve stars, symbolizing his father Jacob (Israel), his mother Rachel, and the twelve tribes of Israel. This imagery directly echoes Revelation 12:1, connecting the woman to the nation of Israel through whom the Messiah was born.

Others, particularly within Catholic tradition, interpret the woman more literally as Mary, the mother of Jesus. This view finds resonance in her role in the nativity and in spiritual motherhood.

However, most evangelical and prophetic scholars favor the symbolic identification of the woman as Israel, especially in light of the broader narrative involving Tribulation, persecution, and end-time preservation.

Some also suggest that the woman may be seen as a composite figure, reflecting multiple prophetic layers:

- Israel's role in birthing the Messiah,
- Her future suffering and protection during the Tribulation,
- And even the Church's eschatological identity as the Bride of Christ.

This multi-dimensional interpretation allows the text to remain faithful to both historical fulfillment and future prophetic unfolding.

The Male Child: Jesus, the Church—or Both?

> And she brought forth a Man Child, who was to rule all nations with a rod of iron: and her Child was caught up unto God, and to His throne. (Revelation 12:5)

Traditionally, the Male Child in Revelation 12:5 has been interpreted as Jesus Christ. This is strongly supported by the phrase, "to rule all nations with a rod of iron"—a direct reference to Psalm 2:9 and Revelation 19:15, both messianic in nature:

> You shalt break them with a rod of iron; You shalt dash them in pieces like a potter's vessel. (Psalm 2:9)

> And out of His mouth goes a sharp sword, that with it He should smite the nations: and He shall rule them with a rod of iron: and He treads the winepress of the fierceness and wrath of Almighty God. (Revelation 19:15)

However, in recent years, many prophecy scholars and watchers have proposed a dual fulfillment. The Greek word for "caught up" (*harpazo*) is the same word used in 1 Thessalonians 4:17 to describe the Rapture of the Church. This raises the possibility that the Male Child may also represent the faithful remnant of the Church—those who will be raptured before the Tribulation Age begins.

This interpretation gains traction particularly in light of the Revelation 12 Sign observed on September 23, 2017, where astronomical alignments mirrored the imagery of the woman, Child, and dragon. If the woman is a collective symbol (Israel, and possibly the Church), and the dragon represents a global satanic system, then it's reasonable to explore a corporate meaning for the "Male Child" as well.

Thus, while Jesus Christ remains the primary and literal fulfillment, the raptured body of believers—the Church in union with Christ—may represent a secondary, prophetic layer in this text.

The Dragon: Satan and the End-Time Beast System

> And there appeared another wonder in heaven; and behold a great red dragon, having seven heads and ten horns, and seven crowns upon his heads. (Revelation 12:3)

The dragon is later identified in Revelation 12:9 as "that old serpent, called the Devil, and Satan," making it unmistakably clear who this figure represents. His grotesque form—seven heads, ten horns, and seven crowns—mirrors the beast in Revelation 13, signaling more than personal evil: it reflects a satanic system that is geopolitical, religious, and economic in nature. This alignment points to the rise of an antichrist empire, animated by Satan and hostile to God's people and purposes.

The image of the dragon's tail drawing a third of the stars of heaven and casting them to the earth is widely interpreted as the rebellion of Satan, when a third of the angels fell and become demonic forces. But this is more than a past celestial mutiny—it signifies an ongoing cosmic war that extends into the earthly realm. This war is not only among angels, but also between kingdoms, ideologies, and eternal souls.

The War in Heaven and the End-Time Conflict—The events of Revelation 12 serve as a bridge between the heavenly realm and earthly history. The dragon's attempt to devour the Male Child at birth reflects Satan's ongoing effort to thwart God's redemptive plan—seen historically in Pharaoh's slaughter of Hebrew infants, Herod's massacre in Bethlehem, and prophetically in the future persecution of the saints during the Tribulation Age.

The sequence of the Child being caught up, the woman fleeing into the wilderness, and the dragon being cast down sets the stage for a cosmic war, described vividly in Revelation 12:7–9, where Michael and his angels battle the dragon and his forces.

This eschatological conflict is not merely symbolic; it signals a spiritual war with global consequences, where celestial signs, biblical prophecy, and geopolitical unrest intersect. The reference to 1,260 days (Revelation 12:6) corresponds precisely to 3½ years, or time, times, and half a time—a prophetic period echoed in Daniel 7:25, Daniel 12:7, and Revelation 11:2–3, commonly understood as the second half of the Tribulation—the Great Tribulation.

Why This Was a Once-in-Human-History Alignment

Among the multitude of celestial events that fill our night skies, few—if any—have matched the prophetic precision, symbolic detail, and historical rarity of what occurred on September 23, 2017. The alignment described in Revelation

12:1–2 was not just an astronomical curiosity; it was a divine appointment woven into the fabric of time since the foundations of the world. The convergence of prophetic elements on that date created a once-in-human-history celestial proclamation that should not be dismissed.

NASA Star Maps Confirmed the Rarity—NASA's publicly accessible astronomy software, including JPL's Solar System Simulator and programs like Stellarium, have made it possible to rewind and fast-forward celestial movements. Using these resources, prophecy researchers and astronomers alike have confirmed that the exact configuration described in Revelation 12:1–2—with the woman (Virgo) clothed in the sun, the moon at her feet, and crown of twelve stars—has never before occurred in this specific arrangement with such remarkable precision.

While similar configurations have happened in portions or fragments, never has all the following occurred simultaneously:

- The sun positioned directly over Virgo's shoulder, clothing her.
- The moon beneath her feet, in perfect alignment.
- Twelve stars above her head formed by the nine stars of Leo combined with Mercury, Mars, and Venus.
- And most remarkably, the planet Jupiter—often called the "King Planet"—undergoing a retrograde motion inside Virgo's womb for approximately 42 weeks, mimicking the human gestation period, before exiting.

No Previous Alignment Matches the Full Picture—Many skeptics claim that similar celestial formations have happened before. But a careful comparison shows that previous alignments have either lacked Jupiter's extended stay in the womb, the presence of all twelve stars, or the perfect positioning of the sun and moon. According to astronomical records, even a partial resemblance of this event has not occurred for thousands of years—possibly not since the time of Genesis 1–3 and the days of Adam and Eve.

The last time a similar celestial configuration even came close was approximately 5,932 years ago, which aligns closely with biblical estimates for the age of early humanity. But even then, it lacked the complete prophetic signature that defines the 2017 alignment.

A Unique Prophetic Sequence—What sets the 2017 Revelation 12 Sign apart from any other celestial alignment in history is the remarkable prophetic sequence that leads up to it and surrounding it. The 2014–2015 blood moon tetrad—a rare series of total lunar eclipses, all falling on Jewish feast days (Passover and

Sukkot)—served as a global wake-up call, prophetically preparing the way for what would follow.

Then, just two days before the Revelation 12 Sign appeared in the heavens, the Feast of Trumpets was observed—an appointed time long associated with the resurrection of the dead, the Rapture of the Church, and coronation of the King.

Most strikingly, the first blood moon of the tetrad occurred exactly 1,260 days before September 23, 2017. This number appears repeatedly in biblical prophecy (Revelation 12:6; Daniel 7:25; and Revelation 11:2–3), representing 3½ years—the length of Israel's protection in the wilderness and the duration of the Great Tribulation, often identified as the second half of the Tribulation Age.

No other known alignment in recorded history carries such mathematical precision, feast-day alignment, and symbolic fulfillment—woven together with such intentionality. This level of orchestration defies randomness. It bears the fingerprint of the Creator of the cosmos, speaking through the heavens to a generation poised on the edge of prophetic fulfillment.

The "Woman in Travail" and Prophetic Pregnancy—The imagery in Revelation 12 is not abstract poetry. It tells a specific story: a woman laboring in pain to deliver a Child, opposed by a red dragon, and surrounded by celestial signs. This prophetic narrative aligns with the exact behavior of Jupiter, which, from our earthly view, entered Virgo's womb in November 2016 and remained there in retrograde motion until September 9, 2017—a total of nearly 280 days, the average duration of a full-term pregnancy.

This is not coincidence; it is prophetic pregnancy symbolism written in the stars. The constellation Virgo (the virgin) symbolized Israel, or perhaps Mary, and by extension, the faithful remnant of believers. The Male Child born and "caught up to God and His throne" (Revelation 12:5) points to Jesus, but also to the Church, which sprang forth from Israel and will be caught up (raptured) before the time of wrath.

This celestial drama mirrored the Genesis 3:15 prophecy: the Seed of the woman would crush the serpent's head. The 2017 alignment acted as a cosmic echo of that ancient promise, reminding us that God's redemptive plan is nearing its climactic fulfillment.

Interpretations and Theological Debate

The Revelation 12 alignment that unfolded on September 23, 2017, has ignited intense theological discussion and divergent interpretations within both prophecy circles and the broader Christian community. Was it merely an interesting astronomical phenomenon? Or was it a divine sign—perhaps even the most significant in modern history—marking the beginning of prophetic acceleration?

Though the heavens clearly aligned in stunning and unprecedented fashion, what exactly the 2017 celestial sign meant continues to be a subject of prayer, debate, and study.

A Sign of the Birth of the Church—Some interpreters, drawing from both historical and prophetic theology, suggest that Revelation 12:1–5 speaks of the birth of the Church through Jesus Christ. In this view, the "woman clothed with the sun" represents Israel, who gave birth to the Messiah (Jesus), and the "Man Child" who was "caught up unto God" reflects Christ's ascension and the subsequent birth of His body—the Church.

From this angle, the 2017 sign commemorates and affirms the central role of the Church in the final phase of human history. It may mark a prophetic reminder of the Church's origin, mission, and soon-coming transformation, as the faithful are gathered to meet Christ.

A Warning of the Approaching Tribulation or Rapture?—Others interpret the sign as a heavenly trumpet blast—a warning that the Tribulation period is near, or perhaps that the Rapture of the Church is imminent. Because the sign occurred just days after the Feast of Trumpets in 2017—a feast long associated with the "last trumpet" (1 Corinthians 15:52)—some believe it may have signaled the beginning of a countdown to the Rapture or to Daniel's 70th Week.

> In a moment, in the twinkling of an eye, at the last trump: for the trumpet shall sound, and the dead shall be raised incorruptible, and we shall be changed. (1 Corinthians 15:52)

Though the Rapture did not occur in 2017, many prophecy teachers emphasize that signs often precede fulfillment. For example, Noah entered the Ark seven days before the Flood began (Genesis 7:10), and Joseph interpreted Pharaoh's dream seven years before the famine struck (Genesis 41:29–30). Similarly, the Revelation 12 Sign on September 23, 2017, may serve not as the fulfillment itself, but as a prophetic warning—a celestial heads-up of what is to come.

Seven years later, in 2024, a pivotal shift occurs: Donald Trump is re-elected, which some view as a sign of a divinely appointed window for both America and the Church. Prophetic interpreters suggest that this may represent a final season of warning and preparation—a pause before judgment, revival, or Christ's return. If this interpretation holds, the year 2028/2029 could mark not only the conclusion of Trump's term, but also the culmination of a significant prophetic cycle.

A Call to Spiritual Awakening and Repentance—Many theologians and watchmen agree that—regardless of one's eschatological interpretation—the

Revelation 12 Sign was undoubtedly a call to spiritual alertness. Like the wise virgins in Jesus' parable (Matthew 25), believers are exhorted to trim their lamps, keep watch, and remain ready for the Bridegroom's return.

The celestial alignment served as a wake-up call from Heaven—a moment when the skies declared the voice of God to a world increasingly deafened by distraction. It was not merely an astronomical curiosity, but a divine summons: an invitation to examine one's walk, return to the Word, and prepare spiritually for the days ahead.

A Prophetic Time Marker: The Beginning of the Final Countdown?—Another widely held view is that the 2017 Revelation 12 Sign marked a transition point—a visible, measurable, time-stamped signal initiating the final countdown toward the fulfillment of end-time prophecy. Some describe it as a "Genesis moment" of the end times, when God's prophetic clock shifted gears and entered its final phase.

Revelation 12 itself moves from the birth and ascension of the Man Child to the woman fleeing into the wilderness for 1,260 days—a period tied directly to the Great Tribulation. It is entirely plausible that the sign not only depicted past redemption, but also served as a prophetic time stamp pointing toward future judgment.

In that light, the Revelation 12 Sign may be seen as God's megaphone to the world, declaring:

The time is short. Prepare. Watch. Repent.

Connection to Other Signs: Eclipses, Tetrads, and Trumpets

The Revelation 12 Sign of September 23, 2017 did not appear in isolation. Rather, it unfolded within a larger prophetic sequence—a sweeping tapestry of celestial signs that include solar eclipses, blood moon tetrads, and planetary alignments. Together, these events seem to form a divine narrative, written not in ink, but in starlight—one that proclaims God's timeline with both precision and poetic intensity.

Like chapters in a prophetic book, each astronomical sign builds upon the last, revealing a message that is not random, but deliberately layered, calling the world to watch, discern, and respond.

A Broader Pattern of Heavenly Warnings—In Genesis 1:14, God declared that the sun, moon, and stars were placed in the heavens "for signs, and for seasons, and for days, and years." These lights are not random or merely decorative—they are part of God's cosmic messaging system, declaring His sovereignty and guiding His people through prophetic seasons.

The Revelation 12 Sign fits squarely within this divine pattern, echoing and amplifying the many celestial signs that preceded it. The years leading up to September 2017 were marked by a series of historic astronomical events, seemingly designed to awaken the spiritually alert and prepare the Bride of Christ:

- The blood moon tetrads of 2014–2015—a rare sequence in which four total lunar eclipses fell on major Jewish feast days—Passover and *Sukkot*—two years in a row.
- Two solar eclipses: one on Nisan 1 (March 20, 2015), and another on Tishri 1 (September 13, 2015)—bookending the tetrads and aligning precisely with the biblical calendar's religious and civil New Year's.
- The Great American Eclipse on August 21, 2017—just a month before the Revelation 12 Sign—cut across the United States from west to east, and began exactly at sunset in Jerusalem.

Each of these signs was not isolated, but part of a larger, interconnected prophetic pattern, signaling that the heavens are not silent. They are declaring: God is speaking. Are we listening?

A Complement to the Great American Eclipses—Many believe the Revelation 12 Sign was divinely timed to complement the prophetic message of the Great American Eclipses—the first in 2017, the second in 2024. Together, these total solar eclipses trace a massive "X" across the United States, with the paths intersecting directly over the New Madrid Seismic Zone, a region historically prone to geological instability. This celestial "marking" is widely seen as a sobering warning to the Gentile nations—and especially to America—to repent and return to God.

The Revelation 12 alignment, appearing exactly one month after the first eclipse and just prior to the Feast of Trumpets, forms a prophetic bridge between two realms of warning:

- A literal solar warning directed toward the nations, and
- A symbolic "birth sign" in the heavens directed toward Israel and the Church.

Together, these events signal a convergence of signs—calling both the Gentile world and God's covenant people to spiritual urgency, repentance, and readiness.

Blood Moons as Precursors to the Celestial Birth—The 2014–2015 blood moon tetrads can be seen as precursor events—early labor pains, so to speak—leading up to the Revelation 12 Sign. Each of these lunar eclipses, falling precisely on the biblical feast days of Passover and *Sukkot*, appeared to set the prophetic stage for what would follow: a celestial portrayal of a woman in travail, laboring to give birth.

This striking progression—from blood moons aligned with feast days to an astronomical depiction of birth—presents a stunning prophetic timeline. It echoes both the natural rhythms of the heavens and the supernatural cadence of God's redemptive plan, reinforcing the idea that God speaks through the sky—not just symbolism, but in seasons and sequence.

Layered Signs as Progressive Revelation—God often speaks in layers—using patterns, types, and shadows to reveal truth progressively. Just as the tabernacle pointed to Christ, and the biblical feasts foreshadowed future fulfillments, so too may these astronomical signs serve as prophetic guideposts along His redemptive timeline.

Each event—whether a blood moon, supermoon, or solar eclipse—is not random, but a thread in a larger tapestry, revealing both the precision and the poetry of God's unfolding plan. Together, they trace a pattern that proclaims His sovereignty and anticipates the climax of the age.

The Revelation 12 Sign is best understood not in isolation, but as part of this divinely orchestrated sequence. It weaves together prophetic Scripture, Jewish feast days, celestial alignments, and biblical numerology to deliver a singular, resounding message: The time is short. God's people must prepare.

The afternoon sun slanted through the stained glass of Irene's study, casting warm amber tones across the open pages of her Bible. Outside, leaves rustled like whispers from another world. Inside, a different stirring—quieter, weightier—settled in the room: the hush of revelation drawing near.

Irene leaned forward in her armchair, her fingers still resting on the thin paper where Revelation 12 lay open—like a wound of glory, pulsing with mystery. I sat opposite her, teacup in hand, watching the furrow deepen in her brow.

Irene's thoughts.

"I can't shake it. That celestial alignment in 2017—Virgo, Jupiter, the crown of twelve stars. It wasn't just a marvel. It was a message. But what if it was more than that? What if it was an intervention?"

I broke the silence, nodding slowly.

"The sign in the heavens . . . Yes, September 23, 2017. It had all the markings of something divine. Virgo clothed with the sun, the moon beneath her feet, and twelve stars above her head. Jupiter in retrograde—like a child in the womb—for exactly nine months."

Irene's voice lowered, almost reverent.

"It matched Revelation 12:1–2 with eerie precision. The imagery wasn't abstract—it was exact. People were watching the skies, expecting something. The Rapture. The Tribulation. A breaking point. But then . . . nothing. No trumpet. No chaos. Just another day."

She paused, eyes fixed on the golden edges of her Bible.

"And that's what got me digging. That's when I stumbled on Maurice Sklar's 2018 vision."

I leaned forward, the porcelain teacup now forgotten in my hand.

"The heavenly courtroom. I've read it too. Powerful stuff."

I let the moment breathe before continuing, my tone thoughtful.

"You know, I've always found it fascinating—how God uses music as a channel for the prophetic. Maurice isn't just a theologian with visions—he's a world-class violinist. Trained at Juilliard and the Curtis Institute, I believe. His music carries this unusual weight—like it's soaked in both classical discipline and Heaven's voice."

Irene nodded slowly, as if remembering a melody only her spirit could hear.

I went on, "It reminds me of Kim Clement, honestly. He had that same fusion—a prophetic anointing woven into music. Except Kim was on the piano, flowing with spontaneous worship, while Maurice draws the bow across strings like he's unlocking another realm. Both of them—messengers who didn't just preach, but played Heaven's heartbeat."

My voice softened.

"What part struck you the most?"

Irene's eyes glistened, distant but focused.

"Everything about it gripped me. But especially the setting. It wasn't some mystical blur—it was specific. A Supreme Court in Heaven. Twelve elders seated beside the Father. Six on His right: Enoch, Abraham, Moses, David, Elijah, Daniel. And six on His left: John the Baptist, Peter, James, John, Andrew, and Paul."

I let out a slow breath, the weight of her words settling over us like incense.

"That's no ordinary council. That's law, covenant, kingship, prophetic fire . . . apostleship and testimony. All in one room. It's not just a vision—it's Heaven's highest government assembled."

Irene's voice lowered, her words carrying a reverent weight.

"Exactly. And there, at the center of that celestial courtroom, stood Satan—brazen, bold, unrepentant. He laid claim to the earth, invoking the 6,000-year lease given to Adam. 'My time has come,' he argued. 'The Tribulation must begin. The earth is mine to rule.'"

I leaned in, heart pounding.

"But then—Jesus stood. The Defense rose. Not to argue. Not to plead. But to present the evidence—His own blood. The Lamb did not refute the claim; He overruled it with the Cross."

Irene's eyes shimmered, caught between awe and urgency.

"Yes. Sklar wrote that when Jesus stood, all of Heaven bowed—every elder, every angel, every realm. And He didn't speak like a defense attorney. He spoke as the Lamb who had already overcome. 'I have taken the death penalty for every fallen soul,' He declared. 'I now strip Satan of the Church—the overcoming Church of the Living God.'"

I set my teacup down, the moment too sacred for anything casual.

"And then . . . He petitioned the court. Not to cancel the judgment—but to delay it. A holy pause. He said, 'This Gospel of the Kingdom must be preached in all nations.' A plea—not for escape, but for harvest."

Irene's voice dropped to a whisper, as if afraid to disturb the weight of what she was saying.

"That's the moment that froze me. What if that really was what happened in 2018? And what if the Revelation 12 Sign in 2017 wasn't the beginning of catastrophe—but Heaven's visual marker of what could have unfolded . . . if not for a divine pause—a mercy delay—granted when the court ruled differently?"

I felt a chill—not of fear, but of awe.

"A mercy interruption," I said slowly. "Not a false alarm, but a divine placeholder. A visible pause in judgment. Jesus didn't just ask for delay—He pleaded for the souls of the nations. For China. For Africa. For the Middle East . . . even for America."

Irene's voice trembled—not from doubt, but reverence.

"He cited the blood of the martyrs—those crying out from the soil of China, Africa, the Middle East. Then, He requested the unveiling of hidden scrolls—documents Satan had never seen, sealed before time itself. Scrolls that spoke of a coming harvest—millions destined to be saved during the Tribulation."

I swallowed hard, the weight of it settling deep.

"But then He made one final plea—'My Church should not go through the Tribulation.' That line . . . that burden. It didn't just convict me—it *shook* me."

Irene's eyes lift to the portrait on the wall—scales held aloft by a blindfolded figure. A hush seems to settle over the room.

She whispers, "And then Lady Justice stepped forward—the angel. Blinded. The scales in her hand tipped heavily toward sin. But on the other side . . . were the prayers of the saints."

My thoughts swirl.

"Our prayers weren't just cries in the dark—they were courtroom evidence. Every whispered plea, every intercession, was entered into the record. They didn't just comfort. They counted."

I spoke softly.

"And then, after the deliberation, the court voted. And the Father decreed: 'An extension of time has been granted.' Not a cancellation. Not a change in prophecy. But a pause. A window of mercy. A divine delay so the Gospel could reach the ends of the earth."

Irene leaned back slightly, her voice quiet but firm.

"But the decree came with a warning: 'The birth pangs will not stop. The time of grace is almost over.'"

I nodded, the truth settling between us like the fading light on the page.

"Yes. And that's the sobering part. The pause wasn't permission to grow complacent—it was a summons. A divine call to prepare. To preach. To warn. To stand in the gap for America—and for the world."

Irene sighs, her voice soft but steady.

"I think we've misunderstood the Revelation 12 Sign in 2017. It wasn't pointing to what *would* happen—it was marking what *was* averted."

The room falls still. Outside, a dove coos on the windowsill, the breeze carrying the scent of approaching rain. Irene closes her Bible with reverence, the pages whispering shut like the echo of Heaven's silence.

She speaks again, almost to herself.

"If we're living on borrowed time, we can't waste a second. The next time the courtroom convenes . . . there may be no more extensions left."

I meet her gaze, a resolve rising in my chest.

"Then let's make this pause count. Preach like the sky is about to split. Pray like the scales our still tipping. And live like we've already taken the witness stand before the Judge."

Irene bows her head, her whisper barely audible. "Amen."

THE THIRD HARBINGER HAS SOUNDED

Heaven Is Declaring, Are We Listening?

From the beginning, God set the sun, moon, and stars not only to give light but to give warning. Long before telescopes, satellites, and star maps, the heavens served as God's cosmic billboard—flashing signs to those who would watch, listen, and understand. These signs are not astrology. They are astronomy submitting to the Author of time. They are not superstition—they are supernatural communication.

The third harbinger is not just in motion—it has appeared, high above us, unfolding one celestial event after another. The sky has become a scroll, and God is writing His final warnings in brilliant light and blood-red moons. These aren't imaginative guesses or vague omens. These are verified, astronomical precise alignments, falling on exact biblical feast days, and mirroring prophetic scriptures written thousands of years ago.

The blood moons, the solar eclipses, the Revelation 12 Sign—they are not isolated. They are layered, deliberate, divine. They form a prophetic mosaic—each piece revealing more of the full picture. And when viewed together, they declare with urgency: The King is coming.

This is not the time for passive curiosity. This is the time for prophetic clarity. The moon has turned to blood. The sun has gone dark. The stars have aligned. And every voice of Heaven is saying, "Look up!" The heavens are not silent. They are shouting.

- The calendars have spoken.
- The sky is testifying.
- The Bride must awaken.

These signs are Heaven's sirens—urgent, visible, and undeniable. They are God's way of reaching through the noise of this age and shaking us awake. The third harbinger is not just a sky event—it is a divine convergence. A warning wrapped in mercy. A countdown marked in stars.

We are not watching random beauty. We are witnessing a rehearsal for the return of the King. Every blood moon is a trumpet. Every eclipse is a drumbeat. Every alignment is a reminder: He is not delayed. He is deliberate.

This is the final boarding call to a Church lulled by comfort and distracted by culture. It's time to rise from slumber and step into synchronization with God's calendar, God's signs, and God's urgency.

What must we do?

We must tune our hearts to the heavens.
We must repent, realign, and return.

We must see the stars not as background—but as a biblical broadcast
We must stop waiting for more signs and realize: The sky is already full of them.

- God's covenant with Israel is visible in the moon.
- God's warning to the nations is written in the sun.
- God's call to His Church is shining in the stars.

This is not mythology. This is Messiah's timeline. And the question is not whether the third harbinger has appeared—it's whether we are watching.

The moon will turn to blood.
The sun will go dark.
The King will split the sky.
Are you ready?

The third harbinger has appeared.
The heavens are declaring.
And Jesus is coming.

Are you listening?
Are you watching?
Are you awake?

CHAPTER SUMMARY

Chapter 7 unveils the Third Harbinger: The Signs in the Heavens, calling attention to the skies as divine scrolls written by the hand of God. Long before telescopes and calendars, the Creator etched His redemptive plan into the stars—from Virgo (the virgin) to Leo (the Lion)—foretelling the Gospel through celestial symbols known and studied since ancient times.

This chapter traces how the sun, moon, and stars have functioned as prophetic timekeepers. From blood moons and supermoons falling precisely on biblical feast days, to solar eclipses marking spiritual pivot points, the heavens have signaled moments of divine intervention. Especially striking are the Great American Eclipses of 2017 and 2024, total solar eclipses seven years apart, crossing the continental U.S. and forming an unmistakable "X" (or Cross) over the land—raising urgent questions about America's spiritual trajectory.

Central to this harbinger is the Revelation 12 Sign, a rare astronomical alignment on September 23, 2017, depicting a woman clothed with the sun, the moon under her feet, and a crown of twelve stars. The convergence, involving the constellation Virgo, Jupiter's 9-month retrograde, and neighboring planets in Leo, stunned both prophecy watchers and astronomers alike. Some interpret this sign as a symbol of the Rapture, the birth of the Church, or a divine countdown to the final prophetic events.

Together, these signs are not coincidence—they are convergence. The chapter presents compelling evidence that God is speaking through layered, timed, and increasingly urgent signs in the heavens, aligning with Scripture, history, and Israel's destiny. The message is unmistakable: look up—your redemption draws near.

KEY TAKEAWAYS

- The constellations tell the Gospel story—from Virgo (the virgin) to Leo (the Lion)—written by God from the beginning.
- Lunar and solar eclipses often align with biblical feast days, serving as divine warnings and markers of judgment or redemption.
- The Great American Eclipses (2017 and 2024) form a massive "X" across the U.S., separated by seven years, symbolizing possible national reckoning.
- The Revelation 12 Sign is seen by many as a once-in-history celestial event, pointing to the Rapture, Tribulation, or birth of a prophetic era.
- The third harbinger reminds us that the heavens are not silent—they are declaring the glory, warnings, and timing of God's unfolding plan.

Chapter 7 sounds the third harbinger with clarity and urgency: the heavens are speaking. These celestial events—eclipses, blood moons, supermoons, and the Revelation 12 Sign—are not cosmic accidents or poetic curiosities. They are divine communications, meticulously timed with prophetic precision and embedded in the very fabric of the universe. Like clockwork, the sun, moon, and stars continue to mark the appointed times of God, echoing the biblical truth first declared in Genesis 1:14—that the lights in the sky were placed there "for signs, and for seasons, and for days, and years."

From Virgo to Leo, the constellations trace the Gospel story in the stars—beginning with the promise of a virgin-born Savior and culminating in the return of the Lion of Judah. The Revelation 12 Sign reminds us that Heaven speaks not just in words, but in wonders. The Great American Eclipses draw our attention to national repentance, while the blood moons aligned with biblical feast days draw our eyes toward Israel's destiny. All of it converges into a single, resounding message: the time is short.

The third harbinger is not meant to stir fear, but to ignite faith, foster discernment, and inspire alignment with God's purposes in this prophetic hour. It is a clarion call to the Church, to the nations, and to every believer: Look up. Wake up. Trim your lamps. Prepare. The King is coming—not someday in the distant future, but soon. The signs are here, the clock is ticking, and the heavens are roaring with the voice of the Lord. The only question that remains is:

Are we watching?

Chapter 8

The Fourth Harbinger:
The Feasts That Reveal the Future

DIVINE APPOINTMENTS AND PROPHETIC CLUES—What if God had scheduled a series of divine appointments—precise, prophetic events planned before the foundation of the world—and what if most of the world missed them simply because they were looking at the wrong calendar?

Welcome to the Fourth Harbinger: The Feasts That Reveal the Future.

The biblical feasts are not merely cultural traditions or ancient rituals—they are God's appointed times, or *moedim*, sacred markers on His prophetic calendar. These "divine appointments" serve as both memorials of redemption past and dress rehearsals for future fulfillment. They are Heaven's invitations to be in sync with the rhythm of God's redemptive plan.

According to Genesis 1:14, the sun and moon were created "for signs, and for seasons, and for days, and years." But the word "seasons" here isn't referring to spring, summer, fall, or winter. The Hebrew word is *moed*—a term that means "set time" or "appointed meeting." This same word reappears in Leviticus 23:2, where God instructs Moses to tell the children of Israel about the Feasts of the LORD, calling them "holy convocations"—public gatherings for sacred purposes.

> Speak unto the children of Israel, and say unto them, Concerning the Feasts of the LORD, which you shall proclaim to be holy convocations, even these are My feasts. (Leviticus 23:2)

In other words, God embedded His prophetic calendar into Creation itself.

Yet over time, this sacred calendar was replaced. The world now operates largely on the Gregorian calendar—created by Julius Caesar (45 BC) and later refined by Pope Gregory XIII (1582 AD)—a purely solar system that has no regard for God's timetable. Even the Islamic calendar, based solely on lunar cycles, deviates from the divine rhythm established in the beginning. Meanwhile, God's calendar is a biblical blend of lunar and solar cycles, aligning perfectly with His feasts and fasts, each bursting with prophetic meaning.

Proverbs 25:2 tells us that:

> It is the glory of God to conceal a thing: but the honor of kings is to search out a matter. (Proverbs 25:2)

God has hidden treasure chests of revelation throughout the Scriptures—truths that can only be unlocked when we align ourselves with His appointed times. These feasts, embedded like glittering keys in the pages of the Bible, unlock the mysteries of what God has done, is doing, and will yet do in the earth.

Over the last several decades, I've discovered some of these treasures—biblical keys that connect ancient feast days with monumental events in history and precise prophetic fulfillments to the very day and hour. I'm inviting you to join me on this treasure hunt. We're not here to predict dates—we're here to understand the patterns, recognize the times and seasons, and prepare our hearts for what's ahead.

Because the truth is: God doesn't operate on man's clock. He operates on His own timepiece, one that ticks with prophetic precision. If we want to know where we are in the story, we need to get back on God's schedule.

Let's begin.

GOD'S PROPHETIC CALENDAR:
A KEY TO END-TIME UNDERSTANDING

The Importance of Aligning with God's Calendar

If you want to understand what God is doing in the world today—and what He is about to do—you must first understand the calendar He uses. God's prophetic schedule is not random. It is ordered, precise, and deeply rooted in the rhythms of Creation and covenant. Every significant event in redemptive history, from the Exodus to the outpouring of the Holy Spirit at Pentecost, has occurred on an appointed day—a *moed*—on God's calendar. And that calendar was never meant to be discarded or replaced.

Many believers today eagerly study biblical prophecy, attend conferences, and comb through current events for signs of the times. Yet astonishingly, many do so while remaining completely disconnected from God's actual timekeeping system. They try to interpret end-time prophecy through a Western, manmade calendar that was never part of the biblical framework. It's like trying to read a map with the wrong compass—it will leave you spiritually disoriented.

Getting on God's calendar is like putting on spiritual 3D glasses. Suddenly, the Bible isn't just a storybook—it's a living roadmap with prophetic markers clearly laid out. And when you learn to track those markers, you will begin to see how His hand has been orchestrating world events all along—down to the very day.

How the Sun and Moon Determined Biblical Appointments

From the very first chapter of Genesis, God established how humanity was to tell time in a spiritual sense:

> And God said, Let there be lights in the firmament of the heaven to divide the day from the night; and let them be for signs, and for seasons, and for days, and years. (Genesis 1:14)

This verse, often skimmed over as poetic language, actually holds a crucial key. The Hebrew word translated "seasons" is *moedim*—appointed times. These are not climate seasons but fixed divine encounters. The sun and moon were created not just to light our world, but to signal when these appointments would take place.

In Leviticus 23, God reiterates that His feast days are "appointed times" (*moedim*) that must be proclaimed and observed. These are not optional Jewish traditions. They are set appointments by the Creator Himself. He placed celestial bodies in motion not just for astronomy, but for theology—for prophecy—for meeting with His people on holy ground in holy time.

Contrast with the Gregorian and Islamic Calendars

Unfortunately, most of the modern world operates on entirely different calendars. The Gregorian calendar—established by Julius Caesar and refined by Pope Gregory XIII—is purely solar. It was never designed to align with God's schedule. In fact, it replaced many biblical observances with manmade traditions and pagan holidays.

On the other side of the spectrum is the Islamic calendar, which is strictly lunar. It accurately follows the phases of the moon but excludes solar synchronization. While this system works well for Islamic observance, it is not the calendar of Scripture, which relies on a combined solar-lunar rhythm to keep the feasts aligned with their appointed seasons.

God's calendar, revealed in the Torah and upheld by the Jewish people to this day, is both lunar and solar. Months begin with the new moon (*Rosh Chodesh*), and leap months are periodically added to keep the festivals in their correct seasons—Passover in spring, Tabernacles in autumn. This adjustment system preserves the prophetic precision of God's divine appointments.

Daniel 7:25 and the Change of Times and Laws by the Enemy

It should come as no surprise that the adversary would seek to disrupt God's calendar. In Daniel 7:25, we are given a sobering prophecy about a future ruler who will "speak great words against the Most High" and "think to change times and laws." This isn't merely about adjusting civil ordinances—it is a direct attack on God's prophetic calendar and appointed times.

> And he shall speak great words against the Most High, and shall wear out the saints of the Most High, and think to change times and laws: and they shall be given into his hand until a time and times and the dividing time. (Daniel 7:25)

This verse is widely interpreted as a description of the Antichrist during the Great Tribulation—the final 3½ years of the Tribulation Age.

Through a combination of ignorance, assimilation, and antisemitism, many believers have been cut off from the feasts, fasts, and seasons God ordained. The Church replaced Passover with Easter, disconnected Pentecost from *Shavuot*, and largely ignored the fall feasts altogether—feasts that hold keys to the Second Coming of the Messiah.

If we are to be a prophetic people, we must return to God's timing. We must realign our hearts, our celebrations, and our understanding with the divine appointments laid out in Scripture. These are not relics of a bygone era. They are rehearsals for eternity—and every one of us has a role to play in the final act.

THE SEVEN FEASTS OF THE LORD (LEVITICUS 23)

Leviticus 23 is often referred to as God's prophetic calendar of redemption—a divine itinerary that spans from Creation to consummation. In this single chapter, God outlines seven appointed feasts, or *moedim*, which serve as sacred convocations—holy appointments preordained by Heaven. These are not manmade festivals or cultural traditions. God calls them "My feasts"—a clear declaration that they belong to Him, and that they are intended for all His people, both Jew and Gentile.

Each feast carries historical meaning, rooted in Israel's deliverance and agricultural life. But more than that, each feast is prophetically charged, serving as a dress rehearsal for future kingdom events. These appointed times were designed by God as spiritual training grounds, enabling His people to prepare for what was—and still is—to come.

The first four feasts—Passover, Unleavened Bread, Firstfruits, and *Shavuot* (Pentecost)—were fulfilled with supernatural precision at Yeshua's (Jesus') First Coming. They foretold the exact days of His sacrificial death, His burial, His resurrection, and the outpouring of the Holy Spirit. Each occurred not just in principle, but in practice—on the exact day of the feast, just as God had ordained.

The final three feasts—*Yom Teruah* (Feast of Trumpets), *Yom Kippur* (Day of Atonement), and *Sukkot* (Feast of Tabernacles)—remain unfulfilled. These fall feasts offer a prophetic glimpse into the Messiah's Second Coming. They forecast the return of the King with the blast of the trumpet, the national repentance of Israel, final judgment, and the ultimate joy of God dwelling among His people once again.

These seven feasts are not merely observances—they are God's holy rehearsals, prophetic stage performances set in motion since Genesis. They lead us to the most anticipated events in human history: the coronation of the Messiah, the marriage supper of the Lamb, and the eternal tabernacling of God with man. To ignore them is to overlook the calendar God uses to communicate His plan.

Every feast also reveals the heart of God—His protection, provision, and promises. When seen together, these sacred appointments form a theological framework and a prophetic timeline that helps us discern the times and seasons we are living in. They invite us to see the Bible not just as a record of the past, but as a roadmap to the future.

So now, let's walk through each of these feasts—one by one—uncovering how they were established, how they were fulfilled or foreshadowed, and how they prophetically point us toward the unfolding of God's final, glorious acts.

1. Passover (Pesach): The First Vanishing— The Lamb Slain from the Foundation of the World

Long before Israel cried out for deliverance, and long before Rome raised a Cross, God had already planned the death and resurrection of His Son. Revelation 13:8 tells us that the Lamb was "slain from the foundation of the world." That means Passover was not simply a historical event—it was a prophetic shadow, a carefully choreographed dress rehearsal scripted by the Master of Time. The slaying of the Messiah wasn't a last-minute plan—it was the first vanishing, the first divine appointment in God's redemptive calendar.

> And all that dwell upon the earth shall worship him (the Antichrist), whose names are not written in the Book of Life of the Lamb slain from the foundation of the world. (Revelation 13:8)

The Pattern of Passover—The Hebrew word *Pesach* means "to pass over," and it refers to the miraculous night recorded in Exodus 12 when the Lord passed over the homes of the Israelites whose doorposts were covered in the blood of a perfect lamb. It was the tenth and final plague, striking down the firstborn sons of Egypt and finally forcing Pharaoh's hand to let God's people go.

But it wasn't just a night of deliverance—it was a night of judgment and justice. Each of the plagues leading up to Passover was a strike against the false gods of Egypt (Exodus 12:12). Pharaoh thought himself divine; but God exposed Egypt's idols, rendering them powerless before His outstretched hand.

The blood on the doorposts was a sign. Exodus 12:13 declares, "When I see the blood, I will pass over you." That sign of blood—the life of the lamb—stood between the people and death. And as Revelation 12:11 later echoes, "They overcame . . . by the blood of the Lamb."

The Prophetic Fulfillment in Yeshua—Yeshua (Jesus) is the fulfillment of this feast. John the Baptist declared it plainly: "Behold the Lamb of God who takes away the sin of the world" (John 1:29). He was the sinless, unblemished Lamb—slain not just for Israel, but for the world. Every detail of His death matched the prophetic blueprint of the Passover.

> In the fourteenth day of the first month at evening is the LORD's Passover. (Leviticus 23:5)

On the 14th of Nisan, the very day ordained in Leviticus 23:5 and practiced for over 1,500 years, Messiah was crucified. The timing was precise:

- 9:00 AM—*The Third Hour*: According to Mark 15:25, this is when Yeshua was nailed to the Cross—the exact hour of the morning sacrifice.
- At the same time, in the Temple, the Passover lamb was being bound to the altar—as the people sang the *Hallel*, a set of Psalms (113–118) traditionally sung at Passover. Psalm 118:27, likely sung at that moment, reads: "Bind the sacrifice with cords, even to the horns of the altar."
- 12:00 PM—*The Sixth Hour*: A supernatural darkness fell over the land, lasting until 3:00 PM, as recorded in all three Synoptic Gospels (Matthew 27:45; Mark 15:33; Luke 23:44). This midday darkness was not a natural eclipse but a divine sign—marking the weight of judgment and the suffering of the Lamb of God as He bore the sins of the world.
- 3:00 PM—*The Ninth Hour*: At the hour of the evening sacrifice, Yeshua gave up His Spirit (Matthew 27:46). The final Lamb was slain, fulfilling the feast to the very hour.

But it doesn't end there.

The Soundtrack of the Crucifixion—After The Last Supper, Yeshua and His disciples sang a hymn (Matthew 26:30). What did they sing? Most scholars agree it was the *Hallel* Psalms—particularly Psalm 118, traditionally sung at Passover. As Jesus was nailed to the Cross, the voices of pilgrims filled the air:

> The LORD is my strength and song, and is become my salvation. The voice of rejoicing and salvation is in the tabernacles of the righteous: the right hand of the LORD does valiantly. The right hand of the LORD is exalted: the right hand of the LORD does valiantly. (Psalm 118:14–16)

Yeshua, whose very name means "salvation," was being exalted—lifted up before the world—as those prophetic words echoed through Jerusalem. It was no coincidence. It was divine orchestration.

A thousand years earlier, King David had unknowingly composed the Messiah's funeral hymns. And on that very day of the crucifixion, Heaven and earth sang them in unison—fulfilling prophecy written a millennium before.

The Father's Grief and the Tearing of the Veil—When Jesus died, the veil of the Temple was torn from top to bottom (Matthew 27:51). This was not more than symbolism—it echoed a deeply personal act of grief. In Jewish tradition, *keriah* is the tearing of one's garment to mourn the death of a close relative. In that sacred moment, it was as if God the Father Himself performed *keriah*—rending the veil, not just to open the way to His presence, but to express a Father's anguish.

> And, behold, the veil of the Temple was rent (torn) in twain (two) from the top to the bottom; and the earth did quake, and the rocks rent. (Matthew 27:51)

God was not distant at the Cross. He was the mourning Parent—His heart torn as His Son breathed His final breath.

A River of Blood and Water—According to historical records, during Passover in Yeshua's day, over 250,000 lambs were sacrificed. Each lamb produced roughly a quart of blood—more than 60,000 gallons poured out at the base of the Temple altar in a single day. But where did it all go?

A hidden drainage system beneath the Temple channeled the blood and water through the Dung Gate, down into the Hinnom Valley—the ancient site of burning refuse and judgment. Since the Temple faced east, the Hinnom Valley lay at its right side.

Now consider John 19:34:

> But one of the soldiers with a spear pierced His side, and forthwith came there out blood and water. (John 19:34)

Just as blood and water flowed from the right side of the Temple, so too did they pour from the right side of the true Temple—Messiah Himself. This was not coincidence. It was divine choreography. The symbolism is unmistakable, the foreshadowing undeniable. The Lamb of God had taken His place at the altar. And from Him flowed a river—not into the valley of refuse, but into the valley of redemption.

The Passover Seder: A Living Memorial—When Yeshua said, "Do this in remembrance of Me" (Luke 22:19), He wasn't establishing a brand-new ritual—He was revealing the fulfillment of an ancient one. The Passover Seder, with its rich symbols—the *matzah* (unleavened bread), the four cups, and the *Afikomen* (a Greek word meaning "I have come," represented by the broken, hidden, and found piece of *matzah*)—had always pointed to Him.

- The third cup, the *Cup of Redemption*, is the one He lifted when declaring, "This cup is the New Covenant in My blood" (Luke 22:20).
- The *Afikomen*, broken, and hidden, then found and eaten at the end of the meal, literally means "I came" in Greek—a stunning picture of Messiah's death, burial, and resurrection.
- The four cups are drawn from God's promises in Exodus 6:6–7: *Sanctification*, *Deliverance*, *Redemption*, and *Acceptance*. Each is fulfilled in Christ, who is both the Lamb and the Liberator.

Wherefore say unto the children of Israel, I am the LORD, and I will bring you out (*cup of sanctification*) from under the burdens of the Egyptians, and I will rid you out of their bondage (*cup of deliverance*), and I will redeem you (*cup of redemption—Luke 22:20*) with a stretched out arm, and with great judgments: And I will take you to Me for a people (*cup of acceptance—or praise*), and I will be to you a God: and you shall know that I am the LORD your God, which brings you out from under the burdens of the Egyptians. (Exodus 6:6–7)

What Yeshua did that night wasn't a departure from Jewish tradition—it was its divine crescendo.

Why It Matters Today—Passover isn't just about ancient Egypt—it's about God's justice, mercy, timing, and love. It's the story of a Lamb slain before the foundation of the world, so that you and I could be passed over when judgment comes.

When we honor the Passover, we're not just recalling history—we're aligning with God's prophetic rhythm, remembering our past deliverance and anchoring our hearts in a future hope.

Yeshua didn't just fulfill Passover by dying—He fulfilled it on the exact day, at the exact hour, while the exact songs were being sung. Why? Because He is the perfect Lamb, and God never misses His appointments.

2. Feast of Unleavened Bread (Hag HaMatzot):
The Hidden King—The Unleavened Bread Mystery

Just as Passover points us to the Lamb who was slain, the Feast of Unleavened Bread points us to what came next—the Lamb who was buried. This second feast on God's prophetic calendar doesn't just speak of death; it reveals the mystery of concealment—of the sinless King hidden in the earth.

It is the Feast of the Hidden King: Yeshua's sinless body, symbolized by unleavened bread, lay in the tomb—silent, untouched by decay, while prophecy and eternity advanced toward resurrection. His burial wasn't absence—it was anticipation. A countdown set in motion by Heaven itself.

The Timing and Command—According to Leviticus 23:6–8, the Feast of Unleavened Bread begins on the 15th of Nisan, immediately after the LORD's Passover on the 14th. For seven days, the Israelites were commanded to eat unleavened bread (*matzah*) and to remove all leaven from their homes. The first and seventh days of the feast were to be treated as Sabbaths, regardless of which day of the week they fell on.

This detail sheds light on a commonly misunderstood verse—John 19:31— where the Sabbath following Yeshua's crucifixion is often assumed to be the regular weekly Sabbath. But Scripture clarifies it was a "high Sabbath"—the first day of Unleavened Bread, a feast-day Sabbath, not necessarily a Saturday.

> The Jews, therefore, because it was the Preparation Day, that the bodies should not remain upon the cross on the Sabbath day, (for that Sabbath day was a high day), besought Pilate that their legs might be broken, and that they might be taken away. (John 19:31)

Understanding this distinction is critical. During the week of Passover and Unleavened Bread, there could be multiple Sabbaths: the weekly Sabbath, and one or more feast-day Sabbaths. In some years, within just two weeks, there could be up to four Sabbaths.

This nuance holds profound prophetic weight: While the Egyptians were burying their firstborn (Numbers 33:3–4), the Firstborn over all creation (Colossians 1:15) was being buried in the earth—on the very day the Feast of Unleavened Bread began.

The Symbolism of *Matzah*: Sinless and Pierced—In Scripture, leaven is often a symbol of sin (Luke 12:1; 1 Corinthians 5:6–8). By removing leaven during the Feast of Unleavened Bread, God's people were rehearsing a deeper truth: the Messiah would come without sin.

> He had done no violence, neither was any deceit in His mouth. (Isaiah 53:9)

> For He has made Him to be sin for us, who knew no sin; that we might be made the righteousness of God in Him. (2 Corinthians 5:21)

Matzah—unleavened bread—was to be eaten for seven days, a visible, edible declaration of purity and sinlessness. But its appearance tells the story too: it is striped, pierced, and bruised—a silent sermon that echoes Isaiah's prophecy:

> By His stripes we are healed. (Isaiah 53:5)

It's no coincidence Yeshua declared, "I am the Bread of Life" (John 6:35). He is the Unleavened One—sinless, pierced, buried like a sheaf in the ground, and raised to life, to give life to the world.

The Hidden King in the Earth—On the 15th of Nisan, while Egypt mourned its firstborn sons, Yeshua's sinless body was placed in the tomb. The imagery is profound: the Lamb who had been slain was now hidden in the earth, fulfilling the Feast of Unleavened Bread with exact prophetic precision.

> For You will not leave my soul in Sheol (Hell); neither will You suffer Your Holy One to see corruption. (Psalm 16:10)

Yeshua's burial was not a sign of defeat—it was a sign of fulfillment. The Feast of Unleavened Bread is not merely about bread without yeast; it's about a King without sin, hidden temporarily, only to conquer death and rise in glory.

> For we have not a High Priest which cannot be touched with the feeling of our infirmities (weaknesses); but was in all points tempted like as we are, yet without sin. (Hebrews 4:15)

This is why, during the feast, homes are cleansed of leaven. Traditionally, this culminates in a symbolic ritual the night before Passover: by candlelight, the father searches the home for remaining crumbs, gently sweeping them onto a wooden spoon with a goose feather, and placing them in a bag to be burned the next morning.

It's more than tradition—it's a picture of inner cleansing. An invitation to search our hearts, remove hidden sin, and prepare ourselves for communion with the Unleavened One—Messiah Himself.

A Pilgrimage of Purity—The Feast of Unleavened Bread is one of three pilgrimage feasts (Deuteronomy 16:16), during which all Jewish males were commanded to come to Jerusalem to appear before the LORD. But this was more than a physical journey—it was a pilgrimage of purity, a call to holiness, separation, and readiness.

The apostle Paul echoes this call for believers:

Therefore let us keep the feast, not with old leaven, neither with the leaven of malice and wickedness; but with the unleavened bread of sincerity and truth. (1 Corinthians 5:8)

Yeshua, our Unleavened Bread, was buried on the very day of this feast—a detail that underscores the perfection of God's timing and the precision of His prophetic plan. His burial wasn't incidental—it fulfilled the feast not only in symbol, but in sequence.

The Bread Hidden, Yet Not Forgotten—In every traditional Passover Seder, a piece of *matzah* called the *Afikomen* is broken, hidden, later found, redeemed for a price, and eaten at the end of the meal. Many believe this tradition points directly to Messiah—broken at the Cross, hidden in the tomb, redeemed, and received again by His people.

Remarkably, *Afikomen*—a Greek word—means "I came."

The Feast of Unleavened Bread becomes, then, a celebration of the Hidden King—the sinless One, laid in the earth on a holy appointed day, waiting to rise as the Firstfruits of resurrection. It is the second step in God's prophetic calendar, and the second act in the greatest redemptive drama ever written.

Let us not forget: this was God's appointment—kept with flawless precision, down to the day and the hour. The burial of the Messiah was not incidental—it was intentional. He was the sheaf hidden in the ground, awaiting the appointed time to rise.

And when He does—everything changes.

3. Feast of Firstfruits (Yom HaBikkurim/Reishit):
The Resurrection Rapture—The Firstfruits Blueprint

If Passover reveals the Lamb who was slain, and Unleavened Bread conceals the King who was buried, then the Feast of Firstfruits unveils the King who has risen—and with Him, the first glimmers of the Resurrection Rapture yet to come.

Known in Hebrew as *Yom HaBikkurim* ("Day of Firstfruits") or *Reishit* ("Beginning/First"), this third feast on God's prophetic calendar establishes the pattern of resurrection—a divine blueprint not only of Messiah's victory over the grave, but of our own future rising when He returns. It is the promise that death is not the end, and that those who belong to Him will also be raised—in order and in season—as the prophetic harvest unfolds.

Timing and Meaning of Firstfruits—The Feast of Firstfruits occurred during the week of Unleavened Bread, specifically on the day after the Sabbath (Leviticus 23:10–11). On this day, the priest was commanded to wave a sheaf of the first ripe barley harvest before the LORD. This simple agricultural act carried profound prophetic meaning: it was an offering of promise—a declaration that the rest of the harvest was guaranteed to follow.

But which Sabbath does this refer to? For over 3,000 years, scholars and rabbis have debated: does it mean the weekly Sabbath (Saturday) or the feast-day Sabbath of Unleavened Bread (Nisan 15)? Based on Scripture and prophetic pattern, many believe that Firstfruits falls on the Sunday following the weekly Sabbath during Passover week.

If so, Yeshua rose from the dead on Firstfruits itself, most likely sometime after sunset on Saturday night, fulfilling the feast with exact prophetic precision.

> And very early in the morning the first day of the week, they came unto the sepulcher (tomb) at the rising of the sun. (Mark 16:2)

As the women approached the tomb at dawn, they found it already empty. Messiah had risen! The first sheaf had been lifted, and with it, the promise of a greater harvest—the resurrection of all who belong to Him.

Yeshua: The First Sheaf of the Resurrection—The apostle Paul declares:

> But now is Christ risen from the dead, and become the firstfruits of them that slept. (1 Corinthians 15:20)

Yeshua Himself foretold this moment in John 12:24:

> Unless a grain of wheat falls into the ground and dies, it remains alone. But if it dies, it produces much fruit. (John 12:24)

Like a seed buried in the earth, He died, was hidden, and now—on the Feast of Firstfruits—He rose again as the first sheaf of a greater harvest: the resurrection of the righteous.

The imagery is stunning.

That very morning, thousands of Israelites brought the first and best of their barley harvest to the Temple. As the Levitical priest lifted the sheaf before the altar, Yeshua ascended to the heavenly Temple, presenting Himself before the Father as the Firstfruits—the beginning of a new creation.

While the earthly priest waved grain, the true High Priest was waving Himself—the fulfillment of what had been rehearsed for generations. It wasn't just a ritual. It was a dress rehearsal, now fulfilled with divine precision.

Resurrection Sunday: The Day Everything Changed—Let's walk through that morning. According to biblical reckoning, the first day of the week begins at sunset on Saturday (Genesis 1:5). While Scripture doesn't record the exact moment Yeshua rose, it clearly states the tomb was already empty before dawn.

- Mary Magdalene and the other women came early and found the stone rolled away (John 20:1).
- Peter and John ran to the tomb, entering to find only the linen cloths left behind (John 20:3–10).
- Mary lingered—and encountered a man she mistook for the gardener, until He gently called her by name (John 20:16).
- That evening, as the disciples mourned in confusion and fear, Yeshua appeared among them—risen, tangible, and gloriously alive (Luke 24:36–43).

From confusion to conviction, from mourning to awe—the resurrection of Yeshua turned sorrow into joy and fear into faith. And it happened exactly as God appointed it—on the Feast of Firstfruits, the day when the first of the harvest is lifted up in thanksgiving.

This was the turning point of history.

The Lamb who was slain had become the Firstborn from the dead—ushering in the promise of resurrection for all who follow Him.

The Resurrection Blueprint: Our Future Hope—Yeshua rose on the Feast of Firstfruits, on the third day, just as foretold.

- He died on Passover (Nisan 14).
- He was buried on Unleavened Bread (Nisan 15).
- He rose on Firstfruits (Nisan 16).

The apostle Paul affirms this divine pattern sequence:

> For as in Adam all die, even so in Christ shall all be made alive. But every man in his own order: Christ the firstfruits; afterward they that are Christ's at His coming. (1 Corinthians 15:22–23)

Firstfruits isn't just a feast—it's a prophetic promise. Because Messiah rose, we will too. His resurrection is not only our example—it's our guarantee. The waving of the sheaf was not the conclusion—it was the inauguration. The harvest is coming. The Rapture is coming. Resurrection is coming.

> Marvel not at this: for the hour is coming, in the which all that are in the graves shall hear His voice, and shall come forth; they that have done good, unto the resurrection of life; and they that have done evil, unto the resurrection of damnation. (John 5:28–29)

The blueprint has been set. The Firstfruits has risen. And because He lives, so shall we.

Fascinating Connections and Historical Echoes—Many other biblical milestones occurred on or around the Feast of Firstfruits, each echoing the themes of resurrection, renewal, and redemptive breakthrough:

- Joshua 5:10–12—The manna ceased, and the Israelites ate the produce of the Promised Land for the first time, marking their transition from wilderness to inheritance.
- Esther 5:1—On this very day, Queen Esther risked her life and approached the king, setting in motion the deliverance of her people.
- Luke 24:44–47—The risen Yeshua opened the Scriptures to His disciples, revealing how the Law, the Prophets, and the Psalms all pointed to Him.

Each moment carries the same prophetic fingerprint: a pattern of resurrection, a step of faith, and a revelation that transforms the future.

Firstfruits: Rarely Observed, Eternally Significant—Today, *Reishit*—the Feast of Firstfruits—is rarely observed in traditional Jewish life. But for followers of Yeshua, it is nothing less than Resurrection Day—the most important day in history. What once marked the beginning of a barley harvest now announces the arrival of a coming kingdom.

And it invites us to live as firstfruits people—set apart, purified, and ready for the trumpet blast that will call us from the earth.

Yeshua didn't just fulfill Firstfruits.

He embodied it.

4. Feast of Weeks (Shavuot/Pentecost): The Harvest and the Holy Spirit

If Passover reveals the Lamb slain, Unleavened Bread conceals the King buried, and Firstfruits unveils the King risen, then *Shavuot*—the Feast of Weeks—marks the Spirit poured out. Known in Greek as Pentecost, this fourth feast on God's prophetic calendar celebrates both the giving of the Torah at Mount Sinai and the giving of the Holy Spirit in Jerusalem fifty days after Yeshua's resurrection. It is the Feast of Harvest and empowerment, where fire fell from heaven—first on stone, then on hearts—birthing a New Covenant people equipped to reap the coming harvest of souls.

God's Appointed Time: Counting the Omer—In Leviticus 23:15–17, God commanded His people to count fifty days from "the day after the Sabbath" following Passover—that is, from the Feast of Firstfruits. This period, known as the Counting of the Omer, culminates in the Feast of *Shavuot* (Hebrew for "weeks"), also known by its Greek name, Pentecost, meaning "fiftieth."

Shavuot was one of the three pilgrimage feasts (Deuteronomy 16:16), during which all Jewish males were required to appear before the LORD in Jerusalem.

To ancient Israel, *Shavuot* was a harvest celebration—a day of rejoicing over the firstfruits of the wheat crop, the beginning of the summer grain harvest. But it was also a day of revelation. According to Jewish tradition, it was on this very day that God gave the Torah—the first five books of the Bible—at Mount Sinai: Fire fell, God's voice thundered, and a covenant was sealed—etched into stone tablets, forging Israel's national identity and spiritual destiny (Exodus 19–20).

A Jewish Feast with a Prophetic Future

> And when the Day of Pentecost had fully come, they were all with one accord in one place. (Acts 2:1)

While many Christians associate Pentecost solely with Acts 2, it's vital to remember that this divine appointment had been rehearsed for 1,500 years before the events in the Upper Room—or rather, as Acts 2 implies, the Temple courts.

On that day, devout Jews from every nation were gathered in Jerusalem (Acts 2:5). Why? Because they were commanded to be there for *Shavuot*. This wasn't a spontaneous revival among pagans—it was a sacred feast day, a divine appointment set by God and faithfully kept by His people.

The disciples weren't hiding out—they were in God's house, gathered at the appointed time. It was the third hour of the day (9:00 AM), the hour of the morning sacrifice (Acts 2:15). And just as fire descended at Mount Sinai, now tongues of fire appeared, and the Holy Spirit was poured out—ushering in the birth of the Church and the beginning of the New Covenant Age (Jeremiah 31:31; Hebrews 9:14–15).

Whereas the Old Covenant Age shaped the period covered in the Old Testament, the New Covenant Age defines the spiritual reality unveiled in the New Testament. The Testaments are the sacred books of Scripture; the Covenants are the divine agreements God made with His people—first through the Law, and now through grace in Christ.

This was no accident. It was a perfect fulfillment: the harvest feast became the launch of the harvest age—a new era of outpouring, evangelism, and Spirit-empowered mission.

The First Pentecostals Were Devout Jews—That moment in Acts 2 was a harvest unlike any other. Peter stood up, filled with the Holy Spirit, and boldly declared the prophecy of Joel had been fulfilled—God was pouring out His Spirit on all flesh (Joel 2:28–32). And right on time, 3,000 souls were added to their number (Acts 2:41). Shortly after, another 5,000 believed (Acts 4:4). By Acts 6:7, even a great company of priests—sons of Aaron themselves—became obedient

to the faith, all while continuing to serve in the Temple for another forty years. Talk about a Feast of Harvest!

And yet, how many today realize that Pentecost is Jewish? That the first Pentecostals were devout Jews—faithfully keeping the Feast of Weeks (*Shavuot*), just as they had for generations? That the Spirit didn't fall into a cultural vacuum—it descended in the context of biblical prophecy and feast-day fulfillment.

Shavuot was always a rehearsal, a holy convocation, preparing God's people for something greater. In Leviticus 23:20–21, the priest was commanded to wave two leavened loaves before the LORD—striking, since leaven often represents sin. Could this be a prophetic foreshadowing? A picture of Jew and Gentile, both imperfect, being made one in Messiah's Spirit-filled body?

Night Watches and Ancient Patterns—To this day, observant Jews commemorate *Shavuot* by staying awake all night to read and study the Torah, in a practice known as *Tikkun Leil Shavuot*. Central readings include Exodus 19–20, recounting the giving of the Law at Sinai; Ezekiel 1, the prophet's fiery vision of God's glory; and Ezekiel 3, where the Spirit lifts Ezekiel with the sound of a rushing wind—foreshadowing the dramatic outpouring in Acts 2.

The Book of Ruth is also read—a story of redemption, harvest, and grafting in. Ruth, the Gentile bride brought into covenant with the Jewish people, becomes a prophetic picture of the Church, brought into the promises of Israel. Her journey from barley to wheat harvest parallels the spiritual transition from Passover (redemption) to Pentecost (empowerment)—a vivid metaphor for the Church Age birthed at *Shavuot*.

Fulfilled to the Day and Hour—Consider the awe-inspiring precision: Yeshua ascended to Heaven on the fortieth day of the Counting of the Omer (Acts 1:3). In obedience to His command, the disciples waited in Jerusalem—not in hiding, but in continual worship at the Temple (Luke 24:52–53), while also gathering in the Upper Room for prayer and fellowship (Acts 1:13–14). For ten days they remained steadfast. Then, on the fiftieth day, the day of *Shavuot*—the Feast of Harvest—the Holy Spirit was poured out, not in confusion or secrecy, but in complete prophetic fulfillment. Likely gathered in the Temple courts—the only place large enough for thousands to witness what happened—the disciples became vessels of fire, launching the Church Age exactly when God appointed it.

We must not overlook the order and accuracy of God's timeline. If the spring feasts—Passover, Unleavened Bread, Firstfruits, and Pentecost—were each fulfilled to the exact day and in some cases to the very hour at Yeshua's First

Coming, then how much more should we trust that the fall feasts will be fulfilled with the same prophetic precision at His Second Coming?

A Challenge to the Modern Church—Do we truly discern the times and seasons—or have we settled for comfort-driven Christianity, unaware of the appointed feasts on God's prophetic calendar? The early Church was birthed from a people who knew the Scriptures, honored the feasts, and recognized their fulfillment in real time.

If we believe that God is the same yesterday, today, and forever, then we must also accept that His calendar has not changed. He fulfilled the spring feasts with stunning precision at His First Coming. He will fulfill the fall feasts with equal precision at His Second Coming.

This isn't just sacred history—it's living prophecy. And it's not just an ancient narrative—it's an invitation to align your life with the divine timeline. Will we recognize the signs, or miss them like many did before?

5. Feast of Trumpets (Yom Teruah/Rosh HaShanah)—
The Awakening Blast: Heralding the Return of the King

The Feast of Trumpets, or *Yom Teruah* in Hebrew—the Day of the Awakening Blast—is the first of the three fall feasts and signals a dramatic prophetic turn on God's calendar. Celebrated on the first day of the seventh month (Tishri), this feast is unlike the spring appointments tied to agricultural harvests. Instead, it functions as a divine announcement—the sounding of the shofar to proclaim the arrival of the King.

Uniquely, it is the only feast that begins on a new moon, when the sky is dark and the moon just begins to reappear. This timing underscores its themes of mystery, hiddenness, and sudden appearance—a perfect parallel to the coming of the Lord "like a thief in the night."

In Leviticus 23, no explicit reason is given for this feast, aside from the commands to rest, assemble, and blow the trumpets. That silence is prophetic. While the spring feasts revealed Messiah's First Coming and redemptive work, *Yom Teruah* foreshadows His sudden return, the resurrection of the righteous (the Rapture), and the initiation of divine judgment (the Tribulation).

A Call to Wake Up and Prepare—The word *Teruah* means "a shout" or "a blast of war, alarm, or joy." It's more than ceremonial—it's a wake-up call, both literal and spiritual. The piercing cry of the shofar breaks through routine and distraction, calling God's people to awaken from spiritual slumber and return to Him.

In Jewish tradition, the month leading up to *Yom Teruah*—the month of Elul—is a time of deep reflection and repentance. But when the feast arrives, it is ushered in with 100 blasts of the trumpet, each one escalating in urgency, culminating in what's called the *Tekiah Gedolah*—the "great blast."

This series of trumpet blasts echoes the apostle Paul's words in 1 Thessalonians 4:16–17:

> For the Lord Himself shall descend from Heaven with a shout, with the voice of the archangel, and with the trump of God: and the dead in Christ shall rise first. Then we who are alive and remain shall be caught up together with them in the clouds, to meet the Lord in the air: and so shall we ever be with the Lord. (1 Thessalonians 4:16–17)

In this light, *Yom Teruah* becomes a prophetic rehearsal of the Rapture—a divine summons for the faithful, not dictated by human calendars but aligned perfectly with God's appointed time. The trumpet is not just a sound—it's a signal. A call. A countdown.

Divine Mystery: "No One Knows the Day or the Hour"—Of all God's appointed feasts, *Yom Teruah*—the Feast of Trumpets—is uniquely wrapped in mystery. In ancient rabbinic tradition, it came to be known as the "feast of which no one knows the day or the hour." Why? Because it is the only feast that begins on a new moon—a phase that must be visually confirmed by the first sliver of the crescent moon. Since weather or atmospheric conditions could obscure its sighting, the feast might begin on one of two possible days, depending on when the new moon is actually observed.

This uncertainty gave rise to a common idiom among the Jewish people: "No one knows the day or the hour."

So when Jesus said in Matthew 24:36:

> But of that day and hour knows no man, no, not the angels of heaven, but My Father only. (Matthew 24:36)

He was not simply speaking in vague mystery—He was pointing to *Yom Teruah*. To His Jewish audience, that phrase would have immediately evoked the Feast of Trumpets. In using it, Jesus wasn't hiding the timeline—He was revealing it. He was signaling that His return would be tied to this very feast, a moment both long-awaited and divinely concealed, just like the hidden crescent moon.

A Day of Judgment and Coronation—*Yom Teruah* is more than a trumpet blast—it is the opening note of a divine drama. It begins the "Ten Days of Awe," a solemn period leading to *Yom Kippur* (the Day of Atonement). In Jewish tradition, this day marks the opening of the books of judgment, when God reviews every life, weighs every heart, and extends an invitation to repentance. The shofar doesn't just call the assembly—it summons the soul to the heavenly courtroom.

In Jewish tradition, *Yom Teruah* is also known as the "Coronation of the King." It is the day the shofar announces that the King is seated on His throne, the Judge is in session, and the books are opened.

From a prophetic lens, this imagery points forward to the return of Messiah—when Yeshua, the King of kings, will take His throne, judge the nations, and gather His Bride. It is a day of awe, accountability, and anticipation—one that calls not only for repentance, but also for readiness.

God's Calendar vs. Man's Calendar—In God's divine design, the Feast of Trumpets is strategically placed in the seventh month—the biblical number of completion and perfection. This placement stands in stark contrast to the world's timekeeping systems. The Gregorian calendar, used by most of the modern world, is solar-based. The Islamic calendar is strictly lunar. But God's calendar—the one that governs His *moedim* (appointed times)—is lunar-solar, uniquely attuned to both the sun and the moon as described in Genesis 1:14.

Scripture warns us that the enemy would attempt to distort God's timekeeping. In Daniel 7:25, it is prophesied that he will "think to change times and laws," subtly removing God's holy appointments from the awareness of His people.

By restoring *Yom Teruah* and the biblical feasts to our spiritual lives, we do more than honor tradition—we realign with Heaven's rhythm. We awaken to the prophetic calendar of God, and in doing so, we position ourselves to rightly interpret the end-time timeline. This is not legalism—it is preparation.

A Dress Rehearsal for the Second Coming—Just as Passover was fulfilled in the exact timing of Yeshua's death, and Firstfruits in His resurrection, the Feast of Trumpets still awaits its glorious fulfillment—the return of the Lord *for* His people. It is more than a historical commemoration; it is a divinely appointed rehearsal for the Rapture, the resurrection of the dead, the awakening of the spiritually slumbering, and the royal announcement of the King's arrival.

This is not merely a Jewish holiday. It is God's *moedim*—His prophetic appointments on Heaven's calendar. And if God fulfilled the spring feasts with perfect precision at Messiah's First Coming, can we not be absolutely certain that He will fulfill the fall feasts—beginning with *Yom Teruah* (the Feast of Trumpets)—with the same prophetic accuracy?

The Feast of Trumpets: The Awakening Blast and Beyond—Before we move on to the next feast, we must pause and reflect on the deeper prophetic layers embedded in *Yom Teruah*. This sacred appointment is not defined solely by trumpets and timing—it is infused with multi-dimensional meaning that reveals the very heart of God's redemptive design.

In Jewish tradition, the Feast of Trumpets is known by several profound titles, each offering a prophetic key to understanding the return of the Messiah:

1. *Yom HaDin*—The Day of Judgment
2. *Yom HaKeseh*—The Hidden Day
3. *Ha Kiddushin/Nesuin*—The Wedding of the Messiah
4. *HaMelech*—The Coronation of the King

Even Jesus' allusion to His return "as a thief in the night" draws from the mystery surrounding this appointed time.

These titles are not arbitrary—they are spirit-filled metaphors that unveil the layers of God's plan for His Bride, His kingdom, and His final return. Let us now examine each name closely, as we encounter the glorious mystery of the Awakening Blast—and all that lies beyond it.

1. *Yom HaDin*—The Day of Judgment

In Jewish tradition, the Feast of Trumpets (*Yom Teruah*) is also known as *Yom HaDin*, The Day of Judgment. This isn't merely symbolism—it represents a divine courtroom scene. On this appointed day, Jewish sages teach that the Books of Life and Death are opened, and Heaven's court convenes. Every soul is brought before the Judge of all the earth. Our deeds, our words, and even our intentions are examined.

This ancient teaching finds its echo in the New Testament:

> For we must all appear before the Judgment Seat of Christ; that every one may receive the things done in his body, according to that he has done, whether it be good or bad. (2 Corinthians 5:10)

But the verdict is not rendered in a single day. *Yom HaDin* initiates the Ten Days of Awe, a grace-filled window between *Yom Teruah* and *Yom Kippur* (the Day of Atonement). These ten days offer a sacred invitation to *teshuvah*—deep repentance and realignment with God. The blast of the shofar is Heaven's alarm clock, rousing sleepy hearts to spiritual self-examination.

This divine pattern of judgment is consistent throughout Scripture:

- Daniel 7:10–11—"The books were opened . . . the judgment was set."
- Revelation 20:11–12—"The dead were judged . . . out of those things which were written in the books."

What's at stake is not merely our temporal well-being—but eternal standing. The Feast of Trumpets foreshadows the future Great White Throne Judgment, where the righteous are distinguished from the wicked. And apart from the righteousness of Christ, the books will testify against us.

2. *Yom HaKeseh*—The Hidden Day

Another profound name for the Feast of Trumpets is *Yom HaKeseh*, The Hidden Day. This title reflects a literal and prophetic truth: it is the only feast celebrated on a new moon, when the moon is concealed from view. In ancient Israel, the precise timing of the new moon required the testimony of two reliable witnesses. Until the crescent was sighted, the feast could not begin. As a result, the exact day or hour could not be known in advance—making this feast unique among the LORD's appointed times.

It is within this context that Jesus' words take on deeper meaning:

> But of that day and hour knows no man, no, not the angels of heaven, but My Father only. (Matthew 24:36)

This statement was not merely about mystery—it was idiomatic language understood by His Jewish listeners to be a clear reference to *Yom Teruah*. It hinted at the timing of His return and underscored the call to readiness.

Yom HaKeseh is not only about hiddenness in the heavens—it also speaks of spiritual concealment and divine shelter. As Psalm 27:5 proclaims:

> For in the time of trouble He shall hide me in His pavilion: in the secret place of His tabernacle shall He hide me; He shall set me up upon a rock. (Psalm 27:5)

This theme continues in the words of the prophets:

- Zephaniah 1:14–18 warns of the Day of the LORD—a day of trumpet blasts, darkness, and divine judgment.
- Zephaniah 2:1–3 exhorts God's people to gather in repentance, seek righteousness, and perhaps be "hidden" in the Day of the LORD's anger.

Even recent history echoes this prophetic motif. The 2005 Gaza evacuation took place on *Tisha B'Av* (the 9th of Av)—a date long associated with catastrophe in Jewish history, including the destruction of both Temples. Many saw that withdrawal as a prophetic foreshadowing of Zephaniah's warnings about judgment and desolation, particularly concerning Gaza ("Gaza shall be forsaken"—Zephaniah 2:4).

> For Gaza shall be forsaken, and Ashkelon a desolation: they shall drive out Ashdod at the noon day, and Ekron shall be rooted up. (Zephaniah 2:4)

Ashkelon, Ashdod, and Ekron were ancient Philistine cities located along the coastal plain of what is now modern-day Israel and the Gaza Strip. They were among the five major Philistine city-states mentioned frequently in the Bible: Gaza, Ashkelon, Ashdod, Ekron, and Gath.

Though the names *Philistine* and *Palestinian* sound similar, they refer to entirely different peoples, cultures, and time periods. The Philistines were an ancient Aegean sea-faring people who settled along the coastal plain of Canaan around the 12th century BC, known for their conflict with Israel in the Old Testament.

In contrast, Palestinians today are an Arab people group, largely descendants of various indigenous and regional populations who lived in the land during and after the Islamic conquests of the 7th century AD. The term "Palestine" was later popularized by the Romans in the 2nd century AD—long after the Philistines had vanished—to erase the Jewish identity of the land.

While modern political narratives often link the two for symbolic reasons, there is no direct ethnic or historical connection between the ancient Philistines and today's Palestinian population.

Then, on 22 Tishri 5784 AM (October 7, 2023)—*Shemini Atzeret/Simchat Torah*, a sacred day meant to celebrate the joy of God's Word—Hamas launched a brutal and coordinated surprise attack on Israel, resulting in the worst massacre of Jews since the Holocaust.

The timing was more than tragic—it was prophetically sobering. In Hebrew, the word "*hamas*" literally means "violence." It's the same word used in Genesis 6:11, describing the days of Noah: "The earth also was corrupt before God, and the earth was filled with violence (*hamas*)." That era of unchecked wickedness and lawlessness provoked God's judgment through the Flood.

> Whereby the world that then was, being overflowed with water, perished: But the heavens and the earth, which are now, by the same word are kept in store, reserved unto fire against the day of judgment and perdition of ungodly men. (2 Peter 3:6–7)

Verse 6 refers to God's first global judgment by water—the great Flood in the days of Noah. Verse 7 shifts the focus to a future judgment by fire, prophesied to come at the end of the age. Many interpret this as unfolding during or following the Great Tribulation—particularly the final 3½ years—culminating in the Day of the Lord and the final judgment. Just as the earth was once cleansed by water, it will one day be purged by fire, according to God's unchanging Word.

To many watching through a biblical lens, the parallels are chilling. Just as violence preceded divine judgment in Noah's time, so too does our generation appear to be spiraling into global chaos and depravity. The eruption of such violence—on a feast day meant for dancing with the Torah—struck many as a divine warning.

These events are not isolated. When viewed together, the Gaza evacuation of 2005—which occurred on *Tisha B'Av*, the 9th of Av, a date historically associated with destruction and exile—and the October 7, 2023 Hamas attack, which fell on *Shemini Atzeret/Simchat Torah* (Tishri 22), a day traditionally linked with joy, renewal, and prophetic new beginnings—appear to serve as prophetic bookends.

Spanning nearly twenty years, this period—two decades (2 + 0 = 2)—reveals a pattern of escalating divine warnings, as if Heaven has moved from a whisper to a shout: The Day of the Lord is drawing near.

> But, beloved, be not ignorant of this one thing, that one day is with the Lord as a thousand years, and a thousand years as one day. (2 Peter 3:8)

Viewed together, *Tisha B'Av* 2005 and *Simchat Torah* 2023 are more than historical markers. They form a prophetic pattern—a divinely timed warning echoing through two sacred dates. One rooted in exile and loss. The other, in joy and renewal. Heaven may be signaling that *Yom Adonai*, the Day of the Lord, is no longer a distant concept—but an approaching reality.

3. ***Ha Kiddushin/Nesuin***—The Wedding of the Messiah

The Feast of Trumpets is intimately tied to the wedding customs of ancient Israel—customs that offer profound insight into the return of the Messiah. This is not merely poetic imagery; it's a prophetic framework that mirrors the ancient Hebrew wedding process:

- The Bridegroom (Messiah) departs to prepare a place for His Bride—"I go to prepare a place for you" (John 14:1–4).
- The Bride (the faithful Church) remains watchful, keeping her lamp burning in anticipation—"At midnight there was a cry made, behold, the Bridegroom comes" (Matthew 25:6–7).
- The shofar blast and a shout announce the arrival of the groom—"For the Lord Himself shall descend from Heaven with a shout, with the voice of the archangel, and with the trump of God" (1 Thessalonians 4:16).
- The couple enters the wedding chamber (*chuppah*) for a time of union and protection—"Come, My people, enter you into your chambers, and shut your doors about you" (Isaiah 26:20).
- Finally, the celebration culminates in the marriage supper of the Lamb—"For the marriage of the Lamb is come, and His wife has made herself ready." (Revelation 19:7–9).

This is the prophetic blueprint of our redemption story—a divine love story that ends in eternal union:

> For as a young man marries a virgin, so shall your sons marry you (Jerusalem/Zion): and as the Bridegroom rejoices over the Bride, so shall your God rejoice over you (Jerusalem/Zion). (Isaiah 62:5)

Even Joel 2 echoes this wedding language, calling both Bride and Bridegroom to sacred assembly. The message is clear: redemption climaxes in a wedding—the covenantal union of Messiah with His spotless Bride.

4. *HaMelech*—The Coronation of the King

The Feast of Trumpets is also known as *HaMelech*, "The King," because it marks the day when God is recognized and crowned as King. This coronation theme is drawn most powerfully from Psalm 47, often called the Coronation Psalm:

- Verses 1–4—The nations clap, shout, and rejoice in a global celebration of God's kingship.
- Verse 5—"God is gone up with a shout, the LORD with the sound of a trumpet."
- Verses 6–9—All creation joins in praise as the King takes His throne.

Tradition also holds that Adam was created on *Yom Teruah*, giving mankind a unique role: to recognize, declare, and honor the sovereignty of the Creator. Thus, the coronation of the King is not only heavenly but also deeply human—inviting our response.

The coronation elements echo both royal ceremony and prophetic fulfillment:

- Issuing the Decree—God's redemptive plan is announced.
- Ascent to the Throne—Messiah takes His rightful place as King of kings.
- Acclamation—Heaven and earth proclaim His reign with trumpet blasts and praise.
- Pledging Allegiance—The Bride, the faithful, acknowledge and submit to His rule.

Sing praises to God, sing praises: sing praises unto our King, sing praises. For God is the King of all the earth: sing you praises with understanding. (Psalm 47:6–7)

This prophetic picture points to the return of Yeshua the Messiah—not only as Savior, but as Sovereign. Just as the spring feasts were fulfilled in exact detail at His First Coming, the fall feasts rehearse His soon-coming coronation. Every year, as believers gather for *Yom Teruah*, we rehearse this heavenly scene, longing for the moment when the King will be crowned before all creation.

As a Thief in the Night—To Whom? Many assume that Messiah will return "as a thief in the night" to all. But Scripture tells a different story—this phrase is not a universal warning, but one reserved for the unprepared.

- Revelation 3:1–3—To the *dead church* at Sardis, Jesus warns, "If you do not watch, I will come upon you as a thief."
- Revelation 3:17–18—To the *lukewarm and blind* Laodicean church, He exposes their spiritual poverty and warns of judgment and shame.
- Revelation 16:15—The blessing is clearly directed to those who are awake and watching: "Blessed is he that watches, and keeps his garments (righteousness)."

This warning is not aimed at the faithful Bride, but rather at those who are spiritually asleep, distracted, or complacent.

Jesus reinforces this in His parables:

- Matthew 25:8–13—The foolish virgins were not ready; their lamps had gone out, and they missed the Bridegroom's arrival.
- Luke 12:35–46—A clear distinction is made between watchful servants who are rewarded, and careless ones who are caught off guard.
- Matthew 16:3—The Pharisees are rebuked for not discerning the "signs of the times."

The apostle Paul also draws a sharp contrast between the faithful and the unaware:

> But you, brethren, are not in darkness, that that day should overtake you as a thief. You are all the children of light, and the children of the day: we are not of the night, nor of darkness. (1 Thessalonians 5:4–5)

Those who understand God's *moedim*—His appointed times—are not surprised. The thief comes to the house that is unguarded, not the one that is watching and prepared.

> But know this, that if the goodman of the house had known in what watch the thief would come, he would have watched, and would not have suffered his house to be broken up. (Matthew 24:43)

Final Warning: Watch, Remember, Proclaim—The message is clear: stay awake, stay ready, and rehearse the feasts—they are God's appointed dress rehearsals for what is to come.

- Stay awake—Proverbs 7 urges us to guard ourselves from deception by keeping God's commandments and His Torah close—like frontlets before our eyes. This section closes with a startling prophetic image: a seductive harlot lures the unwise while the "goodman" (a prophetic picture of Jesus) is away on a long journey, only to return on "the day appointed." This phrase in Hebrew is *yom moed*—a direct reference to an appointed feast day, widely understood as *Yom Teruah*.

- Stay ready—Acts 3:21 affirms that Jesus must remain in Heaven "until the times of restitution of all things." This includes the restoration of God's calendar, His feasts, and the rhythm of divine appointments that the early Church knew and honored.

- Rehearse the feasts—Matthew 22:3–9 portrays the wedding invitation going forth. Many reject or ignore it—too busy, too distracted—but the faithful hear and respond. The wedding feast is being prepared. The King is coming. Are we ready?

Conclusion: A Day Like No Other—The Feast of Trumpets is far more than a celebration—it is a divine alarm, a wedding rehearsal, a court summons, and a coronation ceremony all rolled into one. It is the only appointed feast uniquely known as the day "no man knows the day or hour," perfectly mirroring the mystery and majesty of Messiah's return.

On this sacred day, Heaven and earth hold their breath. Believers look up. They listen for the sound of the shofar. They wait for the sky to split and the King to descend.

Will you be watching? Will you be ready?

Or will the trumpet catch you unaware?

6. Day of Atonement (Yom Kippur): After the Vanishing Mystery

Among the seven Feasts of the LORD outlined in Leviticus 23, *Yom Kippur* stands apart as the most solemn, sacred, and awe-inspiring day on God's prophetic calendar. As the sixth appointed time, it follows the Feast of Trumpets and precedes the Feast of Tabernacles, forming a bridge between judgment and joy, repentance and restoration.

The Hebrew word *Yom* means "day," and *Kippur* comes from the root word *kaphar*, meaning "to cover, to purge, or to reconcile." In Hebrew, the name is plural—*Yom HaKippurim*, the Day of Atonements—because on this day, atonement was made for the high priest, the sanctuary, the altar, the priests, and the entire congregation of Israel (Leviticus 16:33).

But this day is far more than ancient ritual. It is a prophetic rehearsal, pointing to the moment when Israel will recognize her Messiah and the veil over all nations will be lifted (Isaiah 25:7). *Yom Kippur* embodies the paradox of judgment and mercy, of deep repentance and complete restoration.

In Jewish tradition, *Yom Kippur* is also known as "Face to Face," for it is the only time of year when the high priest entered the Holy of Holies, standing before the very presence of God on behalf of the people. This moment foreshadows a coming day when all will stand face to face with the King of kings, and the true meaning of atonement will be fulfilled—not just covered, but completed in the person of Yeshua, our eternal High Priest (Hebrews 9:11–12).

The Day the High Priest Enters the Holy of Holies—On *Yom Kippur*, the holiest man in Israel entered the holiest place on earth to declare the holiest Name of God. Dressed not in his ornate priestly garments, but in simple white linen (Leviticus 16:4), the high priest modeled purity and humility.

He began by offering a bull as a sin offering for himself and his household. Then came two goats—one for the LORD, the other as the scapegoat (*Azazel*). Lots were cast to determine their roles (Leviticus 16:7–10). The goat for the LORD was sacrificed, its blood sprinkled upon the mercy seat inside the Holy of Holies. The scapegoat, bearing the sins of the people, was led into the wilderness, symbolically removing Israel's iniquity (Leviticus 16:21–22).

Meanwhile, the people fasted, prayed, and afflicted their souls (Leviticus 23:26–32). The Book of Jonah was read aloud, reminding them of God's vast mercy and forgiveness. Jewish tradition held that a scarlet thread tied to the Temple door would turn white—if their sins were forgiven (Isaiah 1:18). All of this sacred imagery pointed forward to a greater fulfillment: a final atonement, not repeated yearly, but offered once and for all by Messiah Yeshua, our eternal High Priest (Hebrews 9:12, 10:10).

Jesus and the Fulfillment of *Yom Kippur*—When Yeshua (Jesus) died on the Cross, the veil in the Temple was torn from top to bottom (Luke 23:44–46), symbolizing that access to the Holy of Holies—God's presence—was no longer limited to the high priest once a year. Through His own blood, He made a way for all who believe.

The Book of Hebrews proclaims Jesus as our Great High Priest, who entered not an earthly tabernacle, but Heaven itself, offering His own blood for eternal redemption (Hebrews 9:11–28). No longer would the blood of bulls and goats be required year after year. He became both the perfect sacrifice and the scapegoat, bearing the iniquity—deep moral corruption, sin, and wickedness—of us all and removing our sin as far as the east is from the west.

When Jesus (Yeshua) stood in the synagogue in Nazareth and read from Isaiah 61:2, proclaiming "the acceptable Year of the LORD" (Luke 4:18–21), He was announcing a spiritual Jubilee—a divine season of liberty, release, and restoration. His declaration echoed the heart of *Yom Kippur* and Jubilee themes.

But in a striking parallel to the scapegoat ritual of the Day of Atonement, the people rose up in anger and attempted to cast Him off a cliff (Luke 4:29), unknowingly reenacting the imagery of rejection and removal that was central to Israel's atonement ceremony (Leviticus 16:10, 21–22).

Yet Yeshua stopped short of completing the prophecy. He did not read the next line from Isaiah 61:2—"and the Day of Vengeance of our God"—because that part was not yet fulfilled. It is reserved for His Second Coming, when He will return not only as Redeemer but also as Judge. In His First Coming, He fulfilled the atonement. In His Second Coming, He will execute judgment. *Yom Kippur* thus bridges both comings—mercy then, vengeance to come.

The First *Yom Kippur*: Moses and the Golden Calf—The roots of *Yom Kippur* can be traced back to one of Israel's darkest moments—the sin of the golden calf (Exodus 32). After the people broke covenant with God, Moses ascended Mount Sinai to intercede on their behalf, fasting for forty days (Deuteronomy 9:18). His act of deep repentance and petitioning culminated in the 10th day of the seventh month—the very day that would later become *Yom Kippur*.

On that day, Moses descended from the mountain with the second set of tablets (the Ten Commandments), not in wrath but in restoration (Exodus 34:29–30). Alongside the new tablets came God's forgiveness, a renewed covenant, and instructions to build the Tabernacle, a dwelling place for God's presence among His people (Exodus 35:4–7).

This moment became the blueprint for *Yom Kippur*: intercession, atonement, and divine indwelling. It marked the first national "Day of Atonement," revealing God's mercy and desire to restore relationship even after grievous sin.

The Prophetic Meaning: Israel's National Redemption—*Yom Kippur* was instituted specifically for the nation of Israel (Exodus 19:6)—a kingdom of priests and a holy nation. It is Israel's national Day of Atonement, whereas, Passover represents individual redemption. According to God's divine order, the national cleansing on *Yom Kippur* was to prepare Israel to fulfill her priestly role five days later during *Sukkot* (Feast of Tabernacles), when seventy bulls were sacrificed on behalf of the seventy nations listed in Genesis 10 (Numbers 29:13–32).

This feast points prophetically to a future day when the veil over Israel's heart will be lifted. As Zechariah 12:10 declares, "They shall look upon Me whom they have pierced, and they shall mourn for Him . . ." And Romans 11:26 assures, "And so all Israel shall be saved." That moment of national repentance, restoration, and reconciliation will take place on a future *Yom Kippur*—when Israel finally sees her Messiah face to face.

Revelation: The Heavenly *Yom Kippur*—The Book of Revelation mirrors the prophetic imagery of *Yom Kippur*, presenting a heavenly version of the most sacred day on God's calendar.

In Revelation 6, the souls under the altar cry out for justice—much like the high priest interceded with pleas for mercy on behalf of the people (Revelation 6:9–11). Then in Revelation 8, incense and prayers rise before the throne of God (Revelation 8:3–6), paralleling the high priest offering incense in the Holy of Holies on *Yom Kippur*.

Revelation 11:19 unveils the Ark of the Covenant in Heaven—a direct reference to the Holy of Holies, visible only once a year on this appointed day. Later, in Revelation 15:8, the heavenly temple is filled with smoke, and no one may enter until the judgments are completed—echoing Leviticus 16:17, where no man was permitted in the Tabernacle while the high priest performed the atonement rites.

Finally, in Revelation 19, the Messiah appears in a blood-stained garment, riding forth in judgment. The armies following Him are clothed in fine white linen (Revelation 19:13–15), reflecting both righteousness and the simple linen garments of the high priest. This scene recalls Isaiah 63, where Messiah treads the winepress of judgment alone on the Day of Vengeance.

Jubilee: The Proclamation of Liberty—According to Leviticus 25:9, liberty was to be proclaimed throughout the land on *Yom Kippur* in the Year of Jubilee. This was not only a time of physical restoration—land returned, debts forgiven—but also a spiritual foreshadowing of ultimate redemption.

When Jesus stood in the synagogue and read from Isaiah 61:2, proclaiming "the acceptable Year of the LORD," He was declaring a spiritual Jubilee—a divine proclamation of freedom, healing, and restoration (Luke 4:17–21).

The prophet Hosea offers a profound prophetic framework for understanding God's redemptive timeline. In Hosea 5:15–6:2, the LORD declares that after "two days" He will revive Israel, and "on the third day" they shall live in His sight.

> I will go and return to My place, till they acknowledge their offense, and seek My face: in their affliction they will seek Me early. Come, and let us return unto the LORD: for He has torn, and He will heal us; He has smitten, and He will bind us up. After two days will He revive us: in the third day He will raise us up, and we shall live in His sight. (Hosea 5:15–6:2)

If, as 2 Peter 3:8 reminds us, "one day is with the Lord as a thousand years," then these "two days" symbolically represent two thousand years. This period aligns with the Church Age, now nearing its close.

As we approach the end of this second "day," we stand at the threshold of the third—ushering in the Tribulation, followed by the Millennial Kingdom. This "third day" points to the resurrection of Israel, the return of the Messiah, and the dawning of the Millennial Kingdom.

More than a prophetic milestone, it also echoes the ultimate fulfillment of the final and 115th Jubilee and Year 5800 AM—a divine convergence. The 115th Jubilee—a span of fifty years multiplied 115 times—lands prophetically on the year 5800 AM (*Anno Mundi*) on the biblical Creation calendar. This is not a coincidence, but a culmination. Jubilee, by definition, is a time of release, restoration, and return. When multiplied out (50 x 115 = 5750), and the fiftieth year Jubilee cycle is added, it completes at 5800 AM, signaling a fullness of time—a divine rest on a cosmic scale.

The numeric symbolism adds another prophetic layer: $1 + 1 + 5 = 7$, the number of divine perfection and completion. The 5800th year, therefore, marks not only the 115th Jubilee but potentially the final Jubilee, pointing forward to the Messianic reign, the restoration of Israel, and the dawning of the Millennial Kingdom.

This convergence is more than mathematical—it's Heaven's proclamation of liberty. (More on this in the Fifth Harbinger: The Shemitah Cycles chapter.)

A Day of Vengeance and Reward—*Yom Kippur* is not only a Day of Atonement—it is also a day of divine judgment and righteous reward. While *Rosh HaShanah* marks the opening of the books, *Yom Kippur* seals the verdict. This ten-day period, known as the Days of Awe, culminates in the most solemn of appointments between God and His people.

Revelation 11:18 gives a striking summary of this moment:

> And the nations were angry, and Your wrath is come, and the time of the dead, that they should be judged, and that You should give reward unto Your servants the prophets, and to the saints, and them that fear Your name, small and great; and should destroy them which destroy the earth. (Revelation 11:18)

This verse captures the dual nature of *Yom Kippur*: judgment for the wicked and reward for the righteous. On this day, destinies are finalized, justice is executed, and redemption is extended to those who are written in the Book of Life.

Removing the Veil: Seeing Face to Face—Isaiah 25:7 declares:

> And He will destroy in this mountain the face of the covering cast over all people, and the veil that is spread over all nations. (Isaiah 25:7)

This veil—spiritual blindness and partial understanding—has long obscured the fullness of God's redemptive plan. On *Yom Kippur*, the veil of the Temple was temporarily removed once a year, allowing the high priest to enter the Holy of Holies and meet with God face to face (Leviticus 16).

In the same way, (Ezekiel 20:33–35) prophesies that God will bring Israel into the "wilderness of the peoples" and plead with them face to face, just as He did in the days of Egypt. And 1 Corinthians 13:12 reminds us:

> For now we see through a glass, darkly; but then face to face: now I know in part; but then shall I know even as also I am known. (1 Corinthians 13:12)

Both Jews and Christians currently "see in part," but the time is coming when the veil will be lifted, and the Bride will behold the Bridegroom in full glory—no longer through shadows, but in the radiance of unveiled truth.

Restoration of All Things—Acts 3:19–21 teaches that Jesus will not return until the restoration of all things spoken by the prophets of old. This restoration is not merely spiritual—it includes the recovery of God's divine calendar and the prophetic meaning embedded within His appointed feasts.

> Repent you therefore, and be converted, that your sins may be blotted out, when the times of refreshing shall come from the presence of the Lord. And He shall send Jesus Christ, which before was preached unto you: whom the heaven must receive until the times of restitution of all things, which God has spoken by the mouth of all His holy prophets since the world began. (Acts 3:19–21).

To fully embrace this restoration, the Church must awaken to its true identity—grafted into the commonwealth of Israel (Romans 11). It's not about replacing Israel, but recognizing the Jewish roots of our faith and the Messiah we follow. The feasts are not relics of the past; they are rehearsals of future glory, embedded in God's timeline for redemption. As we align ourselves with His appointed times, we participate in the unfolding of His eternal plan.

Misunderstanding the Jewish Messiah—Many Jewish people do not recognize Yeshua (Jesus) as the Messiah—not because He fails to meet the Messianic criteria, but because He has often been presented in a Gentile framework, divorced from His Jewish identity and Torah observance. Over the centuries, church traditions have redefined Him in ways foreign to His first-century Jewish context.

Deuteronomy 13 warns explicitly against prophets who lead others away from the commandments of God. From a Jewish perspective, when Yeshua is portrayed as having rejected the Torah—or when churches teach that He abolished the Law—it becomes a theological disqualification. But this portrayal is inaccurate. In His own words, Jesus declared:

> Think not that I am come to destroy the Law, or the Prophets (Old Testament): I am not come to destroy, but to fulfill. For verily I say unto you, Till heaven and earth pass, one jot or one tittle shall in no means pass from the Law, till all be fulfilled. (Matthew 5:17–18).

To bridge this misunderstanding, it is vital that the Church return to the authentic, Torah-honoring Messiah of Scripture—Yeshua the Jew—who came not to erase the commandments, but to embody and fulfill them perfectly.

> Master, which is the great commandment in the Law? Jesus said unto him, You shalt love the LORD your God with all your heart, and with all your soul, and with all your mind. This is the first and great commandment. And the second is like unto it, You shalt love your neighbor as yourself. On these two commandments hang all the Law and the Prophets. (Matthew 22:36–40)

Jesus' summary of the commandments in Matthew 22:36–40 captures the essence of the entire moral Law given in the Torah. The first four of the Ten Commandments center on loving God—having no other gods, avoiding idolatry, honoring His name, and keeping the Sabbath. The remaining six focus on loving others—honoring parents, refraining from murder, adultery, theft, false witness, and coveting. By distilling these into two commandments—Love the LORD your God and love your neighbor as yourself—Jesus showed that love is the foundation of all divine instruction. Everything in the Law and the Prophets rests upon this dual command of wholehearted devotion and relational integrity.

The Joseph Parallel: Hidden in Egypt—In Genesis 42, Joseph's brothers stood before him but did not recognize him—he looked, spoke, and ruled like an Egyptian. To them, he was a stranger veiled in a foreign identity. But in Genesis 45, Joseph could no longer restrain himself. He sent everyone away and revealed his true identity to his brothers in private. In that moment, there was weeping—not of condemnation, but of reunion, forgiveness, and restoration.

In the same way, Yeshua (Jesus) remains hidden from much of Israel. Clothed in the "garments" of Gentile tradition and misunderstood across generations, He is often unrecognizable to His own brethren. Yet a day is coming when He will reveal Himself—not as a foreigner, but as their long-lost Brother, the true Son of David. There will be mourning (Zechariah 12:10), but it will lead to a revelation of love, national repentance, and prophetic restoration.

Conclusion: The Holiest Day in Prophetic Perspective—*Yom Kippur* is a day of paradox and promise—solemn yet hopeful, marked by both judgment and mercy, confession and cleansing, mourning and renewal. As the Day of Atonement, it points beyond ancient rituals to a prophetic future when Israel will be purified, the nations will be judged, and the earth will be restored.

The veil will be lifted. The scapegoat will be recognized. And the Great High Priest will return—not with the blood of bulls and goats, but robed in garments stained with His own blood (Isaiah 63:1–3; Revelation 19:13)—to tread the winepress of wrath and complete the final atonement.

This sacred day is not just a remembrance—it is a rehearsal. A divine dress rehearsal for the day when books are sealed, destinies are finalized, and eternity begins.

Let us, therefore, afflict our souls, turn from sin, and prepare our hearts to meet the King face to face. For on some future *Yom Kippur*, the court of Heaven will convene one final time . . . and the verdict will echo through eternity.

Blessed be His glorious Name.

7. Feast of Tabernacles (Sukkot): God Dwelling With Us Again

The Feast of Tabernacles—*Sukkot*—is the seventh and final appointed time in the annual cycle of God's *moedim* (appointed festivals) listed in Leviticus 23:33–43. It's placement in the seventh month is no coincidence. In Scripture, the number seven symbolizes completion, perfection, and divine fulfillment, and *Sukkot* prophetically marks the culmination of God's redemptive plan—His desire to dwell with His people forever.

Also known as the Feast of Booths, the Feast of Ingathering, the Season of Our Joy, and prophetically, the Feast of the Nations, *Sukkot* is both historical and prophetic. It commemorates the forty years Israel spent living in temporary shelters (*sukkot*) under God's care and provision in the wilderness (Nehemiah 8:14–17). At the same time, it points forward to the coming Messianic Kingdom, when Messiah will reign on earth and God will tabernacle among His people (Revelation 21:3).

What makes this feast uniquely joyous is that God commands celebration. It is the only feast where the people are explicitly instructed:

> And you shall rejoice before the LORD your God seven days. (Leviticus 23:40)

In essence, *Sukkot* is God's way of saying, "No whining allowed!" It is a mandatory celebration of God's provision, presence, and promise of eternal fellowship. This feast becomes even more profound when seen in its future prophetic dimensions—a rehearsal for the day when God Himself will dwell with mankind in the New Jerusalem, and sorrow will be no more.

The Joy of Temporary Dwelling—The *sukkah*—a fragile booth made of wood, branches, and open to the sky—reminds us of a powerful truth: our lives are temporary. Just as Israel lived in makeshift shelters during their wilderness journey, we, too, dwell in temporary vessels as we journey toward eternity. The apostle Paul echoes this in 2 Corinthians 5:1, describing our earthly bodies as "tabernacles"—tents destined to be replaced by a permanent, heavenly dwelling. Likewise, Peter refers to his own body as a tabernacle he would soon put off (2 Peter 1:13–14), signaling an imminent transition from the earthly to the eternal.

Living in booths during *Sukkot* is not merely a remembrance of Israel's past but a prophetic rehearsal. It teaches that God chooses to dwell with us now, even in our fragile, temporary condition. But one day, we will be clothed with glory, transformed, and made ready to dwell with Him forever. Building and inhabiting the *sukkah* becomes a living parable—one that anticipates the day when we will no longer dwell in temporal bodies, but in the eternal kingdom, face to face with our Creator.

Messiah's Birth: The Word Tabernacled Among Us—John 1:14 declares, "And the Word was made flesh, and dwelt among us." The Greek word used for "dwelt" is *skenoo*, which literally means "to tabernacle," "to pitch a tent," or "to encamp." This is no coincidence. It points directly to *Sukkot*, the Feast of Tabernacles. Yeshua didn't arrive in the dead of winter—He came during a season of rejoicing, fulfilling the prophetic symbolism of God dwelling with His people.

All signs support this timing:

- Shepherds were in the fields watching their flocks by night (Luke 2:8), something that would have been unlikely during the cold Judean winter.
- Bethlehem and Jerusalem were overcrowded, not because of a Roman census in isolation, but because two million pilgrims had flooded the region for the fall feasts, making it nearly impossible to find lodging.
- The crowds would have been singing Psalm 118, including verse 15: "The voice of rejoicing and salvation is in the tabernacles of the righteous: the right hand of the LORD does valiantly." The very name "Yeshua" means salvation—He was born amid the tabernacles of rejoicing.
- Yeshua was born under the stars, likely in a *sukkah* (temporary shelter), and wrapped in priestly swaddling cloths, traditionally used for sacrificial lambs—foreshadowing His mission as the Lamb of God.

On the eighth day, a time known as *Shemini Atzeret*, He was circumcised and named Yeshua (Jesus), fulfilling both Genesis 17:10–12 and Luke 2:21. It was the perfect convergence: the Lamb of God, entering the covenant of Abraham, in the Temple of God, at the appointed time.

This birth narrative doesn't just fulfill prophecy—it inhabits it. Messiah's arrival during *Sukkot* illustrates the ultimate divine desire: to dwell with His people, both then and forevermore.

The Light of the World and the Living Water—two powerful ceremonies marked the climactic days of *Sukkot* in Temple times, both saturated with messianic expectation:

1. **The Illumination Ceremony**—In the Court of the Women, four towering lampstands—each about 75-feet high—were erected, their massive flames lighting up the entire city of Jerusalem. The wicks were fashioned from the worn-out linen garments of the priests. It was during this spectacular festival of light that Yeshua stood and declared:

   I am the Light of the World: he that follows Me shall not walk in darkness, but shall have the light of life. (John 8:12)

This declaration wasn't random—it was a direct fulfillment of the prophetic symbolism of the festival. The Light had come to dwell among men.

2. **The Water Libation Ceremony**—Each morning during *Sukkot*, priests would descend to the Pool of Siloam, draw "living water," and carry it back to the Temple. There, they would pour it out on the altar along with wine—an appeal for rain, provision, and messianic redemption. This act was accompanied by great rejoicing, and the singing of Isaiah 12 and Psalm 118.

It was on the last and greatest day of the feast, as the people recited: "With joy shall you draw water out of the wells of salvation" (Isaiah 12:3), that Yeshua stood and cried out:

   If any man thirst, let him come unto Me, and drink. He that believes on Me, as the Scripture has said, out of his belly shall flow rivers of living water. (John 7:37–38)

The people were literally singing about "the wells of Yeshua," the Hebrew word for *salvation*, as the embodiment of that very salvation stood in their midst. The Holy One of Israel was with them—tabernacling among them—and yet, many did not recognize Him.

Zechariah's Prophecy: Tabernacles in the Messianic Kingdom—Zechariah 14 reveals a stunning truth: after Messiah returns and defeats the nations, all who survive will be required to come up to Jerusalem year after year to celebrate the Feast of Tabernacles (*Sukkot*). This is no symbolic gesture. Scripture says that those who refuse will suffer divine consequence: no rain will fall on their land (Zechariah 14:16–19).

This isn't presented as a quaint tradition—it's a commanded observance in the coming kingdom. It confirms that God's appointed times (*moedim*) are not obsolete or mere "Old Testament" legalism. Rather, they are eternal signposts of His redemptive plan. The Feast of Tabernacles, in particular, celebrates His greatest promise: to dwell with His people forever—past, present, and future. What was once a rehearsal will be the reality of His presence among the nations.

A Prophetic War and a Covenant Meal—During *Sukkot*, many Jewish communities read from Ezekiel 38–39 and Zechariah 12–14, powerful prophetic passages that foretell the climactic battle of Gog and Magog and the return of Messiah. Ezekiel describes a great earthquake and a divine summons to the birds of the air to gather for a feast—a covenant meal of judgment—to consume the flesh of kings and mighty men (Ezekiel 39:17–20), paralleled explicitly in Revelation 19:17–18.

This battle represents more than military conflict. It is a confrontation between human pride—symbolized by Gog, which in Hebrew carries the root meaning of "roof" or exaltation—and humble dependence on God, depicted in the *sukkah*. While a roof offers manmade security, the *sukkah* is fragile, temporary, and open to the heavens. It is a shelter of trust and surrender, reminding us that our true covering is the presence of God, not the strength of man.

Rejoicing in the Torah and the Living Word—The final and climactic day of the fall feasts is *Shemini Atzeret*—the Eighth Day Assembly—which is also celebrated as *Simchat Torah*, the Rejoicing of the Torah. On this day, the scroll of God's Word is paraded, kissed, and danced with in jubilant celebration. It is a declaration that God's Word is life and joy.

In John 8:6–11, Yeshua—the Word made flesh, the Living Torah—was teaching in the Temple. Ironically, while the people were to be rejoicing in the Torah, the religious leaders attempted to weaponize it. They brought before Him a woman caught in adultery, hoping to trap the very Author of the Law.

Instead, Yeshua stooped and wrote in the dust—a possible allusion to Jeremiah 17:13, which says, "Those who turn away from You shall be written in the dust." As each accuser slipped away in shame, the woman remained, alone before the only One with the authority to condemn. But He spoke life instead: "Neither do I condemn you: go, and sin no more."

On the day when they were meant to celebrate the Torah, they twisted it to condemn. Yet the Torah incarnate used it to redeem. This moment captures the heart of *Simchat Torah*—not just the joy of receiving the Word, but the joy of encountering the Redeemer who fulfills it.

Dwelling with God Forever—The Feast of Tabernacles is not merely a historical observance—it is God's yearly invitation and prophetic reminder that His greatest desire is to dwell with His people. From Eden's garden to Israel's wilderness journey, from the Tabernacle of Moses to the incarnation of Messiah, from the Millennial reign to the unveiling of the New Jerusalem—this is the heartbeat of Scripture.

Revelation 21:3 proclaims the glorious fulfillment: "Behold, the tabernacle of God is with men, and He will dwell with them."

This is the ultimate *Sukkot*—the eternal indwelling of God among His redeemed. Every layer of redemptive history—from Genesis to Revelation, from Exodus to Bethlehem, from the earthly tabernacle to the heavenly temple—points to this climactic truth: God with us. Emmanuel.

God's Appointed Times: A Visual Recap on the Seven Feasts of the LORD

To bring clarity to this rich and layered material, the following chart has been included. It visually summarizes the Holy Days of the LORD. Whether you are new to these truths or deeply familiar with them, this visual is meant to serve as a final reflection for this section—a way to internalize the pattern of God's feasts and the prophetic rehearsal they offer for what is to come.

Let this chart anchor the message of this section:

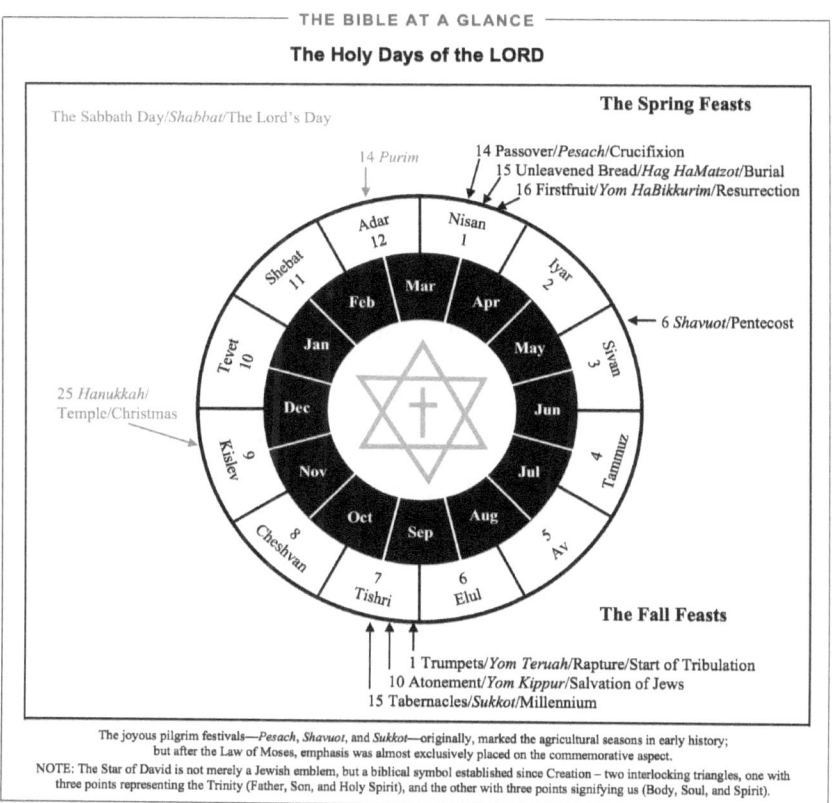

Figure 7 – The Holy Days of the LORD

This section has taken us on a prophetic journey through the seven Feasts of the LORD, also called *moedim*—divinely appointed times that reveal God's redemptive calendar for humanity. These feasts are not merely Jewish cultural traditions or ancient agricultural celebrations. They are God's holy convocations, established in Leviticus 23, designed to point us to Messiah's mission—past, present, and future.

While all seven feasts are sacred and prophetic, three of them—Passover (*Pesach*), Pentecost (*Shavuot*), and Tabernacles (*Sukkot*)—are known as the *Shalosh Regalim*, or pilgrimage festivals, when all Israelite males were commanded to appear before the LORD in Jerusalem (Deuteronomy 16:16). Originally tied to harvest seasons, these feasts have since taken on commemorative significance after the giving of the Torah. Each now marks a pivotal moment in Israel's story, foreshadowing even greater moments in God's eternal plan.

The remaining four feasts—Unleavened Bread (*Hag HaMatzot*), Firstfruits (*Yom HaBikkurim*), the Feast of Trumpets (*Yom Teruah*), and the Day of Atonement (*Yom Kippur*)—are no less significant. Together, these seven feasts form a sacred cycle: beginning with personal deliverance, moving through national redemption, and culminating in global restoration.

We are not aimless wanderers in time—God has given us a calendar, a compass, and a covenant. The feasts are not only shadows of what was, and what is, but brilliant previews of what shall be.

———◆◆◆———

The afternoon sun filtered through the stained-glass windows of Irene's study, scattering dappled colors across a walnut writing desk cluttered with open books, notecards, and a steaming cup of cinnamon tea. The kaleidoscope of light caught the gold-edged pages of her Bible, opened midway through the Book of John. Outside, the rustle of early autumn leaves whispered like echoes of another realm—earth and Heaven brushing shoulders in the quiet.

A stillness settled over the room. It wasn't just the peace of an undisturbed afternoon, but something weightier. A gentle pressing. A spiritual nudge. Revelation was near, hovering like a flame just out of reach, ready to illuminate.

"Ann, as we've been diving into the Feasts of the LORD and their prophetic implications, I keep wondering about two other celebrations—*Hanukkah* and *Purim*. I remember they were mentioned briefly under the Second Harbinger: The Biblical Calendars, but they aren't part of the original seven feasts in Leviticus 23. Still, didn't Jesus observe at least one of them?"

I leaned forward.

"You're absolutely right, Irene. Let's start with *Hanukkah*, also known as the Feast of Dedication. It's not one of the Levitical feasts, but it's mentioned in John 10:22. Scripture says, 'Then came the Feast of Dedication at Jerusalem. It was winter, and Jesus was in the temple area, walking in Solomon's Colonnade.' That alone tells us something powerful: Yeshua Himself honored this feast."

Irene, nodding slowly.

"So what exactly does *Hanukkah* commemorate?"

I smiled, the kind of smile that carried reverence as much as affection—like someone remembering a miracle firsthand.

"Historically," I said, gently, "*Hanukkah* marks the rededication of the Temple in 165 BC, after one of the darkest moments in Jewish history. The Seleucid king, Antiochus Epiphanes, had defiled the sacred altar by sacrificing a pig—an unclean animal—on it. He even poured the pig's blood over the sacred scrolls. His goal wasn't just political control. It was spiritual erasure. He wanted to wipe out Jewish worship entirely, replacing it with Hellenistic paganism."

I paused, letting the weight of history settle in the space between us.

I continued.

"But God wasn't silent. Out of the shadows rose the Maccabees—a small band of Jewish warriors led by Mattathias and his son Judah. They fought back against impossible odds. And through divine intervention, they reclaimed Jerusalem and the desecrated Temple. Then came the moment of rededication—*Hanukkah*, which literally means 'dedication.'"

The fireplace across the study crackled softly, as if in quiet agreement, echoing the courage and consecration of generations past.

Irene furrowed her brow, a hint of unease shadowing her thoughtful expression.

"That sounds eerily familiar—like something that could happen again."

I gave a solemn nod, sensing the gravity of her realization.

"Exactly! That's what makes *Hanukkah* more than just a historical commemoration—it's a prophetic dress rehearsal. Antiochus Epiphanes wasn't merely a villain of the past; he was a foreshadow, a living blueprint of the Antichrist to come."

I leaned forward, lowering my voice as if to underscore the weight of it.

"Antiochus tried to erase truth by defiling what was sacred, not through mass extermination, but through forced assimilation. He outlawed Torah observance, desecrated the Temple, and seduced God's people into compromise. That same pattern will unfold again. The Antichrist won't come at first with open violence—he'll come with persuasion. Deception. Reframing good as evil and evil as good."

Irene's eyes widened slightly, a spark of recognition behind them. She was connecting the dots.

I continued, "Where Haman in the *Purim* story sought instant annihilation, Antiochus—and prophetically, the Antichrist—uses the slow erosion of truth. It's not just about persecution—it's about reprogramming, reshaping righteousness, and inviting God's people to bow in subtle stages. That's what makes the deception so deadly."

Irene let out a slow breath, her voice hushed with realization.

"Wow . . . I've always thought of *Hanukkah* as a kind of Jewish Christmas. The menorah, the dreidel, the gifts—but now I see it points to something so much deeper."

I smiled gently, heartened by her awakening insight.

"It really does. That oil in the menorah—the miracle that it lasted eight days—isn't just a charming tradition. It represents God's presence—His sustaining power in the darkest hour, when logic said the flame should've gone out. But it didn't."

Pausing, I met her gaze.

"That's the deeper meaning. The faithful remnant didn't just win a battle—they rededicated the Temple. And God responded by keeping the light burning. In the days ahead, believers will face the same test. The call won't be to physical war, but to spiritual resolve. To rededicate our hearts, to reject compromise, and to remain faithful—even when doing so costs us everything."

Irene leaned forward, the flicker of insight bright in her eyes.

"And the number symbolizes dedication, right? Like circumcision on the eighth day, or the eighth day of Tabernacles when Solomon's Temple was dedicated?"

I nodded, the connection settling like a warm thread between us.

"Precisely. The number eight shows up again and again at moments of new beginnings and holy dedication. It's no accident. It's God's fingerprint on the timeline of redemptive history."

I paused, letting the weight of it linger before continuing.

"Even Daniel's visions—of Antiochus Epiphanes, the little horn—weren't just history lessons. They were prophetic templates. Daniel saw the same events from multiple angles: a towering statue, four beasts rising from the sea, a ram and a goat locked in conflict. Each was a new layer of the same warning."

My voice dropped slightly, more reflective.

"It's as if God is saying, 'Pay attention—I'm going to show this to you until you recognize it when it comes again.' And Ecclesiastes 1:9 confirms it: 'There is nothing new under the sun.' These aren't ancient fables. They are rehearsals of what's coming."

Irene's brow furrowed as the pieces began to align.

"So *Hanukkah* is not just historical—it's prophetic. It actually helps us interpret what Jesus meant when He warned about the abomination of desolation in Matthew 24."

I met her gaze with a quiet intensity.

"Exactly. When Yeshua spoke those words, His disciples would've immediately thought back to *Hanukkah*. They understood Antiochus's desecration of the Temple not as distant history, but as a lens—a warning of what would come again."

My tone grew more solemn.

"Just like then, we'll face a season of persecution wrapped in the illusion of peace. There will be pressure to assimilate, to compromise, to redefine righteousness. And the sobering truth is—many believers are already bending to modern-day Antiochus systems. They think they can mix truth with error, merge worship with idolatry. But history, and prophecy, warn us: that path leads to spiritual ruin."

Irene tilted her head, a flicker of curiosity in her voice.

"That's sobering. Now what about *Purim*? It seems more festive—like a Jewish Mardi Gras. But surely there's more to it than costumes and cookies?"

I offered a knowing smile.

"Oh, there's so much more. *Purim* is the Feast of Lots, commemorating one of the most dramatic reversals in Jewish history. Haman cast *purim*—lots—to determine the day the Jews would be wiped out. But God's hidden hand was at work the entire time."

Leaning forward slightly, I continued.

"Through Queen Esther's boldness and Mordecai's unshakable integrity, Haman's wicked plot was unraveled. In a divine twist, he was executed on the very gallows he built for God's people. *Purim* reminds us that even when God's name isn't mentioned—like in the Book of Esther—His presence is powerfully active, orchestrating redemption behind the scenes."

Irene's brow furrowed thoughtfully.

"So if *Hanukkah* is a warning about assimilation, then *Purim* is a celebration of survival?"

I nodded, the weight of the contrast settling in.

"That's a good way to frame it. But even more than survival, *Purim* reveals the paradox of final reversal."

I paused, letting the truth sink in before continuing.

"God is never explicitly named in the Book of Esther, and yet His fingerprints are unmistakable—woven through every twist of the plot. What Satan intended for destruction, God turned into deliverance. That's not just history—it's theology. It's the pattern of the Cross."

My voice softened.

"*Purim* is prophetic too. It reminds us that even when God appears silent, He is never absent. He's sovereign. He's setting the stage for redemption, often in ways we don't see until the final act."

Irene's eyes glistened, her voice soft with reflection.

"I love that. It gives hope, especially when the world feels upside down."

I offered a gentle smile, the warmth of her faith anchoring the moment.

"And there's one more key difference worth noticing."

I leaned forward slightly, letting the weight of history speak.

"Haman wanted extermination—total, indiscriminate annihilation of the Jewish people. That was the raw, unmasked spirit of Satan at work: destroy, erase, obliterate."

"But Antiochus?" I continued.

"He was more subtle. He didn't demand that Jews stop being Jewish. He just wanted them to stop worshiping the God of Israel—to blend in, to compromise, to let go of obedience in the name of progress. That's the spirit of Antichrist. And honestly, it's far more dangerous. Because it doesn't just kill the body—it erodes the soul."

Irene's voice caught slightly, her brow furrowed in concern.

"That really hits home. We're seeing that kind of pressure right now—believers being told to compromise in the name of peace or tolerance."

I nodded, the gravity of her words settling between us.

"Exactly. And Paul warned us—2 Thessalonians 2, describes the Antichrist as the 'lawless one'—*anomos* in Greek—someone completely opposed to God's Law, His Torah, His ways."

I paused, letting that sink in.

"Those who don't love the truth, Scripture says, will be handed over to a strong delusion. That's not just deception from the outside—it's surrender from within."

Irene folded her hands tightly in her lap, listening intently.

"That's why *Hanukkah* and *Purim* matter so deeply," I continued.

"They're more than stories. They're blueprints for the faithful—reminders to be bold like the Maccabees, resisting assimilation at all costs, and wise like Esther, standing courageously in the gap. Both feasts call us to the same posture: faithful in persecution, courageous in obedience."

Irene leaned back slowly, her eyes thoughtful.

"So while they're not Levitical feasts, they're still crucial—essential, really—to understanding the end times."

I offered a quiet, affirming smile.

"Absolutely. *Hanukkah* opens our eyes to the Antichrist's strategy: deception cloaked in assimilation. And *Purim*? It's God's reminder that even when evil seems to have the upper hand, His deliverance is already in motion."

My voice softened, though the message held firm.

"Together, they prepare us for what's coming—persecution, pressure, even moments of seeming silence. But they also teach us to endure. And more than that—they teach us how to triumph."

Irene folded her hands in her lap, her voice low and resolute.

"Then may we be like Esther, like the Maccabees, like those wise virgins with oil in their lamps—watching, faithful, and ready."

A quiet stillness followed her words, like the settling of truth in the air.

"Amen, Irene," I whispered, the weight of the moment not lost on either of us. "The days of dedication and deliverance are returning. The question is—will we stand or will we bow?"

I looked toward the window, where the last golden rays of sun filtered through the glass, casting a flame-like shimmer on the floor.

"God's people must be set apart," I said softly, "filled with His light—and ready for the final reversal."

THE SABBATH AND THE *SHABBAT* INVITATION

The Sabbath—*Shabbat* in Hebrew—is not merely one of God's appointed times; it is the very first one He sanctified (Genesis 2:1–3; Leviticus 23:1–3). Before there was sin, before there was Israel, before the Tabernacle, even before commandments were etched in stone—there was *Shabbat*. Not a place, not a people, but a day was made holy. This sets the Sabbath apart as foundational, a cornerstone woven into the very architecture of Creation.

More than a break from labor, the Sabbath is a weekly return to Eden, a rhythm of rest that echoes forward to the coming Messianic Age, when perfect peace will reign. It is both a commemoration and a prophecy—remembering what was and anticipating what will be.

In a culture consumed with striving, producing, and achieving, the Sabbath dares to declare: "God is enough—and I can rest." It is a holy interruption. A defiant act of trust. To honor *Shabbat* is to remember our Creator, to realign ourselves with His rhythm, and to proclaim our identity not in what we produce, but in whose image we bear.

God didn't bless the seventh day because of what was done on it, but because of what ceased. It was not marked by activity, but by presence. The Sabbath is a divine invitation to step out of chaos and into communion, to lay down our burdens and take up His rest. It is God's weekly love letter. Reminding us: Your worth is not found in doing, but in dwelling—with Me.

Practical Tips for Ushering in Shabbat

Ushering in *Shabbat* is a blessing—it's not a rule to be followed, but a rhythm to be embraced. Far from being rigid or legalistic, the Sabbath is a weekly invitation to breathe, to remember who we are, and to step out of the frenzy of life into the arms of peace. Below are simple yet profound ways to make your *Shabbat* meaningful, restful, and joy-filled.

1. **Prepare Ahead—Create Space for Peace**. Just as God prepared Creation before He rested, we too can prepare our hearts and homes. Finish your errands, tidy up your space, light a candle, and prepare a simple, nourishing meal. This preparation honors the holiness of what is to come.

2. **Mark the Moment—Welcome the Light**. As sundown approaches, light two candles—symbolizing "remember" (*zachor*) and "observe" (*shamor*) the Sabbath. Take communion—bless the wine (or grape juice), the bread (*challah*), and your loved ones. These ancient rituals are not empty gestures—they are gateways into the sacred.

   For many believers, *Shabbat* is also a beautiful moment to take Communion, remembering that Jesus is Lord of the Sabbath and the fulfillment of all God's promises. As you bless the bread and the cup, you are not only welcoming the light of *Shabbat* but also proclaiming the greater light of Messiah, who gave His body and blood for our redemption. This simple act weaves together rest and redemption, making the Sabbath meal both a time of physical refreshment and spiritual renewal.

3. **Disconnect to Reconnect**. Put away the noise. Turn off screens. Unplug from the digital world so you can fully connect—with God, with your family, with your soul. The Sabbath invites presence over productivity, stillness over striving.

4. **Read, Reflect, and Pray**. Begin your *Shabbat* with Scripture. Read from Genesis, the Psalms, or the Gospels. Reflect on the weekly Torah portion or a passage from the New Testament. Sing a hymn or a psalm. Let your soul feast on the Word.

5. **Rest and Rejoice**. Let *Shabbat* be different. Take a nap, go for a walk, share stories at the dinner table. Rejoice in the simplicity of being. Bless your children. Laugh. Eat slowly. Don't chase tasks—delight in presence.

6. **Close with Gratitude—The *Havdalah* Bridge**. As *Shabbat* ends at sundown on Saturday, consider closing with *Havdalah*—a brief but powerful ceremony that marks the separation between the sacred and the ordinary. With candlelight, sweet spices, and wine, this ceremony honors the holiness you've just lived and carries its spark into the week ahead.

Havdalah: A Bridge of Blessing into the New Week

Havdalah—meaning "separation" in Hebrew—is far more than a ritual to close the Sabbath. It is a sacred bridge that gently carries us from the sanctity of *Shabbat* into the rhythm of the week, reminding us that holy time doesn't simply end—it reverberates forward, shaping the days ahead with light, joy, and intention. Where *Shabbat* is cathedral in time, *Havdalah* is its doorway back into the world—graceful, fragrant, and luminous.

This ceremony is not a goodbye, but a whispered benediction: "Take the peace of *Shabbat* with you." It acknowledges that while the sun sets on the Sabbath, its beauty continues to shine within us. *Havdalah* marks the transition between the sacred and the secular, the holy and the ordinary, not with a jolt, but with reverence and joy.

The deeper purpose—*Havdalah* flows from the Hebrew root "*badal*," meaning to divide or distinguish. It is a spiritual act of discernment—of honoring the boundary between what is set apart and what is every day. As God separated light from darkness and set apart the seventh day in Creation, so too do we follow that divine example by separating *Shabbat* from the workweek through this meaningful pause.

To participate in *Havdalah* is to say:

"I have been with God, and now I will carry His peace with me."

The Four Core Elements of *Havdalah*—The ceremony is elegant in its simplicity yet rich in symbolism. It consists of four blessings, three physical elements, and one spiritual declaration:

1. **Wine (or Grape Juice)**—Symbolizes joy and sanctity. Blessing: *Borei p'ri hagafen*—"Who creates the fruit of the vine."

2. **Spices (*Besamim*)**—Symbolize comfort and the soul's refreshment as *Shabbat* departs. Blessing: *Borei minei besamim*—"Who creates varieties of spices."

3. *Havdalah* **Candle**—A braided, multi-wick flame that represents Creation, distinction, and the light that leads us into a new week. Blessing: *Borei me'orei ha'esh*—"Who creates the lights of fire."

4. **The *Havdalah* Blessing**—A poetic declaration thanking God for the distinctions He has made between: holy and secular, light and darkness, Israel and the nations, the seventh day and the six days of labor.

Ritual Actions and Symbolism—Each act in *Havdalah* holds layers of meaning:

- Candlelight Reflection—Many look at their fingernails in the flame's glow, symbolizing the gift of sight and the transition from *Shabbat's* inner light to the world outside.
- Passing the Spices—The fragrant spice box is shared, offering comfort to the soul as the sweetness of *Shabbat* departs.
- Extinguishing the Flame—The candle is often dipped in the leftover wine, symbolizing the end of holy time and the start of something new.
- Final Words—The ceremony closes with the joyful Hebrew phrase: "*Shavua Tov!*"—"Have a good week!" Sometimes, singing and dancing follow as joy overflows from sacred time into sacred living.

Havdalah is not an ending—it's a beginning. It infuses the mundane with meaning. It transforms routine with remembrance. It reminds us that we are not leaving God's presence—we are carrying it with us. In a world that rushes from one moment to the next, *Havdalah* invites us to pause, to remember, and to go forth with blessing.

> Behold, God is my salvation; I will trust, and not be afraid: for the LORD JEHOVAH is my strength and my song; He also is become my salvation. Therefore with joy shall you draw water out of the wells of salvation. (Isaiah 12:2–3)

Let the light of *Shabbat* guide your footsteps. Let the fragrance of rest linger in your spirit. Let the joy of the Sabbath overflow into your week.

The Weekly Torah Portion: A Rhythm of Revelation

One of the most beautiful and unifying traditions in both Jewish and Messianic communities is the weekly Torah portion, or *Parashat HaShavua*. This ancient practice involves reading a specific section of the Torah—Genesis through Deuteronomy—each week, completing the entire Torah within one year. It's a sacred rhythm that spans continents, cultures, and centuries, connecting millions of people through the shared meditation on God's Word.

Each Torah portion has a distinct name, usually drawn from one of the first significant Hebrew words in the text. These names—like *Bereishit* (In the Beginning), *Noach*, or *Lech-Lecha*—form a spiritual roadmap through the narrative of Israel and the foundation of all Scripture. The weekly reading typically spans three to five chapters and is accompanied by two additional readings: one from the Prophets (*Haftarach*) and one from the New Covenant (*B'rit Hadashah*) for those following Yeshua as Messiah. These three layers of Scripture beautifully echo and confirm one another, revealing the unity of God's redemptive plan.

The cycle begins anew each year on *Simchat Torah*, the day following the Feast of Tabernacles (*Sukkot*), reminding us that God's Word is not a book we "finish" but a living, breathing story we are invited to step into again and again. Most communities follow the annual cycle (54 portions in total), while some groups, particularly in antiquity or among certain traditional circles, observe a triennial cycle, dividing the Torah readings over three years.

Here is a complete list of the 54 Torah portions (*Parashot*) in the annual cycle, traditionally read each *Shabbat* (Sabbath) in synagogues around the world. These portions span the entire five Books of Moses and begin anew on *Simchat Torah*, immediately following *Sukkot*:

Book of Genesis (*Bereshit*)
1. *Bereshit*—Genesis 1:1–6:8
2. *Noach*—Genesis 6:9–11:32
3. *Lech-Lecha*—Genesis 12:1–17:27
4. *Vayeira*—Genesis 18:1–22:24
5. *Chayei Sarah*—Genesis 23:1–25:18
6. *Toldot*—Genesis 25:19–28:9
7. *Vayetzei*—Genesis 28:10–32:3
8. *Vayishlach*—Genesis 32:4–36:43
9. *Vayeishev*—Genesis 37:1–40:23
10. *Miketz*—Genesis 41:1–44:17
11. *Vayigash*—Genesis 44:18–47:27

12. *Vayechi*—Genesis 47:28–50:26

Book of Exodus (*Shemot*)

13. *Shemot*—Exodus 1:1–6:1
14. *Va'eira*—Exodus 6:2–9:35
15. *Bo*—Exodus 10:1–13:16
16. *Beshalach*—Exodus 13:17–17:16
17. *Yitro*—Exodus 18:1–20:23
18. *Mishpatim*—Exodus 21:1–24:18
19. *Terumah*—Exodus 25:1–27:19
20. *Tetzaveh*—Exodus 37:20–30:10
21. *Ki Tisa*—Exodus 30:11–34:35
22. *Vayakhel*—Exodus 35:1–38:20
23. *Pekudei*—Exodus 38:21–40:38

Book of Leviticus (*Vayikra*)

24. *Vayikra*—Leviticus 1:1–5:26
25. *Tzav*—Leviticus 6:1–8:36
26. *Shemini*—Leviticus 9:1–11:47
27. *Tazria*—Leviticus 12:1–13:59
28. *Metzora*—Leviticus 14:1–15:33
29. *Acharei Mot*—Leviticus 16:1–18:30
30. *Kedoshim*—Leviticus 19:1–20:27
31. *Emor*—Leviticus 21:1–24:23
32. *Behar*—Leviticus 25:1–26:2
33. *Bechukotai*—Leviticus 26:3–27:34

Book of Numbers (*Bamidbar*)

34. *Bamidbar*—Numbers 1:1–4:20
35. *Naso*—Numbers 4:21–7:89
36. *Beha'alotcha*—Numbers 8:1–12:16
37. *Shelach*—Numbers 13:1–15:41
38. *Korach*—Numbers 16:1–18:32
39. *Chukat*—Numbers 19:1–22:1
40. *Balak*—Numbers 22:2–25:9
41. *Pinchas*—Numbers 25:10–30:1
42. *Matot*—Numbers 30:2–32:42
43. *Masei*—Numbers 33:1–36:13

Book of Deuteronomy (*Devarim*)

44. *Devarim* —Deuteronomy 1:1–3:22

45. *Va'etchanan*— Deuteronomy 3:23–7:11
46. *Eikev*— Deuteronomy 7:12–11:25
47. *Re'eh*— Deuteronomy 11:26–16:17
48. *Shoftim*— Deuteronomy 16:18–21:9
49. *Ki Teitzei*— Deuteronomy 21:10–25:19
50. *Ki Tavo*— Deuteronomy 26:1–29:8
51. *Nitzavim*— Deuteronomy 29:9–30:20
52. *Vayelech*— Deuteronomy 31:1–31:30
53. *Ha'Azinu*— Deuteronomy 32:1–32:52
54. *V'Zot HaBerachah*— Deuteronomy 33:21–34:12 read on *Simchat Torah*

But this weekly rhythm is more than academic study or religious ritual. It is a sacred appointment—an invitation to hear from God, reflect on our identity, and align our lives with His purposes. Through the Torah portion, we are reintroduced weekly to the God who speaks, who guides, and who calls His people into covenant faithfulness.

For believers in Messiah, these readings come alive with even deeper meaning. The *B'rit Hadashah* (New Testament) readings reveal how Yeshua fulfilled the promises and patterns of the Torah (Old Testament). The shadows become substance. The prophecies find their person. The scroll comes alive.

To engage in the weekly Torah portion is to say: "I choose to walk in God's rhythm. I choose to listen, to learn, and to grow with the generations who have walked this path before me." It is not a duty—it is a delight.

If you're wondering what this week's portion is, just look up *Parashat HaShavua* for the current date—or start your own journey through the Torah and discover the eternal truths waiting to unfold in your life.

Understanding the Annual Torah Cycle and the Jewish Calendar—The Jewish annual Torah reading cycle consists of 54 portions (*parashot*) that are read each Sabbath over the course of a year. This cycle begins and ends on *Simchat Torah*—"Rejoicing in the Torah"—immediately following *Sukkot* (the Feast of Tabernacles). It is an integral part of Jewish worship and aligns beautifully with the rhythm of the biblical calendar and its appointed festivals.

Unlike the Gregorian calendar, which has a fixed 52-week structure, the Jewish calendar varies, typically including between 50 and 54 Sabbaths per year. This variation is due to the Hebrew calendar being lunisolar, meaning it is based on both the moon's phases and the solar year, with leap years adding an extra month to maintain alignment with the seasons.

To accommodate the full cycle of 54 Torah portions:

- In longer years (with 54 Sabbaths), each weekly portion is read individually.
- In shorter years (with fewer Sabbaths), some portions are combined and read together. Common pairings include *Vayakhel–Pekudei, Tazria– Metzora, Acharei Mot–Kedoshim, Behar–Bechukotai.*

This dynamic structure ensures that the entirety of the Torah is publicly read each year, regardless of the calendar's length. It is a sacred rhythm, inviting the community to journey through the foundational narrative of Scripture—week by week—anchoring their lives in the unfolding story of God and His people.

Sabbath: A Divine Gift, Not a Burden

The Sabbath is not a legalistic burden—it is a sacred gift. From the very beginning, God designed *Shabbat* as a blessing for humanity, not just for Israel. As Jesus said in Mark 2:27, "And He said unto them, The Sabbath was made for man, and not man for the Sabbath." It was woven into the fabric of Creation itself—set apart before sin, before Israel, before even the tabernacle or temple, there was *Shabbat*—the first thing God ever called holy (Genesis 2:1–3). And He still calls us into it today.

> Thus the heavens and the earth were finished, and all the host of them. And on the seventh day God ended His work which He had made; and He rested on the seventh day from all His work which He had made. And God blessed the seventh day, and sanctified it: because that in it He had rested from all His work which God created and made. (Genesis 2:1–3)

The holy day is not about rigid rules, but about rhythm, rest, and relationship. It's an invitation to cease striving, to step off the treadmill of performance, and to remember that God is enough. *Shabbat* calls us back to Eden and forward to the kingdom—a rehearsal for eternal peace. God is still inviting us into His rest. The only question is: Will we accept the invitation?

Honoring the Sabbath: A Prophetic Connection to the Future

The Sabbath is more than a sacred day of rest rooted in the past—it is a prophetic signpost pointing toward our eternal destiny. *Shabbat* holds within it the echoes of Eden and the rhythms of the Messianic Kingdom to come. Scripture reveals that this weekly observance not only commemorates God's Creation but also anticipates His final restoration.

A Prophetic Pattern: From Creation to the Millennial Reign—In Hebrews 4, the writer speaks of a Sabbath rest that still awaits the people of God. This is not merely poetic language—it is prophetic. Just as God established six days of labor followed by a seventh day of rest, the same pattern overlays human history: six thousand years of toil followed by one thousand years of peace under Messiah's reign—the "seventh day" or Millennial Kingdom.

This thousand-year reign of Messiah, referenced six times in Revelation 20, is more than a period of global peace—it is the ultimate fulfillment of *Shabbat*. Just as the seventh day capped off the week of Creation with rest and sanctity, the seventh millennium—after six thousand years of human history—ushers in a divine era of justice, healing, and holy governance.

In this prophetic Sabbath of time, the earth will rest from war, the curse will be lifted, and Messiah will reign from Jerusalem with righteousness. The creation that once groaned will now rejoice. *Shabbat* was always pointing forward to this: a millennial rest for all creation, under the King of kings.

The Millennial Temple and Eternal Calendar—Ezekiel 46:1 provides a powerful glimpse into the future Temple in the Messianic Age. It declares that the gates of the inner court will be open on the Sabbath and on the new moon—God's sacred calendar will still be observed. This reveals a profound truth: God's appointed times are not obsolete—they are eternal.

Similarly, Isaiah 66:22–23 states:

> For as the new heavens and the new earth, which I will make, shall remain before Me, says the LORD, so shall your seed and your name remain. And it shall come to pass, that from one new moon to another, and from one Sabbath to another, shall all flesh come to worship before Me, says the Lord. (Isaiah 66:22–23)

This vision of worship in the age to come affirms that the Sabbath is not a relic of the past or merely a "Jewish custom." It is a divine rhythm embedded in the very architecture of Creation and woven into the eternal future.

Just as the new heavens and new earth remain before God, so too will His appointed times—from one new moon to another, and from one *Shabbat* to another. These sacred moments are not temporary shadows but everlasting signposts pointing to God's unchanging nature and His desire for communion with His people.

The Sabbath is a perpetual covenant that transcends time, culture, and covenantal eras. It was sanctified at Creation, codified at Sinai, honored by Messiah, and prophesied to endure into the Millennial Kingdom and beyond.

In the Millennial Temple, and even into the new creation described in Isaiah 66, *Shabbat* will continue to be honored by *all flesh*. It is not only a memorial of what God has done but also a prophetic rehearsal of what is to come—a holy appointment that eternally connects Heaven and earth.

Sabbath as Prophetic Resistance—There is also a spiritual warfare dimension to *Shabbat* observance. In Daniel 7:25, the prophet warns of a future ruler—the Antichrist—who will "think to change times and laws." This is a direct assault on God's calendar and covenant rhythm.

When we honor *Shabbat*, we are doing more than resting—we are bearing prophetic witness. We are declaring, "God is the Lord of time, not man, not governments, not beasts." Each Sabbath becomes a countercultural act of alignment with Heaven's Kingdom and a prophetic resistance against the systems of this world.

The "Lord's Day" in Revelation—In Revelation 1:10, John writes:

> I was in the Spirit on the Lord's Day, and heard behind me a great voice, as of a trumpet. (Revelation 1:10)

While this phrase is often associated with Sunday in modern tradition, its original Hebraic context likely pointed back to *Shabbat*—the day already declared holy and set apart by God in Genesis 2:1–3. It was on this sacred day that prophets, priests, and kings historically received divine revelation.

Living the Future in the Present—When we welcome the Sabbath each week, we are not simply remembering Eden—we are rehearsing for the kingdom. *Shabbat* becomes a sanctuary in time, a prophetic preview of what is to come.

To keep *Shabbat* is to affirm that the King is coming, the kingdom is near, and we are already living in its light.

The Shabbat Invitation: A Cathedral in Time

The renowned Jewish theologian Abraham Joshua Heschel described *Shabbat* as a "cathedral in time." Unlike the temples of stone we build with our hands, this sanctuary is crafted by the rhythm of Creation itself. While we spend most of our lives conquering space—building, buying, achieving—God invites us to sanctify time.

Shabbat is not a relic of religious legalism. It is grace woven into the calendar—a weekly reminder that we are not defined by what we produce, but by whose we are. It is a holy pause, an intentional retreat into God's presence where striving ceases and identity is restored.

Every Friday night, as the sun sets and the world slows, Heaven leans low and gently whispers: "Welcome to My holy day. Come away and be with Me. You are not a slave. You are not what you do. You are My beloved. Rest." To accept the *Shabbat* invitation is to return to Eden, taste the kingdom to come, and trust that God is enough.

THE FAST DAYS: MOURNING THAT WILL BECOME JOY

In Zechariah 8:18–19, the Lord issues a powerful and hope-filled promise:

> And the Word of the LORD of hosts came unto me, saying, Thus says the LORD of hosts; The fast of the fourth month, and the fast of the fifth, and the fast of the seventh, and the fast of the tenth, shall be to the house of Judah joy and gladness, and cheerful feasts; therefore love the truth and peace. (Zechariah 8:18–19)

These four fasts, each tied to moments of national mourning in Jewish history, were originally instituted to commemorate destruction and exile— particularly events surrounding the fall of Jerusalem and the Temple. But here, God promises a stunning transformation: days marked by sorrow will become days of joy, gladness, and cheerful feasts.

This is not a denial of past suffering. Rather, it is the fulfillment of a prophetic reversal—a divine act of redemption that reframes pain into purpose. What once mourned ruin will celebrate restoration. In God's redemptive plan, even the darkest days are not final.

Just as the resurrection transformed the shame of the Cross into victory and glory, these fasts will one day stand as declarations of God's justice, mercy, and faithfulness. In His appointed time, He turns mourning into dancing—not by erasing history, but by redeeming it.

These feasts will not just be celebratory—they will be testimonies. Each one will proclaim: God restores. God redeems. God keeps His promises.

And the call at the end of the passage is just as relevant for us today: "Therefore love the truth and peace" (Zechariah 8:19). In the face of despair, God invites us to anchor ourselves in truth. In a world of strife, He invites us to cling to peace. These are not just moral virtues—they are prophetic postures that prepare us to receive joy when He turns the fast into a feast.

Historical Tragedies Remembered: The Four Fast Days

The Jewish calendar solemnly commemorates four national fasts—days of deep mourning for pivotal tragedies that scarred Israel's collective memory. These are not merely days of historical reflection but prophetic milestones, woven into God's covenantal dealings with His people. Though rooted in devastation, each fast day carries a hidden promise of redemption—a reminder that God is still writing Israel's story.

1. **17th of Tammuz**—The Breach of Jerusalem's Walls

On the 17th of Tammuz, the protective walls of Jerusalem were breached—not once, but twice. First by the Babylonians in 586 BC, and centuries later by the Romans in AD 70. This critical breach initiated the chain of events that led to the destruction of the Holy Temple.

According to Jewish tradition, other calamities occurred on this day: the cessation of the daily offerings, the burning of the Torah by Apostomos, and the erection of an idol in the Temple. This day symbolizes vulnerability and defeat—a warning that no human wall can stand when God's presence departs. It invites us to humility, repentance, and renewed dependence on the only true Stronghold.

2. **9th of Av (*Tisha B'Av*)**—National Destruction and Exile

Tisha B'Av is the most mournful day in the Jewish year. On this date, both the First and Second Temples were destroyed—first by the Babylonians, then by the Romans—nearly 650 years apart. But the sorrow surrounding this day echoes even deeper:

- The expulsion of the Jews from England (1290).
- The expulsion from Spain (1492).
- The outbreak of World War I (1914), laying the groundwork for the Holocaust.

Tisha B'Av encapsulates generational grief, exile, and unfulfilled longing. Yet, through the ashes, a prophetic light glimmers: the same day that has held such sorrow will one day be transformed into rejoicing—when the Third Temple is filled with the glory of Messiah.

3. **3rd of Tishri**—The Assassination of Gedaliah

This lesser-known fast remembers the murder of Gedaliah ben Ahikam, a righteous leader appointed by the Babylonians to govern Judah after the fall of Jerusalem. His assassination (recorded in Jeremiah 41) crushed the final vestiges of Jewish autonomy and provoked renewed exile and bloodshed.

This day is a solemn reminder that internal betrayal can be just as devastating as external attack. It warns of the danger of disunity, factionalism, and the breakdown of trust among God's people.

4. **10th of Tevet**—The Beginning of the Siege of Jerusalem

On the 10th day of the tenth month (Tevet), Nebuchadnezzar of Babylon laid siege to Jerusalem (2 Kings 25:1). The city didn't fall that day, but it was the beginning of the end. The slow stranglehold of judgment had begun.

This fast teaches a profound spiritual truth: judgment often starts quietly, before its impact is fully visible. Just as a siege tightens gradually, spiritual decline often begins subtly. It's a call to vigilance—to recognize the early signs of compromise and to return to God before the walls fall.

Looking Ahead: From Mourning to Joy

These fast days, of Tevet, Tammuz, Av, and Tishri, though anchored in historical sorrow, are not meant to remain as monuments to grief. They are prophetic markers—reminders that even in loss, God is at work. As Zechariah 8:19 declares, the fasts will be transformed into "joy and gladness, and cheerful feasts" under the righteous reign of Messiah.

These solemn days speak of a covenantal journey—from breach to restoration, from exile to return, from mourning to dancing (Psalm 30:11). Each fast whispers a deeper truth: God is not finished with His people. He will rebuild what was torn down. He will restore what was scattered. And He will reign from Zion in peace and glory.

Anticipating Joy on the Other Side of Mourning

These fasts are like shadows, long and dark, cast by the fiery promises of a God who never breaks His Word. They remind us of pain—but also of promise. Zechariah assures us that the day is coming when these fasts will become feasts, when sorrow will be swallowed by joy, and when Jerusalem will be called "The City of Truth" once more (Zechariah 8:3).

> Thus says the LORD; I am returned unto Zion, and will dwell in the midst of Jerusalem: and Jerusalem shall be called the City of Truth; and the mountain of the LORD of hosts the Holy Mountain. (Zechariah 8:3)

Until that day arrives, we fast with hope.
We mourn with faith, not despair.
And we stand as watchmen on the wall—watching for the dawn.

The King is coming.
And every tear will turn to praise.

THE FOURTH HARBINGER HAS AWAKENED

The Feasts Have Been Sounding—Will We Hear the Final Trumpet?

From the very beginning, God embedded His timeline into Creation through the *moedim*—His appointed feasts. These sacred convocations were never meant to be viewed as relics of Judaism or cultural traditions. They are Heaven's rehearsals for redemption, blueprints that chart the course of human history and Messiah's mission. The fourth harbinger is not written in the stars this time—it pulses through the seasons of God's calendar. It beats in the rhythm of sacred time. The feasts are not optional or symbolic—they are strategic, prophetic markers that declare what was, what is, and what is to come.

Each feast reveals a specific act in the divine drama of salvation. Passover was fulfilled in Messiah's death. Unleavened Bread marked His sinless burial. Firstfruits declared His victorious resurrection. Pentecost (*Shavuot*) was fulfilled with the outpouring of the Holy Spirit. These spring feasts were fulfilled to the very day and hour, without deviation. Can we not expect the same divine precision with the fall feasts still awaiting their fulfillment?

Yom Teruah, the Feast of Trumpets, is not merely a celebration—it is the appointed time for the trumpet of God to sound, the dead in Messiah to rise, and the King to return *for* His Bride. *Yom Kippur*, the Day of Atonement, is more than a ritual of national repentance—it is the opening of Heaven's books, the gathering before the Judge, and the revelation of Messiah as High Priest and King. *Sukkot*, the Feast of Tabernacles, is not just about temporary shelters—it points to the coming kingdom when God will once again dwell with man, when the wedding feast of the Lamb becomes reality and joy floods the earth like never before.

The Fourth Harbinger is Not in the Sky—It's in the Calendar

The fourth harbinger is subtle—easily missed by a Church detached from its Hebraic roots and God's prophetic calendar. Yet it is just as loud to those with ears to hear. While the third harbinger unfolded in the heavens, this fourth warning is written in time itself. It speaks through the forgotten Sabbaths, the neglected holy convocations, and the misunderstood feasts that hold eternal significance. The Church has too often exchanged God's calendar for convenience, treating His appointed times as legalistic or irrelevant. But they are anything but. They are prophetic rehearsals for the very events we await: the Rapture, the return of the King, and the reign of the Messiah.

This is not a time for casual observation—it is a time for prophetic alignment. God's calendar is not background noise—it is the symphony to which the end-time Church must tune its heart. We are not on the edge of some vague spiritual awakening. We are standing on the threshold of the King's return. And the feasts are not silent—they are declaring it with every passing season. The feasts have spoken. The calendar is warning. And the hour is late.

Now is the time to reclaim God's appointed times. To return to the rhythm of redemption. To walk in sync with the season of His appearing. The fourth harbinger is calling the Bride to prepare—not for rehearsal this time, but for the wedding itself. These are the days of Elijah. The clock is striking midnight. The dress rehearsal is over. The King is coming.

The signs have already sounded. The feasts have been fulfilled in part—and will soon be fulfilled in full. The calendar is shaking. The trumpet is trembling. And time is running out.

The fourth harbinger has sounded.
The feasts are declaring.
And Jesus is coming.

Are you aligned?
Are you watching?
Are you ready?

CHAPTER SUMMARY

Chapter 8 unveils the Fourth Harbinger: The Feasts That Reveal the Future, shifting the prophetic spotlight from the heavens to God's sacred calendar. Long before the Church existed, before nations had calendars of their own, God established seven divine appointments—His *moedim*—as prophetic rehearsals for the redemptive plan of history. These appointed times, outlined in Leviticus 23, are more than ancient Jewish rituals; they are Heaven's clock—ticking toward the return of the King.

This chapter explores how the spring feasts—Passover, Unleavened Bread, Firstfruits, and Pentecost—were fulfilled with astonishing accuracy at Jesus' First Coming. From His crucifixion to His burial to His resurrection and the outpouring of the Holy Spirit, every holy convocation aligned perfectly with Yeshua's redemptive mission. Likewise, the fall feasts—Feast of Trumpets, Day of Atonement, and Feast of Tabernacles—are understood as shadows yet to be fulfilled in the Messiah's Second Coming.

The feasts are not legalistic leftovers—they are prophetic guideposts. The chapter revisits the Sabbath (*Shabbat*) as the foundational feast, reminding readers that time, not space or matter, was the first thing God declared holy. Honoring the Sabbath connects believers to the divine rhythm, preparing them for the eternal rest to come. The fast days of Israel, too—days of national mourning like *Tisha B'Av*—hold hidden clues to God's restoration plan, as prophesied in Zechariah 8:19.

Ultimately, this fourth harbinger challenges readers to realign their spiritual calendars with God's. The biblical feasts are not optional traditions; they are prophetic blueprints—revealing the Messiah's work, God's covenant with Israel, and the Church's place in His unfolding plan. The feasts are not only sacred history—they are sacred rehearsal for the coming glory.

KEY TAKEAWAYS

- The seven Feasts of the LORD are not just past traditions but future-oriented rehearsals, prophetically fulfilled in Christ's First Coming and pointing to His return.
- The spring feasts were fulfilled by Yeshua's death, burial, resurrection, and the outpouring of the Holy Spirit—down to the day and hour.
- The fall feasts hold prophetic clues about the Rapture, final judgment, and God dwelling with humanity in the Messianic Kingdom.
- The Sabbath (*Shabbat*) was the first thing God sanctified in time, and honoring it aligns believers with His rhythm and rest.
- The fast days of Israel—like the 9th of Av—represent national mourning that will one day be turned into joy, redemption, and restoration.
- God's calendar is not just history—it's prophecy in motion, revealing the urgency of the hour and the nearness of the Messiah's return.

Chapter 8 sounds the fourth harbinger with clarity and sacred weight: God's feasts are more than religious observances—they are prophetic declarations, pre-written appointments with destiny. As the Church shakes off its slumber and looks to the sky, it must also look at the calendar—the one God wrote in Leviticus, fulfilled in the Gospels, and waiting to be completed in Revelation.

The feasts are not finished.

The next divine appointment is near.

The question is—are we aligned?

Chapter 9

The Fifth Harbinger:
The Shemitah Cycles

THE RHYTHM OF RECKONING—What if the Creator of time didn't just set the days and seasons but built the very rhythm of world history into a repeating pattern—seven-year cycles of warning, reckoning, and renewal?

Welcome to the Fifth Harbinger: The Shemitah Cycles.

Where the Feasts of the LORD mark appointed days, the Shemitah marks appointed years—prophetic seasons woven into God's covenant with His people and echoed in the rise and fall of civilizations.

First revealed in Leviticus 25, Shemitah—meaning "release"—was a year of rest for the land, the canceling of debts, and the freeing of captives. But it was never merely an agricultural instruction. It is a prophetic cycle—a divine reset that strikes every seven years, bringing blessing to nations that honor God and warnings to those that turn away.

Through the ages, these seven-year markers have aligned with seasons of economic collapse, political upheaval, societal resets, and spiritual awakenings. From the fall of empires to the shaking of modern markets, the Shemitah has proven to be more than an ancient ordinance—it is a prophetic signal that the God who measures nations is still keeping time by His calendar, not ours.

History speaks in patterns. The Bible speaks in cycles. And the Shemitah is one of God's clearest prophetic rhythms. From 9/11 in 2001, to the market crash of 2008, to the blood moons of 2014–2015, to the global shaking of 2022—each cycle has sounded a note in this divine timekeeper. These were not random events. They were prophetic tremors—warnings, judgments, and reminders that God's timepiece is still ticking.

We are now in the current Shemitah cycle: 2022/2023 to 2028/2029.

(Why two years? Because the biblical civil year begins in the fall—1 Tishri— and extends into the following Gregorian year.)

Many believe this may be the final Shemitah before the Tribulation begins. If so, we are not merely watching the clock—we are standing on the threshold of eternity.

The question is not *whether* God is sounding the alarm.

The question is—are we listening?

In this chapter, we will explore the Shemitah's divine origins, its prophetic warnings, and its remarkable alignment with world events from the dawn of history to today. We will follow this pattern from the first year of the Hebrew calendar 1 AM to the current Hebrew year 5785 AM (spanning October 2024 to September 2025)—a timeline that stretches from Creation itself to the accelerating events of our own generation.

Across millennia, each Shemitah cycle has served as both a *reset* and a *revelation*—a countdown marker in God's redemptive plan. And as the signs converge, the rhythm grows faster, pointing toward the most extraordinary moment in history yet to come: the Rapture of the Church.

This is not speculation. It is Scripture. It is history. And it is a countdown.

The rhythm is accelerating. The signs are converging. The time is now.

Let's begin.

WHERE ARE WE ON GOD'S TIMELINE?

If we want to know where we are in prophetic history, we must stop watching the world's clock and start watching God's. The nations may keep time by the Gregorian calendar, but Heaven's timepiece has never changed. From the first days of Creation, God embedded a rhythm into the universe—a sacred calendar pulsing with appointed days, seven-year cycles, and seasons of reckoning.

This is not man's system. This is the schedule by which God measures kingdoms, marks turning points, and sets the countdown to the return of His Son. And if we understand this divine rhythm, we can see exactly where we stand—on the edge of a prophetic convergence unlike any in history.

The Origin of the Biblical Calendar

According to Jewish tradition, Creation began in the fall of 3761 BC. This moment marks the first year of the Hebrew calendar—Year 1 AM (*Anno Mundi*), meaning "Year of the World." Rooted in the genealogies and chronologies of Scripture, this dating system has measured time from the dawn of history.

Unlike the Gregorian calendar—established by Pope Gregory XIII in 1582 AD and based solely on the solar cycle—God's calendar is lunisolar, blending the sun and moon into a rhythm that aligns agricultural seasons with divine feasts, fasts, and prophetic appointments. This sacred system fulfills the pattern set in Genesis 1:14, where God declared the sun and moon to be "for signs, and for seasons—*moedim*—and for days, and years."

The Hebrew calendar is not just a way to mark time—it is the framework of prophecy, the divine schedule by which God orders His redemptive plan.

God's 6,000-Year Redemptive Blueprint

From the beginning, God established a pattern for time: six days of labor followed by a seventh day of rest (Genesis 2:1–3). The apostle Peter confirms this prophetic scale, declaring:

> But, beloved, be not ignorant of this one thing, that one day is with the Lord as a thousand years, and a thousand years as one day. (2 Peter 3:8)

This reveals a divine framework:

- 6,000 years of human history—six prophetic "days" of man's labor on the earth.
- 1,000 years of Sabbath rest—the Millennial Kingdom (Revelation 20:1–6).

This is not symbolic poetry. It is God's prophetic architecture—a precise blueprint for the unfolding of redemption.

Where Are We Now?

To understand our prophetic position, we must anchor ourselves to God's calendar, not man's. According to the biblical reckoning of time, 1 AM (*Anno Mundi*)—"Year of the World"—began in the fall of 3761–3760 BC, marking Creation as the starting point of God's redemptive timeline. From that point, the years have been counted forward in a continuous rhythm, unfolding exactly as Scripture declared.

By this measure, we now stand in 5785 AM, a year that began at sunset on October 2, 2024, and will end at sunset on September 22, 2025. This is not just another year on the Hebrew calendar—it is a prophetic marker. It places us in the closing stretch of the sixth millennium, standing on the edge of 6000 AM—a threshold many Bible scholars and prophecy teachers believe will open into the most dramatic chapter in human history.

If this prophetic framework is correct, we are living in the final moments of the sixth "day" of man's labor before the arrival of the seventh "day"—the thousand-year Sabbath rest known as the Millennial Kingdom (Revelation 20:1–6). This would mean we are approaching a convergence of events foretold in Scripture: the Rapture of the Church, the rise of the Antichrist, the seven-year Tribulation, and the triumphant return of Jesus Christ to reign as King.

The significance is staggering. We are not merely counting years—we are counting down. Every festival, every Shemitah cycle, every prophetic sign in the heavens, and every shaking of the nations now carries heightened meaning. God's calendar is advancing toward a fixed and appointed hour, and that hour may be closer than most imagine.

The Urgency of Alignment

If we are indeed nearing the close of the sixth prophetic day, the implications are staggering. The Shemitah cycles—God's seven-year rhythms of reckoning and release—are not ancient agricultural relics. They are prophetic countdown markers, charting where we stand and signaling what is to come.

To discern the times, we must stop measuring history by man's calendar and start aligning our vision with God's. His appointed times are not suggestions. They are sacred summons—to return, to awaken, to prepare.

If you want to know where we are in the story of redemption, you will not find the answer in January 1st or December 31st. You will find it in the cycles of Scripture—in the *moedim*, in the Shemitah, and in the unchanging heartbeat of Heaven.

———◆◆◆———

A quiet afternoon settled over Irene's study. Golden light filtered through linen curtains, casting long shadows across the room. The table was strewn with open Bibles, commentaries, and archaeological timelines. In the background, a kettle whistled softly.

Irene flipped through the worn pages of her timeline chart, brow furrowed in concentration. A second teacup sat untouched across from her.

I entered with my Bible in one hand and a notepad in the other—calm, composed, familiar with the look in her eyes. I had been here before—on the brink of confusion, but walking in revelation.

Irene glanced up from the chart, eyes narrowed.

"Ann, I've got to be honest—something isn't adding up. The traditional Hebrew calendar says Creation happened in the fall of 3761 BC. But when I trace the genealogies—Genesis 5 and 10, 1 and 2 Chronicles—factoring in the lifespans and chronology, I land closer to 4000 BC. That's over a 200-year gap. And that's not even considering the variances between the Masoretic text, the Septuagint, and the Samaritan Pentateuch. So . . . which is it?"

I smiled gently and set my notes down.

"You're not alone, Irene. A lot of scholars have wrestled with that exact question. The Hebrew calendar—anchored in Tishri 1, 3761 BC—was formalized much later, probably around the 4th century AD by Jewish sages. It's more theological than it is strictly chronological. But if you build a timeline using the Bible itself, especially the genealogies in Genesis, yes—it brings us to a Creation date much closer to 4000 BC."

Irene leaned back, tapping a pencil on the desk. "Exactly. Adam's life, then Seth, Enosh, Mahalalel . . . if you track from Adam to Abraham using Genesis 5 and 10, you land pretty confidently around 2000 BC for Abraham and 4000 BC for Creation. So why would rabbinic tradition shift it earlier?"

I nodded. "It's a great question—and the key lies in how time was calculated. The traditional Jewish calendar, beginning in 3761 BC, is based on a compressed chronology known as the *Seder Olam Rabbah*. It was compiled around the second century by Jewish sages who attempted to build a timeline from Adam to their day, using selected biblical events. But in doing so, they compressed certain historical periods—especially the Persian era."

Irene frowned. "But Genesis gives us detailed genealogies. Shouldn't that be enough to calculate how long humanity has been on earth?"

I smiled. "Exactly—and that's why scholars like Archbishop James Ussher relied heavily on Genesis 5 and 10. Those chapters don't just list names—they give lifespans and ages when each father bore the next son. When you add it all up, the numbers point to a Creation date around 4004 BC to 4000 BC."

I paused, then added gently.

"It's also a matter of intent. The rabbinic timeline may have been shaped to reflect theological symbolism or even to distance Jewish reckoning from emerging Christian narratives. Plus, they may have compressed the intertestamental period—the 400 silent years between the Old and New Testaments. But more broadly, we have to recognize the limits of ancient chronology. Some genealogies are telescoped—skipping names for thematic emphasis. Some reigns overlap. And some historical gaps were simply unknown to those compiling the records."

Irene nodded slowly. "So, we're dealing with two timelines—one prophetic and symbolic, the other more literal and genealogical. The civil calendar follows a traditional interpretation, the other a direct reading of Scripture?"

"Exactly," I said. "The rabbinic calendar was intentionally compressed to fit theological and even sociopolitical needs—especially during times of persecution and exile. But when we follow the Genesis genealogies literally, starting around 4000 BC, it aligns much more closely with the plain sense of Scripture."

I smiled, recognizing the connection.

"Yes. Six days of Creation followed by a Sabbath rest. Likewise, six thousand years of human rule—Adam's lease, if you will—followed by one thousand years of divine rule under Messiah. That's why this isn't just a calendar debate—it's a prophetic alignment."

I picked up my pen and began sketching a rough timeline on the notepad between us.

"Here's how I think of it. Before 4000 BC, we enter what I call the Age Before Time—a realm beyond human chronology. That's when the angels were created and the rebellion in Heaven took place. Then, from around 4000 BC, God initiates the Agriculture Age—the moment Adam and Eve are placed in Eden to cultivate and steward the earth. That's the starting point of human history as we can track it."

Irene leaned in, curious. "So what would that look like—mapped out?"

I began sketching. "Here's the arc of time as I see it—not just through history, but through a prophetic lens."

- Before Time—*The Angelic Age*. A realm beyond our time. Ends with Lucifer's rebellion and expulsion (Isaiah 14; Revelation 12).
- 4000 BC—Creation of Adam: *The Agricultural Age* begins. Humanity's stewardship of the earth begins in Eden (Genesis 1:1–3).
- 4000–3300 BC—*The Stone Age*. Early tools and civilization. 3313 BC—the earliest writing—Sumerian cuneiform—emerges.
- 3500–2300 BC—*The Copper Age*. Pure metals in use. 3500 BC—Sumerians build the first cities in Mesopotamia. 2464 BC—God calls Noah 120 years before the Flood (Genesis 6). 2344 BC—The Great Flood. 2213 BC—Tower of Babel and dispersion (Genesis 11). 2052 BC—Abraham is called at age 75.
- 3300–1200 BC—*The Bronze Age*. Alloyed tools and weaponry. 1446 BC—Moses leads the Exodus at age 80.
- 1200–600 BC—*The Iron Age*. Assyria, Babylon, and Israel's monarchy rise. 1051–931 BC—United monarchy—Saul, David, Solomon—each reign 40 years. 931–586 BC—Divided kingdom era.

- 600 BC–100 AD—*The Classical Age.* 586–516 BC—Babylonian exile (70 years). 400 BC–AD 1—Intertestamental period: 400 years of silence. 4 BC–1 AD—Birth of Christ. AD 30–33—crucifixion, burial, resurrection, outpouring of the Holy Spirit.
- 100–1500 AD—*The Medieval Age.* Rise of the Church, the Dark Ages, and preservation of Scripture.
- 1500–1800 AD—*Reformation and Renaissance Age.* Printing press, Protestant Reformation, global exploration.
- 1800–1945 AD—*The Industrial Age.* Machines reshape societies. Steam engines, revolutions, colonial empires.
- 1945–2000 AD—*Atomic and Technological Age.* Nuclear power, world wars, space exploration.
- 2000–Present—*The Information Age.* Instant communication, artificial intelligence, digital globalization. And possibly . . . the threshold of the *Messianic Age.*

Irene's eyes widened. "So these ages aren't just secular history—they reflect spiritual movements too?"

"Absolutely," I said, nodding. "Each age tracks mankind's response to divine revelation—from innocence in Eden to rebellion in Babel, from the Law under Moses to grace through Christ—and now, we're living at the edge of eternity. Every historical shift echoes the divine narrative."

"So history really is His story."

"Yes," I said. "And our story only makes sense because of His."

WHAT IS A SHEMITAH?

The word Shemitah comes from the Hebrew root (*shamat*), meaning to release, to let drop, to fall away. In Scripture, it is far more than an ancient agricultural term—it is a God-ordained cycle of time that governs both the physical and spiritual realms. Established by the LORD Himself in the Law of Moses, the Shemitah occurs every seventh year and is woven into the very fabric of Israel's covenant with God.

In its most basic form, the Shemitah was a year when the land was to rest, debts were to be forgiven, and slaves were to be set free (Leviticus 25; Deuteronomy 15). But beyond its practical commands, the Shemitah is a prophetic pattern—a divine reset button on God's calendar. When honored, it brought blessing and renewal. When ignored, it became a time of reckoning and judgment.

Throughout history, the Shemitah has marked turning points for nations—periods of release, collapse, realignment, and restoration. It is a rhythm that still beats today, echoing across millennia, measuring economies, kingdoms, and even the destiny of the world.

The Shemitah is not a relic of the past. It is a living signpost on God's timeline—a recurring reminder that the earth is the Lord's, and we are stewards under His authority. Understanding it is not optional for those who want to discern the days we are living in.

The Biblical Foundation: Leviticus 25

The word Shemitah means "release," and its origin is found in Leviticus 25 as part of God's covenant with Israel. It marks a divinely ordained seven-year cycle, where every seventh year was set apart as a year of rest for the land, the cancellation of debts, and the release of those bound in servitude.

> But in the seventh year there shall be a Sabbath of solemn rest for the land, a Sabbath to the LORD; you shalt neither sow your field nor prune your vineyard. (Leviticus 25:4)

In this sacred year, fields were to lie uncultivated, debts were to be forgiven, and slaves were to be set free. The Shemitah was God's way of resetting the economic and social order, ensuring that mercy, rest, and restoration were woven into the fabric of the nation's life.

But the Shemitah was never meant to be merely agricultural. It was a spiritual reset—a call to repentance, humility, and renewed trust in God as the true provider. When honored, it opened the windows of blessing. When ignored or defied, it became a doorway to judgment.

The Jubilee: The Grand Shemitah

Even greater than the Shemitah is the Jubilee year (*Yovel*)—the "grand" Shemitah that came once every fifty years, after seven full Shemitah cycles (7 x 7 = 49). The fiftieth year was a sacred climax, announced by the blowing of the shofar on *Yom Kippur*, declaring complete restoration to the nation:

> And you shall hallow (consecrate) the fiftieth year, and proclaim liberty throughout all the land unto all the inhabitants thereof. (Leviticus 25:10)

In the Jubilee year:

- Property returned to its original family owners.
- Slaves were permanently set free.
- The entire nation experienced a God-ordained economic reset.

The Jubilee is the ultimate picture of redemption and restoration—a prophetic foreshadowing of the Messianic Age, when Jesus, our true Jubilee, will return to proclaim liberty to the captives and restore all things (Luke 4:18–19; Acts 3:21).

Just as the Jubilee reset every debt and restored every inheritance, so will the return of Christ bring the greatest restoration in history—healing the land, freeing the oppressed, and reclaiming what sin and Satan have stolen.

Shemitah: Economic, Spiritual, and Prophetic

Though first given to Israel, the Shemitah principle reveals a universal pattern in God's dealings with both nations and history itself. Its echoes are found far beyond ancient Israel's borders—resonating in global events, economic shifts, and prophetic signs.

- Economically—Shemitah years have often aligned with major financial upheavals: market crashes, recessions, debt crises, and global economic resets.
- Spiritually—They have mirrored seasons of revival, repentance, and renewal—or, when ignored, periods of moral decline and divine judgment.
- Prophetically—The Shemitah functions as a countdown marker, pointing toward the ultimate release: the Rapture of the Church and the Day of the Lord.

The Shemitah is not a relic of the past. It is a prophetic rhythm—a divine timepiece ticking through time, measuring the rise and fall of nations, and reminding the world that God is still in control. It calls kings and commoners alike to return to Him before the final trumpet sounds.

SHEMITAH: GOD'S CYCLICAL ALARM CLOCK

From the ancient fields of Israel to the turbulent trading floors of Wall Street, the Shemitah has always been more than an agricultural ordinance—it is God's built-in alarm system, a recurring call to return, reset, and realign with His purposes. Every seventh year, as commanded in Leviticus 25, the land was to rest, debts were to be released, and lives were to be recalibrated around God's provision and sovereignty.

Yet the Shemitah's reach extends far beyond the soil of Israel. It is a spiritual pattern woven into the fabric of history—a divine rhythm of warning, judgment, mercy, and renewal. Like the piercing blast of the shofar, each cycle carries the potential for repentance or for reckoning—depending on whether the call is heeded.

Modern Echoes of the Shemitah

In recent decades, the Shemitah rhythm has continued to reverberate across the world stage—its cycles marked by disruption, awakening, or both:

- 2001 (5761 AM)—The 9/11 attacks claimed thousands of lives, shattered the illusion of national security, and ushered in an era of perpetual war and mass surveillance.
- 2008 (5768 AM)—The global financial collapse ignited the Great Recession, shaking the very foundations of the world economy.
- 2015 (5775 AM)—A rare blood moon tetrad aligned precisely with biblical feast days, accompanied by deepening geopolitical instability and unmistakable spiritual warning signs.
- 2022 (5782 AM)—In the aftermath of COVID-19, the world saw escalating political division, unprecedented digital surveillance, war in Europe, and the rapid rise of global control systems.

These were not random crises. They were prophetic pulses—divine signals in sync with God's seven-year cycle, reminding us that He is still directing the course of human history. Each Shemitah year becomes a crossroads: a chance for repentance and realignment, or a step closer to judgment.

Twenty-First Century Shemitah Timeline

The current Hebrew century—5701–5800 AM (1940–2039 AD)—has been marked by intense prophetic activity, with each Shemitah year echoing the seven-year rhythm established by God:

- 1945—End of World War II; birth pains of a new world order.
- 1952—Global alliances rise; Cold War tensions escalate.
- 1959—Seeds of cultural and moral revolution take root.
- 1966—Prayer removed from schools; spiritual decline deepens.
- 1973—*Roe v. Wade* legalizes abortion; covenant breach in America.
- 1980—Rise of radical Islam; Middle East unrest intensifies.
- 1987—"Black Monday" market crash shakes global economies.
- 1994—Oslo Accords pressure Israel into land-for-peace deals.
- 2001—The 9/11 attacks strike America; national wake-up call.
- 2008—The Great Recession delivers a global economic warning.
- 2015—Blood moon tetrad aligns with Passover and *Sukkot*—while Obama administration celebrates same-sex marriage ruling.
- 2022—Post-pandemic upheaval with war in Europe, digital surveillance, and rising global control systems.

- 2029—*Possible* Rapture of the Church; global chaos and judgment.
- 2036—*Possible* Armageddon; end of the seven-year Tribulation.

If this prophetic pattern continues, 2029 and 2036 could become two of the most pivotal years in history—years when the Shemitah cycle may intersect with the final events of the age.

Jubilee Years: The Grand Shemitah

Every fiftieth year in God's calendar is a Jubilee (*Yovel*)—a "super-Shemitah" of liberation, restoration, and return. While exact calculations can vary, many prophecy scholars identify the following modern events as possible Jubilee markers:

- 1917—The Balfour Declaration becomes the first official statement of international support for a Jewish homeland—exactly fifty years before the liberation of Jerusalem.
- 1967—In the Six-Day War, Israel regains control of Jerusalem for the first time in nearly 2,000 years.
- 2017—Marks both 100 years since the Balfour Declaration and fifty years since Jerusalem's reunification.

If these alignments are more than mere coincidence—and many believe they are—they reveal the hand of God weaving modern geopolitics into His ancient prophetic tapestry. The Jubilee remains a signpost of His covenant faithfulness, reminding us that history is not random—it is ordered by the One who declares "the end from the beginning" (Isaiah 46:10).

SHEMITAH AND THE COMING TRIBULATION

We are living in a Shemitah cycle that many believe could mark the final countdown before the Tribulation Age—the unparalleled time of global upheaval described in the Book of Revelation. This current seven-year span, 2022/2023 to 2028/2029 (5783–5789 AM), has already been marked by post-pandemic unrest, escalating wars, the rapid expansion of surveillance technologies, and unprecedented spiritual division.

Could it also be preparing the stage for the Rapture of the Church?

Is 2028/2029 the Pivotal Year?

While no one knows the exact day or hour, believers are commanded to discern the times and seasons (1 Thessalonians 5:1–6). Many prophetic scholars have noted the potential alignment of 2028/2029 with the Feast of Trumpets—the appointed time historically tied to the gathering of God's people, the awakening trumpet blast, and the coronation of the King. The sequence of the fall feasts—Trumpets, Atonement, and Tabernacles—points prophetically to end-time fulfillment.

Could the fall feasts of 2028 or 2029 signal the Rapture, the beginning of the Tribulation, or even both events in rapid succession?

Daniel's 70 Weeks and the Prophetic Blueprint

Daniel's prophecy of the Seventy Weeks (Daniel 9:24–27) outlines a precise, God-ordained timeline: sixty-nine weeks of years leading to Messiah's First Coming, with one final "week" of years—a seven-year period—reserved for the end times. This Seventieth Week is defined by a covenant with many, a midpoint abomination, and a final climax in divine judgment.

If the Tribulation were to begin in the fall of 2029/2030, the beginning of a new Shemitah cycle, then:

- Midpoint—when the Antichrist breaks the covenant and the Great Tribulation begins—would fall around 2032/2033.
- Conclusion—the return of Christ and the establishment of the Millennial Kingdom—would occur around fall 2035/2036, allowing for slight adjustments depending on the exact start date within the Shemitah framework.

This is not sensational speculation—it is pattern recognition rooted in Scripture. God's timeline is not random. He works in cycles, appointed times, and prophetic shadows brought to their ultimate fulfillment.

PROPHETIC PROOF THROUGH THE FEASTS AND ECLIPSES

Biblical prophecy is not only fulfilled in the events of history—it is written in the heavens and aligned with God's appointed calendar. From the ministry of Jesus to the blood moons and eclipses of our own generation, the Shemitah has consistently marked turning points in God's plan.

Jesus and the Shemitah Transition

In Isaiah 61, the prophet declares: "The Spirit of the Sovereign LORD is upon me . . . to proclaim the acceptable Year of the LORD . . . and the Day of Vengeance of our God." When Jesus read from this very passage in the synagogue (Luke 4:16–21), He stopped mid-verse—announcing the acceptable year, but leaving the Day of Vengeance for a future moment. Many scholars believe His public ministry began at the turn of a Shemitah year (26/27 AD), a prophetic hinge between cycles of favor and judgment.

Eclipses on Appointed Days: Divine Clocks in the Sky

Fast forward to the 2014–2015 Shemitah cycle: two rare solar eclipses fell exactly on the first day of each biblical New Year.

- March 20, 2015—Total solar eclipse on 1 Nisan 5775 AM, the biblical religious New Year, closing the Shemitah cycle 5769–5775 AM.
- September 13, 2015—Partial solar eclipse on 1 Tishri 5776 AM, the civil New Year (*Rosh HaShanah*), opening the next Shemitah cycle 5776–5782 AM.

Two eclipses. Two New Years. One Shemitah transition. Astronomically, the odds are staggering; spiritually, the meaning is unmistakable. These were divine timestamps—heavenly alarm clocks announcing that the prophetic clock had struck a new hour.

CONNECTING THE DOTS: FROM CREATION TO COUNTDOWN

When we step back far enough, the view changes. What at first looks like isolated events begins to form a breathtaking pattern—precise, divine, and unmistakably prophetic. From 1 AM (*Anno Mundi*)—the biblical year of Creation—to our present age, God has woven seven-year Shemitah cycles into the very fabric of time.

These are far more than agricultural laws. They are a heavenly timekeeper, steadily ticking forward toward the ultimate redemption.

God Has Written History in Advance

Scripture declares that God knows "the end from the beginning" (Isaiah 46:10). These Shemitah cycles are not random—they are signposts that mark the rise and fall of kingdoms, the deliverance of God's people, and even the return of Messiah.

> Declaring the end from the beginning, and from ancient times the things that are not yet done, saying, My counsel shall stand, and I will do all My pleasure. (Isaiah 46:10)

From Creation to the Flood, from the Exodus to the building of the Temples, from Jesus' ministry to the destruction of the Second Temple in 70 AD, and from the rebirth of Israel in 1948 to the recapture of Jerusalem in 1967—each has fallen within the divine rhythm.

When the pattern is plotted from 1 AM to 5831 AM, the alignment of biblical prophecy and world history is nothing short of astonishing.

A Living Timeline: The Shemitah Chart

The chart that follows is the Creation/Shemitah Calendar, mapping the timeline from 1 AM (*Anno Mundi*, "Year of the World") to the present. It integrates biblical years with corresponding Gregorian calendar dates, marking each Shemitah cycle, identifying Shemitah years, and noting Jubilee years. Together, these layers form a visual framework of God's appointed cycles, revealing how His calendar has unfolded from Creation to today with prophetic precision.

A Quick Note Before You Study the Chart—I know the chart print in this book is small—that's intentional to conserve space. But I want you to have a full-size version for deeper study. I'm offering the Shemitah Cycles and Jubilee Years Since Creation (1AM) Chart as a free resource.

Simply email me at:
Vanishing@GuardiansOfBiblicalTruth.com with the subject line:
Request for Shemitah Cycles and Jubilee Years Chart.

You'll receive an 8½ x 11, easy-to-read version—because we're not just reading, we're training for reigning.

THE BIBLE AT A GLANCE

Shemitah Cycles and Jubilee Years Since Creation (1 AM)

Shemitah 1 1 AM–7 AM 3761/3760–3755/3754	Shemitah Year 14 8 AM–14 AM 3754/3753–3748/3747	Shemitah Year 21 15 AM–21 AM 3747/3746–3741/3740	Shemitah Year 28 22 AM–28 AM 3740/3739–3734/3733	Shemitah Year 35 29 AM–35 AM 3733/3732–3727/3726	Shemitah Year 42 36 AM–42 AM 3726/3725–3720/3719	Shemitah Year 49 43 AM–49 AM 3719/3718–3713/3712
1st Jubilee 50 50 AM–56 AM 3712/3711–3706/3705	Shemitah Year 63 57 AM–63 AM 3705/3704–3699/3698	Shemitah Year 70 64 AM–70 AM 3698/3697–3692/3691	Shemitah Year 77 71 AM–77 AM 3691/3690–3685/3684	Shemitah Year 84 78 AM–84 AM 3684/3683–3678/3677	Shemitah Year 91 85 AM–91 AM 3677/3676–3671/3670	Shemitah Year 98 92 AM–98 AM 3670/3669–3664/3663
2nd Jubilee 100 99 AM–105 AM 3663/3662–3657/3656	Shemitah Year 112 106 AM–112 AM 3656/3655–3650/3649	Shemitah Year 119 113 AM–119 AM 3649/3648–3643/3642	Shemitah Year 126 120 AM–126 AM 3642/3641–3636/3635	Shemitah Year 133 127 AM–133 AM 3635/3634–3629/3628	Shemitah Year 140 134 AM–140 AM 3628/3627–3622/3621	Shemitah Year 147 141 AM–147 AM 3621/3620–3615/3614
3rd Jubilee 150 148 AM–154 AM 3614/3613–3608/3607	Shemitah Year 161 155 AM–161 AM 3607/3606–3601/3600	Shemitah Year 168 162 AM–168 AM 3600/3599–3594/3593	Shemitah Year 175 169 AM–175 AM 3593/3592–3587/3586	Shemitah Year 182 176 AM–182 AM 3586/3585–3580/3579	Shemitah Year 189 183 AM–189 AM 3579/3578–3573/3572	Shemitah Year 196 190 AM–196 AM 3572/3571–3566/3565
4th Jubilee 200 197 AM–203 AM 3565/3564–3559/3558	Shemitah Year 210 204 AM–210 AM 3558/3557–3552/3551	Shemitah Year 217 211 AM–217 AM 3551/3550–3545/3544	Shemitah Year 224 218 AM–224 AM 3544/3543–3538/3537	Shemitah Year 231 225 AM–231 AM 3537/3536–3531/3530	Shemitah Year 238 232 AM–238 AM 3530/3529–3524/3523	Shemitah Year 245 239 AM–245 AM 3523/3522–3517/3516
5th Jubilee 250 246 AM–252 AM 3516/3515–3510/3509	Shemitah Year 259 253 AM–259 AM 3509/3508–3503/3502	Shemitah Year 266 260 AM–266 AM 3502/3501–3496/3495	Shemitah Year 273 267 AM–273 AM 3495/3496–3489/3488	Shemitah Year 280 274 AM–280 AM 3488/3487–3482/3481	Shemitah Year 287 281 AM–287 AM 3481/3480–3475/3474	Shemitah Year 294 288 AM–294 AM 3474/3473–3468/3467
6th Jubilee 300 295 AM–301 AM 3467/3466–3461/3460	Shemitah Year 308 302 AM–308 AM 3460/3459–3454/3453	Shemitah Year 315 309 AM–315 AM 3453/3452–3447/3446	Shemitah Year 322 316 AM–322 AM 3446/3445–3440/3439	Shemitah Year 329 323 AM–329 AM 3439/3438–3433/3432	Shemitah Year 336 330 AM–336 AM 3432/3431–3426/3425	Shemitah Year 343 337 AM–343 AM 3425/3424–3419/3418
7th Jubilee 350 344 AM–350 AM 3418/3417–3412/3411	Shemitah Year 357 351 AM–357 AM 3411/3410–3405/3404	Shemitah Year 364 358 AM–364 AM 3404/3403–3398/3397	Shemitah Year 371 365 AM–371 AM 3397/3396–3391/3390	Shemitah Year 378 372 AM–378 AM 3390/3389–3384/3383	Shemitah Year 385 379 AM–385 AM 3383/3382–3377/3376	Shemitah Year 392 386 AM–392 AM 3376/3375–3370/3369
8th Jubilee 400	Shemitah Year 406	Shemitah Year 413	Shemitah Year 420	Shemitah Year 427	Shemitah Year 434	Shemitah Year 441

393 AM–399 AM 3369/3368–3363/3362	400 AM–406 AM 3362/3361–3356/3355	407 AM–413 AM 3355/3354–3349/3348	414 AM–420 AM 3348/3347–3342/3341	421 AM–427 AM 3341/3340–3335/3334	428 AM–434 AM 3334/3333–3328/3327	435 AM–441 AM 3327/3326–3321/3320
9th Jubilee 450 442 AM–448 AM 3320/3319–3314/3313	Shemitah Year 455 449 AM–455 AM 3313/3312–3307/3306	Shemitah Year 462 456 AM–462 AM 3306/3305–3300/3299	Shemitah Year 469 463 AM–469 AM 3299/3298–3293/3292	Shemitah Year 476 470 AM–476 AM 3292/3291–3286/3285	Shemitah Year 483 477 AM–483 AM 3285/3284–3279/3278	Shemitah Year 490 484 AM–490 AM 3278/3277–3272/3271
10th Jubilee 500 491 AM–497 AM 3271/3270–3265/3264	Shemitah Year 504 498 AM–504 AM 3264/3263–3258/3257	Shemitah Year 511 505 AM–511 AM 3257/3256–3251/3250	Shemitah Year 518 512 AM–518 AM 3250/3249–3244/3243	Shemitah Year 525 519 AM–525 AM 3243/3242–3237/3236	Shemitah Year 532 526 AM–532 AM 3236/3235–3230/3229	Shemitah Year 539 533 AM–539 AM 3229/3228–3223/3222
11th Jubilee 550 540 AM–546 AM 3222/3221–3216/3215	Shemitah Year 553 547 AM–553 AM 3215/3214–3209/3208	Shemitah Year 560 554 AM–560 AM 3208/3207–3202/3201	Shemitah Year 567 561 AM–567 AM 3201/3200–3195/3194	Shemitah Year 574 568 AM–574 AM 3194/3193–3188/3187	Shemitah Year 581 575 AM–581 AM 3187/3186–3181/3180	Shemitah Year 588 582 AM–588 AM 3180/3179–3174/3173
12th Jubilee 600 589 AM–595 AM 3173/3172–3167/3166	Shemitah Year 602 596 AM–602 AM 3166/3165–3160/3159	Shemitah Year 609 603 AM–609 AM 3159/3158–3153/3152	Shemitah Year 616 610 AM–616 AM 3152/3151–3146/3145	Shemitah Year 623 617 AM–623 AM 3145/3144–3139/3138	Shemitah Year 630 624 AM–630 AM 3138/3137–3132/3131	Shemitah Year 637 631 AM–637 AM 3131/3130–3125/3124
13th Jubilee 650 638 AM–644 AM 3124/3123–3118/3117	Shemitah Year 651 645 AM–651 AM 3117/3116–3111/3110	Shemitah Year 658 652 AM–658 AM 3110/3109–3104/3103	Shemitah Year 665 659 AM–665 AM 3103/3102–3097/3096	Shemitah Year 672 666 AM–672 AM 3096/3095–3090/3089	Shemitah Year 679 673 AM–679 AM 3089/3088–3083/3082	Shemitah Year 686 680 AM–686 AM 3082/3081–3076/3075
14th Jubilee 700 687 AM–693 AM 3075/3074–3069/3068	Shemitah Year 700 694 AM–700 AM 3068/3067–3062/3061	Shemitah Year 707 701 AM–707 AM 3061/3060–3055/3054	Shemitah Year 714 708 AM–714 AM 3054/3053–3048/3047	Shemitah Year 721 715 AM–721 AM 3047/3046–3041/3040	Shemitah Year 728 722 AM–728 AM 3040/3039–3034/3033	Shemitah Year 735 729 AM–735 AM 3033/3032–3027/3026
15th Jubilee 750 736 AM–742 AM 3026/3025–3020/3019	Shemitah Year 749 743 AM–749 AM 3019/3018–3013/3012	Shemitah Year 756 750 AM–756 AM 3012/3011–3006/3005	Shemitah Year 763 757 AM–763 AM 3005/3004–2999/2998	Shemitah Year 770 764 AM–770 AM 2998/2997–2992/2991	Shemitah Year 777 771 AM–777 AM 2991/2990–2985/2984	Shemitah Year 784 778 AM–784 AM 2984/2983–2978/2977
16th Jubilee 800 785 AM–791 AM 2977/2976–2971/2970	Shemitah Year 798 792 AM–798 AM 2970/2969–2964/2963	Shemitah Year 805 799 AM–805 AM 2963/2962–2957/2956	Shemitah Year 812 806 AM–812 AM 2956/2955–2950/2949	Shemitah Year 819 813 AM–819 AM 2949/2948–2943/2942	Shemitah Year 826 820 AM–826 AM 2942/2941–2936/2935	Shemitah Year 833 827 AM–833 AM 2935/2934–2929/2928
17th Jubilee 850 834 AM–840 AM 2928/2927–2922/2921	Shemitah Year 847 841 AM–847 AM 2921/2920–2915/2914	Shemitah Year 854 848 AM–854 AM 2914/2913–2908/2907	Shemitah Year 861 855 AM–861 AM 2907/2906–2901/2900	Shemitah Year 868 862 AM–868 AM 2900/2899–2894/2893	Shemitah Year 875 869 AM–875 AM 2893/2892–2887/2886	Shemitah Year 882 876 AM–882 AM 2886/2885–2880/2879
18th Jubilee 900 883 AM–889 AM 2879/2878–2873/2872	Shemitah Year 896 890 AM–896 AM 2872/2871–2866/2865	Shemitah Year 903 897 AM–903 AM 2865/2864–2859/2858	Shemitah Year 910 904 AM–910 AM 2858/2857–2852/2851	Shemitah Year 917 911 AM–917 AM 2851/2850–2845/2844	Shemitah Year 924 918 AM–924 AM 2844/2843–2838/2837	Shemitah Year 931 925 AM–931 AM 2837/2836–2831/2830
19th Jubilee 950 932 AM–938 AM 2830/2829–2824/2823	Shemitah Year 945 939 AM–945 AM 2823/2822–2817/2816	Shemitah Year 952 946 AM–952 AM 2816/2815–2810/2809	Shemitah Year 959 953 AM–959 AM 2809/2808–2803/2802	Shemitah Year 966 960 AM–966 AM 2802/2801–2796/2795	Shemitah Year 973 967 AM–973 AM 2795/2794–2789/2788	Shemitah Year 980 974 AM–980 AM 2788/2787–2782/2781
20th Jubilee 1000 981 AM–987 AM 2781/2780–2775/2774	Shemitah Year 994 988 AM–994 AM 2774/2773–2768/2767	Shemitah Year 1001 995 AM–1001 AM 2767/2766–2761/2760	Shemitah Year 1008 1002 AM–1008 AM 2760/2759–2754/2753	Shemitah Year 1015 1009 AM–1015 AM 2753/2752–2747/2746	Shemitah Year 1022 1016 AM–1022 AM 2746/2745–2740/2739	Shemitah Year 1029 1023 AM–1029 AM 2739/2738–2733/2732
21st Jubilee 1050 1030 AM–1036 AM 2732/2731–2726/2725	Shemitah Year 1043 1037 AM–1043 AM 2725/2724–2719/2718	Shemitah Year 1050 1044 AM–1050 AM 2718/2717–2712/2711	Shemitah Year 1057 1051 AM–1057 AM 2711/2710–2705/2704	Shemitah Year 1064 1058 AM–1064 AM 2704/2703–2698/2697	Shemitah Year 1071 1065 AM–1071 AM 2697/2696–2691/2690	Shemitah Year 1078 1072 AM–1078 AM 2690/2689–2684/2683
22nd Jubilee 1100 1079 AM–1085 AM 2683/2682–2677/2676	Shemitah Year 1092 1086 AM–1092 AM 2676/2675–2670/2669	Shemitah Year 1099 1093 AM–1099 AM 2669/2668–2663/2662	Shemitah Year 1106 1100 AM–1106 AM 2662/2661–2656/2655	Shemitah Year 1113 1107 AM–1113 AM 2655/2654–2649/2648	Shemitah Year 1120 1114 AM–1120 AM 2648/2647–2642/2641	Shemitah Year 1127 1121 AM–1127 AM 2641/2640–2635/2634
23rd Jubilee 1150 1128 AM–1134 AM 2634/2633–2628/2627	Shemitah Year 1141 1135 AM–1141 AM 2627/2626–2621/2620	Shemitah Year 1148 1142 AM–1148 AM 2620/2619–2614/2613	Shemitah Year 1155 1149 AM–1155 AM 2613/2612–2607/2606	Shemitah Year 1162 1156 AM–1162 AM 2606/2605–2600/2599	Shemitah Year 1169 1163 AM–1169 AM 2599/2598–2593/2592	Shemitah Year 1176 1170 AM–1176 AM 2592/2591–2586/2585
24th Jubilee 1200 1177 AM–1183 AM 2585/2584–2579/2578	Shemitah Year 1190 1184 AM–1190 AM 2578/2577–2572/2571	Shemitah Year 1197 1191 AM–1197 AM 2571/2570–2565/2564	Shemitah Year 1204 1198 AM–1204 AM 2564/2563–2558/2557	Shemitah Year 1211 1205 AM–1211 AM 2557/2556–2551/2550	Shemitah Year 1218 1212 AM–1218 AM 2550/2549–2544/2543	Shemitah Year 1225 1219 AM–1225 AM 2543/2542–2537/2536
25th Jubilee 1250 1226 AM–1232 AM 2536/2535–2530/2529	Shemitah Year 1239 1233 AM–1239 AM 2529/2528–2523/2522	Shemitah Year 1246 1240 AM–1246 AM 2522/2521–2516/2515	Shemitah Year 1253 1247 AM–1253 AM 2515/2514–2509/2508	Shemitah Year 1260 1254 AM–1260 AM 2508/2507–2502/2501	Shemitah Year 1267 1261 AM–1267 AM 2501/2500–2495/2494	Shemitah Year 1274 1268 AM–1274 AM 2494/2493–2488/2487

26th Jubilee 1300 1275 AM–1281 AM 2487/2486–2481/2480	Shemitah Year 1288 1282 AM–1288 AM 2480/2479–2474/2473	Shemitah Year 1295 1289 AM–1295 AM 2473/2472–2467/2466	Shemitah Year 1302 1296 AM–1302 AM 2466/2465–2460/2459	Shemitah Year 1309 1303 AM–1309 AM 2459/2458–2453/2452	Shemitah Year 1316 1310 AM–1316 AM 2452/2451–2446/2445	Shemitah Year 1323 1317 AM–1323 AM 2445/2444–2439/2438
27th Jubilee 1350 1324 AM–1330 AM 2438/2437–2432/2431	Shemitah Year 1337 1331 AM–1337 AM 2431/2430–2425/2424	Shemitah Year 1344 1338 AM–1344 AM 2424/2423–2418/2417	Shemitah Year 1351 1345 AM–1351 AM 2417/2416–2411/2410	Shemitah Year 1358 1352 AM–1358 AM 2410/2409–2404/2403	Shemitah Year 1365 1359 AM–1365 AM 2403/2402–2397/2396	Shemitah Year 1372 1366 AM–1372 AM 2396/2395–2390/2389
28th Jubilee 1400 1373 AM–1379 AM 2389/2388–2383/2382	Shemitah Year 1386 1380 AM–1386 AM 2382/2381–2376/2375	Shemitah Year 1393 1387 AM–1393 AM 2375/2374–2369/2368	Shemitah Year 1400 1394 AM–1400 AM 2368/2367–2362/2361	Shemitah Year 1407 1401 AM–1407 AM 2361/2360–2355/2354	Shemitah Year 1414 1408 AM–1414 AM 2354/2353–2348/2347	Shemitah Year 1421 1415 AM–1421 AM 2347/2346–2341/2340
29th Jubilee 1450 1422 AM–1428 AM 2340/2339–2334/2333	Shemitah Year 1435 1429 AM–1435 AM 2333/2332–2327/2326	Shemitah Year 1442 1436 AM–1442 AM 2326/2325–2320/2319	Shemitah Year 1449 1443 AM–1449 AM 2319/2318–2313/2312	Shemitah Year 1456 1450 AM–1456 AM 2312/2311–2306/2305	Shemitah Year 1463 1457 AM–1463 AM 2305/2304–2299/2298	Shemitah Year 1470 1464 AM–1470 AM 2298/2297–2292/2291
30th Jubilee 1500 1471 AM–1477 AM 2291/2290–2285/2284	Shemitah Year 1484 1478 AM–1484 AM 2284/2283–2278/2277	Shemitah Year 1491 1485 AM–1491 AM 2277/2276–2271/2270	Shemitah Year 1498 1492 AM–1498 AM 2270/2269–2264/2263	Shemitah Year 1505 1499 AM–1505 AM 2263/2262–2257/2256	Shemitah Year 1512 1506 AM–1512 AM 2256/2255–2250/2249	Shemitah Year 1519 1513 AM–1519 AM 2249/2248–2243/2242
31st Jubilee 1550 1520 AM–1526 AM 2242/2241–2236/2235	Shemitah Year 1533 1527 AM–1533 AM 2235/2234–2229/2228	Shemitah Year 1540 1534 AM–1540 AM 2228/2227–2222/2221	Shemitah Year 1547 1541 AM–1547 AM 2221/2220–2215/2214	Shemitah Year 1554 1548 AM–1554 AM 2214/2213–2208/2207	Shemitah Year 1561 1555 AM–1561 AM 2207/2206–2201/2200	Shemitah Year 1568 1562 AM–1568 AM 2200/2199–2194/2193
32nd Jubilee 1600 1569 AM–1575 AM 2193/2192–2187/2186	Shemitah Year 1582 1576 AM–1582 AM 2186/2185–2180/2179	Shemitah Year 1589 1583 AM–1589 AM 2179/2178–2173/2172	Shemitah Year 1596 1590 AM–1596 AM 2172/2171–2166/2165	Shemitah Year 1603 1597 AM–1603 AM 2165/2164–2159/2158	Shemitah Year 1610 1604 AM–1610 AM 2158/2157–2152/2151	Shemitah Year 1617 1611 AM–1617 AM 2151/2150–2145/2144
33rd Jubilee 1650 1618 AM–1624 AM 2144/2143–2138/2137	Shemitah Year 1631 1625 AM–1631 AM 2137/2136–2131/2130	Shemitah Year 1638 1632 AM–1638 AM 2130/2129–2124/2123	Shemitah Year 1645 1639 AM–1645 AM 2123/2122–2117/2116	Shemitah Year 1652 1646 AM–1652 AM 2116/2115–2110/2109	Shemitah Year 1659 1653 AM–1659 AM 2109/2108–2103/2102	Shemitah Year 1666 1660 AM–1666 AM 2102/2101–2096/2095
34th Jubilee 1700 1667 AM–1673 AM 2095/2094–2089/2088	Shemitah Year 1680 1674 AM–1680 AM 2088/2087–2082/2081	Shemitah Year 1687 1681 AM–1687 AM 2081/2080–2075/2074	Shemitah Year 1694 1688 AM–1694 AM 2074/2073–2068/2067	Shemitah Year 1701 1695 AM–1701 AM 2067/2066–2061/2060	Shemitah Year 1708 1702 AM–1708 AM 2060/2059–2054/2053	Shemitah Year 1715 1709 AM–1715 AM 2053/2052–2047/2046
35th Jubilee 1750 1716 AM–1722 AM 2046/2045–2040/2039	Shemitah Year 1729 1723 AM–1729 AM 2039/2038–2033/2032	Shemitah Year 1736 1730 AM–1736 AM 2032/2031–2026/2025	Shemitah Year 1743 1737 AM–1743 AM 2025/2024–2019/2018	Shemitah Year 1750 1744 AM–1750 AM 2018/2017–2012/2011	Shemitah Year 1757 1751 AM–1757 AM 2011/2010–2005/2004	Shemitah Year 1764 1758 AM–1764 AM 2004/2003–1998/1997
36th Jubilee 1800 1765 AM–1771 AM 1997/1996–1991/1990	Shemitah Year 1778 1772 AM–1778 AM 1990/1989–1984/1983	Shemitah Year 1785 1779 AM–1785 AM 1983/1982–1977/1976	Shemitah Year 1792 1786 AM–1792 AM 1976/1975–1970/1969	Shemitah Year 1799 1793 AM–1799 AM 1969/1968–1963/1962	Shemitah Year 1806 1800 AM–1806 AM 1962/1961–1956/1955	Shemitah Year 1813 1807 AM–1813 AM 1955/1954–1949/1948
37th Jubilee 1850 1814 AM–1820 AM 1948/1947–1942/1941	Shemitah Year 1827 1821 AM–1827 AM 1941/1940–1935/1934	Shemitah Year 1834 1828 AM–1834 AM 1934/1933–1928/1927	Shemitah Year 1841 1835 AM–1841 AM 1927/1926–1921/1920	Shemitah Year 1848 1842 AM–1848 AM 1920/1919–1914/1913	Shemitah Year 1855 1849 AM–1855 AM 1913/1912–1907/1906	Shemitah Year 1862 1856 AM–1862 AM 1906/1905–1900/1899
38th Jubilee 1900 1863 AM–1869 AM 1899/1898–1893/1892	Shemitah Year 1876 1870 AM–1876 AM 1892/1891–1886/1885	Shemitah Year 1883 1877 AM–1883 AM 1885/1884–1879/1878	Shemitah Year 1890 1884 AM–1890 AM 1878/1877–1872/1871	Shemitah Year 1897 1891 AM–1897 AM 1871/1870–1865/1864	Shemitah Year 1904 1898 AM–1904 AM 1864/1863–1858/1857	Shemitah Year 1911 1905 AM–1911 AM 1857/1856–1851/1850
39th Jubilee 1950 1912 AM–1918 AM 1850/1849–1844/1843	Shemitah Year 1925 1919 AM–1925 AM 1843/1842–1837/1836	Shemitah Year 1932 1926 AM–1932 AM 1836/1835–1830/1829	Shemitah Year 1939 1933 AM–1939 AM 1829/1828–1823/1822	Shemitah Year 1946 1940 AM–1946 AM 1822/1821–1816/1815	Shemitah Year 1953 1947 AM–1953 AM 1815/1814–1809/1808	Shemitah Year 1960 1954 AM–1960 AM 1808/1807–1802/1801
40th Jubilee 2000 1961 AM–1967 AM 1801/1800–1795/1794	Shemitah Year 1974 1968 AM–1974 AM 1794/1793–1788/1787	Shemitah Year 1981 1975 AM–1981 AM 1787/1786–1781/1780	Shemitah Year 1988 1982 AM–1988 AM 1780/1779–1774/1773	Shemitah Year 1995 1989 AM–1995 AM 1773/1772–1767/1766	Shemitah Year 2002 1996 AM–2002 AM 1766/1765–1760/1759	Shemitah Year 2009 2003 AM–2009 AM 1759/1758–1753/1752
41st Jubilee 2050 2010 AM–2016 AM 1752/1751–1746/1745	Shemitah Year 2023 2017 AM–2023 AM 1745/1744–1739/1738	Shemitah Year 2030 2024 AM–2030 AM 1738/1737–1732/1731	Shemitah Year 2037 2031 AM–2037 AM 1731/1730–1725/1724	Shemitah Year 2044 2038 AM–2044 AM 1724/1723–1718/1717	Shemitah Year 2051 2045 AM–2051 AM 1717/1716–1711/1710	Shemitah Year 2058 2052 AM–2058 AM 1710/1709–1704/1703
42nd Jubilee 2100 2059 AM–2065 AM 1703/1702–1697/1696	Shemitah Year 2072 2066 AM–2072 AM 1696/1695–1690/1689	Shemitah Year 2079 2073 AM–2079 AM 1689/1688–1683/1682	Shemitah Year 2086 2080 AM–2086 AM 1682/1681–1676/1675	Shemitah Year 2093 2087 AM–2093 AM 1675/1674–1669/1668	Shemitah Year 2100 2094 AM–2100 AM 1668/1667–1662/1661	Shemitah Year 2107 2101 AM–2107 AM 1661/1660–1655/1654
43rd Jubilee 2150 2108 AM–2114 AM	Shemitah Year 2121 2115 AM–2121 AM 1647/1646–1641/1640	Shemitah Year 2128 2122 AM–2128 AM 1640/1639–1634/1633	Shemitah Year 2135 2129 AM–2135 AM 1633/1632–1627/1626	Shemitah Year 2142 2136 AM–2142 AM 1626/1625–1620/1619	Shemitah Year 2149 2143 AM–2149 AM 1619/1618–1613/1612	Shemitah Year 2156 2150 AM–2156 AM 1612/1611–1606/1605

1654/1653–1648/1647

44th Jubilee 2200 2157 AM–2163 AM 1605/1604–1599/1598	Shemitah Year 2170 2164 AM–2170 AM 1598/1597–1592/1591	Shemitah Year 2177 2171 AM–2177 AM 1591/1590–1585/1584	Shemitah Year 2184 2178 AM–2184 AM 1584/1583–1578/1577	Shemitah Year 2191 2185 AM–2191 AM 1577/1576–1571/1570	Shemitah Year 2198 2192 AM–2198 AM 1570/1569–1564/1563	Shemitah Year 2205 2199 AM–2205 AM 1563/1562–1557/1556
45th Jubilee 2250 2206 AM–2212 AM 1556/1555–1550/1549	Shemitah Year 2219 2213 AM–2219 AM 1549/1548–1543/1542	Shemitah Year 2226 2220 AM–2226 AM 1542/1541–1536/1535	Shemitah Year 2233 2227 AM–2233 AM 1535/1534–1529/1528	Shemitah Year 2240 2234 AM–2240 AM 1528/1527–1522/1521	Shemitah Year 2247 2241 AM–2247 AM 1521/1520–1515/1514	Shemitah Year 2254 2248 AM–2254 AM 1514/1513–1508/1507
46th Jubilee 2300 2255 AM–2261 AM 1507/1506–1501/1500	Shemitah Year 2268 2262 AM–2268 AM 1500/1499–1494/1493	Shemitah Year 2275 2269 AM–2275 AM 1493/1492–1487/1486	Shemitah Year 2282 2276 AM–2282 AM 1486/1485–1480/1479	Shemitah Year 2289 2283 AM–2289 AM 1479/1478–1473/1472	Shemitah Year 2296 2290 AM–2296 AM 1472/1471–1466/1465	Shemitah Year 2303 2297 AM–2303 AM 1465/1464–1459/1458
47th Jubilee 2350 2304 AM–2310 AM 1458/1457–1452/1451	Shemitah Year 2317 2311 AM–2317 AM 1451/1450–1445/1444	Shemitah Year 2324 2318 AM–2324 AM 1444/1443–1438/1437	Shemitah Year 2331 2325 AM–2331 AM 1437/1436–1431/1430	Shemitah Year 2338 2332 AM–2338 AM 1430/1429–1424/1423	Shemitah Year 2345 2339 AM–2345 AM 1423/1422–1417/1416	Shemitah Year 2352 2346 AM–2352 AM 1416/1415–1410/1409
48th Jubilee 2400 2353 AM–2359 AM 1409/1408–1403/1402	Shemitah Year 2366 2360 AM–2366 AM 1402/1401–1396/1395	Shemitah Year 2373 2367 AM–2373 AM 1395/1394–1389/1388	Shemitah Year 2380 2374 AM–2380 AM 1388/1387–1382/1381	Shemitah Year 2387 2381 AM–2387 AM 1381/1380–1375/1374	Shemitah Year 2394 2388 AM–2394 AM 1374/1373–1368/1367	Shemitah Year 2401 2395 AM–2401 AM 1367/1366–1361/1360
49th Jubilee 2450 2402 AM–2408 AM 1360/1359–1354/1353	Shemitah Year 2415 2409 AM–2415 AM 1353/1352–1347/1346	Shemitah Year 2422 2416 AM–2422 AM 1346/1345–1340/1339	Shemitah Year 2429 2423 AM–2429 AM 1339/1338–1333/1332	Shemitah Year 2436 2430 AM–2436 AM 1332/1331–1326/1325	Shemitah Year 2443 2437 AM–2443 AM 1325/1324–1319/1318	Shemitah Year 2450 2444 AM–2450 AM 1318/1317–1312/1311
 2451 AM–2457 AM 1311/1310–1305/1304	Shemitah Year 2464 2458 AM–2464 AM 1304/1303–1298/1297	Shemitah Year 2471 2465 AM–2471 AM 1297/1296–1291/1290	Shemitah Year 2478 2472 AM–2478 AM 1290/1289–1284/1283	Shemitah Year 2485 2479 AM–2485 AM 1283/1282–1277/1276	Shemitah Year 2492 2486 AM–2492 AM 1276/1275–1270/1269	Shemitah Year 2499 2493 AM–2499 AM 1269/1268–1263/1262
50th Jubilee 2500 2500 AM–2506 AM 1262/1261–1256/1255	Shemitah Year 2513 2507 AM–2513 AM 1255/1254–1249/1248	Shemitah Year 2520 2514 AM–2520 AM 1248/1247–1242/1241	Shemitah Year 2527 2521 AM–2527 AM 1241/1240–1235/1234	Shemitah Year 2534 2528 AM–2534 AM 1234/1233–1228/1227	Shemitah Year 2541 2535 AM–2541 AM 1227/1226–1221/1220	Shemitah Year 2548 2542 AM–2548 AM 1220/1219–1214/1213
51st Jubilee 2550 2549 AM–2555 AM 1213/1212–1207/1206	Shemitah Year 2562 2556 AM–2562 AM 1206/1205–1200/1199	Shemitah Year 2569 2563 AM–2569 AM 1199/1198–1193/1192	Shemitah Year 2576 2570 AM–2576 AM 1192/1191–1186/1185	Shemitah Year 2583 2577 AM–2583 AM 1185/1184–1179/1178	Shemitah Year 2590 2584 AM–2590 AM 1178/1177–1172/1171	Shemitah Year 2597 2591 AM–2597 AM 1171/1170–1165/1164
52nd Jubilee 2600 2598 AM–2604 AM 1164/1163–1158/1157	Shemitah Year 2611 2605 AM–2611 AM 1157/1156–1151/1150	Shemitah Year 2618 2612 AM–2618 AM 1150/1149–1144/1143	Shemitah Year 2625 2619 AM–2625 AM 1143/1142–1137/1136	Shemitah Year 2632 2626 AM–2632 AM 1136/1135–1130/1129	Shemitah Year 2639 2633 AM–2639 AM 1129/1128–1123/1122	Shemitah Year 2646 2640 AM–2646 AM 1122/1121–1116/1115
53rd Jubilee 2650 2647 AM–2653 AM 1115/1114–1109/1108	Shemitah Year 2660 2654 AM–2660 AM 1108/1107–1102/1101	Shemitah Year 2667 2661 AM–2667 AM 1101/1100–1095/1094	Shemitah Year 2674 2668 AM–2674 AM 1094/1093–1088/1087	Shemitah Year 2681 2675 AM–2681 AM 1087/1086–1081/1080	Shemitah Year 2688 2682 AM–2688 AM 1080/1079–1074/1073	Shemitah Year 2695 2689 AM–2695 AM 1073/1072–1067/1066
54th Jubilee 2700 2696 AM–2702 AM 1066/1065–1060/1059	Shemitah Year 2709 2703 AM–2709 AM 1059/1058–1053/1052	Shemitah Year 2716 2710 AM–2716 AM 1052/1051–1046/1045	Shemitah Year 2723 2717 AM–2723 AM 1045/1044–1039/1038	Shemitah Year 2730 2724 AM–2730 AM 1038/1037–1032/1031	Shemitah Year 2737 2731 AM–2737 AM 1031/1030–1025/1024	Shemitah Year 2744 2738 AM–2744 AM 1024/1023–1018/1017
55th Jubilee 2750 2745 AM–2751 AM 1017/1016–1011/1010	Shemitah Year 2758 2752 AM–2758 AM 1010/1009–1004/1003	Shemitah Year 2765 2759 AM–2765 AM 1003/1002–997/996	Shemitah Year 2772 2766 AM–2772 AM 996/995–990/989 BC	Shemitah Year 2779 2773 AM–2779 AM 989/988–983/982 BC	Shemitah Year 2786 2780 AM–2786 AM 982/981–976/975 BC	Shemitah Year 2793 2787 AM–2793 AM 975/974–969/968 BC
56th Jubilee 2800 2794 AM–2800 AM 968/967–962/961	Shemitah Year 2807 2801 AM–2807 AM 961/960–955/954 BC	Shemitah Year 2814 2808 AM–2814 AM 954/953–948/947 BC	Shemitah Year 2821 2815 AM–2821 AM 947/946–941/940 BC	Shemitah Year 2828 2822 AM–2828 AM 940/939–934/933 BC	Shemitah Year 2835 2829 AM–2835 AM 933/932–927/926 BC	Shemitah Year 2842 2836 AM–2842 AM 926/925–920/919 BC
57th Jubilee 2850 2843 AM–2849 AM 919/918–913/912	Shemitah Year 2856 2850 AM–2856 AM 912/911–906/905 BC	Shemitah Year 2863 2857 AM–2863 AM 905/904–899/898 BC	Shemitah Year 2870 2864 AM–2870 AM 898/897–892/891 BC	Shemitah Year 2877 2871 AM–2877 AM 891/890–885/884 BC	Shemitah Year 2884 2878 AM–2884 AM 884/883–878/877 BC	Shemitah Year 2891 2885 AM–2891 AM 877/876–871/870 BC
58th Jubilee 2900 2892 AM–2898 AM 870/869–864/863	Shemitah Year 2905 2899 AM–2905 AM 863/862–857/856 BC	Shemitah Year 2912 2906 AM–2912 AM 856/855–850/849 BC	Shemitah Year 2919 2913 AM–2919 AM 849/848–843/842 BC	Shemitah Year 2926 2920 AM–2926 AM 842/841–836/835 BC	Shemitah Year 2933 2927 AM–2933 AM 835/834–829/828 BC	Shemitah Year 2940 2934 AM–2940 AM 828/827–822/821 BC
59th Jubilee 2950 2941 AM–2947 AM 821/820–815/814	Shemitah Year 2954 2948 AM–2954 AM 814/813–808/807 BC	Shemitah Year 2961 2955 AM–2961 AM 807/806–801/800 BC	Shemitah Year 2968 2962 AM–2968 AM 800/799–794/793 BC	Shemitah Year 2975 2969 AM–2975 AM 793/792–787/786 BC	Shemitah Year 2982 2976 AM–2982 AM 786/785–780/779 BC	Shemitah Year 2989 2983 AM–2989 AM 779/778–773/772 BC
60th Jubilee 3000	Shemitah Year 3003 2997 AM–3003 AM	Shemitah Year 3010 3004 AM–3010 AM	Shemitah Year 3017 3011 AM–3017 AM	Shemitah Year 3024 3018 AM–3024 AM	Shemitah Year 3031 3025 AM–3031 AM	Shemitah Year 3038 3032 AM–3038 AM

2990 AM–2996 AM 772/771–766/765	765/764–759/758 BC	758/757–752/751 BC	751/750–745/744 BC	744/743–738/737 BC	737/736–731/730 BC	730/729–724/723 BC
61st Jubilee 3050 3039 AM–3045 AM 723/722–717/716	Shemitah Year 3052 3046 AM–3052 AM 716/715–710/709 BC	Shemitah Year 3059 3053 AM–3059 AM 709/708–703/702 BC	Shemitah Year 3066 3060 AM–3066 AM 702/701–696/695 BC	Shemitah Year 3073 3067 AM–3073 AM 695/694–689/688 BC	Shemitah Year 3080 3074 AM–3080 AM 688/687–682/681 BC	Shemitah Year 3087 3081 AM–3087 AM 681/680–675/674 BC
62nd Jubilee 3100 3088 AM–3094 AM 674/673–668/667	Shemitah Year 3101 3095 AM–3101 AM 667/666–661/660 BC	Shemitah Year 3108 3102 AM–3108 AM 660/659–654/653 BC	Shemitah Year 3115 3109 AM–3115 AM 653/652–647/646 BC	Shemitah Year 3122 3116 AM–3122 AM 646/645–640/639 BC	Shemitah Year 3129 3123 AM–3129 AM 639/638–633/632 BC	Shemitah Year 3136 3130 AM–3136 AM 632/631–626/625 BC
63rd Jubilee 3150 3137 AM–3143 AM 625/624–619/618	Shemitah Year 3150 3144 AM–3150 AM 618/617–612/611 BC	Shemitah Year 3157 3151 AM–3157 AM 611/610–605/604 BC	Shemitah Year 3164 3158 AM–3164 AM 604/603–598/597 BC	Shemitah Year 3171 3165 AM–3171 AM 597/596–591/590 BC	Shemitah Year 3178 3172 AM–3178 AM 590/589–584/583 BC	Shemitah Year 3185 3179 AM–3185 AM 583/582–577/576 BC
64th Jubilee 3200 3186 AM–3192 AM 576/575–570/569	Shemitah Year 3199 3193 AM–3199 AM 569/568–563/562 BC	Shemitah Year 3206 3200 AM–3206 AM 562/561–556/555 BC	Shemitah Year 3213 3207 AM–3213 AM 555/554–549/548 BC	Shemitah Year 3220 3214 AM–3220 AM 548/547–542/541 BC	Shemitah Year 3227 3221 AM–3227 AM 541/540–535/534 BC	Shemitah Year 3234 3228 AM–3234 AM 534/533–528/527 BC
65th Jubilee 3250 3235 AM–3241 AM 527/526–521/520	Shemitah Year 3248 3242 AM–3248 AM 520/519–514/513 BC	Shemitah Year 3255 3249 AM–3255 AM 513/512–507/506 BC	Shemitah Year 3262 3256 AM–3262 AM 506/505–500/499 BC	Shemitah Year 3269 3263 AM–3269 AM 499/498–493/492 BC	Shemitah Year 3276 3270 AM–3276 AM 492/491–486/485 BC	Shemitah Year 3283 3277 AM–3283 AM 485/484–479/478 BC
66th Jubilee 3300 3284 AM–3290 AM 478/477–472/471	Shemitah Year 3297 3291 AM–3297 AM 471/470–465/464 BC	Shemitah Year 3304 3298 AM–3304 AM 464/463–458/457 BC	Shemitah Year 3311 3305 AM–3311 AM 457/456–451/450 BC	Shemitah Year 3318 3312 AM–3318 AM 450/449–444/443 BC	Shemitah Year 3325 3319 AM–3325 AM 443/442–437/436 BC	Shemitah Year 3332 3326 AM–3332 AM 436/435–430/429 BC
67th Jubilee 3350 3333 AM–3339 AM 429/428–423/422	Shemitah Year 3346 3340 AM–3346 AM 422/421–416/415 BC	Shemitah Year 3353 3347 AM–3353 AM 415/414–409/408 BC	Shemitah Year 3360 3354 AM–3360 AM 408/407–402/401 BC	Shemitah Year 3367 3361 AM–3367 AM 401/400–395/394 BC	Shemitah Year 3374 3368 AM–3374 AM 394/393–388/387 BC	Shemitah Year 3381 3375 AM–3381 AM 387/386–381/380 BC
68th Jubilee 3400 3382 AM–3388 AM 380/379–374/373	Shemitah Year 3395 3389 AM–3395 AM 373/372–367/366 BC	Shemitah Year 3402 3396 AM–3402 AM 366/365–360/359 BC	Shemitah Year 3409 3403 AM–3409 AM 359/358–353/352 BC	Shemitah Year 3416 3410 AM–3416 AM 352/351–346/345 BC	Shemitah Year 3423 3417 AM–3423 AM 345/344–339/338 BC	Shemitah Year 3430 3424 AM–3430 AM 338/337–332/331 BC
69th Jubilee 3450 3431 AM–3437 AM 331/330–325/324	Shemitah Year 3444 3438 AM–3444 AM 324/323–318/317 BC	Shemitah Year 3451 3445 AM–3451 AM 317/316–311/310 BC	Shemitah Year 3458 3452 AM–3458 AM 310/309–304/303 BC	Shemitah Year 3465 3459 AM–3465 AM 303/302–297/296 BC	Shemitah Year 3472 3466 AM–3472 AM 296/295–290/289 BC	Shemitah Year 3479 3473 AM–3479 AM 289/288–283/282 BC
70th Jubilee 3500 3480 AM–3486 AM 282/281–276/275	Shemitah Year 3493 3487 AM–3493 AM 275/274–269/268 BC	Shemitah Year 3500 3494 AM–3500 AM 268/267–262/261 BC	Shemitah Year 3507 3501 AM–3507 AM 261/260–255/254 BC	Shemitah Year 3514 3508 AM–3514 AM 254/253–248/247 BC	Shemitah Year 3521 3515 AM–3521 AM 247/246–241/240 BC	Shemitah Year 3528 3522 AM–3528 AM 240/239–234/233 BC
71st Jubilee 3550 3529 AM–3535 AM 233/232–227/226	Shemitah Year 3542 3536 AM–3542 AM 226/225–220/219 BC	Shemitah Year 3549 3543 AM–3549 AM 219/218–213/212 BC	Shemitah Year 3556 3550 AM–3556 AM 212/211–206/205 BC	Shemitah Year 3563 3557 AM–3563 AM 205/204–199/198 BC	Shemitah Year 3570 3564 AM–3570 AM 198/197–192/191 BC	Shemitah Year 3577 3571 AM–3577 AM 191/190–185/184 BC
72nd Jubilee 3600 3578 AM–3584 AM 184/183–178/177	Shemitah Year 3591 3585 AM–3591 AM 177/176–171/170 BC	Shemitah Year 3598 3592 AM–3598 AM 170/169–164/163 BC	Shemitah Year 3605 3599 AM–3605 AM 163/162–157/156 BC	Shemitah Year 3612 3606 AM–3612 AM 156/155–150/149 BC	Shemitah Year 3619 3613 AM–3619 AM 149/148–143/142 BC	Shemitah Year 3626 3620 AM–3626 AM 142/141–136/135 BC
73rd Jubilee 3650 3627 AM–3633 AM 135/134–129/128	Shemitah Year 3640 3634 AM–3640 AM 128/127–122/121 BC	Shemitah Year 3647 3641 AM–3647 AM 121/120–115/114 BC	Shemitah Year 3656 3648 AM–3656 AM 114/113–108/107 BC	Shemitah Year 3661 3655 AM–3661 AM 107/106–101/100 BC	Shemitah Year 3668 3662 AM–3668 AM 100/99–94/93 BC	Shemitah Year 3675 3669 AM–3675 AM 93/92–87/86 BC
74th Jubilee 3700 3676 AM–3682 AM 86/85–80/79	Shemitah Year 3689 3683 AM–3689 AM 79/78–73/72 BC	Shemitah Year 3696 3690 AM–3696 AM 72/71–66/65 BC	Shemitah Year 3703 3697 AM–3703 AM 65/64–59/58 BC	Shemitah Year 3710 3704 AM–3710 AM 58/57–52/51 BC	Shemitah Year 3717 3711 AM–3717 AM 51/50–45/44 BC	Shemitah Year 3724 3718 AM–3724 AM 44/43–38/37 BC
75th Jubilee 3750 3725 AM–3731 AM 37/36–31/30 BC	Shemitah Year 3738 3732 AM–3738 AM 30/29–24/23 BC	Shemitah Year 3745 3739 AM–3745 AM 23/22–17/16 BC	Shemitah Year 3752 3746 AM–3752 AM 16/15–10/9 BC	Shemitah Year 3759 3753 AM–3759 AM 9/8–3/2 BC	Shemitah Year 3766 3760 AM–3766 AM 3/2 BC–5/6 AD	Shemitah Year 3773 3767 AM–3773 AM 6/7–12/13 AD
76th Jubilee 3800 3774 AM–3780 AM 13/14–19/20 AD	Shemitah Year 3787 3781 AM–3787 AM 20/21–26/27 AD	Shemitah Year 3794 3788 AM–3794 AM 27/28–33/34 AD	Shemitah Year 3801 3795 AM–3801 AM 34/35–40/41 AD	Shemitah Year 3808 3802 AM–3808 AM 41/42–47/48 AD	Shemitah Year 3815 3809 AM–3815 AM 47/48–54/55 AD	Shemitah Year 3822 3816 AM–3822 AM 55/56–61/62 AD
77th Jubilee 3850 3823 AM–3829 AM 62/63–68/69	Shemitah Year 3836 3830 AM–3836 AM 69/70–75/76 AD	Shemitah Year 3843 3837 AM–3843 AM 76/77–82/83 AD	Shemitah Year 3850 3844 AM–3850 AM 83/84–89/90 AD	Shemitah Year 3857 3851 AM–3857 AM 90/91–96/97 AD	Shemitah Year 3864 3858 AM–3864 AM 97/98–103/104 AD	Shemitah Year 3871 3865 AM–3871 AM 104/105–110/111 AD

78th Jubilee 3900 3872 AM–3878 AM 111/112–117/118	Shemitah Year 3885 3879 AM–3885 AM 118/119–124/125 AD	Shemitah Year 3892 3886 AM–3892 AM 125/126–131/132 AD	Shemitah Year 3899 3893 AM–3899 AM 132/133–138/139 AD	Shemitah Year 3906 3900 AM–3906 AM 139/140–145/146 AD	Shemitah Year 3913 3907 AM–3913 AM 146/147–152/153 AD	Shemitah Year 3920 3914 AM–3920 AM 153/154–159/160 AD
79th Jubilee 3950 3921 AM–3927 AM 160/161–166/167	Shemitah Year 3934 3928 AM–3934 AM 167/168–173/174 AD	Shemitah Year 3941 3935 AM–3941 AM 174/175–180/181 AD	Shemitah Year 3948 3942 AM–3948 AM 181/182–187/188 AD	Shemitah Year 3955 3949 AM–3955 AM 188/189–194/195 AD	Shemitah Year 3962 3956 AM–3962 AM 195/196–201/202 AD	Shemitah Year 3969 3963 AM–3969 AM 202/203–208/209 AD
80th Jubilee 4000 3970 AM–3976 AM 209/210–215/216	Shemitah Year 3983 3977 AM–3983 AM 216/217–222/223 AD	Shemitah Year 3990 3984 AM–3990 AM 223/224–229/230 AD	Shemitah Year 3997 3991 AM–3997 AM 230/231–236/237 AD	Shemitah Year 4004 3998 AM–4004 AM 237/238–243/244 AD	Shemitah Year 4011 4005 AM–4011 AM 244/245–250/251 AD	Shemitah Year 4018 4012 AM–4018 AM 251/252–257/258 AD
81st Jubilee 4050 4019 AM–4025 AM 258/259–264/265	Shemitah Year 4032 4026 AM–4032 AM 265/266–271/272 AD	Shemitah Year 4039 4033 AM–4039 AM 272/273–278/279 AD	Shemitah Year 4046 4040 AM–4046 AM 279/280–285/286 AD	Shemitah Year 4053 4047 AM–4053 AM 286/287–292/293 AD	Shemitah Year 4060 4054 AM–4060 AM 293/294–299/300 AD	Shemitah Year 4067 4061 AM–4067 AM 300/301–306/307 AD
81st Jubilee 4100 4068 AM–4074 AM 307/308–313/314	Shemitah Year 4081 4075 AM–4081 AM 314/315–320/321 AD	Shemitah Year 4088 4082 AM–4088 AM 321/322–327/328 AD	Shemitah Year 4095 4089 AM–4095 AM 328/329–334/335 AD	Shemitah Year 4102 4096 AM–4102 AM 335/336–341/342 AD	Shemitah Year 4109 4103 AM–4109 AM 342/343–348/349 AD	Shemitah Year 4116 4110 AM–4116 AM 349/350–355/356 AD
82nd Jubilee 4150 4117 AM–4123 AM 356/357–362/363	Shemitah Year 4130 4124 AM–4130 AM 363/364–369/370 AD	Shemitah Year 4137 4131 AM–4137 AM 370/371–376/377 AD	Shemitah Year 4144 4138 AM–4144 AM 377/378–383/384 AD	Shemitah Year 4145 4145 AM–4151 AM 384/385–390/391 AD	Shemitah Year 4158 4152 AM–4158 AM 391/392–397/398 AD	Shemitah Year 4165 4159 AM–4165 AM 398/399–404/405 AD
83rd Jubilee 4200 4166 AM–4172 AM 405/406–411/412	Shemitah Year 4179 4173 AM–4179 AM 412/413–418/419 AD	Shemitah Year 4186 4180 AM–4186 AM 419/420–425/426 AD	Shemitah Year 4193 4187 AM–4193 AM 426/427–432/433 AD	Shemitah Year 4200 4194 AM–4200 AM 433/434–439/440 AD	Shemitah Year 4207 4201 AM–4207 AM 440/441–446/447 AD	Shemitah Year 4214 4208 AM–4214 AM 447/448–453/454 AD
84th Jubilee 4250 4215 AM–4221 AM 454/455–460/461	Shemitah Year 4228 4222 AM–4228 AM 461/462–467/468 AD	Shemitah Year 4235 4229 AM–4235 AM 468/469–474/475 AD	Shemitah Year 4242 4236 AM–4242 AM 475/476–481/482 AD	Shemitah Year 4249 4243 AM–4249 AM 482/483–488/489 AD	Shemitah Year 4256 4250 AM–4256 AM 489/490–495/496 AD	Shemitah Year 4263 4257 AM–4263 AM 496/497–502/503 AD
85th Jubilee 4300 4264 AM–4270 AM 503/504–509/510	Shemitah Year 4277 4271 AM–4277 AM 510/511–516/517 AD	Shemitah Year 4284 4278 AM–4284 AM 517/518–523/524 AD	Shemitah Year 4291 4285 AM–4291 AM 524/525–530/531 AD	Shemitah Year 4298 4292 AM–4298 AM 531/532–537/538 AD	Shemitah Year 4305 4299 AM–4305 AM 538/539–544/545 AD	Shemitah Year 4312 4306 AM–4312 AM 545/546–551/552 AD
86th Jubilee 4350 4313 AM–4319 AM 552/553–558/559	Shemitah Year 4326 4320 AM–4326 AM 559/560–565/566 AD	Shemitah Year 4333 4327 AM–4333 AM 566/567–572/573 AD	Shemitah Year 4340 4334 AM–4340 AM 573/574–579/580 AD	Shemitah Year 4347 4341 AM–4347 AM 580/581–586/587 AD	Shemitah Year 4354 4348 AM–4354 AM 587/588–593/594 AD	Shemitah Year 4361 4355 AM–4361 AM 594/595–600/601 AD
87th Jubilee 4400 4362 AM–4368 AM 601/602–607/608	Shemitah Year 4375 4369 AM–4375 AM 608/609–614/615 AD	Shemitah Year 4382 4376 AM–4382 AM 615/616–621/622 AD	Shemitah Year 4389 4383 AM–4389 AM 622/623–628/629 AD	Shemitah Year 4396 4390 AM–4396 AM 629/630–635/636 AD	Shemitah Year 4403 4397 AM–4403 AM 636/637–642/643 AD	Shemitah Year 4410 4404 AM–4410 AM 643/644–649/650 AD
88th Jubilee 4450 4411 AM–4117 AM 650/651–656/657	Shemitah Year 4424 4418 AM–4424 AM 657/658–663/664 AD	Shemitah Year 4431 4425 AM–4431 AM 664/665–670/671 AD	Shemitah Year 4438 4432 AM–4438 AM 671/672–677/678 AD	Shemitah Year 4445 4439 AM–4445 AM 678/679–684/685 AD	Shemitah Year 4452 4446 AM–4452 AM 685/686–691/692 AD	Shemitah Year 4459 4453 AM–4459 AM 692/693–698/699 AD
89th Jubilee 4500 4460 AM–4466 AM 699/700–705/706	Shemitah Year 4473 4467 AM–4473 AM 706/707–712/713 AD	Shemitah Year 4480 4474 AM–4480 AM 713/714–719/720 AD	Shemitah Year 4487 4481 AM–4487 AM 720/721–726/727 AD	Shemitah Year 4494 4488 AM–4494 AM 727/728–733/734 AD	Shemitah Year 4501 4495 AM–4501 AM 734/735–740/741 AD	Shemitah Year 4508 4502 AM–4508 AM 741/742–747/748 AD
90th Jubilee 4550 4509 AM–4515 AM 748/749–754/755	Shemitah Year 4522 4516 AM–4522 AM 755/756–761/762 AD	Shemitah Year 4529 4523 AM–4529 AM 762/763–768/769 AD	Shemitah Year 4536 4530 AM–4536 AM 769/770–775/776 AD	Shemitah Year 4543 4537 AM–4543 AM 776/777–782/783 AD	Shemitah Year 4550 4544 AM–4550 AM 783/784–789/790 AD	Shemitah Year 4557 4551 AM–4557 AM 790/791–796/797 AD
91st Jubilee 4600 4558 AM–4564 AM 797/798–803/804	Shemitah Year 4571 4565 AM–4571 AM 804/805–810/811 AD	Shemitah Year 4578 4572 AM–4578 AM 811/812–817/818 AD	Shemitah Year 4585 4579 AM–4585 AM 818/819–824/825 AD	Shemitah Year 4592 4586 AM–4592 AM 825/826–831/832 AD	Shemitah Year 4599 4593 AM–4599 AM 832/833–838/839 AD	Shemitah Year 4606 4600 AM–4606 AM 839/840–845/846 AD
92nd Jubilee 4650 4607 AM–4613 AM 846/847–852/853	Shemitah Year 4620 4614 AM–4620 AM 853/854–859/860 AD	Shemitah Year 4627 4621 AM–4627 AM 860/861–866/867 AD	Shemitah Year 4634 4628 AM–4634 AM 867/868–873/874 AD	Shemitah Year 4641 4635 AM–4641 AM 874/875–880/881 AD	Shemitah Year 4648 4642 AM–4648 AM 881/882–887/888 AD	Shemitah Year 4655 4649 AM–4655 AM 888/889–894/895 AD
93rd Jubilee 4700 4656 AM–4662 AM 895/896–901/902	Shemitah Year 4669 4663 AM–4669 AM 902/903–908/909 AD	Shemitah Year 4676 4670 AM–4676 AM 909/910–915/916 AD	Shemitah Year 4683 4677 AM–4683 AM 916/917–922/923 AD	Shemitah Year 4690 4684 AM–4690 AM 923/924–929/930 AD	Shemitah Year 4697 4691 AM–4697 AM 930/931–936/937 AD	Shemitah Year 4704 4698 AM–4704 AM 937/938–943/944 AD
94th Jubilee 4750 4705 AM–4711 AM	Shemitah Year 4718 4712 AM–4718 AM 951/952–957/958 AD	Shemitah Year 4725 4719 AM–4725 AM 958/959–964/965 AD	Shemitah Year 4732 4726 AM–4732 AM 965/966–971/972 AD	Shemitah Year 4739 4733 AM–4739 AM 972/973–978/979 AD	Shemitah Year 4746 4740 AM–4746 AM 979/980–985/986 AD	Shemitah Year 4753 4747 AM–4753 AM 986/987–992/993 AD

944/945–950/951

95th Jubilee 4800 4754 AM–4760 AM 993/994–999/1000	Shemitah Year 4767 4761 AM–4767 AM 1000/1001–1006/1007	Shemitah Year 4774 4768 AM–4774 AM 1007/1008–1013/1014	Shemitah Year 4781 4775 AM–4781 AM 1014/1015–1020/1021	Shemitah Year 4788 4782 AM–4788 AM 1021/1022–1027/1028	Shemitah Year 4795 4789 AM–4795 AM 1028/1029–1034/1035	Shemitah Year 4802 4796 AM–4802 AM 1035/1036–1041/1042
96th Jubilee 4850 4803 AM–4809 AM 1042/1043–1048/1049	Shemitah Year 4816 4810 AM–4816 AM 1049/1050–1055/1056	Shemitah Year 4823 4817 AM–4823 AM 1056/1057–1062/1063	Shemitah Year 4830 4824 AM–4830 AM 1063/1064–1069/1070	Shemitah Year 4837 4831 AM–4837 AM 1070/1071–1076/1077	Shemitah Year 4844 4838 AM–4844 AM 1077/1078–1083/1084	Shemitah Year 4851 4845 AM–4851 AM 1084/1085–1090/1091
97th Jubilee 4900 4852 AM–4858 AM 1091/1092–1097/1098	Shemitah Year 4865 4859 AM–4865 AM 1098/1099–1104/1105	Shemitah Year 4872 4866 AM–4872 AM 1105/1106–1111/1112	Shemitah Year 4879 4873 AM–4879 AM 1112/1113–1118/1119	Shemitah Year 4886 4880 AM–4886 AM 1119/1120–1125/1126	Shemitah Year 4893 4887 AM–4893 AM 1126/1127–1132/1133	Shemitah Year 4900 4894 AM–4900 AM 1133/1134–1139/1140
4901 AM–4907 AM 1140/1141–1146/1147	Shemitah Year 4914 4908 AM–4914 AM 1147/1148–1153/1154	Shemitah Year 4921 4915 AM–4921 AM 1154/1155–1160/1161	Shemitah Year 4928 4922 AM–4928 AM 1161/1162–1167/1168	Shemitah Year 4935 4929 AM–4935 AM 1168/1169–1174/1175	Shemitah Year 4942 4936 AM–4942 AM 1175/1176–1181/1182	Shemitah Year 4949 4943 AM–4949 AM 1182/1183–1188/1189
98th Jubilee 4950 4950 AM–4956 AM 1189/1190–1195/1196	Shemitah Year 4963 4957 AM–4963 AM 1196/1197–1202/1203	Shemitah Year 4970 4964 AM–4970 AM 1203/1204–1209/1210	Shemitah Year 4977 4971 AM–4977 AM 1210/1211–1216/1217	Shemitah Year 4984 4978 AM–4984 AM 1217/1218–1223/1224	Shemitah Year 4991 4985 AM–4991 AM 1224/1225–1230/1231	Shemitah Year 4998 4992 AM–4998 AM 1231/1232–1237/1238
99th Jubilee 5000 4999 AM–5005 AM 1238/1239–1244/1245	Shemitah Year 5012 5006 AM–5012 AM 1245/1246–1251/1252	Shemitah Year 5019 5013 AM–5019 AM 1252/1253–1258/1259	Shemitah Year 5026 5020 AM–5026 AM 1259/1260–1265/1266	Shemitah Year 5033 5027 AM–5033 AM 1266/1267–1272/1273	Shemitah Year 5040 5034 AM–5040 AM 1273/1274–1279/1280	Shemitah Year 5047 5041 AM–5047 AM 1280/1281–1286/1287
100th Jubilee 5050 5048 AM–5054 AM 1287/1288–1293/1294	Shemitah Year 5061 5055 AM–5061 AM 1294/1295–1300/1301	Shemitah Year 5068 5062 AM–5068 AM 1301/1302–1307/1308	Shemitah Year 5075 5069 AM–5075 AM 1308/1309–1314/1315	Shemitah Year 5082 5076 AM–5082 AM 1315/1316–1321/1322	Shemitah Year 5089 5083 AM–5089 AM 1322/1323–1328/1329	Shemitah Year 5096 5090 AM–5096 AM 1329/1330–1335/1336
101st Jubilee 5100 5097 AM–5103 AM 1336/1337–1342/1343	Shemitah Year 5110 5104 AM–5110 AM 1343/1344–1349/1350	Shemitah Year 5117 5111 AM–5117 AM 1350/1351–1356/1357	Shemitah Year 5124 5118 AM–5124 AM 1357/1358–1363/1364	Shemitah Year 5131 5125 AM–5131 AM 1364/1365–1370/1371	Shemitah Year 5138 5132 AM–5138 AM 1371/1372–1377/1378	Shemitah Year 5145 5139 AM–5145 AM 1378/1379–1384/1385
102nd Jubilee 5150 5146 AM–5152 AM 1385/1386–1391/1392	Shemitah Year 5159 5153 AM–5159 AM 1392/1393–1398/1399	Shemitah Year 5166 5160 AM–5166 AM 1399/1400–1405/1406	Shemitah Year 5173 5167 AM–5173 AM 1406/1407–1412/1413	Shemitah Year 5180 5174 AM–5180 AM 1413/1414–1419/1420	Shemitah Year 5187 5181 AM–5187 AM 1420/1421–1426/1427	Shemitah Year 5194 5188 AM–5194 AM 1427/1428–1433/1434
103rd Jubilee 5200 5195 AM–5201 AM 1434/1435–1440/1441	Shemitah Year 5208 5202 AM–5208 AM 1441/1442–1447/1448	Shemitah Year 5215 5209 AM–5215 AM 1448/1449–1454/1455	Shemitah Year 5222 5216 AM–5222 AM 1455/1456–1461/1462	Shemitah Year 5229 5223 AM–5229 AM 1462/1463–1468/1469	Shemitah Year 5236 5230 AM–5236 AM 1469/1470–1475/1476	Shemitah Year 5243 5237 AM–5243 AM 1476/1477–1482/1483
104th Jubilee 5250 5244 AM–5250 AM 1483/1484–1489/1490	Shemitah Year 5257 5251 AM–5257 AM 1490/1491–1496/1497	Shemitah Year 5264 5258 AM–5264 AM 1497/1498–1503/1504	Shemitah Year 5271 5265 AM–5271 AM 1504/1505–1510/1511	Shemitah Year 5278 5272 AM–5278 AM 1511/1512–1517/1518	Shemitah Year 5285 5279 AM–5285 AM 1518/1519–1524/1525	Shemitah Year 5292 5286 AM–5292 AM 1525/1526–1531/1532
105th Jubilee 5300 5293 AM–5299 AM 1532/1533–1538/1539	Shemitah Year 5306 5300 AM–5306 AM 1539/1540–1545/1546	Shemitah Year 5313 5307 AM–5313 AM 1546/1547–1552/1553	Shemitah Year 5320 5314 AM–5320 AM 1553/1554–1559/1560	Shemitah Year 5327 5321 AM–5327 AM 1560/1561–1566/1567	Shemitah Year 5334 5328 AM–5334 AM 1567/1568–1573/1574	Shemitah Year 5341 5335 AM–5341 AM 1574/1575–1580/1581
106th Jubilee 5350 5342 AM–5348 AM 1581/1582–1587/1588	Shemitah Year 5355 5349 AM–5355 AM 1588/1589–1594/1595	Shemitah Year 5362 5356 AM–5362 AM 1595/1596–1601/1602	Shemitah Year 5369 5363 AM–5369 AM 1602/1603–1608/1609	Shemitah Year 5376 5370 AM–5376 AM 1609/1610–1615/1616	Shemitah Year 5383 5377 AM–5383 AM 1616/1617–1622/1623	Shemitah Year 5390 5384 AM–5390 AM 1623/1624–1629/1630
107th Jubilee 5400 5391 AM–5397 AM 1630/1631–1636/1637	Shemitah Year 5404 5398 AM–5404 AM 1637/1638–1643/1644	Shemitah Year 5411 5405 AM–5411 AM 1644/1645–1650/1651	Shemitah Year 5418 5412 AM–5418 AM 1651/1652–1657/1658	Shemitah Year 5425 5419 AM–5425 AM 1658/1659–1664/1665	Shemitah Year 5432 5426 AM–5432 AM 1665/1666–1671/1672	Shemitah Year 5439 5433 AM–5439 AM 1672/1673–1678/1679
108th Jubilee 5450 5440 AM–5446 AM 1679/1680–1685/1686	Shemitah Year 5453 5447 AM–5453 AM 1686/1687–1692/1693	Shemitah Year 5460 5454 AM–5460 AM 1693/1694–1699/1700	Shemitah Year 5467 5461 AM–5467 AM 1700/1701–1706/1707	Shemitah Year 5474 5468 AM–5474 AM 1707/1708–1713/1714	Shemitah Year 5481 5475 AM–5481 AM 1714/1715–1720/1721	Shemitah Year 5488 5482 AM–5488 AM 1721/1722–1727/1728
109th Jubilee 5500 5489 AM–5495 AM 1728/1729–1734/1735	Shemitah Year 5502 5496 AM–5502 AM 1735/1736–1741/1742	Shemitah Year 5509 5503 AM–5509 AM 1742/1743–1748/1749	Shemitah Year 5516 5510 AM–5516 AM 1749/1750–1755/1756	Shemitah Year 5523 5517 AM–5523 AM 1756/1757–1762/1763	Shemitah Year 5530 5524 AM–5530 AM 1763/1764–1769/1770	Shemitah Year 5537 5531 AM–5537 AM 1770/1771–1776/1777
110th Jubilee 5550 5538 AM–5544 AM 1777/1778–1783/1784	Shemitah Year 5551 5545 AM–5551 AM 1784/1785–1790/1791	Shemitah Year 5558 5552 AM–5558 AM 1791/1792–1797/1798	Shemitah Year 5565 5559 AM–5565 AM 1798/1799–1804/1805	Shemitah Year 5572 5566 AM–5572 AM 1805/1806–1811/1812	Shemitah Year 5579 5573 AM–5579 AM 1812/1813–1818/1819	Shemitah Year 5586 5580 AM–5586 AM 1819/1820–1825/1826
111th Jubilee 5600	Shemitah Year 5600 5594 AM–5600 AM	Shemitah Year 5607 5601 AM–5607 AM	Shemitah Year 5614 5608 AM–5614 AM	Shemitah Year 5621 5615 AM–5621 AM	Shemitah Year 5628 5622 AM–5628 AM	Shemitah Year 5635 5629 AM–5635 AM

5587 AM–5593 AM 1826/1827–1832/1833	1833/1834–1839/1840	1840/1841–1846/1847	1847/1848–1853/1854	1854/1855–1860/1861	1861/1862–1867/1868	1868/1869–1874/1875
112th Jubilee 5650 5636 AM–5642 AM 1875/1876–1881/1882	Shemitah Year 5649 5643 AM–5649 AM 1882/1883–1888/1889	Shemitah Year 5656 5650 AM–5656 AM 1889/1890–1895/1896	Shemitah Year 5663 5657 AM–5663 AM 1896/1897–1902/1903	Shemitah Year 5670 5664 AM–5670 AM 1903/1904–1909/1910	Shemitah Year 5677 5671 AM–5677 AM 1910/1911–1916/1917	Shemitah Year 5684 5678 AM–5684 AM 1917/1918–1923/1924
113th Jubilee 5700 5685 AM–5691 AM 1924/1925–1930/1931	Shemitah Year 5698 5692 AM–5698 AM 1931/1932–1937/1938	Shemitah Year 5705 5699 AM–5705 AM 1938/1939–1944/1945	Shemitah Year 5712 5706 AM–5712 AM 1945/1946–1951/1952	Shemitah Year 5713 5713 AM–5719 AM 1952/1953–1958/1959	Shemitah Year 5726 5720 AM–5726 AM 1959/1960–1965/1966	Shemitah Year 5733 5727 AM–5733 AM 1966/1967–1972/1973
114th Jubilee 5750 5734 AM–5740 AM 1973/1974–1979/1980	Shemitah Year 5747 5741 AM–5747 AM 1980/1981–1986/1987	Shemitah Year 5754 5748 AM–5754 AM 1987/1988–1993/1994	Shemitah Year 5761 5755 AM–5761 AM 1994/1995–2000/2001	Shemitah Year 5768 5762 AM–5768 AM 2001/2002–2007/2008	Shemitah Year 5775 5769 AM–5775 AM 2008/2009–2014/2015	Shemitah Year 5782 5776 AM–5782 AM 2015/2016–2021/2022
115th Jubilee 5800 5783 AM–5789 AM 2022/2023–2028/2029	Shemitah Year 5796 5790 AM–5796 AM 2029/2030–2035/2036	Shemitah Year 5803 5797 AM–5803 AM 2036/2037–2042/2043	Shemitah Year 5810 5804 AM–5810 AM 2043/2044–2049/2050	Shemitah Year 5817 5811 AM–5817 AM 2050/2051–2056/2057	Shemitah Year 5818 5818 AM–5824 AM 2057/2058–2063/2064	Shemitah Year 5831 5825 AM–5831 AM 2064/2065–2070/2071

Figure 8 – Shemitah Cycles and Jubilee Years Since Creation (1 AM)

In Summary: The 115th Jubilee and the Creation Calendar

In biblical reckoning, the Jubilee is a sacred fiftieth-year cycle established by God, symbolizing liberty, restoration, and a divine reset. According to Leviticus 25:9–10, every fiftieth year is proclaimed as a Jubilee—marked by the sounding of the shofar on *Yom Kippur* and the declaration of freedom throughout the land.

Counting from Year 1 AM (*Anno Mundi*, "Year of the World") using a strict fifty-year cycle, the 115th Jubilee would fall in 5750 AM (50 x 115 = 5750).

However, many prophetic scholars and Hebrew roots researchers propose a refined model, aligning the 120th Jubilee with 6000 AM—reflecting the prophetic pattern of 6,000 years of mankind's history followed by 1,000 years of Messianic reign. In this view, the 115th Jubilee would occur in 5800 AM, not 5750 AM.

This alternate reckoning may:

- Begin counting Jubilees after Israel entered the Promised Land.
- Adjust for Jubilees not observed during the Babylonian exile.
- Integrate prophetic symbolism into the calculation, emphasizing God's redemptive timeline.

Under this framework, the 5800 AM marker is more than mathematics—it is prophetic theology, pointing to the nearness of the final Jubilee and the ultimate restoration. This Jubilee cycle is not just a way of measuring time—it is a prophetic key that connects liberty, redemption, and the return of Messiah. As the cycles approach their completion, the calendar is no longer simply counting years—it is revealing the patterns of God's plan and announcing that the end of the age is drawing near.

334 | THE VANISHING

THE FIFTH HARBINGER HAS BEEN ACTIVATED

The Shemitah Is Sounding—Mercy or Judgment? The Choice Is Yours

The Shemitah is not a relic of agricultural law—it is a prophetic alarm clock, a divine rhythm pulsing through human history. Every seventh year, God sounds the warning: reset, release, return. But when nations refuse to listen, the Shemitah transforms from a Sabbath of rest into a storm of reckoning. It is not a one-time event, but a recurring cycle of warning and mercy, judgment and restoration. It is God's way of shaking the nations, reordering economies, humbling leaders, and calling His people to repentance before greater judgment arrives.

The fifth harbinger is more than a whisper—it is a roar. Through every Shemitah cycle, God issues His terms: "Return to Me, and I will return to you." But we have turned to idols, to self, to security in what can be shaken. So He shakes it. Again and again. 2001. 2008. 2015. 2022. These were not economic coincidences or geopolitical accidents. They were prophetic pulses, echoing the pattern of Shemitah—warnings wrapped in mercy.

This isn't fearmongering—it's a wake-up call. The time is now. Paul wrote in 2 Corinthians 6:2, "Behold, now is the accepted time; behold, now is the day of salvation." This is not *chronos* time—measured by clocks and calendars. This is *kairos* time—God's appointed moment. You don't want to miss it. You don't want to sleep through the Vanishing, to ignore the sound of the trumpet because your ears were tuned to the noise of the world.

The fifth harbinger asks you plainly: Are you in the Ark or still mocking Noah? Are you living in prophetic ignorance or urgent expectancy? The Shemitah is a siren, not a lullaby. It is not meant to soothe—it is meant to stir. The days of comfort are over. The days of divine confrontation are here. And soon, the doors will close. The King will come. And the window of mercy will slam shut.

We are now in the midst of the 2022–2029 Shemitah cycle—a span that may hold one of the most climactic moments in prophetic history: the Rapture of the Church (2028/2029) or the opening of Daniel's 70th Week (possibly in 2029/2030). If this sequence unfolds as anticipated, the midpoint of the Tribulation could arrive in 2032/2033, culminating in Armageddon and the Return of the King as early as the fall of 2035/2036.

The warnings are accelerating.
The cycles are converging.
The countdown is ticking.

This is not a drill.
This is not a rehearsal.
This could be the final Shemitah before everything changes.

CHAPTER SUMMARY

Chapter 9 unveils the Fifth Harbinger: The Shemitah Cycles of judgment and mercy, shifting the prophetic lens from the Feasts of the LORD to the divine rhythm of seven-year resets. Long before Wall Street collapsed or global wars erupted, God had already encoded a pattern into the very soil of Israel—a Sabbath for the land, a Sabbath for nations, a Sabbath for warning. The Shemitah, outlined in Leviticus 25, was not only agricultural—it was spiritual, national, and prophetic.

This chapter traces the Shemitah from its original purpose as a year of rest and release, to its prophetic function as a cycle of correction and realignment. When Israel obeyed, the land flourished. When they rebelled, judgment followed. That same pattern echoes through modern history—seen in the crashes of 2001, 2008, and 2015, and the global tremors of 2022. These were not isolated events; they were part of God's cyclical alarm clock, warning that time is running out.

The chapter also unlocks the mystery of the Jubilee—the fiftieth year that follows seven Shemitah cycles. Could the 115th Jubilee—where 1 + 1 + 5 equals seven, the biblical number of perfection and divine completion—be the final Jubilee on God's calendar? With the 2022–2029 Shemitah cycle now in motion, the question grows sharper: could 2028 or 2029 mark the Rapture of the Church, or the opening of Daniel's 70th Week in 2029/2030? The convergence of fall feasts, prophetic midpoints, and overlapping timelines only intensifies the urgency of this possibility.

From Creation to the present *Information Age*, the chapter sketches the biblical epochs—distinct periods in time—that lead us to today's prophetic brink. These aren't just historical ages—they are spiritual dispensations and divine milestones, each reflecting mankind's response to revelation and God's mercy.

Ultimately, the Shemitah is more than a historical pattern—it is a living, breathing harbinger still speaking today. It warns. It resets. It invites repentance. And it prepares the world for the next great shaking.

KEY TAKEAWAYS

- The Shemitah—God's seven-year cycle of release, warning, and realignment—first given to Israel, yet echoed in the rise and fall of nations throughout history.

- Historic convergence—Major economic, geopolitical, and spiritual turning points in 2001, 2008, 2015, and 2022 all align with Shemitah years, underscoring the cycle's ongoing relevance.

- The 115th Jubilee (2022/2023 to 2028/2029)—1 + 1 + 5 = 7, the biblical number of perfection and divine completion—potentially marking the final Jubilee on God's calendar.
- The current cycle (2022–2029)—May witness the Rapture, the start of the Tribulation (Daniel's 70th Week), or both—placing us on the threshold of prophetic fulfillment.
- Not a fear tactic—The Shemitah is a mercy cycle, designed to awaken hearts, reset priorities, and turn people back to Christ before greater judgment comes.
- From Creation to now—This chapter connects biblical epochs and Shemitah cycles into a single prophetic roadmap, revealing God's timetable for the end of the age.

Chapter 9 sounds the fifth harbinger with unmistakable force: The Shemitah is not just history—it's prophecy in motion. It is God's pattern for mercy before judgment, reset before collapse, and alignment before return.

The cycles are converging.
The clock is ticking.
The King is coming.

The Shemitah is sounding.
The countdown has begun.

Are you watching?
Are you ready?

Chapter 10

The Sixth Harbinger:
Daniel's 70th Week Trigger

THE FINAL COUNTDOWN HAS BEGUN—Of all the prophetic revelations in Scripture, none match the mathematical precision and apocalyptic weight of Daniel's Seventy Weeks prophecy. Given during Israel's captivity in Babylon, this revelation is unlike any other: a divine countdown that began with a royal decree to rebuild Jerusalem and will end with the return of the Messiah.

It is God's blueprint for history's climax—a celestial stopwatch that has been running for more than two millennia.

In Daniel 9:24–27, the angel Gabriel delivers a time-bound prophecy so precise that it not only foretold the coming of the Messiah, but pinpointed the very day of crucifixion.

Daniel's 70 Weeks (490 years):

> Seventy weeks are determined upon your people and upon your Holy City, to finish the transgression, and to make an end of sins, and to make reconciliation for iniquity, and to bring in everlasting righteousness, and to seal up the vision and prophecy, and to anoint the Most Holy. (Daniel 9:24)

Daniel's 69 Weeks (483 years):

> Know therefore and understand, that from the going forth of the commandment to restore and to build Jerusalem unto the Messiah the Prince shall be seven

weeks, and threescore and two weeks: the streets shall be built again, and the wall, even in troublous times. (Daniel 9:25)

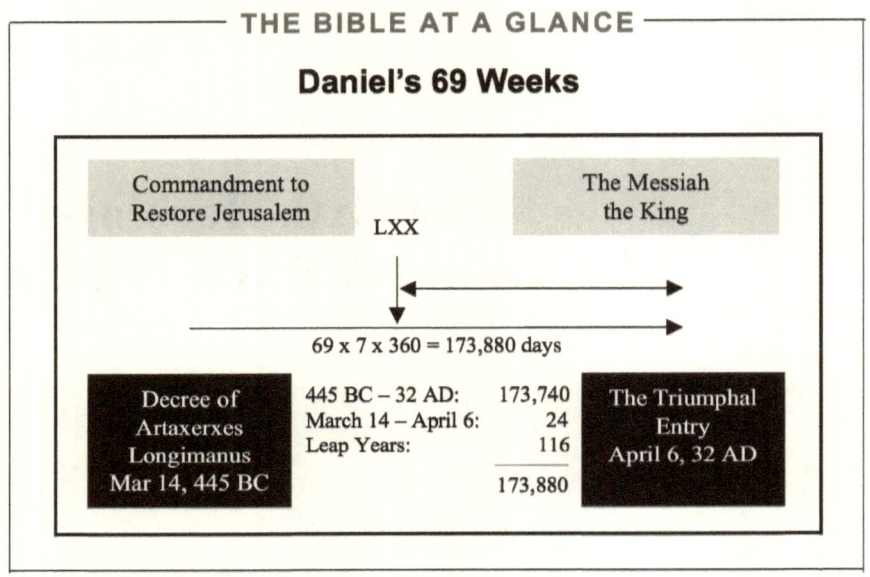

Figure 9 – Daniel's 69 Weeks

The first sixty-nine weeks—483 prophetic years—were fulfilled with supernatural precision, culminating in the triumphal entry of Jesus into Jerusalem. But the countdown did not end at the Cross. One week remains—seven prophetic years—still suspended over the world like a drawn sword, ready to fall.

This is not ancient trivia; it is the structural framework of the end times. The first sixty-nine weeks have already been fulfilled with breathtaking accuracy. The final, seventieth week is yet to come—and when it begins, it will set in motion the events that bring this present age to its dramatic and inevitable close.

The Gap After the 69th Week

And after threescore and two weeks shall Messiah be cut off, but not for Himself: and the people of the prince that shall come shall destroy the city and the sanctuary; and the end thereof shall be with a flood, and unto the end of the war desolations are determined. (Daniel 9:26)

This verse implies a prophetic gap between the sixty-ninth and seventieth weeks—the Church Age, a mystery later revealed in the New Testament

(Ephesians 3:3–9). During this period, God is gathering a people for His name until "the fullness of the Gentiles comes in" (Romans 11:25). After that, He turns again to Israel in the final week.

Daniel's 70th Week: The Tribulation Age (7 Years)

> And he (the Antichrist) shall confirm the covenant with many for one week: and in the midst of the week he shall cause the sacrifice and the oblation to cease, and for the overspreading of abominations he shall make it desolate, even until the consummation, and that determined shall be poured upon the desolate. (Daniel 9:27)

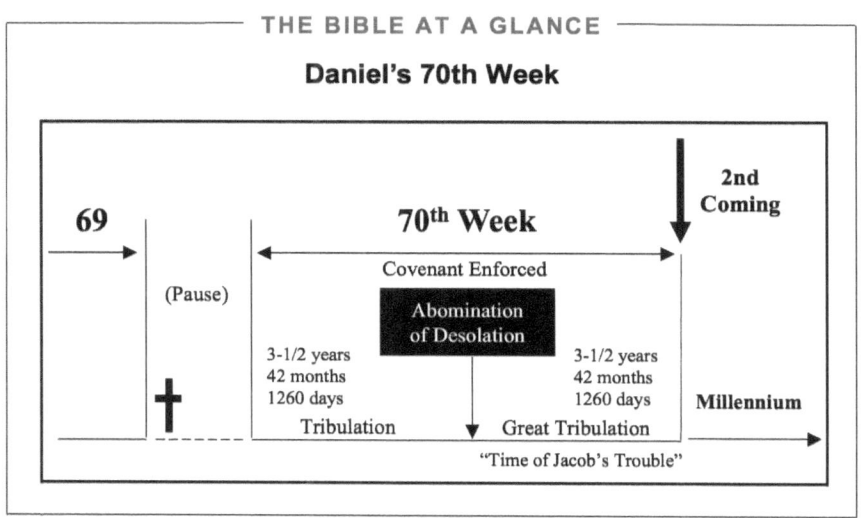

THE BIBLE AT A GLANCE

Daniel's 70th Week

Figure 10 – Daniel's 70th Week

This final week is not about the Church; it centers on Israel, judgment, and redemption as God's decree unfolds at the end of the age. The pause between the sixty-ninth and seventieth weeks marks the Church Age—a mystery hidden in ages past. That pause is nearly over. And as the world accelerates toward global upheaval, financial collapse, religious apostasy, and geopolitical realignment, we are not waiting for the clock to start—we are watching it wind to zero.

This seven-year period aligns precisely with other prophetic timelines:

- "Time, times, and half a time" (3½ years)—Daniel 7:25, 12:7.
- 42 months and 1,260 days—Revelation 11–13.

Known as the Tribulation and "the time of Jacob's trouble" (Jeremiah 30:7), it culminates in the Second Coming of Jesus Christ.

The sixth harbinger is the trigger—the beginning of the final prophetic week. It will arrive not with a whisper, but with a trumpet. The prophecy has already been fulfilled once—with flawless precision. Shall it not be fulfilled again?

The seventieth week is waiting.

The harbinger is sounding.

And the clock is about to strike the final seven.

Are you watching?

DANIEL'S CLOCK AND THE MISSED SHEMITAHS

The Prophetic Pattern Hidden in Cycles of Rest and Judgment

The foundation of Daniel's Seventy Weeks prophecy isn't just numbers—it's timing rooted in obedience, rest, and judgment. Long before Daniel ever received his vision of seventy sevens, Israel had already broken a divine rhythm. For 490 years, the nation failed to honor the Shemitah—the sabbatical year of rest for the land commanded in Leviticus 25. The result? Seventy missed Shemitah years. Seventy years of exile in Babylon. One year of captivity for every cycle of disobedience. So:

- 1 week = 7 years.
- 70 weeks x 7 years = 490 years total.

That's why Daniel's prophetic timeline is inseparably tied to the Shemitah. What began as a national punishment became the very structure of a messianic countdown.

Seventy "weeks" of years—seventy cycles of seven—were decreed not only as a roadmap to Messiah's First Coming but also as a framework for Israel's future. The first sixty-nine "weeks" (483 years) ended with Messiah's arrival. But the seventieth? It still awaits fulfillment. And just like the judgment that birthed it, the final "week" must begin at the head of a Shemitah cycle. Prophetic timing is not arbitrary—it's appointed.

That brings us to the present. We are now living in the Shemitah cycle of 2022/2023 to 2028/2029. Looking ahead, the next cycle—beginning in the fall of 2029/2030—places *Rosh HaShanah* as a compelling candidate for the launch of Daniel's 70th Week. This date is more than symbolic; it is strategically aligned with God's prophetic calendar. Known as "the day no one knows," *Rosh HaShanah*—the Feast of Trumpets—foreshadows the coronation of the King and may sound the call that sets the final seven years in motion: the Tribulation Age.

The same prophetic clock that once counted down to the Messiah's sacrifice is poised to start again—this time ticking toward His return. The Shemitah cycle set the rhythm, and Daniel was given divine insight into its sequence. Today, we stand in the pause between prophecy declared and prophecy fulfilled. As the final "week" approaches, the question is not whether time is moving—it is whether we are watching. Are you counting the moments?

TIMING CLUES: WHO WON'T KNOW THE DAY OR HOUR?

One of the most misunderstood concepts in end-time prophecy is the idea that "no one knows the day or the hour." Many use this as proof that attempting to understand God's prophetic timeline is futile. Yet a closer reading of Scripture reveals something different—and far more sobering.

In Matthew 25, Jesus describes ten virgins awaiting the Bridegroom. Only five were wise, prepared with oil in their lamps. The other five—the foolish— were caught off guard when the Bridegroom arrived.

> And while they went to buy, the Bridegroom came; and they that were ready went in with Him to the marriage: and the door was shut. Afterward came also the other virgins, saying, Lord, Lord, open to us. But He answered and said, Verily I say unto you, I know you not. (Matthew 25:10–12)

Notice whom Jesus rebukes: "Verily I say unto you, I know you not." It wasn't the watchful who were in the dark. It was the unprepared. Likewise, in Luke 12, Jesus commends the "faithful and wise" servants who stayed ready, but warns of the servant who says in his heart, "My master delays his coming." That servant is the one surprised, judged, and cut off.

> But and if that servant say in his heart, My lord delays his coming; and shall begin to beat the menservants and maidens, and to eat and drink, and to be drunken; The lord of that servant will come in a day when he looks not for him, and at an hour when he is not aware, and will cut him in sunder, and will appoint him his portion with the unbelievers. (Luke 12:45–46)

So who won't know the day or the hour? The foolish. The complacent. The willfully blind. Jesus wasn't warning His faithful Bride to remain ignorant; He was warning the careless not to be caught sleeping.

That raises a sobering question: Does today's Church understand the prophetic hour as clearly as the Adversary does? Satan seems to recognize the appointed times, aligning world events, culture, and deception with uncanny precision. Meanwhile, much of the Church has dismissed prophecy as irrelevant or unknowable. But God never intended His calendar to be hidden from those who watch.

For those who understand the *moedim*—God's appointed times—the season of Messiah's return is not a surprise. Just as the spring feasts were fulfilled in exact detail at Jesus' First Coming, the fall feasts will be fulfilled with the same precision at His Second Coming. *Rosh HaShanah*, the Feast of Trumpets, is more than symbolic—it is the appointed day for the trumpet to sound and the King to be revealed.

The signs are sounding. The calendar is speaking. The only question is: Will we be found wise enough to hear and ready enough to act?

PROPHETIC LAYERS IN PROVERBS AND PARABLES

Scripture often hides prophetic depth beneath its surface—patterns, symbols, and metaphors that echo across time and connect seemingly unrelated passages. One striking example emerges when we compare Revelation 17's harlot—symbol of the end-time system of spiritual seduction—with the adulterous woman in Proverbs 7. Both portray a force of deception that draws the unsuspecting away from truth at a critical moment.

In Proverbs 7:18–20, the woman tempts a "young man void of understanding" with secret pleasures while her husband is away. The prophetic hint comes in verse 20:

> Come, let us take our fill of love until the morning: let us solace ourselves with loves. For the goodman (her husband) is not at home, he is gone a long journey: he has taken a bag of money with him, and will come home at the day appointed (new moon, full moon, or appointed time). (Proverbs 7:18–20)

This apparent contradiction resolves when we look at the original Hebrew word *keseh*, which can mean "new moon," "full moon," or "appointed time," and is linked to the idea of concealment. In Jewish tradition, *keseh* is associated with hiddenness and royal enthronement.

Read through a Hebraic lens, the language points toward a *moed*—a fixed, appointed time on God's calendar. The clearest candidate is *Rosh HaShanah* (Feast of Trumpets), the only biblical feast that begins on the new moon. This two-day feast starts while the moon is hidden from sight, awaiting the first visible sliver—hence its title, "the day no one knows."

In Jewish tradition, *Rosh HaShanah* carries coronation imagery, but prophetically it represents the moment when the Bridegroom comes *for* His Bride—the Rapture of the Church. His public coronation as King of kings will not occur until the Second Coming, at the close of the Tribulation Age, pictured in the Feast of Tabernacles. At that time, He will return *with* His Bride and the holy angels to rule and reign on the earth.

In this light, Proverbs 7 is more than moral instruction—it is a prophetic warning. The harlot's assurance that the husband's return is far off mirrors the complacency of the foolish servant and the unprepared virgins. Yet the truth is that the appointed day is fixed and will arrive suddenly—at the concealed new moon—when the Bridegroom returns *for* His Bride, bringing the Church Age to a close.

The takeaway is sobering: what appears to be an everyday proverb may contain a prophetic calendar marker. God's Word is layered with meaning, and the wise will search out these timing clues rather than dismiss them.

THE DRESS REHEARSAL FOR THE BRIDEGROOM'S ARRIVAL

Every year, without fail, a divine appointment is rehearsed across the earth—often overlooked by much of the Church, but never forgotten in Heaven. *Rosh HaShanah*, also called the Feast of Trumpets, is far more than a Jewish holiday. It is the annual dress rehearsal for the Bridegroom's return—a prophetic preview of the day Messiah will come *for* His Bride.

Just as the spring feasts were fulfilled with exact precision—Passover marking the crucifixion, Unleavened Bread the burial, Firstfruits the resurrection, and *Shavuot* (Pentecost) the outpouring of the Holy Spirit—so the fall feasts will also be fulfilled in their appointed order. God's redemptive plan is not random; His *moedim*—appointed times—are fixed, and His calendar reveals His plan.

Rosh HaShanah is unique among the feasts in that it begins on the new moon, when the first sliver is sighted and the exact day and hour cannot be predicted—hence its title, "the day no one knows." On that future appointed day, when the shofar blast sounds, the Bridegroom will appear *for* His Bride, fulfilling the imagery of the ancient Galilean wedding. The dead in Messiah will rise, the living faithful will be caught up, the Church Age will close, and the Tribulation will begin.

Prophetically, the Tribulation Age serves as the dress rehearsal for *Yom Kippur*—the Day of Atonement—which falls between the Feast of Trumpets and the Feast of Tabernacles in God's fall feast sequence. *Yom Kippur* pictures Israel's national repentance and reconciliation with her Messiah, a fulfillment that will occur at His Second Coming.

What has been rehearsed for millennia will suddenly become reality. For those who have been watching and ready, the change will be instantaneous—one moment on earth, the next in the presence of the Bridegroom they have longed awaited.

THE DRESS REHEARSAL FOR THE CROWNING OF THE KING

While *Rosh HaShanah* prophetically points to the Bridegroom's arrival *for* His Bride, the imagery of the crowning of the King finds its ultimate fulfillment seven years later—at the Second Coming of Messiah, pictured in the Feast of Tabernacles (*Sukkot*).

In Jewish tradition, *Rosh HaShanah* carries coronation themes, but prophetically, Messiah's public enthronement as King of kings does not take place until His return *with* His Bride and the armies of Heaven at the end of the Tribulation. At that time, He will defeat His enemies, judge the nations, and take His rightful place on David's throne to rule the earth in righteousness for a thousand years.

The Feast of Tabernacles foreshadows this moment of victory and glory. It celebrates God dwelling with His people and marks the beginning of Messiah's Millennial reign. The coronation imagery embedded in the fall feasts finds its fullest expression here, when the King takes His throne—not in a heavenly meeting *with* His Bride, but in a public, global manifestation of His authority over every kingdom and nation.

Just as the rehearsal for the Bridegroom's arrival keeps us ready for the Rapture, the rehearsal for the King's coronation keeps us longing for the day when He will reign in person—restoring the earth and fulfilling every promise of His Word.

SEVEN KINGDOMS: FROM PHARAOH TO THE FINAL TRUMPET

The biblical prophetic timeline is not random—it's a structured sequence of kingdoms that have either ruled over or directly impacted God's covenant people. From the first oppression in Egypt to the final global power before Messiah's return, Scripture reveals a connected chain of empires. Daniel's visions (Daniel 2 and 7) anchor this sequence, showing the progression of human dominion until the establishment of God's everlasting kingdom.

1. **Egypt**—The First Oppressor

Egypt enslaved God's people under Pharaoh, initiating the long conflict between God's redemptive plan and human empire. Though absent from Daniel's statue vision, Egypt remains foundational to prophecy as the first great oppressor—and the first from which God delivered His people through miraculous intervention in 1446 BC.

Why is Egypt missing from Daniel's vision? Because Daniel's prophetic sequence begins during his own lifetime, under Babylonian rule. The statue in Daniel 2 depicts the success of Gentile kingdoms from Babylon forward—those that would dominate Jerusalem until Messiah's return (Luke 21:24). Egypt's role was already part of Israel's history, not its prophetic future from Daniel's perspective.

> Therefore they did set over them taskmasters to afflict them with their burdens. And they built for Pharaoh supply cities, Pithom and Raamses. (Exodus 1:11)

> I am the LORD your God, which have brought you out of the land of Egypt, out of the house of bondage. (Exodus 20:2)

2. **Assyria**—The Scattering Empire

Assyria followed Egypt as the next major power to dominate the biblical world. In 722 BC, the Assyrian armies besieged and captured Samaria, capital of the northern kingdom of Israel. This marked the tragic dispersion of the ten northern tribes—a scattering that continues to this day. The prophets Isaiah and Nahum condemned Assyria's pride, violence, and idolatry, portraying it as a tool of God's judgment but also as an example of the fate awaiting arrogant nations.

> Then the king of Assyria came up throughout all the land, and went up to Samaria, and besieged it three years. In the ninth year of Hoshea the king of Assyria took Samaria, and carried Israel away into Assyria, and placed them in Halah and in Habor by the river of Gozan, and in the cities of the Medes. (2 Kings 17:5–6)

3. **Babylon**—The Prophetic Countdown Begins

With Assyria's fall in 609 BC, Babylon rose as the dominant world power. Under King Nebuchadnezzar, Babylon's armies swept into Judah, destroying Jerusalem and the Temple in 586 BC. The people of Judah—the two southern tribes—were taken into captivity, fulfilling Jeremiah's prophecy of a seventy-year exile (Jeremiah 25:11–12).

Daniel, taken as a young man in the first wave of deportations (Daniel 1:1–6), interpreted Nebuchadnezzar's dream of the great statue, identifying Babylon as the head of gold (Daniel 2:37–38). This vision marked the start of the "times of the Gentiles" (Luke 21:24), when foreign powers would dominate Jerusalem until Messiah's return.

During the exile, Daniel received the Seventy Weeks prophecy (Daniel 9:24–27), a divine countdown to Messiah's First Coming and Israel's ultimate redemption. This period in history was not merely political—it was prophetic, placing Babylon at the starting line of God's end-time timeline.

> Now the rest of the people that were left in the city, and the fugitives that fell away to the king of Babylon, with the remnant of the multitude, did Nebuzaradan the capital of the guard (a servant of the king) carry away. (2 Kings 25:11)

4. **Medo-Persia**—The Decree to Return

Symbolized by the chest and arms of silver in Daniel's statue (Daniel 2:32, 39), the Medo-Persian Empire was a dual kingdom made of the Medes and the Persians. Under the leadership of King Cyrus II (Cyrus the Great), they overthrew the Babylonian Empire in 539 BC during the reign of King Belshazzar, as recorded in Daniel 5.

This conquest was swift and strategic. According to both Scripture and historical counts, the Medo-Persian forces diverted the Euphrates River, lowering the water level so their troops could enter Babylon under the city walls. That very night, while Babylon celebrated with feasting, the city was taken without a prolonged battle.

King Cyrus, recognized in prophecy more than a century before his birth (Isaiah 44:28, 45:1), later issued a decree allowing the Jewish exiles to return to Jerusalem and rebuild the Temple. This fulfilled the words of Isaiah and Jeremiah and restarted the prophetic clock toward Messiah's First Coming.

> That says of Cyrus, He is My shepherd, and shall perform all My pleasure: Even saying to Jerusalem, You shalt be built; and to the Temple, your foundation shall be laid. (Isaiah 44:28)

5. **Greece**—The Swift Conqueror

Represented by the belly and thighs of bronze in Daniel's statue (Daniel 2:32, 39), the Greek Empire rose under Alexander the Great, whose lightning-fast military campaigns toppled the Medo-Persian Empire in 331 BC. Daniel foresaw this centuries earlier in a vision (Daniel 8), depicting a "rough goat" coming from the west with unmatched speed, striking down the Medo-Persian ram.

Alexander, the "great horn" in Daniel's prophecy, united Greece and expanded his empire across the known world in just over a decade. But at the height of his power, Alexander died suddenly at age 32, fulfilling Daniel 8:22— "Now that being broken . . ."

His empire did not pass to his descendants but was divided among four of his generals: Cassander, Lysimachus, Seleucus, and Ptolemy. From the Seleucid line merged Antiochus IV Epiphanes, a cruel ruler who desecrated the Temple in Jerusalem. Antiochus became a prophetic foreshadow of the coming Antichrist—the "abomination of desolation" (Daniel 11:31; Matthew 24:15)—showing how past events mirror the final rebellion before Messiah's return.

> The ram which you saw having two horns are the kings of Media and Persia. And the rough goat is the king of Greece: and the great horn that is between his eyes is the first king. Now that being broken, whereas four stood up for it, four kingdoms shall stand up out of the nation, but not in his power. (Daniel 8:20–22)

6. **Rome**—The Empire of Iron

Symbolized by the legs of iron in Nebuchadnezzar's statue (Daniel 2:33, 40), the Roman Empire emerged as the most dominate military and political power of the ancient world. Rising from the small city-state of Rome in the 8th century BC, it grew through disciplined legions, advanced engineering, and an unmatched system of law and governance. Rome first expanded across the Italian peninsula, then absorbed Greece and the remnants of Alexander's divided empire, and finally conquered territories from Britain to the Middle East.

By 63 BC, under General Pompey, Rome had brought Judea—the territory that roughly corresponded to the land of the tribe of Judah (and parts of Benjamin), with Jerusalem as its capital—under its control. This set the stage for the fulfillment of messianic prophecy during the reign of Caesar Augustus, when Jesus was born (Luke 2:1). Under Roman authority, Pontius Pilate presided over Jesus' trial and crucifixion (John 19:15–16).

> And it came to pass in those days, that there went out a decree from Caesar Augustus, that all the world should be taxed. (Luke 2:1)

> But they cried out, Away with Him, away with Him, crucify Him. Pilate says unto them, Shall I crucify your King? The chief priests answered, We have no king but Caesar. Then delivered he Him therefore unto them to be crucified. And they took Jesus, and led Him away. (John 19:15–16)

Rome's legacy was not only in its iron military power but also the persecution of early Christians and the destruction of Jerusalem in 70 AD—carried out by the Romans under Titus, the son of Emperor Vespasian—fulfilling Jesus' prophecy in Luke 21:24.

> And they shall fall by the edge of the sword, and shall be led away captive into all nations: and Jerusalem shall be trodden down of the Gentiles, until the times of the Gentiles be fulfilled. (Luke 21:24)

The final form of the Roman system is seen in Daniel 2:41–43—iron mixed with clay—representing a divided, partly strong and partly brittle end-time power. Many interpreters see modern parallels in America and other Western nations, which echo Rome's architecture, governance, military might, and moral decline.

7. **Mystery Babylon**—The Final Global Power

Revelation 17–18 portrays Mystery Babylon as a wealthy, influential, and spiritually corrupt superpower in the last days. She is clothed in purple and scarlet, adorned with gold, jewels, and pearls—symbols of her opulence and dominance. She holds a golden cup filled with abominations, representing her idolatry, immorality, and spiritual compromise.

Many Bible teachers and watchmen see striking parallels between Mystery Babylon and modern America—both marked by unprecedented wealth, global influence, military dominance, and moral decline. Whether this final kingdom is America herself or a global system that operates from her, the Bible is clear: she will fall suddenly and catastrophically before Messiah's return.

> And the woman was arrayed in purple and scarlet color, and decked with gold and precious stones and pearls, having a golden cup in her hand full of abominations and filthiness of her fornication: And upon her forehead was a name written, MYSTERY, BABYLON THE GREAT, THE MOTHER OF HARLOTS AND ABOMINATION OF THE EARTH. (Revelation 17:4–5)

Her destruction will be swift and final:

> Therefore shall her plagues come in one day, death, and mourning, and famine; and she shall be utterly burned with fire: for strong is the Lord GOD who judges her. (Revelation 18:8)

This prophetic warning parallels Old Testament passages about Babylon's sudden fall (Isaiah 47:7–15; Jeremiah 50–51). The unifying theme is that her judgment is inevitable, unstoppable, and divinely decreed.

From Pharaoh to the final trumpet, every empire has risen and fallen according to God's prophetic timeline. These kingdoms form the backdrop against which the ultimate King will return. The patterns are clear, the clock is ticking, and the question remains: are we watching and ready?

——◆◆◆——

"Ann, before we continue, I think we need to pause for a moment. Let's step back and consider the broader context—during the Tribulation, Satan's empire doesn't emerge overnight. It's been developing throughout history strategically building toward this moment."

"Yes! And it's not random, Irene. Revelation 13:1 describes a beast with seven heads and ten horns—imagery packed with meaning. The seven heads symbolize seven world empires influenced by Satan, a truth confirmed in Revelation 17:9–10, which outlines these kingdoms across prophetic history."

> And here is the mind which has wisdom. The seven heads are seven mountains, on which the woman sits. And there are seven kings: five are fallen, and one is, and the other is not yet come; and when he comes, he must continue a short space. (Revelation 17:9–10)

Irene nodded.

"So, what are these seven heads? And what do the seven super-kingdoms of Satan represent?"

"Let's walk through them—are you ready?"

Irene gave a quick nod.

"Absolutely. Let's do it."

"First—Egypt. That's where it all began. Egypt enslaved God's people, trying to crush the covenant before it could take root. Remember Pharaoh? God raised up Moses to confront him."

"Exactly. Egypt tried to destroy the seed. Satan was aiming to abort Israel's destiny before it could be fulfilled."

I continued.

"Second—Assyria. Ruthless and brutal. After the deaths of King David and his son Solomon, Israel split into two kingdoms: the northern kingdom consisting of ten tribes, and the southern kingdom of Judah and Benjamin. In 722 BC, the Assyrians conquered the northern kingdom and scattered the ten tribes throughout their empire. Once again, Satan struck at God's people—trying to erase the Abrahamic covenant promise before it could be fulfilled."

"And third?"

"Babylon. It wasn't just military conquest—it was spiritual seduction. Idolatry, sorcery, and paganism saturated the culture. They exiled Judah and defiled the Temple."

"And Babylon becomes more than history—it's a prophetic symbol. Revelation's 'Mystery Babylon' picks up the thread of end-time deception."

"Exactly, Irene. Fourth—Medo-Persia. Though God used the Medes and Persians to bring the Jews back home, Satan still moved behind the scenes. Remember Haman's plot in Esther?"

Irene nodded.

"A satanic attempt at genocide. But once again, God intervened and preserved His covenant people."

"Fifth was Greece," I continued. "Under Alexander the Great, the world was swept up in philosophy, culture, and human wisdom. Satan used it to elevate intellect over truth—subtly replacing God's revelation with prideful reasoning."

"And then comes Rome—number six."

"Yes. Rome was the iron empire. It ruled during Christ's First Coming—it crucified Jesus and persecuted the early Church with unrelenting force. Revelation 17:10 says:"

And there are seven kings: five are fallen, and one is, and the other is not yet come; and when he comes, he must continue a short space. (Revelation 17:10)

I continued.

"That 'one is'—that's Rome. John was living under its dominion when he wrote this."

Irene leaned forward.

"That's six. What's number seven?"

I took a breath.

"The seventh head . . . is America."

Irene blinked.

"Seriously? I thought the Antichrist's empire would be based in the Middle East or Europe."

I nodded.

"It will be—but that's part of the complexity. Revelation 17:10 says, 'five are fallen, one is, and the other is not yet come; and when he comes, he must continue a short space.' Rome was the sixth—John lived under it. The seventh is the next great superpower with global dominance."

Irene sat back.

"And you think that's the United States?"

"Think about it. America may not be ancient like Egypt or Babylon, but her reach is global—militarily, economically, culturally. She has her tentacles in every continent, every conflict. She's the only empire in history with military bases in over 70 nations and the power to influence worldwide decisions."

Irene nodded slowly.

"And only 250 years old," she said.

> Your mother shall be sore confounded; she that bare you shall be ashamed: behold, the hindermost of the nations shall be a wilderness, a dry land, and a desert. (Jeremiah 50:12)

I nodded. "Yes, the phrase 'hindermost of the nations' can be translated as 'the youngest of the nations.' Some watchmen interpret this as a reference to a nation that rises late in history compared to ancient empires. This has been applied to the United States, which is young compared to Babylon, Rome, or Israel."

"If so, who is America's mother?" Irene asked.

"In historical terms," I continued, "America was born out of British colonies, making Great Britain the logical "mother" in this interpretation."

I continued.

"Compared to the centuries of millennia of the other empires, America's dominance is brief—a 'short space,' just like Revelation says."

Irene furrowed her brow. "But where does the Antichrist fit into this? Isn't his power base in the Middle East?"

I pulled out my Bible to Revelation 17, reading aloud:

> And the ten horns which you saw are ten kings, which have received no kingdom as yet; but receive power as kings one hour with the beast. These have one mind, and shall give their power and strength unto the beast. (Revelation 17:12–13)

"That's the twist. The Antichrist's empire—the ten-horn coalition—is a subset of the beast. It's likely formed from Middle Eastern and European regions, yes. But post-Rapture, after the sixth seal and the first four trumpets, the whole world changes."

Irene looked intrigued.

"You mean geologically?"

"Exactly," I said. "The sixth seal causes a global earthquake—every mountain and island moved. That's followed by trumpet judgments that burn up a third of the earth, oceans, rivers, and sky. It's like God is reclaiming and reshaping the planet—burning away what doesn't belong."

Irene leaned forward again.

"So you're saying the lower third of the Pangaea landmass (Genesis 1) is destroyed, and the landmass is restored to the Bible Lands?"

I nodded, pulling out my maps I used in *Trumpet I* and *Trumpet II*.

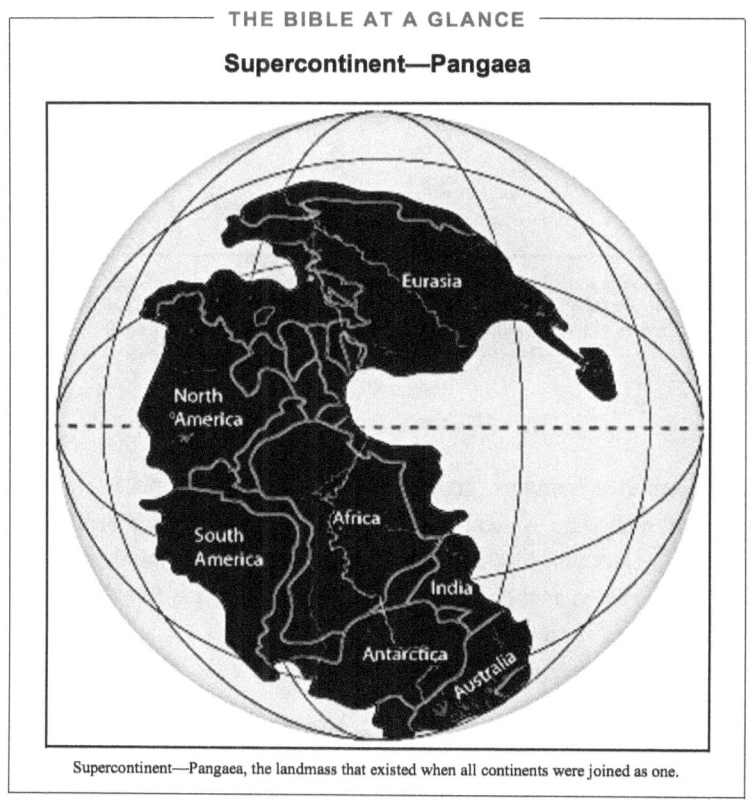

THE BIBLE AT A GLANCE

Supercontinent—Pangaea

Supercontinent—Pangaea, the landmass that existed when all continents were joined as one.

Figure 11 – Supercontinent—Pangaea (Genesis 1:9)

And God said, Let the waters under the heaven be gathered together unto one place, and let the dry land appear: and it was so. (Genesis 1:9)

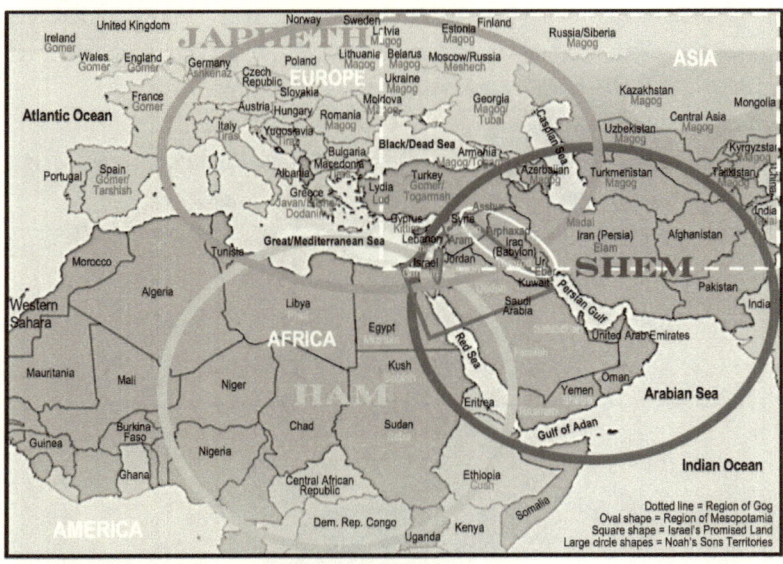

The large circles show the Bible Lands. The central square marks the full covenant land God promised to Abraham's descendants (Genesis 15:18–21). This promise remains unfulfilled and awaits its future fulfillment during the Messianic Kingdom (Ezekiel 47–48).

Figure 12 – North America and Eurasia

"Yes. America remains geographically, but the world's attention and structure shift east. The Antichrist's kingdom will be centered around Israel—what the Bible calls the 'pleasant land'—but it will carry global authority. And America, having ruled as the seventh head, gives way to the final beast system."

Irene was quiet for a moment.

"So America's rise wasn't random—it was strategic. A final empire before the real endgame begins."

I looked solemn.

"She offers peace, security, even prosperity—but in the end, she's part of the beast system. She will fall before the King returns."

Irene tilted her head.

"But wait—can we really call the Antichrist's empire a world empire? Doesn't he just make a covenant with Israel and a few nations at first?"

I nodded.

"Exactly. That's what makes this so deceptive. For the first 3½ years of the Tribulation, his influence is mostly regional. Daniel 9:27 says he confirms a covenant with *many*, but not necessarily the whole world."

Irene leaned in, curiosity flickering in her eyes.

"So his kingdom doesn't start globally?"

I shook my head.

"No. It begins small—likely rooted in a Middle Eastern or European alliance. But after the Rapture, the world is thrown into chaos. That vacuum of power? He steps right into it. That's why Scripture calls him a 'beast rising from the sea'— he emerges from the swirling chaos of nations."

Irene folded her arms, thinking it over.

"But his reign . . . it's only seven years."

"Exactly," I said. "Daniel's prophecy gives him just one week of years. The first 3½ years, his influence is mainly regional—consolidating power."

Irene's brow furrowed.

"So what changes at the midpoint?"

"That's when everything shifts," I said.

"Satan is cast down to the earth—and he possesses the Antichrist. Then the Antichrist walks into the rebuilt Third Temple and commits the abomination of desolation."

Her eyes widened.

"And that's when the False Prophet shows up?"

"Yes," I nodded.

"Then the False Prophet—under satanic control—forces the world to worship the beast. He launches the mark of the beast system so no one can buy or sell without it."

I took a breath.

"From that moment, Revelation says he's given authority over every tribe, language, and nation. That's the Great Tribulation—the last 3½ years—when the entire world falls under his grip."

I leaned back.

"And compared to every major empire in history, seven years is nothing. That's why it's so striking—he has immense power, but it's brief. The Bible never compares his rule to the length or stability of Babylon or Rome."

Irene's expression tightened.

"So then . . . why is America so important in this?"

I hesitated.

"Because America has acted like a global empire—without calling herself one. Think about it. She's overthrown governments, installed puppet leaders, and shaped entire regions through military, economic, and intelligence influence."

Irene's eyes narrowed.

"Regime changes."

I nodded.

"Exactly. From Latin America to the Middle East. And when she declines—or faces judgment—the vacuum she leaves will be enormous. The Antichrist will step into that space, offering the world a new hope, a new order."

Irene frowned.

"But it's a lie."

"Yes," I said.

"A deadly one. America is the seventh head of the beast. The Antichrist's ten-king coalition is the final phase—the beast's horns. He won't rule the entire globe overnight. At first, he'll rule by deception, by proxy, and through crisis."

Irene's voice was quiet.

"And then it all comes crashing down."

I leaned forward and whispered, "Right before the King returns."

Irene furrowed her brow.

"So, Ann, let me recap: Egypt, Assyria, Babylon, Medo-Persia, Greece, Rome, and America. That's seven. But why do so many scholars still say the seventh kingdom is a revised or revived Rome?"

I nodded slowly.

"That's the big debate. And here's the thing—it's not about geography, it's about ideology. America may not be Rome in location, but in function? She mirrors it almost perfectly."

Irene tilted her head.

"How so?"

"Think about it," I said.

"Rome may have collapsed as a political empire, but its operating system never died. Law, government, military strategy, even how cities are built—those ideas didn't vanish. They evolved, moved, and found new hosts. And today, America is their primary face to the world."

Irene was quiet, processing.

"So . . . America is a kind of revived imperial power?"

I nodded.

"Exactly. Not with legions marching across Europe, but with influence that circles the globe. America's dominance is economic, technological, military, and cultural—its reach flows through Hollywood's films, Silicon Valley's code, Wall Street's capital, and Washington's policy. That's not just influence. That's empire without borders."

Irene looked up.

"But it's not ruling by land conquest."

I smiled.

"Right. It's ruling by systems. America projects its power through finance, media, technology, even moral ideology—reshaping nations without ever moving a border. That's imperialism in a modern suit. It's not armies—it's algorithms. Not territories—it's bandwidth. And that's exactly why it fits Revelation 17:10: 'five have fallen, one is, and the other has not yet come.'"

Irene leaned forward.

"So America is the 'one that has not yet come'—the seventh head?"

I nodded.

"Yes. She's the final head before the Antichrist's ten-king coalition emerges—the horn phase of the beast. The heads mark successive world empires; the horns mark its last, violent surge of power. America's dominance is the bridge—she holds the seat until the beast's horns rise to take it."

Irene shook her head slowly.

"Wow. So scholars aren't wrong to call it 'revived Rome'—they just missed who revived it."

I smiled.

"Exactly. Rome was the blueprint. America became the builder. And just as Revelation foretold, her reign is for 'a short space.'"

I leaned in slightly.

"If this glimpse into the Book of Revelation has stirred your spirit, I've poured the full picture into two in-depth studies. *The Trumpet I* covers Revelation chapters 1–11. *The Trumpet II* explores chapters 12–22."

The Trumpet I: The Ancient Prophecy That Reveals America's Final Hour

The Trumpet II: The Prophecy Continues—America's Final Hour Unveiled

"Together, they unpack these mysteries verse by verse, with Irene and Ann in tow—eye-opening, timely, and impossible to read without sensing the urgency of the hour."

———◆◆◆———

THE SIXTH HARBINGER HAS BEEN TRIGGERED

Daniel's Final Week Is Approaching—Will You Be Found Watching?

The Seventy Weeks of Daniel are not just theological trivia—they are Heaven's countdown clock, precision-tuned by the hand of God. From the rebuilding of Jerusalem to the cutting off of the Messiah, every tick of Daniel's prophetic timeline has landed with supernatural accuracy. Now, only one week remains. One final period of seven years—the seventieth week—is all that separates us from the fulfillment of every end-time prophecy.

This isn't guesswork. It's Scripture. It's math. It's divine design.

Daniel's prophecy was birthed from the ashes of missed Shemitahs—seventy Sabbath cycles ignored by a rebellious people. So God sent them into seventy years of captivity. But what began as judgment became a blueprint. Those seventy years unlocked Daniel's Seventy Weeks. And the final week? It must begin where it all began—with the start of a Shemitah cycle.

The current Shemitah cycle spans 2022/2023 to 2028/2029. And as we approach the Feast of Trumpets in the fall of the final year of this cycle—2028/2029—all signs point to a prophetic convergence of appointed times: the Rapture of the Church, the start of the Tribulation with the beginning of the next Shemitah cycle in 2029/2030, and the coronation of the King at the close of that cycle in the fall of 2035/2036. This is not speculation—it is alignment with God's calendar.

Yet the church sleeps.

The foolish virgins will be caught off guard. The evil servants will be swept away by judgment. But the wise—the watchful—will know. They will discern the seasons. They will hear the trumpet before the world even knows it's blowing.

Proverbs. Parables. Prophecies. They all point to the same moment. The seductress of Mystery Babylon still calls to the simple—promising peace when sudden destruction is near. But the faithful hear a different voice. The voice of the Goodman—the Husband—returning at the appointed time. The voice of the Bridegroom at midnight. The voice of the King coming to claim His throne.

Rosh HaShanah—the Feast of Trumpets—is not just a holiday. It's a rehearsal for the Bride. Every year, the heavens gather in sacred assembly—rehearsing for the Feast of Tabernacles, the enthronement of Messiah. One year, exactly seven years apart, the rehearsals will end. The reality will begin. The trumpet will sound—not in symbolism, but in summoning. And only those who have watched will rise at the Feast of Trumpets.

Daniel's Seventieth Week isn't a theory—it's the final page of this age. The kingdoms of man have risen and fallen, just as God declared. Egypt. Assyria. Babylon. Medo-Persia. Greece. Rome. And now, America—the modern

Babylon—stands at the threshold, paving the way for the Antichrist's rise to global rule.

The Adversary knows the timing. He's preparing. Is the Church?

Daniel's prophecy demands a response. You can't opt out. You can only choose where you'll stand when the clock strikes. With the foolish or the wise. With the seductress or the Savior. With the world or with the Word.

This is not alarmism. This is alignment.

The sixth harbinger is sounding.

The Seventieth Week is near.

The King is returning.

And the time to choose your side . . . is now.

CHAPTER SUMMARY

Chapter 10 unveils the Sixth Harbinger: Daniel's 70th Week Trigger—the most precise prophetic timeline in Scripture. Daniel 9:24–27 outlines a divine countdown from Israel's restoration to Messiah's arrival, followed by a pause—the Church Age. That pause is ending. The final "week" (seven years) will resume, likely at the start of a Shemitah cycle. With the current cycle running from 2022/2023 to 2028/2029, fall 2029 (*Rosh HaShanah*) emerges as a key marker for the Tribulation's onset.

This chapter connects missed Shemitah years in Israel's past to the structure of Daniel's prophecy, showing that the final countdown must align with God's Sabbath rhythms. It also clarifies that only the *foolish virgins* and *evil servants* are caught off guard—those watching will discern the times.

Prophetic clues in Proverbs 7 link the seductive woman to Revelation's harlot, while Hebrew insights into the word *keseh* reveal *Rosh HaShanah* as the "appointed time" for Messiah's return *for* His Bride. As the spring feasts were fulfilled to the day, so too will the fall feasts—starting with *Rosh HaShanah*: the resurrection and the beginning of Daniel's 70th Week.

Finally, the prophetic journey through world empires—Egypt, Assyria, Babylon, Medo-Persia, Greece, Rome, and now America—confirms the accuracy of Daniel's vision. America, echoing Roman traits, may be the final extension before the last kingdom emerges.

Chapter 10 sounds the sixth harbinger: the prophetic clock is ticking once again.

KEY TAKEAWAYS

- Daniel's Seventy Weeks prophecy is the most precise countdown in Scripture—sixty-nine weeks (483 years) were fulfilled at Messiah's First Coming, leaving one "week" (seven years) remaining.
- That final week—the Tribulation— must begin at the start of a Shemitah cycle. The current cycle (2022–2029) places fall 2029 as a *possible* trigger point.
- Jesus' warnings about not knowing the day or hour were directed at the foolish and unwatchful, not the wise. The appointed time will not be a mystery to those who are watching.
- Proverbs. Parables. Feasts. All point to *Rosh HaShanah*—the Feast of Trumpets—as the appointed season for the Rapture of the Church and the beginning Tribulation. Seven years later, Messiah will be crowned at His return.
- Daniel's five kings mirror five modern movements of judgment and redemption, possibly including President Donald Trump as a Cyrus-type liberator.
- The prophetic succession of empires reveals we are living in the final phase of Daniel's vision—on the edge of fulfillment.

Chapter 10 sounds the sixth harbinger and prophetic intensity: the clock that once counted down to Messiah's sacrifice is about to resume—this time, counting down to His return. The warnings are not vague. The timeline is not guesswork. The end is not far, the Seventieth Week is on the horizon and the trigger may already be in motion.

Chapter 11

The Seventh Harbinger:
The War Prophecies

THE RISING STORM—"And you shall hear of wars and rumors of wars: see that you be not troubled: for all these things must come to pass, but the end is not yet. For nation shall rise against nation, and kingdom against kingdom: and there shall be famines, and pestilences, and earthquakes, in diverse places" (Matthew 24:6–7). And John saw:

> And there went out another horse that was red: and power was given to him that sat thereon to take peace from the earth, and that they should kill one another: and there was given unto him a great sword. (Revelation 6:4)

We are living in a time when conflict is no longer just political—it is prophetic. The growing hostility in the Middle East, the shifting alliances of global powers, and the sharpening rhetoric against Israel are not simply signs of instability. They are the fulfillment of ancient war prophecies—warnings God declared long before today's headlines.

Scripture does not merely hint at wars as vague end-time signs. It names them. It locates them. It sequences them. From the confederacy of hatred in Psalm 83, to the destruction of Damascus in Isaiah 17, to the northern invasion of Ezekiel 38–39, these prophecies form a divine pattern—each one a step toward the climactic return of Christ.

In this chapter, we will explore these three prophetic war theaters—distinct in geography, alliances, and outcomes—yet united in purpose: to usher in the final era of human history before the King comes.

The Psalm 83 War—The Ancient Hatred Revived

Psalm 83 describes a confederacy of ancient enemies—Edom, Moab, Ammon, Amalek, Philistia, Tyre—united by a single purpose: the annihilation of Israel. These territories align today with modern Jordan, Lebanon, Gaza, and other surrounding Arab nations. This is not a war waged from across continents, but a regional storm gathering at Israel's very borders.

Psalm 83:4 captures their intent with chilling clarity:

> They have said, Come, and let us cut them off from being a nation; that the name of Israel may be no more in remembrance. (Psalm 83:4)

This is not ancient rhetoric—it is the present-day voice of Hamas, the rallying cry of *jihad*, and the calculated hostility of Israel's neighbors: ancient enmity fused with modern strategy, all aimed at the same unchanging goal.

Isaiah 17—The Destruction of Damascus

Few prophecies are as chilling as Isaiah 17:1:

> The burden of Damascus. Behold, Damascus is taken away from being a city, and it shall be a ruinous heap. (Isaiah 17:1)

This has never been fulfilled in its entirety. Damascus—recognized as the world's oldest continually inhabited city—still stands, but it teeters on the edge of collapse. Years of civil war, foreign occupation, and proxy battles have reduced it to a shadow of its former self. Yet Scripture predicts a single, decisive moment when Damascus will be utterly removed from the map—no longer functioning as a city at all.

This prophecy places Damascus on a prophetic fault line. Its destruction could ignite a chain reaction of Middle Eastern conflict, destabilizing the region and setting the geopolitical stage for the war that follows. It's not just a headline we might wake up to—it's a trigger event God has already recorded in His Word.

Ezekiel 38–39—The Gog and Magog War

The Gog and Magog War, foretold in Ezekiel 38–39, stands as one of the most dramatic and decisive end-times prophecies—a global confrontation that will end, not by the might of armies, but by the direct hand of God.

In Ezekiel's vision, a northern coalition led by Gog of the land of Magog—often interpreted by many prophecy scholars as Russia—advances against Israel.

They are joined by Persia (modern-day Iran), Cush (Sudan), Put (Libya), and the regions of Gomer and Beth Togarmah (associated with Turkey and parts of Central Asia). These ancient names point to nations that, in our time, are aligning in open hostility toward Israel—an alliance both improbable in history and undeniable in today's headlines.

This war will not be decided through peace treaties or human negotiation. The LORD Himself will intervene, shaking the nations with a great earthquake, sending torrential hail, raining fire, and sowing confusion that causes the invading armies to turn on one another. The outcome will be so unmistakably divine that the world will be forced to acknowledge:

> Thus will I magnify Myself, and sanctify Myself; and I will be known in the eyes of many nations, and they shall know that I am the LORD. (Ezekiel 38:23)

It is crucial to understand that this is not the battle of Armageddon. Rather, it appears to be a pre-tribulation conflict—likely unfolding shortly before or in the opening years of Daniel's Seventieth Week—setting the stage for the rise of the Antichrist and the unprecedented events of the Tribulation period.

Why These Wars Matter Now

Many prophecy students fix their attention on Ezekiel's Gog and Magog War, but the Bible gives us a sequence, not just a single event. Psalm 83 may depict a regional conflict in which Israel defeats her surrounding enemies, resulting in a temporary "peace and safety" (1 Thessalonians 5:3). This false calm could open the door for the global coalition of Ezekiel 38–39 to strike.

> For when they shall say, Peace and safety; then sudden destruction comes upon them, as travail upon a woman with child; and they shall not escape. (1 Thessalonians 5:3)

The destruction of Damascus in Isaiah 17 could be the spark that ignites this chain reaction—a geopolitical flashpoint that escalates into the wider conflicts foretold by the prophets.

Taken together, these three prophecies form a chilling roadmap:

- Psalm 83—a local but devastating confederacy against Israel.
- Isaiah 17—the overnight eradication of one of the world's oldest cities.
- Ezekiel 38–39—a worldwide invasion met by God's direct, miraculous intervention.

Each war intensifies the scope, the alliances, and the supernatural nature of the events, leading humanity ever closer to the return of Christ.

The Harbinger Has Spoken

We've watched history unfold before our eyes; most recently: 1948, 1967, 1973, 1991, 2008–2009, 2014, 2023. Again and again, Israel has been surrounded, outnumbered, and attacked by overwhelming forces . . . yet each time, she has not only survived but miraculously prevailed.

But these victories were only previews—dress rehearsals for a final storm unlike anything the world has ever seen.

Now, as we enter the era of the seventh harbinger, the headlines are no longer random. They are fulfilling the very pages of Scripture. War is no longer a distant possibility—it is prophetically inevitable.

The red horse is rising.

The confederacies are gathering.

And the Lord of hosts is preparing to defend His name on the battlefield of the nations.

Are you watching?

THE PSALM 83 WAR: THE WAR OF ANNIHILATION

Not all prophetic wars are the same—nor do they all erupt on a global stage. Psalm 83 describes what many scholars believe is a distinct, earlier conflict: a regional war fueled by deep-rooted hatred and unrelenting territorial hostility.

Unlike the sweeping coalition of Ezekiel 38–39, this prophecy zeroes in on Israel's immediate neighbors. These nations form a confederacy with a singular, chilling objective—erasing Israel from existence:

> They have said, Come, and let us cut them off from being a nation; that the name
> of Israel may be no more in remembrance. (Psalm 83:4)

This is not a border dispute. It is not a political negotiation. It is a cry for genocide. While some view Psalm 83 as merely a historical plea, its described coalition mirrors—with stunning precision—the alliances we see aligning today. What was once ancient hostility is now reinforced by modern ideology and geopolitical ambition, making this prophecy as urgent as tomorrow's headlines.

Ancient Enemies and Their Modern Counterparts

Psalm 83 lists a confederacy of ancient peoples, each rooted in Israel's biblical history yet still present in the modern geopolitical landscape under new national identities:

- Edom, Moab, Ammon—Correspond to parts of present-day Jordan.
- Amalek—Historically tied to the southern regions of Israel and the Sinai Peninsula.

- Philistia—Modern Gaza Strip, now under the control of Hamas.
- Tyre—Present-day Lebanon, a stronghold of Hezbollah.
- Assyria—Regions of northern Iraq and Syria, often aligned with Iranian proxy forces.
- Ishmaelites and Hagarenes—Ancient Arab tribes that may prophetically point to Saudi Arabia and other Gulf states.

Taken together, this alliance forms a prophetic picture: Israel encircled by immediate neighbors—bound not by shared economics or distant treaties, but by a unified, deep-seated hatred. Just as in ancient days, the cry is not for compromise but for complete eradication.

A Prelude to Gog and Magog?

Unlike the far-reaching coalition of Ezekiel 38–39—drawing its power from distant nations—Psalm 83 describes a close-proximity, Arab-centric assault. This is an attack from Israel's immediate neighbors, not from the ends of the earth.

Many scholars see this war as a prelude to Ezekiel's prophecy—a decisive regional conflict that reshapes Israel's borders and shifts the geopolitical balance. Its outcome could create the very conditions Paul describes:

> For when they shall say, Peace and safety: then sudden destruction comes upon them, as travail upon a woman with child; and they shall not escape. (1 Thessalonians 5:3)

In this view, Psalm 83 represents the battle Israel wins outright—expanding her territory. Securing temporary regional dominance, and entering a season of perceived security. Yet that peace would be short-lived, for it sets the stage for the next—and far greater—storm: the global strike from the north foretold in Ezekiel 38–39.

Seven Historical Echoes: 1948, 1967, 1973, 1991, 2008–2009, 2014, 2023

This mindset of annihilation in Psalm 83 is not a relic of the ancient world—it has echoed across the battlefields of modern Israel:

- 1948—The War of Independence—On the very day Israel declared statehood, six Arab nations invaded, intent on erasing the newborn nation from the map.
- 1967—The Six-Day War—Surrounded on all sides and outnumbered, Israel struck preemptively and secured a miraculous victory, reclaiming Jerusalem, the Golan Heights, and the West Bank.

- 1973—The *Yom Kippur* War—On their holiest day, Israel was ambushed by a coordinated Arab assault but prevailed against overwhelming odds.
- 1991—The Gulf War—Iraq launched Scud missiles toward Israel in an attempt to provoke retaliation and fracture the U.S.-led coalition. Though heavily targeted, Israel refrained from striking back—yet was miraculously spared from mass casualties.
- 2008–2009—Operation Cast Lead—After years of rocket fire from Gaza, Israel launched a three-week military campaign targeting Hamas' infrastructure. The operation sought to halt the bombardment of civilian areas in southern Israel and severely weakened Hamas' capabilities, though global condemnation followed.
- 2014—Operation Protective Edge—Triggered by the abduction and murder of three Israeli teenagers and an intensification of rocket attacks from Gaza, this fifty-day conflict was one of the most intense in recent history. Israel targeted Hamas' tunnel network and rocket launchers, engaging in heavy urban combat while under relentless international scrutiny.
- 2023—Swords of Iron War—On October 7, 2023—exactly fifty years and one day after the outbreak of the 1973 *Yom Kippur* War—Hamas launched *Operation Al-Aqsa Flood*, a surprise, multi-pronged assault on Israel from Gaza. This unprecedented attack came during the festival of *Simchat Torah*, and the close of the High Holy Days, when much of the nation was at rest and off guard. The assault combined mass rocket barrages, coordinated ground infiltrations, and targeted massacres in civilian communities, marking the deadliest day for Jews since the Holocaust. Israel responded by initiating Operation Swords of Iron, plunging the region into a full-scale war that continues to reshape the Middle East's geopolitical and prophetic landscape.

Each of these events carried the same underlying battle cry of Psalm 83: "Come, and let us cut them off from being a nation." Yet time after time, God preserved His covenant people, demonstrating that His promises are not bound by the odds of war.

The Storm at Israel's Gates

Psalm 83 isn't just an ancient lament—it's a prophecy whose shadow may already be stretching over our headlines. The confederacy it describes reads like a spiritual blueprint: surrounding nations uniting with one goal—erasing Israel from the map. From Gaza to Lebanon, from Damascus to Amman, the echoes are unmistakable.

1. **The Unfulfilled View: Still to Come**—Many prophetic scholars maintain that Psalm 83 points to a distinct, future war—one in which *every* ancient territory listed (Edom, Moab, Ammon, Amalek, Philistia, Tyre, Assyria) will be fully engaged in a coordinated assault.

   While the October 7, 2023, attack and subsequent fighting match the *spirit* of Psalm 83, not all the ancient players have yet entered the battlefield.

   In this view, Israel ultimately wins this war—decisively defeating the surrounding coalition. Only later, in the Gog and Magog War of Ezekiel 38–39, does God Himself step in supernaturally, ending that global invasion with overwhelming judgment.

2. **The Historical View: Pattern Repeating**— Some interpret Psalm 83 as a record of Israel's past conflicts rather than a future script.

   From this perspective, the events of 2023–2025 are not *the* fulfillment but a recurring pattern—ancient enmity playing out in modern form.

   The same geography, the same hostility, the same desire to "cut them off from being a nation" (Psalm 83:4).

3. **The Staging-Ground View: Foreshadowing Gog and Magog**—In this interpretation, the Psalm 83 conflict is not the final war itself but a prelude—a smaller, regional showdown that reshapes Israel's borders and security before the global storm of Ezekiel 38–39.

   Psalm 83 may see Israel achieve a decisive military victory, weakening her immediate neighbors and setting the stage for the larger northern coalition to gather.

   When that later war comes, Israel will not prevail by force of arms. God Himself will intervene, ending the Gog and Magog invasion with unmistakable supernatural acts so that "the nations shall know that I am the LORD" (Ezekiel 38:23).

Whether we are watching the *foreshadowing*, the *repetition*, or the *early stages* of Psalm 83, one truth remains: this is not ultimately about politics or land—it is about identity, covenant, and the God who neither slumbers nor forsakes His people. Israel will not be annihilated. Her enemies, however, may face a very different fate.

THE ISAIAH 17 PROPHECY: THE DESTRUCTION OF DAMASCUS

Few prophecies are as chilling—or as specific—as Isaiah 17:1:

> The burden of Damascus. Behold, Damascus is taken away from being a city, and it shall be a ruinous heap. (Isaiah 17:1)

This verse points to an event still waiting for its full fulfillment. Damascus—one of the world's oldest continually inhabited cities—has endured invasions, sieges, and civil war, yet it has never been entirely erased from the map. Isaiah's prophecy is not about partial ruin or temporary devastation; it foretells the city's total and irreversible destruction.

In a single moment, Damascus will cease to function as a city—its centuries-old streets silenced, its skyline reduced to rubble. Whether this comes through war, weapons of mass destruction, or divine intervention, Scripture makes it clear: the day is coming when Damascus will be no more.

Syria's Strategic Importance and Ongoing Instability

Syria remains one of the most volatile flashpoints in the Middle East—a fractured nation where civil war, foreign military occupation, and entrenched terror networks converge. Damascus, its ancient capital, is caught in a tightening vise of regional hostility.

Iranian weapons convoys snake their way through the countryside. Hezbollah strongholds lie entrenched just across the border. Russian military assets operate alongside Syrian forces. Layered atop this is Israel's ongoing campaign of targeted airstrikes into Syrian territory—preempting Iranian advances and neutralizing threats before they can erupt into open war.

Yet, as destabilizing as these strikes may be, Isaiah 17 foresees something far more catastrophic. This prophecy does not speak of incremental damage or temporary setbacks—it envisions an event so sudden, so complete, that Damascus will vanish from the map, reduced to a silent ruin.

How Might It Happen? Sudden and Catastrophic

Isaiah's vision offers no hint of a prolonged siege or slow erosion—it speaks of a single, decisive moment. Damascus' destruction will be swift, shocking, and irreversible. How could such a moment unfold?

- A nuclear or chemical strike that vaporizes the city in an instant.
- A massive Israeli preemptive assault targeting a perceived existential threat.
- A staged "false flag" operation designed to ignite a wider regional war.

- A direct act of divine judgment, perfectly timed with God's prophetic clock.

Whatever the trigger, the result will be unlike anything seen in modern warfare—an ancient capital erased in one stroke, sending geopolitical shockwaves across the Middle East and reverberating throughout the world.

Solar Eclipses as Prophetic Markers: 2017, 2024, and 2026

Throughout Scripture, celestial events have served as God's "billboards" in the sky—public signs that most will see but only the spiritually watchful will understand. Joel 2:31 warns, "The sun shall be turned into darkness, and the moon into blood, before the great and terrible Day of the LORD come." Jesus Himself spoke of "signs in the sun, and in the moon, and in the stars" (Luke 21:25) as precursors to climactic prophetic events. In this light, the solar eclipses of 2017, 2024, and 2026 may not be random astronomical events, but synchronized prophetic markers—divine timestamps in the heavens.

The American Cross: 2017 and 2024—Two total solar eclipses—August 21, 2017 and April 8, 2024—have traced a giant "X" over the heart of the United States, intersecting in southern Illinois, a region historically called "Little Egypt." In Scripture, Egypt often symbolizes bondage, idolatry, and rebellion against God. The fact that this celestial Cross marks a place with such a name is more than coincidence—it may be a prophetic warning etched in the heavens.

The 2017 eclipse swept from Oregon to South Carolina; the 2024 eclipse reversed that path from Texas to Maine. At the crossing point lies a land between the Ohio and Mississippi Rivers, surrounded by cities and towns with some having biblically resonate names: Carbondale, *Cairo, Marion*, Murphysboro, Harrisburg, *Metropolis*. To the watchful believer, the "X" is a message—a divine summons for America to choose between repentance and judgment, between turning back to God or crossing a line from which there is no return.

The Middle Eastern Eclipse: 2026—On August 12, 2026, a total solar eclipse will shadow Europe, North Africa, and the Middle East, sweeping over nations already at the center of biblical prophecy. This path will darken skies above Spain, northern Africa, and the Arab world, passing directly over Damascus—the very city Isaiah 17 declares will one day be reduced to "a ruinous heap."

In prophetic context, the timing is sobering. This eclipse arrives at a moment when the region simmers with hostility, alliances are aligning as foretold in Ezekiel 38–39, and the spark for the Psalm 83 War could ignite at any time. For prophecy watchers, the shadow over Damascus is not a poetic flourish—it may be a cosmic countdown to the fulfillment of Isaiah's vision, a prelude to cascading events that will draw the world into the wars of the last days.

A Synchronized Warning System—When viewed together, these eclipses appear to form a twofold prophetic message:

- To America—A warning marked by the 2017 and 2024 "X" across the land, calling for repentance before judgment falls.
- To the Middle East—A shadow crossing volatile, biblically significant lands in 2026, potentially marking the onset of prophetic wars and divine intervention.

Jesus rebuked the Pharisees for failing to "discern the signs of the times" (Matthew 16:3). In our day, the heavens may be declaring more than beauty—they may be declaring urgency, judgment, and the nearness of events that will shake the nations.

Damascus on the Brink

Isaiah 17 is not a parable. It is not an allegory. It is not the language of exaggeration. It is a laser-focused prophecy aimed at one city—Damascus—foretelling an event so sudden and complete that it will erase the world's longest continually inhabited capital from the map. For thousands of years, Damascus has stood through wars, empires, and upheavals, but Scripture declares there will come a single moment when it will no longer exist as a functioning city. That day has not yet come—but the stage is being set before our eyes.

Today, Syria sits at the crossroads of chaos. The civil war has left deep scars. Foreign powers, terror networks, and militias use its territory as a chessboard for regional dominance. Damascus itself is a powder keg—hosting Iranian arms shipments, Hezbollah command centers, and Russian military positions. Israeli intelligence watches it constantly, striking at weapons convoys and military sites to preempt threats. And yet, Isaiah's prophecy describes something far beyond these targeted raids—something cataclysmic, instantaneous, and irreversible.

The geopolitical climate could not be more volatile. Israel's enemies are emboldened, alliances are shifting, and the shadow of regional war grows longer by the day. In this environment, one trigger—whether an act of terrorism, a preemptive strike, or even a supernatural act of divine judgment—could unleash the destruction foretold in Isaiah 17:1. This would not merely be a headline; it would be a prophetic earthquake with aftershocks that would ripple across the globe.

Once Damascus falls, the balance of power in the Middle East will change overnight. Israel's security strategy will shift. Borders could be redrawn. The international community will scramble to respond. Economies will tremble as energy markets react. And perhaps most significantly, the prophetic clock will tick loudly toward the next sequence of end-time events—Psalm 83, Ezekiel 38–39, and beyond.

When that day comes, the world will remember that God's Word spoke of it long before it happened. And nothing—nothing—will ever be the same again.

THE GOG AND MAGOG WAR: EZEKIEL 38–39

Among the most dramatic and sobering prophecies in all of Scripture is the war described in Ezekiel chapters 38 and 39—an apocalyptic confrontation often called the Gog and Magog War. This is no ordinary clash of armies. It is a divinely scheduled moment in history when a vast coalition of nations will rise against Israel, only to face the full, unrestrained power of the LORD. Far from being just another geopolitical crisis it is a supernatural showdown in which God Himself orchestrates the battle's outcome, turning the forces of darkness into instruments for revealing His glory.

The Coalition of Nations

Ezekiel's prophecy pinpoints a future moment in the "latter days" when a powerful alliance of nations will set their sights on Israel. These nations are named in ancient terms, yet their modern counterparts align with startling precision:

- Gog—widely understood as a leader or spiritual ruler over the land of Magog, often identified with modern-day Russia.
- Persia—unmistakably Iran, whose enmity toward Israel is openly declared.
- Cush—generally linked to regions in Sudan and Ethiopia, both with historical and modern connections to Islamic alliance.
- Put—associated with Libya, a nation long marked by instability and militant factions.
- Gomer and Beth Togarmah—pointing toward parts of Turkey and Central Asia, regions that bridge East and West and hold strategic influence in any Middle Eastern conflict.

In Ezekiel's day, these territories had little political cohesion. Yet, in recent years, we have witnessed an improbable realignment—nations once separated by culture, language, and distance now finding common cause. Most notable is the emerging cooperation between Russia, Iran, and Turkey—a trio specifically named in this ancient prophecy. Their military coordination in Syria, joint economic ventures, and shared strategic goals against Western influence signal that Ezekiel's vision is not a relic of the past—it's unfolding in real time.

Timing and Strategy

Ezekiel 38:11 paints a startling picture: the invasion will strike when Israel is "dwelling safely." This phrase does not necessarily imply an era of absolute peace, but rather a season of perceived security—a moment when the nation feels insulated from major threats. This could be the result of diplomatic treaties, military superiority, or even a false sense of stability born from regional agreements and strategic deterrence.

> And you shalt say, I will go up to the land of unwalled villages; I will go to them that are at rest, that dwell safely, all of them dwelling without walls, and having neither bars nor gates. (Ezekiel 38:11)

Whatever the source of this confidence, Israel's enemies will see it as the perfect opportunity to launch their assault. Yet they will underestimate both the resolve of Israel and, more importantly, the intervention of Israel's God.

The prophetic nuance here is crucial: while the coalition believes it has chosen the ideal time to strike, it is actually stepping into God's appointed time— a trap set by divine sovereignty. Their campaign will not unfold according to their plans, but according to the timetable of the Almighty, leading to their own destruction.

A Supernatural Showdown

This will not be an ordinary war, nor will it end through the strength of Israel's military or the cleverness of her leaders. When the coalition advances, it will be walking straight into the hands of the Almighty. The battle will quickly escalate beyond the realm of human strategy and into the arena of divine intervention.

The prophet Ezekiel describes the scene in unmistakably apocalyptic terms:

- A massive earthquake will rip through the land, shaking not only Israel but the nations involved (Ezekiel 38:19).
- Panic and confusion will seize the invaders, causing them to turn their weapons against each other in chaos (Ezekiel 38:21).
- Torrential rains, hailstones, and fire mingled with brimstone will descend from the heavens, devastating the armies and annihilating their plans (Ezekiel 38:22).
- The destruction will be so overwhelming that it will take Israel seven months to bury the dead (Ezekiel 39:12).

This is God's war. It will serve as an undeniable declaration that no weapon formed against Israel will prosper—not because of her might, but because of her Covenant-Keeping God who defends her. In this moment, the world will see that the God of Abraham, Isaac, and Jacob still reigns over the nations and still fulfills His promises.

The Purpose Revealed

Ezekiel leaves no room for misunderstanding about God's motive in orchestrating this dramatic intervention. In Ezekiel 38:23, the LORD declares:

> Thus will I magnify Myself, and sanctify Myself; and I will be known in the eyes of many nations, and they shall know that I am LORD. (Ezekiel 38:23)

This is the prophetic climax—the moment when the fog of politics, religion, and human pride is burned away by the undeniable reality of God's sovereignty. The Gog and Magog War is not about shifting borders or temporary alliances. It is not a mere skirmish for resources or influence. It is about God's name, His holiness, and His covenant being publicly vindicated before the eyes of a watching world.

In this divine confrontation, God reintroduces Himself on the global stage—not as a distant concept, but as the living God of Abraham, Isaac, and Jacob. Nations will be forced to reckon with His justice, His power, and His faithfulness to Israel. The outcome will be an unmistakable reminder that history is not random; it is unfolding exactly as He decreed, and every event—even the schemes of hostile nations—serves His ultimate purpose.

When the dust settles, the world will know: the God of Israel is not merely a chapter in ancient history—He is the Author of all history, and He will have the final word.

ISRAEL'S HISTORIC WARS: PATTERNS OF DIVINE INTERVENTION

From the moment Israel reemerged as a sovereign nation on May 14, 1948, she has been under almost constant threat from neighbors who have sworn to erase her from the map. Human logic and military science would say her survival is improbable—if not impossible—given her size, population, and the sheer number of enemies surrounding her. Yet, time and again, Israel has not only survived these trials but emerged stronger, reclaiming land, advancing security, and strengthening her national resolve.

These victories are not merely the result of clever military strategy or advanced technology—though Israel has often displayed both in abundance. They point to a deeper, supernatural reality. In every major conflict since 1948, there is an observable pattern: Israel faces overwhelming odds, suffers an initial moment of vulnerability, and then—often suddenly and in ways that defy explanation—the tide turns. The survival and success of Israel in these moments mirror the biblical accounts of deliverance found in the days of Moses, Joshua, and the Judges, where divine intervention determined the outcome.

Far from being isolated historical events, these modern battles serve as prophetic signposts. They echo the promises of God to Abraham, Isaac, and Jacob, reminding the world that the covenant still stands and the Keeper of Israel neither slumbers nor sleeps (Psalm 121:4). They foreshadow a time yet to come, when God will act openly and unmistakably on behalf of His people, as described in prophecies like Ezekiel 38–39.

> Behold, He that keeps Israel shall neither slumber nor sleep. (Psalm 121:4)

1948: War of Independence

On May 14, 1948, David Ben-Gurion read Israel's Declaration of Independence in Tel Aviv, restoring Jewish sovereignty after nearly two thousand years of exile. The ink was barely dry when six Arab nations—Egypt, Transjordan (Jordan), Syria, Lebanon, Iraq, and Saudi Arabia—launched a coordinated invasion, vowing to drive the Jews into the sea.

From a military standpoint, the odds were impossible. Israel had no standing army, only the Haganah militia, and a handful of poorly trained underground fighters, many of them Holocaust survivors still bearing the physical and emotional scars of Nazi persecution. They possessed only a few thousand rifles, some makeshift armored cars, and an assortment of smuggled weapons—many outdated and unreliable. Ammunition was so scarce that in some battles soldiers were issued just 10–15 bullets each.

Yet in the face of annihilation, the tide turned. Against all logic, Israel not only repelled the invasion but gained territory beyond the UN Partition Plan's original boundaries. Even seasoned military historians admit the outcome defies explanation.

From a prophetic perspective, the war is nothing short of a modern Exodus moment—a living testimony that the same God who brought His people back into the land (Isaiah 66:8) would also be the One to defend it. Psalm 44:3 captures the essence of this miracle:

> For they got not the land in possession by their own sword, neither did their own arm save them: but it was Your right hand, and Your arm, and the light of Your countenance, because You had a favor unto them. (Psalm 44:3)

The War of Independence set the prophetic stage for everything that would follow—demonstrating from day one that Israel's survival would not depend on her own strength, but on the covenant faithfulness of the God of Abraham, Isaac, and Jacob.

1967: The Six-Day War

By the summer of 1967, Israel stood on the brink of annihilation. The armies of Egypt, Syria, and Jordan massed along her borders, their leaders openly declaring their intent to wipe Israel off the map. The threat was not merely military—it was existential. Outnumbered in soldiers, tanks, and aircraft, and surrounded on three fronts, Israel faced a crisis that echoed the desperate moments of ancient biblical battles.

In a move that stunned the world, Israel launched a preemptive strike on June 5, 1967. In the opening hours, Israeli pilots destroyed nearly the entire Egyptian Air Force while it sat vulnerable on the tarmac, granting Israel immediate and decisive air superiority. What followed was a lightning campaign so swift and coordinated that historians still struggle to explain its efficiency. In just six days, Israel reclaimed the Golan Heights from Syria, the West Bank from Jordan, the Gaza Strip from Egypt, and—most significantly—East Jerusalem, including the Old City and the Temple Mount.

For the Jewish people, the return to Jerusalem was not just a strategic victory—it was a moment of prophetic weight. The words of the psalmist seemed to come alive:

> If I forget you, O Jerusalem let my right hand forget her cunning. (Psalm 137:5)

After nearly two thousand years of exile, the city of David was once again under Jewish sovereignty. To many believers, this was a step toward the fulfillment of Zechariah 12:6, which foretells that Judah will be "like a hearth of fire among the wood," consuming the surrounding nations.

> In that day will I make the governors of Judah like an hearth of fire among the wood, and like a torch of fire in a sheaf; and they shall devour all the people round about, on the right hand and on the left: and Jerusalem shall be inhabited again in her own place, even in Jerusalem. (Zechariah 12:6)

From a purely military perspective, Israel's victory seemed impossible. Outnumbered more than two to one and facing the combined might of multiple Arab states, her survival should have been in question—yet the war ended with Israel controlling territory more than three times its original size. The speed and decisiveness of the campaign defied conventional logic. To those who look through the lens of Scripture, the explanation is clear: the God of Abraham, Isaac, and Jacob was still keeping His covenant promises.

This war was not merely another chapter in Israel's modern history—it was a prophetic pivot point. By restoring Jerusalem to Jewish control, the Six-Day War moved the clock of biblical prophecy forward, setting the stage for the events described by the prophets and echoed in the pages of the New Testament. In those six extraordinary days, the world witnessed a modern-day echo of Joshua's conquests, a reminder that no coalition of nations can thwart the purposes of the Almighty.

1973: The Yom Kippur War

On October 6, 1973, the Day of Atonement—*Yom Kippur*—dawned in Israel with an unusual stillness. It was the holiest day in the Jewish calendar, a day when businesses closed, traffic stopped, and families gathered in fasting and prayer. Yet as Israel sought the LORD in sacred assembly, her enemies sought her destruction. In a coordinated surprise attack, Egypt struck across the Suez Canal and Syria stormed down from the Golan Heights, catching the nation completely off guard. Many soldiers of the Israel Defense Forces (IDF) were not even at their posts, having been released to observe the solemn day.

In the opening hours, Israel's situation appeared desperate. Egyptian forces overran the Bar Lev Line along the canal, while Syrian tanks poured through the Golan, threatening to sweep into the Galilee. For a moment, it seemed as though the prophecy of Psalm 83—nations conspiring to "cut them off from being a nation"—was playing out before the world's eyes.

But the God of Israel had not abandoned His people. Though the cost was high and casualties heavy, a fierce counteroffensive began. On the Syrian front, Israel managed to halt the advance and push enemy forces back beyond the pre-war lines. In the south, a daring maneuver led by General Ariel Sharon crossed the Suez Canal into Egyptian territory, encircling the Egyptian Third Army and forcing a ceasefire.

From a military perspective, the turnaround was extraordinary. Within days, Israel shifted from near collapse to holding positions deep in enemy territory. But for those who view history through the lens of prophecy, this was more than battlefield strategy—it was another chapter in the enduring testimony that Israel's survival is not secured by her own arm, but by the Covenant-Keeping God who has promised her a future.

The *Yom Kippur* War was a sobering reminder that Israel's enemies often strike during times of perceived vulnerability. Yet, time and again, divine strength has turned the tide. Just as in the days of Jehoshaphat, when the LORD said, "The battle is not yours, but God's" (2 Chronicles 20:15), Israel's deliverance in 1973 stands as a modern witness that His hand still shields His people.

> And He said, Hearken you, all Judah, and you inhabitants of Jerusalem, and you king Jehoshaphat, Thus says the LORD unto you, Be not afraid nor dismayed by reason of this great multitude; for the battle is not yours, but God's. (2 Chronicles 20:15)

1991: The Gulf War

In January 1991, as the world's attention was fixed on the U.S.-led coalition's efforts to liberate Kuwait from Saddam Hussein's Iraq, Israel suddenly found herself under direct attack—without firing a single shot in the conflict. Over the course of the war, Saddam Hussein launched 41 Scud missiles into the heart of Israel's civilian population centers, targeting Tel Aviv, Haifa, and other cities. His goal was clear: provoke Israel into retaliating, fracture the coalition, and shift the war into a wider Middle East conflict.

The damage was staggering. Over 5,000 homes were destroyed or severely damaged, entire apartment buildings were reduced to rubble, and countless others were left uninhabitable. Yet, against all expectations, the death toll was astonishingly low—only two fatalities were recorded from all the missile strikes. Military analysts, engineers, and rescue workers searched for a rational explanation, but even the most seasoned experts admitted the numbers didn't add up.

How could missiles, some carrying large high-explosive warheads, obliterate entire buildings and yet spare so many lives? Some point to timing and coincidence; others quietly acknowledge what many believers see plainly: the invisible shield of divine protection. Whether through angelic intervention, the sovereign hand of God, or a combination of both, the outcome was undeniable— Israel was spared catastrophic loss of life.

This event became another marker in the ongoing pattern of Israel's supernatural preservation. It was a modern echo of Psalm 91:7—"A thousand shall fall at your side, and ten thousand at your right hand; but it shall not come near you." The Gulf War reminded the world that even in conflict Israel did not start, the Covenant-Keeping God still watches over His people, ensuring that, though targeted by her enemies, she remains standing.

2008–2009: Operation Cast Lead

Between December 27, 2008, and January 18, 2009, Israel undertook Operation Cast Lead—a decisive military campaign launched after years of relentless rocket fire from Gaza. For over eight years, Hamas had fired Kassam and Grad rockets into southern Israel, terrorizing cities like Sderot, Ashkelon, and Beersheba. The months leading up to the operation were particularly intense: in just the six months preceding the war, over 750 rockets and mortars had been launched at civilian communities.

Despite repeated ceasefire agreements, Hamas repeatedly violated them, using the lulls not to seek peace, but to rearm and strengthen its military infrastructure. By late 2008, the security situation had become untenable, and Israel acted. The operation targeted weapons caches, rocket launch sites, smuggling tunnels, and Hamas leadership—carefully distinguishing between combatants and civilians, even though Hamas embedded itself in densely populated neighborhoods.

While the battles raged in the heart of urban Gaza, Israel's Iron Dome defense system (in its early stages) and well-drilled civilian evacuation protocols kept mass casualties on the Israeli side remarkably low. This was not only a demonstration of military precision, but also of Israel's ethical warfare doctrine—restraining fire when civilians were in harm's way, even at the risk of losing the element of surprise or strategic advantage.

For many believers, Operation Cast Lead was another chapter in Israel's prophetic story—a reminder that God's covenant promises still hold. Israel once again faced an existential threat and emerged standing, echoing Psalm 125:2, "As the mountains are round about Jerusalem, so the LORD is round about His people from henceforth even forever." The war underscored both the necessity of vigilance and the reality of divine preservation, even in the modern age.

2014: Operation Protective Edge

In July 2014, a chain of escalating events ignited a fifty-day conflict that would test Israel's resolve yet again. The war began after the kidnapping and brutal murder of three Israeli teenagers by Hamas operatives—an act that shocked the nation and drew international condemnation. But beneath the surface, another threat had been quietly growing for years: the terror tunnels.

Hamas had invested immense resources into building a sprawling network of sophisticated underground passages stretching from Gaza into Israeli territory. Some tunnels reached over a mile in length, equipped with electricity, rail tracks, and reinforced walls. Many ended just beneath Israeli civilian areas—some under kindergartens—designed for mass abductions and large-scale terror raids.

When Israel launched Operation Protective Edge, the mission was not only to stop the relentless rocket fire (over 4,500 rockets during the conflict) but also to uncover and destroy this subterranean threat. In total, Israel located and demolished 32 terror tunnels, many of which could have facilitated catastrophic attacks had they remained undiscovered.

Despite fierce urban combat and a relentless rocket barrage, Israel employed extraordinary measures to minimize civilian casualties in Gaza—often at the cost of operational surprise. These included the controversial yet humanitarian roof knock warnings, where small, non-lethal munitions were dropped on a building to warn residents before a targeted strike. This ethical approach drew criticism from detractors and praise from supporters, but it underscored Israel's doctrine of restraint even in the face of existential danger.

The outcome was both military and moral. Israel emerged battered but unbroken, its citizens reminded that vigilance is a constant necessity and that its survival often hinges on both human courage and divine providence. For those who view modern events through a prophetic lens, Operation Protective Edge was yet another echo of Psalm 121:4—"Behold, He that keeps Israel shall neither slumber nor sleep."

2023: Swords of Iron War

On October 7, 2023, during *Simchat Torah*—a joyous festival marking the completion of the annual Torah reading cycle and a time when Jewish communities celebrate with dancing and singing—Israel was plunged into its darkest day in decades. In a meticulously planned and shockingly brutal assault, Hamas launched a multi-front attack that shattered the nation's sense of security.

From the early morning hours, over 3,000 rockets rained down on southern and central Israel, unleashing chaos and fear. But the rockets were only the opening act. Heavily armed terrorists breached Israel's borders, infiltrating towns, *kibbutzim* (collective agricultural communities), and even a music festival in the Negev desert. What followed defied comprehension: more than 1,200 civilians were murdered—men, women, children, and the elderly. Entire families were executed in their homes, hostages were dragged into Gaza, and atrocities were committed so barbaric they stunned even veteran war correspondents.

The chilling parallel to Genesis 6:11–13 could not be ignored: "The earth also was corrupt before God, and the earth was filled with violence (Hebrew: *hamas*)." The very name of the terrorist group—Hamas—is the same biblical term used to describe the depravity and lawlessness of Noah's day, when judgment loomed on the horizon.

> The earth also was corrupt before God, and the earth was filled with violence. And God looked upon the earth, and, behold, it was corrupt; for all flesh had corrupted his way upon the earth. And God said unto Noah, The end of all flesh

is come before Me; for the earth is filled with violence through them; and, behold, I will destroy them with the earth. (Genesis 6:11–13)

Yet even in the face of such carnage, Israel's survival defied the odds. Within hours, the nation mobilized under Operation Iron Swords, reclaiming lost ground, striking militant infrastructure, and targeting the vast network of terror tunnels under Gaza. The swiftness and precision of Israel's counteroffensive testified to a resilience that was as much spiritual as it was strategic.

The massacre became a turning point—not only militarily, but prophetically. Jewish communities worldwide rallied in solidarity, and discussions surged about whether this was the spark that could ignite the prophetic war cycle outlined in Psalm 83, Isaiah 17, and Ezekiel 38–39. For many watchers of biblical prophecy, October 7th was not an isolated act of terror, but potentially the trigger that will set into motion events leading to Daniel's 70th Week.

Above the grief and rage, one truth remained unshaken: "He that keeps Israel shall neither slumber nor sleep" (Psalm 121:4). Even when surrounded by enemies and drenched in mourning, Israel stood—wounded, but unbroken—under the shadow of the Covenant-Keeping God.

Prophetic Significance

Throughout modern history, Israel's wars reveal a striking and recurring prophetic pattern:

1. **The Attack Comes Suddenly—Often in Holy Seasons**. Enemies strike during times of rest, worship, or celebration—moments Israel least expects conflict.

2. **Global Condemnation Follows**—The international community often turns against Israel, framing her defense as aggression.

3. **Victory Against All Odds**—Outnumbered, outgunned, and surrounded, Israel emerges not only intact but strengthened.

4. **A Supernatural Signature**—These victories bear marks of divine restraint, precision, and preservation that defy human explanation.

When viewed through the lens of prophecy, these conflicts function as *birth pangs*—foreshocks leading toward the greater end-times wars of Psalm 83, Isaiah 17, and Ezekiel 38–39. Each battle carries the same divine fingerprint: impossible odds met with supernatural deliverance.

Enemies plan, nations rage, missiles fly—yet Israel stands. These aren't mere stories of survival; they are living testimonies of a Covenant-Keeping God. The same God who split the Red Sea (Exodus 14:13–31) and later parted the Jordan

River (Joshua 3–4), who rained manna in the wilderness (Exodus 16), and brought down Jericho's walls (Joshua 6:20), still moves on behalf of His people. And one day—just as surely as He acted then—He will act again. Ezekiel 38:23, promises a moment when His intervention will be so direct, so unmistakable, that the nations will have no choice but to know: "I am the LORD."

THE SEVENTH HARBINGER IS SOUNDING

The Storm of War Is Rising—Will You Be Found Standing?

The world's wars are not chaos—they are choreography. What appears to be global disorder is, in truth, divine order unfolding on the stage of human history. Psalm 83. Isaiah 17. Ezekiel 38–39. These are not vague predictions; they are distinct prophetic milestones, each marking a step toward Messiah's return.

Three different wars—one unstoppable timeline:

- Psalm 83—A war of annihilation, where Israel's surrounding neighbors rise in hatred to erase her name forever.
- Isaiah 17—A sudden, surgical strike—the destruction of Damascus, the oldest continuously inhabited city in the world.
- Ezekiel 38–39—An unprecedented assault led by Gog of Magog, where God Himself—not Israel's military, not the UN—intervenes with earthquakes, fire, hail, and confusion.

Each conflict escalates the tension. Each sets the stage for the next. Together, they form the drumbeat of the Seventh Harbinger: The War Prophecies.

The headlines match the prophets. Ancient enemies are reemerging under new flags. Russia, Iran, Turkey unite in an unnatural alliance. Arab nations encircle Israel again. Terror strikes. Missiles fly. Beneath the soil of every battlefield lies a prophecy waiting for its fulfillment.

The signs are overlapping. The solar eclipses of 2017 and 2024 carved an "X" over the United States. Earthquakes rumble. Disasters multiply. Ancient alliances form. The sword is being sharpened. Just as in Ezekiel's vision, God will make Himself known—not through human diplomacy or military brilliance, but through supernatural acts of judgment and deliverance.

This is not fearmongering—it is forewarning. With every harbinger comes an invitation: repent, return, and ready yourself.

The seventh harbinger is not just about war—it is about the God of War: the Holy One of Israel, the Covenant-Keeper, the One who declares the end from the beginning. Soon, the nations will know His name.

The harbinger has sounded.

The alliances are forming.

The judgments are aligning.

And the King is coming.

The time to choose your allegiance is not later. It is now.

———◆◆◆———

Late afternoon sunlight streamed through the tall-pane glass windows of my study, bathing the room in a warm, amber glow. Dust motes danced lazily in the slanted light, suspended between Heaven and earth like prayers waiting for an answer. The atmosphere was quiet, but it wasn't peaceful—it was thick with anticipation. The kind of stillness that doesn't calm, but warns.

Irene sat across from me at the small round table—our usual spot for Bible study and end-time discussions—but today, her demeanor was more agitated than reflective. Her Bible lay unopened beside a stack of freshly printed news articles. I could see the headlines from where I sat:

> Iran and Hezbollah Threaten Retaliation
> Jordan's King Calls Emergency Summit
> Hamas Vows Continued Resistance

The print still smelled like ink.

Her brow was furrowed, her finger tapping an anxious rhythm on the edge of the paper. Finally, she broke the silence.

"Ann, I don't get it," she said, shaking her head.

"Everywhere I turn—podcasts, prophecy conferences, even the Sunday sermons—it's all about Gog and Magog. Ezekiel 38 and 39. But no one seems to mention Psalm 83 or Isaiah 17. Why is that? Aren't those wars just as important?"

I looked up from my open Bible, the thin pages ruffling slightly as the air shifted from the vent above. I smiled gently, but my eyes met hers with deliberate seriousness.

"That's a great question, Irene. And one that more people need to be asking."

I closed my Bible just long enough to lean forward, pressing my hands together in thought.

"The reason Psalm 83 and Isaiah 17 don't get the same attention as Ezekiel's war is because it doesn't have the same apocalyptic flash. Ezekiel's prophecy is filled with supernatural interventions—fire falling from Heaven, earthquakes, nations turned upside down. It feels like something out of a Hollywood script. But Psalm 83? Isaiah 17? They're more subtle. More personal. And that's what makes it dangerous."

She raised an eyebrow, leaning in.

I continued, "You see, Psalm 83 and Isaiah 17 aren't global. They're regional. They don't involve distant superpowers—they involve Israel's immediate neighbors. The ones with a generational grudge. And the disturbing part is, while Ezekiel's war may still be on the horizon, both Psalm 83 and Isaiah 17 might already be unfolding—right now—before our very eyes."

Irene leaned forward, her interest visibly piqued.

I slid my Bible toward her and flipped it open to a familiar passage. The thin pages crackled faintly as I turned them.

"Listen to this," I said, reading aloud:

> They have said, Come, and let us cut them off from being a nation; that the name of Israel may be no more in remembrance. For they have consulted together with one consent: they are confederate against you. (Psalm 83:4–5)

I paused, then tapped the next verses with my finger.

> The tabernacles of Edom, and the Ishmaelites; of Moab, and the Hagarenes; Gebal, and Ammon, and Amalek; the Philistines with the inhabitants of Trye; Assyria also is joined with them: they have helped the children of Lot. Selah. (Psalm 83:6–8)

"Here's the list of nations. Edom, Moab, Ammon, Amalek, the Philistines, Gebal, Tyre, and Assyria."

Lifting my gaze, I watched Irene's brow crease as she followed along. I offered the translation.

"In modern terms? Edom, Moab, and Ammon now fall within the borders of Jordan. Amalek is often associated with the Negev—southern Israel itself. The Philistines, of course, point to Gaza. Gebal and Tyre correspond to Lebanon. And Assyria? That's the territory covering much of modern northern Iraq, northeastern Syria, and parts of southeastern Turkey—an empire that at times extended its control over Damascus and the surrounding regions."

Irene's eyes widened in astonishment.

"That's literally the map of every single nation that surrounds Israel today. And most of them are hostile right now."

I nodded again, more somber this time.

"Exactly. Psalm 83 isn't about some far-off coalition from distant continents—it's about Israel's immediate neighbors. Nations that have, for millennia, sought her destruction and still harbor that ambition. This isn't just prophecy—it's a repeating pattern."

Irene's eyes widened.

"And Isaiah 17? Damascus isn't a distant symbol—it's a real city, still standing today, right in the heart of Syria. And God says its destruction will be sudden and complete."

I leaned back slightly, the weight of the Scripture settling between us like a stone dropped in still water.

"This isn't random," I said.

"It's strategic. It's prophetic. And it's personal—for God."

Irene's fingers tightened around the edges of the articles in her lap.

"So then . . . Psalm 83 and Isaiah 17 aren't just history repeating—they're prophecy in motion?"

I gave a slow, solemn nod.

"Yes. And if they unfold as many scholars anticipate, they could serve as the spark—the match that ignites the larger conflagration of Ezekiel 38. Psalm 83 sets the stage, Isaiah 17 delivers a sudden blow, and Ezekiel 38 brings the nations against Israel in a war that only God Himself will end."

Irene looked down at the articles she had brought—headlines about rocket fire from Gaza, rising tensions in Lebanon, border skirmishes with Jordan, and Hezbollah's growing arsenal. Her voice was low, almost a whisper.

"It feels like Psalm 83 is less a prophecy and more a playbook."

I nodded slowly, letting the weight of her words settle.

"That's exactly what many Bible scholars have come to believe. Psalm 83 isn't just poetic lament—it's a tactical outline. A forecast. And if it is prophetic, then it's not just history on repeat—it's the prelude to something much bigger."

I paused, then added, "Think about it. Psalm 83 involves Israel's immediate neighbors—those most likely to strike first. It would make sense for a short, brutal regional war to erupt—one where Israel is forced to neutralize its closest threats. Only then, once Israel is dwelling in a false sense of security, does the Ezekiel 38 alliance strike from afar."

Irene sat back, eyes scanning the invisible map in her mind, tracing the jagged borders of the Middle East as if she could feel the tension pulsing along each line.

"So Psalm 83 clears the ground. Isaiah 17 delivers the decisive blow. Ezekiel 38 ignites the stage for a global confrontation."

"Exactly," I said.

"It's strategic. It's sequential. And if we're watching closely, we may be seeing it all unfold right now."

"So," Irene whispered, "if Psalm 83 comes first, then we're not just watching prophecy unfold—we're standing in the middle of it."

I looked at her, my voice low but unwavering.

"I believe we are, Irene. October 7, 2023 wasn't just another headline—it was a prophetic tremor. The brutality of Hamas, the escalating threats from Hezbollah, the Houthis seizing the moment—it's all Iran's proxies, stirred to strike. And now, Iran itself has crossed the line and launched a direct attack."

I paused, letting the weight of it settle.

"And if that weren't enough, the final piece of the Psalm 83 puzzle—Syria— is stirring. Israel just struck Damascus in defense of the Druze population along the Golan Heights, who have been targeted by Islamist militias. It's as if every border is erupting at once. And through it all, the cry of Psalm 83 still echoes: 'Let us wipe them off from being a nation; that the name of Israel may be no more in remembrance.'"

I leaned forward, my tone sharpening.

"This isn't just politics—it's a confederacy of hatred, rooted in ancient enmity and revived through modern alliances. It's the Psalm 83 spirit—alive, dangerous, and rising again."

Irene's eyes welled, but I continued gently.

"And yet, we've seen this before—1948, 1967, 1973, 1991, 2008, 2014, and 2023. Surrounded. Outnumbered. Written off. But God has never broken His covenant. And He will not start now."

Irene looked up slowly, her voice trembling.

"But this time . . . it feels different."

I nodded, my expression grave.

"You're right. In the past, Israel has fought massive wars and witnessed miraculous deliverance—but there were always gaps. Some borders stayed quiet. Some enemies held back."

"October 7, 2023, changed that," I continued.

"For the first time in modern history, Israel was surrounded on every side— north, south, east, and west—at the same time. Gaza erupted in brutality. Hezbollah rained rockets from Lebanon. Syria stirred with fire from its borders. The Houthis launched missiles from Yemen. Iran orchestrated from the shadows. Even Jordan simmered with unrest."

I took a breath.

"It wasn't just an attack—it was an encirclement, the kind Psalm 83 describes. A tightening noose of hatred, ancient in its origin, modern in its methods."

I paused and turned back to Psalm 83, running my finger down the verses.

"It's all here, Irene—ancient names wearing modern faces. A confederacy fueled by hatred, united by one purpose: 'Let us wipe them out as a nation.' And for the first time in history, the map perfectly matches the prophecy."

Irene leaned back, her eyes locked on the pages in front of her, her voice barely above a whisper.

"So you're saying . . . we're not just reading prophecy anymore—we're standing inside it?"

I met her gaze, my voice heavy with certainty.

"I believe we're in the midst of the Psalm 83 War right now. This isn't a rehearsal for the last days—it's curtain time. The timing, the players, the intensity—everything lines up. This isn't a preview. This is the performance."

She glanced at the headlines again, her brow furrowing.

"And Damascus? The reports said Israel struck near the capital just days ago . . ."

I held her gaze.

"Yes. And that single event inching us closer to the Isaiah 17 prophecy: 'Behold, Damascus will cease to be a city, and will become a ruinous heap.' It's the kind of prophecy that could be fulfilled in a single night—and I believe the ground is already trembling beneath it."

Irene's brows furrowed.

"But Israel's been defending itself. Will they win these wars?"

"They will," I answered without hesitation.

"Psalm 83 and Isaiah 17—Israel will prevail militarily. God has preserved them time and again. But the next war—Ezekiel's Gog and Magog War—that's different. Israel won't win that one by its own strength."

I reached across the table and tapped her Bible.

"That war, Irene . . . God Himself steps in. Earthquakes will shake the land. Hailstones will fall. Fire will rain down. Confusion will grip the armies until they turn on each other. And it's not just about saving Israel—it's about making Himself known. Ezekiel 38:23 declares, 'Thus will I magnify Myself, and sanctify Myself; and I will be known in the eyes of many nations, and they shall know that I am the LORD.'"

Irene's voice trembled.

"And you're saying we're already watching that war gather on the horizon?"

"Yes," I said.

"The nations named in Ezekiel 38 and 39—Russia, Iran, Turkey—they're already aligning. The hostility is in place. The alliances are tightening. It's the next prophetic layer, and when it happens, it will be undeniable."

She turned toward the window, as if seeing the world for the first time.

"And after that war?"

I drew a slow breath.

"That war won't end in treaties—it will end in awe. The world will be shaken . . . then seduced. A false peace will settle over the nations, a momentary sigh of relief. And in that calm, the Antichrist will make his move. He'll confirm a covenant with Israel, offering protection. But it will be a lie. And that's the spark that ignites the final seven years—the Tribulation—just as Daniel 9:27 foretold."

Irene was quiet.

Then finally, she whispered, "It's all happening."

I nodded, my voice low but firm.

"And the clock is ticking."

CHAPTER SUMMARY

Chapter 11 unveils the Seventh Harbinger: The War Prophecies—the scriptural blueprint of coming military conflicts that culminate in divine judgment and global awakening. From Psalm 83 to Isaiah 17, from Ezekiel 38–39 to Israel's own war history, this chapter exposes the ancient forecasts driving today's headlines. These wars are not random—they are revelations unfolding in real time.

This chapter distinguishes three major prophetic wars: the Psalm 83 war, a regional assault by Israel's immediate neighbors bent on her annihilation; the Isaiah 17 prophecy, forecasting the sudden obliteration of Damascus; and the Gog and Magog War of Ezekiel 38–39, describing a vast, multinational invasion met by direct supernatural intervention. Together, these conflicts form a sequential pattern—escalating from localized hostility to global warfare and culminating in divine glory.

The chapter also recounts Israel's modern miracles of survival—seven victories that defy human explanation. From the *1948 War of Independence* to the lightning triumph of the *1967 Six-Day War*; from the surprise attack during the *1973 Yom Kippur War* to the miraculous protection from Saddam Hussein's missile barrage in the *1991 Gulf War*; from the targeted campaigns of *2008–2009's Operation Cast Lead* to *2014's Operation Protective Edge*—and now, the *Swords of Iron War* sparked by Hamas' brutal October 7, 2023 assault. Again and again, against overwhelming odds, Israel not only endures but prevails. It is not by might, nor by power, but by the unmistakable hand of the Covenant-Keeping God who still watches over His people.

Yet the signs are not confined to the battlefield—they are also written in the heavens. The solar eclipses of 2017, 2024, and 2026 appear to form a synchronized prophetic message: a giant "X" traced across America in 2017 and

2024, intersecting over a region known as "Little Egypt," and a shadow in 2026 passing over volatile, biblically significant lands in the Middle East—including Damascus. These celestial alignments echo Genesis 1:14's declaration that the sun, moon, and stars were appointed "for signs, and seasons" and may serve as divine timestamps pointing to America's urgent call to repentance and the Middle East's looming prophetic wars. The wise watch. The faithful will prepare. And the world, whether ready or not, will soon see that the same hand that governs the heavens also governs the destiny of nations.

Ultimately, the seventh harbinger reveals that the God of Israel remains the Defender of Israel. The wars foretold are not just judgments on her enemies, but signs to the world that the King is coming. The alliances have formed. The warnings are manifesting. And America, too, stands under the shadow of judgment for its own rebellion.

KEY TAKEAWAYS

- The Psalm 83 War is likely a distinct regional conflict involving Israel's immediate Arab neighbors and may precede the larger Gog Magog conflict.
- Isaiah 17 prophesies the sudden, total destruction of Damascus—an event that may ignite broader conflict in the Middle East.
- The Gog and Magog War of Ezekiel 38–39 describes a vast coalition—Russia, Iran, Turkey, and others—invading Israel, only to be defeated by divine intervention.
- Israel's miraculous modern victories (1948, 1967, 1973, 1991, 2008–2009, 2014, 2023) form a prophetic pattern of supernatural preservation, affirming her covenant role in God's plan.
- The solar eclipses of 2017, 2024, and 2026 may serve as prophetic markers: 2017 and 2024 form an "X" across America, possibly warning of judgment, while the 2026 crosses the Middle East, including Damascus, hinting at Isaiah 17's prophecy.
- The seventh harbinger is not simply about war—it's about the revelation of God's power, His unbreakable covenant with Israel, and the soon return of Christ.

Chapter 11 sounds the seventh harbinger: the wars of prophecy are aligning. The alliances are in motion. The divine response is imminent. And the choice of allegiance—between the kingdoms of this world and the coming King—must be made now.

Chapter 12

The Final Countdown:
The Last Days Before Forever

THE FINAL TURN OF THE HOURGLASS—From the very beginning, God did not simply create time—He consecrated it. Time was never meant to be a passive measurement of passing moments. It was designed as a sacred vessel, a divine container for eternal purpose. In the hands of man, time becomes a calendar. In the hands of God, time becomes a covenant. It is prophetic, not neutral. It moves toward a consummation—when all things will be brought under the dominion of Christ.

Everything we've covered—the harbingers, the empires, the signs in the heavens, the appointed feasts, the rising wars—points to one unavoidable truth: we are living in the final turn of the hourglass. The sand is almost gone. This moment is not merely another crisis in history—it is the convergence of prophecy.

One of Scripture's most overlooked revelations is what many prophetic scholars call the 6,000-year clock—a divine timeline woven from Genesis to Revelation. Jewish tradition, early Church teaching, and biblical patterns all point to this truth: God's plan for humanity spans seven millennia—six thousand years of man's rule under sin, followed by one thousand years of rest, when Christ will reign from Jerusalem in righteousness.

The blueprint is embedded in Creation itself: six days of work, one day of rest. As Psalm 90:4 reminds us, "A thousand years in Your sight are like a day that has just gone by." From Adam to Christ spans 4,000 years of patriarchs, prophets, and covenant promise. From Christ until now, another 2,000 years—the Church Age, a season of grace. But grace, while abundant, is not infinite. Its appointed time is almost complete. The seventh millennium—the Sabbath rest for the earth—is drawing near.

History itself has been divided into dispensations—eras of God's governance, each ending in judgment and transition. From Eden's innocence to Sinai's Law, from Calvary's grace to the present age, every dispensation has moved us toward this final shift: the close of the Church Age and the arrival of the Day of the Lord. This change will not be gradual—it will be sudden.

God's clock is measured not by human calendars but by covenants, Shemitahs, Jubilees, genealogies, and appointed feasts. It measures faithfulness as much as time. And by every measure—ancient and modern—the time of mortal man is expiring. The dominion of nations is about to give way to the dominion of Christ. The trumpet is about to sound.

This final chapter is not only a revelation—it is an invitation. Time is sacred. The question is no longer, "What time is it?" but "What will I do with the time that remains?" Because in the turning of this hourglass lies more than prophecy—it holds your calling, your commission, and your eternal crossroads.

The clock is not just ticking.

It is trembling.

The last days before forever are nearly upon us.

THE COUNTDOWN TO THE SABBATH KINGDOM

From the beginning, God set a sacred rhythm into motion—a prophetic countdown woven into the fabric of Creation. Six days of work. One day of rest. This was never just the pattern of the week; it was a divine clock measuring the entire span of human history.

According to Scripture and echoed in both Jewish tradition and the early Church, history is mapped across seven millennia: six thousand years of mankind's rule under the curse of sin, followed by one thousand years of rest and restoration under the reign of Christ—the Sabbath kingdom.

The Bible itself gives us the time key. Psalm 90:4 declares, "For a thousand years in Your sight are but as yesterday when it is past, and as a watch in the night," and Peter confirms it: "But, beloved, be not ignorant of this one thing, that one day is with the Lord as a thousand years, and a thousand years as one day" (2 Peter 3:8). These are not just poetic musings—they are prophetic timecodes.

The Age of Promise—4,000 Years

The first four "days" stretch from Adam to the First Coming of Jesus Christ—4,000 years marked by patriarchs, covenants, prophets, and the Law. From Eden's fall, God wove a scarlet thread of redemption through every generation, pointing toward the Messiah who would come to save.

The Age of Grace—2,000 Years

The next two "days" span from the Cross to today—2,000 years of the Church Age. This is the era of global evangelism, where salvation through Christ is offered freely to Jew and Gentile alike. But grace, though abundant, has a set season. It will not extend forever.

The Age of Glory—1,000 Years

That final "day" is still to come—a thousand years when Christ Himself will rule from Jerusalem in righteousness. This is the Millennial Kingdom described in Revelation 20—the global Sabbath, when Creation itself rests and all is set right.

> Come, and let us return unto the LORD: for He has torn, and He will heal us; He has smitten, and He will bind us up. After two days will He revive us: in the third day He will raise us up, and we shall live in His sight. (Hosea 6:1–2)

Hosea 6:1–2 offers a striking prophecy: "After two days He will revive us; on the third day He will raise us up, that we may live in His sight." After two prophetic days—2,000 years—God will restore His people. The third day—the seventh millennium—ushers in resurrection, renewal, and divine presence.

We are now standing at the threshold of that seventh day. The sixth day is fading; the seventh is dawning. History has never been random—it has been rhythmic, each age moving us toward this moment. Six days belong to man. The seventh belongs to the Lord. And the countdown is almost over.

Sunlight spilled through the western window of my study, bathing the bookshelf-lined walls in gold. The quiet tick of the antique clock on the mantel was the only sound for a moment, except for the rustling of paper as Irene settled into the tufted chair across from me. Her Bible was opened on her lap, a pen tucked behind her ear, her eyes bright with the kind of curiosity that often precedes revelation.

She leaned forward, her voice low but animated. "Ann, I read something fascinating the other day—it was about how the seven days of Creation in Genesis mirror seven thousand years of human history. And now this. I had no idea there was such a prophetic parallel!"

I smiled, heartened by her discovery. The joy of unfolding Scripture never dulled for either of us.

"Yes!" I said, nodding. "It's an incredible insight—and it's rooted in Scripture. Second Peter 3:8 says, 'With the Lord one day is as a thousand years, and a thousand years as one day.' The early Church fathers, Jewish rabbis, and prophetic scholars have long believed that each day of Creation prophetically points to 1,000 years of God's plan for mankind."

I paused, watching her take it in.

"It's as if," I continued, "God embedded the blueprint of all human history into the very rhythm of the first week."

Irene's eyes lit up as she leaned back, thinking aloud.

"That would mean humanity has a 7,000-year story arc—from Creation to the New Earth?"

I nodded slowly, the corners of my mouth lifting in a quiet smile.

"Exactly, Irene. It's breathtaking when you realize it. God embedded the entire story of redemption right into the rhythm of Creation itself. That's why every civilization on Earth, regardless of culture or religion, follows a seven day week. There's no astronomical basis for it—nothing from the sun, moon, or stars that dictates that rhythm. It's divinely appointed. A sacred echo from Eden that still governs our lives."

She sat silently for a moment, absorbing the weight of that truth, as the light in the study dimmed into early evening.

Irene leaned in again, curiosity dancing in her expression.

"So day one would parallel the first 1,000 years after Adam?"

I nodded, turning a page in my Bible and tapping gently on Genesis 1.

"Yes. On day one, God separated light from darkness. And in the first millennium, Adam—after the fall—was separated from God. That was the moment spiritual darkness entered the human story. What began as perfect communion was broken by sin. So the prophetic mirror is clear: the first 'day' of history reflects the beginning of man's spiritual exile from divine light."

Irene's brow furrowed thoughtfully. "And day two?"

I closed my eyes for a brief moment, recalling the Scripture.

"On day two, God separated the waters above from the waters below," I said slowly. "It was a dividing line—Heaven from earth, judgment from mercy. And prophetically, that division came to life in the second millennium. The Flood of Noah was not just a historical event—it was divine judgment in liquid form. Water poured out, above and below. The earth was baptized in death before it could begin again."

Irene leaned in, her curiosity growing.

"Wow. And what about day three?"

I turned a few pages of my Bible, pausing with reverence.

"On the third day," I began, "God caused the dry land to appear—and in Hebrew, the word for land is *eretz*. It's the same word used for the land of Israel."

I let that settle before continuing.

"In the third millennium, something prophetic unfolded: Joshua led the Israelites into *Eretz Yisrael*, the Promised Land. It was the fulfillment of the covenant God made with Abraham centuries earlier. A people, a promise, and a piece of land—finally joined."

Irene nodded slowly, the weight of the timeline beginning to dawn on her.

Irene's voice dropped, almost reverently.

"That's powerful. So day four is the one the rabbis believed pointed to the coming of the Messiah?"

I nodded, the candlelight flickering between us as if echoing the theme.

"Exactly. On day four, God created the sun, moon, and stars—greater light to govern the day, and the lesser to govern the night. And in the fourth millennium, Jesus—the Light of the World—entered human history."

I opened my Bible gently, turning to one of my favorite verses.

Then spoke Jesus again unto them, saying, I am the Light of the World: he that follows Me shall not walk in darkness, but shall have the light of life. (John 8:12)

"He fulfilled hundreds of prophecies, shattered the darkness, and brought salvation not only to Israel, but to all mankind. Just like the sun governs the day, He came to rule in righteousness and truth."

Irene exhaled slowly, her fingers resting on the rim of her teacup.

"That gives me chills, Ann. What about day five? That one sounds a bit more symbolic."

I nodded thoughtfully, tapping my Bible with a gentle rhythm.

"Yes, it is—but symbolism doesn't mean it lacks meaning. On day five, God created the birds of the air and the fish of the sea. In Scripture, birds can carry layered symbolism—often dark. In Joseph's interpretation of the baker's dream, birds came to devour the bread from the baskets on the man's head. It was a prophecy of death and judgment—Pharaoh would execute him, and the birds would feast on his flesh."

I turned to another passage, the parable of the sower.

And He spoke many things unto them in parables, saying, Behold, a sower went forth to sow; And when He sowed, some seeds fell by the way side, and the fowls came and devoured them up: Some fell upon stony places, where they had not much earth: and forthwith they sprung up, because they had no deepness of earth: And when the sun was up, they were scorched; and because they had no root, they withered away. And some fell among thorns; and the thorns sprung up, and choked them: But others fell into good ground, and brought forth fruit, some a hundredfold, some sixtyfold, some thirtyfold. Who has ears to hear, let him hear. (Matthew 13:3–9)—*The Parable of the Sower*

Hear you therefore the parable of the sower. When any one hears the Word of the kingdom, and understands it not, then comes the wicked one (Satan), and catches away that which was sown in the heart. This is he which received seed by the way side. But he that received the seed into stony places, the same is he that hears the Word, and immediately with joy receives it; yet has he no root in himself, but endures only for a while: for when tribulation or persecution arises because of the Word, by and by he is offended. He also that received seed among the thorns is he that hears the Word; and the care of this world, and the deceitfulness of riches, choke the Word, and he becomes unfruitful. But he that received seed into the good ground is he that hears the Word, and understands it; which also bears fruit, and brings forth, some a hundredfold, some sixty, some thirty. (Matthew 13:18–23)—*Jesus' Explanation*

"Jesus told of birds snatching up the seeds before they could take root. And when the disciples asked what it meant, He said it represented Satan—stealing the Word before it could grow. That symbolism becomes striking when you look at the fifth millennium."

I leaned in slightly, my voice lower.

"This was the age when the institutional Church was increasingly compromised. Doctrines of demons crept in. Corruption festered. The Crusades, the Inquisition, the silencing and persecution of true believers—it was a spiritual battleground. The birds were indeed circling."

Irene sat quietly for a moment, absorbing the weight of it.

She leaned forward, her brows furrowed with intensity. "And day six would be the age of man?"

I nodded slowly.

"Exactly. On the sixth day, God created man. Biblically, the number six has always been associated with humanity—our limitations, our striving, and ultimately, our rebellion. Ancient Jewish rabbis and early Christian theologians believed that mankind was allotted six thousand years to rule the earth. It's like a divine lease—temporary, probationary."

I paused for effect.

"And that lease is almost up. We're not just in the sixth day, Irene—we're living at the very end of it. The final hours of the age of man are ticking down."

She whispered, almost to herself, "That means the next day is . . ."

Irene's eyes widened. "That means Jesus could return at any moment. The seventh millennium would be the day of rest—the Sabbath Millennium?"

I smiled gently.

"Exactly. Just as God rested on the seventh day, the seventh millennium will be a time of divine rest—Christ's millennial reign. It will be a thousand years of peace, justice, and worship. Zechariah 14 even says that during this time, all the nations will go up to Jerusalem to celebrate the Feast of Tabernacles."

> And it shall come to pass, that every one that is left of all the nations which came against Jerusalem shall even go up from year to year to worship the King, the LORD of hosts, and to keep the Feast of Tabernacles. (Zechariah 14:16)

I looked at her and added softly, "It's as if God is saying, 'This is the Sabbath of human history.' A thousand-year rest after six thousand years of human striving. The Kingdom Age is coming, Irene—and it's closer than we think."

Irene leaned back, her expression thoughtful.

"So the seven days of Creation weren't just the beginning—they're the map. From Genesis to Revelation, the timeline is there."

I nodded, a quiet smile forming.

"Exactly. God gave us a prophetic calendar from the very start. We're not living in random times—we're living in prophetic times. And soon, the eternal Sabbath rest will begin."

My voice softened.

"But right now is still man's day. And we need to be ready—before the clock runs out."

She looked at me, resolute.

"Then let's live like people who know what time it is."

"Amen," I whispered.

"The hour is late—but the hope is eternal."

GOD'S TIMELINE: FROM CREATION TO ETERNITY

From before the first ray of light touched the void to the eternal dawn that will never fade, God's dealings with mankind have followed a deliberate, divinely appointed order. These seasons—known as dispensations—are not random divisions of history. They are stages in the great drama of redemption, each marked by a fresh revelation of God's will, a unique stewardship entrusted to humanity, a test of obedience, and an inevitable worldwide judgment when that stewardship is broken.

Every dispensation tells two stories: the faithfulness of God and the failure of man. And each one moves us closer to the restoration of all things, when God will dwell with His people in righteousness forever.

Eternity Past—Before time began, before earth was formed, before the first angel took flight, God existed in perfect, infinite communion—Father, Son, and Holy Spirit—dwelling in unapproachable light (John 17:5; Ephesians 1:4; 1 Timothy 6:16). The entire plan of redemption was already complete in His mind. Christ was "the Lamb slain from the foundation of the world" (Revelation 13:8). What was yet to unfold in human history had already been settled in the counsels of eternity.

1. The Age of Innocence—Creation to the Fall

4000 BC–3970 BC—God created mankind in His image, placing Adam and Eve in Eden, a paradise without death, disease, or decay. Their stewardship was simple: tend the garden, enjoy its abundance, and abstain from the fruit of one forbidden tree. There was no sin, no shame, and no separation from God—only innocence and intimate fellowship (Genesis 1:26–31, 2:15–17).

Worldwide Divine Judgment: The Curse—When Adam and Eve disobeyed, sin entered the human story, bringing death, toil, pain, and separation from the presence of God (Genesis 3:14–19; Romans 5:12). The earth itself was placed under a curse, and mankind's innocence was forever lost.

2. The Age of Conscience—Fall to the Flood

3970 BC–2348 BC—Without written law, humanity lived under the moral compass of conscience, aware of good and evil but without direct governance from God. Yet, instead of pursuing righteousness, mankind descended rapidly into violence, corruption, and depravity. The testimony of Cain's murder of Abel became the pattern for generations that followed (Genesis 4:3–7; Romans 2:14–15).

Worldwide Divine Judgment: The Flood—God, grieved by the depth of human wickedness, sent a global deluge that destroyed all life except for Noah, his family, and the animals preserved in the Ark (Genesis 6:5–7; 2 Peter 2:5). The earth was cleansed, but sin remained in the human heart.

3. The Age of Human Government—Post-Flood to Abraham

2348 BC–2000 BC—After the Flood, God established human authority as a means to restrain evil, uphold justice, and preserve order in society. Mankind was charged with multiplying, spreading across the earth, and upholding God's moral order (Genesis 9:1–7). Alongside this charge, God gave humanity a universal moral code—later known as the Seven Noahic Laws—which included: prohibition of idolatry, blasphemy, murder, sexual immorality, theft, eating flesh taken from a living animal, and the requirement to establish courts of justice.

Instead, humanity united in defiance at Babel, seeking to make a name for themselves apart from God.

Worldwide Divine Judgment: The Confusion of Tongues—At the Tower of Babel, God confounded their languages and scattered them across the face of the earth (Genesis 11:1–9), birthing the nations and laying the groundwork for the redemptive story through Israel.

4. The Age of the Old Covenant—Abraham to the End of the OT

2000 BC–33 AD—God called Abraham and his descendants to be a covenant people, set apart to carry His promises, the Law, and the hope of the coming Messiah. Through the patriarchs, judges, prophets, and kings, God revealed His holiness and the need for atonement (Genesis 12:1–3; Exodus 19:5–6; Deuteronomy 7:6–9).

Worldwide Divine Judgment: The Cross—In the fullness of time, Jesus Christ came as Israel's promised Messiah. But the nation rejected Him, leading to His crucifixion—a judgment that fell as both a curse upon unbelieving Israel (Matthew 27:25; Luke 19:41–44) and a blessing to all who would believe (Galatians 3:13–14).

5. The Church Age (Age of Grace)—Pentecost to the Rapture

33 AD–possibly 2028/2029—Following Christ's resurrection and ascension, the Holy Spirit was poured out at Pentecost, ushering in an age where salvation is freely offered to Jew and Gentile alike by grace through faith. This era, spanning nearly two thousand years, is a season of mercy, but not without limit. Grace is a window, not a wall, and that window is closing (Acts 2:1–4; Ephesians 3:2–6).

Worldwide Divine Judgment: The Rapture—In a moment, the true Church will be caught up to meet the Lord in the air (1 Thessalonians 4:16–17). For those left behind, sudden destruction will fall as the world plunges into the Tribulation Age (1 Thessalonians 5:2–3).

6. The Tribulation Age—Seven Years of Global Judgment

Following the Rapture, possibly 2029/2030—This will be the most severe period of judgment in human history, as seals, trumpets, and bowls of wrath are poured out upon the earth. The Antichrist will rise, deceiving the nations, and unprecedented persecution will fall upon believers and Israel (Daniel 9:27; Revelation 6–19).

Worldwide Divine Judgment: The Second Coming of Christ—At the height of global rebellion, Jesus will return in glory, destroying His enemies and judging the nations (Revelation 19:11–21; Matthew 25:31–46).

7. The Millennial Kingdom Age—1,000-Year Reign of Christ

Following the Tribulation—Christ will reign from Jerusalem, fulfilling God's promises to Israel and bringing global peace. The curse upon Creation will be lifted, justice will prevail, and the knowledge of the Lord will cover the earth as the waters cover the sea (Revelation 20:1–6; Isaiah 2:2–4).

Worldwide Divine Judgment: The Great White Throne Judgment—After Satan's final rebellion is crushed, all unbelievers of all ages will be resurrected to stand before God, judged according to their works, and cast into the Lake of Fire (Revelation 20:11–15).

Eternity Future—The Eternal Age—new heaven, new earth, and New Jerusalem. When the old heavens and earth pass away, God will create a new heaven and new earth, where righteousness dwells. The New Jerusalem will descend, and God Himself will dwell among His people. There will be no more death, sorrow, crying, or pain—only unending joy in the presence of God the Father and our Lord Jesus Christ. This is the final restoration, the eternal Sabbath, and the true beginning of forever (Isaiah 65:17, 66:22; 2 Peter 3:13; Revelation 21:1).

THE FINAL CONVERGENCE:
WHY 2028/2029 MAY MARK THE TURNING POINT

The years 2028 and 2029 may represent far more than dates on a calendar—they could signal the closing of the Church Age and the opening of the Tribulation Age leading to the Kingdom Age. We are seeing a prophetic alignment of Scripture, cycles, signs, and global agendas that is too exact to ignore.

1. The Prophetic Generation

"The days of our years are threescore years and ten; and if by reason of strength they be fourscore years, yet is their strength labor and sorrow; for it is soon cut off, and we fly away" (Psalm 90:10). When Israel was reborn in 1948 (Matthew 24:32–34), the prophetic clock started for the "generation" that would witness the end-time events. A biblical lifespan of 70–80 years places the outer limit around 2028. This means we are approaching the end of the fig tree generation—and with it, the culmination of God's prophetic plan.

> Now learn a parable of the fig tree (Israel); When his branch is yet tender, and puts forth leaves, you know that summer is near. So likewise you, when you shall see all these things, know that it is near, even at the doors. Verily I say unto you, This generation shall not pass, till all these things be fulfilled. (Matthew 24:32–34)

2. Shemitah Cycles and Daniel's Timeline

The current seven-year Shemitah cycle began in fall 2022/2023 and ends in fall 2028/2029. Daniel 9:27 shows the Tribulation as a seven-year period beginning with a covenant and ending with the return of the King. For this to align with the next Shemitah cycle (2029/2030–2035/2036), the covenant could be confirmed in or near fall 2029/2030—marking the prophetic pivot from grace to judgment.

3. Feasts and Appointed Times

Jesus fulfilled the spring feasts of Leviticus 23 at His First Coming. The fall feasts—Trumpets, Atonement, and Tabernacles—await fulfillment. Many watchmen believe the Feast of Trumpets may mark the Rapture or Tribulation's start. In 2029, the Feast of Trumpets falls on September 9–11 (*Rosh HaShanah*), perfectly aligned with the Shemitah transition. This could be the very feast Paul described when "the trumpet shall sound" (1 Corinthians 15:52):

> In a moment, in the twinkling of an eye, at the last trump: for the trumpet shall sound, and the dead shall be raised incorruptible, and we shall be changed. (1 Corinthians 15:52)

4. Economic Harbingers

On God's biblical calendar, Elul 29—the final day of the civil year—has often served as a prophetic marker for financial upheaval. In 2001, a Shemitah year, the markets plunged sharply after reopening from the September 11 attacks, with the Dow dropping 14 percent in a single week. Seven years later, in 2008, also a Shemitah year, the collapse of Lehman Brothers on September 15 triggered the steepest market fall since the Great Depression.

The next Elul 29 Shemitah year falls on September 9, 2029, immediately before the Feast of Trumpets. This alignment is striking—it places a potential economic reset or global financial crisis right on the prophetic threshold of a new season. If history is any indication, this could be more than coincidence; it may be a divine signal that the world is on the brink of dramatic change.

5. Cosmic and Celestial Signs

From the Shoemaker-Levy comet's dramatic collision with Jupiter in 1994—a planetary warning shot seen by the whole world—to the striking blood moon tetrad of 2014–2015, which aligned perfectly with the biblical feast days (Passover, *Sukkot*, Passover, *Sukkot*), the heavens have continued to declare the warnings prophesied in Joel 2:31 and Revelation 6:12: "The sun shall be turned into darkness, and the moon into blood, before the great and terrible Day of the Lord come."

The total solar eclipses of 2017 and 2024 etched an unmistakable "X" across the American heartland—interpreted by many as both a national warning and a divine marker in time. In 2026, another total solar eclipse will cut directly across the Middle East, passing over Damascus—an ominous reminder of Isaiah 17, which foretells the city's sudden and utter destruction.

Looking ahead, one of the most publicized celestial events of the century will occur on April 13, 2029, when the massive asteroid 99942 Apophis will make an extraordinarily close pass by Earth—closer than many satellites in orbit. While NASA currently rules out an impact during this approach, its proximity and timing have fueled speculation in prophetic circles, with some linking it to the "great star" called Wormwood in Revelation 8:10–11, which poisons a third of Earth's waters. Whether Apophis fulfills this prophecy or merely foreshadows it, its appearance underscores the vulnerability of our world and the certainty of divine judgment to come.

The skies also hold another prophetic appointment: the next blood moon tetrad in 2032–2033. This series of four total lunar eclipses is rare in occurrence and prophetic in timing, with two of them falling exactly on major biblical feast days:

- April 25, 2032—Total lunar eclipse
- October 18, 2032—Total lunar eclipse
- April 14, 2033—Total lunar eclipse (Passover)
- October 8, 2033—Total lunar eclipse (Feast of Tabernacles)

Notably, a total solar eclipse will also occur mid-sequence on March 30, 2033, amplifying the prophetic weight of this tetrad.

When viewed together—the comet strike of 1994, the feast-aligned tetrads, the Cross-shaped eclipses over America, the Middle Eastern eclipse of 2026, the close flyby of Apophis in 2029, and the feast-aligned tetrad of 2032–2033—a prophetic tapestry emerges. These celestial harbingers are not random; they are signs written in the heavens, reminding us that God's clock is advancing and that the appointed hour is drawing near.

6. Global Political Agenda

The world is rapidly moving toward an era of unprecedented centralization—politically, economically, and ideologically. The United Nations' Agenda 2030, adopted in 2015—a Shemitah year—outlines seventeen Sustainable Development Goals (SDGs) aimed at reshaping global priorities by the end of this decade.

While presented as a blueprint for peace, equality, and environmental stewardship, its framework points toward a unified global governance model—one in which national sovereignty is gradually diminished in favor of a centralized authority that sets universal standards for economics, climate policy, healthcare, technology, and even cultural values.

This agenda is not unfolding in a vacuum. Scripture warns that in the end-times, the world will come under the control of a singular system—political, economic, religious, and militarily—ultimately ruled by the Antichrist. Revelation 13 depicts a "beast" with authority over "all kindreds, and tongues, and nations," enforcing allegiance and economic compliance through the infamous "mark" without which no one can buy or sell. The prophetic description of this beast system parallels today's increasing calls for digital identification systems, centralized banking oversight, and global regulatory frameworks.

Agenda 2030's emphasis on global equity, resource redistribution, and environmental mandates mirrors the kind of universal control that will characterize the Antichrist's regime. Its timeline—culminating around 2030—sits uncomfortably close to many biblical prophecy watchers' projections for the end of the Church Age and the dawn of the Tribulation Age. This convergence of political will, technological readiness, and spiritual deception could very well set the stage for the beast system to rise fully into power once the restraining influence of the Holy Spirit—working through the Church—is removed at the Rapture.

What may appear to the world as a noble, humanitarian vision could, in reality, be the scaffolding for the most oppressive system in human history. As these globalist structures tighten, believers must discern the difference between man's utopian promises and God's prophetic truth. The stage is being set, the actors are in place, and the final act of history—as foretold in the Bible—is preparing to unfold.

A Watchman's Warning

This is not about date-setting—it is about discernment. God's Word calls His people to watch, to be alert, and to recognize the season when the signs He foretold begin to converge. The years 2028 and 2029 are not isolated numbers; they form an extraordinary intersection of prophetic markers. We see the generational window from the rebirth of Israel in 1948 drawing to a close. We see the Shemitah cycles aligning perfectly with the conclusion of an 80-year biblical generation. We see appointed feast days on the biblical calendar falling into place. Layered on top are the growing tremors in the global economy, dramatic celestial events that mirror Scripture's warnings, and the relentless march toward centralized global governance. No single sign tells the whole story—but together, they form a prophetic mosaic that cannot be ignored.

Like the watchmen of ancient Israel who stood upon the walls to sound the trumpet at the first sign of danger, we are compelled to lift our voices. The patterns are converging; the pace is accelerating. What was once theory is becoming reality before our eyes. Now is the time to anchor ourselves in Christ, to live with urgency, and to proclaim the gospel while the door remains open. For the One who promised to return is faithful, and the signs are telling us His return is near.

> And when these things begin to come to pass, then look up, and lift up your heads; for your redemption draws near. (Luke 21:28)

THE FEASTS OF THE LORD: DRESS REHEARSALS FOR THE KINGDOM

While the world marks time by manmade calendars, God's prophetic clock runs on *moedim*—appointed times—established from Creation itself. These are not quaint traditions or relics of an ancient religion. They are sacred rehearsals, set by the Lord, to reveal His redemptive plan from the first Passover to the final trumpet blast.

Every feast carries a dual nature: a commemoration of God's past acts and a prophetic blueprint for His future promises. Together, they tell the full story of the Messiah—His First Coming, His return in glory, and His eternal reign.

The Spring Feasts—Fulfilled in the First Coming

The first four feasts were fulfilled with astonishing precision during the ministry, death, burial, and resurrection of Jesus Christ:

- Passover (*Pesach*)—Jesus, the spotless Lamb of God, was crucified on the very day Israel sacrificed their Passover lambs (Exodus 12; John 1:29). His blood delivers us from God's judgment.
- Unleavened Bread (*Hag HaMatzot*)—His sinless body was laid in the grave, fulfilling the picture of removing leaven (sin) from the home and heart (1 Corinthians 5:7–8).
- Firstfruits (*Bikkurim*)—On the very day Israel offered the firstfruits of the harvest, Jesus rose from the dead as "the firstfruits of those who have fallen asleep" (1 Corinthians 15:20), guaranteeing the resurrection of His people.
- Pentecost (*Shavuot*)—On the day Israel celebrated God's giving of the Law, the Holy Spirit was poured out (Acts 2), writing God's Law on human hearts and birthing the Church.

These were not symbolic coincidences—they were divine appointments fulfilled on the exact days and in the exact ways foretold.

The Fall Feasts: Prophetic Blueprints of His Second Coming

Just as the spring feasts were fulfilled in His First Coming, the fall feasts foreshadow His Second Coming and the consummation of the kingdom:

- Feast of Trumpets (*Yom Teruah*)—Known as the "day no man knows" because it begins at the sighting of the new moon, this feast pictures a sudden, divine summons (1 Thessalonians 4:16–17; Matthew 24:36). Many connect it to the Rapture or the start of the Tribulation. It calls God's people to repentance, readiness, and watchfulness.
- Day of Atonement (*Yom Kippur*)—A solemn day pointing to Israel's national repentance when they "look upon Me whom they have pierced" (Zechariah 12:10). It is a day of judgment and cleansing, foreshadowing the moment when Messiah returns and redeems His people.
- Feast of Tabernacles (*Sukkot*)—A joyful celebration picturing the Millennial Kingdom, when Messiah will "tabernacle" among His people (Zechariah 14:16–19; Revelation 21:3). It speaks of restored relationship, abundance, and peace.

Cycles, Patterns, and Prophetic Urgency

The Feasts of the LORD are not simply historical markers—they are prophetic cycles. Every year they return, like the steady sweep of a divine clock hand, reminding God's people that the next act in His redemptive drama is approaching. The spring feasts prove He came once exactly as promised. The fall feasts guarantee He will return in like manner—on time, in order, and in glory.

We are not rehearsing in vain. One year, the trumpet will not signal a practice—it will announce the King. And when it does, the "appointed time" will have arrived. The only question will be whether we were ready.

THE GREAT INVITATION: WILL YOU BE AT THE WEDDING?

Heaven is not preparing for a conference or a committee meeting—it is preparing for a wedding. The invitations have been sent. The banquet is being prepared. The music is about to begin. And the Groom Himself wants to know—will you be there?

In Matthew 22, Jesus told of a king who arranged a wedding feast for his son. The invitations went out, but many ignored them—too busy, too distracted, too self-absorbed. Others scoffed and even turned violent against the king's messengers. So the king threw open the doors, inviting anyone who would come—good and bad alike—until the wedding hall was full. But when he entered the room, he saw one guest without wedding clothes. "Friend," the king asked, "how did you get in here without a wedding garment?" Speechless, the man was cast into outer darkness.

This isn't about fashion—it's about righteousness. The wedding garment is the righteousness of Christ, given only to those who are truly born again (Isaiah 61:10; Revelation 19:8). You can't borrow it. You can't fake it. Church attendance, ministry work, or religious heritage will not replace it. If the Groom does not know you personally, you will hear the most devastating words a soul could ever hear: "I never knew you" (Matthew 7:23).

Jesus' parable of the ten virgins in Matthew 25 drives the warning even deeper. All ten were waiting for the Bridegroom. All had lamps. But only five carried extra oil. When the midnight cry rang out, the wise went in, and the door was shut. The foolish arrived too late, crying, "Lord, Lord," but the answer came: "I do not know you."

This is not a story for someone else—it's a mirror for you and me. Is your lamp burning brightly with the oil of the Holy Spirit, or are you coasting on yesterday's flame? Have you clothed yourself with Christ (Romans 13:14), or are you relying on your own garments?

The wedding feast will happen. The trumpet will sound. The Bridegroom will arrive. But once the door closes, it will not open again. The only question is—when that moment comes, will you be found inside, rejoicing at the table . . . or outside, pounding on a door that will never again open?

CONCLUSION: CHOOSE THIS DAY

We have not simply arrived at the last page of a chapter—we have reached the last pages of this book, standing at the very threshold of eternity's unfolding drama. Everything you've read has been leading here. The prophetic patterns, the cycles, the appointed times, the converging signs—they are not academic curiosities. They are God's mercy alarms, sounding for a generation drifting toward the edge.

This journey was never meant to leave you as you were. It was meant to awaken you. To help you see that history is not random, that the chaos is not unplanned, and that God's Word is not silent in our time. From Genesis to Revelation, the Author has been pointing to this exact moment—your moment—to choose whom you will serve.

Two Urgent Realignments

First, get on God's calendar. The Feasts of the LORD are not relics of an ancient faith; they are the prophetic heartbeat of Heaven. The spring feasts were fulfilled with pinpoint accuracy at Jesus' First Coming. The fall feasts will be fulfilled in the same exact manner when He returns in glory. The Shemitah cycles and Jubilee years are not obscure theological puzzles—they are God's time signatures, counting down redemptive seasons and setting the stage for His next move. Align yourself with His clock, not the world's, so you will be found ready when the final trumpet pierces the sky.

Second, stand with Israel. God's covenant with Israel has never expired. The Jewish people are still the apple of His eye, and the land is still His gift to them. Do not be deceived by the lies of replacement theology or the shifting winds of public opinion. In the days to come, the dividing line between truth and deception will be drawn with increasing clarity, and it will run straight through the question of Israel. Where you stand will reveal whose Word you trust.

The Invitation Before the Trumpet

This is not a time for hesitation. The prophetic clock is seconds from striking midnight. The wedding invitations have gone out, and the Groom is on His way. But the door will not stay open forever.

Jesus is still knocking (Revelation 3:20). Still inviting (Matthew 22:4). Still warning: "The time is fulfilled, the Kingdom of God is at hand. Repent, and believe the gospel" (Mark 1:15).

You were born for such a time as this. Not to blend into the shadows, but to shine as one of the wise who know the times. The next voice you hear might not be the anchor on the news or the hum of your daily life—it might be the shout of the archangel and the trumpet of God.

The Final Word

When that moment comes, there will be no time to prepare—only time to be revealed for who you already are. That is why the call is urgent: Choose this day whom you will serve. Because when the trumpet sounds, your eternity will already be decided.

The book ends here. The story of your choice does not.

CHAPTER SUMMARY

Chapter 12—The Final Countdown: The Last Days Before Forever—reminds us that time is not random but unfolding according to a divine plan set from Creation. From Genesis to the threshold of the Millennial Kingdom, God's appointed times, feasts, and prophetic markers have been leading to this present moment.

At its core is the 6,000-year blueprint: six "days" of man's rule, followed by one "day" of rest under Christ. History moves through the Age of Promise (Adam to Christ), the Age of Grace (Christ to now), and the soon-coming Age of Glory (Christ's reign). We stand at the razor's edge of that final shift.

Signs converge in the late 2020s—Israel's 80-year prophetic generation, Shemitah and Jubilee cycles, economic collapses, eclipses, blood moons, and even the world's 2030 reset agenda—aligning with God's calendar. The Feasts of the LORD remain exact prophetic appointments, with the fall feasts yet to be fulfilled.

Jesus' parables warn us: the wedding feast is near, the door is about to close, and only those clothed in His righteousness will enter. This is not about religion—it's about knowing the Bridegroom before the trumpet sounds.

KEY TAKEAWAYS

- Time is prophetic—a sacred rhythm set at Creation to reveal God's plan of redemption.
- The 6,000-year model points to the imminent close of man's rule and the beginning of Christ's 1,000-year reign.
- The Age of Grace is ending; the Day of the Lord approaches—bringing both judgment and glory.
- 2028/2029 aligns with prophetic patterns, feast days, Shemitah cycles, and global events.
- The Feasts of the LORD are God's calendar—fulfilled in exact order past and future.
- Intimacy with Christ—not religion—secures your place at the wedding feast.
- The invitation is still open, but the door is about to close.

Chapter 12 is the final call. The prophetic calendar is not speculation—it's God's countdown. The sands of the hourglass are almost gone. The Bridegroom is at the door. Come to the wedding . . . while there's still time.

Afterword: The Invitation

THE CHOICE BEFORE YOU—The late afternoon sun slanted through the blinds, laying golden stripes across the table where our Bibles lay open. Irene leaned forward, her elbows resting on the edge, eyes fixed on me.

"Ann," she began, her voice deliberate, "have you thought about what the 6,000-year lease means? Six days for man's rule . . . then one day—1,000 years—of Christ's reign."

I nodded slowly, my finger tracing the familiar words of Psalm 90:4.

"It's the full picture—7,000 years in all. And we're standing right at the edge of that final day—the Millennium."

Her brow furrowed. "And in that thousand years . . . not everyone is glorified, right?"

"Right," I said. "The sheep who survive the Tribulation will still carry the sin nature. They'll marry, raise children—maybe twelve, fifteen generations. Some will follow the Shepherd . . . some will rebel. That's why the Millennium exists—God's final separation before eternity. The Father's holiness can't be exposed to sin."

Irene's eyes softened, but her voice was firm. "Then why give a full thousand years?"

I looked up, my voice low. "Because He's patient. Because He wants none to perish. John 3:16 still stands—right up to the end."

She smiled faintly, then leaned back. "We only know in part . . . but it feels like God's speaking more clearly now—through prophets, watchers, teachers. But there's so much noise. How do we guard against that?"

I smiled knowingly. "We think in layers. We test everything by the Word. Even if a Bible-based message isn't all accurate, the parts confirmed by Scripture are true—and God can use them to speak directly to us. But we have to shut out the world's noise."

Her head tilted. "Replace it with what?"

"All things of the kingdom," I said without hesitation. "Surround yourself with His voice. Relationship with God—not religion. In the kingdom, there are no denominations. In the Millennium and the new earth, we'll live under the Gospel of the Kingdom—pure, whole."

Her eyes locked on mine. "Ann . . . our souls never die. Heaven is real. Hell is real. So . . . when's the right time to decide?"

I felt my throat tighten. "Now. Not later. Later isn't guaranteed. One heartbeat, one accident—and your eternity is set forever."

Irene glanced down, then looked back up. "Jesus warned—many will say, 'Lord, Lord,' and He'll reply, 'I never knew you.' People have had chances—church services, weddings, funerals, even a Bible in their home. The question is, did they ignore them? God sees His Word as gold—more valuable than anything we could hold. It's our food. And Jesus—He's our drink. Without Him, we starve spiritually. Without Him, we die eternally."

The room went still. I closed my Bible, the weight of her words hanging heavy like a final call.

She exhaled. "So . . . the choice is Heaven or Hell."

"Yes," I whispered. "And eternity is forever."

THE INVITATION THAT MATTERS MOST

If you've read this far, then perhaps you feel it—the undeniable pull of God's Spirit on your heart. The truths you've just encountered are not meant to inform you only, but to transform you. Every prophecy, every sign, every page of this book points to one central reality: Jesus Christ is coming again—and you must be ready.

The Bible says, "It is appointed unto men once to die, but after this the judgment" (Hebrews 9:27). There is no second chance once the door is shut. Eternity is not decided by good intentions, religious rituals, or family heritage. It is decided by one thing alone—whether you have a living, personal relationship with the Son of God.

Jesus Himself declared, "I am the way, the truth, and the life: no man comes to the Father, but by Me" (John 14:6). There are not many roads to Heaven. There is only one—and His name is Jesus.

If you've never surrendered your life to Him, or if you've wandered and know you're not ready to meet Him, today is the day. The Bible says, "Now is the accepted time; behold, now is the day of salvation" (2 Corinthians 6:2).

(For He says, I have heard you in a time accepted, and in the day of salvation have I helped you: behold, now is the accepted time; behold, now is the day of salvation.) (2 Corinthians 6:2)

The Gospel in Simple Terms

1. God loves you and created you for relationship with Him (John 3:16).

For God so loved the world, that He gave His only begotten Son, that whosoever believes in Him should not perish, but have everlasting life. (John 3:16)

2. Sin separates us from God, and we've all sinned (Romans 3:23).

For all have sinned, and come short of the glory of God. (Romans 3:23)

3. Jesus paid the price for your sins by dying on the Cross and rising again (Romans 5:8).

But God commends His love toward us, in that, while we were yet sinners, Christ died for us. (Romans 5:8)

4. You must personally receive Him as Lord and Savior (Romans 10:9–10).

That if you shalt confess with your mouth the Lord Jesus, and shalt believe in your heart that God has raised Him from the dead, you shalt be saved. For with the heart man believes unto righteousness; and with the mouth confession is made unto salvation. (Romans 10:9–10)

A Prayer to Surrender Your Life to Jesus

This is not magic words—it's the cry of your heart. If you mean it sincerely, pray something like this:

Lord Jesus, I believe You are the Son of God. I believe You died for my sins and rose again. I confess that I have sinned and need Your forgiveness. Right now, I turn from my sin and place my trust in You alone for salvation. Come into my heart, be my Lord and Savior, and make me the person You want me to be. From this day forward, I choose to follow You. Thank You for saving me. Amen.

If You Prayed That Prayer

If you prayed in faith, welcome to the family of God! Heaven is rejoicing over you right now (Luke 15:7).

> I say unto you, that likewise joy shall be in Heaven over one sinner that repents, more than over ninety and nine just persons, which need no repentance. (Luke 15:7)

Here are your first steps:

- Read the Bible daily, starting with the Gospel of John.
- Pray daily—talk to God like you would a close friend.
- Find a Bible-believing church where you can grow and be baptized.
- Tell someone about your decision—let your light shine (Matthew 5:16).

> Let your light so shine before men, that they may see your good works, and glorify your Father which is in heaven. (Matthew 5:16)

The prophecies in this book point to one truth: the clock is running out. But if you belong to Jesus, you can face the future with peace, knowing your name is written in the Lamb's Book of Life. The Bridegroom is coming—live ready.

The hourglass is almost empty.
The Bridegroom is at the door.
And if you listen closely, the next sound you hear . . . might be the trumpet.

FROM THE AUTHOR

Thank you for taking this prophetic journey through *The Vanishing* with me.

My prayer is that these pages have stirred your spirit, deepened your hunger for truth, and awakened within you a greater urgency to walk closely with the Lord while the window of grace is still open.

We are living in prophetic days. The signs that Jesus spoke of are converging all around us, and the Rapture of the Church is no longer a distant hope—it is an imminent reality.

The journey of Irene and Ann mirrors are own—watching, discerning, preparing. These dialogues may be fiction, but they carry truths drawn from God's Word and the world we see unfolding before our eyes. They are reminders that what is coming is not just a story, but our future.

If you're ready to go deeper, *The Trumpet I: The Ancient Prophecy That Reveals America's Final Hour* and *The Trumpet II: The Prophecy Continues—America's Final Hour Unveiled* explore the Book of Revelation in detail and reveal America's prophetic role in these end times.

Together with *The Vanishing*, they offer a complete picture: where we are now, what's coming next, and how to live prepared. If *The Vanishing* is your pre-flight checklist—ensuring your heart and life are ready for lift-off—*The Trumpet* series is your in-flight manual, guiding you through the rest of the prophetic journey until we arrive at the King's return.

There is more prophecy to be fulfilled.
More truth to be revealed.
More calls to readiness to answer.

Until the Vanishing occurs—and even more so afterward—we are called to be faithful watchmen on the wall, proclaiming what we see and living as if we could meet our King today.

The time is short.
The warnings are sounding.
The King is coming.
Will you be ready?

In His service,
Lori Ann Moeszinger

Continue the Journey Into Kingdom Living

If this book has stirred your heart, don't stop here. Take the next step into God's prophetic calling with the powerful companion volume . . .

THE

VANISHING

A PROPHETIC GUIDE TO LIFE AFTER THE
SINNER'S PRAYER

You prayed the prayer. You believe. Now what?

This life-changing guide takes you beyond the moment of salvation into the radical, world-shaking life Jesus calls you to live. Too many stop at the starting line—this book shows you how to run the race.

Inside, you will:

- Discover what it means to live as a citizen of Heaven in the last days.
- Unpack the weekly Sabbaths, annual Feasts, and biblical calendars—and why they matter today.
- Explore Shemitah cycles, Jubilee years, solar and lunar eclipses, and their prophetic significance.
- See God's plan unfold through charts, timelines, and visual summaries; many drawn directly from *The Vanishing: The Day Will Begin Like Any Other—Until the RAPTURE Silences the World.*

This is more than a study guide. It's a call to discipleship, holiness, and kingdom living in a world racing toward its prophetic climax.

You've read the headlines. You've seen the signs. Now learn to live with urgency, faith, and purpose—before it's too late.

Order your copy today and continue the journey.

THE RIDGE

PUBLISHING GROUP

Acknowledgments

THANK YOU, LORD JESUS CHRIST—You are the Author of all things, the Giver of truth, and the One who opens our eyes in due season. Every word in this book was written by Your grace, for Your glory, and in obedience to the burden You placed on my heart. *The Vanishing* could not have been written without Your voice speaking first. I give You all the praise and all the glory.

To my beloved husband, Eric—your strength, support, and unwavering belief in my calling have carried me through every page. Your patience, your love, and your faithfulness in our shared walk with Christ inspire me daily. You are my partner in life, in purpose, and in promise. I am so thankful God gave me you.

To my sons—Matthew, John, and Jared—each of you reflects a different dimension of God's love for me. You are the treasures of my heart, and the reason I surrendered to God's call. It is my prayer that this book will be part of your legacy—a witness to the truth and urgency of our time. May you always stand firm in faith, watching, and ready for His return.

To Pastors John and Brenda Kilpatrick and Church of His Presence—thank you for being a voice of revival and a refuge for seekers. Your sermons, prayers, and boldness in preaching truth have watered the soil of this message. I am grateful to be part of a body that is watching, worshiping, and preparing.

To the teachers, preachers, and watchmen who have helped sharpen my understanding of the Word—Evangelist Tiff Shuttlesworth, Pastor Steve Cioccolanti, Brandon and Diana Biggs, and others too numerous to name—thank you for sounding the alarm, for teaching truth in season and out, and for helping equip this generation for what lies ahead.

To those who prayed, encouraged, or simply believed in this message—thank you. Every conversation, every confirmation, and every moment of grace helped bring this book to completion. Your presence mattered more than you know.

To the reader—*you* are the reason this book was written. It is not by accident that you're holding these pages. The warnings in *The Vanishing* are not meant to frighten, but to awaken. You were born for this time, chosen for this hour, and called to be ready.

May the Holy Spirit speak to your heart as you read, and may the Word of God stir you to action.

The trumpet will sound. The vanishing will come.

And the time to prepare . . . is now.

To God alone be the glory.

Author Photo © 2023 Edwin Wolfe

ABOUT THE AUTHOR—Lori Ann Moeszinger, affectionately known as "L," is the founder and creative force behind The Ridge Publishing Group and its family of imprints. A prolific American author, blogger, and publisher, Lori brings a passion for clarity, truth, and inspiration to everything she writes. Nestled in the lakeside beauty of Coeur d'Alene, Idaho, she draws daily inspiration from God's Creation, her husband's unwavering support, and the quiet companionship of their two beloved dogs.

Holding a Juris Doctorate in Law, along with an Associate's degree in Paralegal Studies, and a Bachelor's degree in Business Administration, Lori transitioned from a legal career to full-time authorship and publishing, embracing the freedom to pursue her calling. Since 2016, she has devoted her life to the study of biblical prophecy and Scripture, bringing both depth and urgency to her writing.

Under the byline L. A. Moeszinger, she writes extensively on business, law, and the publishing industry, helping authors bring their dreams to life. Under her full name, Lori Ann Moeszinger, she explores biblical truths, prophetic insights, and personal reflections rooted in faith. Her New Youniversity Chronicles and The Manhattan Diaries series showcase her versatile storytelling gifts across multiple genres and voices.

At the heart of all she writes is a deep conviction: that faith is the foundation for life, that blessings are to be shared, and that diligence is a divine calling. Her books are more than words—they are invitations to prepare, to believe, and to live with eternal purpose.

LATEST RELEASES

For More Information . . .

If you would like to explore more of what you've read in *The Vanishing*—or dive deeper into related teachings, prophetic studies, biblical insights, and the call to prepare for Christ's return—or if you're seeking salvation, discipleship, or a deeper understanding of God's end-time purposes, you are warmly invited to connect further. Write to:

The Ridge Publishing Group
P.O. Box 549
Coeur d'Alene, Idaho 83816

You can also discover the multifaceted worlds Lori Ann Moeszinger has woven through her books, blogs, and ministries. Each platform is designed to equip, inspire, and walk alongside you in your journey of faith, purpose, and readiness.

Parent Platforms:

RidgePublishingGroup.com—Home base for all Lori's imprints, books, publishing updates, and new releases.

PublisherAndHerWorld.com—Blog site offering publishing insights, author tools, and faith-based reflections for Christian writers.

Ministry Platforms:

GuardiansofBiblicalTruth.com—Focused on Bible teaching, prophecy, and end-time preparation.

Jesus-Says.com—Home of *Coffee with God*, featuring daily inspiration, personal testimonies, and Scripture-rooted teachings.

Author Platforms:

LAMoeszinger.com—Lori's personal author site with theological writings, spiritual reflections, and upcoming projects.

NewYouniversityChronicles.com—A movement for faith-driven personal growth through the *New Youniversity Chronicles* and *The Manhattan Diaries* book series.

ManhattanChronicles.com—Where urban life, cultural reflection, and spiritual depth meet.

Publishing and Writer Support Platforms:

AuthorsDoor.com—Tools, training, and encouragement for indie authors.

AuthorsRedDoor.com—A blog site for writers pursuing excellence in publishing, marketing and writing—offering wisdom, strategies, and encouragement.

Children, Young Adult, and Family Adventures:

EthanFoxBooks.com—Enter the world of Ethan Fox, where wonder meets character-building adventure.

KidsStagram.com—Creative content and blog posts for young readers and families.

STAY CONNECTED

We invite you to join our online communities and become part of a growing network of watchmen, believers, writers, seekers, and young adventurers preparing for what lies ahead. Explore, engage, and grow deeper through our private Facebook groups and social spaces:

- Ethan Fox KidsStagram Fan Zone—A creative and inspiring space for young readers, families, and fans of Ethan Fox's adventures.
- Publisher and Her World Forum—A supportive community for writers and publishing entrepreneurs seeking guidance, encouragement, and industry insights.

- Guardians of Biblical Truth Forum—A gathering place for believers to study Scripture, explore prophecy, share testimonies, and strengthen their walk with Christ.
- AuthorsDoor Strategy Forum—A mastermind group for authors and independent publishers dedicated to writing, marketing, and publishing strategies that make an impact.

You can find links to these private groups, as well as *free* newsletter subscriptions, resources, and more across our websites.

EXPLORE OUR YOUTUBE CHANNELS

Discover a rich library of content across nine unique YouTube channels under The Ridge Publishing Group umbrella. From biblical teaching and prophetic insight to author features and publishing resources, our channels include:

- Publisher Website
  - Publisher and Her World at Ridge Publishing Group
- Author Website
  - Live with LAM #Shorts
- Guardians of Biblical Truth
  - Guardians of Biblical Truths
  - Coffee with God! Jesus-Says #Shorts
- AuthorsDoor Group
  - AuthorsDoor Group
  - Authors Red Door #Shorts
- Ethan Fox Books
  - Ethan Fox Live
  - Ethan Fox KidsStagram Book Club Circle
  - KidsStagram Ethan Fox Books #Shorts

Each channel offers curated videos designed to inform, encourage, and equip viewers for deeper spiritual understanding and creative inspiration. Subscribe and journey with us through truth, storytelling, and timeless wisdom.

Stay watchful. Stay ready. Stay connected.